IC En

FOURTH EDITION

About the Author

V. GANESAN currently working as Professor Emeritus in the Department of Mechanical Engineering, Indian Institute of Technology Madras, is the recipient of Anna University National Award for Outstanding Academic for the Year 1997. He was the Head of the Department of Mechanical Engineering, at Indian Institute of Technology Madras between October 2000 and June 2002. He was also the Dean (Academic Research) at Indian Institute of Technology Madras between January 1998 and October 2000. He has so far published more than 350 research papers in national and international journals and conferences and has guided 20 M.S. and 40 Ph.D.s.

Among other awards received by him are the Babcock Power Award for the best fundamental scientific paper of Journal of Energy (1987), the Institution of Engineers Merit Prize and Citation (1993), SVRCET Surat Prize (1995), Sri Rajendra Nath Mookerjee Memorial Medal (1996), Automobile Engineer of the Year by the Institution of Automobile Engineers (India) (2001), Institution of Engineers (India), Tamil Nadu Scientist Award (TANSA) – 2003 by Tamil Nadu State Council for Science and Technology, ISTE Periyar Award for Best Engineering College Teacher (2004), N K Iyengar Memorial Prize (2004) by Institution of Engineers (India), SVRCET Surat Prize (2004), Khosla National Award (2004), Bharat Jyoti Award (2006), UWA Outstanding Intellectuals of the 21st Century Award by United Writers Association, Chennai (2006), 2006 SAE Cliff Garrett Turbomachinery Engineering Award by SAE International, USA, Sir Rajendra Nath Mookerjee Memorial Prize (2006) by Institution of Engineers, Environmental Engineering Design Award 2006 by The Institution of Engineers (India), 2006 SAE Cliff Garrett Turbomachinery Engineering Award (2007), Excellence in Engineering Education (Triple "E") Award by SAE International, USA (2007), Rashtriya Gaurav Award in the field of Science and Technology by India International Friendship Society (2012), and Best Citizens of India Award by International Publishing House New Delhi (2012). He is the Fellow of Indian National Academy of Engineering, National Environmental Science Academy, Fellow of SAE International, USA, and Institution of Engineers (India). He has also been felicitated by International Combustion Institute Indian Section for lifetime contribution in the field of I C engines and combustion.

Dr. Ganesan has authored several other books on *Gas Turbines, Computer Simulation of Four-Stroke Spark-Ignition Engines* and *Computer Simulation of Four-Stroke Compression-Ignition Engines* and has also edited several proceedings. He was formerly the Chairman of Combustion Institute (Indian Section) and is currently the Chairman of Engineering Education Board of SAE (India), besides being a member of many other professional societies.

Dr. Ganesan is actively engaged in a number of sponsored research projects and is a consultant for various industries and R&D organizations.

IC Engines

FOURTH EDITION

V Ganesan
Professor Emeritus
Department of Mechanical Engineering
Indian Institute of Technology Madras
Chennai

McGraw Hill Education (India) Private Limited
NEW DELHI

McGraw Hill Education Offices
New Delhi New York St Louis San Francisco Auckland Bogotá Caracas
Kuala Lumpur Lisbon London Madrid Mexico City Milan Montreal
San Juan Santiago Singapore Sydney Tokyo Toronto

McGraw Hill Education (India) Private Limited

Published by McGraw Hill Education (India) Private Limited
P-24, Green Park Extension, New Delhi 110 016

IC Engines

Tenth reprint 2015
DZCYYRXVRQXAY

ISBN (13 digit): 978-1-25-900619-7
ISBN (10 digit): 1-25-900619-0

Managing Director: *Kaushik Bellani*
Head—Higher Education (Publishing and Marketing): *Vibha Mahajan*
Publishing Manager—SEM & Tech. Ed.: *Shalini Jha*
Sr Editorial Researcher: *Harsha Singh*
Executive—Editorial Services: *Sohini Mukherjee*
Sr Production Manager: *Satinder S Baveja*
Production Executive: *Anuj K Shriwastava*
Marketing Manager—Higher Education: *Vijay Sarathi*

General Manager—Production: *Rajender P Ghansela*
Manager—Production: *Reji Kumar*

Typeset at Tej Composers, WZ 391, Madipur New Delhi 110 063 and
text and cover printed at Rajkamal Electric Press, Plot No. 2, Phase-IV, Kundli, Haryana.

Visit us at: www.mheducation.co.in

DEDICATED TO MY BELOVED MOTHER

L. SEETHA AMMAL

FOREWORD

Focussing on the need of a first level text book for the undergraduates, postgraduates and a professional reference book for practicing engineers, the author of this work Dr. V. Ganesan has brought forth this volume using his extensive teaching and research experience in the field of internal combustion engineering. It is a great pleasure to write a foreword to such a book which satisfies a long-felt requirement.

For selfish reasons alone, I wish that this book would have come out much earlier for the benefit of several teachers like me who have finished their innings a long time ago. For me, this would have been just the required text book for my young engineering students and engineers in the transportation and power fields. The style of the book reflects the teaching culture of premier engineering institutions like IITs, since a vast topic has to be covered in a comprehensive way in a limited time. Each chapter is presented with elegant simplicity requiring no special prerequisite knowledge of supporting subjects. Self-explanatory sketches, graphs, line schematics of processes and tables have been generously used to curtail long and wordy explanations. Numerous illustrated examples, exercises and problems at the end of each chapter serve as a good source material to practice the application of the basic principles presented in the text. SI system of units has been used throughout the book which is not so readily available in the currently-used books.

It is not a simple task to bring out a comprehensive book on an all-encompassing subject like internal combustion engines. Over a century has elapsed since the discovery of the diesel and gasoline engines. Excluding a few developments of rotary combustion engines, the IC engines has still retained its basic anatomy. As a descendent of the steam engine, it is still crystallized into a standard piston-in-cylinder mechanism, reciprocating first in order to rotate finally. The attendant kinematics requiring numerous moving parts are still posing dynamic problems of vibration, friction losses and mechanical noise. Empiricism has been the secret of its evolution in its yester years.

As our knowledge of engine processes has increased, these engines have continued to develop on a scientific basis. The present day engines have to satisfy the strict environmental constraints and fuel economy standards in addition to meeting the competitiveness of the world market. Today, the IC engine has synthesized the basic knowledge of many disciplines — thermodynamics, fluid flow, combustion, chemical kinetics and heat transfer as applied to a system with both spatial and temporal variations in a state of non-equilibrium. With the availability of sophisticated computers, art of multi-dimensional mathematical modelling and electronic instrumentation have added new refinements to the engine design. From my personal knowledge, Dr. Ganesan has himself made many original contributions in these intricate areas. It is a wonder for me how he has modestly kept out these details from the text as it is beyond the scope of this book. However, the reader is not denied the benefits of these investigations. Skillfully the overall findings and updated information have been summarized as is reflected in topics on combustion and flame propagation, engine heat transfer, scavenging processes and engine emissions – to name a few examples. Indeed, it must have been a difficult task to summarize the best of the wide ranging results of combustion engine research and compress them in an elegant simple way in this book. The author has also interacted with the curriculum development cell so that the contents of the book will cater to the needs of any standard accredited university.

I congratulate the author, Dr. V. Ganesan on bringing out this excellent book for the benefit of students in IC engines. While many a student will find it rewarding to follow this book for his class work, I also hope that it will motivate a few of them to specialize in some key areas and take up combustion engine research as a career. With great enthusiasm, I recommend this book to students and practicing engineers.

B. S. Murthy
Former Professor, IIT Madras

PREFACE

We are bringing out the fourth edition of the book after the third edition has undergone fifteen reprints. Just to recall the history, the first edition of this book, published in 1994, had 15 Chapters which were framed in such a way that it will be useful to both academia and industry. Based on the feedback and response from the students and teachers the book was revised in 2003 with the addition of five more chapters taking into account the recent developments in engine technology and management. Again, the feedback from academia helped me to revise the book in 2007 for the second time with the addition of multiple choice questions. It is gratifying to note that all the three editions have received overwhelming response and appreciation from the students, teachers and practicing engineers.

I am extremely happy to receive the continuous positive feedback from the students and teachers. The review of the third edition by eminent reviewers has prompted me to revise the book to bring out this edition. In this, I have included a new chapter on Nonconventional Engines, which brings out the modern trends in the I C Engine development. The topics included are:

- Common Rail Direct Injection (CRDI) Engine
- Dual fuel and Multi-fuel Engine
- Free Piston Engine
- Gasoline Direct Injection (GDI) Engine
- Homogeneous charge Compression Ignition (HCCI) Engine
- Lean Burn Engine
- Stirling Engine
- Stratified Charge Engine
- Variable Compression Ratio(VCR) Engine
- Wankel Engine

I am sure that this will satisfy the long felt need of teachers, students and practicing engineers to understand the latest developments. Further, I have included the topic on vegetable oil and biodiesel in the chapter on alternate fuels which is the latest trend in engine fuel research. Additional materials, wherever appropriate, have been added in various chapters. Almost all the chapters have been thoroughly revised.

In writing this book, I have kept in mind the tremendous amount of material which the students and practicing engineers of today are expected to cover. On this count, the chapters have been organized to form a continuous logical narrative. Maximum care has been taken to minimize the errors and typing mistakes. I would be obliged to the readers for informing me any such errors and mistakes and will be thankful for bringing them to my notice. I am grateful to all those who are supporting this book.

It would be impossible to refer in detail, to the many persons whom I have consulted in the compilation of this work. I take this opportunity to thank all those who have helped me directly or indirectly in bringing out this book. This edition would not have been brought to this perfection but for the sincere and dedicated efforts of Ms. Vijayashree, who has helped me in compiling this book. My thanks are due to the Centre for Continuing Education of IIT Madras for their support under book writing scheme.

I hope this edition will also receive the same continued overwhelming support from academia and practicing engineers. I will be thankful for any constructive criticism for improvements in the future edition of the book.

V GANESAN

Contents

NOMENCLATURE

A

a_1	constant
$amep$	mean effective pressure required to drive the auxiliary components
A	piston area [Chp.1]
A	TEL in ml/gal of fuel [Chp.5]
A	area of heat transfer [Chp.14]
A	average projected area of each particles [Chp.15]
A_1	cross-sectional area at inlet of the carburettor
A_2	cross-sectional area at venturi of the carburettor
A_{act}	actual amount of air in kg for combustion per kg of fuel
A_f	area of cross-section of the fuel nozzle [Chp.7]
A_f	area of fin [Chp.14]
A_e	effective area
A_{th}	theoretical amount of air in kg per kg of fuel
A/F	air-fuel ratio

B

b_1	constant
bp	brake power
bhp	brake horsepower
$bmep$	brake mean effective pressure
$bsfc$	brake specific fuel consumption
BDC	Bottom Dead Centre

C

$cmep$	mean effective pressure required to drive the compressor or scavenging pump
C	velocity [Chp.7]
C_d	coefficient of discharge for the orifice [Chp.7]
C_{da}	coefficient of discharge for the venturi
C_{df}	coefficient of discharge for fuel nozzle
C_f	fuel velocity at the nozzle exit
C_p	specific heat of gas at constant pressure
C_{rel}	relative charge
C_v	specific heat at constant volume
CV	calorific value of the fuel

D

d	cylinder bore diameter [Chp.1]
d	diameter of orifice [Chp.7]
D	brake drum diameter

E

e	expansion ratio
E	enrichment [Chp.7]
EVC	Exhaust Valve Closing
EVO	Exhaust Valve Opening

F

f	coefficient of friction
$fmep$	frictional mean effective pressure
fp	frictional power
F	force
F/A	fuel-air ratio
F_R	relative fuel-air ratio

G

g	acceleration due to gravity
g_c	gravitational constant
gp	gross power

H

h	specific enthalpy
h	pressure difference [Chp.7]
h	convective heat transfer coefficient [Chp.13]
H	enthalpy

I

ip	indicated power
$imep$	indicated mean effective pressure
$isfc$	indicated specific fuel consumption
I	intensity
IDC	Inner Dead Centre
IVC	Inlet Valve Closing
IVO	Inlet Valve Opening

K

k	thermal conductivity of gases
k_1	constant [Chp.3]
K	number of cylinders
K_{ac}	optical absorption coefficient

L

l	characteristic length
l	distance [Chp.15]

L	stroke
L_ℓ	length of the light path

M

m	mass
m	exponent [Chp.13]
mep	mean effective pressure
$mmep$	mechanical mean effective pressure
$\dot{m}_a$	mass flow rate of air
$\dot{m}_{act}$	actual mass flow rate of air
$\dot{m}_{th}$	theoretical mass flow rate of air
M_{del}	mass of fresh air delivered
M_f	molecular weight of the fuel
M	molecular weight
M_{ref}	reference mass

N

n	number of power strokes
n	number of soot particles per unit volume [Chp.15]
N	speed in revolutions per minute
N_i	number of injections per minute [Chp.8]

O

ODC	Outer Dead Centre
ON	Octane Numbers

P

p	pressure
$pmep$	charging mean effective pressure
pp	pumping power
p_{ar}	pure air ratio
p_{bm}	brake mean effective pressure
p_e	exhaust pressure
p_i	inlet pressure
p_{im}	indicated mean effective pressure
p_m	mean effective pressure
P_{cyl}	pressure of charge inside the cylinder
P_{inj}	fuel pressure at the inlet to injector
P_l	pressure loss coefficient
P_s	specific power output
PN	performance number

Q

q	heat transfer
$\dot{q}$	rate of heat transfer

Q_R	heat rejected
Q_S	heat supplied

R

r	compression ratio
rpn	relative performance number
r_c	cut-off ratio
r_p	pressure ratio
R	length of the moment arm
R	delivery ratio [Chp.19]
$\overline{R}$	universal gas constant
R_{del}	delivery ratio

S

$\overline{s}_p$	mean piston speed
sfc	specific fuel consumption
S	spring scale reading

T

t	time
T	absolute temperature
T	torque [Chp.15]
TDC	Top Dead Centre
T_b	black body temperature
T_f	friction torque
T_g	mean gas temperature
T_l	load torque

U

u	specific internal energy
U	internal energy
U_c	chemical energy
U_s	stored energy

V

v	specific volume
V	volume
V_{ch}	volume of cylinder charge
V_{cp}	volume of combustion products
V_{del}	volume of air delivered
V_f	fuel jet velocity
V_{pure}	volume of pure air
V_{ref}	reference volume
V_{res}	volume of residual gas
V_{ret}	volume of retained air or mixture

V_s	displacement volume
V_s	swept volume
V_{short}	short circuiting air
V_{tot}	total volume
V_C	clearance volume
V_T	volume at bottom dead centre

W

w	specific weight
w	work transfer [Chp.7]
W	net work
W	weight [Chp.15]
W	number of quartz windows [Chp.15]
W	load [Chp.12]
WOT	Wide Open Throttle
W_C	compressor work
W_T	turbine work
W_x	external work

Z

z	height of the nozzle exit [Chp.7]
Z	constant

GREEK

α	air coefficient
γ	ratio of specific heats
Δp	pressure difference
ΔT	temperature difference between the gas and the wall
ϵ	heat exchanger efficiency
η	efficiency
$\eta_{air\ std}$	air standard efficiency
η_{bth}	brake thermal efficiency
η_c	compressor efficiency
η_{ch}	charging efficiency
η_{ith}	indicated thermal efficiency
η_m	mechanical efficiency
η_{rel}	relative efficiency
η_{sc}	scavenging efficiency
η_t	turbine efficiency
η_{th}	thermal efficiency
η_{trap}	trapping efficiency
η_v	volumetric efficiency
θ	crank angle [Chp.11]
θ	specific absorbance per particle [Chp.15]
λ	wave length [Chp.15]
λ	excess air factor [Chp.19]

μ	kinematic viscosity of gases
ν	dynamic viscosity
ρ	density
ρ_f	density of fuel
ϕ	equivalence ratio
ψ	magnetic field strength
ω	angular velocity

1

INTRODUCTION

1.1 ENERGY CONVERSION

The distinctive feature of our civilization today, one that makes it different from all others, is the wide use of mechanical power. At one time, the primary source of power for the work of peace or war was chiefly man's muscles. Later, animals were trained to help and afterwards the wind and the running stream were harnessed. But, the great step was taken in this direction when man learned the art of energy conversion from one form to another. The machine which does this job of energy conversion is called an engine.

1.1.1 Definition of 'Engine'

An engine is a device which transforms one form of energy into another form. However, while transforming energy from one form to another, the efficiency of conversion plays an important role. Normally, most of the engines convert thermal energy into mechanical work and therefore they are called 'heat engines'.

1.1.2 Definition of 'Heat Engine'

Heat engine is a device which transforms the chemical energy of a fuel into thermal energy and utilizes this thermal energy to perform useful work. Thus, thermal energy is converted to mechanical energy in a heat engine.

Heat engines can be broadly classified into two categories:

(i) Internal Combustion Engines (IC Engines)

(ii) External Combustion Engines (EC Engines)

1.1.3 Classification and Some Basic Details of Heat Engines

Engines whether Internal Combustion or External Combustion are of two types:

(i) Rotary engines (ii) Reciprocating engines

A detailed classification of heat engines is given in Fig.1.1. Of the various types of heat engines, the most widely used ones are the reciprocating internal combustion engine, the gas turbine and the steam turbine. The steam engine is slowly phased out nowadays. The reciprocating internal combustion engine enjoys some advantages over the steam turbine due to the absence of heat exchangers in the passage of the working fluid (boilers and condensers in steam turbine plant). This results in a considerable mechanical simplicity and improved power plant efficiency of the internal combustion engine.

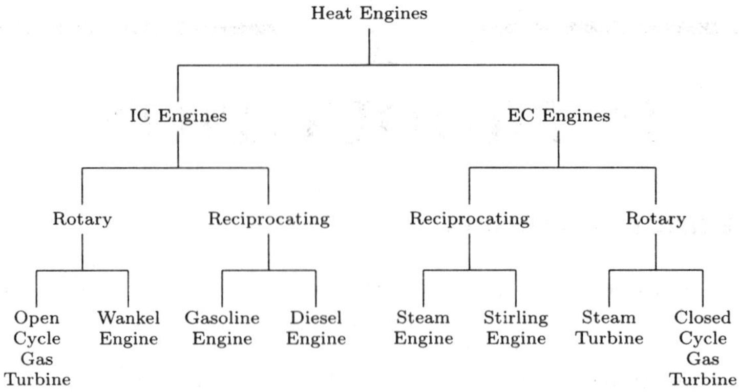

Fig. 1.1 Classification of heat engines

Another advantage of the reciprocating internal combustion engine over the other two types is that all its components work at an average temperature which is much below the maximum temperature of the working fluid in the cycle. This is because the high temperature of the working fluid in the cycle persists only for a very small fraction of the cycle time. Therefore, very high working fluid temperatures can be employed resulting in higher thermal efficiency.

Further, in internal combustion engines, higher thermal efficiency can be obtained with moderate maximum working pressure of the fluid in the cycle, and therefore, the weight to power ratio is quite less compared to steam turbine power plant. Also, it has been possible to develop reciprocating internal combustion engines of very small power output (power output of even a fraction of a kilowatt) with reasonable thermal efficiency and cost.

The main disadvantage of this type of engine is the problem of vibration caused by the reciprocating components. Also, it is not possible to use a variety of fuels in these engines. Only liquid or gaseous fuels of given specification can be effectively used. These fuels are relatively more expensive.

Considering all the above factors the reciprocating internal combustion engines have been found suitable for use in automobiles, motor-cycles and scooters, power boats, ships, slow speed aircraft, locomotives and power units of relatively small output.

1.1.4 External Combustion and Internal Combustion Engines

External combustion engines are those in which combustion takes place outside the engine whereas in internal combustion engines combustion takes place within the engine. For example, in a steam engine or a steam turbine, the heat generated due to the combustion of fuel is employed to generate high pressure steam which is used as the working fluid in a reciprocating engine or a turbine. In case of gasoline or diesel engines, the products of combustion generated by the combustion of fuel and air within the cylinder form the working fluid.

1.2 BASIC ENGINE COMPONENTS AND NOMENCLATURE

Even though reciprocating internal combustion engines look quite simple, they are highly complex machines. There are hundreds of components which have to perform their functions effectively to produce output power. There are two types of engines, viz., spark-ignition (SI) and compression-ignition (CI) engine. Let us now go through some of the important engine components and the nomenclature associated with an engine.

1.2.1 Engine Components

A cross section of a single cylinder spark-ignition engine with overhead valves is shown in Fig.1.2. The major components of the engine and their functions are briefly described below.

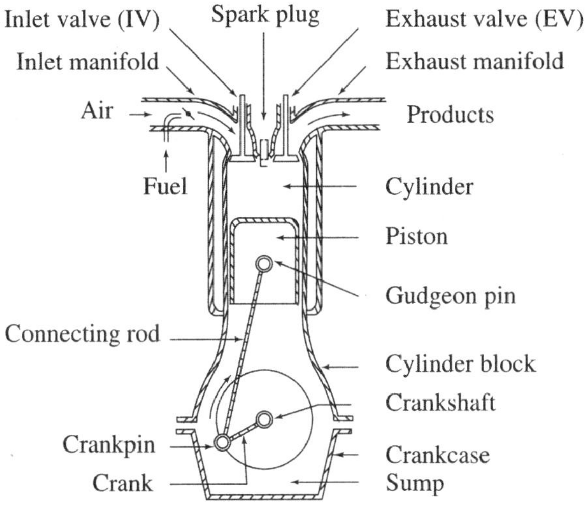

Fig. 1.2 Cross-section of a spark-ignition engine

Cylinder Block : The cylinder block is the main supporting structure for the various components. The cylinder of a multicylinder engine are cast as a single unit, called cylinder block. The cylinder head is mounted on the cylinder block. The cylinder head and cylinder block are provided with water jackets in the case of water cooling or with cooling fins in the case of air cooling. Cylinder head gasket is incorporated between the cylinder block and cylinder head. The cylinder head is held tight to the cylinder block by number of bolts or studs. The bottom portion of the cylinder block is called crankcase. A cover called crankcase which becomes a sump for lubricating oil is fastened to the bottom of the crankcase. The inner surface of the cylinder block which is machined and finished accurately to cylindrical shape is called bore or face.

Cylinder : As the name implies it is a cylindrical vessel or space in which the piston makes a reciprocating motion. The varying volume created in the cylinder during the operation of the engine is filled with the working fluid and subjected to different thermodynamic processes. The cylinder is supported in the cylinder block.

Piston : It is a cylindrical component fitted into the cylinder forming the moving boundary of the combustion system. It fits perfectly (snugly) into the cylinder providing a gas-tight space with the piston rings and the lubricant. It forms the first link in transmitting the gas forces to the output shaft.

Combustion Chamber : The space enclosed in the upper part of the cylinder, by the cylinder head and the piston top during the combustion process, is called the combustion chamber. The combustion of fuel and the consequent release of thermal energy results in the building up of pressure in this part of the cylinder.

Inlet Manifold : The pipe which connects the intake system to the inlet valve of the engine and through which air or air-fuel mixture is drawn into the cylinder is called the inlet manifold.

Exhaust Manifold : The pipe which connects the exhaust system to the exhaust valve of the engine and through which the products of combustion escape into the atmosphere is called the exhaust manifold.

Inlet and Exhaust Valves : Valves are commonly mushroom shaped poppet type. They are provided either on the cylinder head or on the side of the cylinder for regulating the charge coming into the cylinder (inlet valve) and for discharging the products of combustion (exhaust valve) from the cylinder.

Spark Plug : It is a component to initiate the combustion process in Spark-Ignition (SI) engines and is usually located on the cylinder head.

Connecting Rod : It interconnects the piston and the crankshaft and transmits the gas forces from the piston to the crankshaft. The two ends of the connecting rod are called as small end and the big end (Fig.1.3). Small end is connected to the piston by gudgeon pin and the big end is connected to the crankshaft by crankpin.

Crankshaft : It converts the reciprocating motion of the piston into useful rotary motion of the output shaft. In the crankshaft of a single cylinder engine there are a pair of crank arms and balance weights. The balance weights are provided for static and dynamic balancing of the rotating system. The crankshaft is enclosed in a crankcase.

Piston Rings : Piston rings, fitted into the slots around the piston, provide a tight seal between the piston and the cylinder wall thus preventing leakage of combustion gases (refer Fig.1.3).

Gudgeon Pin : It links the small end of the connecting rod and the piston.

Camshaft : The camshaft (not shown in the figure) and its associated parts control the opening and closing of the two valves. The associated parts are push rods, rocker arms, valve springs and tappets. This shaft also provides the drive to the ignition system. The camshaft is driven by the crankshaft through timing gears.

Cams : These are made as integral parts of the camshaft and are so designed to open the valves at the correct timing and to keep them open for the necessary duration (not shown in the figure).

Fly Wheel : The net torque imparted to the crankshaft during one complete cycle of operation of the engine fluctuates causing a change in the angular velocity of the shaft. In order to achieve a uniform torque an inertia mass in the form of a wheel is attached to the output shaft and this wheel is called the flywheel (not shown in the figure).

1.2.2 Nomenclature

Cylinder Bore (d) **:** The nominal inner diameter of the working cylinder is called the cylinder bore and is designated by the letter d and is usually expressed in millimeter (mm).

Piston Area (A) **:** The area of a circle of diameter equal to the cylinder bore is called the piston area and is designated by the letter A and is usually expressed in square centimeter (cm^2).

Stroke (L) **:** The nominal distance through which a working piston moves between two successive reversals of its direction of motion is called the stroke and is designated by the letter L and is expressed usually in millimeter (mm).

Stroke to Bore Ratio : L/d ratio is an important parameter in classifying the size of the engine. If $d < L$, it is called under-square engine. If $d = L$, it is called square engine. If $d > L$, it is called over-square engine.

An over-square engine can operate at higher speeds because of larger bore and shorter stroke.

Dead Centre : The position of the working piston and the moving parts which are mechanically connected to it, at the moment when the direction of the piston motion is reversed at either end of the stroke is called the dead centre. There are two dead centres in the engine as indicated in Fig.1.3. They are:

(i) Top Dead Centre (ii) Bottom Dead Centre

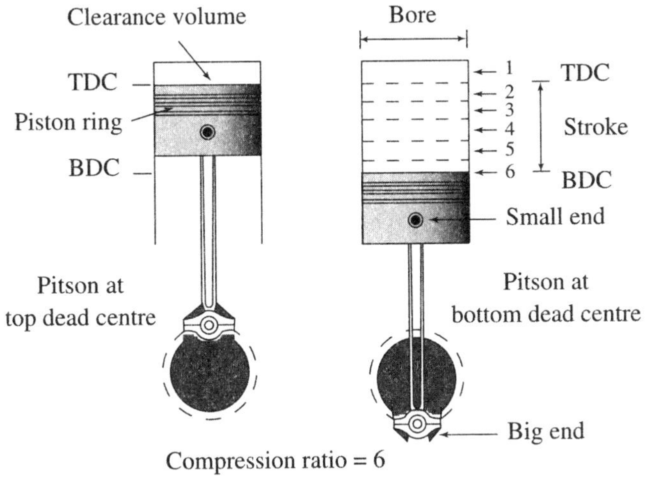

Fig. 1.3 Top and bottom dead centres

(i) *Top Dead Centre* (TDC) : It is the dead centre when the piston is farthest from the crankshaft. It is designated as TDC for vertical engines and Inner Dead Centre (IDC) for horizontal engines.

(ii) *Bottom Dead Centre (BDC) :* It is the dead centre when the piston is nearest to the crankshaft. It is designated as BDC for vertical engines and Outer Dead Centre (ODC) for horizontal engines.

Displacement or Swept Volume (V_s) **:** The nominal volume swept by the working piston when travelling from one dead centre to the other is called the displacement volume. It is expressed in terms of cubic centimeter (cc) and given by

$$V_s = A \times L = \frac{\pi}{4} d^2 L \tag{1.1}$$

Cubic Capacity or Engine Capacity : The displacement volume of a cylinder multiplied by number of cylinders in an engine will give the cubic capacity or the engine capacity. For example, if there are K cylinders in an engine, then

$$\text{Cubic capacity} = V_s \times K$$

Clearance Volume (V_C) **:** The nominal volume of the combustion chamber above the piston when it is at the top dead centre is the clearance volume. It is designated as V_C and expressed in cubic centimeter (cc).

Compression Ratio (r) **:** It is the ratio of the total cylinder volume when the piston is at the bottom dead centre, V_T, to the clearance volume, V_C. It is designated by the letter r.

$$r = \frac{V_T}{V_C} = \frac{V_C + V_s}{V_C} = 1 + \frac{V_s}{V_C} \tag{1.2}$$

1.3 THE WORKING PRINCIPLE OF ENGINES

If an engine is to work successfully then it has to follow a cycle of operations in a sequential manner. The sequence is quite rigid and cannot be changed. In the following sections the working principle of both SI and CI engines is described. Even though both engines have much in common there are certain fundamental differences.

The credit of inventing the spark-ignition engine goes to Nicolaus A. Otto (1876) whereas compression-ignition engine was invented by Rudolf Diesel (1892). Therefore, they are often referred to as Otto engine and Diesel engine.

1.3.1 Four-Stroke Spark-Ignition Engine

In a four-stroke engine, the cycle of operations is completed in four strokes of the piston or two revolutions of the crankshaft. During the four strokes, there are five events to be completed, viz., suction, compression, combustion, expansion and exhaust. Each stroke consists of 180° of crankshaft rotation and hence a four-stroke cycle is completed through 720° of crank rotation. The cycle of operation for an ideal four-stroke SI engine consists of the following four strokes : (i) suction or intake stroke; (ii) compression stroke; (iii) expansion or power stroke and (iv) exhaust stroke.

The details of various processes of a four-stroke spark-ignition engine with overhead valves are shown in Fig.1.4 (a-d). When the engine completes all the five events under ideal cycle mode, the pressure-volume (p-V) diagram will be as shown in Fig.1.5.

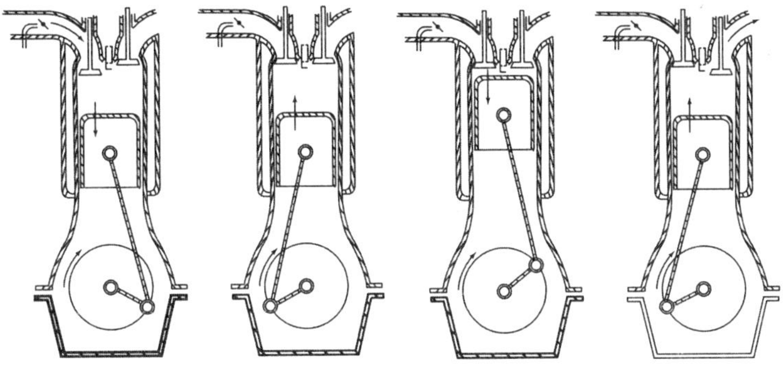

Fig. 1.4 Working principle of a four-stroke SI engine

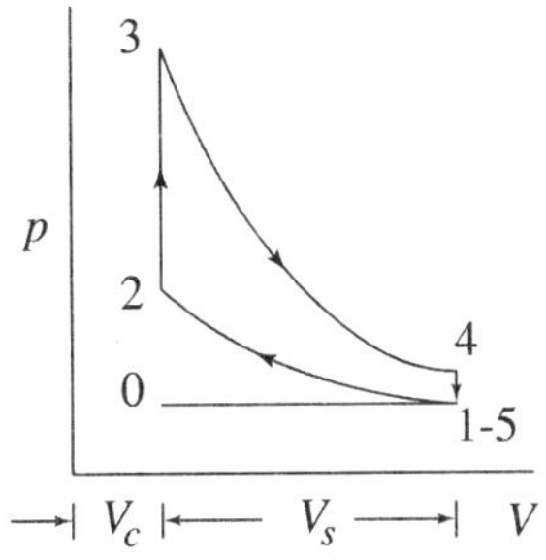

Fig. 1.5 Ideal p-V diagram of a four-stroke SI engine

(i) *Suction or Intake Stroke :* Suction stroke $0 \rightarrow 1$ (Fig.1.5) starts when the piston is at the top dead centre and about to move downwards. The inlet valve is assumed to open instantaneously and at this time the exhaust valve is in the closed position, Fig.1.4(a). Due to the suction created by the motion of the piston towards the bottom dead centre, the charge consisting of fuel-air mixture is drawn into the cylinder. When the piston reaches the bottom dead centre the suction stroke ends and the inlet valve closes instantaneously.

(ii) *Compression Stroke :* The charge taken into the cylinder during the suction stroke is compressed by the return stroke of the piston $1 \rightarrow 2$, (Fig.1.5). During this stroke both inlet and exhaust valves are in closed position, Fig.1.4(b). The mixture which fills the entire cylinder volume is now compressed into the clearance volume. At the end of the compression stroke the mixture is ignited with the help of a spark plug located on the cylinder head. In ideal engines it is assumed that burning takes place instantaneously when the piston is at the top dead centre and hence the burning process can be approximated as heat addition at constant volume. During the burning process the chemical energy of the fuel is converted into heat energy producing a temperature rise of about 2000 °C (process 2→3), Fig.1.5. The pressure at the end of the combustion process is considerably increased due to the heat release from the fuel.

(iii) *Expansion or Power Stroke :* The high pressure of the burnt gases forces the piston towards the *BDC*, (stroke 3→4) Fig.1.5. Both the valves are in closed position, Fig.1.4(c). Of the four-strokes only during this stroke power is produced. Both pressure and temperature decrease during expansion.

(iv) *Exhaust Stroke :* At the end of the expansion stroke the exhaust valve opens instantaneously and the inlet valve remains closed, Fig.1.4(d). The pressure falls to atmospheric level a part of the burnt gases escape. The piston starts moving from the bottom dead centre to top dead centre (stroke 5→0), Fig.1.5 and sweeps the burnt gases out from the cylinder almost at atmospheric pressure. The exhaust valve closes when the piston reaches *TDC*. at the end of the exhaust stroke and some residual gases trapped in the clearance volume remain in the cylinder.

These residual gases mix with the fresh charge coming in during the following cycle, forming its working fluid. Each cylinder of a four-stroke engine completes the above four operations in two engine revolutions, first revolution of the crankshaft occurs during the suction and compression strokes and the second revolution during the power and exhaust strokes. Thus for one complete cycle there is only one power stroke while the crankshaft makes two revolutions. For getting higher output from the engine the heat addition (process 2→3) should be as high as possible and the heat rejection (process 3→4) should be as small as possible. Hence, one should be careful in drawing the ideal p-V diagram (Fig.1.5), which should depict the processes correctly.

1.3.2 Four-Stroke Compression-Ignition Engine

The four-stroke CI engine is similar to the four-stroke SI engine but it operates at a much higher compression ratio. The compression ratio of an SI engine is between 6 and 10 while for a CI engine it is from 16 to 20. In the CI engine during suction stroke, air, instead of a fuel-air mixture, is inducted. Due to higher compression ratios employed, the temperature at the end of the compression stroke is sufficiently high to self ignite the fuel which is injected into the combustion chamber. In CI engines, a high pressure fuel pump and an injector are provided to inject the fuel into the combustion chamber. The carburettor and ignition system necessary in the SI engine are not required in the CI engine.

The ideal sequence of operations for the four-stroke CI engine as shown in Fig.1.6 is as follows:

(i) *Suction Stroke :* Air alone is inducted during the suction stroke. During this stroke inlet valve is open and exhaust valve is closed, Fig.1.6(a).

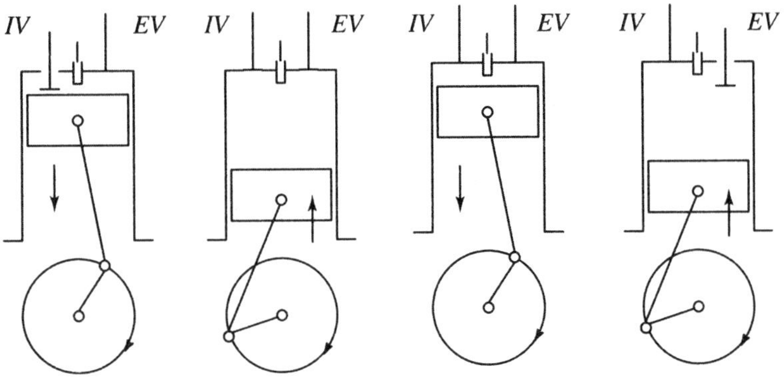

(a) Suction (b) Compression (c) Expansion (d) Exhaust

Fig. 1.6 Cycle of operation of a CI engine

(ii) *Compression Stroke :* Air inducted during the suction stroke is compressed into the clearance volume. Both valves remain closed during this stroke, Fig.1.6(b).

(iii) *Expansion Stroke :* Fuel injection starts nearly at the end of the compression stroke. The rate of injection is such that combustion maintains the pressure constant in spite of the piston movement on its expansion stroke increasing the volume. Heat is assumed to have been added at constant pressure. After the injection of fuel is completed (i.e. after cut-off) the products of combustion expand. Both the valves remain closed during the expansion stroke, Fig.1.6(c).

(iv) *Exhaust Stroke :* The piston travelling from BDC to TDC pushes out the products of combustion. The exhaust valve is open and the intake valve is closed during this stroke, Fig.1.6(d). The ideal p-V diagram is shown in Fig.1.7.

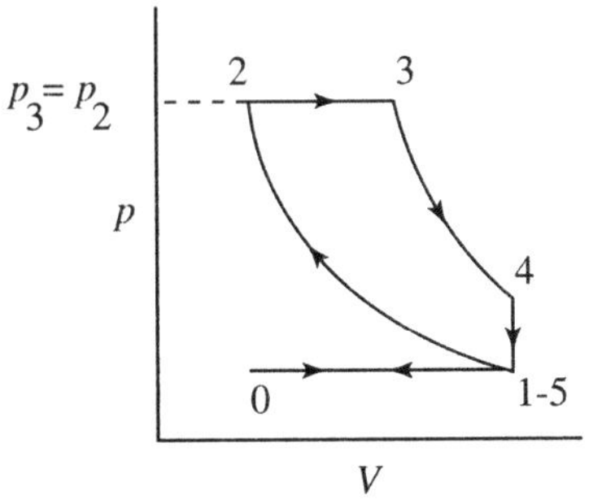

Fig. 1.7 Ideal p-V diagram for a four-stroke CI engine

Due to higher pressures in the cycle of operations the CI engine has to be sturdier than a SI engine for the same output. This results in a CI engine being heavier than the SI engine. However, it has a higher thermal efficiency on account of the high compression ratio (of about 18 as against about 8 in SI engines) used.

1.3.3 Four-stroke SI and CI Engines

In both SI and CI four-stroke engines, there is one power stroke for every two revolutions of the crankshaft. There are two non-productive strokes of exhaust and suction which are necessary for flushing the products of combustion from the cylinder and filling it with the fresh charge respectively. If this purpose could be served by an alternative arrangement, without involving the piston movement, then it is possible to obtain a power stroke for every revolution of the crankshaft increasing the output of the engine. However, in both SI and CI engines operating on four-stroke cycle, power can be obtained only in every two revolution of the crankshaft. Since both SI and CI engines have much in common, it is worthwhile to compare them based on important parameters like basic cycle of operation, fuel induction, compression ratio etc. The detailed comparison is given in Table 1.1.

1.3.4 Two-Stroke Engine

As already mentioned, if the two unproductive strokes, viz., the suction and exhaust could be served by an alternative arrangement, especially without the movement of the piston then there will be a power stroke for each revolution of the crankshaft. In such an arrangement, theoretically the power output of the engine can be doubled for the same speed compared to a four-stroke engine. Based on this concept, Dugald Clark (1878) invented the two-stroke engine.

In two-stroke engines the cycle is completed in one revolution of the crankshaft. The main difference between two-stroke and four-stroke engines is in the method of filling the fresh charge and removing the burnt gases from the cylinder. In the four-stroke engine these operations are performed by the engine piston during the suction and exhaust strokes respectively. In a two-stroke engine, the filling process is accomplished by the charge compressed in crankcase or by a blower. The induction of the compressed charge moves out the product of combustion through exhaust ports. Therefore, no separate piston strokes are required for these two operations. Two strokes are sufficient to complete the cycle, one for compressing the fresh charge and the other for expansion or power stroke. It is to be noted that the effective stroke is reduced.

Figure 1.8 shows one of the simplest two-stroke engines, viz., the crankcase scavenged engine. Figure 1.9 shows the ideal p-V diagram of such an engine. The air-fuel charge is inducted into the crankcase through the spring loaded inlet valve when the pressure in the crankcase is reduced due to upward motion of the piston during compression stroke. After the compression and ignition, expansion takes place in the usual way.

During the expansion stroke the charge in the crankcase is compressed. Near the end of the expansion stroke, the piston uncovers the exhaust ports and the cylinder pressure drops to atmospheric pressure as the combustion products leave the cylinder. Further movement of the piston uncovers the

Table 1.1 Comparison of SI and CI Engines

Description	SI Engine	CI Engine
Basic cycle	Works on Otto cycle or constant volume heat addition cycle.	Works on Diesel cycle or constant pressure heat addition cycle.
Fuel	Gasoline, a highly volatile fuel. Self-ignition temperature is high.	Diesel oil, a non-volatile fuel. Self-ignition temperature is comparatively low.
Introduction of fuel	A gaseous mixture of fuel-air is introduced during the suction stroke. A carburettor and an ignition system are necessary. Modern engines have gasoline injection.	Fuel is injected directly into the combustion chamber at high pressure at the end of the compression stroke. A fuel pump and injector are necessary.
Load control	Throttle controls the quantity of fuel-air mixture to control the load.	The quantity of fuel is regulated to control the load. Air quantity is not controlled.
Ignition	Requires an ignition system with spark plug in the combustion chamber. Primary voltage is provided by either a battery or a magneto.	Self-ignition occurs due to high temperature of air because of the high compression. Ignition system and spark plug are not necessary.
Compression ratio	6 to 10. Upper limit is fixed by antiknock quality of the fuel.	16 to 20. Upper limit is limited by weight increase of the engine.
Speed	Due to light weight and also due to homogeneous combustion, they are high speed engines.	Due to heavy weight and also due to heterogeneous combustion, they are low speed engines.
Thermal efficiency	Because of the lower CR, the maximum value of thermal efficiency that can be obtained is lower.	Because of higher CR, the maximum value of thermal efficiency that can be obtained is higher.
Weight	Lighter due to comparatively lower peak pressures.	Heavier due to comparatively higher peak pressures.

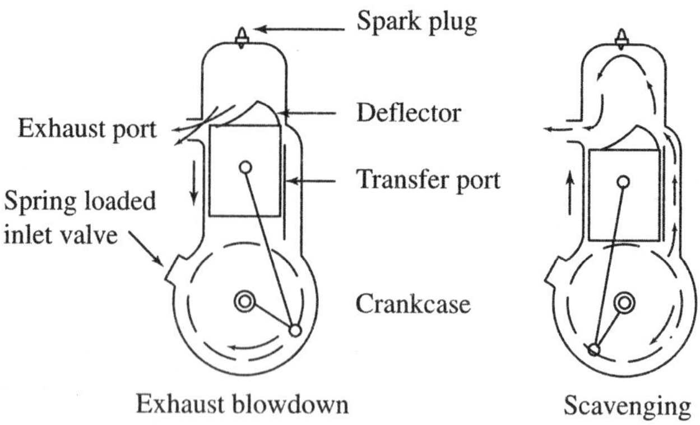

Fig. 1.8 Crankcase scavenged two-stroke SI engine

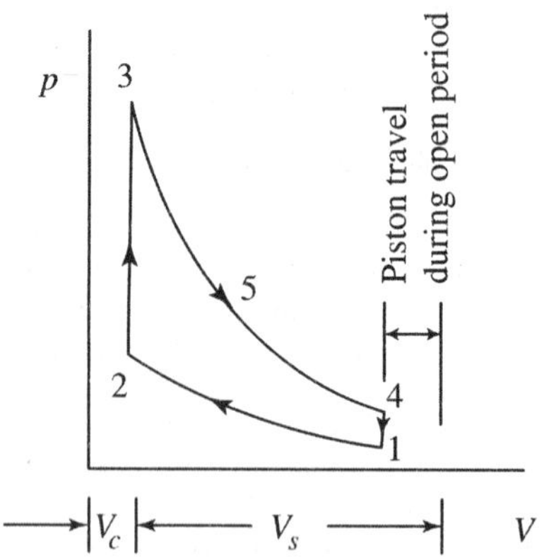

Fig. 1.9 Ideal p-V diagram of a two-stroke SI engine

transfer ports, permitting the slightly compressed charge in the crankcase to enter the engine cylinder. The piston top usually has a projection to deflect the fresh charge towards the top of the cylinder preventing the flow through the exhaust ports. This serves the double purpose of scavenging the combustion products from the upper part of the cylinder and preventing the fresh charge from flowing out directly through the exhaust ports.

The same objective can be achieved without piston deflector by proper shaping of the transfer port. During the upward motion of the piston from *BDC* the transfer ports close first and then the exhaust ports, thereby the effective compression of the charge begins and the cycle is repeated.

1.3.5 Comparison of Four-Stroke and Two-Stroke Engines

The two-stroke engine was developed to obtain higher output from the same size of the engine. The engine has no valves and valve actuating mechanism making it mechanically simpler. Almost all two-stroke engines have no conventional valves but only ports (some have an exhaust valve). This makes the two-stroke engine cheaper to produce and easy to maintain. Theoretically a two-stroke engine develops twice the power of a comparable four-stroke engine because of one power stroke every revolution (compared to one power stroke every two revolutions of a four-stroke engine). This makes the two-stroke engine more compact than a comparable four-stroke engine. In actual practice power output is not exactly doubled but increased by only about 30% due to

(i) reduced effective expansion stroke and

(ii) increased heating caused by increased number of power strokes which limits the maximum speed.

The other advantages of two-stroke engines are more uniform torque on crank-shaft and comparatively less exhaust gas dilution. However, when applied to the spark-ignition engine the two-stroke cycle has certain disadvantages which have restricted its application to only small engines suitable for motor cycles, scooters, lawn mowers, outboard engines etc. In the SI engine, the incoming charge consists of fuel and air. During scavenging, as both inlet and exhaust ports are open simultaneously for some time, there is a possibility that some of the fresh charge containing fuel escapes with the exhaust. This results in high fuel consumption and lower thermal efficiency. The other drawback of two-stroke engine is the lack of flexibility, viz., the capacity to operate with the same efficiency at all speeds. At part throttle operating condition, the amount of fresh mixture entering the cylinder is not enough to clear all the exhaust gases and a part of it remains in the cylinder to contaminate the charge. This results in irregular operation of the engine.

The two-stroke diesel engine does not suffer from these defects. There is no loss of fuel with exhaust gases as the intake charge in diesel engine is only air. The two-stroke diesel engine is used quite widely in many high output engines which work on this cycle. A disadvantage common to all two-stroke engines, gasoline as well as diesel, is the greater cooling and lubricating oil requirements due to one power stroke in each revolution of the crankshaft. Consumption of lubricating oil is high in two-stroke engines due to higher temperature. A detailed comparison of two-stroke and four-stroke engines is given in Table 1.2.

1.4 ACTUAL ENGINES

Actual engines differ from the ideal engines because of various constraints in their operation. The indicator diagram also differs considerably from the ideal indicator diagrams. Typical indicator diagrams of actual two-stroke and four-stroke SI engines are shown in Figs.1.10(a) and (b) respectively. The various processes are indicated in the respective figures.

1.5 CLASSIFICATION OF IC ENGINES

Internal combustion engines are usually classified on the basis of the thermodynamic cycle of operation, type of fuel used, method of charging the cylinder, type of ignition, type of cooling and the cylinder arrangement etc. Details are given in Fig.1.11.

Table 1.2 Comparison of Four and Two-Stroke Cycle Engines

Four-Stroke Engine	Two-Stroke Engine
The thermodynamic cycle is completed in four strokes of the piston or in two revolutions of the crankshaft. Thus, one power stroke is obtained in every two revolutions of the crankshaft.	The thermodynamic cycle is completed in two strokes of the piston or in one revolution of the crankshaft. Thus there is one power stroke for every revolution of the crankshaft.
Because of the above, turning moment is not so uniform and hence a heavier flywheel is needed.	Because of the above, turning moment is more uniform and hence a lighter flywheel can be used.
Again, because of one power stroke for two revolutions, power produced for same size of engine is less, or for the same power the engine is heavier and bulkier.	Because of one power stroke for every revolution, power produced for same size of engine is twice, or for the same power the engine is lighter and more compact.
Because of one power stroke in two revolutions lesser cooling and lubrication requirements. Lower rate of wear and tear.	Because of one power stroke in one revolution greater cooling and lubrication requirements. Higher rate of wear and tear.
Four-stroke engines have valves and valve actuating mechanisms for opening and closing of the intake and exhaust valves.	Two-stroke engines have no valves but only ports (some two-stroke engines are fitted with conventional exhaust valve or reed valve).
Because of comparatively higher weight and complicated valve mechanism, the initial cost of the engine is more.	Because of light weight and simplicity due to the absence of valve actuating mechanism, initial cost of the engine is less.
Higher volumetric efficiency due to more time for mixture intake.	Lower volumetric efficiency due to lesser time for mixture intake.
Thermal efficiency is higher; part load efficiency is better.	Thermal efficiency is lower; part load efficiency is poor.
Used where efficiency is important, viz., in cars, buses, trucks, tractors, industrial engines, aero planes, power generation etc.	Used where low cost, compactness and light weight are important, viz., in mopeds, scooters, motorcycles, hand sprayers etc.

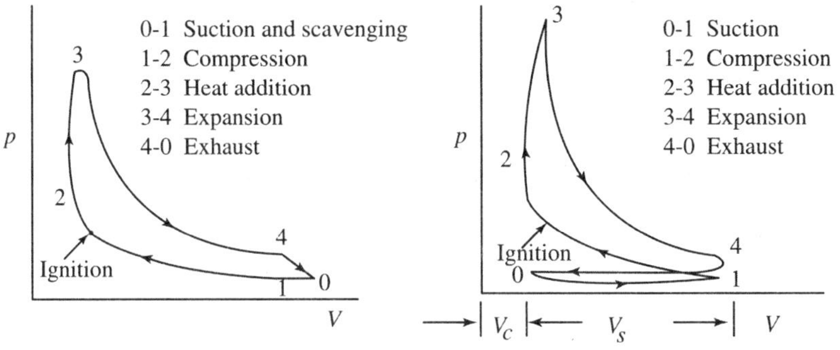

(a) Two-stroke engine (b) Four-stroke engine

Fig. 1.10 Actual p-V diagrams

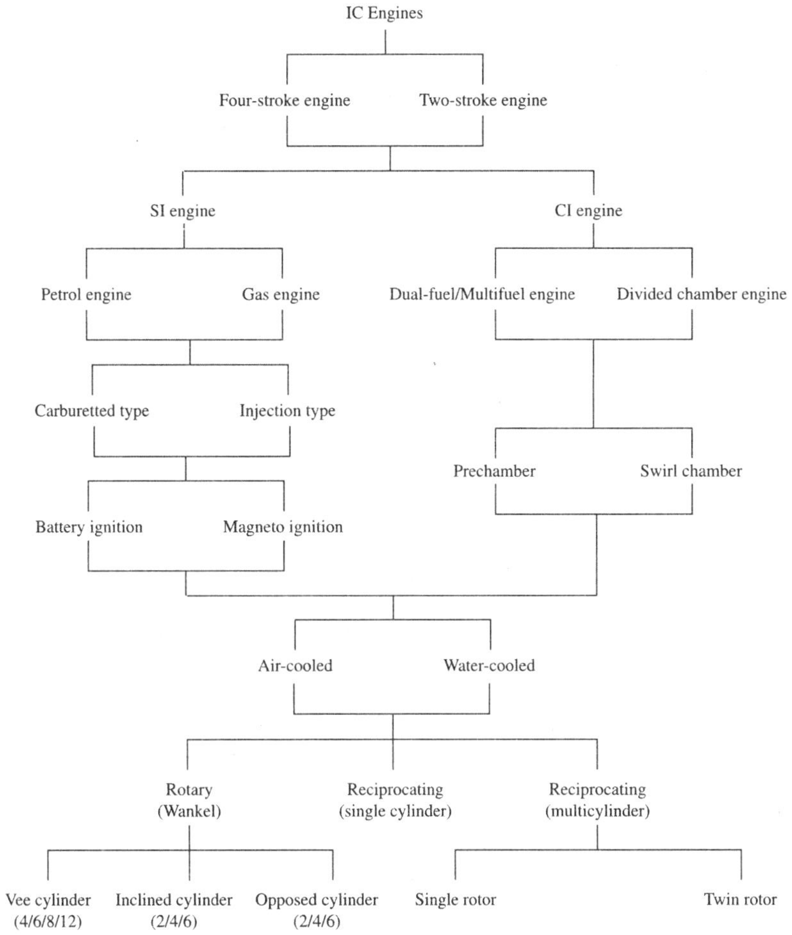

Fig. 1.11 Classification of internal combustion engines

1.5.1 Cycle of Operation

According to the cycle of operation, IC engines are basically classified into two categories.

(i) Constant volume heat addition engine or Otto cycle engine. It is also called a Spark-Ignition engine, SI engine or Gasoline engine.

(ii) Constant-pressure heat addition engine or Diesel cycle engine. It is also called a compression-ignition engine, CI engine or Diesel engine.

1.5.2 Type of Fuel Used

Based on the type of fuel used engines are classified as

(i) Engines using volatile liquid fuels, For example, gasoline, alcohol, kerosene, benzene etc.
The fuel is generally mixed with air to form a homogeneous charge in a carburettor outside the cylinder and drawn into the cylinder in its suction stroke. The charge is ignited near the end of the compression stroke by an externally applied spark and therefore these engines are called spark-ignition engines.

(ii) Engines using gaseous fuels like Compressed Natural Gas (CNG), Liquefied Petroleum Gas (LPG), blast furnace gas and biogas. Gaseous fuels are comparatively better compared to liquid fuels because of the reduced ignition delay.
The gas is mixed with air and the mixture is introduced into the cylinder during the suction process. Working of this type of engine is similar to that of the engines using volatile liquid fuels (SI gas engine).

(iii) Engine using solid fuels like charcoal, powdered coal etc.
Solid fuels are generally converted into gaseous fuels outside the engine in a separate gas producer and the engine works as a gas engine.

(iv) Engines using viscous (low volatility at normal atmospheric temperatures) liquid fuels like heavy and light diesel oils.
The fuel is generally introduced into the cylinder in the form of minute droplets by a fuel injection system near the end of the compression process. Combustion of the fuel takes place due to its coming into contact with the high temperature compressed air in the cylinder. Therefore, these engines are called compression-ignition engines.

(v) Engines using two fuels.
A gaseous fuel or a highly volatile liquid fuel is supplied along with air during the suction stroke or during the initial part of compression through a gas valve in the cylinder head and the other fuel (a viscous liquid fuel) is injected into the combustion space near the end of the compression stroke. These are called dual-fuel engines .

1.5.3 Method of Charging

According to the method of charging, the engines are classified as

(i) Naturally aspirated engines : Admission of air or fuel-air mixture at near atmospheric pressure.

(ii) Supercharged Engines : Admission of air or fuel-air mixture under pressure, i.e., above atmospheric pressure.

1.5.4 Type of Ignition

Spark-ignition engines require an external source of energy for the initiation of spark and thereby the combustion process. A high voltage spark is made to jump across the spark plug electrodes. In order to produce the required high voltage there are two types of ignition systems which are normally used. They are :

(i) battery ignition system (ii) magneto ignition system.

They derive their name based on whether a battery or a magneto is used as the primary source of energy for producing the spark.

In the case of CI engines there is no need for an external means to produce the ignition. Because of high compression ratio employed, the resulting temperature at the end of the compression process is high enough to self-ignite the fuel when injected. However, the fuel should be atomized into very fine particles. For this purpose a fuel injection system is used.

1.5.5 Type of Cooling

Cooling is very essential for the satisfactory running of an engine. There are two types of cooling systems used in engines, viz.,

(i) air-cooled engine (ii) water-cooled engine

1.5.6 Cylinder Arrangements

Another common method of classifying reciprocating engines is by the cylinder arrangement. The cylinder arrangement is only applicable to multicylinder engines. Two terms used in connection with cylinder arrangements must be defined first.

(i) *Cylinder Row :* An arrangement of cylinders in which the centreline of the crankshaft journals is perpendicular to the plane containing the centrelines of the engine cylinders.

(ii) *Cylinder Bank :* An arrangement of cylinders in which the centreline of the crankshaft journals is parallel to the plane containing the centrelines of the engine cylinders.

A number of cylinder arrangements popular with designers are described below. The details of various cylinder arrangements are shown in Fig.1.12.

In-line Engine : The in-line engine is an engine with one cylinder bank, i.e. all cylinders are arranged linearly, and transmit power to a single crankshaft.

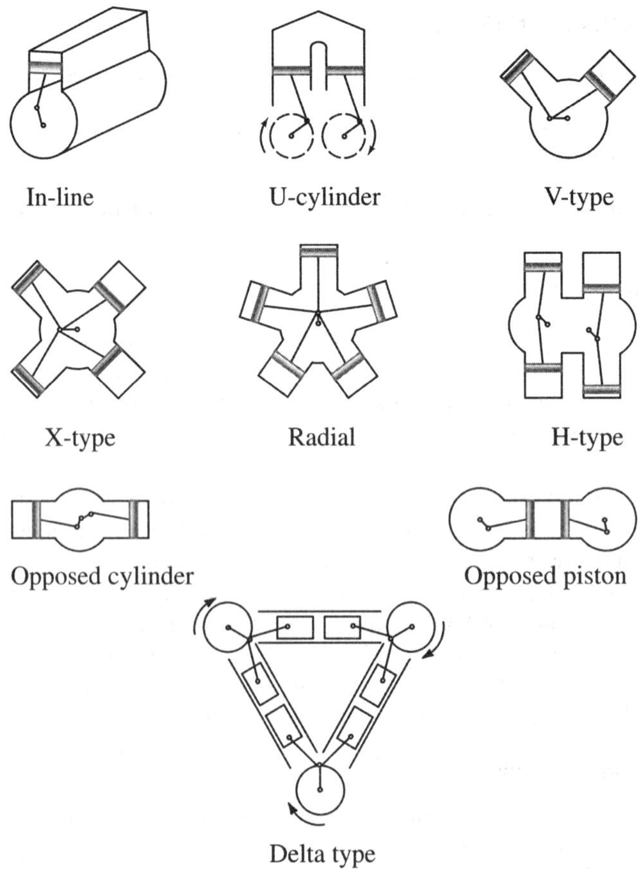

Fig. 1.12 Engine classification by cylinder arrangements

This type is quite common with automobile engines. Four and six cylinder in-line engines are popular in automotive applications.

'V' Engine : In this engine there are two banks of cylinders (i.e., two in line engines) inclined at an angle to each other and with one crankshaft. Most of the high powered automobiles use the 8 cylinder 'V' engine, four in-line on each side of the 'V'. Engines with more than six cylinders generally employ this configuration.

Opposed Cylinder Engine : This engine has two cylinder banks located in the same plane on opposite sides of the crankshaft. It can be visualized as two ' in-line' arrangements 180 degrees apart. It is inherently a well balanced engine and has the advantages of a single crankshaft. This design is used in small aircrafts.

Opposed Piston Engine : When a single cylinder houses two pistons, each of which driving a separate crankshaft, it is called an opposed piston engine. The movement of the pistons is synchronized by coupling the two crankshafts. Opposed piston arrangement, like opposed cylinder arrangement, and is inherently well balanced. Further, it has the advantage of requiring no cylinder head. By its inherent features, this engine usually functions on the principle of two-stroke engines.

Radial Engine : Radial engine is one where more than two cylinders in each row are equally spaced around the crankshaft. The radial arrangement of cylinders is most commonly used in conventional air-cooled aircraft engines where 3, 5, 7 or 9 cylinders may be used in one bank and two to four banks of cylinders may be used. The odd number of cylinders is employed from the point of view of balancing. Pistons of all the cylinders are coupled to the same crankshaft.

'X' Type Engine : This design is a variation of 'V' type. It has four banks of cylinders attached to a single crankshaft.

'H' Type Engine : The 'H' type is essentially two 'Opposed cylinder' type utilizing two separate but interconnected crankshafts.

'U' Type Engine : The 'U' type is a variation of opposed piston arrangement.

Delta Type Engine : The delta type is essentially a combination of three opposed piston engine with three crankshafts interlinked to one another.

In general, automobile and general purpose engines utilize the 'in-line' and 'V' type configuration or arrangement. The 'radial' engine was used widely in medium and large aircrafts till it was replaced by the gas turbine. Small aircrafts continue to use either the 'opposed cylinder' type or 'in-line' or 'V' type engines. The 'opposed piston' type engine is widely used in large diesel installations. The 'H' and 'X' types do not presently find any application, except in some diesel installations. A variation of the 'X' type is referred to as the 'pancake' engine.

1.6 APPLICATION OF IC ENGINES

The most important application of IC engines is in transport on land, sea and air. Other applications include industrial power plants and as prime movers for electric generators. Table 1.3 gives, in a nutshell, the applications of both IC and EC engines.

1.6.1 Two-Stroke Gasoline Engines

Small two-stroke gasoline engines are used where simplicity and low cost of the prime mover are the main considerations. In such applications a little higher fuel consumption is acceptable. Very small two-stroke engines (¡50 cc)are used in mopeds and lawn mowers. Scooters and motor cycles, the commonly used two wheeler transport, have generally 100-150 cc, two-stroke gasoline engines developing a maximum brake power of about 5 kW at 5500 rpm. High powered motor cycles have generally 250 cc gasoline engines developing a maximum brake power of about 10 kW at 5000 rpm. Gasoline engines are used in very small electric generating sets, pumping sets, and outboard motor boats. However, their specific fuel consumption is higher due to the loss of fuel-air charge in the process of scavenging and because of high speed of operation

Table 1.3 Application of Engines

IC Engine		EC Engine	
Type	Application	Type	Application
Gasoline engines	Automotive, Marine, Aircraft	Steam Engines	Locomotives, Marine
Gas engines	Industrial power	Stirling Engines	Experimental Space Vehicles
Diesel engines	Automotive, Railways, Power,Marine	Steam Turbines	Power, Large Marine
Gas turbines	Power, Aircraft, Industrial, Marine	Close Cycle Gas Turbine	Power, Marine

for which such small engines are designed. It may be noted that four-stroke engines are slowly replacing the two-stroke engines used in two-wheelers.

1.6.2 Two-Stroke Diesel Engines

Very high power diesel engines used for ship propulsion are commonly two-stroke diesel engines. In fact, all engines between 400 to 900 mm bore are loop scavenged or uniflow type with exhaust valves (see Figs.19.8 and 19.9). The brake power on a single crankshaft can be upto 37000 kW. Nordberg, 12 cylinder 800 mm bore and 1550 mm stroke, two-stroke diesel engine develops 20000 kW at 120 rpm. This speed allows the engine to be directly coupled to the propeller of a ship without the necessity of reduction gear.

1.6.3 Four-Stroke Gasoline Engines

The most important application of small four-stroke gasoline engines is in automobiles. A typical automobile is powered by a four-stroke four cylinder engine developing an output in the range of 30-60 kW at a speed of about 4500 rpm. American automobile engines are much bigger and have 6 or 8 cylinder engines with a power output upto 185 kW. However, the oil crisis and air pollution from automobile engines have reversed this trend towards smaller capacity engines.

Once four-stroke gasoline engines were used for buses and trucks. They were generally 4000 cc, 6 cylinder engines with maximum brake power of about 90 kW. However, nowadays gasoline engines have been practically replaced by diesel engines. The four-stroke gasoline engines have also been used in high power motor cycles with side cars. Another application of four-stroke gasoline engine is in small pumping sets and mobile electric generating sets.

Smaller aircrafts normally employ four-stroke gasoline (SI) radial engines. Engines having maximum power output from 400 kW to 4000 kW have been used in aircraft. An example is the Bristol Contours 57, 18 cylinder two row, sleeve valve, air-cooled radial engine developing, a maximum brake power of about 2100 kW.

1.6.4 Four-Stroke Diesel Engines

The four-stroke diesel engine is one of the most efficient and versatile prime movers. It is manufactured in sizes from 50 mm to more than 1000 mm of cylinder diameter and with engine speeds ranging from 100 to 4500 rpm while delivering outputs from 1 to 35000 kW.

Small diesel engines are used in pump sets, construction machinery, air compressors, drilling rigs and many miscellaneous applications. Tractors for agricultural application use about 30 kW diesel engines whereas jeeps, buses and trucks use 40 to 100 kW diesel engines. Generally, the diesel engines with higher outputs than about 100 kW are supercharged. Earth moving machines use supercharged diesel engines in the output range of 200 to 400 kW. Locomotive applications require outputs of 600 to 4000 kW. Marine applications, from fishing vessels to ocean going ships use diesel engines from 100 to 35000 kW. Diesel engines are used both for mobile and stationary electric generating plants of varying capacities. Compared to gasoline engines, diesel engines are more efficient and therefore manufacturers have come out with diesel engines even in personal transportation. However, the vibrations from the engine and the unpleasant odour in the exhaust are the main drawbacks.

1.7 THE FIRST LAW ANALYSIS OF ENGINE CYCLE

Before a detailed thermodynamic analysis of the engine cycle is done, it is desirable to have a general picture of the energy flow or energy balance of the system so that one becomes familiar with the various performance parameters. Figure 1.13 shows the energy flow through the reciprocating engine and Fig.1.14 shows its block diagram as an open system.

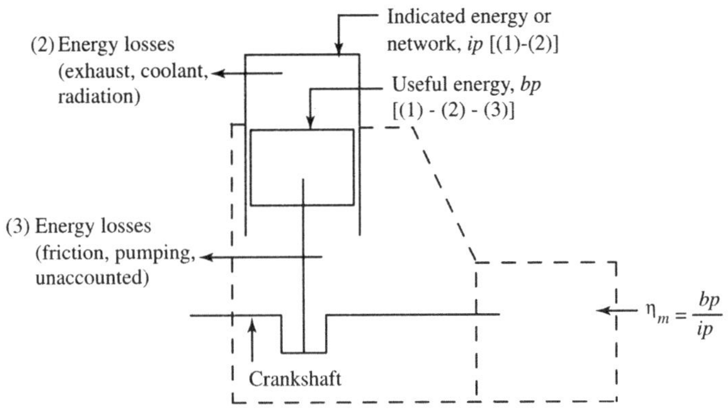

Fig. 1.13 Energy flow through reciprocating engine

According to the first law of thermodynamics, energy can neither be created nor destroyed. It can only be converted from one form to another. Therefore, there must be an energy balance between input and output of the system. In a reciprocating internal combustion engine the fuel is fed into the combustion chamber where it burns in air converting chemical energy of the fuel into heat. The liberated heat energy cannot be totally utilized for

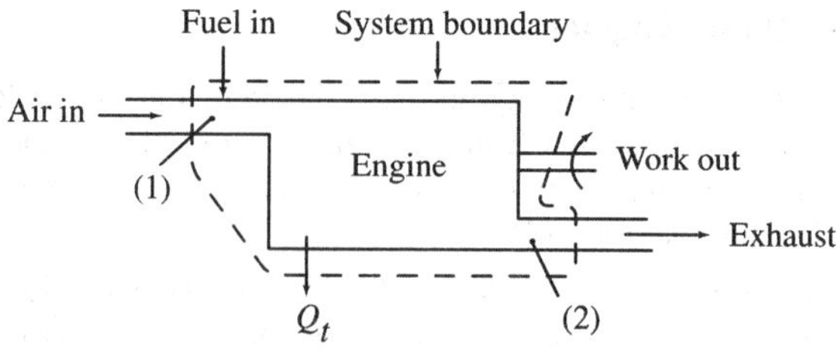

Fig. 1.14 Reciprocating engine as an open system

driving the piston as there are losses through the engine exhaust, to the coolant and due to radiation. The heat energy which is converted to power at this stage is called the *indicated power*, *ip* and it is utilized to drive the piston. The energy represented by the gas forces on the piston passes through the connecting rod to the crankshaft. In this transmission there are energy losses due to bearing friction, pumping losses etc. In addition, a part of the energy available is utilized in driving the auxiliary devices like feed pump, valve mechanisms, ignition systems etc. The sum of all these losses, expressed in units of power is termed as *frictional power*, *fp* . The remaining energy is the useful mechanical energy and is termed as the *brake power*, *bp* . In energy balance, generally, frictional power is not shown separately because ultimately this energy is accounted in exhaust, cooling water, radiation, etc.

1.8 ENGINE PERFORMANCE PARAMETERS

The engine performance is indicated by the term *efficiency*, η. Five important engine efficiencies and other related engine performance parameters are:

(i)	Indicated thermal efficiency	(η_{ith})
(ii)	Brake thermal efficiency	(η_{bth})
(iii)	Mechanical efficiency	(η_m)
(iv)	Volumetric efficiency	(η_v)
(v)	Relative efficiency or Efficiency ratio	(η_{rel})
(vi)	Mean effective pressure	(p_m)
(vii)	Mean piston speed	$(\overline{s}_p)$
(viii)	Specific power output	(P_s)
(ix)	Specific fuel consumption	(sfc)
(x)	Inlet-valve Mach Index	(Z)
(x)	Fuel-air or air-fuel ratio	$(F/A$ or $A/F)$
(xi)	Calorific value of the fuel	(CV)

Figure 1.15 shows the diagrammatic representation of energy distribution in an IC engine.

1.8.1 Indicated Thermal Efficiency (η_{ith})

Indicated thermal efficiency is the ratio of energy in the indicated power, *ip*, to the input fuel energy in appropriate units.

$$\eta_{ith} = \frac{ip \text{ [kJ/s]}}{\text{energy in fuel per second [kJ/s]}} \tag{1.3}$$

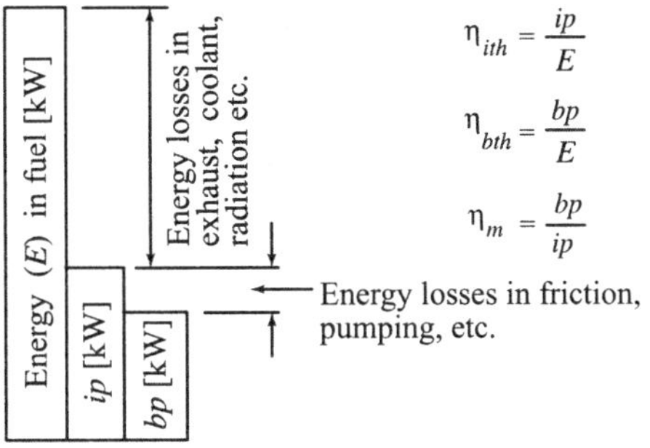

Fig. 1.15 Energy distribution

$$= \frac{ip}{\text{mass of fuel/s} \times \text{calorific value of fuel}} \tag{1.4}$$

1.8.2 Brake Thermal Efficiency (η_{bth})

Brake thermal efficiency is the ratio of energy in the brake power, bp, to the input fuel energy in appropriate units.

$$\eta_{bth} = \frac{bp}{\text{Mass of fuel/s} \times \text{ calorific value of fuel}} \tag{1.5}$$

1.8.3 Mechanical Efficiency (η_m)

Mechanical efficiency is defined as the ratio of brake power (delivered power) to the indicated power (power provided to the piston) or can be defined as the ratio of the brake thermal efficiency to the indicated thermal efficiency.

$$\eta_m = \frac{bp}{ip} = \frac{bp}{bp + fp} \tag{1.6}$$

$$fp = ip - bp \tag{1.7}$$

1.8.4 Volumetric Efficiency (η_v)

This is one of the very important parameters which decides the performance of four-stroke engines. Four-stroke engines have distinct suction stroke, volumetric efficiency indicates the breathing ability of the engine. It is to be noted that the utilization of the air is that determines the power output of the engine. Intake system must be designed in such a way that the engine must be able to take in as much air as possible.

Volumetric efficiency is defined as the ratio of actual volume flow rate of **air** into the intake system to the rate at which the volume is displaced by the system.

$$\eta_v = \frac{\dot{m}_a/\rho_a}{V_{\text{disp}} N/2} \tag{1.8}$$

where ρ_a is the inlet density.

An alternative equivalent definition for volumetric efficiency is

$$\eta_v = \frac{\dot{m}_a}{\rho_a V_d} \tag{1.9}$$

It is to be noted that irrespective of the engine whether SI, CI or gas engine, *volumetric rate of air flow is what to be taken into account* and not the mixture flow.

If ρ_a is taken as the atmospheric air density, then η_v is the pumping performance of the entire inlet system. If it is taken as the air density in the inlet manifold, then η_v is the pumping performance of the inlet port and valve only.

The normal range of volumetric efficiency at full throttle for SI engines is between 80 to 85% where as for CI engines it is between 85 to 90%. Gas engines have much lower volumetric efficiency since gaseous fuel displaces air and therefore the breathing capacity of the engine is reduced.

1.8.5 Relative Efficiency or Efficiency Ratio (η_{rel})

Relative efficiency or efficiency ratio is the ratio of thermal efficiency of an actual cycle to that of the ideal cycle. The efficiency ratio is a very useful criterion which indicates the degree of development of the engine.

$$\eta_{rel} = \frac{\text{Actual thermal efficiency}}{\text{Air-standard efficiency}} \tag{1.10}$$

1.8.6 Mean Effective Pressure (p_m)

Mean effective pressure is the average pressure inside the cylinders of an internal combustion engine based on the calculated or measured power output. It increases as manifold pressure increases. For any particular engine, operating at a given speed and power output, there will be a specific indicated mean effective pressure, *imep*, and a corresponding brake mean effective pressure, *bmep*. They are derived from the indicated and brake power respectively. For derivation see Chapter 16. Indicated power can be shown to be

$$ip = \frac{p_{im} LAnK}{60 \times 1000} \tag{1.11}$$

then, the indicated mean effective pressure can be written as

$$p_{im} = \frac{60000 \times ip}{LAnK} \tag{1.12}$$

Similarly, the brake mean effective pressure is given by

$$p_{bm} = \frac{60000 \times bp}{LAnK} \tag{1.13}$$

where ip = indicated power (kW)
p_{im} = indicated mean effective pressure (N/m^2)
L = length of the stroke (m)
A = area of the piston (m^2)
N = speed in revolutions per minute (rpm)
n = Number of power strokes
$N/2$ for 4-stroke and N for 2-stroke engines
K = number of cylinders

Another way of specifying the indicated mean effective pressure p_{im} is from the knowledge of engine indicator diagram (p-V diagram). In this case, p_{im}, may be defined as

$$p_{im} = \frac{\text{Area of the indicator diagram}}{\text{Length of the indicator diagram}}$$

where the length of the indicator diagram is given by the difference between the total volume and the clearance volume.

1.8.7 Mean Piston Speed ($\overline{s}_p$)

An important parameter in engine applications is the mean piston speed, $\overline{s}_p$. It is defined as

$$\overline{s}_p = 2LN$$

where L is the stroke and N is the rotational speed of the crankshaft in rpm. It may be noted that $\overline{s}_p$ is often a more appropriate parameter than crank rotational speed for correlating engine behaviour as a function of speed.

Resistance to gas flow into the engine or stresses due to the inertia of the moving parts limit the maximum value of $\overline{s}_p$ to within 8 to 15 m/s. Automobile engines operate at the higher end and large marine diesel engines at the lower end of this range of piston speeds.

1.8.8 Specific Power Output (P_s)

Specific power output of an engine is defined as the power output per unit piston area and is a measure of the engine designer's success in using the available piston area regardless of cylinder size. The specific power can be shown to be proportional to the product of the mean effective pressure and mean piston speed.

$$\text{Specific power output, } P_s = bp/A \tag{1.14}$$

$$= \text{constant} \times p_{bm} \times \overline{s}_p \tag{1.15}$$

As can be seen the specific power output consists of two elements, viz., the force available to work and the speed with which it is working. Thus, for the same piston displacement and *bmep*, an engine running at a higher speed will give a higher specific output. It is clear that the output of an engine can be increased by increasing either the speed or the *bmep*. Increasing the speed involves increase in the mechanical stresses of various engine components. For increasing the *bmep* better heat release from the fuel is required and this will involve more thermal load on engine cylinder.

1.8.9 Specific Fuel Consumption (sfc)

The fuel consumption characteristics of an engine are generally expressed in terms of specific fuel consumption in kilograms of fuel per kilowatt-hour. It is an important parameter that reflects how good the engine performance is. It is inversely proportional to the thermal efficiency of the engine.

$$\text{sfc} = \frac{\text{Fuel consumption per unit time}}{\text{Power}} \tag{1.16}$$

Brake specific fuel consumption and indicated specific fuel consumption, abbreviated as $bsfc$ and $isfc$, are the specific fuel consumptions on the basis of bp and ip respectively.

1.8.10 Inlet-Valve Mach Index (Z)

In a reciprocating engine the flow of intake charge takes place through the intake valve opening which is varying during the induction operation. Also, the maximum gas velocity through this area is limited by the local sonic velocity. Thus gas velocity is finally chosen by the following equation,

$$u = \frac{A_p}{C_i A_i} V_p \tag{1.17}$$

where u = gas velocity through the inlet valve at smallest flow area
A_p = piston area
A_i = nominal intake valve opening area
C_i = inlet valve flow co-efficient

and

$$\frac{u}{\alpha} = \frac{A_p}{A_i}\frac{V_p}{C_i \alpha} = \left(\frac{b}{D_i}\right)^2 \frac{V_p}{C_i \alpha} = Z \tag{1.18}$$

where b = cylinder diameter
D_i = inlet valve diameter
V_p = mean piston speed
α = inlet sonic velocity
C_i = inlet valve average flow co-efficient
Z = inlet valve Mach index.

Large number of experiments have been conducted on CFR single cylinder engine with gaseous mixtures and short induction pipe lengths, at fixed valve timing and fixed compression ratio, but varying inlet valve diameter and lift. The results are quite revealing as regards the relationship of volumetric efficiency versus Mach index are concerned. From Fig.1.16, it could be seen that the maximum volumetric efficiency is obtainable for an inlet Mach number of 0.55. Therefore, engine designers must take care of this factor to get the maximum volumetric efficiency for their engines.

1.8.11 Fuel-Air (F/A) or Air-Fuel Ratio (A/F)

The relative proportions of the fuel and air in the engine are very important from the standpoint of combustion and the efficiency of the engine. This is

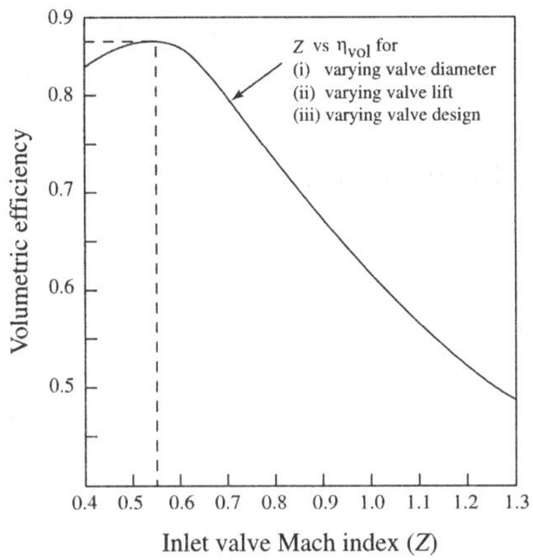

Fig. 1.16 Inlet-valve mach index

expressed either as a ratio of the mass of the fuel to that of the air or vice versa.

In the SI engine the fuel-air ratio practically remains a constant over a wide range of operation. In CI engines at a given speed the air flow does not vary with load; it is the fuel flow that varies directly with load. Therefore, the term fuel-air ratio is generally used instead of air-fuel ratio.

A mixture that contains just enough air for complete combustion of all the fuel in the mixture is called a chemically correct or stoichiometric fuel-air ratio. A mixture having more fuel than that in a chemically correct mixture is termed as rich mixture and a mixture that contains less fuel (or excess air) is called a lean mixture. For most of the hydrocarbon fuels, the stoichiometric air-fuel ratio is around 15:1. SI engines operate around this ratio during normal operation. The air-fuel ratio for CI engines vary from 18:1 to 80:1 from full load to no load.

The ratio of actual fuel-air ratio to stoichiometric fuel-air ratio is called equivalence ratio and is denoted by ϕ.

$$\phi = \frac{\text{Actual fuel-air ratio}}{\text{Stoichiometric fuel-air ratio}} \tag{1.19}$$

Accordingly, $\phi = 1$ means stoichiometric (chemically correct) mixture, $\phi < 1$ means lean mixture and $\phi > 1$ means rich mixture.

1.8.12 Calorific Value (CV)

Calorific value of a fuel is the thermal energy released per unit quantity of the fuel when the fuel is burned completely and the products of combustion are cooled back to the initial temperature of the combustible mixture. Other terms used for the calorific value are heating value and heat of combustion.

When the products of combustion are cooled to 25 °C practically all the water vapour resulting from the combustion process is condensed. The heating value so obtained is called the higher calorific value or gross calorific value of the fuel. The lower or net calorific value is the heat released when water vapour in the products of combustion is not condensed and remains in the vapour form.

1.9 DESIGN AND PERFORMANCE DATA

Engine ratings usually indicate the highest power at which manufacturers expect their products to give reasonably good performance. The performance parameters usually takes into account satisfactory economy, reliability, and durability under service conditions. The speed at which the maximum torque is achieved, is also usually given. It may be noted that both these quantities depend on displacement volume. Therefore, for comparative analysis between engines of different displacements in a given engine category normalized performance parameters are preferred and they are most useful.

Typical design and performance data for SI and CI engines used in different applications are summarized in Table 1.4. As can be seen the four-stroke cycle dominates except in the smallest and largest engines. The larger engines are usually turbocharged or supercharged. As the engine size increases, the maximum rated engine speed decreases, maintaining the maximum mean piston speed in the range of about 8 to 15 m/sis maintained. The maximum *bmep* for turbocharged and supercharged engines is higher compared to naturally aspirated engines. Because the maximum fuel-air ratio for SI engines is higher than for CI engines, their naturally aspirated maximum *bmep* levels are higher. As the engine size increases, brake specific fuel consumption decreases and fuel conversion efficiency increases due to the reduced heat losses and friction. For the large CI engines, brake thermal efficiencies of about 40% and indicated thermal efficiencies of about 50% can be obtained in modern engines.

The various operating conditions that should be taken into account are

(i) maximum or normal rated operation,

(ii) full throttle or full load operation, and

(iii) long period operation.

For (i) the most important performance parameters are mean piston speed, brake mean effective pressure, power per unit piston area, specific weight, and specific volume. For (ii) the most important performance parameters is bmep only and for (iii) they are brake specific fuel consumption, and brake specific fuel emissions.

Table 1.4 *Typical Design and Performance Data for Modern Internal Combustion Engines*

	Operating cycle (Stroke)	Compression ratio	Bore (m)	Stroke/ bore ratio	Rated Maximum Speed (rev/min)	Rated Maximum *bmep* (atm)	Weight/ Power ratio (kg/kW)	Approx. best *bsfc* (g/kW h)
Spark-ignition engines								
Small (e.g. motorcycles)	2/4	6–10	0.05–0.085	1.2–0.9	4500–7500	4–10	5.5–2.5	350
Passenger cars	4	8–10	0.07–0.1	1.1–0.9	4500–6500	7–10	4–2	270
Trucks	4	7–9	0.09–0.13	1.2–0.7	3600–5000	6.5–7	6.5–2.5	300
Large gas engines	2/4	8–12	0.22–0.45	1.1–1.4	300–900	6.8–12	23–35	200
Wankel engines	4	≈ 9	0.57 dm^3 per chamber		6000–8000	9.5–10.5	1.6–0.9	300
Compression-ignition engines								
Passenger cars	4	16–20	0.075–0.1	1.2–0.9	4000–5000	5–7.5	5–2.5	250
Trucks	4	16–20	0.1–0.15	1.3–0.8	2100–4000	6–9	7–4	210
Locomotive	4/2	16–18	0.15–0.4	1.1–1.3	425–1800	7–23	6–18	190
Large engines	2	10–12	0.4–1	1.2–3.0	110–400	9–17	12–50	180

Worked out Examples

1.1 The cubic capacity of a four-stroke over-square spark-ignition engine is 245 cc. The over-square ratio is 1.1. The clearance volume is 27.2 cc. Calculate the bore, stroke and compression ratio of the engine.

Solution

$$\text{Cubic capacity, } V_s = \frac{\pi}{4}d^2L = \frac{\pi}{4}\frac{d^3}{1.1} = 245$$

$$d^3 = 343$$

$$\text{Bore, } d = \mathbf{7\ cm} \qquad \Leftarrow \text{Ans}$$

$$\text{Stroke, } L = \frac{7}{1.1} = \mathbf{6.36\ cm} \qquad \Leftarrow \text{Ans}$$

$$\text{Compression ratio, } r = \frac{V_s + V_c}{V_c}$$

$$= \frac{245 + 27.2}{27.2} = \mathbf{10} \qquad \Leftarrow \text{Ans}$$

1.2 The mechanical efficiency of a single-cylinder four-stroke engine is 80%. The frictional power is estimated to be 25 kW. Calculate the indicated power (*ip*) and brake power (*bp*) developed by the engine.

Solution

$$\frac{bp}{ip} = 0.8$$

$$ip - bp = 25$$

$$ip - 0.8 \times ip = 25$$

$$\text{Indicated power, } ip = \frac{25}{0.2} = \mathbf{125\ kW} \qquad \Leftarrow \text{Ans}$$

$$\text{Brake power, } bp = ip - fp = 125 - 25 = \mathbf{100\ kW} \qquad \Leftarrow \text{Ans}$$

1.3 A 42.5 kW engine has a mechanical efficiency of 85%. Find the indicated power and frictional power. If the frictional power is assumed to be constant with load, what will be the mechanical efficiency at 60% of the load?

Solution

$$ip = \frac{bp}{\eta_m} = \frac{42.5}{0.85} = \mathbf{50\ kW} \qquad \Leftarrow \text{Ans}$$

$$\text{Frictional power, } fp = ip - bp = 50 - 42.5 = \mathbf{7.5\ kW} \quad \overset{\text{Ans}}{\Longleftarrow}$$

$$\text{Brake power at 60\% load} = 42.5 \times 0.6 = 25.5 \text{ kW}$$

$$\text{Mechanical efficiency } \eta_m = \frac{bp}{bp + fp} = \frac{25.5}{25.5 + 7.5}$$

$$= 0.773 = \mathbf{77.3\%} \quad \overset{\text{Ans}}{\Longleftarrow}$$

1.4 Find out the speed at which a four-cylinder engine using natural gas can develop a brake power of 50 kW working under following conditions. Air-gas ratio 9:1, calorific value of the fuel = 34 MJ/m^3, Compression ratio 10:1, volumetric efficiency = 70%, indicated thermal efficiency = 35% and the mechanical efficiency = 80% and the total volume of the engine is 2 litres.

Solution

$$\text{Total volume/cylinder, } V_{tot} = \frac{2000}{4} = 500 \text{ cc}$$

$$\text{Swept volume/cylinder,} V_s = \frac{9}{10} \times 500 = 450 \text{ cc}$$

$$\text{Volume of air taken in/cycle} = \eta_v \times V_s = 0.7 \times 450 = 315 \text{ cc}$$

$$\text{Volume of gas taken in/cycle} = \frac{315}{9} = 35 \text{ cc}$$

$$\text{Energy supplied/cylinder, } E = 35 \times 10^{-6} \times 34 \times 10^3$$

$$= 1.19 \text{ kJ} \qquad (1)$$

$$\text{Indicated thermal efficiency, } \eta_{ith} = \frac{bp/\eta_m}{\text{Energy supplied/cylinder/s}}$$

$$\text{Energy supplied/cylinder/s,} E_1 = \frac{50/0.8}{0.35 \times 4} = 44.64 \text{ kJ}$$

Now, energy supplied per cylinder in kJ $= \dfrac{E_1}{N/120}$

$$= \frac{44.64 \times 120}{N} = \frac{5356.8}{N} \qquad (2)$$

$$\text{Equating (1) and (2) } \frac{5356.8}{N} = 1.19$$

$$N \approx \mathbf{4500\ rpm} \quad \overset{\text{Ans}}{\Longleftarrow}$$

1.5 A four-stroke, four-cylinder diesel engine running at 2000 rpm develops 60 kW. Brake thermal efficiency is 30% and calorific value of fuel (CV)

is 42 MJ/kg. Engine has a bore of 120 mm and stroke of 100 mm. Take $\rho_a = 1.15$ kg/m^3, air-fuel ratio = 15:1 and $\eta_m = 0.8$. Calculate (i) fuel consumption (kg/s); (ii) air consumption (m^3/s); (iii) indicated thermal efficiency; (iv) volumetric efficiency; (v) brake mean effective pressure and (vi) mean piston speed

Solution

$$\text{Fuel consumption, } \dot{m}_f = \frac{bp}{\eta_{bth} \times CV} = \frac{60}{0.3 \times 42000}$$

$$= \mathbf{4.76 \times 10^{-3}\ kg/s} \qquad \text{Ans}$$

$$\text{Air consumption} = \frac{\dot{m}_f}{\rho_a}\frac{A}{F} = \frac{4.76 \times 10^{-3}}{1.15} \times 15$$

$$= \mathbf{62.09 \times 10^{-3}\ m^3/\,s} \qquad \text{Ans}$$

$$\text{Air flow rate/cylinder} = \frac{62.09 \times 10^{-3}}{4} = 15.52 \times 10^{-3}\ \text{m}^3/\text{s}$$

$$\text{Indicated power} = \frac{bp}{\eta_m} = \frac{60}{0.8} = 75\ \text{kW}$$

$$\eta_{ith} = \frac{75}{4.76 \times 10^{-3} \times 42000}$$

$$= 0.37515 = \mathbf{37.51\%} \qquad \text{Ans}$$

Volumetric efficiency =

$$\frac{\text{Actual volume flow rate of air}}{\text{Volume flow rate of air corresponding to displacement volume}} \times 100$$

$$\eta_v = \frac{15.52 \times 10^{-3}}{\frac{\pi}{4} \times 0.12^2 \times 0.10 \times \frac{2000}{2 \times 60}} \times 100$$

$$= \mathbf{82.3\%} \qquad \text{Ans}$$

Brake mean effective pressure,

$$p_{bm} = \frac{bp}{LAnK}$$

$$= \frac{60}{0.1 \times \frac{\pi}{4} \times 0.12^2 \times \frac{2000}{2 \times 60} \times 4} \times 10^3$$

$$= 7.96 \times 10^5\ \text{N/m}^2 = \mathbf{7.96\ bar} \qquad \text{Ans}$$

$$\text{Mean piston speed} = \frac{2 \times 0.1 \times 2000}{60} = 6.67\ \text{m/s} \qquad \text{Ans}$$

1.6 A single-cylinder, four-stroke hydrogen fuelled spark-ignition engine delivers a brake power of 20 kW at 6000 rpm. The air-gas ratio is 8:1 and the calorific value of fuel is 11000 kJ/m^3. The compression ratio is 8:1. If volumetric efficiency is 70%, indicated thermal efficiency is 33% and the mechanical efficiency is 90%, calculate the cubic capacity of the engine.

Solution

$$\text{Energy input} = \frac{bp/\eta_m}{\eta_{ith}} = \frac{20}{0.8 \times 0.33}$$

$$= 75.76 \text{ kJ/s}$$

$$\text{Number of power strokes/s} = \frac{N}{2 \times 60} = \frac{6000}{120} = 50$$

$$\text{Energy input/power stroke} = \frac{75.76}{50} = 1.52 \text{ kJ}$$

$$\text{Actual volume of H}_2 \times CV = 1.52$$

$$\text{Actual volume of hydrogen taken in} = \frac{1.52 \times 10^6}{11000} = 138.18 \text{ cc}$$

$$\text{Actual volume of air take in} = \frac{A}{F} \times 138.18 = 8 \times 138.18$$

$$= 1105.44 \text{ cc}$$

$$\text{Swept volume, } V_s = \frac{\text{Actual volume of air taken in}}{\eta_v}$$

$$= \frac{1105.44}{0.7} = 1579.2 \text{ cc}$$

$$\text{Cubic capacity of the engine} = V_s \times K = 1579.2 \times 1$$

$$= \mathbf{1579.2 \text{ cc}}$$ Ans ⟸

1.7 Consider two engines with the following details:

Engine I: Four-stroke, four-cylinder, SI engine, indicated power is 40 kW, mean piston speed 10 m/s.

Engine II: Two-stroke, two-cylinder, SI engine, indicated power is 10 kW.

Assume that mean effective pressure of both the engine to be same. Ratio of bore of the engine I:II = 2:1. Show that the mean piston speed of engine II is same as that of engine I.

Solution

$$ip = \frac{P_m LAnK}{60000}$$

$n = \frac{N}{2}$ *for four-stroke engine and* $n = N$ *for two-stroke engine.*

$$\text{Maximum speed, } \bar{s}_p = 2LN$$

$$\text{For engine I: } 40 = \frac{P_{mI} \times A_I \times \frac{\bar{s}_{pI}}{4} \times 4}{60000}$$

$$\text{For engine II: } 10 = \frac{P_{mII} \times A_{II} \times \frac{\bar{s}_{pII}}{2} \times 2}{60000}$$

$$\frac{40}{10} = \frac{A_I}{A_{II}} \times \frac{10}{\bar{s}_{pII}}$$

$$\bar{s}_{pII} = \frac{A_I}{A_{II}} \times \frac{10}{4} = \left(\frac{d_1}{d_2}\right)^2 \times 2.5$$

$$= \left(\frac{2}{1}\right)^2 \times 2.5 = 10 \text{ m/s}$$

$$\bar{s}_{pII} = \bar{s}_{pI} = \mathbf{10\ m/s}$$ Ans ⟸

1.8 An one-litre cubic capacity, four-stroke, four-cylinder SI engine has a brake thermal efficiency of 30% and indicated power is 40 kW at full load. At half load, it has a mechanical efficiency of 65%. Assuming constant mechanical losses, calculate: (i) brake power (ii) frictional power (iii) mechanical efficiency at full load (iv) indicated thermal efficiency. If the volume decreases by eight-fold during the compression stroke, calculate the clearance volume.

Solution

Let the brake power at full load be bp and the frictional power be fp.

$$bp + fp = 40 \text{ kW} \quad (1)$$

$$\text{At half load, } bp = 0.5 \times bp \text{ at full load}$$

$$\eta_m = 0.65 = \frac{0.5\ bp}{0.5\ bp + fp}$$

$$0.5\ bp = 0.65 \times (0.5 \times bp + fp)$$

$$= 0.325 \times bp + 0.65 \times fp$$

$$fp = \frac{0.175}{0.65} \times bp = 0.27bp \quad (2)$$

$$\text{Using (2) in (1)} \quad bp = \frac{40}{1.27} = \mathbf{31.5\ kW}$$ Ans ⟸

$$fp = 31.5 \times 0.27 = \mathbf{8.5\ kW}$$ Ans ⟸

$$\eta_m \text{ at full load} = \frac{31.5}{40} = 0.788 = \mathbf{78.8\%} \quad \stackrel{\text{Ans}}{\Longleftarrow}$$

$$\eta_{ith} = \frac{\eta_{bth}}{\eta_m} = \frac{30}{78.8} \times 100 = \mathbf{38\%} \quad \stackrel{\text{Ans}}{\Longleftarrow}$$

$$\text{Swept volume/cylinder} = \frac{1000}{4} = 250 \text{ cc}$$

$$r = \frac{V_s + V_c}{V_c} = 1 + \frac{V_s}{V_c} = 8$$

$$V_c = \frac{250}{7} = \mathbf{35.71 \ cc} \quad \stackrel{\text{Ans}}{\Longleftarrow}$$

1.9 A four-stroke petrol engine at full load delivers 50 kW. It requires 8.5 kW to rotate it without load at the same speed. Find its mechanical efficiency at full load, half load and quarter load?

Also find out the volume of the fuel consumed per second at full load if the brake thermal efficiency is 25%, given that calorific value of the fuel = 42 MJ/kg and specific gravity of petrol is 0.75. Estimate the indicated thermal efficiency.

Solution

Mechanical efficiency at full load $= \dfrac{bp}{bp + fp}$

$$= \frac{50}{50 + 8.5} = 0.8547 = \mathbf{85.47\%} \quad \stackrel{\text{Ans}}{\Longleftarrow}$$

Mechanical efficiency at half load

$$= \frac{25}{25 + 8.5} = 0.7462 = \mathbf{74.62\%} \quad \stackrel{\text{Ans}}{\Longleftarrow}$$

Mechanical efficiency at quarter load

$$= \frac{12.5}{12.5 + 8.5} = 0.5952 = \mathbf{59.52\%} \quad \stackrel{\text{Ans}}{\Longleftarrow}$$

$$\dot{m}_f = \frac{bp}{\eta_{bth} \times CV} = \frac{50}{0.25 \times 42000}$$

$$= 4.76 \times 10^{-3} \text{ kg/s}$$

$$\text{Volume flow rate of fuel} = \frac{4.76 \times 10^{-3}}{750} = \mathbf{6.34 \times 10^{-6} \ m^3/s} \quad \stackrel{\text{Ans}}{\Longleftarrow}$$

Indicated thermal efficiency at full load

$$\eta_{ith} = \frac{\eta_{bth}}{\eta_m} = \frac{0.25}{0.8547} = 0.2925$$

$$= \mathbf{29.25\%} \quad \stackrel{\text{Ans}}{\Longleftarrow}$$

1.10 The indicated thermal efficiency of four-stroke engine is 32% and its mechanical efficiency is 78%. The fuel consumption rate is 20 kg/h running at a fixed speed. The brake mean pressure developed is 6 bar and the mean piston speed is 12 m/s. Assuming it to be a single cylinder square engine, calculate the crank radius and the speed of the engine. Take $CV = 42000$ kJ/kg.

Solution

$$\text{Brake thermal efficiency, } \eta_{bth} = \eta_{ith} \times \eta_m = 0.32 \times 0.78$$

$$= 0.2496 = 24.96\%$$

$$\text{Rate of energy input from fuel} = \frac{20}{3600} \times 42000 = 233.33 \text{ kW}$$

$$\text{Brake power, } bp = \eta_{bth} \times 233.33$$

$$= 0.2496 \times 233.33 = 58.24 \text{ kW}$$

Since it is a square engine, $d = L$.

$$p_{bm} = \frac{bp \times 60000}{LAnK}$$

$$= \frac{58.24 \times 60000}{\frac{\pi}{4}L^3 \times n \times 1} = 6 \times 10^5$$

$$L^3 n = 7.415 \qquad (1)$$

Note L is in m and N in per minute. Now,

$$\bar{s}_p = 12 = \frac{2LN}{60}$$

$$LN = 360 \qquad (2)$$

Dividing (1) by (2), gives,

$$L^2 \frac{n}{N} = 0.0206$$

For a four-stroke engine $n/N = \frac{1}{2}$.

$$L = \sqrt{0.0206 \times 2} = 0.203 \text{ m}$$

$$= 203 \text{ mm}$$

$$\text{Crank radius} = \frac{203}{2} = 101.5 \text{ mm}$$

$$\text{Speed, } N = \frac{360}{L} = \frac{360}{0.203}$$

$$= \mathbf{1773.4 \text{ rpm}}$$

Ans ⟸

Review Questions

1.1 Define the following : (i) engine and (ii) heat engine.

1.2 How are heat engines classified?

1.3 Explain the basic difference in their work principle?

1.4 Give examples of EC and IC engines.

1.5 Compare EC and IC engines.

1.6 What are the important basic components of an IC engine? Explain them briefly.

1.7 Draw the cross-section of a single cylinder spark-ignition engine and mark the important parts.

1.8 Define the following :

(i)	*bore*	*(iv)*	*clearance volume*
(ii)	*stroke*	*(v)*	*compression ratio*
(iii)	*displacement volume*	*(vi)*	*cubic capacity*

Mention the units in which they are normally measured.

1.9 What is meant by TDC and BDC? In a suitable sketch mark the two dead centres.

1.10 What is meant by cylinder row and cylinder bank?

1.11 With neat sketches explain the working principle of four-stroke spark-ignition engine.

1.12 Classify the internal combustion engine with respect to

(i)	*cycle of operation*	*(iv)*	*type of ignition*
(ii)	*cylinder arrangements*	*(v)*	*type of fuels used*
(iii)	*method of charging the cylinder*	*(vi)*	*type of cooling*

1.13 In what respects four-stroke cycle CI engine differ from that of an SI engine?

1.14 What is the main reason for the development of two-stroke engines and what are the two main types of two-stroke engines?

1.15 Describe with a neat sketch the working principle of a crankcase scavenged two-stroke engine.

1.16 Draw the ideal and actual indicator diagrams of a two-stroke SI engine. How are they different from that of a four-stroke cycle engine?

1.17 Compare four-stroke and two-stroke cycle engines. Bring out clearly their relative merits and demerits.

1.18 Discuss in detail the application of various types of IC engines.

1.19 Give an account of the first law analysis of an internal combustion engine.

1.20 Compare SI and CI engines with respect to

(i)	*basic cycle*	*(v)*	*compression ratio*
(ii)	*fuel used*	*(vi)*	*speed*
(iii)	*introduction of fuel*	*(vii)*	*efficiency*
(iv)	*ignition*	*(viii)*	*weight*

1.21 Show by means of a diagram the energy flow in a reciprocating IC engine.

1.22 What is meant by mean piston speed? Explain its importance.

1.23 Discuss briefly the design performance data of SI and CI engines.

1.24 Define the following efficiencies :

(i)	*indicated thermal efficiency*	*(iv) relative efficiency*
(ii)	*brake thermal efficiency*	*(v) volumetric efficiency*
(iii)	*mechanical efficiency*	

1.25 Explain briefly

(i)	*mean effective pressure*	*(iv)*	*fuel-air ratio*
(ii)	*specific output*	*(v)*	*heating value of the fuel*
(iii)	*specific fuel consumption*	*(vi)*	*inlet valve Mach index*

Exercise

1.1 A diesel engine has a brake thermal efficiency of 30 per cent. If the calorific value of the fuel is 42000 kJ/kg. Find its brake specific fuel consumption. *Ans:* 0.2857 kg/kW h

1.2 A gas engine having a cylinder 250 mm bore and 450 mm stroke has a volumetric efficiency of 80%. Air-gas ratio equals 9:1, calorific value of fuel 21000 kJ per m^3 at NTP. Calculate the heat supplied to the engine per working cycle. If the compression ratio is 5:1, what is the heat value of the mixture per working stroke per m^3 of total cylinder volume? *Ans:* (i) 36.08 kJ (ii) 1306.8 kJ/m^3

1.3 A certain engine at full load delivers a brake power of 36.8 kW at certain speed. It requires 7.36 kW to overcome the friction and to rotate the engine without load at the same speed. Calculate its mechanical efficiency. Assuming that the mechanical losses remain constant, what will be the mechanical efficiency at half load and quarter load. *Ans:* (i)83.33% (ii) 71.42% (iii) 55.55%

1.4 An engine develops a brake power of 3.68 kW. Its indicated thermal efficiency is 30%, mechanical efficiency is 80%, calorific value of the fuel is 42 MJ/kg and its specific gravity = 0.875. Calculate (i) the fuel consumption of the engine in (a) kg/h (b) litres/h (ii) indicated specific fuel consumption and (iii) brake specific fuel consumption. *Ans:* (i) (a)1.31 kg/h (b)1.5017 l/h (ii) 0.2856 kg/kW h (iii) 0.3571 kg/kW h

1.5 A two-stroke CI engine develops a brake power of 368 kW while its frictional power is 73.6 kW. Its fuel consumption is 180 kg/h and works with an air-fuel ratio of 20:1. The heating value of the fuel is 42000 kJ/kg. Calculate (i) indicated power (ii) mechanical efficiency (iii) air consumption per hour (iv) indicated thermal efficiency and (v) brake thermal efficiency.
Ans: (i) 441.6 kW (ii) 83.3% (iii) 3600 kg/h (iv) 21% (v) 17.5%

1.6 Compute the brake mean effective pressure of a four-cylinder, four-stroke diesel engine having 150 mm bore and 200 mm stroke which develops a brake power of 73.6 kW at 1200 rpm. *Ans:* 5.206 bar

1.7 Compute the *bmep* of a four-cylinder, two-stroke engine, 100 mm bore 125 mm stroke when it develops a torque of 490 Nm. *Ans:* 7.84 bar

1.8 Find the brake thermal efficiency of an engine which consumes 7 kg of fuel in 20 minutes and develops a brake power of 65 kW. The fuel has a heating value of 42000 kJ/kg. *Ans:* 26.53%

1.9 Find the mean piston speed of a diesel engine running at 1500 rpm. The engine has a 100 mm bore and L/d ratio is 1.5. *Ans:* 7.5 m/s

1.10 An engine is using 5.2 kg of air per minute while operating at 1200 rpm. The engine requires 0.2256 kg of fuel per hour to produce an indicated power of 1 kW. The air-fuel ratio is 15:1. Indicated thermal efficiency is 38% and mechanical efficiency is 80%. Calculate (i) brake power and (ii) heating value of the fuel. *Ans:* (i) 73.7 kW (ii) 41992.89 kJ/kg

1.11 A four-cylinder, four-stroke, spark-ignition engine has a bore of 80 mm and stroke of 80 mm. The compression ratio is 8. Calculate the cubic capacity of the engine and the clearance volume of each cylinder. What type of engine is this?
Ans: (i) 1608.4 cc (ii) 57.4 cc (iii) Square engine

1.12 A four-stroke, compression-ignition engine with four cylinders develops an indicated power of 125 kW and delivers a brake power of 100 kW. Calculate (i) frictional power (ii) mechanical efficiency of the engine.
Ans: (i) 25 kW (ii) 80%

1.13 An engine with 80 per cent mechanical efficiency develops a brake power of 30 kW. Find its indicated power and frictional power. If frictional power is assumed to be constant, what will be the mechanical efficiency at half load. *Ans:* (i) 37.5 kW (ii) 7.5 kW (iii) 66.7%

1.14 A single-cylinder, compression-ignition engine with a brake thermal efficiency of 30% uses high speed diesel oil having a calorific value of 42000 kJ/kg. If its mechanical efficiency is 80 per cent, calculate (i) *bsfc* in kg/kW h (ii) *isfc* in kg/kW h
Ans: (i) 0.286 kg/kW h (ii) 0.229 kg/kW h

1.15 A petrol engine uses a fuel of calorific value of 42000 kJ/kg and has a specific gravity of 0.75. The brake thermal efficiency is 24 per cent and mechanical efficiency is 80 per cent. If the engine develops a brake power of 29.44 kW, calculate (i) volume of the fuel consumed per second (ii) indicated thermal efficiency *Ans:* (i) 2.92×10^{-3} kg/s (ii) 30%

1.16 A single-cylinder, four-stroke diesel engine having a displacement volume of 790 cc is tested at 300 rpm. When a braking torque of 49 Nm is applied, analysis of the indicator diagram gives a mean effective pressure of 980 kPa. Calculate the brake power and mechanical efficiency of the engine. *Ans:* (i) 1.54 kW (ii) 79.4%

1.17 A four-stroke SI engine delivers a brake power of 441.6 kW with a mechanical efficiency of 85 per cent. The measured fuel consumption is 160 kg of fuel in one hour and air consumption is 410 kg during one sixth of an hour. The heating value of the fuel is 42000 kJ/kg. Calculate (i) indicated power (ii) frictional power (iii) air-fuel ratio (iv) indicated thermal efficiency (v) brake thermal efficiency.
Ans: (i) 519.5 kW (ii) 77.9 kW (iii) 15.5 (iv) 28.1% (v) 23.9%

1.18 A two-stroke CI engine develops a brake power of 368 kW while 73.6 kW is used to overcome the friction losses. It consumes 180 kg/h of fuel at an air-fuel ratio of 20:1. The heating value of the fuel is 42000 kJ/kg. Calculate (i) indicated power (ii) mechanical efficiency; (iii) Air consumption (iv) indicated thermal efficiency (v) brake thermal efficiency.
Ans: (i) 441.6 kW (ii) 83.3% (iii) 1 kg/s (iv) 21% (v) 17.5%

1.19 A four-stroke petrol engine delivers a brake power of 36.8 kW with a mechanical efficiency of 80%. The air-fuel ratio is 15:1 and the fuel consumption is 0.4068 kg/kW h. The heating value of the fuel is 42000 kJ/kg. Calculate (i) indicated power (ii) frictional power(iii) brake thermal efficiency (iv) indicated thermal efficiency (v) total fuel consumption (vi) air consumption/second.
Ans: (i) 46 kW (ii) 9.2 kW (iii) 21% (iv) 26.25%
(v) 0.0042 kg/s (vi) 0.063 kg/s.

1.20 A spark-ignition engine has a fuel-air ratio of 0.067. How many kg of air per hour is required for a brake power output of 73.6 kW at an overall brake thermal efficiency of 20%? How many m^3 of air is required per hour if the density of air is 1.15 kg/m^3. If the fuel vapour has a density four times that of air, how many m^3 per hour of the mixture is required? The calorific value of the fuel is given as 42000 kJ/kg.
Ans: (i) 470.75 kg/h (ii) 409.35 m^3/h (iii) 416.21 m^3/h

1.21 A four-stroke CI engine having a cylinder diameter of 39 cm and stroke of 28 cm has a mechanical efficiency of 80%. Assume the frictional power as 80 kW. Its fuel consumption is 86 kg/h with an air-fuel ratio of 18:1. The speed of the engine is 2000 rpm. Calculate (i) indicated power (ii) if η_{ith} is 40%, calculate the calorific value of the fuel used (iii) p_{im} (iv) $\dot{m}_a$/hour (v) $\overline{s}_p$. *Ans:* (i) 400 kW (ii) 41860 kJ (iii) 12.13 bar
(iv) 1548 kg/h (v) 18.7 m/s

1.22 A four-stroke LPG engine having a cylinder 250 mm diameter and stroke of 300 mm has a volumetric efficiency of 70% at atmospheric conditions. Gas to air ratio is 8:1. Calorific value of the fuel is 100 MJ/m^3 at atmospheric conditions. Find the heat supplied to the engine per working cycle. If the compression ratio is 10, what is the heat value of the mixture per working stroke per m^3 of the total cylinder volume?
Ans: (i) 128.8 kJ (ii) 7.8 MJ

1.23 A four-cylinder spark-ignition engine has the following dimensions: bore = 680 mm and a crank radius = 375 mm. If the compression ratio is 8:1, determine the (i) stroke length (ii) swept volume (iii) cubic capacity (iv) clearance volume and (v) total volume. If the volumetric efficiency is 80% determine the (vi) actual volume of air aspirated/stroke in each cylinder? *Ans:* (i) 750 mm (ii) 1.088 m^3 (iii) 0.272 m^3 (iv) 0.039 m^3 (v) 0.0311 m^3 (vi) 0.2176 m^3

1.24 An engine with an indicated thermal efficiency of 25% and mechanical efficiency of 75% consumes 25 kg/h of fuel at a fixed speed. The brake mean effective pressure is 5 bar and the mean piston speed is 15 m/s. Assuming it is a single cylinder square engine determine the crank radius and the speed in rpm. Take CV of the fuel = 42 MJ/kg.
Ans: (i) 68.2 mm (ii) 3300 rpm

1.25 A four-cylinder SI engine running at 1200 rpm gives 18.87 kW as brake power. When one cylinder missed firing the average torque was 100 Nm. Calculate the indicated thermal efficiency if the CV of fuel is 42 MJ/kg. The engine uses 0.335 kg of fuel per kW/h. What is the mechanical efficiency of the engine? *Ans:* (i) 34.2% (ii) 74.9%

1.26 A certain engine with a bore of 250 mm has an indicated thermal efficiency of 30%. The $bsfc$ and specific power output are 0.35 kg/kW h and 90 kW/m^2. Find the mechanical efficiency and brake thermal efficiency of the engine. Take the calorific value of the fuel as 42 MJ/kg.
Ans: (i) 81.7% (ii) 24.5%

1.27 A single-cylinder, four-stroke engine having a cubic capacity of 0.7 litre was tested at 200 rpm. From the indicator diagram the mean effective pressure was found to be 10^6 N/m^2 and the mechanical efficiency is 75%. Find the frictional power of the engine if the engine is an over-square engine with a over-square ratio of 0.8. Calculate the bore and stroke.
Ans: (i) 0.29 kW (ii) 41.5 mm (iii) 89.34 mm (iv) 111.68 mm

1.28 In a performance test on a four-stroke engine, the indicator diagram area was found to be 5×10^{-4} m^2 and the length of the indicator diagram was 0.05 m. If the y-axis has a scale of 1 m = 50 MPa, find the $imep$ of the engine given that bore = 150 mm, stroke = 200 mm. The measured engine speed was 1200 rpm. Also calculate the ip and $isfc$ of the engine if the fuel injected per cycle is 0.5 cc with the specific gravity of 0.8.
Ans: (i) 5 bar (ii) 70.68 kW (iii) 203 g/kW h

1.29 A four-stroke, four-cylinder automotive engine develops 150 Nm brake torque at 3000 rpm. Assuming *bmep* to be 0.925 bar, find (i) brake power (ii)displacement volume (iii) stroke (iv) bore. Take $\bar{s}_p = 12$ m/s.
Ans: (i) 47.124 kW (ii) 5.1 $\times 10^{-3}$ m^3 (iii) 120 mm (iv) 233 mm

1.30 A single-cylinder, four-stroke, engine has a $bsfc$ of 1.13×10^{-5} kg/kW h and a fuel consumption rate of 0.4068 kg/h. The specific power output of the engine is 0.33 kW/cm^2. If the engine runs at 3000 rpm find the displacement volume of the cylinder and if the $\bar{s}_p$ is 15 m/s, find the *bmep*. *Ans:* (i) 900 cc (ii) 4.44 bar

Multiple Choice Questions (choose the most appropriate answer)

1. Advantage of reciprocating IC engines over steam turbine is
   (a) mechanical simplicity
   (b) improved plant efficiency
   (c) lower average temperature
   (d) all of the above

2. The intake charge in a diesel engine consists of
   (a) air alone
   (b) air + lubricating oil
   (c) air + fuel
   (d) air + fuel + lubricating oil

3. Disadvantages of reciprocating IC engine are
   (a) vibration
   (b) use of fossil fuels
   (c) balancing problems
   (d) all of the above

4. Gudgeon pin forms the link between
   (a) piston and big end of connecting rod
   (b) piston and small end of connecting rod
   (c) connecting rod and crank
   (d) big end and small end

5. Engines of different cylinder dimensions, power and speed are compared on the basis of
   (a) maximum pressure
   (b) fuel consumption

(c) mean effective pressure
(d) unit power

6. In a four-stroke IC engine cam shaft rotates at

(a) same speed as crankshaft
(b) twice the speed of crankshaft
(c) half the speed of crankshaft
(d) none of the above

7. Thermal efficiency of CI engine is higher than that of SI engine due to

(a) fuel used
(b) higher compression ratio
(c) constant pressure heat addition
(d) none of the above

8. SI engines are of

(a) light weight
(b) high speed
(c) homogeneous charge of fuel and oil
(d) all of the above

9. Compression ratio in diesel engines is of the order of

(a) 5–7
(b) 7–10
(c) 10–12
(d) 14–20

10. Main advantage of a two-stroke engine over four-stroke engine is

(a) more uniform torque on the crankshaft
(b) more power output for the cylinder of same dimensions
(c) absence of valves
(d) all of the above

11. Engines used for ships are normally

(a) four-stroke SI engines of very high power
(b) two-stroke CI engines of very high power
(c) four-stroke CI engines of high speed
(d) two-stroke SI engines of high power

12. An IC engine gives an output of 3 kW when the input is 10,000 J/s. The thermal efficiency of the engine is

    (a) 33.3%
    (b) 30%
    (c) 60%
    (d) 66.6%

13. In a reciprocating engine with a cylinder diameter of D and stroke of L, the cylinder volume is

    (a) $\frac{\pi}{4}D^2L\times$ clearance volume
    (b) $\frac{\pi}{4}D^2L-$ clearance volume
    (c) $\frac{\pi}{4}D^2L+$ clearance volume
    (d) $\frac{\pi}{4}D^2L\div$ clearance volume

14. If L is the stroke and N is the rpm, mean piston speed of two-stroke engine is

    (a) LN
    (b) $\frac{LN}{2}$
    (c) $2LN$
    (d) none of the above

15. Equivalence ratio is

    (a) $\frac{\text{actual fuel/air ratio}}{\text{stoichiometric fuel/air ratio}}$
    (b) $\frac{\text{stoichiometric fuel/air ratio}}{\text{actual fuel/air ratio}}$
    (c) $\frac{\text{stoichiometric fuel/air ratio}}{\text{actual air/fuel ratio}}$
    (d) $\frac{\text{actual air/fuel ratio}}{\text{stoichiometric fuel/air ratio}}$

16. The volumetric efficiency of the SI engine is comparatively

    (a) lower than CI engine
    (b) higher than CI engine
    (c) will be same as CI engine
    (d) none of the above

17. The range of volumetric efficiency of a diesel engine is

    (a) 65 – 75%
    (b) 75 – 85%

(c) 85 – 90%
(d) 90 – 95%

18. Relative efficiency is the ratio of

(a) $\dfrac{\text{actual thermal efficiency}}{\text{mechanical efficiency}}$

(b) $\dfrac{\text{actual thermal efficiency}}{\text{airstandard efficiency}}$

(c) $\dfrac{\text{airstandard efficiency}}{\text{actual thermal efficiency}}$

(d) $\dfrac{\text{mechanical efficiency}}{\text{actual thermal efficiency}}$

19. Brake specific fuel consumption is defined as

(a) fuel consumption per hour
(b) fuel consumption per km
(c) fuel consumption per bp
(d) fuel consumption per brake power hour

20. Engine can be fired with

(a) solid fuel
(b) liquid fuel
(c) gaseous fuel
(d) any of the above fuels

21. Frictional power is given by

(a) $fp = ip + bp$
(b) $fp = ip/bp$
(c) $fp = ip \times bp$
(d) $fp = ip - bp$

22. Specific power of an IC engine is given by

(a) $p_s = ip/A$
(b) $p_s = ip/V$
(c) $p_s = bp/A$
(d) $p_s = bp/V$

23. Carburetor is mainly employed

(a) SI engine
(b) CI engine

(c) gas engine
(d) none of the above

24. In a four-stroke SI engine during suction

(a) only air is sucked
(b) only fuel is sucked
(c) fuel-air mixture is sucked
(d) none of the above

25. Inlet valve Mach index usually relates

(a) mechanical efficiency
(b) volumetric efficiency
(c) brake thermal efficiency
(d) relative efficiency

Ans:	1. – (d)	2. – (a)	3. – (d)	4. – (b)	5. – (c)
	6. – (c)	7. – (b)	8. – (d)	9. – (d)	10. – (d)
	11. – (b)	12. – (b)	13. – (c)	14. – (c)	15. – (b)
	16. – (a)	17. – (c)	18. – (b)	19. – (d)	20. – (d)
	21. – (d)	22. – (c)	23. – (a)	24. – (c)	25. – (b)

2

AIR-STANDARD CYCLES AND THEIR ANALYSIS

2.1 INTRODUCTION

The operating cycle of an internal combustion engine can be broken down into a sequence of separate processes viz., intake, compression, combustion, expansion and exhaust. The internal combustion engine does not operate on a thermodynamic cycle as it involves an open system i.e., the working fluid enters the system at one set of conditions and leaves at another. However, it is often possible to analyze the open cycle as though it were a closed one by imagining one or more processes that would bring the working fluid at the exit conditions back to the condition of the starting point.

The accurate analysis of internal combustion engine processes is very complicated. In order to understand them it is advantageous to analyze the performance of an idealized closed cycle that closely approximates the real cycle. One such approach is the air-standard cycle, which is based on the following assumptions:

(i) The working medium is assumed to be a perfect gas and follows the relation $pV = mRT$ or $p = \rho RT$.

(ii) There is no change in the mass of the working medium.

(iii) All the processes that constitute the cycle are reversible.

(iv) Heat is assumed to be supplied from a constant high temperature source and not from chemical reactions during the cycle.

(v) Some heat is assumed to be rejected to a constant low temperature sink during the cycle.

(vi) It is assumed that there are no heat losses from the system to the surroundings.

(vii) The working medium has constant specific heats throughout the cycle.

(viii) The physical constants viz., C_p, C_v, γ and M of working medium are the same as those of air at standard atmospheric conditions. For example in SI units,

$$C_p = 1.005 \text{ kJ/kg K} \qquad M = 29 \text{ kg/kmol}$$
$$C_v = 0.717 \text{ kJ/kg K} \qquad \gamma = 1.4$$

Due to these assumptions, the analysis becomes over-simplified and the results do not agree with those of the actual engine. Work output, peak pressure, peak temperature and thermal efficiency based on air-standard cycles will be the maximum that can be attained and will differ considerably from those of the actual engine. It is often used, mainly because of the simplicity in getting approximate answers to the complicated processes in internal combustion engines.

In this chapter, we will review the various cycles and also derive the equations for work output, mean effective pressure, efficiency etc. Also, comparison will be made between Otto, Dual and Diesel cycles to see which cycle is more efficient under a set of given operating conditions.

2.2 THE CARNOT CYCLE

Sadi Carnot, a French engineer, proposed a reversible cycle in 1824, in which the working medium receives heat at a higher temperature and rejects heat at a lower temperature. The cycle will consist of two isothermal and two reversible adiabatic processes as shown in Fig.2.1. Carnot cycle is represented as a standard of perfection and engines can be compared with it to judge the degree of perfection. It gives the concept of maximizing work output between two temperature limits.

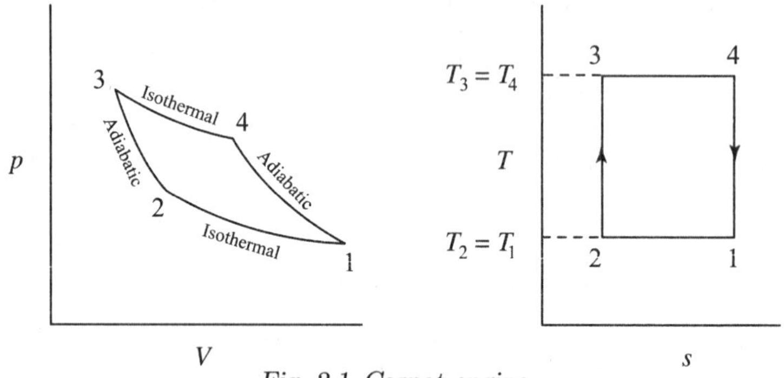

Fig. 2.1 Carnot engine

The working of an engine based on the Carnot cycle can be explained referring to Fig.2.2 which shows a cylinder and piston arrangement working without friction. The walls of cylinder are assumed to be perfect insulators. The cylinder head is so arranged that it can be a perfect heat conductor as well as a perfect heat insulator.

First the heat is transferred from a high temperature source, (T_3), to the working medium in the cylinder and as a result the working medium expands. This is represented by the isothermal process 3→4 in Fig.2.1. Now the cylinder head is sealed and it acts as a perfect insulator. The working medium in the cylinder is now allowed to expand further from state 4 to

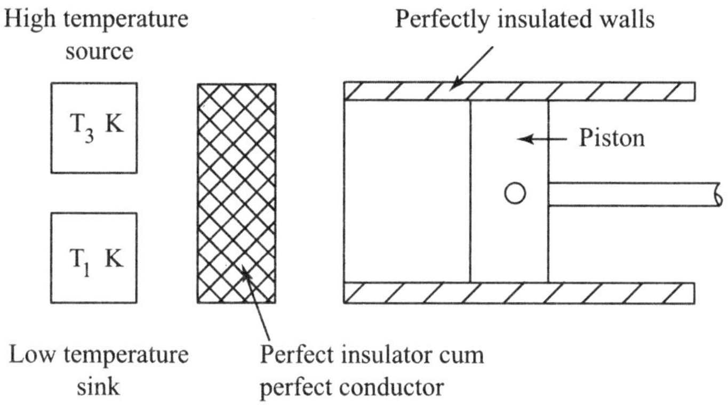

Fig. 2.2 Working principle of a Carnot engine

state 1 and is represented by reversible adiabatic process 4→1 in p-V and T-s diagrams in Fig.2.1. Now the system is brought into contact with a constant low temperature sink, (T_1), as the cylinder head is now made to act as a perfect heat conductor. Some heat is rejected to the sink without altering the temperature of sink and as a result the working medium is compressed from state 1 to 2 which is represented by isothermal line 1→2. Finally the cylinder head is made again to act as a perfect insulator and the working medium is compressed adiabatically from state 2 to 3 which is represented by process 2→3. Thus the cycle is completed.

Analyzing the cycle thermodynamically the efficiency of the cycle can be written as

$$\eta_{Carnot} = \frac{\text{Work done by the system during the cycle } (W)}{\text{Heat supplied to the system during the cycle } (Q_S)}$$

According to the first law of thermodynamics,

$$\text{Work done} = \text{Heat supplied} - \text{Heat rejected}$$

$$W = Q_S - Q_R \tag{2.1}$$

Considering the isothermal processes 1→2 and 3→4, we get

$$Q_R = mRT_1 \log_e \frac{V_1}{V_2} \tag{2.2}$$

$$Q_S = mRT_3 \log_e \frac{V_4}{V_3} \tag{2.3}$$

Considering adiabatic processes 2→3 and 4→1

$$\frac{V_3}{V_2} = \left(\frac{T_2}{T_3}\right)^{\left(\frac{1}{\gamma-1}\right)} \tag{2.4}$$

and

$$\frac{V_4}{V_1} = \left(\frac{T_1}{T_4}\right)^{\left(\frac{1}{\gamma-1}\right)} \tag{2.5}$$

Since $T_1 = T_2$ and $T_4 = T_3$ we have,

$$\frac{V_4}{V_1} = \frac{V_3}{V_2}$$

or

$$\frac{V_4}{V_3} = \frac{V_1}{V_2} = r \quad (say) \tag{2.6}$$

then,

$$\eta_{Carnot} = \frac{mRT_3 \log_e r - mRT_1 \log_e r}{mRT_3 \log_e r} \tag{2.7}$$

$$= \frac{T_3 - T_1}{T_3} = 1 - \frac{T_1}{T_3} \tag{2.8}$$

The lower temperature i.e., sink temperature, T_1, is normally the atmospheric temperature or the cooling water temperature and hence fixed. So the increase in thermal efficiency can be achieved only by increasing the source temperature. In other words, the upper temperature is required to be maintained as high as possible, to achieve maximum thermal efficiency. Between two fixed temperatures Carnot cycle (and other reversible cycles) has the maximum possible efficiency compared to other air-standard cycles. In spite of this advantage, Carnot cycle does not provide a suitable basis for the operation of an engine using a gaseous working fluid because the work output from this cycle will be quite low.

Mean effective pressure, p_m, is defined as that hypothetical constant pressure acting on the piston during its expansion stroke producing the same work output as that from the actual cycle. Mathematically,

$$p_m = \frac{\text{Work Output}}{\text{Swept Volume}} \tag{2.9}$$

It can be shown as

$$p_m = \frac{\text{Area of indicator diagram}}{\text{Length of diagram}} \times \text{constant} \tag{2.10}$$

The constant depends on the mechanism used to get the indicator diagram and has the units, bar/m. These formulae are quite often used to calculate the performance of an internal combustion engine. If the work output is the indicated output then it is called indicated mean effective pressure, p_{im}, and if the work output is the brake output then it is called brake mean effective pressure, p_{bm}.

2.3 THE STIRLING CYCLE

The Carnot cycle has a low mean effective pressure because of its very low work output. Hence, one of the modified forms of the cycle to produce higher mean effective pressure whilst theoretically achieving full Carnot cycle efficiency is the Stirling cycle. It consists of two isothermal and two constant volume processes. The heat rejection and addition take place at constant temperature. The p-V and T-s diagrams for the Stirling cycle are shown in Figs.2.3(a) and 2.3(b) respectively. It is clear from Fig.2.3(b) that the amount of heat addition

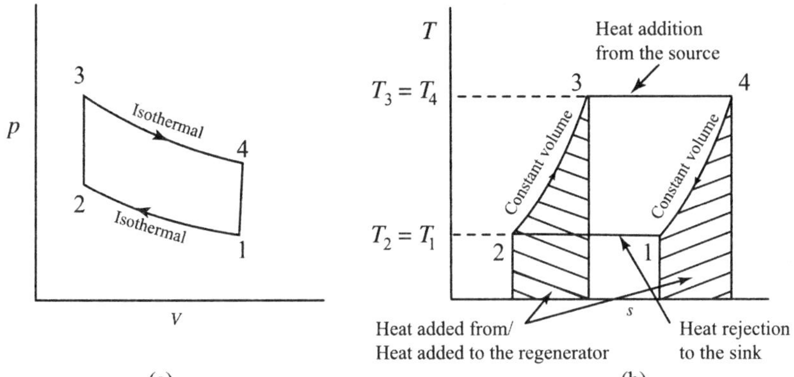

Fig. 2.3 Stirling cycle

and rejection during constant volume processes is same. Hence, the efficiency of the cycle is given as

$$\eta_{Stirling} = \frac{RT_3 \log_e\left(\frac{V_4}{V_3}\right) - RT_1 \log_e\left(\frac{V_1}{V_2}\right)}{RT_3 \log_e\left(\frac{V_4}{V_3}\right)} \tag{2.11}$$

But $V_3 = V_2$ and $V_4 = V_1$

$$\eta_{Stirling} = \frac{T_3 - T_1}{T_3} \tag{2.12}$$

same as Carnot efficiency

The Stirling cycle was used earlier for hot air engines and became obsolete as Otto and Diesel cycles came into use. The design of Stirling engine involves a major difficulty in the design and construction of heat exchanger to operate continuously at very high temperatures. However, with the development in metallurgy and intensive research in this type of engine, the Stirling engine has staged a comeback in practical appearance. In practice, the heat exchanger efficiency cannot be 100%. Hence the Stirling cycle efficiency will be less than Carnot efficiency and can be written as

$$\eta = \frac{R(T_3 - T_1)\log_e r}{RT_3 \log_e r + (1-\epsilon)C_v(T_3 - T_1)} \tag{2.13}$$

where ϵ is the heat exchanger effectiveness.

2.4 THE ERICSSON CYCLE

The Ericsson cycle consists of two isothermal and two constant pressure processes. The heat addition and rejection take place at constant pressure as well as isothermal processes. Since the process 2→3 and 3→4 are parallel to each other on the T-s diagram, the net effect is that the heat need be added only at constant temperature $T_3 = T_4$ and rejected at the constant temperature $T_1 = T_2$.

The cycle is shown on p-V and T-s diagrams in Fig.2.4(a) and 2.4(b) respectively. The advantage of the Ericsson cycle over the Carnot and Stirling cycles is its smaller pressure ratio for a given ratio of maximum to minimum specific volume with higher mean effective pressure.

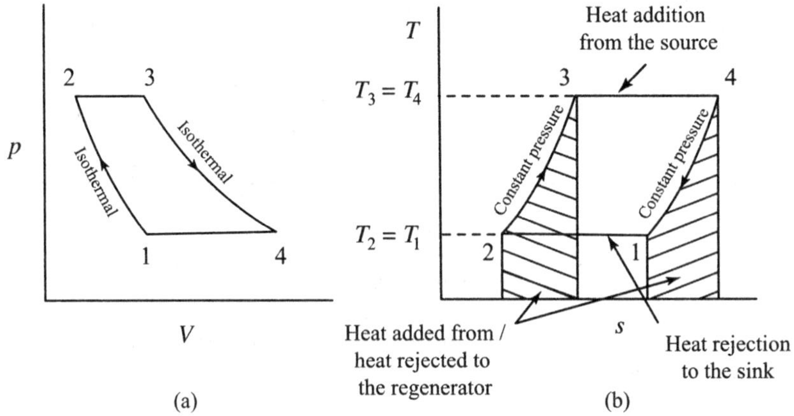

Fig. 2.4 Ericsson cycle

The Ericsson cycle does not find practical application in piston engines but is approached by a gas turbine employing a large number of stages with heat exchangers, insulators and reheaters.

2.5 THE OTTO CYCLE

The main drawback of the Carnot cycle is its impracticability due to high pressure and high volume ratios employed with comparatively low mean effective pressure. Nicolaus Otto (1876), proposed a constant-volume heat addition cycle which forms the basis for the working of today's spark-ignition engines. The cycle is shown on p-V and T-s diagrams in Fig.2.5(a) and 2.5(b) respectively.

When the engine is working on full throttle, the processes 0→1 and 1→0 on the p-V diagram represents suction and exhaust processes and their effect is nullified. The process 1→2 represents isentropic compression of the air when the piston moves from bottom dead centre to top dead centre. During the process 2→3 heat is supplied reversibly at constant volume. This process corresponds to spark-ignition and combustion in the actual engine. The processes 3→4 and 4→1 represent isentropic expansion and constant volume heat rejection respectively.

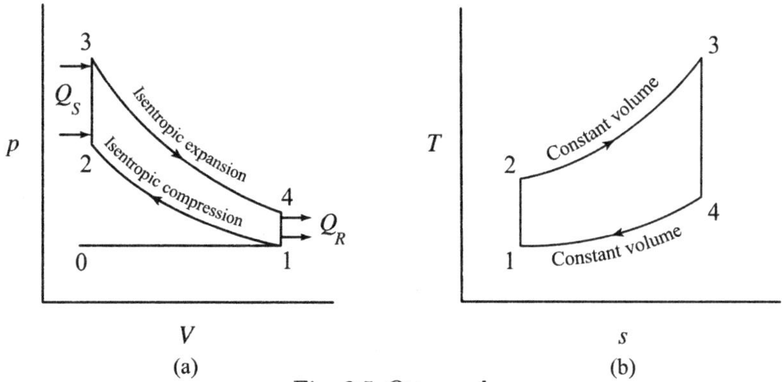

Fig. 2.5 Otto cycle

2.5.1 Thermal Efficiency

The thermal efficiency of Otto cycle can be written as

$$\eta_{Otto} = \frac{Q_S - Q_R}{Q_S} \tag{2.14}$$

Considering constant volume processes 2→3 and 4→1, the heat supplied and rejected of air can be written as

$$Q_S = mC_v(T_3 - T_2) \tag{2.15}$$

$$Q_R = mC_v(T_4 - T_1) \tag{2.16}$$

$$\eta_{Otto} = \frac{m(T_3 - T_2) - m(T_4 - T_1)}{m(T_3 - T_2)}$$

$$= 1 - \frac{T_4 - T_1}{T_3 - T_2} \tag{2.17}$$

Considering isentropic processes 1→2 and 3→4, we have

$$\frac{T_2}{T_1} = \left(\frac{V_1}{V_2}\right)^{(\gamma-1)} \tag{2.18}$$

and

$$\frac{T_3}{T_4} = \left(\frac{V_4}{V_3}\right)^{(\gamma-1)} \tag{2.19}$$

But the volume ratios V_1/V_2 and V_4/V_3 are equal to the compression ratio, r. Therefore,

$$\frac{V_1}{V_2} = \frac{V_4}{V_3} = r \tag{2.20}$$

therefore,

$$\frac{T_2}{T_1} = \frac{T_3}{T_4} \tag{2.21}$$

From Eq.2.21, it can be easily shown that

$$\frac{T_4}{T_3} = \frac{T_1}{T_2} = \frac{T_4 - T_1}{T_3 - T_2} \tag{2.22}$$

$$\eta_{Otto} = 1 - \frac{T_1}{T_2} \tag{2.23}$$

$$= 1 - \frac{1}{\left(\frac{V_1}{V_2}\right)^{(\gamma-1)}} \tag{2.24}$$

$$= 1 - \frac{1}{r^{(\gamma-1)}} \tag{2.25}$$

Note that the thermal efficiency of Otto cycle is a function of compression ratio r and the ratio of specific heats, γ. As γ is assumed to be a constant for any working fluid, the efficiency is increased by increasing the compression ratio. Further, the efficiency is independent of heat supplied and pressure ratio. The use of gases with higher γ values would increase efficiency of Otto cycle. Fig.2.6 shows the effect of γ and r on the efficiency.

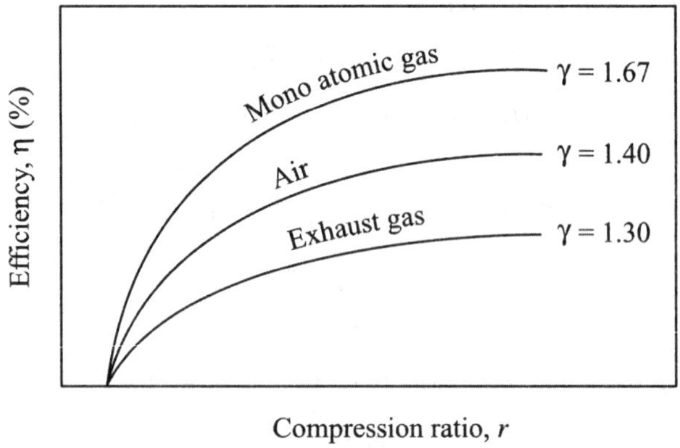

Fig. 2.6 Effect of r and γ on efficiency for Otto cycle

2.5.2 Work Output

The net work output for an Otto cycle can be expressed as

$$W = \frac{p_3V_3 - p_4V_4}{\gamma - 1} - \frac{p_2V_2 - p_1V_1}{\gamma - 1} \tag{2.26}$$

Also

$$\frac{p_2}{p_1} = \frac{p_3}{p_4} = r^{\gamma}$$

$$\frac{p_3}{p_2} = \frac{p_4}{p_1} = r_p \quad \text{(say)} \tag{2.27}$$

$$V_1 = rV_2 \quad \text{and} \quad V_4 = rV_3$$

therefore,

$$W = \frac{p_1V_1}{\gamma - 1}\left(\frac{p_3V_3}{p_1V_1} - \frac{p_4V_4}{p_1V_1} - \frac{p_2V_2}{p_1V_1} + 1\right) \tag{2.28}$$

$$= \frac{p_1V_1}{\gamma - 1}\left(\frac{r_pr^\gamma}{r} - r_p - \frac{r^\gamma}{r} + 1\right)$$

$$= \frac{p_1V_1}{\gamma - 1}\left(r_pr^{\gamma-1} - r_p - r^{\gamma-1} + 1\right)$$

$$= \frac{p_1V_1}{\gamma - 1}(r_p - 1)\left(r^{\gamma-1} - 1\right) \tag{2.29}$$

2.5.3 Mean Effective Pressure

The mean effective pressure of the cycle is given by

$$p_m = \frac{\text{Work output}}{\text{Swept volume}} \tag{2.30}$$

$$\text{Swept volume} = V_1 - V_2 = V_2(r - 1)$$

$$p_m = \frac{\frac{1}{\gamma-1}p_1V_1(r_p - 1)\left(r^{(\gamma-1)} - 1\right)}{V_2(r-1)}$$

$$= \frac{p_1r(r_p - 1)\left(r^{(\gamma-1)} - 1\right)}{(\gamma - 1)(r - 1)} \tag{2.31}$$

Thus, it can be seen that the work output is directly proportional to pressure ratio, r_p. The mean effective pressure which is an indication of the internal work output increases with a pressure ratio at a fixed value of compression ratio and ratio of specific heats. For an Otto cycle, an increase in the compression ratio leads to an increase in the mean effective pressure as well as the thermal efficiency.

2.6 THE DIESEL CYCLE

In actual spark-ignition engines, the upper limit of compression ratio is limited by the self-ignition temperature of the fuel. This limitation on the compression ratio can be circumvented if air and fuel are compressed separately and brought together at the time of combustion. In such an arrangement fuel can be injected into the cylinder which contains compressed air at a higher temperature than the self-ignition temperature of the fuel. Hence the fuel ignites on its own accord and requires no special device like an ignition system in a spark-ignition engine. Such engines work on heavy liquid fuels. These engines are called compression-ignition engines and they work on a ideal cycle known as Diesel cycle. The difference between Otto and Diesel cycles is in the process of heat addition. In Otto cycle the heat addition takes place at constant volume whereas in the Diesel cycle it is at constant pressure. For this reason, the Diesel cycle is often referred to as the constant-pressure cycle. It is better to avoid this term as it creates confusion with Joules cycle. The Diesel cycle is shown on p-V and T-s diagrams in Fig.2.7(a) and 2.7(b) respectively.

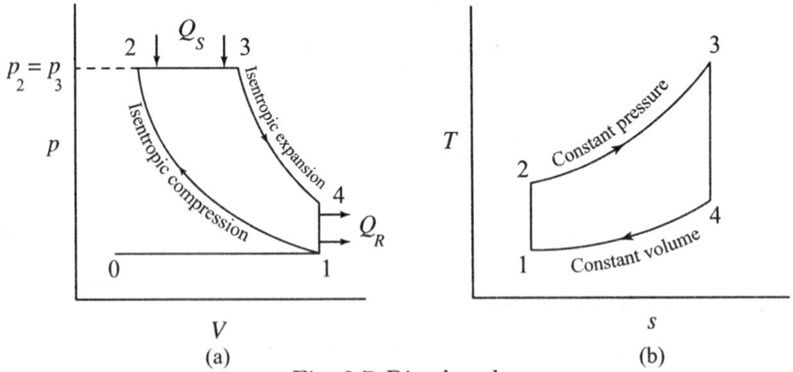

Fig. 2.7 Diesel cycle

To analyze the diesel cycle the suction and exhaust strokes, represented by 0→1 and 1→0, are neglected as in the case of the Otto cycle. Here, the volume ratio $\frac{V_1}{V_2}$ is the compression ratio, r. The volume ratio $\frac{V_3}{V_2}$ is called the cut-off ratio, r_c.

2.6.1 Thermal Efficiency

The thermal efficiency of the Diesel cycle is given by

$$\eta_{Diesel} = \frac{Q_S - Q_R}{Q_S}$$

$$= \frac{mC_p(T_3 - T_2) - mC_v(T_4 - T_1)}{mC_p(T_3 - T_2)} \quad (2.32)$$

$$= 1 - \frac{C_v(T_4 - T_1)}{C_p(T_3 - T_2)}$$

$$= 1 - \frac{1}{\gamma}\left(\frac{T_4 - T_1}{T_3 - T_2}\right) \quad (2.33)$$

Considering the process 1→2

$$T_2 = T_1\left(\frac{V_1}{V_2}\right)^{(\gamma-1)} = T_1 r^{(\gamma-1)} \quad (2.34)$$

Considering the constant pressure process 2→3, we have

$$\frac{V_2}{T_2} = \frac{V_3}{T_3}$$

$$\frac{T_3}{T_2} = \frac{V_3}{V_2} = r_c \quad \text{(say)}$$

$$T_3 = T_2 r_c \tag{2.35}$$

From Eqs.2.34 and 2.35, we have

$$T_3 = T_1 r^{(\gamma-1)} r_c \tag{2.36}$$

Considering process 3→4, we have

$$T_4 = T_3\left(\frac{V_3}{V_4}\right)^{(\gamma-1)} \tag{2.37}$$

$$= T_3\left(\frac{V_3}{V_2} \times \frac{V_2}{V_4}\right)^{(\gamma-1)}$$

$$= T_3\left(\frac{r_c}{r}\right)^{(\gamma-1)} \tag{2.38}$$

From Eqs.2.36 and 2.37, we have

$$T_4 = T_1 r^{(\gamma-1)} r_c \left(\frac{r_c}{r}\right)^{(\gamma-1)} = T_1 r_c^{\gamma}$$

$$\eta_{Diesel} = 1 - \frac{1}{\gamma}\left[\frac{T_1(r_c^{\gamma}-1)}{T_1\left(r^{(\gamma-1)}r_c - r^{(\gamma-1)}\right)}\right]$$

$$= 1 - \frac{1}{\gamma}\left[\frac{(r_c^{\gamma}-1)}{r^{(\gamma-1)}r_c - r^{(\gamma-1)}}\right]$$

$$= 1 - \frac{1}{r^{(\gamma-1)}}\left[\frac{r_c^{\gamma}-1}{\gamma(r_c-1)}\right] \tag{2.39}$$

It may be noted that the efficiency of the Diesel cycle is different from that of the Otto cycle only in the bracketed factor. This factor is always greater than unity. Hence for a given compression ratio, the Otto cycle is more efficient. In diesel engines the fuel cut-off ratio, r_c, depends on output, being maximum for maximum output. Therefore, unlike the Otto cycle the air-standard efficiency of the Diesel cycle depends on output. The higher efficiency of the Otto cycle as compared to the Diesel cycle for the same compression ratio is of no practical importance. In practice the operating compression ratios of diesel engines are much higher compared to spark-ignition engines working on Otto cycle. The normal range of compression ratio for diesel engine is 16 to 20 whereas for spark-ignition engines it is 6 to 10. Due to the higher compression ratios used in diesel engines the efficiency of a diesel engine is more than that of the gasoline engine.

2.6.2 Work Output

The net work output for a Diesel cycle is given by

$$W = p_2(V_3 - V_2) + \frac{p_3V_3 - p_4V_4}{\gamma - 1} - \frac{p_2V_2 - p_1V_1}{\gamma - 1} \tag{2.40}$$

$$= p_2V_2(r_c - 1) + \frac{p_3r_cV_2 - p_4rV_2}{\gamma - 1} - \frac{p_2V_2 - p_1rV_2}{\gamma - 1}$$

$$= V_2\left[\frac{p_2(r_c - 1)(\gamma - 1) + p_3r_c - p_4r - (p_2 - p_1r)}{\gamma - 1}\right]$$

$$= V_2\left[\frac{p_2(r_c - 1)(\gamma - 1) + p_3\left(r_c - \frac{p_4}{p_3}r\right) - p_2\left(1 - \frac{p_1}{p_2}r\right)}{\gamma - 1}\right]$$

$$= p_2V_2\left[\frac{(r_c - 1)(\gamma - 1) + \left(r_c - r_c^{\gamma}r^{(1-\gamma)}\right) - \left(1 - r^{(1-\gamma)}\right)}{\gamma - 1}\right]$$

$$= \frac{p_1V_1r^{(\gamma-1)}\left[\gamma(r_c - 1) - r^{(1-\gamma)}(r_c^{\gamma} - 1)\right]}{\gamma - 1} \tag{2.41}$$

2.6.3 Mean Effective Pressure

The expression for mean effective pressure can be shown to be

$$p_m = \frac{p_1V_1\left[r^{(\gamma-1)}\gamma(r_c - 1) - (r_c^{\gamma} - 1)\right]}{(\gamma - 1)V_1\left(\frac{r-1}{r}\right)} \tag{2.42}$$

$$= \frac{p_1[\gamma r^{\gamma}(r_c - 1) - r(r_c^{\gamma} - 1)]}{(\gamma - 1)(r - 1)} \tag{2.43}$$

2.7 THE DUAL CYCLE

In the Otto cycle, combustion is assumed at constant volume while in Diesel cycle combustion is at constant pressure. In practice they are far from real. Since, some time interval is required for the chemical reactions during combustion process, the combustion cannot take place at constant volume. Similarly, due to rapid uncontrolled combustion in diesel engines, combustion does not occur at constant pressure. The Dual cycle, also called a mixed cycle or limited pressure cycle, is a compromise between Otto and Diesel cycles. Figures 2.8(a) and 2.8(b) show the Dual cycle on p-V and T-s diagrams respectively.

In a Dual cycle a part of the heat is first supplied to the system at constant volume and then the remaining part at constant pressure.

2.7.1 Thermal Efficiency

The efficiency of the cycle may be written as

$$\eta_{Dual} = \frac{Q_S - Q_R}{Q_S} \tag{2.44}$$

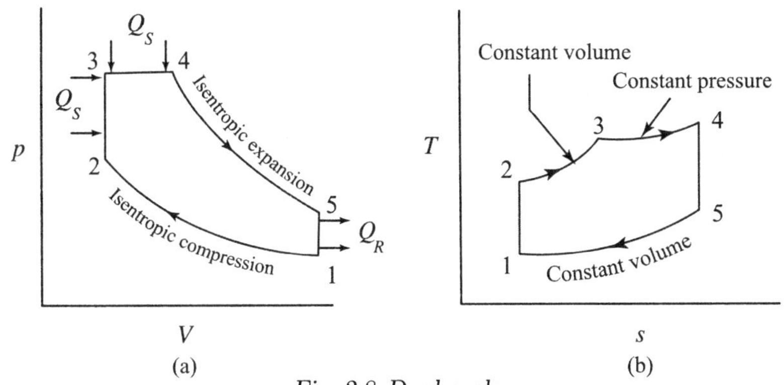

Fig. 2.8 Dual cycle

$$= \frac{mC_v(T_3 - T_2) + mC_p(T_4 - T_3) - mC_v(T_5 - T_1)}{mC_v(T_3 - T_2) + mC_p(T_4 - T_3)}$$

$$= 1 - \frac{T_5 - T_1}{(T_3 - T_2) + \gamma(T_4 - T_3)} \tag{2.45}$$

Now,

$$T_2 = T_1\left(\frac{V_1}{V_2}\right)^{(\gamma-1)} = T_1 r^{(\gamma-1)} \tag{2.46}$$

$$T_3 = T_2\left(\frac{p_3}{p_2}\right) = T_1 r_p r^{(\gamma-1)} \tag{2.47}$$

where r_p is the pressure ratio in the constant volume heat addition process and is equal to $\frac{p_3}{p_2}$.

Cut-off ratio r_c is given by $(\frac{V_4}{V_3})$

$$T_4 = T_3\frac{V_4}{V_3} = T_3 r_c$$

Substituting for T_3 from Eq.2.47

$$T_4 = T_1 r_c r_p r^{(\gamma-1)} \tag{2.48}$$

and

$$T_5 = T_4\left(\frac{V_4}{V_5}\right)^{(\gamma-1)} = T_1 r_p r_c r^{(\gamma-1)}\left(\frac{V_4}{V_5}\right)^{(\gamma-1)} \tag{2.49}$$

Now

$$\frac{V_4}{V_5} = \frac{V_4}{V_1} = \frac{V_4}{V_3} \times \frac{V_3}{V_1} \tag{2.50}$$

$$= \frac{V_4}{V_3} \times \frac{V_2}{V_1} \qquad (\text{since} V_2 = V_3)$$

Therefore,

$$\frac{V_4}{V_5} = \frac{r_c}{r} \tag{2.51}$$

where $\frac{V_4}{V_5}$ is the expansion ratio. Now,

$$\begin{aligned} T_5 &= T_1 r_p r_c r^{\gamma-1}\left(\frac{r_c}{r}\right)^{\gamma-1} \\ &= T_1 r_p r_c^{\gamma} \end{aligned} \tag{2.52}$$

Substituting for T_2, T_3, T_4 and T_5 into Eq.2.45 and simplifying

$$\eta = 1 - \frac{1}{r^{(\gamma-1)}}\left[\frac{r_p r_c^{\gamma} - 1}{(r_p - 1) + r_p\gamma(r_c - 1)}\right] \tag{2.53}$$

It can be seen from the above equation that a value of $r_p > 1$ results in an increased efficiency for a given value of r_c and γ. Thus the efficiency of Dual cycle lies between that of the Otto cycle and the Diesel cycle having same compression ratio.

With $r_c = 1$, it becomes an Otto cycle, and with $r_p = 1$, it becomes a Diesel cycle.

2.7.2 Work Output

The net work output of the cycle is given by

$$\begin{aligned} W &= p_3(V_4 - V_3) + \frac{p_4V_4 - p_5V_5}{\gamma - 1} - \frac{p_2V_2 - p_1V_1}{\gamma - 1} \\ &= \frac{p_1V_1}{\gamma - 1}\left[(\gamma - 1)\left(\frac{p_4V_4}{p_1V_1} - \frac{p_3V_3}{p_1V_1}\right) + \frac{p_4V_4}{p_1V_1} - \frac{p_5V_5}{p_1V_1} - \frac{p_2V_2}{p_1V_1} + 1\right] \\ &= \frac{p_1V_1}{\gamma - 1}\left[(\gamma - 1)\left(r_c r_p r^{\gamma-1} - r_p r^{\gamma-1}\right) + r_c r_p r^{\gamma-1}\right. \\ &\qquad \left. - r_p r_c^{\gamma} - r^{\gamma-1} + 1\right] \\ &= \frac{p_1V_1}{\gamma - 1}\left[\gamma r_c r_p r^{\gamma-1} - \gamma r_p r^{\gamma-1} + r_p r^{\gamma-1} - r_p r_c^{\gamma} - r^{\gamma-1} + 1\right] \\ &= \frac{p_1V_1}{\gamma - 1}\left[\gamma r_p r^{\gamma-1}(r_c - 1) + r^{\gamma-1}(r_p - 1) - (r_p r_c^{\gamma} - 1)\right] \end{aligned} \tag{2.54}$$

2.7.3 Mean Effective Pressure

The mean effective pressure is given by

$$\begin{aligned} p_m &= \frac{\text{Work output}}{\text{Swept volume}} = \frac{W}{V_s} \\ &= \frac{1}{V_1 - V_2}\frac{p_1V_1}{\gamma - 1}\left[\gamma r_p r^{\gamma-1}(r_c - 1) + r^{\gamma-1}(r_p - 1) - (r_p r_c^{\gamma} - 1)\right] \end{aligned}$$

$$= \frac{1}{\left(1-\frac{V_2}{V_1}\right)}\frac{p_1}{(\gamma-1)}\left[\gamma r_p r^{\gamma-1}(r_c-1)+r^{\gamma-1}(r_p-1)\right.$$

$$\left.-(r_p r_c^{\gamma}-1)\right]$$

$$= p_1\frac{[\gamma r_p r^{\gamma}(r_c-1)+r^{\gamma}(r_p-1)-r(r_p r_c^{\gamma}-1)]}{(\gamma-1)(r-1)} \qquad (2.55)$$

2.8 COMPARISON OF THE OTTO, DIESEL AND DUAL CYCLES

The important variable factors which are used as the basis for comparison of the cycles are compression ratio, peak pressure, heat addition, heat rejection and the net work. In order to compare the performance of the Otto, Diesel and Dual combustion cycles some of the variable factors must be fixed. In this section, a comparison of these three cycles is made for the same compression ratio, same heat addition, constant maximum pressure and temperature, same heat rejection and net work output. This analysis will show which cycle is more efficient for a given set of operating conditions.

2.8.1 Same Compression Ratio and Heat Addition

The Otto cycle 1→2→3→4→1, the Diesel cycle 1→2→3′→4′→1 and the Dual cycle 1→2→2″→3″→4″→1 are shown in *p-V* and *T-s* diagrams in Fig.2.9(a) and 2.9(b) respectively for the same compression ratio and heat input.

From the *T-s* diagram, it can be seen that Area 5236 = Area 523′6′ = Area 522″3″6″ as this area represents the heat input which is the same for all cycles.

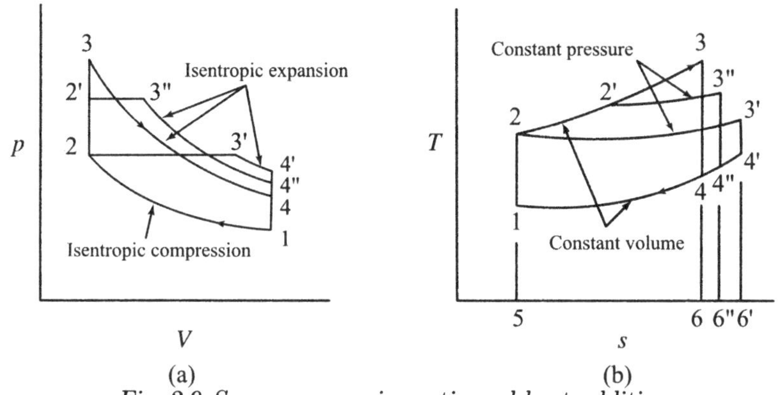

Fig. 2.9 Same compression ratio and heat addition

All the cycles start from the same initial state point 1 and the air is compressed from state 1 to 2 as the compression ratio is same. It is seen from the *T-s* diagram for the same heat input, the heat rejection in Otto cycle (area 5146) is minimum and heat rejection in Diesel cycle (514′6′) is maximum. *Consequently Otto cycle has the highest work output and efficiency. Diesel cycle has the least efficiency and Dual cycle having the efficiency between the two.* For same compression ratio and heat addition, $\eta_{Otto} > \eta_{Dual} > \eta_{Diesel}$.

One more observation can be made i.e., Otto cycle allows the working medium to expand more whereas Diesel cycle is least in this respect. The reason is heat is added before expansion in the case of former (Otto cycle) and the last portion of heat supplied to the fluid has a relatively short expansion in case of the latter (Diesel cycle).

2.8.2 Same Compression Ratio and Heat Rejection

The p-V and T-s diagrams are shown in Figs.2.10(a) and 2.10(b). Now,

$$\eta_{Otto} = 1 - \frac{Q_R}{Q_S}$$

where Q_S is the heat supplied in the Otto cycle and is equal to the area under the curve 2→3 on the T-s diagram [Fig.2.10(b)]. The efficiency of the Diesel cycle is given by

$$\eta_{Diesel} = 1 - \frac{Q_R}{Q'_S}$$

where Q'_S is heat supplied in the Diesel cycle and is equal to the area under the curve 2→3′ on the T-s diagram [Fig.2.10(b)].

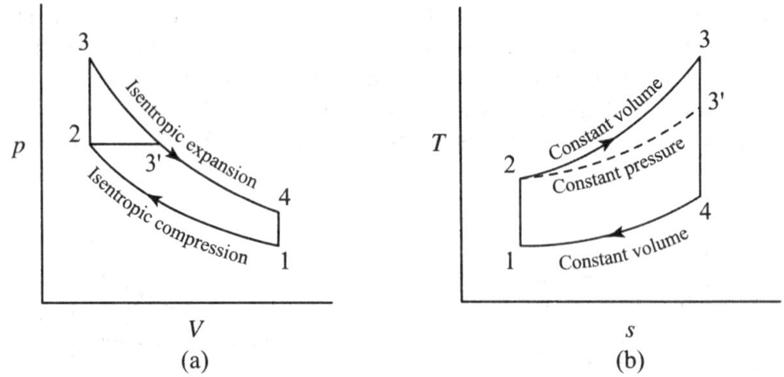

Fig. 2.10 Same compression ratio and heat rejection

From the T-s diagram in Fig.2.10 it is clear that $Q_S > Q'_S$ i.e., heat supplied in the Otto cycle is more than that of the Diesel cycle. *Hence, it is evident that, the efficiency of the Otto cycle is greater than the efficiency of the Diesel cycle for a given compression ratio and heat rejection.* Also, for the same compression ratio and heat rejection, $\eta_{Otto} > \eta_{Dual} > \eta_{Diesel}$.

2.8.3 Same Peak Pressure, Peak Temperature and Heat Rejection

Figures 2.11(a) and 2.11(b) show the Otto cycle 1→2→3→4 and Diesel cycle 1→2′→3→4 on p-V and T-s coordinates, where the peak pressure and temperature and the amount of heat rejected are the same.

The efficiency of the Otto cycle 1→2→3→4 is given by

$$\eta_{Otto} = 1 - \frac{Q_R}{Q_S}$$

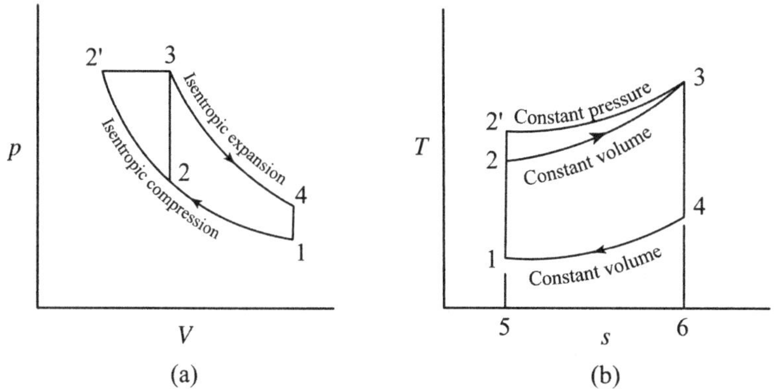

Fig. 2.11 Same peak pressure and temperature

where Q_S in the area under the curve 2→3 in Fig.2.11(b).
The efficiency of the Diesel cycle, 1→2→3′→3→4 is

$$\eta_{Diesel} = 1 - \frac{Q_R}{Q'_S}$$

where Q'_S is the area under the curve 2′→3 in Fig.2.11(b).

It is evident from Fig.2.11 that $Q'_S > Q_S$. Therefore, the Diesel cycle efficiency is greater than the Otto cycle efficiency when both engines are built to withstand the same thermal and mechanical stresses. Also, for the same peak pressure, peak temperature and heat rejection, $\eta_{Otto} > \eta_{Dual} > \eta_{Diesel}$.

2.8.4 Same Maximum Pressure and Heat Input

For same maximum pressure and same heat input the Otto cycle (12341) and Diesel cycle (12′3′4′1) are shown on *p-V* and *T-s* diagrams in Figs.2.12(a) and 2.12(b) respectively.

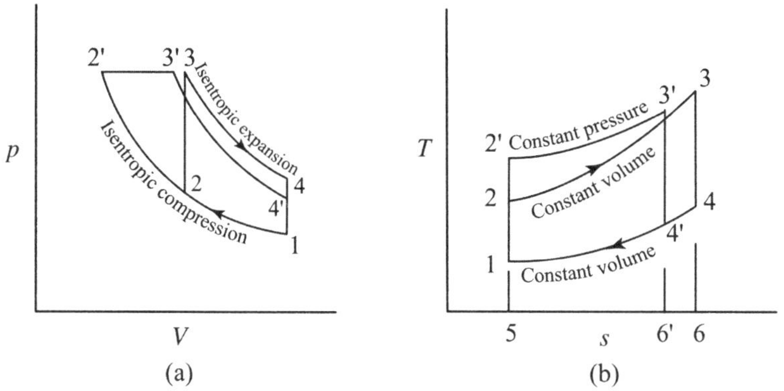

Fig. 2.12 Same maximum pressure and heat input

It is evident from the figure that the heat rejection for Otto cycle (area 1564 on *T-s* diagram) is more than the heat rejected in Diesel cycle (156′4′).

Hence Diesel cycle is more efficient than Otto cycle for the condition of same maximum pressure and heat input. One can make a note that with these conditions the Diesel cycle has higher compression ratio $\frac{V_1}{V_{2'}}$ than that of Otto cycle $\frac{V_1}{V_2}$. One should also note that the cycle which is having higher efficiency allows maximum expansion. The Dual cycle efficiency will be between these two. Hence, for the same maximum pressure and heat input, $\eta_{Otto} > \eta_{Dual} > \eta_{Diesel}$.

2.8.5 Same Maximum Pressure and Work Output

The efficiency, η, can be written as

$$\eta = \frac{\text{Work done}}{\text{Heat supplied}} = \frac{\text{Work done}}{\text{Work done} + \text{Heat rejected}}$$

Refer to T-s diagram in Fig.2.12(b). For same work output the area 1234 (work output of Otto cycle) and area $12'3'4'$ (work output of Diesel cycle) are same. To achieve this, the entropy at 3 should be greater than entropy at $3'$. It is clear that the heat rejection for Otto cycle is more than that of Diesel cycle. Hence, for these conditions the Diesel cycle is more efficient than the Otto cycle. The efficiency of Dual cycle lies between the two cycles. Hence, for the same maximum pressure and work output, $\eta_{Otto} > \eta_{Dual} > \eta_{Diesel}$.

2.9 THE LENOIR CYCLE

The Lenoir cycle consists of the following processes [see Fig.2.13(a)]. Constant volume heat addition (1→2); isentropic expansion (2→3); constant pressure heat rejection (3→1). The Lenoir cycle is used for pulse jet engines.

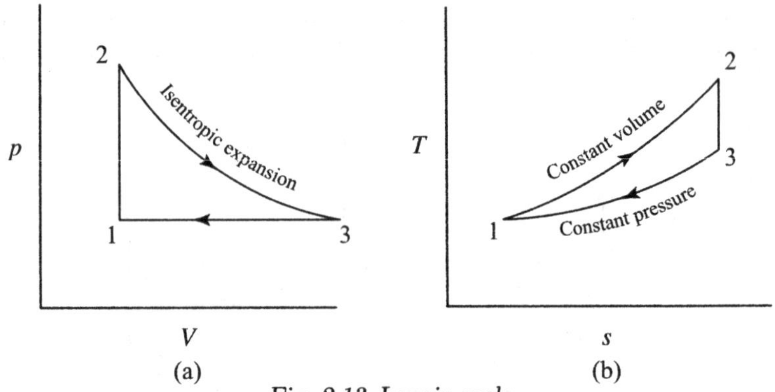

Fig. 2.13 Lenoir cycle

$$\eta_{Lenoir} = \frac{Q_S - Q_F}{Q_S}$$

$$Q_S = mC_v(T_2 - T_1) \tag{2.56}$$

$$Q_R = mC_p(T_3 - T_1) \tag{2.57}$$

$$\eta_{Lenoir} = \frac{mC_v(T_2 - T_1) - mC_p(T_3 - T_1)}{mC_v(T_2 - T_1)} \quad (2.58)$$

$$= 1 - \gamma\left(\frac{T_3 - T_1}{T_2 - T_1}\right)$$

Taking $p_2/p_1 = r_p$, we have $T_2 = T_1 r_p$ and

$$\frac{T_3}{T_2} = \left(\frac{p_3}{p_2}\right)^{\left(\frac{\gamma-1}{\gamma}\right)} \quad (2.59)$$

$$T_3 = T_2\left(\frac{1}{r_p}\right)^{\left(\frac{\gamma-1}{\gamma}\right)} = T_1 r_p \left(\frac{1}{r_p}\right)^{\left(\frac{\gamma-1}{\gamma}\right)} = T_1 r_p^{(1/\gamma)}$$

$$\eta = 1 - \gamma\left(\frac{T_1 r_p^{(1/\gamma)} - T_1}{T_1 r_p - T_1}\right) = 1 - \gamma\left(\frac{r_p^{(1/\gamma)} - 1}{r_p - 1}\right) \quad (2.60)$$

Thus the efficiency of the Lenoir cycle depends upon the pressure ratio as well as the ratio of specific heats, viz., γ.

2.10 THE ATKINSON CYCLE

Atkinson cycle is an ideal cycle for Otto engine exhausting to a gas turbine. In this cycle the isentropic expansion (3→4) of an Otto cycle (1234) is further allowed to proceed to the lowest cycle pressure so as to increase the work output. With this modification the cycle is known as Atkinson cycle. The cycle is shown on p-V and T-s diagrams in Figs.2.14(a) and 2.14(b) respectively.

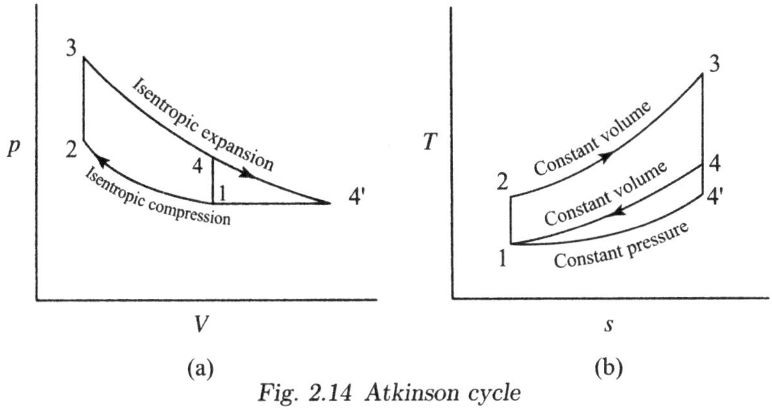

Fig. 2.14 Atkinson cycle

$$\eta_{Atkinson} = \frac{Q_S - Q_R}{Q_S} \quad (2.61)$$

$$= \frac{mC_v(T_3 - T_2) - mC_p(T_{4'} - T_1)}{mC_v(T_3 - T_2)} \quad (2.62)$$

$$= 1 - \gamma\left(\frac{T_{4'} - T_1}{T_3 - T_2}\right) \quad (2.63)$$

the compression ratio, $r = \frac{V_1}{V_2}$ and the expansion ratio $e = \frac{V_{4'}}{V_3}$. Now,

$$\frac{T_2}{T_1} = \left(\frac{V_1}{V_2}\right)^{(\gamma-1)} = r^{(\gamma-1)} \quad (2.64)$$

$$T_2 = T_1 r^{(\gamma-1)} \quad (2.65)$$

$$\frac{T_3}{T_2} = \frac{p_3}{p_2} = \left(\frac{p_3}{p_{4'}} \times \frac{p_{4'}}{p_2}\right) = \left(\frac{p_3}{p_{4'}} \times \frac{p_1}{p_2}\right) \quad (2.66)$$

$$\frac{p_3}{p_{4'}} = \left(\frac{V_{4'}}{V_3}\right)^{\gamma} = e^{\gamma} \quad (2.67)$$

$$\frac{p_1}{p_2} = \left(\frac{V_2}{V_1}\right)^{\gamma} = \frac{1}{r^{\gamma}} \quad (2.68)$$

Substituting Eqs.2.67 and 2.68 in Eq.2.66,

$$\frac{T_3}{T_2} = \frac{e^{\gamma}}{r^{\gamma}} \quad (2.69)$$

$$T_3 = T_2\frac{e^{\gamma}}{r^{\gamma}} = T_1 r^{(\gamma-1)}\frac{e^{\gamma}}{r^{\gamma}} = T_1\frac{e^{\gamma}}{r} \quad (2.70)$$

$$\frac{T_{4'}}{T_3} = \left(\frac{V_3}{V_{4'}}\right)^{(\gamma-1)} = \frac{1}{e^{(\gamma-1)}}$$

$$T_{4'} = T_3\frac{1}{e^{(\gamma-1)}} = T_1\left(\frac{e^{\gamma}}{r}\right)\left(\frac{1}{e^{(\gamma-1)}}\right) \quad (2.71)$$

$$T_{4'} = T_1\frac{e}{r} \quad (2.72)$$

Substituting the values of T_2, T_3, $T_{4'}$ in the Eq.2.63,

$$\eta_{Atkinson} = 1 - \gamma\left[\frac{T_1 e/r - T_1}{T_1 e^{\gamma}/r - T_1 r^{(\gamma-1)}}\right]$$

$$= 1 - \gamma\left[\frac{e - r}{e^{\gamma} - r^{\gamma}}\right] \quad (2.73)$$

2.11 THE BRAYTON CYCLE

Brayton cycle is a theoretical cycle for gas turbines. This cycle consists of two reversible adiabatic or isentropic processes and two constant pressure processes. Figure 2.15 shows the Brayton cycle on p-V and T-s coordinates. The cycle is similar to the Diesel cycle in compression and heat addition. The isentropic expansion of the Diesel cycle is further extended followed by

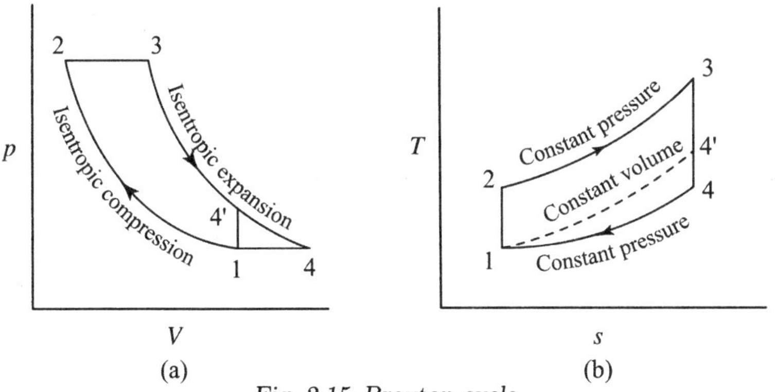

Fig. 2.15 Brayton cycle

constant pressure heat rejection.

$$\eta_{Brayton} = \frac{Q_S - Q_R}{Q_S}$$

$$= \frac{mC_p(T_3 - T_2) - mC_p(T_4 - T_1)}{mC_p(T_3 - T_2)} \tag{2.74}$$

$$= 1 - \frac{T_4 - T_1}{T_3 - T_2}$$

If r is compression ratio i.e., (V_1/V_2) and r_p is the pressure ratio i.e., (p_2/p_1) then,

$$\frac{T_3}{T_4} = \left(\frac{p_3}{p_4}\right)^{\left(\frac{\gamma-1}{\gamma}\right)} = \left(\frac{p_2}{p_1}\right)^{\left(\frac{\gamma-1}{\gamma}\right)} \tag{2.75}$$

$$= \left(\frac{V_1}{V_2}\right)^{(\gamma-1)} = r^{(\gamma-1)} \tag{2.76}$$

$$T_4 = \frac{T_3}{r^{(\gamma-1)}} \tag{2.77}$$

$$T_1 = \frac{T_2}{r^{(\gamma-1)}} \tag{2.78}$$

$$\eta_{Brayton} = 1 - \frac{(T_3/r^{(\gamma-1)}) - (T_2/r^{(\gamma-1)})}{T_3 - T_2}$$

$$= 1 - \frac{1}{r^{(\gamma-1)}} \tag{2.79}$$

$$r = \frac{V_1}{V_2} = \left(\frac{p_2}{p_1}\right)^{\frac{1}{\gamma}} = r_p^{\frac{1}{\gamma}} \tag{2.80}$$

$$= 1 - \frac{1}{\left(r_p^{\frac{1}{\gamma}}\right)^{\gamma-1}} = 1 - \frac{1}{r_p^{\left(\frac{\gamma-1}{\gamma}\right)}} \quad (2.81)$$

From Eq.2.81, it is seen that the efficiency of the Brayton cycle depends only on the pressure ratio and the ratio of specific heat, γ.

$$\text{Network output} = \text{Expansion work} - \text{Compression work}$$

$$= C_p(T_3 - T_4) - C_p(T_2 - T_1)$$

$$= C_pT_1\left(\frac{T_3}{T_1} - \frac{T_4}{T_1} - \frac{T_2}{T_1} + 1\right)$$

$$\frac{W}{C_pT_1} = \frac{T_3}{T_1} - \frac{T_4}{T_3}\frac{T_3}{T_1} - \frac{T_2}{T_1} + 1 \quad (2.82)$$

It can be easily seen from the Eq.2.82 (work output) that, the work output of the cycle depends on initial temperature, T_1, the ratio of the maximum to minimum temperature, $\frac{T_3}{T_1}$, pressure ratio, r_p and γ which are used in the calculation of $\frac{T_2}{T_1}$. Therefore, for the same pressure ratio and initial conditions work output depends on the maximum temperature of the cycle.

Worked out Examples

OTTO CYCLE

2.1 An engine working on Otto cycle has the following conditions : Pressure at the beginning of compression is 1 bar and pressure at the end of compression is 11 bar. Calculate the compression ratio and air-standard efficiency of the engine. Assume $\gamma = 1.4$.

Solution

$$r = \frac{V_1}{V_2} = \left(\frac{p_2}{p_1}\right)^{\left(\frac{1}{\gamma}\right)} = 11^{\frac{1}{1.4}} = \mathbf{5.54} \qquad \stackrel{\text{Ans}}{\Longleftarrow}$$

$$\eta_{\text{air-std}} = 1 - \frac{1}{r^{\gamma-1}} = 1 - \left(\frac{1}{5.54}\right)^{0.4}$$

$$= 0.496 = \mathbf{49.6\%} \qquad \stackrel{\text{Ans}}{\Longleftarrow}$$

2.2 In an engine working on ideal Otto cycle the temperatures at the beginning and end of compression are 50 °C and 373 °C. Find the compression ratio and the air-standard efficiency of the engine.

Solution

$$r = \frac{V_1}{V_2} = \left(\frac{T_1}{T_2}\right)^{\frac{1}{\gamma-1}} = \left(\frac{646}{323}\right)^{\frac{1}{0.4}} = \mathbf{5.66} \qquad \stackrel{\text{Ans}}{\Longleftarrow}$$

$$\eta_{Otto} = 1 - \frac{1}{r^{\gamma-1}} = 1 - \frac{T_1}{T_2}$$

$$= 1 - \frac{323}{646} = 0.5 = \mathbf{50\%} \qquad \stackrel{\text{Ans}}{\Longleftarrow}$$

2.3 In an Otto cycle air at 17 °C and 1 bar is compressed adiabatically until the pressure is 15 bar. Heat is added at constant volume until the pressure rises to 40 bar. Calculate the air-standard efficiency, the compression ratio and the mean effective pressure for the cycle. Assume $C_v = 0.717$ kJ/kg K and $R = 8.314$ kJ/kmol K.

Solution

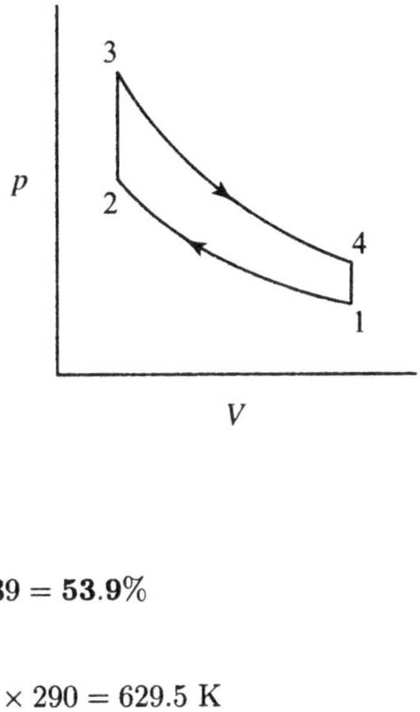

Consider the process 1 – 2

$$p_1 V_1^{\gamma} = p_2 V_2^{\gamma}$$

$$\frac{V_1}{V_2} = r = \left(\frac{p_2}{p_1}\right)^{\frac{1}{\gamma}}$$

$$= \left(\frac{15}{1}\right)^{\frac{1}{1.4}} = 6.91$$

$$\eta = 1 - \left(\frac{1}{r}\right)^{\gamma-1}$$

$$= 1 - \left(\frac{1}{6.91}\right)^{0.4} = 0.539 = \mathbf{53.9\%}$$

$$T_2 = \frac{p_2 V_2}{p_1 V_1} T_1 = \frac{15}{1} \times \frac{1}{6.91} \times 290 = 629.5 \text{ K}$$

Consider the process 2 – 3

$$T_3 = \frac{p_3 T_2}{p_2} = \frac{40}{15} \times 629.5 = 1678.7$$

$$\textit{Heat supplied} = C_v(T_3 - T_2)$$

$$= 0.717 \times (1678.7 - 629.5) = 752.3 \text{ kJ/kg}$$

$$\textit{Work done} = \eta \times q_s = 0.539 \times 752.3 = 405.5 \text{ kJ/kg}$$

$$p_m = \frac{\text{Work done}}{\text{Swept volume}}$$

$$v_1 = \frac{V_1}{m} = M\frac{RT_1}{p_1} = \frac{8314 \times 290}{29 \times 1 \times 10^5} = 0.8314 \text{ m}^3/\text{kg}$$

$$v_1 - v_2 = \frac{5.91}{6.91} \times 0.8314 = 0.711 \text{ m}^3/\text{kg}$$

$$p_m = \frac{405.5}{0.711} \times 10^3 = 5.70 \times 10^5 \text{ N/m}^2$$

$$= \mathbf{5.70 \ bar}$$

Ans ⟸

2.4 Fuel supplied to an SI engine has a calorific value 42000 kJ/kg. The pressure in the cylinder at 30% and 70% of the compression stroke are 1.3 bar and 2.6 bar respectively. Assuming that the compression follows the law $pV^{1.3}$ = constant. Find the compression ratio. If the relative efficiency of the engine compared with the air-standard efficiency is 50%. Calculate the fuel consumption in kg/kW h.

Solution

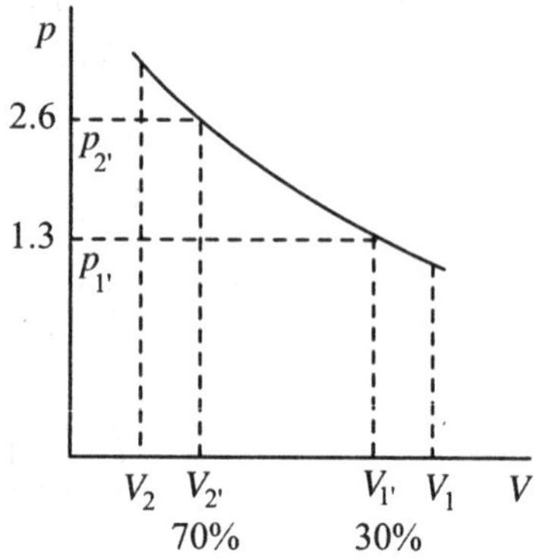

$$V_2 = 1$$

$$V_{1'} = 1 + 0.7(r-1)$$

$$= 0.7r + 0.3$$

$$V_{2'} = 1 + 0.3(r-1)$$

$$= 0.3r + 0.7$$

$$\frac{V_{1'}}{V_{2'}} = \left(\frac{p_2}{p_1}\right)^{\frac{1}{n}}$$

$$= \left(\frac{2.6}{1.3}\right)^{\frac{1}{1.3}} = 1.7$$

$$\frac{0.7r + 0.3}{0.3r + 0.7} = 1.7$$

$$r = \mathbf{4.68}$$

Ans ⟸

$$\eta_{air-std} = 1 - \frac{1}{r^{\gamma-1}}$$

$$= 1 - \frac{1}{4.68^{0.4}} = 0.46 = 46\%$$

$$\text{Relative efficiency} = \frac{\text{Indicated thermal efficiency}}{\text{Air-standard efficiency}}$$

$$\eta_{ith} = 0.5 \times 0.46 = 0.23$$

$$\eta_{th} = \frac{ip}{CV \times \dot{m}}$$

where $\dot{m}$ is in kg/s

$$\frac{\dot{m}}{ip} = \frac{1}{42000 \times 0.23}$$

$$= 1.035 \times 10^{-4} \text{ kg/kW s}$$

$$= 1.035 \times 10^{-4} \times 3600 \text{ kg/kW h}$$

$$isfc = \mathbf{0.373 \text{ kg/kW h}}$$ Ans ⟸

2.5 A gas engine working on the Otto cycle has a cylinder of diameter 200 mm and stroke 250 mm. The clearance volume is 1570 cc. Find the air-standard efficiency. Assume C_p = 1.004 kJ/kg K and C_v = 0.717 kJ/kg K for air.

Solution

$$V_s = \frac{\pi}{4}d^2L = \frac{\pi}{4} \times 20^2 \times 25 = 7853.98 \text{ cc}$$

$$r = 1 + \frac{V_s}{V_c} = 1 + \frac{7853.98}{1570} = 6.00$$

$$\gamma = \frac{C_p}{C_v} = \frac{1.004}{0.717} = 1.4$$

$$\eta_{\text{air-std}} = 1 - \frac{1}{r^{\gamma-1}} = 1 - \frac{1}{6^{(0.4)}} \times 100 = \mathbf{51.2\%}$$ Ans ⟸

2.6 In a S.I. engine working on the ideal Otto cycle, the compression ratio is 5.5. The pressure and temperature at the beginning of compression are 1 bar and 27 °C respectively. The peak pressure is 30 bar. Determine the pressure and temperatures at the salient points, the air-standard efficiency and the mean effective pressure. Assume ratio of specific heats to be 1.4 for air.

Solution

Since $V_2 = V_3 = V_c$

$V_1 = rV_2 = rV_c,$

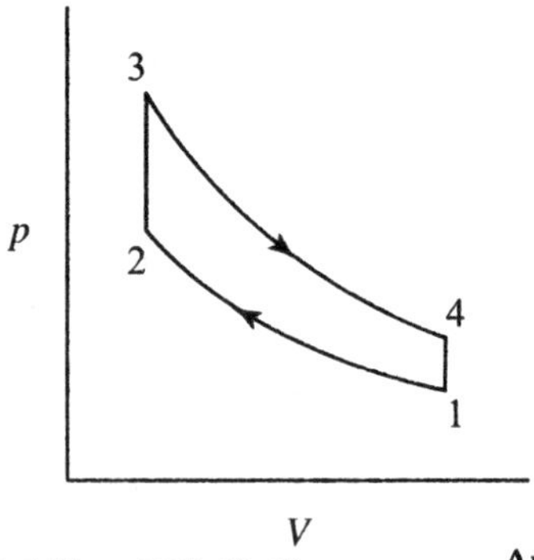

Consider the process 1 – 2,

$$\frac{p_2}{p_1} = r^{\gamma} = 5.5^{1.4} = 10.88$$

$$p_2 = 10.88 \times 1 \times 10^5$$

$$= \mathbf{10.88 \times 10^5\ N/m^2}$$

$$\frac{T_2}{T_1} = r^{\gamma-1} = 5.5^{0.4} = 1.978$$

$$T_2 = 1.978 \times 300 = 593.4\ \text{K} = \mathbf{320.4^\circ\ C} \qquad \underleftarrow{\text{Ans}}$$

Consider the process 2 – 3,

$$p_3 = 30 \times 10^5\ \text{N/m}^2$$

$$\frac{T_3}{T_2} = \frac{p_3}{p_2} = \frac{30}{10.88} = 2.757$$

$$T_3 = 2.757 \times 593.4 = 1636\ \text{K}$$

$$= \mathbf{1363^\circ\ C} \qquad \underleftarrow{\text{Ans}}$$

Consider the process 3 – 4,

$$\frac{p_3}{p_4} = \left(\frac{V_4}{V_3}\right)^{\gamma} = \left(\frac{V_1}{V_2}\right)^{\gamma}$$

$$= r^{\gamma} = 5.5^{1.4} = 10.88$$

$$p_4 = \frac{p_3}{10.88} = \mathbf{2.76 \times 10^5\ N/m^2} \qquad \underleftarrow{\text{Ans}}$$

$$\frac{T_3}{T_4} = r^{\gamma-1} = 5.5^{0.4} = 1.978$$

$$T_4 = \frac{T_3}{1.978} = \frac{1636}{1.978} = 827.1\ \text{K} = \mathbf{554.1^\circ\ C} \qquad \underleftarrow{\text{Ans}}$$

$$\eta_{Otto} = 1 - \frac{1}{r^{(\gamma-1)}} = 1 - \frac{1}{5.5^{0.4}} = 0.4943 = \mathbf{49.43\%} \qquad \underleftarrow{\text{Ans}}$$

$$p_m = \frac{\textit{Indicated work/cycle}}{V_s} = \frac{\textit{Area of p-V diagram 1234}}{V_s}$$

Area 1234 = *Area under 3-4 – Area under 2-1*

$$= \frac{p_3V_3 - p_4V_4}{\gamma - 1} - \frac{p_2V_2 - p_1V_1}{\gamma - 1}$$

$$= \frac{30 \times 10^5 \times V_c - 2.76 \times 10^5 \times 5.5V_c}{0.4}$$

$$- \frac{10.88 \times 10^5 \times V_c - 1 \times 10^5 \times 5.5V_c}{0.4}$$

$$= 23.6 \times 10^5 \times V_c = p_m \times V_s$$

$$p_m = \frac{23.6 \times 10^5 \times V_c}{V_s} = \frac{23.6 \times 10^5 \times V_c}{4.5 \times V_c}$$

$$= 5.24 \times 10^5 \text{ N/m}^2 = \mathbf{5.24 \text{ bar}}$$ Ans $\Longleftarrow$

2.7 A gas engine operating on the ideal Otto cycle has a compression ratio of 6:1. The pressure and temperature at the commencement of compression are 1 bar and 27 °C. Heat added during the constant volume combustion process is 1170 kJ/kg. Determine the peak pressure and temperature, work output per kg of air and air-standard efficiency. Assume C_v = 0.717 kJ/kg K and γ = 1.4 for air.

Solution

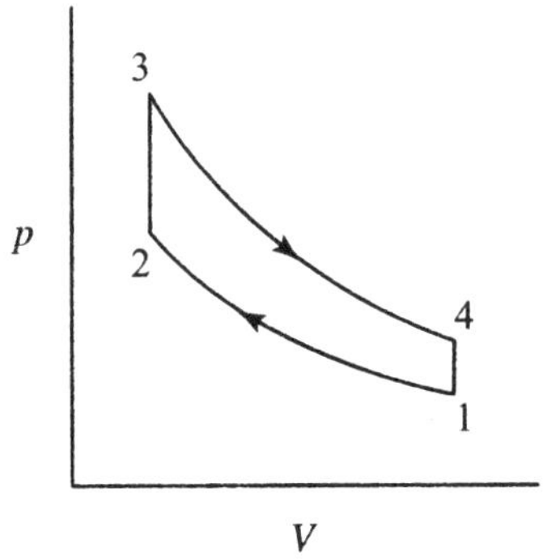

Consider the process 1-2

$$\frac{p_2}{p_1} = r^\gamma = 6^{1.4} = 12.28$$

$$p_2 = 12.28 \times 10^5 \text{ N/m}^2$$

$$\frac{T_2}{T_1} = \left(\frac{V_1}{V_2}\right)^{\gamma-1} = r^{\gamma-1}$$

$$= 6^{0.4} = 2.05$$

$$T_2 = 2.05 \times 300 = 615K = 342° \text{ C}$$

Consider the process 2-3

For unit mass flow

$$q_s = q_{2-3} = C_v(T_3 - T_2) = 1170 \text{ kJ/kg}$$

$$T_3 - T_2 = \frac{1170}{0.717} = 1631.8$$

$$T_3 = 1631.8 + 615 = 2246.8 \text{ K}$$

$$= \mathbf{1973.8° \text{ C}}$$ Ans $\Longleftarrow$

$$\frac{p_3}{p_2} = \frac{T_3}{T_2} = \frac{2246.8}{615} = 3.65$$

$$\text{Peak pressure}, p_3 = 3.65 \times 12.28 \times 10^5$$

$$= 44.82 \times 10^5 \text{ N/m}^2 = \mathbf{44.82\ bar} \quad \xleftarrow{\text{Ans}}$$

$$\text{Work output} = \text{Area of } p\text{-}V \text{ diagram}$$

$$= \text{Area under } (3 - 4) - \text{Area under } (2 - 1)$$

$$= \frac{p_3V_3 - p_4V_4}{\gamma - 1} - \frac{p_2V_2 - p_1V_1}{\gamma - 1}$$

$$= \frac{mR}{\gamma - 1}[(T_3 - T_4) - (T_2 - T_1)]$$

$$R = C_p - C_v = 1.004 - 0.717$$

$$= 0.287 \text{ kJ/kg K}$$

$$\frac{T_3}{T_4} = \left(\frac{V_3}{V_4}\right)^{\gamma-1} = r^{(\gamma-1)} = 6^{0.4} = 2.048$$

$$T_4 = \frac{T_3}{2.048} = \frac{2246.8}{2.048} = 1097.1 \text{ K}$$

$$\text{Work output/kg} = \frac{0.287}{0.4} \times [(2246.8 - 1097.1) - (615 - 300)]$$

$$= \mathbf{598.9\ kJ} \quad \xleftarrow{\text{Ans}}$$

$$\eta_{Otto} = 1 - \frac{1}{r^{(\gamma-1)}} = 1 - \frac{1}{6^{0.4}} 0.5116 = \mathbf{51.16\%} \quad \xleftarrow{\text{Ans}}$$

2.8 A spark-ignition engine working on ideal Otto cycle has the compression ratio 6. The initial pressure and temperature of air are 1 bar and 37 °C. The maximum pressure in the cycle is 30 bar. For unit mass flow, calculate (i) p, V and T at various salient points of the cycle and (ii) the ratio of heat supplied to the heat rejected. Assume $\gamma = 1.4$ and $R =$ 8.314 kJ/kmol K.

Solution

Consider point 1,

$$n = \frac{m}{M} = \frac{1}{29}$$

$$V_1 = \frac{nRT_1}{p_1} = \frac{1 \times 8314 \times 310}{29 \times 10^5} = \mathbf{0.889\ m^3} \quad \xleftarrow{\text{Ans}}$$

Consider point 2,

$$p_2 = p_1\ r^{\gamma} = 10^5 \times 6^{1.4} = 12.3 \times 10^5 \text{ N/m}^2 = \mathbf{12.3\ bar} \quad \xleftarrow{\text{Ans}}$$

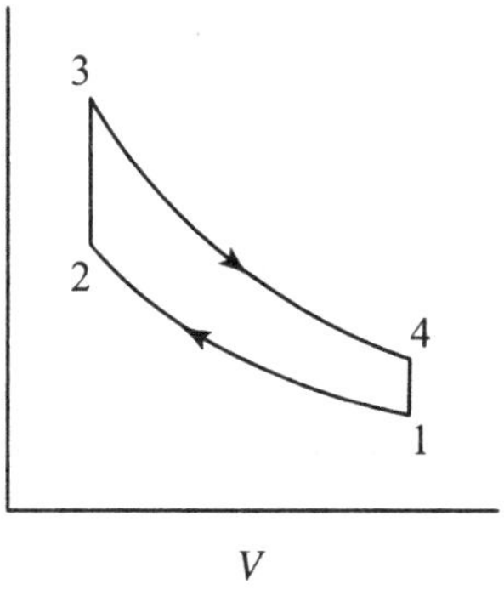

$$V_2 = \frac{V_1}{6} = \frac{0.889}{6}$$

$$= \mathbf{0.148\ m^3} \quad \stackrel{\text{Ans}}{\Longleftarrow}$$

$$T_2 = \frac{p_2 V_2}{p_1 V_1} T_1$$

$$= \frac{12.3 \times 10^5 \times 0.148 \times 310}{1 \times 10^5 \times 0.889}$$

$$= 634.8\ \text{K}$$

$$= \mathbf{361.8^\circ\ C} \quad \stackrel{\text{Ans}}{\Longleftarrow}$$

Consider point 3,

$$V_3 = V_2 = \mathbf{0.148\ m^3} \quad \stackrel{\text{Ans}}{\Longleftarrow}$$

$$p_3 = 30 \times 10^5\ \text{N/m}^2 = \mathbf{30\ bar} \quad \stackrel{\text{Ans}}{\Longleftarrow}$$

$$\frac{p_3}{T_3} = \frac{p_2}{T_2}$$

$$T_3 = \frac{30 \times 10^5}{12.3 \times 10^5} \times 634.8$$

$$= 1548\ \text{K} = \mathbf{1275^\circ\ C} \quad \stackrel{\text{Ans}}{\Longleftarrow}$$

Consider point 4,

$$p_3 V_3^\gamma = p_4 V_4^\gamma$$

$$p_4 = p_3 \left(\frac{V_3}{V_4}\right)^\gamma = 30 \times 10^5 \left(\frac{1}{6}\right)^{1.4}$$

$$= 2.44 \times 10^5\ \text{N/m}^2 = \mathbf{2.44\ bar} \quad \stackrel{\text{Ans}}{\Longleftarrow}$$

$$V_4 = V_1 = \mathbf{0.889\ m^3} \quad \stackrel{\text{Ans}}{\Longleftarrow}$$

$$T_4 = T_1 \frac{p_4}{p_1} = 310 \times \frac{2.44 \times 10^5}{1 \times 10^5}$$

$$= 756.4\ \text{K} = \mathbf{483.4^\circ\ C} \quad \stackrel{\text{Ans}}{\Longleftarrow}$$

$$C_v = \frac{R}{M(\gamma - 1)} \frac{8.314}{29 \times 0.4} = 0.717\ \text{kJ/kg K}$$

For unit mass,

$$\textit{Heat supplied} = C_v(T_3 - T_2)$$

$$= 0.717 \times (1548 - 635.5) = 654.3\ \text{kJ}$$

$$\text{Heat rejected} = C_v(T_4 - T_1)$$

$$= 0.717 \times (756.4 - 310) = 320.1 \text{ kJ}$$

$$\frac{\text{Heat supplied}}{\text{Heat rejected}} = \frac{654.3}{320.1} = \mathbf{2.04}$$ Ans

2.9 In an Otto engine, pressure and temperature at the beginning of compression are 1 bar and 37 °C respectively. Calculate the theoretical thermal efficiency of this cycle if the pressure at the end of the adiabatic compression is 15 bar. Peak temperature during the cycle is 2000 K. Calculate (i) the heat supplied per kg of air (ii) the work done per kg of air and (iii) the pressure at the end of adiabatic expansion. Take $C_v = 0.717$ kJ/kg K and $\gamma = 1.4$.

Solution

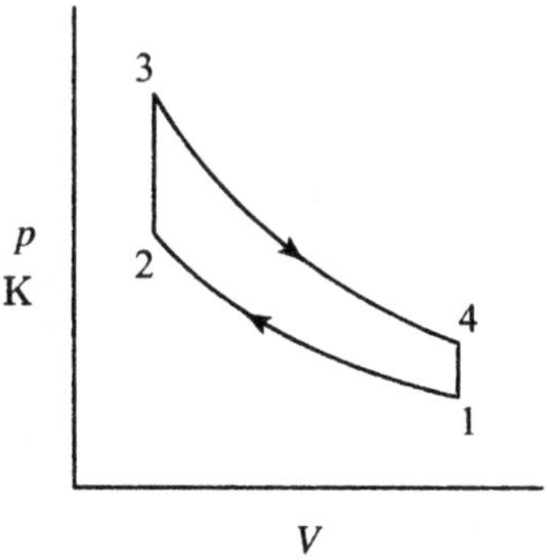

Consider the process 1-2

$$T_2 = T_1\left(\frac{p_2}{p_1}\right)^{\frac{\gamma-1}{\gamma}}$$

$$= 310 \times (15)^{(0.4/1.4)} = 672 \text{ K}$$

$$\eta = 1 - \frac{T_1}{T_2} = 1 - \frac{310}{672}$$

$$= 0.539 = 53.9\%$$

Consider the process 2 – 3

For unit mass flow,

$$q_s = C_v(T_3 - T_2)$$

$$= 0.717 \times (2000 - 672) = \mathbf{952.2 \text{ kJ/kg}}$$ Ans

$$\eta = \frac{\text{Work done per kg of air}}{\text{Heat supplied per kg of air}} = \frac{w}{q_s}$$

$$w = \eta q_s = 0.539 \times 952.2 = \mathbf{513.2 \text{ kJ/kg}}$$ Ans

$$p_3 = p_2\left(\frac{T_3}{T_2}\right) = 15 \times \frac{2000}{672} = 44.64 \text{ bar}$$

Consider the process 3 – 4

$$\frac{p_3}{p_4} = \left(\frac{V_4}{V_3}\right)^{\gamma} = \left(\frac{V_1}{V_2}\right)^{\gamma} = \frac{p_2}{p_1}$$

$$p_4 = p_3\left(\frac{p_1}{p_2}\right) = \frac{44.64 \times 1}{15} = \mathbf{2.98 \text{ bar}}$$ Ans

2.10 Compare the efficiencies of ideal Atkinson cycle and Otto cycle for a compression ratio is 5.5. The pressure and temperature of air at the beginning of compression stroke are 1 bar and 27 °C respectively. The peak pressure is 25 bar for both cycles. Assume $\gamma = 1.4$ for air.

Solution

$$\eta_{Otto} = 1 - \frac{1}{r^{\gamma-1}} = 1 - \frac{1}{5.5^{0.4}} = 49.43\%$$

Refer Fig.2.14

$$\eta_{Atkinson} = 1 - \frac{\gamma(e-r)}{e^{\gamma} - r^{\gamma}}$$

$$r = 5.5$$

$$e = \frac{V_{4'}}{V_3} = \left(\frac{p_3}{p_{4'}}\right)^{\frac{1}{\gamma}} = \left(\frac{25}{1}\right)^{\frac{1}{1.4}} = 9.966$$

$$e^{\gamma} = 9.966^{1.4} = 25$$

$$r^{\gamma} = 5.5^{1.4} = 10.88$$

$$\eta_{Atkinson} = 1 - \frac{1.4 \times (9.966 - 5.5)}{25 - 10.88} = 55.72\%$$

$$\frac{\eta_{Atkinson}}{\eta_{Otto}} = \frac{55.72}{49.43} = \mathbf{1.127}$$

$\underleftarrow{\text{Ans}}$

DIESEL CYCLE

2.11 A Diesel engine has a compression ratio of 20 and cut-off takes place at 5% of the stroke. Find the air-standard efficiency. Assume $\gamma = 1.4$.

Solution

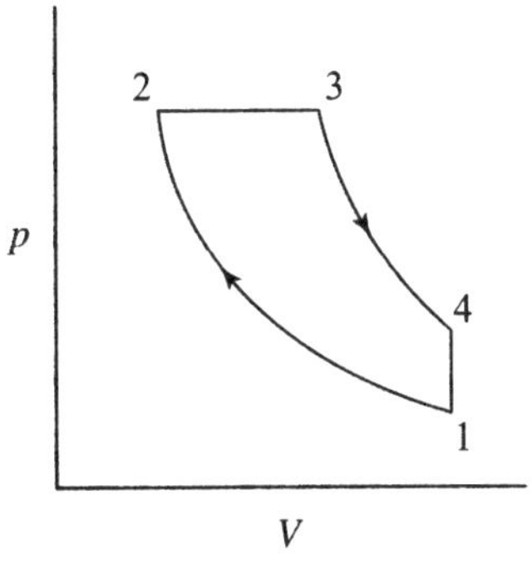

$$r = \frac{V_1}{V_2} = 20$$

$$V_1 = 20V_2$$

$$V_s = 20V_2 - V_2 = 19V_2$$

$$V_3 = 0.05V_s + V_2$$

$$= 0.05 \times 19V_2 + V_2$$

$$= 1.95V_2$$

$$r_c = \frac{V_3}{V_2} = \frac{1.95V_2}{V_2} = 1.95$$

$$\eta = 1 - \frac{1}{r^{\gamma-1}} \frac{r_c^{\gamma} - 1}{\gamma(r_c - 1)}$$

$$= 1 - \frac{1}{20^{0.4}} \times \left[\frac{1.95^{1.4} - 1}{1.4 \times (1.95 - 1)}\right] = 0.649 = \mathbf{64.9\%}$$ Ans

2.12 Determine the ideal efficiency of the diesel engine having a cylinder with bore 250 mm, stroke 375 mm and a clearance volume of 1500 cc, with fuel cut-off occurring at 5% of the stroke. Assume $\gamma = 1.4$ for air.

Solution

$$V_s = \frac{\pi}{4} d^2 \ L = \frac{\pi}{4} \times 25^2 \times 37.5$$

$$= 18407.8 \text{ cc}$$

$$r = 1 + \frac{V_s}{V_c} = 1 + \frac{18407.8}{1500} = 13.27$$

$$\eta = 1 - \frac{1}{r^{\gamma-1}} \frac{r_c^{\gamma} - 1}{\gamma(r_c - 1)}$$

$$r_c = \frac{V_3}{V_2}$$

$$\text{Cut-off volume} = V_3 - V_2 = 0.05V_s = 0.05 \times 12.27V_c$$

$$V_2 = V_c$$

$$V_3 = 1.6135V_c$$

$$r_c = \frac{V_3}{V_2} = 1.6135$$

$$\eta = 1 - \frac{1}{13.27^{0.4}} \times \frac{1.6135^{1.4} - 1}{1.4 \times (1.6135 - 1)}$$

$$= 0.6052 = \mathbf{60.52\%}$$ Ans

2.13 In an engine working on Diesel cycle inlet pressure and temperature are 1 bar and 17 °C respectively. Pressure at the end of adiabatic compression is 35 bar. The ratio of expansion i.e. after constant pressure heat addition is 5. Calculate the heat addition, heat rejection and the efficiency of the cycle. Assume $\gamma = 1.4$, $C_p = 1.004$ kJ/kg K and $C_v = 0.717$ kJ/kg K.

Solution

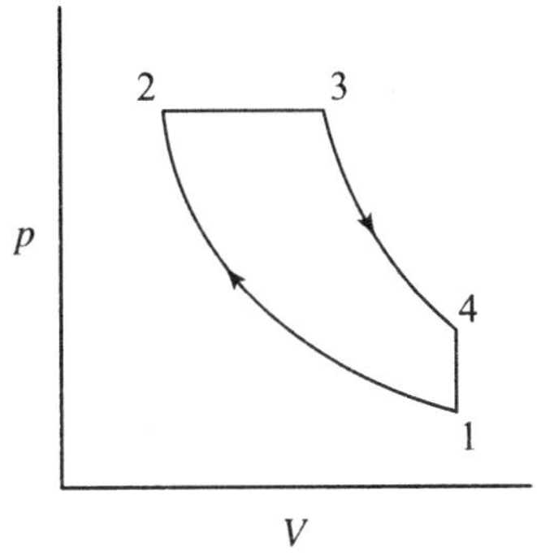

Consider the process 1 – 2

$$\frac{V_1}{V_2} = r$$

$$= \left(\frac{p_2}{p_1}\right)^{\frac{1}{\gamma}}$$

$$= \left(\frac{35}{1}\right)^{\frac{1}{1.4}} = 12.674$$

$$r_c = \frac{V_3}{V_2} = \frac{V_3}{V_1} \times \frac{V_1}{V_2}$$

$$= \frac{\text{Compression ratio}}{\text{Expansion ratio}} = \frac{12.674}{5} = 2.535$$

$$\frac{T_2}{T_1} = \left(\frac{p_2}{p_1}\right)^{\frac{\gamma-1}{\gamma}} = \left(\frac{35}{1}\right)^{0.286} = 2.76$$

$$T_2 = 2.76 \times 290 = 801.7 \text{ K}$$

Consider the process 2 – 3

$$T_3 = T_2\frac{V_3}{V_2} = 801.7 \times \frac{V_3}{V_2} = 801.7 \times 2.535 = 2032.3 \text{ K}$$

Consider the process 3 – 4

$$T_4 = T_3\left(\frac{V_3}{V_4}\right)^{\gamma-1} = 2032.3 \times \left(\frac{1}{5}\right)^{0.4} = 1067.6 \text{ K}$$

$$\textit{Heat added} = C_p(T_3 - T_2) = 1.004 \times (2032.3 - 801.7)$$

$$= \mathbf{1235.5 \text{ kJ/kg}} \quad \overset{\text{Ans}}{\Longleftarrow}$$

$$\textit{Heat rejected} = C_v(T_4 - T_1) = 0.717 \times (1067.6 - 290)$$

$$= \mathbf{557.5 \text{ kJ/kg}} \quad \overset{\text{Ans}}{\Longleftarrow}$$

$$\textit{Efficiency} = \frac{\text{Heat supplied - Heat rejected}}{\text{Heat supplied}}$$

$$= \frac{1235.5 - 557.5}{1235.5} = 0.549 = \mathbf{54.9\%} \quad \overset{\text{Ans}}{\Longleftarrow}$$

2.14 A Diesel engine is working with a compression ratio of 15 and expansion ratio of 10. Calculate the air-standard efficiency of the cycle. Assume $\gamma = 1.4$.

Solution

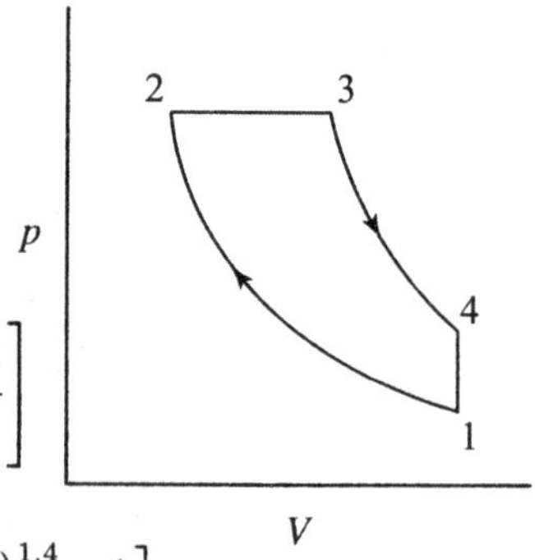

$$r = \frac{V_1}{V_2} = 15$$

$$r_e = \frac{V_4}{V_3} = 10$$

$$\eta = 1 - \frac{1}{\gamma}\frac{1}{r^{\gamma-1}}\left[\frac{\left(\frac{r}{r_e}\right)^{\gamma} - 1}{\left(\frac{r}{r_e}\right) - 1}\right]$$

$$= 1 - \frac{1}{1.4} \times \frac{1}{15^{0.4}} \times \left[\frac{\left(\frac{15}{10}\right)^{1.4} - 1}{\left(\frac{15}{10}\right) - 1}\right] = 0.63 = \mathbf{63\%}$$ Ans

2.15 A Diesel engine works on Diesel cycle with a compression ratio of 15 and cut-off ratio of 1.75. Calculate the air-standard efficiency assuming $\gamma = 1.4$.

Solution

$$\eta = 1 - \frac{1}{r^{\gamma-1}}\frac{1}{\gamma}\left(\frac{r_c^{\gamma} - 1}{r - 1}\right)$$

$$= 1 - \frac{1}{15^{0.4}} \times \frac{1}{1.4} \times \left(\frac{1.75^{1.4} - 1}{1.75 - 1}\right) = 0.617 = \mathbf{61.7\%}$$ Ans

2.16 A Diesel cycle operates at a pressure of 1 bar at the beginning of compression and the volume is compressed to $\frac{1}{16}$ of the initial volume. Heat is supplied until the volume is twice that of the clearance volume. Calculate the mean effective pressure of the cycle. Take $\gamma = 1.4$.

Solution

$$V_1 = 16V_2$$

$$V_3 = 2V_2$$

$$V_s = V_1 - V_2 = (r-1)V_2 = 15\ V_2$$

$$V_2 = \frac{V_s}{15}$$

Consider the process 1 – 2

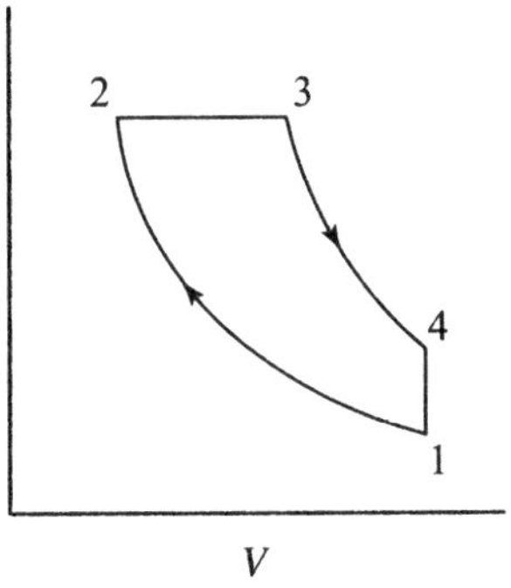

$$p_2 = p_1\left(\frac{V_1}{V_2}\right)^{\gamma}$$

$$= 1 \times 16^{1.4} = 48.5 \text{ bar}$$

$$p_2 = p_3 = 48.5 \text{ bar}$$

$$p_4 = p_3\left(\frac{V_3}{V_4}\right)^{1.4}$$

$$= 48.5 \times \left(\frac{2}{16}\right)^{1.4}$$

$$= \frac{48.5}{8^{1.4}} = 2.64 \text{ bar} \qquad (\text{Since, } V_4 = V_1)$$

$$p_m = \frac{1}{V_s}\left[p_2(V_3 - V_2) + \frac{p_3V_3 - p_4V_4}{\gamma - 1} - \frac{p_2V_2 - p_1V_1}{\gamma - 1}\right]$$

$$= \frac{V_2}{V_s}\left[p_3\left(\frac{V_3}{V_2} - 1\right) + \frac{\left(p_3\frac{V_3}{V_2} - p_4\frac{V_4}{V_2}\right)}{\gamma - 1} - \frac{\left(p_2 - p_1\frac{V_1}{V_2}\right)}{\gamma - 1}\right]$$

$$= \frac{1}{15} \times \left[48.5 \times (2 - 1) + \frac{48.5 \times 2 - 2.64 \times 16}{1.4 - 1} - \frac{48.5 - 1 \times 16}{1.4 - 1}\right]$$

$$= \mathbf{6.94 \text{ bar}}$$

Ans ⟸

2.17 In an engine working on the Diesel cycle the ratios of the weights of air and fuel supplied is 50 : 1. The temperature of air at the beginning of the compression is 60 °C and the compression ratio used is 14 : 1. What is the ideal efficiency of the engine. Calorific value of fuel used is 42000 kJ/kg. Assume $C_p = 1.004$ kJ/kg K and $C_v = 0.717$ kJ/kg K for air.

Solution

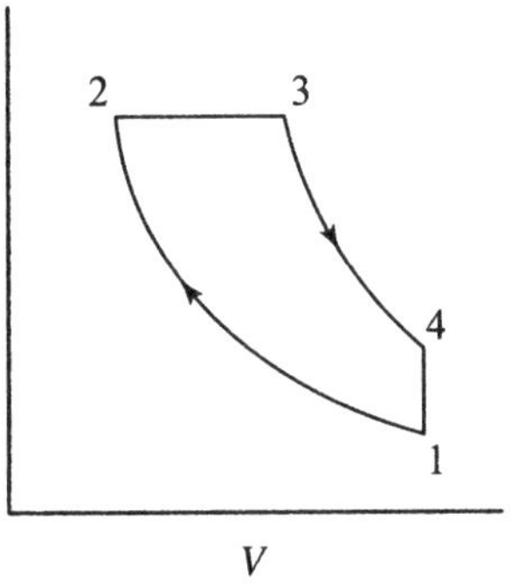

$$\eta = 1 - \frac{1}{r^{\gamma-1}}\,\frac{r_c^{\gamma} - 1}{\gamma(r_c - 1)}$$

$$\gamma = \frac{C_p}{C_v} = \frac{1.004}{0.717} = 1.4$$

$$r_c = \frac{V_3}{V_2} = \frac{T_3}{T_2}$$

Consider the process 1 – 2

$$\frac{T_2}{T_1} = \left(\frac{V_1}{V_2}\right)^{(\gamma-1)} = r^{(\gamma-1)} = 14^{0.4} = 2.874$$

$$T_2 = 2.874 \times 333 = 957.04 \text{ K}$$

Consider the process 2 – 3

$$\textit{Heat added/kg of air} = C_p\,(T_3 - T_2) = F/A \times CV$$

$$T_3 - T_2 = \frac{F/A \times CV}{C_p} = \frac{42000}{50 \times 1.004} = 836.6$$

$$T_3 = 1793.64K$$

$$r_c = \frac{T_3}{T_2} = \frac{1793.64}{957.04} = 1.874$$

$$\eta = 1 - \frac{1}{1.4 \times 14^{0.4}} \times \left(\frac{1.874^{1.4} - 1}{0.874}\right)$$

$$= 0.60 = \mathbf{60\%}$$ Ans

2.18 In an ideal Diesel cycle, the pressure and temperature are 1.03 bar and 27 °C respectively. The maximum pressure in the cycle is 47 bar and the heat supplied during the cycle is 545 kJ/kg. Determine (i) the compression ratio (ii) the temperature at the end of compression (iii) the temperature at the end of constant pressure combustion and (iv) the air-standard efficiency. Assume γ= 1.4 and C_p = 1.004 kJ/kg K for air.

Solution

$$p_2 = p_3 = 47 \times 10^5 \text{ N/m}^2$$

$$\frac{p_2}{p_1} = \left(\frac{V_1}{V_2}\right)^{\gamma} = r^{\gamma}$$

$$r = \left(\frac{p_2}{p_1}\right)^{\left(\frac{1}{\gamma}\right)} = \left(\frac{47}{1.03}\right)^{\left(\frac{1}{1.4}\right)} = \mathbf{15.32}$$ Ans

$$\frac{T_2}{T_1} = \left(\frac{V_1}{V_2}\right)^{(\gamma-1)} = r^{(\gamma-1)} = 15.32^{0.4} = 2.979$$

$$T_2 = 2.979 \times 300 = 893.7 \text{ K} = \mathbf{620.7^\circ\ C}$$ Ans

$$\textit{Heat supplied/kg} = C_p\,(T_3 - T_2) = 545$$

$$T_3 - T_2 = \frac{545}{1.004} = 542.8$$

$$T_3 = 542.8 + 893.7 = 1436.5 \text{ K}\mathbf{1163.5^\circ\ C}$$ Ans

$$\eta = 1 - \frac{1}{r^{\gamma-1}}\frac{r_c^{\gamma}-1}{\gamma(r_c-1)}$$

$$r_c = \frac{V_3}{V_2} = \frac{T_3}{T_2} = \frac{1436.5}{893.7} = 1.61$$

$$\eta_{Diesel} = 1 - \left[\frac{1}{1.4 \times 15.32^{0.4}} \times \left(\frac{1.61^{1.4}-1}{0.61}\right)\right]$$

$$= 0.6275 = \mathbf{62.75\%}$$ Ans

2.19 A diesel engine operating on the air-standard Diesel cycle has six cylinders of 100 mm bore and 120 mm stroke. The engine speed is 1800 rpm. At the beginning of compression the pressure and temperature of air are 1.03 bar and 35 °C. If the clearance volume is 1/8th of the stroke volume, calculate (i) the pressure and temperature at the salient points of the cycle (ii) the compression ratio (iii) the efficiency of the cycle and (iv) the power output if the air is heated to 1500 °C Assume C_p and C_v of air to be 1.004 and 0.717 kJ/kg K respectively.

Solution

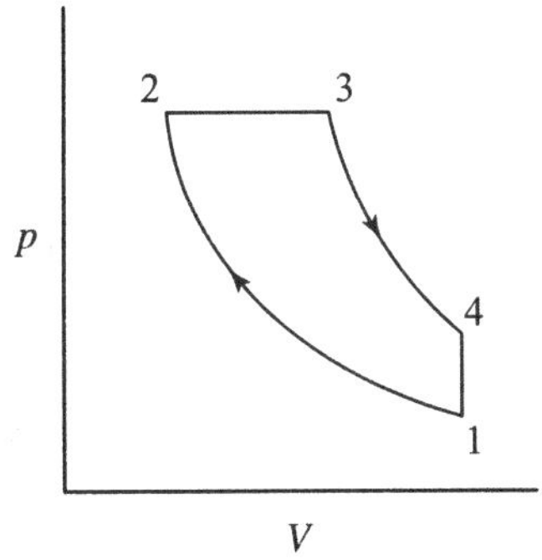

$$r = 1 + \frac{V_s}{V_c}$$

$$= 1 + 8 = \mathbf{9}$$ Ans

Consider the process 1 – 2,

$$\frac{p_2}{p_1} = r^{\gamma} = 9^{1.4} = 21.67$$

$$p_2 = 21.67 \times 1.03 \times 10^5$$

$$= 22.32 \times 10^5 \text{ N/m}^2$$

$$= \mathbf{22.32 \text{ bar}}$$ Ans

Consider the process 3 – 4,

$$\frac{T_3}{T_4} = r_e^{(\gamma-1)}$$

$$\frac{T_2}{T_1} = r^{(\gamma-1)} = 9^{0.4} = 2.408$$

$$T_2 = 308 \times 2.408 = 741.6 \text{ K} = \mathbf{468.6°C}$$ Ans

Consider the process 2 – 3,

$$p_3 = p_2 = 22.32 \times 10^5 \text{ N/m}^2 = \mathbf{22.32 \text{ bar}} \quad \overset{\text{Ans}}{\Longleftarrow}$$

$$T_3 = 1773 \text{ K} = \mathbf{1500° \text{ C}} \quad \overset{\text{Ans}}{\Longleftarrow}$$

$$r_c = \frac{T_3}{T_2} = \frac{1773}{741.6} = 2.39$$

$$r_e = \frac{r}{r_c} = \frac{9}{2.391} = 3.764$$

$$T_4 = \frac{T_3}{1.7} = \frac{1773}{1.7} = 1042.9 \text{ K} = \mathbf{769.9° \text{ C}} \quad \overset{\text{Ans}}{\Longleftarrow}$$

$$\frac{p_3}{p_4} = r_e^{\gamma} = 3.764^{1.4} = 6.396$$

$$p_4 = \frac{p_3}{6.396} = \frac{22.32 \times 10^5}{6.396}$$

$$= 3.49 \times 10^5 \text{ N/m}^2 = \mathbf{3.49 \text{ bar}} \quad \overset{\text{Ans}}{\Longleftarrow}$$

$$\eta_{Cycle} = \frac{\textit{Work output}}{\textit{Heat added}} = 1 - \frac{\textit{Heat rejected}}{\textit{Heat added}}$$

$$= 1 - \frac{q_{4-1}}{q_{2-3}}$$

$$q_{4-1} = C_v (T_4 - T_1)$$

$$= 0.717 \times (1042.9 - 308) = 526.9 \text{ kJ/kg}$$

$$q_{2-3} = C_p (T_3 - T_2)$$

$$= 1.004 \times (1773 - 741.6) = 1035.5 \text{ kJ/kg}$$

$$\eta_{Cycle} = 1 - \frac{526.9}{1035.5} = 0.4912 = \mathbf{49.12\%} \quad \overset{\text{Ans}}{\Longleftarrow}$$

$$\textit{Work output} = q_{2-3} - q_{4-1}$$

$$= 1035.5 - 526.9 = 508.6 \text{ kJ/kg}$$

$$\textit{Power output} = \textit{Work output} \times \dot{m}_a$$

$$\dot{m}_a = \frac{p_1 V_1}{R T_1} \times \frac{N}{2}$$

$$R = C_p - C_v = 0.287 \text{ kJ/kg K}$$

$$V_1 = V_s + V_c = \frac{9}{8} V_s$$

$$V_s = 6 \times \frac{\pi}{4} d^2 \ L = 6 \times \frac{\pi}{4} \times 10^2 \times 12$$

$$= 5654.8 \text{ cc} = 5.65 \times 10^{-3} \text{ m}^3$$

$$V_1 = 5.65 \times 10^{-3} \times \frac{9}{8} = 6.36 \times 10^{-3} \text{ m}^3$$

$$\dot{m}_a = \frac{1.03 \times 10^5 \times 6.36 \times 10^{-3} \times 30}{287 \times 308 \times 2} = 0.111 \text{ kg/s}$$

Power output $= 508.6 \times 0.111 =$ **56.45 kW** Ans

2.20 The mean effective pressure of an ideal Diesel cycle is 8 bar. If the initial pressure is 1.03 bar and the compression ratio is 12, determine the cut-off ratio and the air-standard efficiency. Assume ratio of specific heats for air to be 1.4.

Solution

$$W = p_m \times V_s = \text{Area } 1234$$

$$= \text{Area under } 2-3 + \text{Area under } 3-4 - \text{Area under } 2-1$$

$$= p_2 (V_3 - V_2) + \frac{p_3 V_3 - p_4 V_4}{\gamma - 1} - \frac{p_2 V_2 - p_1 V_1}{\gamma - 1}$$

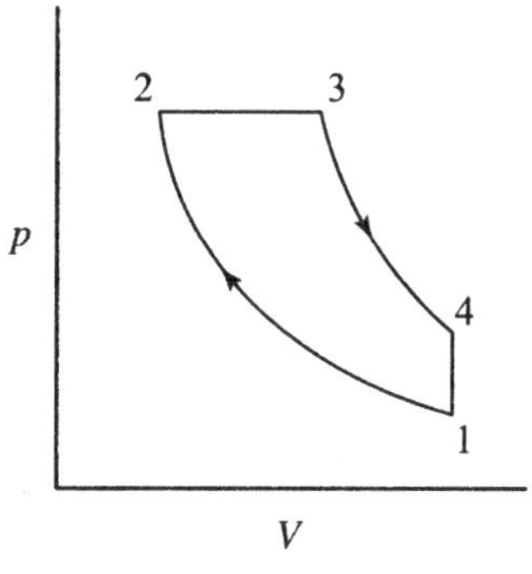

$$r = \frac{V_1}{V_2} = 1 + \frac{V_s}{V_c} = 12$$

$$V_s = 11 V_c$$

$$V_2 = V_c$$

$$V_1 = V_4 = 12 V_2 = 12 V_c$$

$$V_3 = r_c V_2 = r_c V_c$$

$$\frac{p_2}{p_1} = r^{\gamma} = 12^{1.4} = 32.42$$

$$p_2 = 32.42 \times 1.03 \times 10^5 = 33.39 \times 10^5 \text{ N/m}^2 = p_3$$

$$\frac{p_3}{p_4} = \left(\frac{r}{r_c}\right)^{1.4} = \frac{12^{1.4}}{r_c^{1.4}} = \frac{32.42}{r_c^{1.4}}$$

$$p_4 = \frac{33.39}{32.42} \times r_c^{1.4} \times 10^5 = 1.03 r_c^{1.4} \times 10^5$$

$$\text{Area 1234} = 33.39\,(r_cV_c - V_c) + \frac{33.39 \times r_cV_c - 1.03r_c^{1.4} \times 12V_c}{0.4} - \frac{33.39 \times V_c - 1.03 \times 12V_c}{0.4} \times 10^5$$

$$p_m \times V_s = 8 \times 11V_c \times 10^5$$

$$\text{Area 1234} = p_m \times V_s$$

Substituting and simplifying

$$0.672r_c - 0.178r_c^{1.4} = 1$$

Solving by iteration,

$$r_c = \mathbf{2.38} \qquad \underleftarrow{\text{Ans}}$$

$$\eta = 1 - \frac{1}{r^{\gamma-1}}\,\frac{r_c^{\gamma} - 1}{\gamma(r_c - 1)}$$

$$= 1 - \frac{1}{1.4 \times 12^{0.4}} \times \left(\frac{2.38^{1.4} - 1}{1.38}\right) = 0.5466 = \mathbf{54.66\%} \qquad \underleftarrow{\text{Ans}}$$

DUAL CYCLES

2.21 An air-standard Dual cycle has a compression ratio of 10. The pressure and temperature at the beginning of compression are 1 bar and 27 °C. The maximum pressure reached is 42 bar and the maximum temperature is 1500 °C. Determine (i) the temperature at the end of constant volume heat addition (ii) cut-off ratio (iii) work done per kg of air and (iv) the cycle efficiency. Assume C_p = 1.004 kJ/kg K and C_v = 0.717 kJ/kg K for air.

Solution

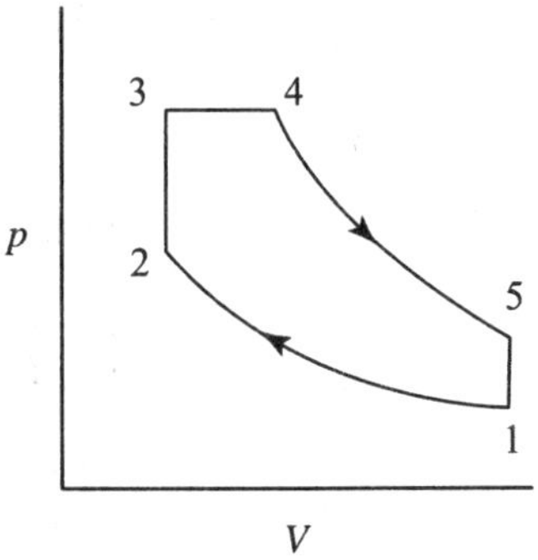

$$\frac{V_s}{V_c} = r - 1 = 9$$

$$V_s = 9V_c$$

$$\gamma = \frac{C_p}{C_v} = \frac{1.004}{0.717} = 1.4$$

Consider the process 1 – 2

$$\frac{T_2}{T_1} = r^{(\gamma-1)} = 10^{0.4} = 2.512$$

$$T_2 = 2.512 \times 300 = 753.6 \text{ K}$$

$$\frac{p_2}{p_1} = r^{\gamma} = 10^{1.4} = 25.12$$

$$p_2 = 25.12 \times 10^5 \text{ N/m}^2$$

Consider the process 3 – 4

$$\frac{T_3}{T_2} = \frac{p_3}{p_2} = \frac{42}{25.12} = 1.672$$

$$T_3 = 1.672 \times 753.6 = 1260 \text{ K} = \mathbf{987° \ C}$$ Ans

$$r_c = \frac{T_4}{T_3} = \frac{1773}{1260} = \mathbf{1.407}$$ Ans

Work done/kg = *Heat supplied - Heat rejected*

$$\textit{Heat supplied/kg} = C_v\,(T_3 - T_2) + C_p\,(T_4 - T_3)$$

$$= 0.717 \times (1260 - 753.6) +$$

$$1.004 \times (1773 - 1260) = \mathbf{878.1 \ kJ}$$ Ans

Consider the process 4 – 5

$$\frac{T_4}{T_5} = \left(\frac{V_5}{V_4}\right)^{(\gamma-1)} = \left(\frac{r}{r_c}\right)^{(\gamma-1)} = \left(\frac{10}{1.407}\right)^{0.4} = 2.191$$

$$T_5 = \frac{T_4}{2.191} = \mathbf{809.2 \ K}$$ Ans

$$\textit{Heat rejected/kg} = C_v\,(T_5 - T_1)$$

$$= 0.717 \times (809.2 - 300) = 365.1 \text{ kJ}$$

$$\textit{Work output/kg} = 878.1 - 365.1 = \mathbf{513 \ kJ}$$ Ans

$$\eta_{Dual} = \frac{\textit{Work output}}{\textit{Heat added}} = \frac{513}{878.1}$$

$$= 0.5842 = \mathbf{58.42\%}$$ Ans

2.22 For an engine working on the ideal Dual cycle, the compression ratio is 10 and the maximum pressure is limited to 70 bar. If the heat supplied is 1680 kJ/kg, find the pressures and temperatures at the various salient points of the cycle and the cycle efficiency. The pressure and temperature of air at the commencement of compression are 1 bar and 100 °C respectively. Assume C_p = 1.004 kJ/kg K and C_v = 0.717 kJ/kg K for air.

Solution

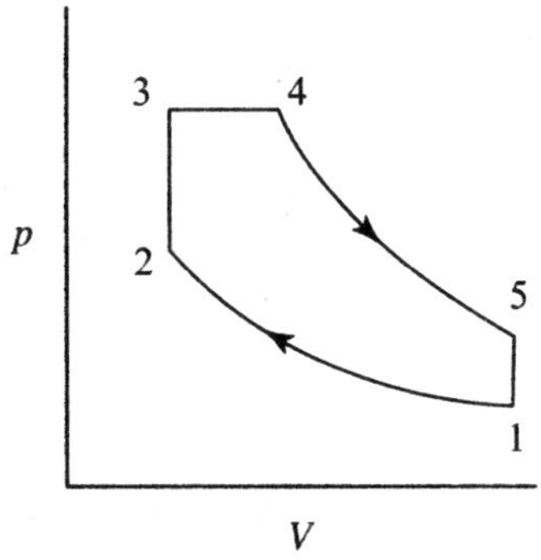

$$\frac{V_s}{V_c} = r - 1 = 9$$

$$\gamma = \frac{C_p}{C_v} = \frac{1.004}{0.717} = 1.4$$

Consider the process 1 – 2

$$\frac{p_2}{p_1} = r^{\gamma} = 10^{1.4} = 25.12$$

$$p_2 = 25.12 \times 10^5 \text{ N/m}^2$$

$$= \mathbf{25.12 \text{ bar}} \quad \overset{\text{Ans}}{\Longleftarrow}$$

$$\frac{T_2}{T_1} = r^{(\gamma-1)} = 10^{0.4} = 2.512$$

$$T_2 = 2.512 \times 373 = 936.9 \text{ K} = \mathbf{663.9^\circ C} \quad \overset{\text{Ans}}{\Longleftarrow}$$

Consider the process 2 – 3 and 3 – 4

$$\frac{T_3}{T_2} = \frac{p_3}{p_2} = \frac{70}{25.12} = 2.787$$

$$T_3 = 2.787 \times 936.9 = 2611.1 \text{ K} = \mathbf{2338^\circ \text{ C}} \quad \overset{\text{Ans}}{\Longleftarrow}$$

Heat added during constant volume combustion

$$= C_v (T_3 - T_2) = 0.717 \times (2611.1 - 936.9)$$

$$= 1200.4 \text{ kJ/kg}$$

$$\textit{Total heat added} = 1680 \text{ kJ/kg}$$

Hence, heat added during constant pressure combustion

$$= 1680 - 1200.4 = 479.6 \text{ kJ/kg}$$

$$= C_p (T_4 - T_3)$$

$$T_4 - T_3 = \frac{479.6}{1.004} = 477.7 \text{ K}$$

$$T_4 = 477.7 + 2611.1$$

$$= 3088.8 \text{ K} = \mathbf{2815.8^\circ \text{ C}} \quad \overset{\text{Ans}}{\Longleftarrow}$$

$$r_c = \frac{V_4}{V_3} = \frac{T_4}{T_3} = \frac{3088.8}{2611.1} = 1.183$$

Consider the process 4 – 5

$$\frac{T_4}{T_5} = \left(\frac{r}{r_c}\right)^{(\gamma-1)} = 8.453^{0.4} = 2.35$$

$$T_5 = \frac{T_4}{2.35} = \frac{3088.8}{2.35} = 1314.4 \text{ K} = \mathbf{1041.4^\circ\ C} \overset{\text{Ans}}{\Longleftarrow}$$

$$\frac{p_4}{p_5} = \left(\frac{r}{r_c}\right)^{\gamma} = 19.85$$

$$p_5 = \frac{p_4}{19.85} = \frac{70 \times 10^5}{19.85}$$

$$= 3.53 \times 10^5 \text{ N/m}^2 = \mathbf{3.53\ bar} \quad \overset{\text{Ans}}{\Longleftarrow}$$

$$\textit{Heat rejected} = C_v(T_5 - T_1)$$

$$= 0.717 \times (1314.4 - 373) = 674.98 \text{ kJ/kg}$$

$$\eta = \frac{1680 - 674.98}{1680} = \mathbf{59.82\%} \quad \overset{\text{Ans}}{\Longleftarrow}$$

2.23 An oil engine works on the Dual cycle, the heat liberated at constant pressure being twice that liberated at constant volume. The compression ratio of the engine is 8 and the expansion ratio is 5.3. But the compression and expansion processes follow the law $pV^{1.3}$ = C. The pressure and temperature at the beginning of compression are 1 bar and 27 °C respectively. Assuming C_p = 1.004 kJ/kg K and C_v = 0.717 kJ/kg K for air, find the air-standard efficiency and the mean effective pressure.

Solution

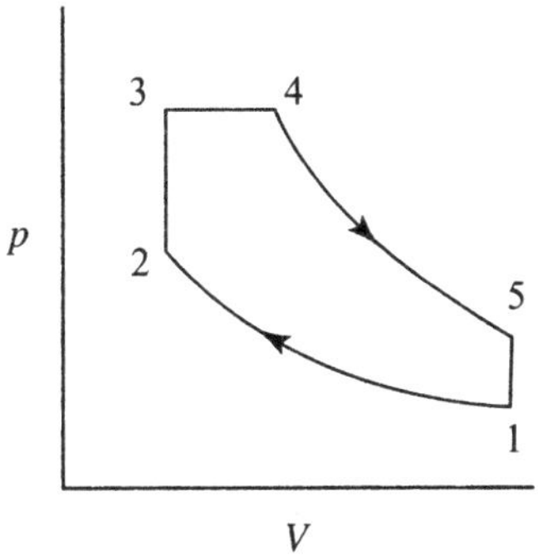

$$\gamma = \frac{C_p}{C_v} = \frac{1.004}{0.717} = 1.4$$

$$\frac{V_s}{V_c} = r - 1 = 7$$

$$V_s = 7V_c$$

$$r_e = \frac{r}{r_c} = 5.3$$

$$r_c = \frac{8}{5.3} = 1.509$$

$$mep = \frac{\text{Area 12345}}{V_s}$$

$$\text{Area 12345} = \text{Area under } 3-4 + \text{Area under } 4-5 - \text{Area under } 2-1$$

$$= p_3(V_3 - V_4) + \frac{p_4V_4 - p_5V_5}{n-1} - \frac{p_2V_2 - p_1V_1}{n-1}$$

$$V_2 = V_3 = V_c$$

$$V_1 = V_5 = rV_c = 8\,V_c$$

$$V_4 = r_cV_3 = 1.509\,V_c$$

$$\frac{T_2}{T_1} = r^{(n-1)} = 8^{0.3} = 1.866$$

$$T_2 = 1.866 \times 300 = 559.82 \text{ K}$$

$$\frac{p_2}{p_1} = r^n = 8^{1.3} = 14.93$$

$$p_2 = 14.93 \times p_1 = 14.93 \times 10^5 \text{ N/m}^2$$

Heat released during constant pressure combustion

= 2 × *Heat released during constant volume combustion*

$$C_p(T_4 - T_3) = 2C_v(T_3 - T_2)$$

$$1.004 \times (T_4 - T_3) = 2 \times 0.717 \times (T_3 - T_2)$$

$$T_4 - T_3 = 1.428 \times (T_3 - T_2)$$

$$\frac{T_4}{T_3} = \frac{V_4}{V_3} = r_c = 1.509$$

$$T_4 = 1.509\,T_3$$

$$1.509\,T_3 - T_3 = 1.428 \times (T_3 - 559.82)$$

$$T_3 = 869.88 \text{ K}$$

$$T_4 = 1312.65 \text{ K}$$

$$\frac{p_3}{p_2} = \frac{T_3}{T_2} = \frac{869.88}{559.82} = 1.554$$

$$p_3 = 1.554 \times 14.93 \times 10^5$$

$$= 23.20 \times 10^5 \text{ N/m}^2 = p_4$$

$$\frac{T_4}{T_5} = r_e^{(n-1)} = 5.3^{0.3} = 1.649$$

$$T_5 = \frac{1312.65}{1.649} = 796.03 \text{ K}$$

$$\frac{p_4}{p_5} = r_e^n = 5.3^{1.3} = 8.741$$

$$p_5 = \frac{p_4}{8.741} = \frac{23.2 \times 10^5}{8.741}$$

$$= 2.654 \times 10^5 \text{ N/m}^2$$

$$\text{Area 12345} = \left[\frac{23.2 \times 1.509V_c - 2.654 \times 8V_c}{0.3} + 23.2 \times (1.509V_c - V_c) - \frac{14.93 \times V_c - 1 \times 8V_c}{0.3}\right] \times 10^5$$

$$= 34.63 \times V_c \times 10^5 \text{ N/m}^2$$

$$V_c = \frac{V_1}{8}$$

$$\text{Area 12345} = p_m \times V_s = p_m \times 7 \times V_c$$

$$p_m = \frac{34.63}{7} = 4.95 \times 10^5 \text{ N/m}^2$$

$$= \mathbf{4.95 \text{ bar}}$$ Ans

$$\eta = \frac{w}{q_s}$$

$$v_1 = \frac{mRT_1}{p_1} = \frac{1 \times 287 \times 300}{1 \times 10^5} = 0.861 \text{ m}^3\text{/kg}$$

$$w = 34.63 \times 10^5 \times \frac{v_1}{8} = 34.63 \times 10^5 \times \frac{0.861}{8}$$

$$= 3.727 \times 10^5 \text{ J/kg} = 372.7 \text{ kJ/kg}$$

Note : Work done should be calculated only from the area ($\int pdv$) for a polytropic process

$$q_s = q(T_3 - T_2) + C_p(T_4 - T_3) = 667.1 \text{ kJ/kg}$$

$$\eta = \frac{372.7}{667.1} \times 100 = \mathbf{55.9\%} \quad \overset{\text{Ans}}{\Longleftarrow}$$

COMPARISON OF CYCLES

2.24 A four-cylinder, four-stroke, spark-ignition engine has a displacement volume of 300 cc per cylinder. The compression ratio of the engine is 10 and operates at a speed of 3000 rev/min. The engine is required to develop an output of 40 kW at this speed. Calculate the cycle efficiency, the necessary rate of heat addition, the mean effective pressure and the maximum temperature of the cycle. Assume that the engine operates on the Otto cycle and that the pressure and temperature at the inlet conditions are 1 bar and 27 °C respectively.
If the above engine is a compression-ignition engine operating on the Diesel cycle and receiving heat at the same rate, calculate efficiency, the maximum temperature of the cycle, the cycle efficiency, the power output and the mean effective pressure. Take $C_v = 0.717$ kJ/kg K and $\gamma = 1.4$.

Solution

Consider the Otto cycle, Fig.2.9(a)

$$\eta = 1 - \frac{1}{r^{\gamma-1}}$$

$$= 1 - \frac{1}{10^{0.4}} = 0.602 = \mathbf{60.2\%} \quad \overset{\text{Ans}}{\Longleftarrow}$$

$$\eta = \frac{\textit{Power output}}{\textit{Heat supplied}}$$

$$\textit{Heat supplied} = \frac{40}{0.602} = 66.5 \text{ kW} = \mathbf{66.5\ kJ/s} \quad \overset{\text{Ans}}{\Longleftarrow}$$

$$\textit{Number of cycles/s} = \frac{3000}{2 \times 60} = 25$$

Net work output per cycle from each cylinder

$$= \frac{40}{4 \times 25} = 0.4 \text{ kJ}$$

$$p_m = \frac{W}{V_s} = \frac{0.4 \times 1000}{300 \times 10^{-6}}$$

$$= \mathbf{13.3 \times 10^5\ N/m^2} \quad \overset{\text{Ans}}{\Longleftarrow}$$

$$T_2 = T_1 \left(\frac{V_1}{V_2}\right)^{\gamma-1} = 300 \times 10^{0.4} = 753.6 \text{ K}$$

Heat supplied/cylinder/cycle (Q_{2-3})

$$= \frac{66.5}{4 \times 25} = 0.665 \text{ kJ}$$

Now,

$$Q_{2-3} = mC_v(T_3 - T_2)$$

$$v_1 = \frac{RT_1}{p_1} = \frac{287 \times 300}{1 \times 10^5}$$

$$= 0.861 \text{ m}^3/\text{kg}$$

This initial volume of air in the cylinder is

$$V_1 = V_2 + V_s = \left(\frac{V_1}{10}\right) + V_s$$

$$0.9V_1 = V_s$$

$$V_1 = \frac{V_s}{0.9} = \frac{300 \times 10^{-6}}{0.9}$$

$$= 333 \times 10^{-6} \text{ m}^3$$

$$m = \frac{V_1}{v_1} = \frac{333 \times 10^{-6}}{0.861}$$

$$= 0.387 \times 10^{-3} \text{ kg}$$

The temperature rise resulting from heat addition is

$$T_3 - T_2 = \frac{Q_{2-3}}{m\ C_v}$$

$$= \frac{0.665}{0.387 \times 10^{-3} \times 0.717} = 2396.6 \text{ K}$$

$$T_3 = T_2 + 2396.6 = 753.6 + 2396.6$$

$$= 3150.2 \text{ K} = \mathbf{2877^\circ\ C}$$ Ans ⟸

Now let us consider the Diesel cycle

T_2 is the same as in the previous case, i.e.

$$T_2 = 753.6$$

Heat supplied per cycle per cylinder is also same, i.e.

$$Q_{2-3'} = 0.665 \text{ kJ}$$

$$Q_{2-3'} = m\ C_p(T_{3'} - T_2)$$

$$T_{3'} - T_2 = \frac{0.665}{0.387 \times 10^{-3}} \times \frac{1}{1.004}$$

$$= 1711.5 \text{ K}$$

$$T_{3'} = 1711.5 + 753.6 = 2465.1 \text{ K}$$

$$= \mathbf{2192.1^\circ\ C} \qquad \stackrel{\text{Ans}}{\Longleftarrow}$$

$$\text{Cut-off ratio, } r_c = \frac{V_3}{V_2} = \frac{T_{3'}}{T_2} = \frac{2465.1}{753.6} = 3.27$$

$$\text{Air-standard efficiency} = 1 - \frac{1}{r^{\gamma-1}}\left[\frac{r_c^\gamma - 1}{\gamma\,(r_c - 1)}\right]$$

$$= 1 - \frac{1}{10^{0.4}} \times \left[\frac{3.27^{1.4} - 1}{1.4 \times (3.27 - 1)}\right]$$

$$= 1 - 0.398 \times 1.338 = 0.467$$

$$= \mathbf{46.7\%} \qquad \stackrel{\text{Ans}}{\Longleftarrow}$$

$$\text{Power output} = \eta \times \textit{total rate of heat added}$$

$$= 0.467 \times 66.5 = 31.1 \text{ kW}$$

$$\text{Power output/cylinder} = \frac{31.1}{4} = 7.76 \text{ kW}$$

$$\text{Work done/cylinder/cycle} = \frac{7.76}{25} = 0.3104 \text{ kJ}$$

$$p_m = \frac{W}{V_s} = \frac{0.3104 \times 1000}{300 \times 10^{-6}}$$

$$= \mathbf{10.35 \times 10^5\ N/m^2} \qquad \stackrel{\text{Ans}}{\Longleftarrow}$$

As discussed in the text, this problem illustrates that for the same compression ratio and heat input Otto cycle is more efficient.

2.25 The compression ratio of an engine is 10 and the temperature and pressure at the start of compression is 37 °C and 1 bar. The compression and expansion processes are both isentropic and the heat is rejected at exhaust at constant volume. The amount of heat added during the cycle is 2730 kJ/kg. Determine the mean effective pressure and thermal efficiency of the cycle if (i) the maximum pressure is limited to 70 bar and heat is added at both constant volume and constant pressure and (ii) if all the heat is added at constant volume. In this case how much additional work per kg of charge would be obtained if it were possible to expand isentropically the exhaust gases to their original pressure of 1 bar. Assume that the charge has the same physical properties as that of air.

Solution

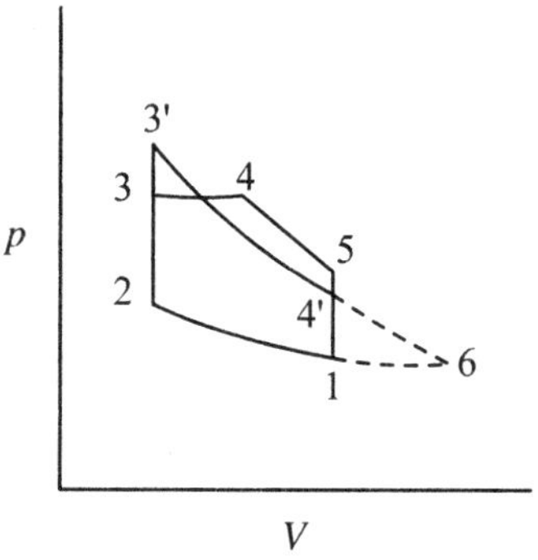

$$v_1 = \frac{V_1}{m} = \frac{RT_1}{p_1}$$

$$= \frac{287 \times 310}{1 \times 10^5} = 0.89 \text{ m}^3/\text{kg}$$

Consider the process 1-2

$$\frac{T_2}{T_1} = \left(\frac{V_1}{V_2}\right)^{\gamma-1}$$

$$= 310 \times 10^{0.4} = 778.7 \text{ K}$$

$$p_2 = p_1\left(\frac{V_1}{V_2}\right)^{\gamma} = 25.12 \text{ bar}$$

Consider the limited pressure cycle (123451)

$$T_3 = T_2\frac{p_3}{p_2} = 778.7 \times \frac{70}{25.12} = 2170 \text{ K}$$

Heat supplied at constant volume

$$= 0.717 \times (2170 - 778.7) = 997.56 \text{ kJ/kg}$$

Heat supplied at constant pressure

$$= 2730 - 997.56 = 1732.44 \text{ kJ/kg}$$

$$1732.4 = 1.004 \times (T_4 - 2170)$$

$$T_4 = 2170 + \frac{1732.4}{1.004} = 3895.5 \text{ K}$$

$$v_4 = v_3 \times \frac{T_4}{T_3} = \frac{0.89}{10} \times \frac{3895.5}{2170} = 0.16 \text{ m}^3/\text{kg}$$

$$T_5 = T_4\left(\frac{v_4}{v_5}\right)^{\gamma-1} = 3895.5 \times \left(\frac{0.16}{0.89}\right)^{0.4} = 1961 \text{ K}$$

$$\textit{Heat rejected} = C_v\,(T_5 - T_1)$$

$$= 0.717 \times (1961 - 310) = 1184 \text{ kJ/kg}$$

$$\textit{Work done} = \textit{Heat supplied} - \textit{Heat rejected}$$

$$= 2730 - 1184 = 1546 \text{ kJ/kg}$$

$$\eta = \frac{w}{q} = \frac{1546}{2730} = 0.57 = \mathbf{57\%}$$ Ans

$$p_m = \frac{w}{v_1 - v_2} = \frac{w}{v_1\left(1 - \frac{1}{r}\right)}$$

$$= \frac{1546 \times 10^3}{0.89 \times \left(1 - \frac{1}{10}\right)}$$

$$= 19.32 \times 10^5 \text{ N/m}^2 = \mathbf{19.32\ bar}$$ Ans

Consider the constant-volume cycle (123′4′1)

$$q_{2-3'} = 2730 \text{ kJ/kg}$$

$$2730 = 0.717 \times (T_{3'} - 778)$$

$$T_{3'} = 4586 \text{ K}$$

$$p_{3'} = T_{3'}\left(\frac{p_2}{T_2}\right) = 4586 \times \frac{25.12}{778.7} = 147.9 \text{ bar}$$

$$\frac{T_{3'}}{T_{4'}} = \left(\frac{V_{4'}}{V_{3'}}\right)^{\gamma-1}$$

$$T_{4'} = 4586 \times \left(\frac{1}{10}\right)^{0.4} = 1852.7$$

$$\textit{Heat rejected} = 0.717 \times (1825.7 - 310) = 1087 \text{ kJ/kg}$$

$$w = 2730 - 1087 = 1643 \text{ kJ}$$

$$\eta = \frac{1643}{2730} = 0.602 = \mathbf{60.2\%}$$ Ans

$$p_m = \frac{1643 \times 10^3}{\left(1 - \frac{1}{10}\right) \times 0.89} = 20.53 \times 10^5 \text{ N/m}^2$$

$$= \mathbf{20.53\ bar}$$ Ans

If the gases were expanded isentropically to their original pressure of 1 bar, then the temperature T_6 at the end of expansion would be

$$T_6 = T_{3'}\left(\frac{p_6}{p_{3'}}\right)^{\frac{\gamma-1}{\gamma}} = 4586 \times \left(\frac{1}{147.9}\right)^{\frac{0.4}{1.4}} = 1100.12$$

Heat rejected at constant pressure

$$= 1.004 \times (1100.12 - 310) = 793.3 \text{ kJ/kg}$$

$$\textit{Work increase} = 1087 - 793.3 = \mathbf{293.7\ kJ/kg}$$ Ans

Review Questions

2.1 *What is the simplest way by which an IC engine cycle can be analyzed? Do IC engines operate on a thermodynamic cycle?*

2.2 *What is the use of air-standard cycle analysis?*

2.3 *Mention the various assumption made in air-standard cycle analysis.*

2.4 *What is Carnot cycle and what is its importance? How is this cycle reversible?*

2.5 *Draw the Carnot cycle on p-V and T-s diagrams. Derive an expression for its efficiency. Comment on the significance of this result as it related to source and sink temperature.*

2.6 *Define mean effective pressure and comment its application in internal combustion engines.*

2.7 *Name the cycles which have the same efficiency of Carnot cycle. Are these cycles reversible in the sense the Carnot cycle is?*

2.8 *Draw the Stirling cycle on p-V and T-s diagrams and show how the cycle is reversible?*

2.9 *Derive the expression for Stirling cycle efficiency and show that the expression is same as that of Carnot cycle.*

2.10 *If you include the efficiency of the heat exchanger show how the expression is modified.*

2.11 *Draw the p-V and T-s diagram of Ericsson cycle and show how it is made reversible.*

2.12 *Compare Carnot, Stirling and Ericsson cycles operating between the same source and sink temperatures and with equal changes in specific volume.*

2.13 *Draw the Otto cycle on p-V and T-s diagrams mark the various processes.*

2.14 *Derive an expression for the efficiency of Otto cycle and comment on the effect of compression ratio on the efficiency with respect of ratio of specific heats by means of a suitable graph.*

2.15 *Obtain an expression for mean effective pressure of an Otto cycle.*

2.16 *What is the basic difference between an Otto cycle and Diesel cycle? Derive the expression for the efficiency and mean effective pressure of the Diesel cycle.*

2.17 *Show that the efficiency of the Diesel cycle is lower than that of Otto cycle for the same compression ratio. Comment why the higher efficiency of the Otto cycle compared to Diesel cycle for the same compression ratio is only of a academic interest and not practical importance.*

2.18 Compare the Otto cycle for the same peak pressure and temperature. Illustrate the cycles on p-V and T-s diagrams.

2.19 Draw the p-V and T-s diagrams of a Dual cycle. Why this cycle is also called limited pressure or mixed cycle?

2.20 Derive the expressions for the efficiency and mean effective pressure of a Dual cycle.

2.21 Compare Otto, Diesel and Dual cycles for the

(i) same compression ratio and heat input

(ii) same maximum pressure and heat input

(iii) same maximum pressure and temperature

(iv) same maximum pressure and work output

2.22 Sketch the Lenoir cycle on p-V and T-s diagrams and obtain an expression for its air-standard efficiency.

2.23 Compare the Otto cycle and Atkinson cycle. Derive the expression for the efficiency of Atkinson cycle.

2.24 Derive an expression for the air-standard efficiency of the Joule cycle in terms of

(i) compression ratio

(ii) pressure ratio.

2.25 Where do the following cycles have applications

(i) Otto cycle

(ii) Diesel cycle

(iii) Dual cycle

(iv) Stirling cycle

(v) Ericsson cycle

(vi) Atkinson cycle

(vii) Lenoir cycle

(viii) Joule cycle

Exercise

2.1 Assume working substance for a Carnot cycle to be air with $C_p = 1$ kJ/kg K and $C_v = 0.717$ kJ/kg K. Temperature at which heat is added is 2000 K and temperature at which heat is rejected is 300 K. The amount of heat added per kg of the working substance is 840 kJ/kg. Calculate for the cycle (i) the maximum pressure developed (ii) the compression ratio assuming adiabatic compression and (iii) the efficiency of the cycle. The pressure at the beginning of isothermal compression is 1 bar. *Ans:* (i) 3304.8 bar (ii) 114.75 (iii) 85%

2.2 An engine operates on Otto cycle between pressures 1 bar and 30 bar. The ratio of pressure at constant volume is 4. The temperature at the end of compression is 200 °C and the law of compression and expansion is $PV^{1.3}$ = constant. If the engine now operates on Carnot cycle for the same range of temperature, find the efficiency of the cycle.
Ans: 84.3%

2.3 An Otto cycle engine having a clearance volume of 250 cc has a compression ratio of 8. The ratio of pressure rise at constant volume is 4. If the initial pressure is 1 bar, find the work done per cycle and the theoretical mean effective pressure. Take $\gamma = 1.4$.
Ans: (i) 1946.1 J/cycle (ii) 11.12 bar

2.4 Find the *mep* for the ideal air-standard Otto cycle having a maximum pressure of 40 bar and minimum pressure of 1 bar. The compression ratio is 5:1. Take $\gamma = 1.4$
Ans: 9.04 bar

2.5 An engine working on ideal Otto cycle, the ratio of temperature at the beginning of compression is 300 K. If the ideal air-standard efficiency = 0.5, calculate the compression ratio of the engine. If the peak temperature of the cycle is 1150 K, calculate the temperature when the piston is at BDC during expansion stroke.
Ans: (i) 5.66 (ii) 575 K

2.6 A 2.7 litre cubic capacity, six-cylinder, four-stroke Otto engine has a compression ratio of 10. The engine develops 138 kW at 5000 rpm. Calculate (i) air-standard efficiency; (ii) the necessary rate of heat addition; (iii) the mean effective pressure of the cycle; (iv) the peak temperature and pressure of the cycle.
Ans: (i) 0.602 (ii) 229.23 kW (iii) 12.26 bar
(iv) 2966 K (v) 98.8 bar

2.7 It is desired to increase the output of an SI engine working on ideal Otto cycle, either by

(i) increasing the compression ratio

(ii) increasing the inlet pressure from 1 to 1.5 bar

which one will give higher peak pressure in the cycle and what is its value? Assume heat supplied at the constant volume process is the same in both the cases which is 420 kJ. Take $T_1 = 27°, p_1 = 1$ bar, $\gamma = 1.4$. Comment on the result.
Ans: (i) Increase in the compression ratio will produce higher peak pressure. (ii) 44.6 bar

2.8 A petrol engine working on Otto cycle has an maximum pressure of 50 bar. Heat supplied is 1000 kJ/kg. If the pressure ratio during compression 12.286, find the compression ratio and also the ratio of peak temperature to inlet temperature. Take $p_1 = 1$ bar and $T_1 = 27°$ C.
Ans: (i) 6 (ii) 8.34

2.9 An Otto cycle takes in air at 300 K. The ratio of maximum to minimum temperature is 6. Find out the optimum compression ratio for the maximum work output of the cycle. *Ans:* 9.39

2.10 The pressure and temperature of a Diesel cycle at the start are 1 bar and 20 °C respectively and the compression ratio is 14. The pressure at the end of expansion is 2.5 bar. Find the percentage of working stroke at which heat is supplied and heat supplied per kg of air. Assume $\gamma =$ 1.4 and $C_p = 1.004$ kJ/kg K. *Ans:* (i) 7.11% (ii) 781.46 kJ/kg

2.11 An oil engine works on Diesel cycle, the compression ratio being 15. The temperature at the start of compression is 17 °C and 700 kJ of heat is supplied at constant pressure per kg of air and it attains a temperature of 417 °C at the end of adiabatic expansion. Find the air-standard efficiency of the cycle. What would be the theoretical work done per kg of air. Take $C_v = 0.717$ kJ/kg K and $\gamma = 1.4$. *Ans:* (i) 59.03% (ii) 413.20 kJ

2.12 An internal combustion engine works on Diesel cycle with a compression ratio of 8 and expansion ratio of 5. Calculate the air-standard efficiency. Assume $\gamma = 1.41$. *Ans:* 52.6 %

2.13 A Diesel engine works on Diesel cycle with a compression ratio of 16 and cut-off ratio of 1.8. Calculate the thermal efficiency assuming $\gamma =$ 1.4. *Ans:* 62.38 %

2.14 An internal combustion engine works on Diesel cycle with a compression ratio of 14 and cut-off takes place at 10 % of the stroke. Find the ratio of cut-off and the air-standard efficiency. *Ans:* (i) 2.3 (ii) 57.8 %

2.15 An ideal Diesel cycle operates on a pressure of 1 bar and a temperature of 27 °C at the beginning of compression and a pressure of 2 bar at the end of adiabatic expansion. Calculate the amount of heat required to be supplied per kg of air if the ideal thermal efficiency is taken as 60 %. Take $C_v = 0.717$ kJ/kg K. *Ans:* 537.75 kJ/kg

2.16 The pressure and temperature of a Diesel cycle at the start are 1 bar and 17 °C. The pressure at the end of compression is 40 bar and that at the end of expansion is 2 bar. Find the air-standard efficiency. Assume $\gamma = 1.4$. *Ans:* 61.14 %

2.17 A Diesel cycle operates at a pressure of 1 bar at the beginning of compression and the volume is compressed to $\frac{1}{15}$ of the initial volume. Heat is then supplied until the volume is twice that of the clearance volume. Determine the mean effective pressure. Take $\gamma = 1.4$. *Ans:* 6.69 bar

2.18 A semi-diesel engine works on dual combustion cycle. The pressure and temperature at the beginning of the compression is 1 bar and 27 °C respectively and the compression ratio being 12. If the maximum pressure is 50 bar and heat received at constant pressure is for $\frac{1}{30}$th of the stroke, find the work done per kg of air and the thermal efficiency. Take $C_v = 0.717$ and $C_p = 1.004$. *Ans:* (i) 476.76 kJ/kg (ii) 61.5 %

2.19 A compression-ignition engine has a compression ratio of 10 and $\frac{2}{3}$ of heat of combustion is liberated at constant volume and the remainder at constant pressure. The pressure and temperature at the beginning are 1 bar and 27 °C and the maximum pressure is 40 bar. Find the temperatures at the end of compression and expansion, if it follows the law $pV^{1.35}$ = constant, and $\gamma = 1.4$. *Ans:* (i) 398.6 °C (ii) 380.3 °C

2.20 A compression-ignition engine works on dual combustion cycle. The pressure and temperature at the beginning of compression are 1 bar and 27 °C respectively and the pressure at the end of compression is 25 bar. If 420 kJ of heat is supplied per kg of air during constant volume heating and the pressure at the end of adiabatic expansion is found to be 3 bar, find the ideal thermal efficiency. Assume $C_p = 1.004$ kJ/kg K and $C_v = 0.717$ kJ/kg K. *Ans:* 41.36%

2.21 The cycle of an internal combustion engine with isochoric heat supply is performed with the compression ratio equal to 8. Find heat supplied to the cycle and the useful work, if the removed heat is 500 kJ/kg and the working fluid is air. *Ans:* (i) 1148.63 kJ/kg (ii) 648.63 kJ/kg

2.22 The initial parameters (at the beginning of compression) of the cycle of an internal combustion engine with isobaric heat supply are 0.1 MPa and 80 °C. The compression ratio is 16 and the heat supplied is 850 kJ/kg. Calculate the parameters at the characteristic points of the cycle and the thermal efficiency, if the working fluid is air.

Ans: (i) $p_2 = 48.5$ bar (ii) $p_3 = 48.5$ bar
(iii) $p_4 = 2.26$ bar (iv) $T_2 = 1070.1$ K
(v) $T_3 = 1916$ K (vi) $T_4 = 797.73$ K
(vii) $\eta_{th} = 62.5\%$

2.23 The pressure ratio $\lambda = 1.5$ in the process of isochoric heat supply for the cycle of an internal combustion engine with a mixed supply of heat = 1034 kJ/kg and the compression ratio = 13. Find the thermal efficiency and temperature at the characteristic points of the cycle if the initial parameters are 0.09 MPa and 70 °C and the working substance is air.

Ans: (i) $\eta_{th} = 57.5\%$ (ii) $T_2 = 956.9$ K
(iii) $T_3 = 1435.5$ K (iv) $T_4 = 2122.86$ K
(v) $T_5 = 890$ K

2.24 The parameters of the initial state of one kilogram of air in the cycle of an internal combustion engine are 0.095 MPa and 65 °C. The compression ratio is 11. Compare the values of the thermal efficiency for isobaric and isochoric heat supply in amounts of 800 kJ, assuming that $k = 1.4$. *Ans:* $\eta_{t_p} = 55.7$ %, $\eta_{t_v} = 61.7\%$

2.25 Find the thermal efficiency of the cycle of an internal combustion engine with a mixed heat supply, if the minimum temperature of the cycle is

85 °C and the maximum temperature is 1700 K. The compression ratio is 15 and the pressure ratio in the process of heat supply is 1.3. The working fluid is air. *Ans:* $\eta_{th} = 65.25$ %

2.26 The pressure ratio during the compression in the cycle of an internal combustion engine with isochoric heat supply is equal to 18. Find the compression ratio, supplied and removed heat, work and efficiency, if during heat removal the temperature drops from 600 to 100 °C and the working fluid is air. Assume $\gamma = 1.4$ and $C_v = 0.717$ kJ/kg K.

Ans: (i) $r = 7.88$ (ii) $q_1 = 818.73$ kJ/kg (iii) $q_2 = 358.5$ kJ/kg (iv) $w = 460.23$ kJ/kg (v) $\eta_{th} = 56.21\%$

2.27 An oil engine working on the dual combustion cycle has a cylinder diameter of 20 cm and stroke of 40 cm. The compression ratio is 13.5 and the explosion ratio 1.42. Cut-off occurs at 5.1% of the stroke. Find the air-standard efficiency. Take $\gamma = 1.4$. *Ans:* 61.32 %

2.28 A compression-ignition engine working on Dual cycle takes in two-fifth of its total heat supply at constant volume and the remaining at constant pressure. Calculate :

(i) The pressure and temperature at the five cardinal points of the cycle.

(ii) The ideal thermal efficiency of the cycle.

Given : compression ratio = 13.1, Maximum pressure in the cycle = 45 bar, air intake at 1 bar and 15 °C, $C_p = 1.004$ kJ/kg K and $C_v = 0.717$ kJ/kg K.

Ans: (i) $p_1 = 1$ bar (ii) $p_2 = 36.3$ bar (iii) $p_3 = 45$ bar (iv) $p_4 = 45$ bar (v) $p_5 = 1.61$ bar (vi) $T_1 = 288$ K (vii) $T_2 = 804.09$ K (viii) $T_3 = 996.88$ K (ix) $T_4 = 1203.4$ K (x) $T_5 = 464.6$ K (xi) $\eta_{th} = 63.36\%$

2.29 An oil engine working on the dual combustion cycle has a cylinder diameter of 25 cm and stroke 35 cm. The clearance volume is 1500 cc and cut-off takes place at 5% of the stroke. The explosion ratio 1.4. Find the air-standard efficiency of the engine. Assume $\gamma = 1.4$ for air. *Ans:* 60.74 %

2.30 A gas turbine unit works on an air-standard Brayton cycle. The pressure ratio across the compression is 6. Air enters the compressor at 1 bar and 27 °C. The maximum temperature of the cycle is 850 °C. Calculate the specific output of the cycle. What will be the power developed by the unit for a mass flow rate of 10 kg/s. Would you recommend this cycle for a reciprocating engine? For air $\gamma = 1.4$ and $C_p = 1.005$ kJ/kg K.

Ans: (i) 250.64 kJ/kg (ii) 2506.4 kW
(iii) The volume of the cylinder will be too large due to high specific volume at state 4, therefore this cycle is not recommended for reciprocating engine.

Multiple Choice Questions (choose the most appropriate answer)

1. The efficiency of Carnot engine is 0.75. If the cycle is reversed, its coefficient of performance as heat refrigerator is

   (a) 0.25
   (b) 0.33
   (c) 1.33
   (d) 4

2. A perfect engine works on the Carnot cycle between 727 °C and 227°C. The efficiency of the engine is

   (a) 0.5
   (b) 2
   (c) $\frac{227}{727}$
   (d) $\frac{500}{727}$

3. Efficiency of stirling cycle is same as

   (a) Otto cycle
   (b) Diesel cycle
   (c) Carnot cycle
   (d) Ericsson cycle

4. The air standard efficiency of Otto cycle is

   (a) $\eta = 1 - r^{\gamma-1}$
   (b) $\eta = 1 - \frac{1}{r^{\gamma-1}}$
   (c) $\eta = 1 - r^{\frac{\gamma-1}{\gamma}}$
   (d) $\eta = 1 - \frac{1}{r^{\frac{\gamma-1}{\gamma}}}$

5. The air standard Otto cycle consists of

   (a) two constant volume and two isentropic processes
   (b) two constant pressure and two isentropic processes
   (c) two constant pressure and two constant volume processes
   (d) none of the above

6. In air standard Diesel cycle at fixed r and fixed γ,

   (a) $\eta_{thermal}$ increases with increase in heat addition and cut-off ratio
   (b) $\eta_{thermal}$ decreases with increase in heat addition and cut=off ratio
   (c) $\eta_{thermal}$ remains the same with increase in heat addition and cut=off ratio
   (d) none of the above

7. Mean effective pressure of Otto cycle is

   (a) inversely proportional to pressure ratio
   (b) directly proportional to pressure ratio
   (c) does not depend on pressure ratio
   (d) proportional to square root of pressure ratio

8. For a given compression ratio the work output of Otto cycle is

   (a) increases with increase in r
   (b) decreases with increase in r
   (c) is not affected
   (d) none of the above

9. For a given value of r, efficiency of Otto cycle

   (a) decreases with compression ratio
   (b) increases with compression ratio
   (c) is not affected
   (d) none of the above

10. For dual combustion cycle for fixed value of heat addition and compression ratio

    (a) *mep* will be greater with increase in r_p and decrease in r_c
    (b) *mep* will be greater with decrease in r_p and decrease in r_c
    (c) *mep* remain the same with increase in r_p and decrease in r_c
    (d) none of the above

11. The normal range of compression ratio for Otto cycle is

    (a) 6 to 10
    (b) 2 to 4
    (c) > 10
    (d) none of the above

12. The normal range of compression ratio for Diesel cycle is
    (a) 4 to 6
    (b) 6 to 8
    (c) 15 to 20
    (d) >25

13. For the same compression ratio and heat addition
    (a) $\eta_{Otto} > \eta_{Diesel} > \eta_{Dual}$
    (b) $\eta_{Diesel} > \eta_{Otto} > \eta_{Dual}$
    (c) $\eta_{Otto} > \eta_{Dual} > \eta_{Diesel}$
    (d) $\eta_{Dual} > \eta_{Diesel} > \eta_{Otto}$

14. For the same compression ratio and heat rejection,
    (a) $\eta_{Otto} > \eta_{Dual} > \eta_{Diesel}$
    (b) $\eta_{Diesel} > \eta_{Dual} > \eta_{Otto}$
    (c) $\eta_{Dual} > \eta_{Diesel} > \eta_{Otto}$
    (d) $\eta_{Dual} > \eta_{Otto} > \eta_{Diesel}$

15. When the engines are built to withstand the same thermal and mechanical stresses
    (a) $\eta_{Diesel} > \eta_{Dual} > \eta_{Otto}$
    (b) $\eta_{Dual} > \eta_{Diesel} > \eta_{Otto}$
    (c) $\eta_{Otto} > \eta_{Dual} > \eta_{Diesel}$
    (d) $\eta_{Otto} > \eta_{Diesel} > \eta_{Dual}$

16. For the same peak pressure and heat input
    (a) $\eta_{Otto} > \eta_{Dual} > \eta_{Diesel}$
    (b) $\eta_{Otto} > \eta_{Diesel} > \eta_{Dual}$
    (c) $\eta_{Diesel} > \eta_{Dual} > \eta_{Otto}$
    (d) $\eta_{Diesel} > \eta_{Otto} > \eta_{Dual}$

17. For the same peak pressure and work output
    (a) $\eta_{Otto} > \eta_{Dual} > \eta_{Diesel}$
    (b) $\eta_{Otto} > \eta_{Diesel} > \eta_{Dual}$
    (c) $\eta_{Diesel} > \eta_{Otto} > \eta_{Dual}$
    (d) $\eta_{Diesel} > \eta_{Dual} > \eta_{Otto}$

18. Lenoir cycle is used in

    (a) SI engines
    (b) CI engines
    (c) pulse jet engines
    (d) gas turbines

19. A Brayton cycle consists of

    (a) two constant volume and two constant pressure processes
    (b) two constant volume and two isentropic processes
    (c) one constant pressure, one constant volume and two isentropic processes
    (d) none of the above

20. Brayton cycle is used in

    (a) Ramjet engines
    (b) gas turbines
    (c) pulse jet engines
    (d) CI engines
    (e) SI engines

Ans:					
	1. – (b)	2. – (a)	3. – (c)	4. – (b)	5. – (a)
	6. – (b)	7. – (b)	8. – (a)	9. – (b)	10. – (a)
	11. – (a)	12. – (c)	13. – (c)	14. – (a)	15. – (a)
	16. – (c)	17. – (d)	18. – (c)	19. – (c)	20. – (b)

3

FUEL–AIR CYCLES AND THEIR ANALYSIS

3.1 INTRODUCTION

In the previous chapter, a detailed discussion of air-standard cycles, particularly for IC engines has been given. The analysis was based on highly simplifying assumptions. Because of this, the estimated engine performance by air-standard cycle analysis is on the higher side compared to the actual performance. For example, the actual indicated thermal efficiency of an SI engine, say with a compression ratio of 8:1, is of the order of 28% whereas the air-standard efficiency is 56.5%. This large deviation may to some extent be attributed to progressive burning of the fuel, incomplete combustion and valve operation etc. However, the main reasons for this may be attributed to the over simplified assumptions made in the analysis.

In an actual engine, the working fluid is a mixture of air, fuel vapour and residual gases from the previous cycle. Further, the specific heats of the working fluid are not constant but increase with temperature. Finally, the products of combustion are subjected to certain dissociation at high temperatures. If the actual physical properties of the gases in the cylinder before and after the combustion are taken into account, reasonably close values to the actual pressures and temperatures existing within the engine cylinder can be estimated. The mean effective pressures and efficiencies, calculated by this analysis, in the case of well designed engines are higher only by a few per cent from the actual values obtained by tests. The analysis based on the actual properties of the working medium viz., fuel and air is called the fuel-air cycle analysis and even this analysis has simplifying assumptions. However, they are more justifiable and close to the actual conditions than those used in the air-standard cycle analysis.

3.2 FUEL–AIR CYCLES AND THEIR SIGNIFICANCE

By air-standard cycle analysis, it is understood how the efficiency is improved by increasing the compression ratio. However, analysis cannot bring out the effect of air-fuel ratio on the thermal efficiency because the working medium was assumed to be air. In this chapter, the presence of fuel in the cylinder is taken into account and accordingly the working medium will be a mixture of fuel and air. By fuel-air cycle analysis it will be possible to bring out the effect of fuel-air ratio on thermal efficiency and also study how the peak pressures and temperatures during the cycle vary with respect to fuel-air ratio. In general, influence of many of the engine operating variables on the pressures and temperatures within the engine cylinder may be better understood by the examination of the fuel-air cycles. The fuel-air cycle analysis takes into account the following :

(i) *The actual composition of the cylinder gases* : The cylinder gases contains fuel, air, water vapour and residual gas. The fuel-air ratio changes during the operation of the engine which changes the relative amounts of CO_2, water vapour, etc.

(ii) *The variation in the specific heat with temperature* : Specific heats increase with temperature except for mono-atomic gases. Therefore, the value of γ also changes with temperature.

(iii) *The effect of dissociation* : The fuel and air do not completely combine chemically at high temperatures (above 1600 K) and this leads to the presence of CO, H_2, H and O_2 at equilibrium conditions.

(iv) *The variation in the number of molecules* : The number of molecules present after combustion depends upon fuel-air ratio and upon the pressure and temperature after the combustion.

Besides taking the above factors into consideration, the following assumptions are commonly made :

(i) There is no chemical change in either fuel or air prior to combustion.

(ii) Subsequent to combustion, the charge is always in chemical equilibrium.

(iii) There is no heat exchange between the gases and the cylinder walls in any process, i.e. they are adiabatic. Also the compression and expansion processes are frictionless.

(iv) In case of reciprocating engines it is assumed that fluid motion can be ignored inside the cylinder. With particular reference to constant-volume fuel-air cycle, it is also assumed that

(v) The fuel is completely vaporized and perfectly mixed with the air, and

(vi) The burning takes place instantaneously at top dead centre (at constant volume).

As already mentioned, the air-standard cycle analysis shows the general effect of only compression ratio on engine efficiency whereas the fuel-air cycle analysis gives the effect of variation of fuel-air ratio, inlet pressure and temperature on the engine performance. It will be noticed that compression ratio and fuel-air ratio are very important parameters of the engine while inlet conditions are not so important.

The actual efficiency of a good engine is about 85 per cent of the estimated fuel-air cycle efficiency. A good estimate of the power to be expected from the actual engine can be made from fuel-air cycle analysis. Also, peak pressures and exhaust temperatures which affect the engine structure and design can be estimated reasonably close to an actual engine. Thus the effect of many variables on the performance of an engine can be understood better by fuel-air cycle analysis.

3.3 COMPOSITION OF CYLINDER GASES

The air-fuel ratio changes during the engine operation. This change in air-fuel ratio affects the composition of the gases before combustion as well as after combustion particularly the percentage of carbon dioxide, carbon monoxide, water vapour etc in the exhaust gases.

In four-stroke engines, fresh charge as it enters the engine cylinder, comes into contact with the burnt gases left in the clearance space of the previous cycle. The amount of exhaust gases in clearance space varies with speed and load on the engine. Fuel-air cycle analysis takes into account this fact and the results are computed for preparing the combustion charts. However, with the availability of fast digital computers, nowadays it is possible to analyze the effect of cylinder gas composition on the performance of the engine by means of suitable numerical techniques. The computer analysis can produce fast and accurate results. Thus, fuel-air cycle analysis can be done more easily through computers rather than through manual calculations.

3.4 VARIABLE SPECIFIC HEATS

All gases, except mono-atomic gases, show an increase in specific heat with temperature. The increase in specific heat does not follow any particular law. However, over the temperature range generally encountered for gases in heat engines (300 K to 2000 K) the specific heat curve is nearly a straight line which may be approximately expressed in the form

$$\left.\begin{aligned} C_p &= a_1 + k_1 T \\ C_v &= b_1 + k_1 T \end{aligned}\right\} \qquad (3.1)$$

where a_1, b_1 and k_1 are constants. Now,

$$R = C_p - C_v = a_1 - b_1 \qquad (3.2)$$

where R is the characteristic gas constant.

Above 1500 K the specific heat increases much more rapidly and may be expressed in the form

$$C_p = a_1 + k_1 T + k_2 T^2 \qquad (3.3)$$

$$C_v = b_1 + k_1 T + k_2 T^2 \qquad (3.4)$$

In Eqn.3.4 if the term T^2 is neglected it becomes same as Eqn.3.1. Many expressions are available even upto sixth order of T (i.e. T^6) for the calculation of C_p and C_v.

The physical explanation for increase in specific heat is that as the temperature is raised, larger fractions of the heat would be required to produce motion of the atoms within the molecules. Since temperature is the result of motion of the molecules, as a whole, the energy which goes into moving the atoms does not contribute to proportional temperature rise. Hence, more heat is required to raise the temperature of unit mass through one degree at higher levels. This heat by definition is the specific heat. The values for C_p and C_v for air are usually taken as

$C_p = 1.005$ kJ/kg K at 300 K $\quad C_v = 0.717$ kJ/kg K at 300 K

$C_p = 1.345$ kJ/kg K at 2000 K $\quad C_v = 1.057$ kJ/kg K at 2000 K

Since the difference between C_p and C_v is constant, the value of γ decreases with increase in temperature. Thus, if the variation of specific heats is taken into account during the compression stroke, the final temperature and pressure would be lower than if constant values of specific heat are used. This point is illustrated in Fig.3.1.

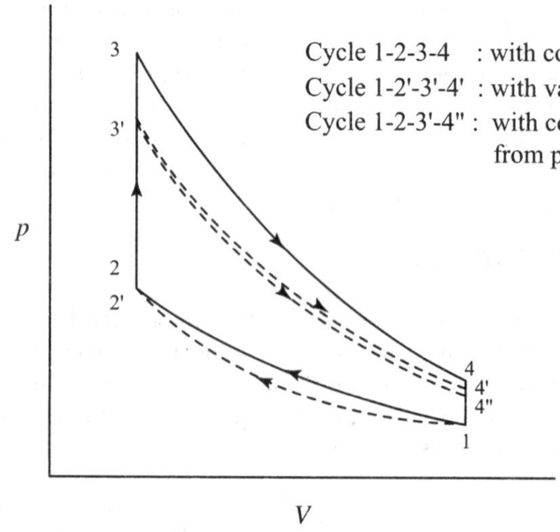

Fig. 3.1 Loss of power due to variation of specific heat

With variable specific heats, the temperature at the end of compression will be $2'$, instead of 2. The magnitude of drop in temperature is proportional to the drop in the value of ratio of specific heats. For the process $1 \rightarrow 2$, with constant specific heats

$$T_2 = T_1 \left(\frac{v_1}{v_2} \right)^{\gamma - 1} \tag{3.5}$$

with variable specific heats,

$$T_{2'} = T_1 \left(\frac{v_1}{v_{2'}} \right)^{k - 1} \tag{3.6}$$

where $k = \frac{C_p}{C_v}$. Note that $v_{2'} = v_2$ and $v_1/v_2 = v_1/v_{2'} = r$.

For given values of T_1, p_1 and r, the magnitude of $T_{2'}$ depends on k. Constant volume combustion, from point $2'$ will give a temperature $T_{3'}$ instead of T_3. This is due to the fact that the rise in the value of C_v because of variable specific heat, which reduces the temperature as already explained.

The process, $2' \rightarrow 3'$ is heat addition with the variation in specific heat. From $3'$, if expansion takes place at constant specific heats, this would result in the process $3' \rightarrow 4''$ whereas actual expansion due to variable specific heat

will result in $3' \to 4'$ and $4'$ is higher than $4''$. The magnitude in the difference between $4'$ and $4''$ is proportional to the reduction in the value of γ.
Consider the process $3'4''$

$$T_{4''} = T_{3'} \left(\frac{v_3}{v_4} \right)^{(k-1)} \tag{3.7}$$

for the process $3'4'$

$$T_{4'} = T_{3'} \left(\frac{v_3}{v_4} \right)^{(\gamma-1)} \tag{3.8}$$

Reduction in the value of k due to variable specific heat results in increase of temperature from $T_{4''}$ to $T_{4'}$.

3.5 DISSOCIATION

Dissociation process can be considered as the disintegration of combustion products at high temperature. Dissociation can also be looked as the reverse process to combustion. During dissociation the heat is absorbed whereas during combustion the heat is liberated. In IC engines, mainly dissociation of CO_2 into CO and O_2 occurs, whereas there is a very little dissociation of H_2O.

The dissociation of CO_2 into CO and O_2 starts commencing around 1000 °C and the reaction equation can be written as

$$CO_2 \rightleftharpoons 2CO + O_2$$

Similarly, the dissociation of H_2O occurs at temperatures above 1300 °C and is written as

$$H_2O \rightleftharpoons 2H_2 + O_2$$

The presence of CO and O_2 in the gases tends to prevent dissociation of CO_2; this is noticeable in a rich fuel mixture, which, by producing more CO, suppresses dissociation of CO_2. On the other hand, there is no dissociation in the burnt gases of a lean fuel-air mixture. This is mainly due to the fact that the temperature produced is too low for this phenomenon to occur. Hence, the maximum extent of dissociation occurs in the burnt gases of the chemically correct fuel-air mixture when the temperatures are expected to be high but decreases with the leaner and richer mixtures.

In case of internal combustion engines heat transfer to the cooling medium causes a reduction in the maximum temperature and pressure. As the temperature falls during the expansion stroke the separated constituents recombine; the heat absorbed during dissociation is thus again released, but it is too late in the stroke to recover entirely the lost power. A portion of this heat is carried away by the exhaust gases.

Figure 3.2 shows a typical curve that indicates the reduction in the temperature of the exhaust gas mixtures due to dissociation with respect to air-fuel ratio. With no dissociation maximum temperature is attained at chemically correct air-fuel ratio. With dissociation maximum temperature is obtained when mixture is slightly rich. Dissociation reduces the maximum temperature by about 300 °C even at the chemically correct air-fuel ratio. In the Fig.3.2, lean mixtures and rich mixtures are marked clearly.

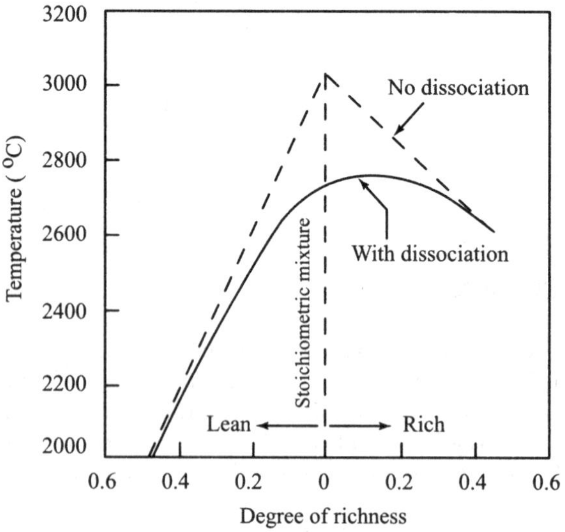

Fig. 3.2 Effect of dissociation on temperature

The effect of dissociation on output power is shown in Fig.3.3 for a typical four-stroke spark-ignition engine operating at constant speed. If there is no dissociation the brake power output is maximum when the mixture ratio is stoichiometric. The shaded area between the brake power graphs shows the loss of power due to dissociation. When the mixture is quite lean there is no dissociation. As the air-fuel ratio decreases i.e., as the mixture becomes rich the maximum temperature raises and dissociation commences. The maximum dissociation occurs at chemically correct mixture strength. As the mixture becomes richer, dissociation effect tends to decline due to incomplete combustion.

Dissociation effects are not so pronounced in a CI engine as in an SI engine. This is mainly due to

(i) the presence of a heterogeneous mixture and

(ii) excess air to ensure complete combustion.

Both these factors tend to reduce the peak gas temperature attained in the CI engine.

Figure 3.4 shows the effect of dissociation on p-V diagram of Otto cycle. Because of lower maximum temperature due to dissociation the maximum pressure is also reduced and the state after combustion will be represented by $3'$ instead of 3. If there was no reassociation due to fall of temperature during expansion the expansion process would be represented by $3' \rightarrow 4''$ but due to reassociation the expansion follows the path $3' \rightarrow 4'$.

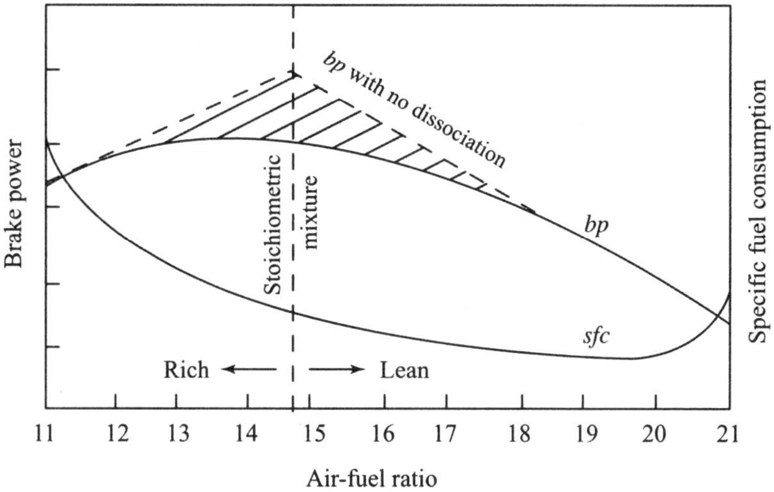

Fig. 3.3 Effect of dissociation on power

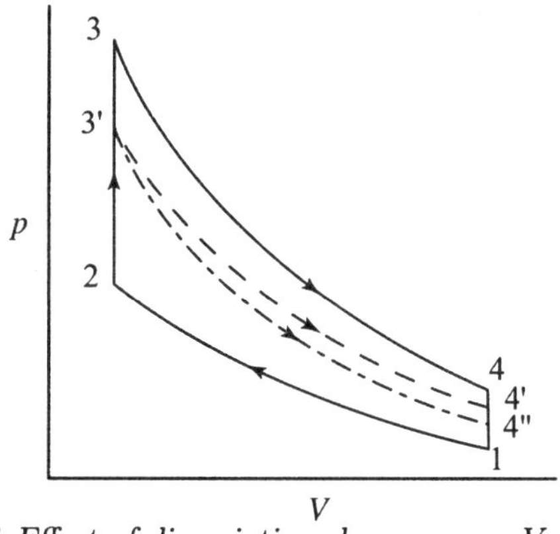

Fig. 3.4 Effect of dissociation shown on a p-V diagram

By comparing with the ideal expansion 3→4, it is observed that the effect of dissociation is to lower the temperature and consequently the pressure at the beginning of the expansion stroke. This causes a loss of power and also efficiency. Though during recombining the heat is given back it is too late to contribute a convincing positive increase in the output of the engine.

3.6 EFFECT OF NUMBER OF MOLES

As already mentioned the number of molecules present in the cylinder after combustion depends upon the fuel-air ratio, type and extend of reaction in the cylinder. According to the gas law

$$pV = N\overline{R}T$$

the pressure depends on the number of molecules or moles present. This has direct effect on the amount of work the cylinder gases can impart on the piston.

3.7 COMPARISON OF AIR–STANDARD AND FUEL–AIR CYCLES

In this section reasons for difference between air-standard cycles and fuel-air cycles is discussed. The magnitude of difference between the two cycles can be attributed to the following factors :

(i) character of the cycle (due to assumptions)

(ii) equivalence ratio (actual $F/A \div$ stoichiometric F/A)

(iii) chemical composition of the fuel

Figure 3.5 shows variation of efficiency with mixture strength of fuel-air cycle relative to that of air cycle showing the gain in efficiency as the mixture becomes leaner. It is seen from Fig.3.5 that the efficiency ratio (fuel-air cycle efficiency/air-standard cycle efficiency) increases as the mixture becomes leaner and leaner tending towards the air-standard cycle efficiency. It is to be noted that this, trend exists at all compression ratios.

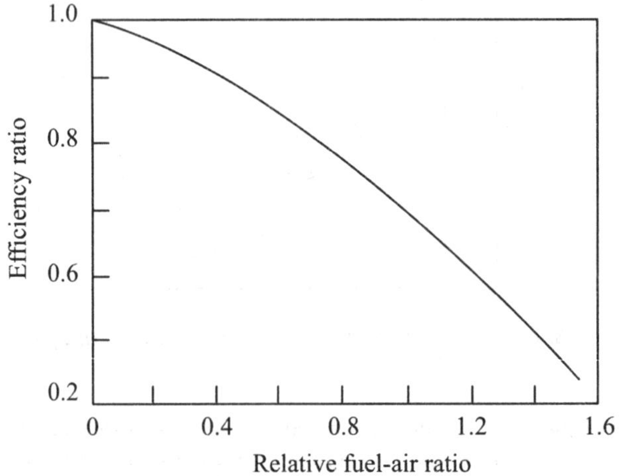

Fig. 3.5 Effect of relative fuel-air ratio on efficiency ratio

At very low fuel-air ratio the mixture would tend to behave like a perfect gas with constant specific heat. Cycles with lean to very lean mixtures tend towards air-standard cycles. In such cycles the pressure and temperature rises. Some of the chemical reactions involved tend to be more complete as the pressure increases. These considerations apply to constant-volume as well as constant-pressure cycles.

The simple air-standard cycle analysis cannot predict the variation of thermal efficiency with mixture strength since air is assumed to be the working medium. However, fuel-air cycle analysis suggests that the thermal efficiency will deteriorate as the mixture supplied to an engine is enriched. This is explained by the increasing losses due to variable specific heats and dissociation as the mixture strength approaches chemically correct values. This is because, the gas temperature goes up after combustion as the mixture strength approaches chemically correct values. Enrichment beyond the chemically correct ratio will lead to incomplete combustion and loss in thermal efficiency. Therefore, it will appear that thermal efficiency will increase as the mixture is made leaner. However, beyond a certain leaning, the combustion becomes erratic with loss of efficiency. Thus the maximum efficiency is within the lean zone very near the stoichiometric ratio. This gives rise to combustion loop, as shown in Fig.3.6 which can be plotted for different mixture strengths for an engine running at constant speed and at a constant throttle setting. This loop gives an idea about the effect of mixture strength on the specific fuel consumption.

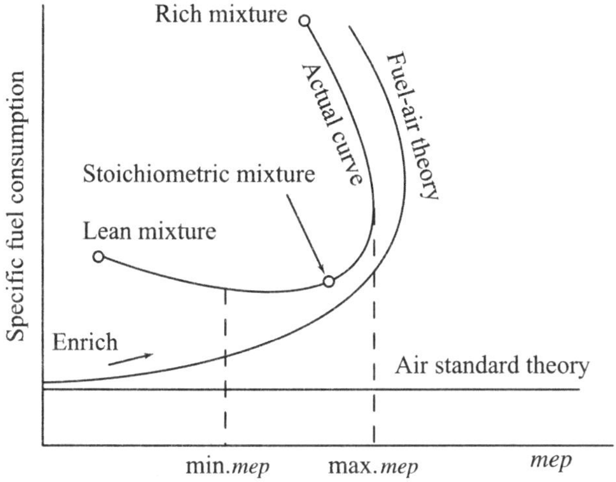

Fig. 3.6 Specific fuel consumption vs. mean effective pressure at constant speed and constant throttle setting

3.8 EFFECT OF OPERATING VARIABLES

The effect of the common engine operating variables on the pressure and temperature within the engine cylinder is better understood by fuel-air cycle analysis. The details are discussed in the following sections.

3.8.1 Compression Ratio

The fuel-air cycle efficiency increases with the compression ratio in the same manner as the air-standard cycle efficiency, principally for the same reason (more scope of expansion work). This is shown in Fig.3.7.

The variation of indicated thermal efficiency with respect to the equivalence ratio for various compression ratios is given in Fig.3.8 The equivalence ratio, ϕ, is defined as ratio of actual fuel-air ratio to chemically correct fuel-air

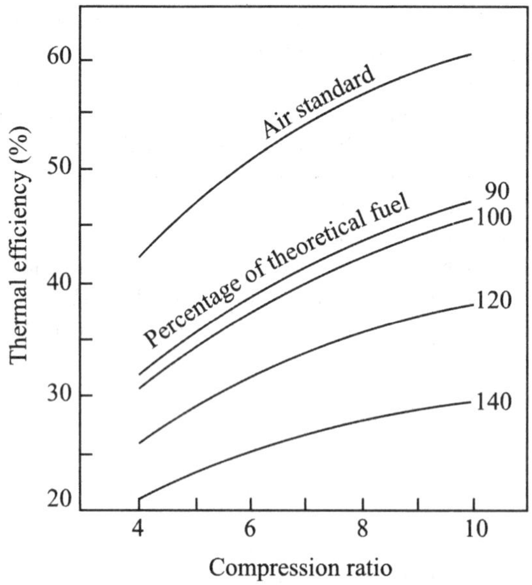

Fig. 3.7 Effect of compression ratio and mixture strength on efficiency

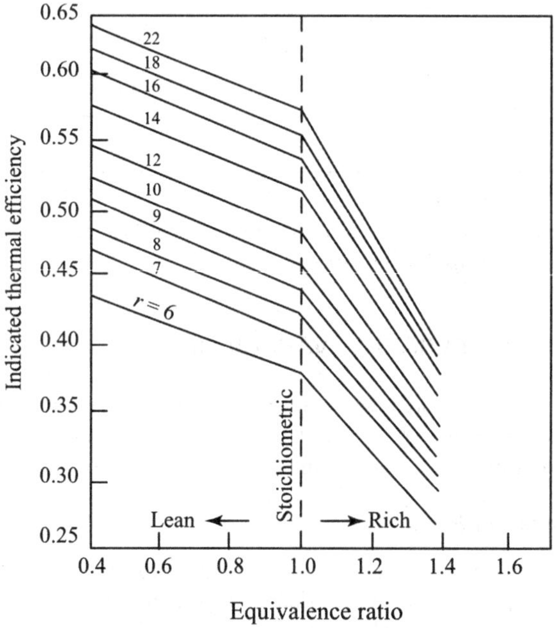

Fig. 3.8 Effect of mixture strength on thermal efficiency for various compression ratios

ratio on mass basis. The maximum pressure and maximum temperature increase with compression ratio since the temperature, T_2, and pressure, p_2, at the end of compression are higher. However, it can be noted from the experimental results (Fig.3.9) that the ratio of fuel-air cycle efficiency to air-standard efficiency is independent of the compression ratio for a given equivalence ratio for the constant-volume fuel-air cycle.

3.8.2 Fuel–Air Ratio

(i) *Efficiency :* As the mixture is made lean (less fuel) the temperature rise due to combustion will be lowered as a result of reduced energy input per unit mass of mixture. This will result in lower specific heat. Further, it will lower the losses due to dissociation and variation in specific heat. The efficiency is therefore, higher and, in fact, approaches the air-cycle efficiency as the fuel-air ratio is reduced as shown in Fig.3.10.

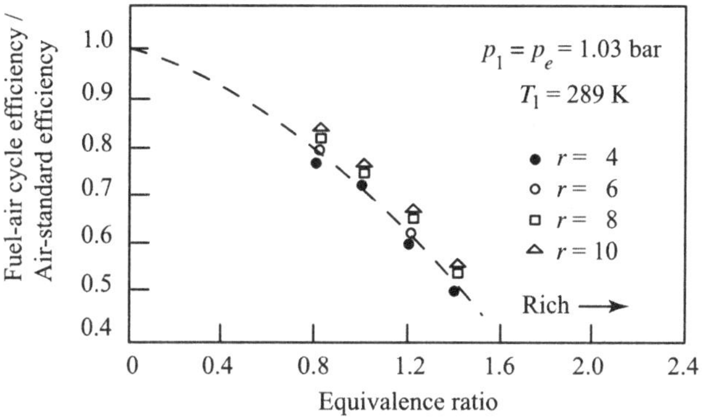

Fig. 3.9 Variation of efficiency with mixture strength for a constant volume fuel-air cycle

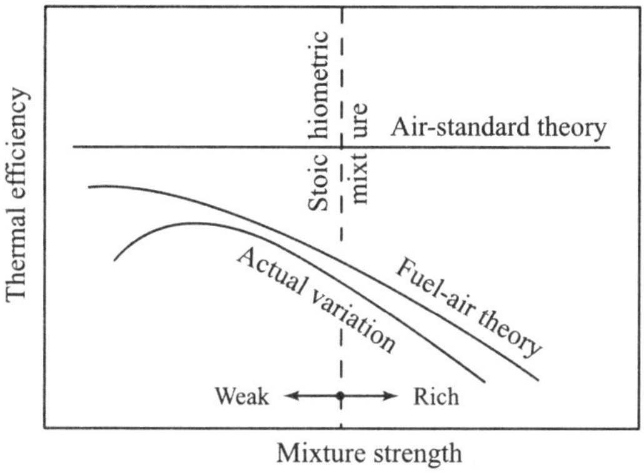

Fig. 3.10 Effect of mixture strength on thermal efficiency

(ii) *Maximum Power :* Fuel-air ratio affects the maximum power output of the engine. The variation is as shown in Fig.3.11. As the mixture becomes richer, after a certain point both efficiency and power output falls as can be seen from the experimental curve (Figs.3.10 and 3.11). This is because in addition to higher specific heats and chemical equilibrium losses, there is insufficient air which will result in formation of CO and H_2 during combustion, which represents a direct wastage of fuel. However, fuel-air cycle analysis cannot exactly imitate the experimental curve due to various simplifying assumptions made.

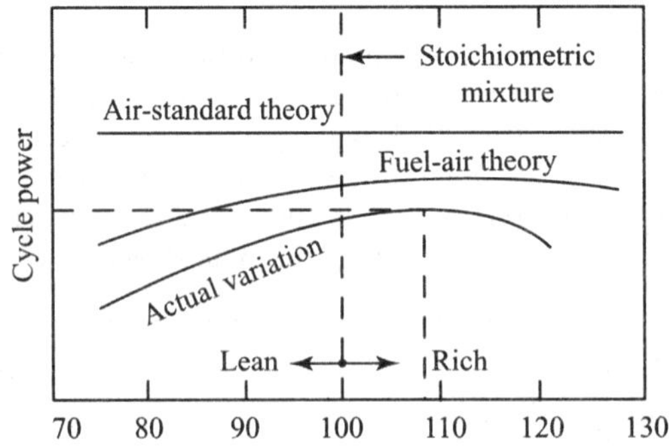

Fig. 3.11 Effect of fuel-air ratio on power

(iii) *Maximum temperature :* At a given compression ratio the temperature after combustion reaches a maximum when the mixture is slightly rich, i.e., around 6% or so ($F/A = 0.072$ or $A/F = 14 : 1$) as shown in Fig.3.12. At chemically correct ratio there is still some oxygen present at the point 3 (in the *p-V* diagram, refer Fig.3.1) because of chemical equilibrium effects a rich mixture will cause more fuel to combine with oxygen at that point thereby raising the temperature T_3. However, at richer mixtures increased formation of CO counters this effect.

(iv) *Maximum Pressure :* The pressure of a gas in a given space depends upon its temperature and the number of molecules The curve of p_3, therefore follows T_3, but because of the increasing number of molecules p_3 does not start to decrease until the mixture is somewhat richer than that for maximum T_3 (at $F/A = 0.083$ or A/F 12 : 1), i.e. about 20 per cent rich (Fig.3.12).

(v) *Exhaust Temperature :* The exhaust gas temperature, T_4 is maximum at the chemically correct mixture as shown in Fig.3.13. At this point the fuel and oxygen are completely used up, as the effect of chemical equilibrium is not significant. At lean mixtures, because of less fuel, T_3 is less and hence T_4 is less. At rich mixtures less sensible energy is developed and hence T_4 is less. That is, T_4 varies with fuel-air ratio in the same manner as T_3 except that maximum T_4 is at the chemically correct fuel-air ratio in place of slightly rich fuel-air ratio (6%) as in case of T_3. However, the behaviour of T_4 with compression ratio is

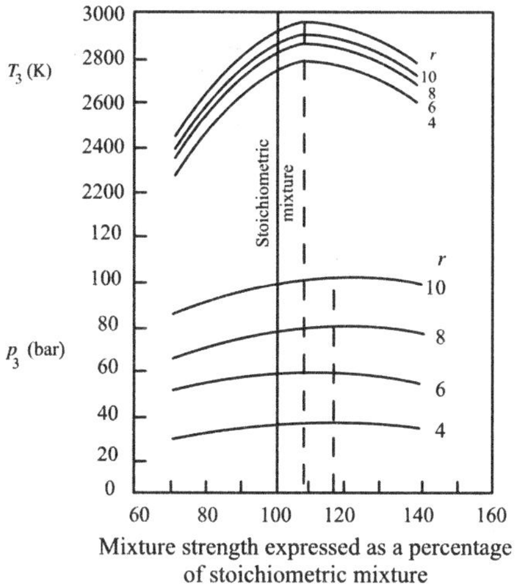

Fig. 3.12 Effect of equivalence ratio on T_3 and p_3

different from that of T_3 as shown in Fig.3.13. Unlike T_3, the exhaust gas temperature, T_4 is lower at high compression ratios, because the increased expansion causes the gas to do more work on the piston leaving less heat to be rejected at the end of the stroke. The same effect is present in the case of air-cycle analysis also.

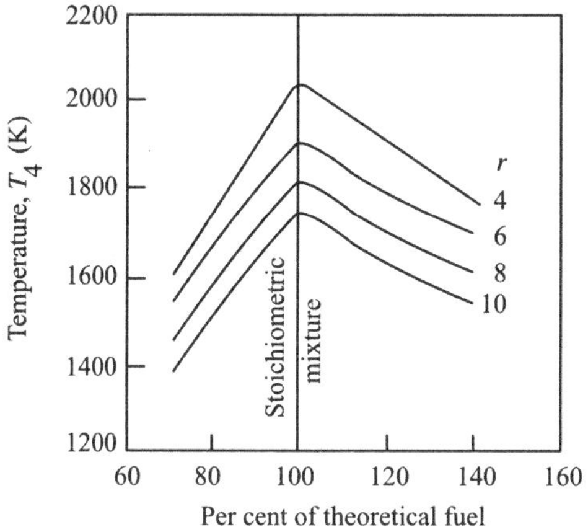

Fig. 3.13 Effect of fuel-air ratio on the exhaust gas temperature

(vi) *Mean Effective Pressure (mep)* : The mean effective pressure increases with compression ratio. It follows the trend of p_3 and p_4 and hence it is maximum at a fuel-air ratio slightly richer than the chemically correct ratio as shown in Fig.3.14. Table 3.1 shows a summary of conditions which give maximum pressure and temperature in a constant-volume cycle assuming fuel-air cycle approximations.

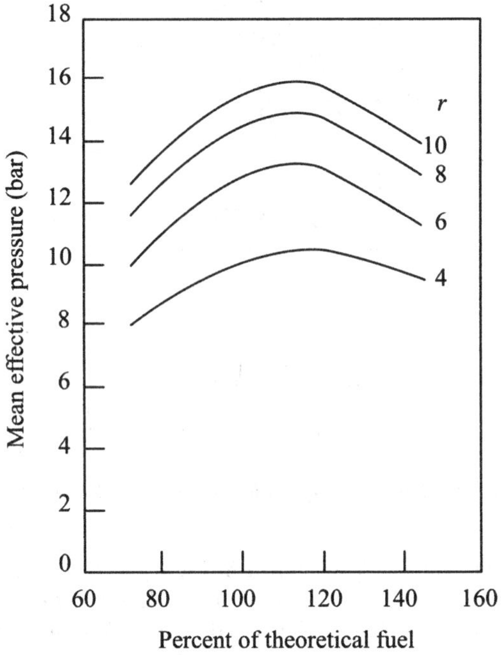

Fig. 3.14 Effect of fuel-air ratio on mep

Table 3.1 Condition for maximum temperature and pressure in a constant volume fuel-air cycle

Variable	Maximum at	Reason
1. Temperature, T_3 (Fig.3.12)	6% rich, $F/A = 0.072$; $A/F = 14:1, \phi = 1.06$	Because of chemical equilibrium some O_2 still present even at chemically correct F/A ratio. More fuel can be burnt. Limit is reached at 6% rich. If > 6% rich CO formation.
2. Pressure, p_3 (Fig.3.12)	20% rich, $F/A = 0.083$; $A/F = 12:1$	$pV = N\overline{R}T$. p depends on T and N
3. Temperature, T_4 (see Fig.3.13)	Chemically correct fuel-air ratio	No effect of chemical equilibrium due to low temperature and incomplete combustion at rich mixture.
4. Mean effective pressure (Fig.3.14)	6% rich, $F/A = 0.0745$; A/F=13.5,ϕ=1.05 to 1.1	*mep* follows the trend of p_3 and p_4.

Worked out Examples

3.1 What will be the effect on the efficiency of an Otto cycle having a compression ratio of 8, if C_v increases by 1.6%?

Solution

$$\eta_{Otto} = 1 - \frac{1}{r^{\gamma-1}}$$

$$C_p - C_v = R \, ; \quad \frac{C_p}{C_v} = \gamma \quad \text{and} \quad \gamma - 1 = \frac{R}{C_v}$$

$$\eta = 1 - \left(\frac{1}{r}\right)^{R/C_v}$$

$$1 - \eta = r^{-R/C_v}$$

$$\ln(1 - \eta) = \frac{-R}{C_v} \ln r$$

Differentiating

$$-\frac{1}{1-\eta} d\eta = \frac{R}{C_v^2} \ln r dC_v$$

$$d\eta = -\frac{(1-\eta) R \ln r}{C_v^2} dC_v$$

$$\frac{d\eta}{\eta} = -\frac{(1-\eta)(\gamma - 1) \ln r}{\eta} \frac{dC_v}{C_v}$$

$$\eta = 1 - \left(\frac{1}{8}\right)^{0.4} = 0.565 = 56.5\%$$

$$\frac{d\eta}{\eta} = -\frac{(1 - 0.565) \times (1.4 - 1) \times \ln 8}{0.565} \times \frac{1.6}{100}$$

$$= \mathbf{-1.025\%}$$

Ans ⟸

3.2 What will be the effect on the efficiency of a diesel cycle having a compression ratio of 20 and a cut-off ratio is 5% of the swept volume, if the C_v increases by 1%. Take $C_v = 0.717$ and $R = 0.287$ kJ/kg K.

Solution

$$\eta_{Diesel} = 1 - \left(\frac{1}{r}\right)^{\gamma-1} \left(\frac{1}{\gamma} \frac{r_c^{\gamma} - 1}{r_c - 1}\right)$$

$$1 - \eta = \frac{1}{\gamma} \frac{r_c^{\gamma} - 1}{r^{\gamma-1}(r_c - 1)}$$

Taking logarithm

$$\ln(1-\eta) = -\ln\gamma + \ln(r_c^\gamma - 1) - \ln(r_c - 1) - (\gamma - 1)\ln r$$

$$\gamma - 1 = \frac{R}{C_v}$$

$$\gamma = \left(1 + \frac{R}{C_v}\right)$$

Substituting this in the above equation

$$\ln(1-\eta) = -\ln\left(\frac{R}{C_v} + 1\right) + \ln\left(r_c^{\left(\frac{R}{C_v}+1\right)} - 1\right) - \ln(r_c - 1) - \frac{R}{C_v}\ln r$$

Differentiating we get,

$$-\frac{d\eta}{\eta} = \frac{\frac{R}{C_v^2}dC_v}{\frac{R}{C_v}+1} - \frac{\frac{R}{C_v^2}\left(r_c^{\left(\frac{R}{C_v}+1\right)}\right)\ln r_c dC_v}{r_c^{\left(\frac{R}{C_v}+1\right)} - 1} + \frac{R}{C_v^2}\ln r dC_v$$

$$\frac{d\eta}{\eta} = -\frac{dC_v}{C_v}\frac{R}{C_v}\left(\frac{1-\eta}{\eta}\right)$$

$$\times \left(\frac{1}{\frac{R}{C_v}+1} + \ln r - \frac{r_c^{\frac{R}{C_v}+1}\ln(r_c)}{r_c^{\frac{R}{C_v}+1} - 1}\right)$$

$$\frac{d\eta}{\eta} = -\frac{dC_v}{C_v}\left(\frac{1-\eta}{\eta}\right)(\gamma - 1)\left[\frac{1}{\gamma} + \ln r - \frac{r_c^\gamma \ln(r_c)}{r_c^\gamma - 1}\right]$$

$$\gamma = 1.4$$

$$\frac{V_1}{V_2} = r = 20$$

$$V_1 = 20V_2$$

$$V_s = 20V_2 - V_2 = 19V_2$$

$$V_3 = 0.05V_s + V_2 = (0.05 \times 19V_2) + V_2 = 1.95V_2$$

$$r_c = \frac{V_3}{V_2} = \frac{1.95V_2}{V_2} = 1.95$$

$$\eta = 1 - \frac{1}{\gamma}\frac{1}{r^{\gamma-1}}\frac{r_c^\gamma - 1}{r_c - 1}$$

$$= 1 - \frac{1}{1.4} \times \left(\frac{1}{20}\right)^{0.4} \times \frac{1.95^{1.4} - 1}{1.95 - 1} = 0.649$$

$$\frac{d\eta}{\eta} = -0.01 \times \frac{1-0.649}{0.649}$$

$$\times 0.4 \times \left[\frac{1}{1.4} + \ln(20) - \frac{1.95^{1.4} \times \ln(1.95)}{1.95^{1.4} - 1}\right]$$

$$= \mathbf{-0.565\%}$$

Ans $\Longleftarrow$

3.3 A petrol engine having a compression ratio of 6 uses a fuel with calorific value of 42 MJ/kg. The air-fuel ratio is 15:1. Pressure and temperature at the start of the suction stroke is 1 bar and 57 °C respectively. Determine the maximum pressure in the cylinder if the index of compression is 1.3 and the specific heat at constant volume is given by $C_v = 0.678 + 0.00013$ T, where T is in Kelvin. Compare this value with that obtained when $C_v = 0.717$ kJ/kg K.

Solution Consider the process 1-2

$$p_2 V_2^n = p_1 V_1^n$$

$$p_2 = p_1 \left(\frac{V_1}{V_2}\right)^n = 1 \times 6^{1.3} = 10.27 \text{ bar}$$

$$T_2 = T_1 \left(\frac{p_2 V_2}{p_1 V_1}\right) = 330 \times \left(\frac{10.27}{1} \times \frac{1}{6}\right) = 565 \text{ K}$$

$$\text{Average temperature during combustion} = \frac{T_3 + T_2}{2}$$

$$C_{v_{mean}} = 0.678 + 0.00013 \times \left(\frac{T_3 + T_2}{2}\right)$$

Assuming unit quantity of air

$$Q_{2-3}/\textit{kg of air} = \frac{42}{15} = 2.8 \text{ MJ}$$

$$\textit{Mass of charge} = 1 + \frac{1}{15} = \frac{16}{15} \text{ kg/kg of air}$$

$$Q_{2-3} = C_{v_{mean}} \dot{m} (T_3 - T_2)$$

$$2.8 \times 10^3 = \left[0.678 + 13 \times 10^{-5} \times \left(\frac{T_3 + 565}{2}\right)\right]$$

$$\times \frac{16}{15} \times (T_3 - 565)$$

$$T_3 = 3375 \text{ K}$$

$$p_3 = p_2 \frac{T_3}{T_2} = 10.27 \times \frac{3375}{565} = \mathbf{61.35\ bar}$$

Ans $\Longleftarrow$

For constant specific heat

$$2.8 \times 10^3 = 0.717 \times \frac{16}{15} \times (T_3 - 565)$$

$$T_3 = 4226$$

$$p_3 = 10.27 \times \frac{4226}{565} = \textbf{76.81 bar}$$ Ans

3.4 The air-fuel ratio of a Diesel engine is 29:1. If the compression ratio is 16:1 and the temperature at the end of compression is 900 K, find at what cylinder volume the combustion is complete? Express this volume as a percentage of stroke. Assume that the combustion begins at the top dead centre and takes place at constant pressure. Take calorific value of the fuel as 42000 kJ/kg, $R = 0.287$ kJ/kg K and $C_v = 0.709 + 0.000028\,T$ kJ/kg K.

Solution

$$C_p = C_v + R$$

$$= (0.709 + 0.000028\ T) + 0.287$$

$$= 0.996 + 0.000028\ T$$

$$dQ = mC_p dT$$

For unit mass, $Q = \int_2^3 C_p dT$

For 1 kg of fuel the total charge is 30 kg

$$Q = \frac{CV}{30} = \frac{42000}{30} = 1400$$

$$= \int_2^3 (0.996 + 0.000028\ T)dT$$

$$= 0.996(T_3 - T_2) + \frac{0.000028}{2}(T_3^2 - T_2^2)$$

$$= 0.996 \times (T_3 - 900) + 0.000014 \times \left(T_3^2 - 900^2\right)$$

$$T_3 = 2246.07 \text{ K}$$

$$V_3 = \frac{T_3}{T_2}V_2 = \frac{2246.07}{900}V_2 = 2.496\ V_2$$

$$V_s = V_1 - V_2 = V_2\left(\frac{V_1}{V_2} - 1\right) = V_2(r-1) = 15\ V_2$$

$$\frac{V_3}{V_s} = \frac{2.496 \times V_2}{15 \times V_2} \times 100 = \textbf{16.64\%}$$ Ans

3.5 An oil engine, working on the dual combustion cycle, has a compression ratio of 13:1. The heat supplied per kg of air is 2000 kJ, half of which is supplied at constant volume and the other half at constant pressure. If the temperature and pressure at the beginning of compression are 100 °C and 1 bar respectively, find (i) the maximum pressure in the cycle and (ii) the percentage of stroke when cut-off occurs. Assume $\gamma = 1.4$, $R = 0.287$ kJ/kg K and $C_v = 0.709 + 0.000028T$ kJ/kg K.

Solution

$$p_1 V_1^\gamma = p_2 V_2^\gamma$$

$$p_2 = p_2 \left(\frac{V_1}{V_2}\right)^\gamma = 1 \times 10^5 \times 13^{1.4} = 36.27 \times 10^5 \text{ N/m}^2$$

$$T_1 V_1^{(\gamma-1)} = T_2 V_2^{\gamma-1}$$

$$T_2 = T_1 r^{(\gamma-1)} = 373 \times 13^{0.4} = 1040.6 \text{ K}$$

For unit mass :
Consider the process 2-3,

$$Q_{2-3} = \frac{1}{2} \times 2000 = 1000 \text{ kJ}$$

$$Q_{2-3} = m \int_2^3 (0.709 + 0.000028T) dT$$

$$1000 = 0.709 \times (T_3 - 1040.6) + \frac{0.000028}{2} \times (T_3^2 - 1040.6^2)$$

$$T_3 = 2362.2 \text{ K}$$

$$p_3 = p_2 \left(\frac{T_3}{T_2}\right) = 36.27 \times \left(\frac{2362.2}{1040.6}\right) \times 10^5$$

$$= \mathbf{82.34 \times 10^5 \ N/m^2}$$ Ans

Consider the process 3-4,

$$Q_{3-4} = \frac{1}{2} \times 1000 = 500 \text{ kJ}$$

$$C_p = C_v + R = 0.996 + 0.000028\ T$$

$$Q_{3-4} = m \int_3^4 dT$$

$$500 = \int_3^4 (0.996 + 0.000028) dT$$

$$= \quad 0.996 \times (T_4 - 2362.2) + \frac{0.000028}{2} \times (T_4^2 - 2362.2^2)$$

$$T_4 = 2830.04 \text{ K}$$

$$V_4 = V_3\left(\frac{T_4}{T_3}\right) = \frac{2830.04}{2362.2}V_3 = 1.198\ V_3$$

$$V_s = V_1 - V_3 = V_3(r-1) = 12\ V_3$$

$$\text{Cut-off \%} = \frac{V_4 - V_3}{V_s} \times 100 = \frac{V_4 - V_3}{12\ V_3} \times 100$$

$$= \frac{1.198 - 1}{12} \times 100 = \mathbf{1.65\%}$$

Ans ⟸

3.6 A petrol engine with a compression ratio of 7 used a mixture of iso-octane and hexane as fuel. The pressure and temperature at the beginning of the compression process is 1 bar and 55.22 °C respectively. If the fuel-air mixture is 19.05% rich and the maximum pressure developed is 115.26 bar then evaluate the composition of the mixture (in percentage weight). Take C_v = 0.717 kJ/kg K, $(CV)_{\text{hexane}}$ = 43 MJ/kg, $(CV)_{\text{iso-octane}}$ = 42 MJ/kg and $pV^{1.31}$ is constant for the expansion and compression processes.

Solution

Suppose every kmol of iso-octane is mixed with x kmols of hexane. The stoichiometric equation is

$$xC_6H_{14} + C_8H_{18} + y(0.21\ O_2 + 0.79\ N_2) \rightarrow$$

$$(8 + 6x)CO_2 + (9 + 7x)\ H_2O + (0.79y)N_2$$

Equating number of oxygen atoms on both sides

$$0.42y = 2 \times (8 + 6x) + (9 + 7x)$$

$$y = \frac{1}{0.42} \times (25 + 19x)$$

As the fuel-air mixture is 19.05% rich, for x moles of hexane and 1 mole of iso-octane, number of moles of air present

$$= \frac{y}{1.1905} = (50 + 38x)$$

The combustion equation may now be written as

$$xC_6H_{14} + C_8H_{18} + (50 + 38x)(0.21\ O_2 + 0.79\ N_2) \rightarrow$$

$$aCO_2 + b\ CO + (9 + 7x)\ H_2O + 0.79(50 + 38x)N_2$$

Equating number of carbon atoms

$$a + b = 6x + 8 \qquad (1)$$

Equating number of oxygen atoms

$$2a + b = 8.96x + 12 \qquad (2)$$

On solving Eqs.(1) and (2)

$$a = 2.96x + 4$$

$$b = 3.04x + 4$$

$$\frac{n_f}{n_i} = \left(\frac{56.5 + 43.02x}{51 + 39x}\right)$$

State 2:

$$p_2 = p_1 r^n = 12.796 \text{ bar}$$

$$T_2 = T_1 r^{n-1} = 600 \text{ K}$$

Now, consider (50 + 38 x) kmols of air

Molecular weight of C_6H_{14} = 86 kg/kmol and molecular weight of C_8H_{18} = 114 kg/kmol. Therefore,

$$\text{Heat added} = 86x \times 43 \times 10^3 + 114 \times 42 \times 10^3$$

$$= (3698x + 4788) \times 10^3 \text{ kJ}$$

$$\textit{Total weight} = 28.97 \times (50 + 38x) + (86x + 114)$$

$$= (1186.86x + 1562.5) \text{ kg}$$

$$Q_s = mC_v(T_3 - T_2)$$

$$(3698x + 4788) \times 10^3 = (1186.86x + 1562.5) \times 0.717 \times (T_3 - T_2)$$

$$T_3 = 600 + \frac{3698x + 4788}{0.851x + 1.120} = \frac{4208.6x + 5460}{0.851x + 1.120}$$

$$p_3 = p_2\left(\frac{T_3}{T_2}\right)\left(\frac{n_f}{n_i}\right)$$

$$115.26 = \frac{12.796}{600} \times \left(\frac{4208.6x + 5460}{0.851x + 1.120}\right) \times \left(\frac{43.02x + 56.5}{39x + 51}\right)$$

Solving this we get $x = 0.1$. Therefore, percentage weight of iso-octane

$$= \left(\frac{114}{114 + 86x}\right) \times 100\% = \mathbf{93\%} \qquad \overset{\text{Ans}}{\Longleftarrow}$$

Percentage weight of hexane

$$= \left(\frac{86x}{114 + 86x}\right) \times 100\% = \mathbf{7\%} \qquad \overset{\text{Ans}}{\Longleftarrow}$$

Review Questions

3.1 Mention the various simplified assumptions used in fuel-air cycle analysis.

3.2 What is the difference between air-standard cycle and fuel-air cycle analysis? Explain the significance of the fuel-air cycle.

3.3 Explain why the fuel-air cycle analysis is more suitable for analyzing through a computer rather than through hand calculations.

3.4 How do the specific heats vary with temperature? What is the physical explanation for this variation?

3.5 Explain with the help of a p-V diagram the loss due to variation of specific heats in an Otto cycle.

3.6 Show with the help of a p-V diagram for an Otto cycle, that the effect of dissociation is similar to that of variation of specific heats.

3.7 Explain by means of suitable graphs the effect of dissociation on maximum temperature and brake power. How does the presence of CO affect dissociation?

3.8 Explain the effect of change of number of molecules during combustion on maximum pressure in the Otto cycle.

3.9 Compare the air-standard cycle and fuel-air cycles based on (i) character of the cycle (ii) fuel-air ratio (iii) chemical composition of the fuel

3.10 Is the effect of compression ratio on efficiency the same in fuel-air cycles also? Explain.

3.11 From the point of view of fuel-air cycle analysis how does fuel-air ratio affect efficiency, maximum power, temperature and pressure in a cycle.

3.12 How does exhaust temperature and mean effective pressure affect the engine performance? Explain.

Exercise

3.1 Find the percentage change in the efficiency of an Otto cycle having a compression ratio of 10, if C_v decreases by 2%. *Ans:* 1.22%

3.2 Find the percentage increase in the efficiency of a Diesel cycle having a compression ratio of 16 and cut-off ratio is 10% of the swept volume, if C_v decreases by 2%. Take $C_v = 0.717$ and $\gamma = 1.4$. *Ans:* 1.23%

3.3 The air-fuel ratio of a Diesel engine is 31:1. If the compression ratio is 15:1 and the temperature at the end of compression is 1000 K, find at what percentage of stroke is the combustion complete if the combustion begins at TDC and continuous at constant pressure. Calorific value of the fuel is 40000 kJ/kg. Assume the variable specific heat, $C_p = a + bT$, where $a = 1$ and $b = 0.28 \times 10^{-4}$. *Ans:* 15.68%

3.4 An engine working on the Otto cycle, uses hexane (C_6H_{14}) as fuel. The engine works on chemically correct air-fuel ratio and the compression ratio is 8. Pressure and temperature at the beginning of compression are 1 bar and 77 °C respectively. If the calorific value of the fuel is 43000 kJ/kg and $C_v = 0.717$ kJ/kg K, find the maximum temperature and pressure of the cycle. Assume the compression follows the law $pV^{1.3} = c$. *Ans:* (i) 4343.6 K (ii) 99.28 bar

3.5 Find the percentage change in efficiency of a dual cycle having compression ratio = 16 and cut-off ratio of 10% of swept volume and if C_v increases by 2%. Given $\frac{T_3}{T_2} = 1.67$. *Ans:* 0.68%

3.6 It is estimated that for air operating in a given engine the γ decreases by 2% from its original value of 1.4. Find the change in efficiency. The pressure at the end of compression is 18 bar. *Ans:* 4.5%

Multiple Choice Questions (choose the most appropriate answer)

1. The actual efficiency of a good engine is about

   (a) 100%
   (b) 85%
   (c) 50%
   (d) 25%

   of the estimated fuel-air cycle efficiency.

2. With dissociation peak temperature is obtained

   (a) at the stoichiometric air-fuel ratio
   (b) when the mixture is slightly lean
   (c) when the mixture is slightly rich
   (d) none of the above

3. With dissociation the exhaust gas temperature

   (a) decreases
   (b) increases
   (c) no effect
   (d) increases upto certain air-fuel ratio and then decreases

4. Fuel-air ratio affects maximum power output of the engine due to

   (a) higher specific heats
   (b) chemical equilibrium losses
   (c) both (a) and (b)
   (d) none of the above

5. Mean effective pressure at a given compression ratio is maximum when the air-fuel ratio is
   (a) higher than stoichiometric
   (b) lower than stoichiometric
   (c) equal to stoichiometric
   (d) none of the above

6. For a compression process with variable specific heat the peak temperature and pressure are
   (a) lower
   (b) higher
   (c) no effect
   (d) none of the above

   compared to constant specific heat

7. Dissociation can be considered as
   (a) disintegration of combustion products at high temperature
   (b) reverse process of combustion
   (c) heat absorption process
   (d) all of the above

8. Cycles with lean to very lean mixture tend towards
   (a) practical cycles
   (b) fuel-air cycles
   (c) air-standard cycles
   (d) none of the above

9. When the mixture is lean
   (a) efficiency is less
   (b) power output is less
   (c) maximum temperature and pressure are higher
   (d) all of the above

10. For a given compression ratio, as the mixture is made progressively rich from lean the mean effective pressure
    (a) increases
    (b) decreases
    (c) initially increases and then decreases
    (d) remains more or less same

Ans:	1. – (b)	2. – (c)	3. – (a)	4. – (c)	5. – (b)
	6. – (a)	7. – (d)	8. – (d)	9. – (b)	10. – (c)

4

ACTUAL CYCLES AND THEIR ANALYSIS

4.1 INTRODUCTION

The actual cycles for IC engines differ from the fuel-air cycles and air-standard cycles in many respects. The actual cycle efficiency is much lower than the air-standard efficiency due to various losses occurring in the actual engine operation. The major losses are due to:

(i) Variation of specific heats with temperature

(ii) Dissociation of the combustion products

(iii) Progressive combustion

(iv) Incomplete combustion of fuel

(v) Heat transfer into the walls of the combustion chamber

(vi) Blowdown at the end of the exhaust process

(vii) Gas exchange process

An estimate of these losses can be made from previous experience and some simple tests on the engines and these estimates can be used in evaluating the performance of an engine.

4.2 COMPARISON OF AIR-STANDARD AND ACTUAL CYCLES

The actual cycles for internal combustion engines differ from air-standard cycles in many respects. These differences are mainly due to:

(i) The working substance being a mixture of air and fuel vapour or finely atomized liquid fuel in air combined with the products of combustion left from the previous cycle.

(ii) The change in chemical composition of the working substance.

(iii) The variation of specific heats with temperature.

(iv) The change in the composition, temperature and actual amount of fresh charge because of the residual gases.

(v) The progressive combustion rather than the instantaneous combustion.

(vi) The heat transfer to and from the working medium.

(vii) The substantial exhaust blowdown loss, i.e., loss of work on the expansion stroke due to early opening of the exhaust valve.

(viii) Gas leakage, fluid friction etc., in actual engines.

Points (i) to (iv), being related to fuel-air cycles have already been dealt in detail in Chapter 4. Remaining points viz. (v) to (viii) are in fact responsible for the difference between fuel-air cycles and actual cycles.

Most of the factors listed above tend to decrease the thermal efficiency and power output of the actual engines. On the other hand, the analysis of the cycles while taking these factors into account clearly indicates that the estimated thermal efficiencies are not very different from those of the actual cycles.

Out of all the above factors, major influence is exercised by

(i) *Time loss factor* i.e. loss due to time required for mixing of fuel and air and also for combustion.

(ii) *Heat loss factor* i.e. loss of heat from gases to cylinder walls.

(iii) *Exhaust blowdown factor* i.e. loss of work on the expansion stroke due to early opening of the exhaust valve.

These major losses which are not considered in the previous two chapters are discussed in the following sections.

4.3 TIME LOSS FACTOR

In air-standard cycles the heat addition is assumed to be an instantaneous process whereas in an actual cycle it is over a definite period of time. The time required for the combustion is such that under all circumstances some change in volume takes place while it is in progress. The crankshaft will usually turn about 30 to 40° between the initiation of the spark and the end of combustion. There will be a time loss during this period and is called time loss factor.

The consequence of the finite time of combustion is that the peak pressure will not occur when the volume is minimum i.e., when the piston is at TDC; but will occur some time after TDC. The pressure, therefore, rises in the first part of the working stroke from b to c as shown in Fig.4.1. The point 3 represents the state of gases had the combustion been instantaneous and an additional amount of work equal to area shown hatched would have been done. This loss of work reduces the efficiency and is called *time loss due to progressive combustion* or merely *time losses.*

The time taken for the burning depends upon the flame velocity which in turn depends upon the type of fuel and the fuel-air ratio and also on the shape and size of the combustion chamber. Further, the distance from the point of ignition to the opposite side of the combustion space also plays an important role.

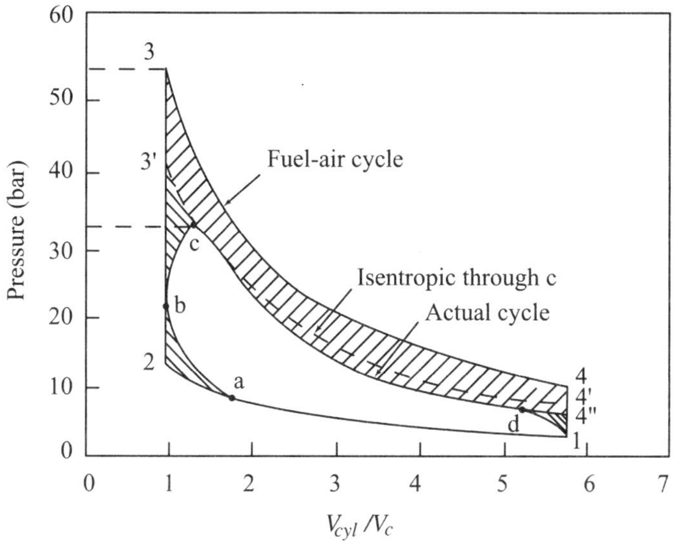

Fig. 4.1 Effect of time losses shown on p-V diagram

Table 4.1 Cycle performance for various ignition timings for $r = 6$ (typical values)

Cycle	Ignition advance	Max. cycle pressure bar	*mep* bar	efficiency %	$\frac{\text{Actual } \eta}{\text{Fuel cycle } \eta}$
Fuel-air cycle	0°	44	10.20	32.2	1.00
Actual cycle	0°	23	7.50	24.1	0.75
"	17°	34	8.35	26.3	0.81
"	35°	41	7.60	23.9	0.74

In order that the peak pressure is not reached too late in the expansion stroke, the time at which the combustion starts is varied by varying the spark timing or spark advance. Figures 4.2 and 4.3 show the effect of spark timing on *p-V* diagram from a typical trial. With spark at *TDC* (Fig.4.2) the peak pressure is low due to the expansion of gases. If the spark is advanced to achieve complete combustion close to *TDC* (Fig.4.3) additional work is required to compress the burning gases.

This represents a direct loss. In either case, viz., with or without spark advance the work area is less and the power output and efficiency are lowered. Therefore, a moderate or optimum spark advance (Fig.4.4) is the best compromise resulting in minimum losses on both the compression and expansion strokes. Table 4.1 compares the engine performance for various ignition timings. Figure 4.5 shows the effect of spark advance on the power output by means of the *p-V* diagram. As seen from Fig.4.6, when the ignition advance is increased there is a drastic reduction in the *imep* and the consequent loss

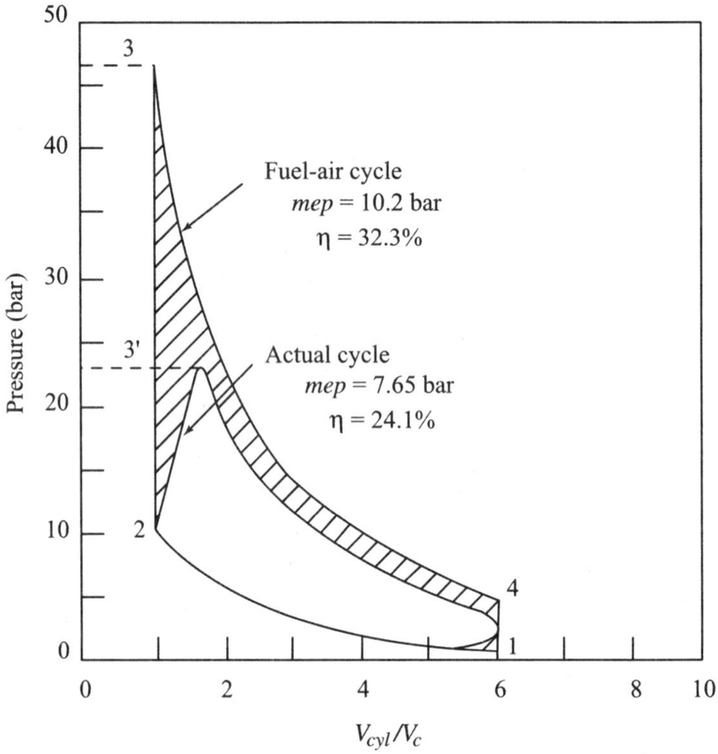

Fig. 4.2 Spark at TDC, advance 0°

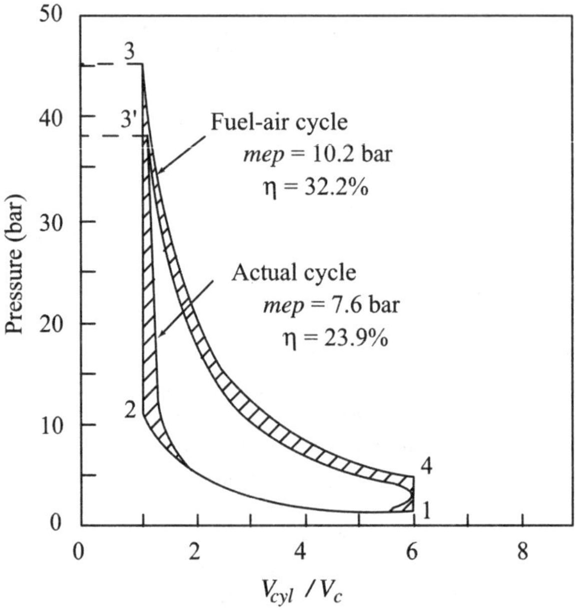

Fig. 4.3 Combustion completed at TDC, advance 35°

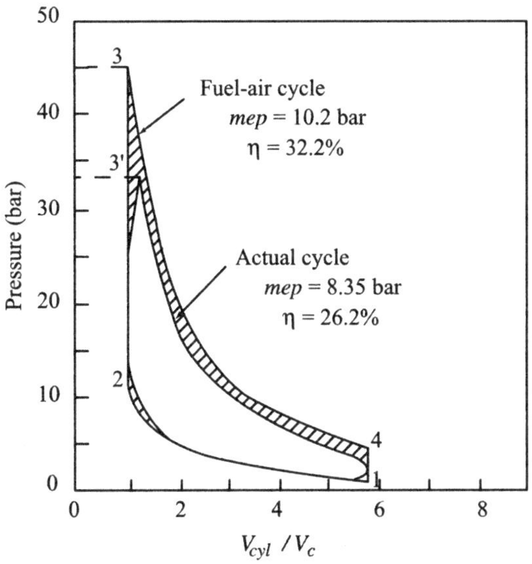

Fig. 4.4 Optimum advance 15° – 30°

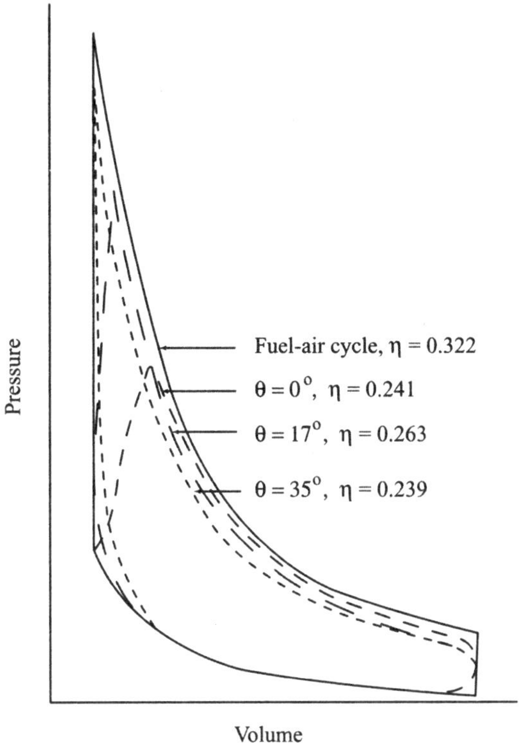

Fig. 4.5 p-V diagram showing power loss due to ignition advance

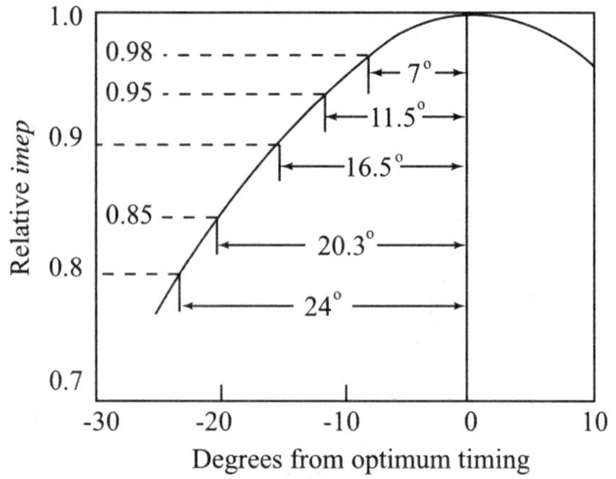

Fig. 4.6 Power loss due to ignition advance

of power. However, some times a deliberate spark retardation from optimum may be necessary in actual practice in order to avoid knocking and to simultaneously reduce exhaust emissions of hydrocarbons and carbon monoxide.

At full throttle with the fuel-air ratio corresponding to maximum power and the optimum ignition advance the time losses may account for a drop in efficiency of about 5 per cent (fuel-air cycle efficiency is reduced by about 2%). These losses are higher when the mixture is richer or leaner when the ignition advance is not optimum and also at part throttle operations the losses are higher. It is impossible to obtain a perfect homogeneous mixture with fuel-vapour and air, since, residual gases from the previous cycle are present in the clearance volume of the cylinder. Further, only very limited time is available between the mixture preparation and ignition. Under these circumstances, it is possible that a pocket of excess oxygen is present in one part of the cylinder and a pocket of excess fuel in another part. Therefore, some fuel does not burn or burns partially to CO and the unused O_2 appears in the exhaust as shown in Fig.4.7 Energy release data show that only about 95% of the energy is released with stoichiometric fuel-air ratios. Energy release in actual engine is about 90% of fuel energy input.

It should be noted that it is necessary to use a lean mixture to eliminate wastage of fuel, while a rich mixture is required to utilize all the oxygen. Slightly leaner mixture would give maximum efficiency but too lean a mixture will burn slowly increasing the time losses or will not burn at all causing total wastage of fuel. In a rich mixture a part of the fuel will not get the necessary oxygen and will be completely lost. Also the flame speed in mixtures more than 10% richer is low, thereby, increasing the time losses and lowering the efficiency. Even if this unused fuel and oxygen eventually combine during the exhaust stroke and burn, the energy which is released at such a late stage cannot be utilized. Imperfect mixing of fuel and air may give different fuel-air ratios during suction stroke or certain cylinders in a multicylinder engine may get continuously leaner mixtures than others.

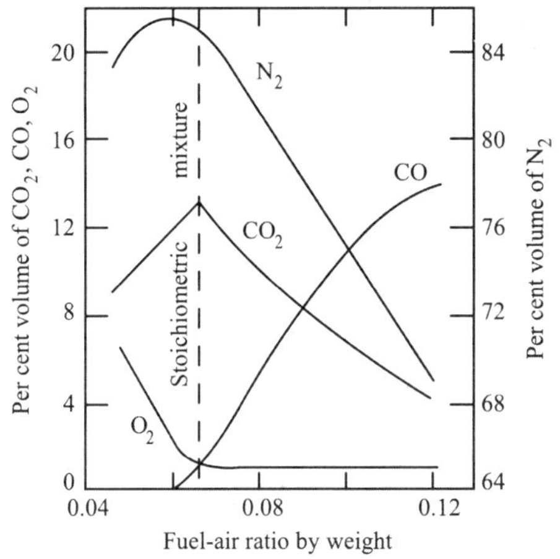

Fig. 4.7 Composition of exhaust gases for various fuel-air ratios

4.4 HEAT LOSS FACTOR

During the combustion process and the subsequent expansion stroke the heat flows from the cylinder gases through the cylinder walls and cylinder head into the water jacket or cooling fins. Some heat enters the piston head and flows through the piston rings into the cylinder wall or is carried away by the engine lubricating oil which splashes on the underside of the piston. The heat loss along with other losses is shown on the p-V diagram in Fig.4.8

Heat loss during combustion will naturally have the maximum effect on the cycle efficiency while heat loss just before the end of the expansion stroke can have very little effect because of its contribution to the useful work is very little. The heat lost during the combustion does not represent a complete loss because, even under ideal conditions assumed for air-standard cycle, only a part of this heat could be converted into work (equal to $Q \times \eta_{th}$) and the rest would be rejected during the exhaust stroke. About 15 per cent of the total heat is lost during combustion and expansion. Of this, however, much is lost so late in the cycle to have contributed to useful work. If all the heat loss is recovered only about 20% of it may appear as useful work. Figure 4.8 shows percentage of time loss, heat loss and exhaust loss in a Cooperative Fuel Research (CFR) engine. Losses are given as percentage of fuel-air cycle work. The effect of loss of heat during combustion is to reduce the maximum temperature and therefore, the specific heats are lower. It may be noted from the Fig.4.8 that of the various losses, heat loss factor contributes around 12%.

4.5 EXHAUST BLOWDOWN

The cylinder pressure at the end of exhaust stroke is about 7 bar depending on the compression ratio employed. If the exhaust valve is opened at the bottom dead centre, the piston has to do work against high cylinder pressures during

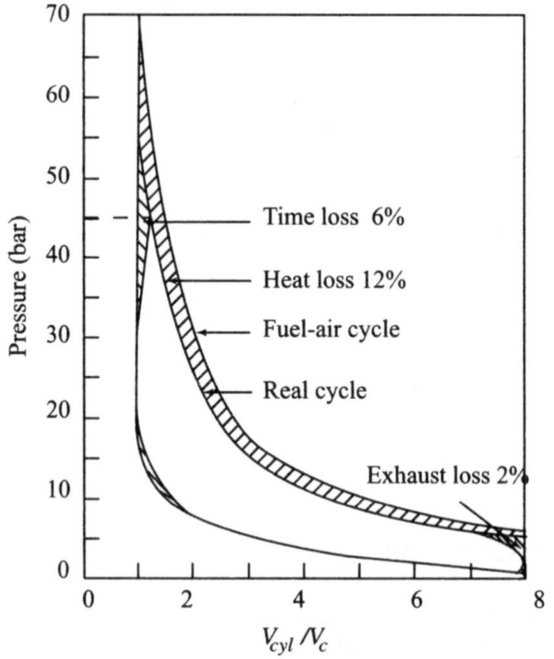

Fig. 4.8 Time loss, heat loss and exhaust loss in petrol engines

the early part of the exhaust stroke. If the exhaust valve is opened too early, a part of the expansion stroke is lost. The best compromise is to open the exhaust valve 40° to 70° before BDC thereby reducing the cylinder pressure to halfway (say 3.5 bar) before the exhaust stroke begins. This is shown in Fig.4.9 by the roundness at the end of the diagram.

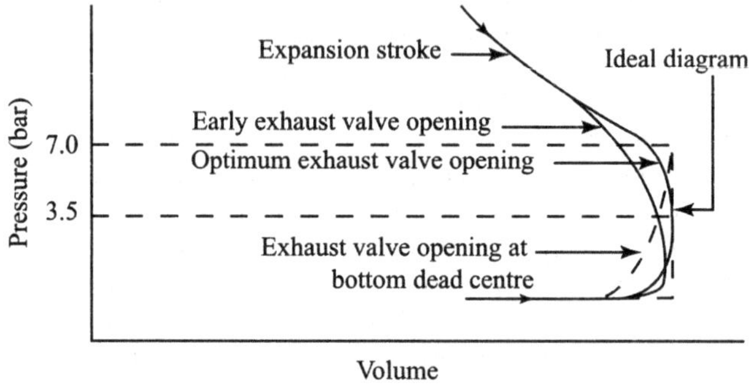

Fig. 4.9 Effect of exhaust valve opening time on blowdown

4.5.1 Loss Due to Gas Exchange Processes

The difference of work done in expelling the exhaust gases and the work done by the fresh charge during the suction stroke is called the pumping work. In other words loss due to the gas exchange process (pumping loss) is due to pumping gas from lower inlet pressure p_i to higher exhaust pressure p_e. *The pumping loss increases at part throttle because throttling reduces the suction pressure.* Pumping loss also increases with speed. The gas exchange processes affect the volumetric efficiency of the engine. The performance of the engine, to a great deal, depends on the volumetric efficiency. Hence, it is worthwhile to discuss this parameter in greater detail here.

4.5.2 Volumetric Efficiency

As already stated in section 1.8.4, volumetric efficiency is an indication of the breathing ability of the engine and is defined as the ratio of the volume of air actually inducted at ambient condition to swept volume. However, it may also be defined on mass basis as the ratio of the actual mass of air drawn into the engine during a given period of time to the theoretical mass which should have been drawn in during that same period of time, based upon the total piston displacement of the engine, and the temperature and pressure of the surrounding atmosphere.

The above definition is applicable only to the naturally aspirated engine. In the case of the supercharged engine, however, the theoretical mass of air should be calculated at the conditions of pressure and temperature prevailing in the intake manifold. The volumetric efficiency is affected by many variables, some of the important ones are:

(i) *The density of the fresh charge* : As the fresh charge arrives in the hot cylinder, heat is transferred to it from the hot chamber walls and the hot residual exhaust gases, raising its temperature. This results in a decrease in the mass of fresh charge admitted and a reduction in volumetric efficiency. The volumetric efficiency is increased by low temperatures (provided there are no heat transfer effects) and high pressure of the fresh charge, since density is thereby increased, and more mass of charge can be inducted into a given volume.

(ii) *The exhaust gas in the clearance volume* : As the piston moves from *TDC* to *BDC* on the intake stroke, these products tend to expand and occupy a portion of the piston displacement greater than the clearance volume, thus reducing the space available to the incoming charge. In addition, these exhaust products tend to raise the temperature of the fresh charge, thereby decreasing its density and further reducing volumetric efficiency.

(iii) *The design of the intake and exhaust manifolds* : The exhaust manifold should be so designed as to enable the exhaust products to escape readily, while the intake manifold should be designed so as to bring in the maximum possible fresh charge. This implies minimum restriction is offered to the fresh charge flowing into the cylinder, as well as to the exhaust products being forced out.

(iv) *The timing of the intake and exhaust valves* : Valve timing is the regulation of the points in the cycle at which the valves are set to open and close. Since, the valves require a finite period of time to open or close for smooth operation, a slight "lead" time is necessary for proper opening and closing. The design of the valve operating cam provides for the smooth transition from one position to the other, while the cam setting determines the timing of the valve.

The effect of the *intake valve* timing on the engine air capacity is indicated by its effect on the air inducted per cylinder per cycle, i.e., the mass of air taken into one cylinder during one suction stroke. Figure 4.10 shows representative intake valve timing for both a low speed and high speed SI engine. In order to understand the effect of the intake valve timing on the charge inducted per cylinder per cycle, it is desirable to follow through the intake process, referring to the Fig.4.10.

While the intake valve should open, theoretically, at TDC, almost all SI engines employ an intake valve opening of a few degrees before TDC on the exhaust stroke. This is to ensure that the valve will be fully open and the fresh charge starts to flow into the cylinder as soon as the piston reaches TDC. In Fig.4.10, the intake valve starts to open 10° before TDC. It may be noted from Fig.4.10 that for a low speed engine, the intake valve closes 10° after BDC, and for a high speed engine, 60° after BDC.

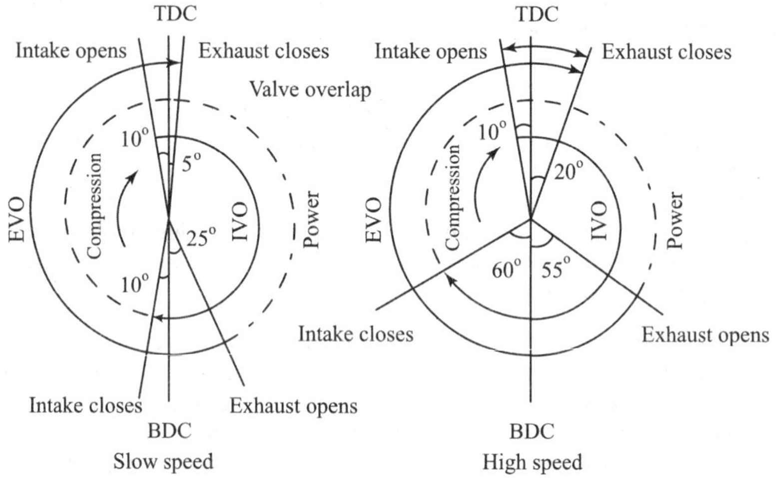

Fig. 4.10 Valve timing diagram of four-stroke engines

As the piston descends on the intake stroke, the fresh charge is drawn in through the intake port and valve. When the piston reaches BDC and starts to ascend on the compression stroke, the inertia of the incoming fresh charge tends to cause it to continue to move into the cylinder. At low engine speeds, the charge is moving into the cylinder relatively slowly, and its inertia is relatively low. If the intake valve were to remain open much beyond BDC, the up-moving piston on the compression stroke would tend to force some of the charge, already in the cylinder back into the intake manifold, with consequent reduction in volumetric efficiency. Hence, the intake valve is closed relatively early after BDC for a slow speed engine. High speed engines, however, bring the charge in through the intake manifold at greater speeds, and the charge has greater inertia. As the piston moves up on the compression stroke, there is a "ram" effect produced by the incoming mixture which tends to pack more charge into the cylinder. In the high speed engine, therefore, the intake valve closing is delayed for a greater period of time after BDC in order to take advantage of this "ram" and induct the maximum quantity of charge.

For either a low speed or a high speed engine operating in its range of speeds, there is some point at which the charge per cylinder per cycle becomes a maximum, for a particular valve setting. If the revolutions of the low speed engine are increased beyond this point, the intake valve in effect close too soon, and the charge per cylinder per cycle is reduced. If the revolutions of the high speed engine are increased beyond this maximum, the flow may be chocked due to fluid friction. These losses can become greater than the benefit of the *ram*, and the charge per cylinder per cycle falls off.

The chosen intake valve setting for an engine operating over a range of speeds must necessarily be a compromise between the best setting for the low speed end of the range and the best setting for the high speed end.

The timing of the *exhaust valve* also affects the volumetric efficiency. The exhaust valve usually opens before the piston reaches BDC on the expansion stroke. This reduces the work done by the expanding gases during the power stroke, but decreases the work necessary to expel the burned products during the exhaust stroke, and results in an overall gain in output.

During the exhaust stroke, the piston forces the burned gases out at high velocity. If the closing of the exhaust valve is delayed beyond TDC, the inertia of the exhaust gases tends to scavenge the cylinder better by carrying out a greater mass of the gas left in the clearance volume, and results in increased volumetric efficiency. Consequently, the exhaust valve is often set to close a few degrees after TDC on the exhaust stroke, as indicated in Fig.4.10. It should be noted that it is quite possible for both the intake and exhaust valves to remain open, or partially open, at the same time. This is termed the *valve overlap*. This overlap, of course, must not be excessive enough to allow the burned gases to be sucked into the intake manifold, or the fresh charge to escape through the exhaust valve.

The reasons for the necessity of valve overlap and valve timings other than at TDC or BDC, has been explained above, taking into consideration only the dynamic effects of gas flow. One must realize, however, that the presence of a mechanical problem in actuating the valves has an influence in the timing of the valves.

The valve cannot be lifted instantaneously to a desired height, but must be opened gradually due to the problem of acceleration involved. If the sudden change in acceleration from positive to negative values are encountered in design of a cam. The cam follower may lose the contact with the cam and then be forced back to close contact by the valve spring, resulting in a blow against the cam. This type of action must be avoided and, hence, cam contours are so designed as to produce gradual and smooth changes in directional acceleration. As a result, the opening of the valve must commence ahead of the time at which it is fully opened. The same reasoning applies for the closing time. It can be seen, therefore, that the timing of valves depends on dynamic and mechanical considerations.

Both the intake and exhaust valves are usually timed to give the most satisfactory results for the average operating conditions of the particular engine, and the settings are determined on the prototype of the actual engine.

4.6 LOSS DUE TO RUBBING FRICTION

These losses are due to friction between the piston and the cylinder walls, friction in various bearings and also the energy spent in operating the auxiliary equipment such as cooling water pump, ignition system, fan, etc. The piston ring friction increases rapidly with engine speed. It also increases to a small extent with increase in mean effective pressure. The bearing friction and the auxiliary friction also increase with engine speed. The efficiency of an engine is maximum at full load and decreases at part loads. It is because the percentage of direct heat loss, pumping loss and rubbing friction loss increase at part loads. The approximate losses for a gasoline engine of high compression ratio, say 8:1 using a chemically correct mixture are given in Table 4.2, as percentage of fuel energy input.

Table 4.2 Typical losses in a gasoline engine for $r = 8$

S.No.	Item	At load	
		Full load	Half load
(a)	Air-standard cycle efficiency ($\eta_{air\text{-}std}$)	56.5	56.5
1.	Losses due to variation of specific heat and chemical equilibrium, %	13.0	13.0
2.	Loss due to progressive combustion, %	4.0	4.0
3.	Loss due to incomplete combustion, %	3.0	3.0
4.	Direct heat loss, %	4.0	5.0
5.	Exhaust blowdown loss, %	0.5	0.5
6.	Pumping loss, %	0.5	1.5
7.	Rubbing friction loss, %	3.0	6.0
(b)	Fuel-air cycle efficiency $= \eta_{air\text{-}std} - (1)$	43.5	43.5
(c)	Gross indicated thermal efficiency (η_{th}) $=$ Fuel-air cycle efficiency (η_{ith}) $-(2+3+4+5)$	32.0	31.0
(d)	Actual brake thermal efficiency $= \eta_{ith} - (6+7)$	28.5	23.5

4.7 ACTUAL AND FUEL-AIR CYCLES OF CI ENGINES

In the diesel cycle the losses are less than in the otto cycle. The main loss is due to incomplete combustion and is the cause of main difference between fuel-air cycle and actual cycle of a diesel engine. This is shown in Fig.4.11. In a fuel-air cycle the combustion is supposed to be completed at the end of the constant pressure burning whereas in actual practice *after burning* continues

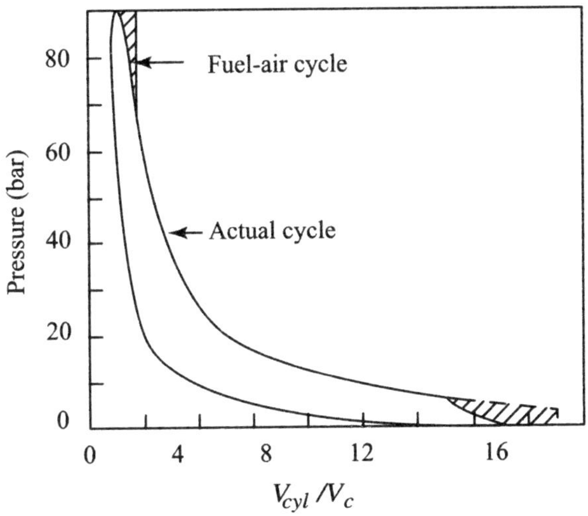

Fig. 4.11 Actual diesel cycle vs equivalent fuel combustion limited pressure cycle for two-stroke diesel engine

up to half of the expansion stroke. The ratio between the actual efficiency and the fuel-air cycle efficiency is about 0.85 in the diesel engines.

In fuel-air cycles, when allowance is made for the presence of fuel and combustion products, there is reduction in cycle efficiency. In actual cycles, allowances are also made for the losses due to phenomena such as heat transfer and finite combustion time. This reduces the cycle efficiency further. For complete analysis of actual cycles, computer models are being developed nowadays. These models are helpful in understanding the various processes that are taking place in an engine. Models are developed for both not only for CI engines but also for SI engines.

Review Questions

4.1 Why the actual cycle efficiency is much lower than the air-standard cycle efficiency? List the major losses and differences in actual engine and air-standard cycles.

4.2 List three principal factors that influence engine performance?

4.3 Briefly explain the following: (i) time loss factor (ii) heat loss factor (iii) exhaust blowdown factor.

4.4 Compare the actual and fuel-air cycles of a gasoline engine.

4.5 How does the composition of exhaust gases vary for various fuel-air ratios in a gasoline engine?

4.6 Discuss the effect of spark advance on the performance of an Otto cycle engine. What is meant by the optimum spark advance?

4.7 Discuss the optimum opening position of exhaust valve to reduce the exhaust blowdown loss.

4.8 Briefly discuss pumping and rubbing friction losses.

4.9 Discuss briefly the loss due to gas exchange process.

4.10 Define volumetric efficiency and discuss the effect of various factors affecting the volumetric efficiency.

Multiple Choice Questions (choose the most appropriate answer)

1. Time loss factor in actual cycle is due to
   (a) progressive combustion
   (b) heat loss through cylinder walls
   (c) gas leakage
   (d) friction

2. If the spark timing is at TDC, the work is less as
   (a) the peak pressure is high
   (b) the peak pressure is low
   (c) the friction is high
   (d) none of the above

3. When the spark is advanced, work output is less as
   (a) the peak pressure is low
   (b) the peak temperature is low
   (c) additional work is required to compress the burning gas
   (d) frictional losses increase

4. Optimum spark timing gives
   (a) higher mean effective pressure
   (b) higher efficiency
   (c) both (a) and (b)
   (d) none of the above

5. The major loss in a SI engine is due to
   (a) exhaust blow down
   (b) pumping
   (c) incomplete combustion
   (d) variation in specific heat and chemical equilibrium

6. Fuel-air cycle efficiency is less than air-standard cycle efficiency by an amount equal to

    (a) pumping loss
    (b) friction loss
    (c) loss due to specific heat variation and chemical equilibrium
    (d) exhaust blow down loss

7. The major loss in a CI engine is

    (a) direct heat loss
    (b) loss due to incomplete combustion
    (c) rubbing friction loss
    (d) pumping loss

8. The ratio of the actual efficiency and the fuel-air cycle efficiency for CI engines is about

    (a) 0.2–0.3
    (b) 0.5–0.6
    (c) 1.0
    (d) 0.6–0.8

9. In an actual SI engine the pumping loss with respect to speed

    (a) decreases
    (b) increases
    (c) remains constant
    (d) nothing to do with speed

10. The volumetric efficiency is affected by

    (a) the exhaust gas in the clearance volume
    (b) the design of intake and exhaust valve
    (c) valve timing
    (d) all of the above

11. In diesel cycles compared to otto cycle, the losses are

    (a) lesser
    (b) more
    (c) equal
    (d) none of the above

12. The timing of the exhaust valve affects

    (a) mechanical efficiency
    (b) volumetric efficiency
    (c) indicated thermal efficiency
    (d) none of the above

13. Valve overlap is the period in which

    (a) intake valve is open while exhaust valve is closed
    (b) intake valve is closed while exhaust valve is open
    (c) both intake and exhaust valves are open
    (d) both intake and exhaust valves are closed

14. With increase in mean effective pressure the ring friction

    (a) remains constant
    (b) increases and then decreases
    (c) decreases
    (d) increases only to a small extent

15. Opening the intake valve before the top dead centre improves

    (a) power output
    (b) brake thermal efficiency
    (c) volumetric efficiency
    (d) all of the above

Ans:					
	1. – (a)	2. – (b)	3. – (c)	4. – (c)	5. – (d)
	6. – (c)	7. – (b)	8. – (d)	9. – (b)	10. – (d)
	11. – (a)	12. – (b)	13. – (c)	14. – (d)	15. – (d)

5

CONVENTIONAL FUELS

5.1 INTRODUCTION

The study of fuels for IC engines has been carried out ever since these engines came into existence. The engine converts heat energy which is obtained from the chemical combination of the fuel with the oxygen, into mechanical energy. Since the heat energy is derived from the fuel, a fundamental knowledge of types of fuels and their characteristics is essential in order to understand the combustion phenomenon. The characteristics of the fuel used have considerable influence on the design, efficiency, output and particularly, the reliability and durability of the engine. Further, the fuel characteristics play a vital role in the atmospheric pollution caused by the engines used in automobiles.

5.2 Fuels

Internal combustion engines can be operated on different types of fuels such as liquid, gaseous and even solid fuels. Depending upon the type of fuel to be used the engine has to be designed accordingly.

5.2.1 Solid Fuels

The solid fuels find little practical application at present because of the problems in handling the fuel as well as in disposing off, the solid residue or ash after combustion. However, in the initial stages of the engine development, solid fuels such as finely powdered coal was attempted. Compared to gaseous and liquid fuels, solid fuels are quite difficult to handle and storage and feeding are quite cumbersome. Because of the complications in the design of the fuel feed systems these fuels have become unsuitable in solid form. Attempts are being made to generate gaseous or liquid fuels from charcoal for use in IC engines.

5.2.2 Gaseous Fuels

Gaseous fuels are ideal and pose very few problems in using them in internal combustion engines. Being gaseous, they mix more homogeneously with air and eliminate the distribution and starting problems that are encountered with liquid fuels. Even though the gaseous fuels are the most ideal for internal combustion engines, storage and handling problems restrict their use in automobiles. Consequently, they are commonly used for stationary power plants located near the source of availability of the fuel. Some of the gaseous fuels can be liquefied under pressure for reducing the storage volume but this arrangement is very expensive as well as risky. Because of the energy crisis in the recent years considerable research efforts are being made to improve the design and performance of gas engines which became obsolete when liquid fuels began to be used.

5.2.3 Liquid Fuels

In most of the modern internal combustion engines, liquid fuels which are the derivatives of liquid petroleum are being used. The three principal commercial types of liquid fuels are benzyl, alcohol and petroleum products. However, petroleum products form the main fuels for internal combustion engines as on today.

5.3 CHEMICAL STRUCTURE OF PETROLEUM

Petroleum as obtained from the oil wells, is predominantly a mixture of many hydrocarbons with differing molecular structure. It also contains small amounts of sulphur, oxygen, nitrogen and impurities such as water and sand. The carbon and hydrogen atoms may be linked in different ways in a hydrocarbon molecule and this linking influences the chemical and physical properties of different hydrocarbon groups. Most petroleum fuels tend to exhibit the characteristics of that type of hydrocarbon which forms a major constituent of the fuel.

The carbon and hydrogen combine in different proportions and molecular structures to form a variety of hydrocarbons. The carbon to hydrogen ratio which is one of the important parameters and their nature of bonding determine the energy characteristics of the hydrocarbon fuels. Depending upon the number of carbon and hydrogen atoms the petroleum products are classified into different groups.

The differences in physical and chemical properties between the different types of hydrocarbon depend on their chemical composition and affect mainly the combustion processes and hence, the proportion of fuel and air required in the engine. The basic families of hydrocarbons, their general formulae and their molecular arrangement are shown in Table 5.1.

Table 5.1 Basic families of hydrocarbons

Family of hydrocarbons	General formula	Molecular structure	Saturated/ Unsaturated	Stability
Paraffin	C_nH_{2n+2}	Chain	Saturated	Stable
Olefin	C_nH_{2n}	Chain	Unsaturated	Unstable
Naphthene	C_nH_{2n}	Ring	Saturated	Stable
Aromatic	C_nH_{2n-6}	Ring	Highly unsaturated	Most unstable

5.3.1 Paraffin Series

The normal paraffin hydrocarbons are of straight chain molecular structure. They are represented by a general chemical formula, C_nH_{2n+2}. The molecular structures of the first few members of the paraffin family of hydrocarbons are shown below.

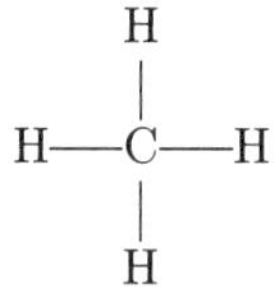

Methane

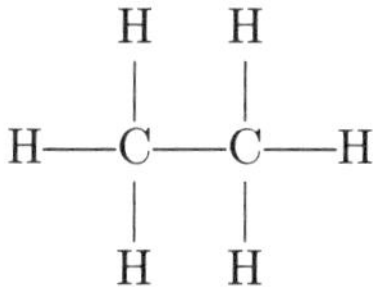

Ethane

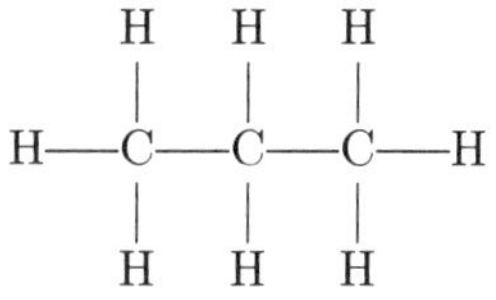

Propane

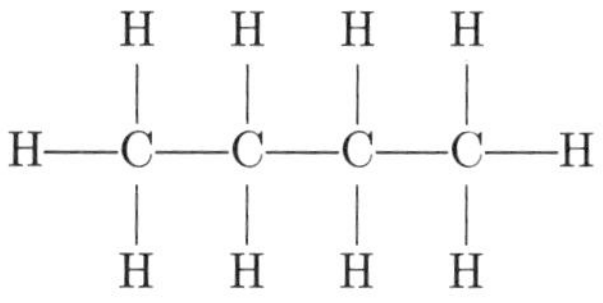

Butane

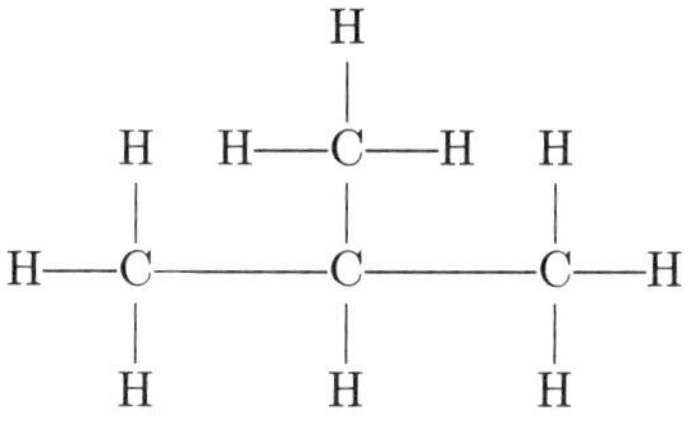

Isobutane

In these hydrocarbons the valency of all the carbon atoms is fully utilized by single bonds with hydrogen atoms. Therefore, the paraffin hydrocarbons are saturated compounds and are characteristically very stable.

A variation of the paraffin family consists of an open chain structure with an attached branch and is usually termed a branched chain paraffin. The hydrocarbons which have the same chemical formulae but different structural formulae are known as isomers.

Isobutane shown above has the same general chemical formula and molecular weight as butane but a different molecular structure and physical characteristics. It is called an isomer of butane and is known as isobutane. Isoparaffins are also stable compounds.

5.3.2 Olefin Series

Olefins are also straight chain compounds similar to paraffins but are unsaturated because they contain one or more double bonds between carbon atoms. Their chemical formula is C_nH_{2n}. Mono-olefins have one double bond whereas diolefin have two in their structure.

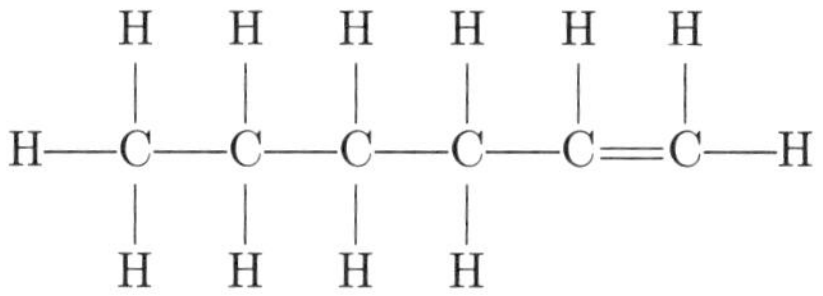

Hexene

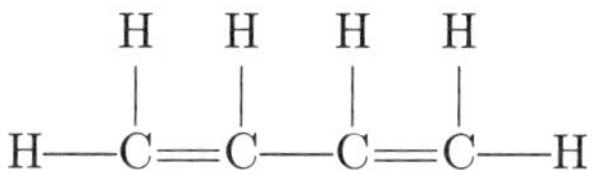

Butadiene

Olefins are not as stable as the single bond paraffins because of the presence of the double bonds in their structure. Consequently, these are readily oxidized in storage to form gummy deposits. Hence, olefin content in certain petroleum products is kept low by specification.

5.3.3 Naphthene Series

The naphthenes have the same chemical formula as the olefin series of hydrocarbons but have a ring structure and therefore, often they are called as cyclo-paraffins. They are saturated and tend to be stable. The naphthenes are saturated compounds whereas olefins are unsaturated. Cyclopentane is one of the compounds in the naphthene series (C_nH_{2n}).

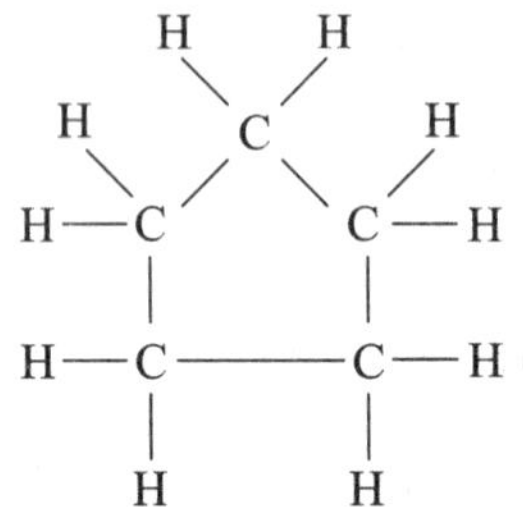

Cyclopentane

5.3.4 Aromatic Series

Aromatic compounds are ring structured having a benzene molecule as their central structure and have a general chemical formula C_nH_{2n-6}. Though the presence of double bonds indicate that they are unsaturated, a peculiar nature of these double bonds causes them to be more stable than the other unsaturated compounds. Various aromatic compounds are formed by replacing one or more of the hydrogen atoms of the benzene molecules with an organic radical such as paraffins, naphthenes and olefins.

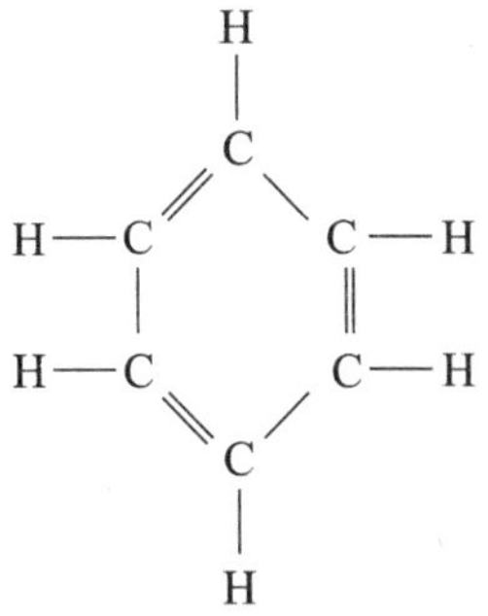

Benzene

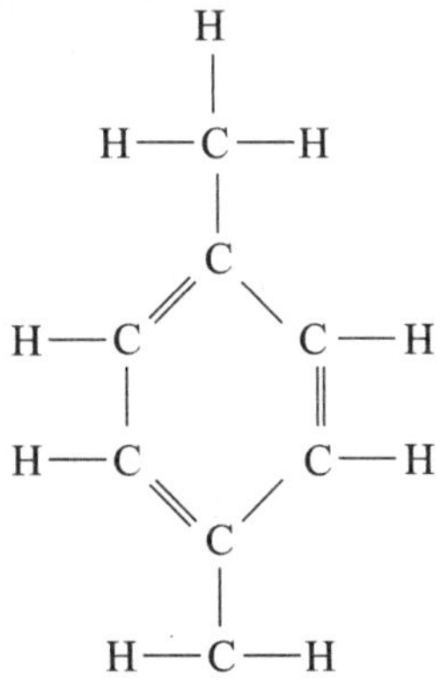

Toluene

By adding a methyl group (CH_3), benzene is converted to toluene ($C_6H_5CH_3$), the base for the preparation of Trinitrotoluene (TNT) which is a highly explosive compound.

The above families of hydrocarbons exhibit some general characteristics due to their molecular structure which are summarized below:

(i) Normal paraffins exhibit the poorest antiknock quality when used in an SI engine. But the antiknock quality improves with the increasing number of carbon atoms and the compactness of the molecular structure. The aromatics offer the best resistance to knocking in SI Engines.

(ii) For CI engines, the order is reversed i.e., the normal paraffins are the best fuels and aromatics are the least desirable.

(iii) As the number of atoms in the molecular structure increases, the boiling temperature increases. Thus fuels with fewer atoms in the molecule tend to be more volatile.

(iv) The heating value generally increases as the proportion of hydrogen atoms to carbon atoms in the molecule increases due to the higher heating value of hydrogen than carbon. Thus, paraffins have the highest heating value and the aromatics the least.

5.4 PETROLEUM REFINING PROCESS

Crude petroleum, as obtained from the oil wells contains gases (mainly methane and ethane) and certain impurities such as water, solids etc. The crude oil is separated into gasoline, kerosene, fuel oil etc. by the process of fractional distillation. This process is based on the fact that the boiling points of various hydrocarbons increase with increase in molecular weight.

Figure 5.1 shows a simple diagram of the refining process of crude petroleum (the diagram does not show the facilities for process utilization, desulphurization etc.). In the first step, the petroleum is passed through a separator in which the gases are removed and a product known as natural gasoline is obtained. The liquid petroleum is then vapourized in a still, at temperatures of 600 °C and the vapour is admitted at the bottom of the fractionating tower. The vapour is forced to pass upwards along a labyrinth-like arrangement of plates which direct the vapour through trays of liquid fuel maintained at different temperatures. The compounds with higher boiling points get condensed out at lower levels while those with lower boiling points move up to higher levels where they get condensed in trays at appropriate temperature. Generally the top fraction is called the straight-run gasoline and the other fractions, kerosene, diesel oil, fuel oils etc. are obtained in the increasing range of boiling temperatures. Details are shown in Fig.5.1. The important products of the refining process are given in Table 5.2

Many processes can be used to convert some of these fractions to compounds for which there is a greater demand. Some of the main refinery processes are as follows:

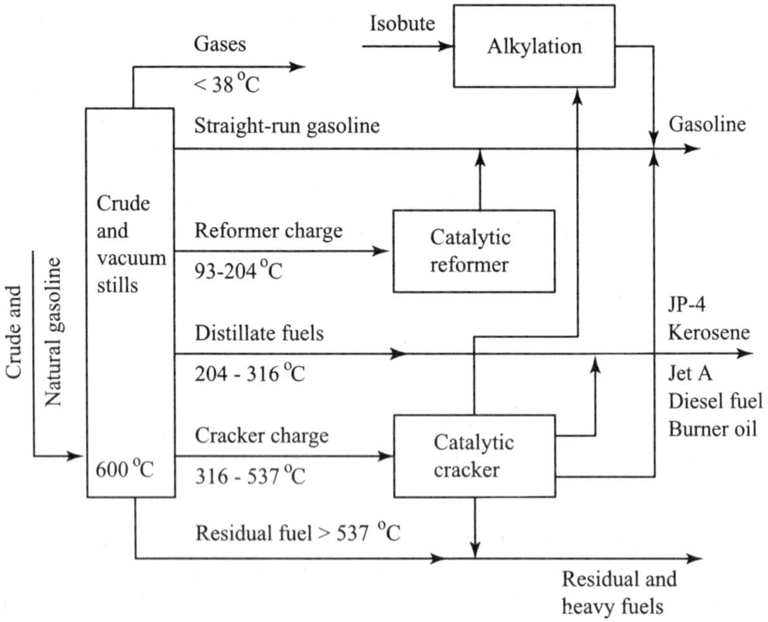

Fig. 5.1 Refining process of petroleum

(i) *Cracking* consists of breaking down large and complex hydrocarbon molecules into simpler compounds. Thermal cracking subjects the large hydrocarbon molecules to high temperature and pressure and they are decomposed into smaller, lower boiling point molecules. Catalytic cracking using catalysts is done at a relatively lower pressure and temperature than the thermal cracking. Due to catalysis, the naphthenes are cracked to olefins; paraffins and olefins to isoparaffins, needed for gasoline. Catalytic cracking gives better antiknock property for gasoline as compared to thermal cracking.

(ii) *Hydrogenation* consists of the addition of hydrogen atoms to certain hydrocarbons under high pressure and temperature to produce more desirable compounds. It is often used to convert unstable compounds to stable ones.

(iii) *Polymerization* is the process of converting olefins, the unsaturated products of cracking, into heavier and stable compounds.

(iv) *Alkylation* combines an olefin with an isoparaffin to produce a branched chain isoparaffin in the presence of a catalyst. Example:

$$\text{isobutylene} + \text{isobutane} \xleftrightarrow{\text{Alkylation}} \text{iso-octane}$$

(v) *Isomerization* changes the relative position of the atoms within the molecule of a hydrocarbon without changing its molecular formula. For example, isomerization is used for the conversion of n-butane into isobutane for alkylation. Conversion of n-pentane and n-hexane into

Table 5.2 Products of petroleum refining process

S.No.	Fraction	App. boiling range, °C	Remarks
1.	Fuel gas	-160 to -44	Methane, ethane and some propane used as refinery fuel
2.	Propane	-40	LPG
3.	Butane	-12 to 30	Blended with motor gasoline to increase its volatility
4.	Light Naphtha	0 to 150	Motor gasoline for catalytic reforming
5.	Heavy Naphtha	150 to 200	Catalytic reforming fuel, blended with light gas oil to form jet fuels
6.	Kerosene – Middle distillate	200 to 300	Domestic, aviation fuels
7.	Light gas oil – Middle distillate	200 to 315	Furnace fuel oil, diesel fuels
8.	Heavy gas oil	315 to 425	Feed for catalytic cracking
9.	Vacuum gas oil	425 to 600	Feed for catalytic cracking
10.	Pitch	>600	Heavy fuel oil, asphalts

isoparaffins to improve knock rating of highly volatile gasoline is another example.

(vi) *Cyclization* joins together the ends of a straight chain molecule to form a ring compound of the naphthene family.

(vii) *Aromatization* is similar to cyclization, the exception being that the product is an aromatic compound.

(viii) *Reformation* is a type of cracking process which is used to convert the low antiknock quality stocks into gasolines of higher octane rating (see section 6.6). It does not increase the total gasoline volume.

(ix) *Blending* is a process of obtaining a product of desired quality by mixing certain products in some suitable proportion.

5.5 IMPORTANT QUALITIES OF ENGINE FUELS

Fuels used in IC engines should possess certain basic qualities which are important for the smooth running of the engines. In this section, the important qualities of fuels for both SI and CI engines are reviewed.

5.5.1 SI Engine Fuels

Gasoline which is mostly used in the present day SI engines is usually a blend of several low boiling paraffins, naphthenes and aromatics in varying proportions. Some of the important qualities of gasoline are discussed below.

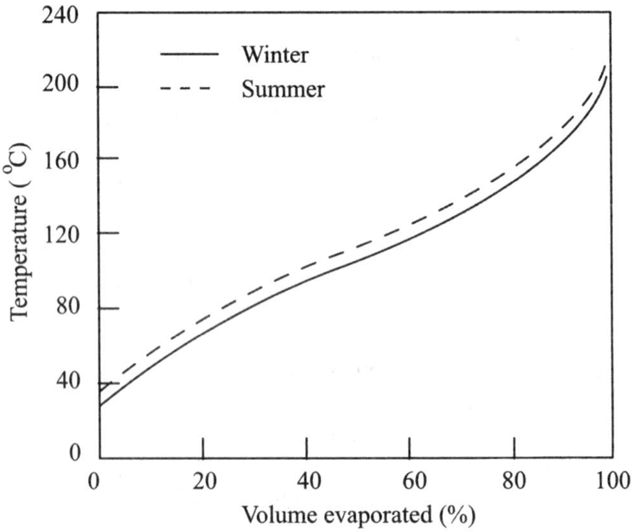

Fig. 5.2 Typical distillation curves of gasoline

(i) *Volatility :* Volatility is one of the main characteristic properties of gasoline which determines its suitability for use in an SI engine. Since gasoline is a mixture of different hydrocarbons, volatility depends on the fractional composition of the fuel. The usual practice of measuring the fuel volatility is the distillation of the fuel in a special device at atmospheric pressure and in the presence of its own vapour. The fraction that boils off at a definite temperature is measured. The characteristic points are the temperatures at which 10, 40, 50 and 90% of the volume evaporates as well as the temperature at which boiling of the fuel terminates. Figure 5.2 shows the fractional distillation curve of gasoline for both winter and summer grade gasoline. The method for measuring volatility has been standardized by the American Society for Testing Materials (ASTM) and the graphical representation of the result of the tests is generally referred to as the ASTM distillation curve. The more important aspects of volatility related to engine fuels are discussed in detail in conjunction with the distillation curve.

(ii) *Starting and Warm up :* A certain part of the gasoline should vapourize at the room temperature for easy starting of the engine. Hence, the portion of the distillation curve between about 0 and 10% boiled off have relatively low boiling temperatures. As the engine warms up, the temperature will gradually increase to the operating temperature. Low distillation temperatures are desirable throughout the range of the distillation curve for best warm-up.

(iii) *Operating Range Performance :* In order to obtain good vapourization of the gasoline, low distillation temperatures are preferable in the engine operating range. Better vapourization tends to produce both more uniform distribution of fuel to the cylinders as well as better acceleration characteristics by reducing the quantity of liquid droplets in the intake manifold.

(iv) *Crankcase Dilution :* Liquid fuel in the cylinder causes loss of lubricating oil (by washing away oil from cylinder walls) which deteriorates the quality of lubrication and tends to cause damage to the engine through increased friction. The liquid gasoline may also dilute the lubricating oil and weaken the oil film between rubbing surfaces. To prevent these possibilities, the upper portion of the distillation curve should exhibit sufficiently low distillation temperatures to insure that all gasoline in the cylinder is vapourized by the time the combustion starts.

(v) *Vapour Lock Characteristics :* High rate of vapourization of gasoline can upset the carburettor metering or even stop the fuel flow to the engine by setting up a vapour lock in the fuel passages. This characteristic, demands the presence of relatively high boiling temperature hydrocarbons throughout the distillation range. Since this requirement is not consistent with the other requirements desired in (a), (b) and (c), a compromise must be made for the desired distillation temperatures.

(vi) *Antiknock Quality :* Abnormal burning or detonation in an SI engine combustion chamber causes a very high rate of energy release, excessive temperature and pressure inside the cylinder adversely affects its thermal efficiency. Therefore, the characteristics of the fuel used should be such that it resists the tendency to produce detonation and this property is called its antiknock property. The antiknock property of a fuel depends on the self-ignition characteristics of its mixture and vary largely with the chemical composition and molecular structure of the fuel. In general, the best SI engine fuel will be that having the highest antiknock property, since this permits the use of higher compression ratios and thus the engine thermal efficiency and the power output can be greatly increased.

(vii) *Gum Deposits :* Reactive hydrocarbons and impurities in the fuel have a tendency to oxidize upon storage and form liquid and solid gummy substances. The gasoline containing hydrocarbons of the paraffin, naphthene and aromatic families forms little gum while cracked gasoline containing unsaturated hydrocarbons is the worst offender. A gasoline with high gum content will cause operating difficulties such as sticking valves and piston rings carbon deposits in the engine, gum deposits in the manifold, clogging of carburettor jets and enlarging of the valve stems, cylinders and pistons. The amount of gum increases with increased concentrations of oxygen, with rise in temperature, with exposure to sunlight and also on contact with metals. Gasoline specifications therefore limit both the gum content of the fuel and its tendency to form gum during storage.

(viii) *Sulphur Content :* Hydrocarbon fuels may contain free sulphur, hydrogen sulphide and other sulphur compounds which are objectionable for several reasons. The sulphur is a corrosive element of the fuel that can corrode fuel lines, carburettors and injection pumps and it will unite with oxygen to form sulphur dioxide that, in the presence of water at low temperatures, may form sulphurous acid. Since sulphur has a low ignition temperature, the presence of sulphur can reduce the self-ignition temperature, then promoting knock in the SI engine.

5.5.2 CI Engine Fuels

(i) *Knock Characteristics :* Knock in the CI engine occurs because of an ignition lag in the combustion of the fuel between the time of injection and the time of actual burning. As the ignition lag increases, the amount of fuel accumulated in the combustion chamber increases and when combustion actually takes place, abnormal amount of energy is suddenly released causing an excessive rate of pressure rise which results in an audible knock. Hence, a good CI engine fuel should have a short ignition lag and will ignite more readily. Furthermore, ignition lag affects the starting, warm up, and leads to the production of exhaust smoke in CI engines. The present day measure in the cetane rating, the best fuel in general, will have a cetane rating sufficiently high to avoid objectionable knock.

(ii) *Volatility :* The fuel should be sufficiently volatile in the operating range of temperature to produce good mixing and combustion. Figure 5.3 is a representative distillation curve of a typical diesel fuel.

(iii) *Starting Characteristics :* The fuel should help in starting the engine easily. This requirement demands high enough volatility to form a combustible mixture readily and a high cetane rating in order that the self-ignition temperature is low.

(iv) *Smoking and Odour :* The fuel should not promote either smoke or odour in the engine exhaust. Generally, good volatility is the first prerequisite to ensure good mixing and therefore complete combustion.

(v) *Viscosity :* CI engine fuels should be able to flow through the fuel system and the strainers under the lowest operating temperatures to which the engine is subjected to.

(vi) *Corrosion and Wear :* The fuel should not cause corrosion and wear of the engine components before or after combustion. These requirements are directly related to the presence of sulphur, ash and residue in the fuel.

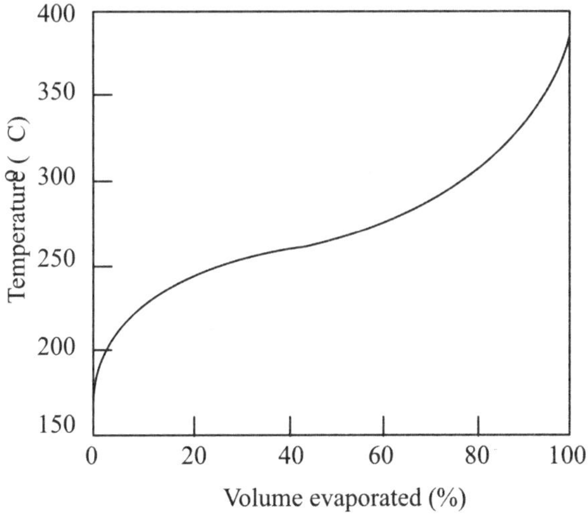

Fig. 5.3 Typical distillation curve for diesel

(vii) *Handling Ease :* The fuel should be a liquid that will readily flow under all conditions that are encountered in actual use. This requirement is measured by the pour point and the viscosity of the fuel. The fuel should also have a high flash point and a high fire point.

5.6 RATING OF FUELS

Normally fuels are rated for their antiknock qualities. The rating of fuels is done by defining two parameters called Octane number and Cetane number for gasoline and diesel oil respectively. The rating of fuels, both for SI and CI engines is discussed in this section.

5.6.1 Rating of SI Engine Fuels

Resistance to knocking is an extremely important characteristic of fuel for spark-ignition engines. These fuels differ widely in their ability to resist knock depending on their chemical composition. A satisfactory rating method for comparing the antiknock qualities of the various fuels has been established. In addition to the chemical characteristics of hydrocarbons in the fuel, other operating parameters such as fuel-air ratio, ignition timing, dilution, engine speed, shape of the combustion chamber, ambient conditions, compression ratio etc. affect the tendency to knock in the engine cylinder. Therefore, in order to determine the knock resistance characteristic of the fuel, the engine and its operating variables must be fixed at standard values.

According to a standard practice, the antiknock value of an SI engine fuel is determined by comparing its antiknock property with a mixture of two reference fuels, iso-octane (C_8H_{18}) and normal heptane (C_7H_{16}). Iso-octane chemically being a very good antiknock fuel, is arbitrarily assigned a rating of 100 octane number. Normal heptane (C_7H_{16}), on the other hand, has very poor antiknock qualities and is given a rating of 0 octane number. *The Octane number fuel is defined as the percentage, by volume, of iso-octane in a mixture of iso-octane and normal heptane, which exactly matches the knocking intensity of the fuel in a standard engine under a set of standard operating conditions.* The addition of certain compounds (e.g. tetraethyl lead) to iso-octane produces fuels of greater antiknock quality (above 100 octane number). The antiknock effectiveness of tetraethyl lead, for the same quantity of lead added, decreases as the total content of lead in the fuel increases. Further, each octane number at the higher range of the octane scale will produce greater antiknock effect compared to the same unit at the lower end of the scale. For instance, octane number increase from 92 to 93 produce greater antiknock effect than a similar increase from 32 to 33 octane number. Because of this non-linear variation, a new scale was derived which expresses the approximate relative engine performance and the units of this scale are known as the Performance Numbers, PN. Octane numbers, ON above 100 can be computed by

$$\text{ON}(>100) = 100 + \frac{28.28A}{1.0 + 0.736A + \sqrt{1.0 + 0.736A - 0.035216A^2}}$$

where A is TEL in ml/gal of fuel, or from the performance number, PN,

$$\text{Octane Number} \quad = \quad 100 + \frac{PN - 100}{3}$$

Laboratory Method: The engine is run at specified conditions with a definite compression ratio and a definite blend of reference fuels. The intensity of knock at these standard conditions is called standard knock. The knock meter is adjusted to give a particular reading under these conditions. The test fuel is now used in the engine and air-fuel ratio is adjusted to give maximum knock intensity. The compression ratio of the engine is gradually changed until the knock meter reading is the same as in the previous run (standard knock). The compression ratio is now fixed and known blends of reference fuels are used in the engine. The blend of reference fuels which gives a knock meter reading equal to the standard value will match the knocking characteristics of the test fuel. Percentage by volume of iso-octane in the particular blend gives the octane number.

5.6.2 Rating of CI Engine Fuels

In compression-ignition engines, the knock resistance depends on chemical characteristics as well as on the operating and design conditions of the engine. Therefore, the knock rating of a diesel fuel is found by comparing the fuel under prescribed conditions of operation in a special engine with primary reference fuels. The reference fuels are normal cetane, $C_{16}H_{34}$, which is arbitrarily assigned a cetane number of 100 and alpha methyl naphthalene, $C_{11}H_{10}$, with an assigned cetane number of 0. *Cetane number of a fuel is defined as the percentage by volume of normal cetane in a mixture of normal cetane and α-methyl naphthalene which has the same ignition characteristics (ignition delay) as the test fuel when combustion is carried out in a standard engine under specified operating conditions.* Since ignition delay is the primary factor in controlling the initial autoignition in the CI engine, it is reasonable to conclude that knock should be directly related to the ignition delay of the fuel. Knock resistance property of diesel oil can be improved by adding small quantities of compounds like amyl nitrate, ethyl nitrate or ether.

Laboratory Method: The test is carried out in a standard single cylinder engine like the CFR diesel engine or Ricardo single cylinder variable compression engine under the conditions shown in Table 5.3. The test fuel is first used in the engine operating at the specified conditions. The fuel pump delivery is adjusted to give a particular fuel-air ratio. The injection timing is also adjusted to give an injection advance of 13 degrees. By varying the compression ratio the ignition delay can be increased or decreased until a position is found where combustion begins at TDC. When this position is found, the test fuel undergoes a 13 degree ignition delay. The cetane number of the unknown fuel

Table 5.3 Conditions for ignition quality test on diesel fuels

Engine speed	900 rpm
Jacket water temperature	100 °C
Inlet air temperature	65.5 °C
Injection advance	Constant at 13° $bTDC$
Ignition delay	13°

can be estimated by noting the compression ratio for 13 degree delay and then referring to a prepared chart showing the relationship between cetane number and compression ratio. However, for accuracy two reference fuel blends differing by not more than 5 cetane numbers are selected to bracket the unknown sample. The compression ratio is varied for each reference blend to reach the standard ignition delay (13 degrees) and, by interpolation of the compression ratios, the cetane rating of the unknown fuel is determined.

Review Questions

5.1 *What are the different kinds of fuels used in an IC engine?*

5.2 *Briefly explain the chemical structure of petroleum.*

5.3 *Give the general chemical formula of the following fuels: (i) paraffin (ii) olefin (iii) diolefin (iv) naphthene(v) aromatic Also state their molecular arrangements and mention whether they are saturated or unsaturated.*

5.4 *Briefly explain the petroleum refining process.*

5.5 *Discuss the significance of distillation curves.*

5.6 *Discuss the important qualities of an SI and CI engine fuel.*

5.7 *What is the effect of high sulphur content on the performance of SI and CI engines?*

5.8 *How are SI and CI engine fuels rated?*

Multiple Choice Questions (choose the most appropriate answer)

1. Advantage of gaseous fuel is that
   (a) it can be stored easily
   (b) it can mix easily with air
   (c) it can displace more air from the engine
   (d) all of the above

2. Paraffins are in general represented by
   (a) C_nH_n
   (b) C_nH_{2n}
   (c) C_nH_{2n+2}
   (d) C_nH_{2n-6}

3. Paraffins have molecular structure of
   (a) chain saturated
   (b) chain unsaturated
   (c) ring saturated
   (d) ring unsaturated

4. Olefins are represented by the formula
   (a) C_nH_{2n}
   (b) C_nH_{2n+2}
   (c) C_nH_{2n-4}
   (d) C_nH_{2n-6}

5. Hydrocarbons are decomposed into smaller hydrocarbons by
   (a) reforming
   (b) refining
   (c) cracking
   (d) polymerization

6. The molecular structure of the straight-run gasoline is changed by
   (a) cracking
   (b) reforming
   (c) refining
   (d) boiling

7. For SI engines fuels most preferred are
   (a) aromatics
   (b) paraffins
   (c) olefins
   (d) napthenes

8. For CI engine fuels most preferred are
   (a) napthenes
   (b) paraffins
   (c) olefins
   (d) aromatics

9. Octane number of iso-octane is
   (a) 0
   (b) 30
   (c) 60
   (d) 100

10. Ignition quality of diesel fuel is indicated by its
    (a) octane number
    (b) cetane number
    (c) flash point
    (d) fire point

11. Iso-octane has
    (a) straight chain structure with 8 carbon atoms
    (b) ring chain structure with 8 carbon atoms
    (c) branched chain structure with 8 carbon atoms
    (d) none of the above

12. An effective method to prevent detonation in SI engines is
    (a) heating of the charge
    (b) cooling of the charge
    (c) increasing the charge pressure
    (d) none of the above

13. The major constituent of natural gas

    (a) butane
    (b) ethane
    (c) methane
    (d) propane

14. Addition of tetraethyl lead in gasoline is being discontinued as

    (a) it has bad odour
    (b) it is costly
    (c) decreases engine efficiency
    (d) blocks the catalytic converter

15. Crude oil is separated into gasoline, kerosene and fuel oil by

    (a) cracking
    (b) heating
    (c) fractional distillation
    (d) reforming

16. Abnormal combustion in a SI engine causes

    (a) high ratio of energy decrease
    (b) excessive rise in pressure and temperature
    (c) reduction in thermal efficiency
    (d) all of the above

17. A good CI engine fuel should have

    (a) high octane number
    (b) very high cetane number
    (c) a short ignition lag
    (d) all of the above

18. Blending of fuel is the process of

    (a) just mixing two fuels
    (b) obtaining a product of desired quality
    (c) mixing of fuel and air for combustion
    (d) none of the above

Ans:					
	1. – (b)	2. – (c)	3. – (a)	4. – (a)	5. – (c)
	6. – (b)	7. – (a)	8. – (b)	9. – (d)	10. – (b)
	11. – (c)	12. – (b)	13. – (c)	14. – (d)	15. – (c)
	16. – (d)	17. – (c)	18. – (b)		

6

ALTERNATE FUELS

6.1 INTRODUCTION

In this century, it is believed that crude oil and petroleum products will become very scarce and costly. Day-to-day, fuel economy of engines is getting improved and will continue to improve. However, enormous increase in number of vehicles has started dictating the demand for fuel. Gasoline and diesel will become scarce and most costly in the near future. With increased use and the depletion of fossil fuels, alternative fuel technology will become more common in the coming decades.

All these years there have always been some IC engines fuelled with non-gasoline or diesel oil fuels. However, their numbers have been relatively very small. Because of the high cost of petroleum products, some developing countries are trying to use alternate fuels for their vehicles.

Another reason motivating the development of alternate fuels for the IC engine is the concern over the emission problems of gasoline and diesel engines. Combined with other air-polluting systems, the large number of automobiles is a major contributor to the air quality problem of the world. Quite a lot of improvements have been made in reducing emissions from automobile engines. If a 35% improvement made over a period of years, it is to be noted that during the same time the number of automobiles in the world increases by 40%, thereby nullifying the improvement. Lot of efforts has gone into for achieving the net improvement in cleaning up automobile exhaust. However, more improvements are needed to bring down the ever-increasing air pollution due to automobile population.

A third reason for alternate fuel development is the fact that a large percentage of crude oil must be imported from other countries which control the larger oil fields. As of now many alternate fuels have been used in limited quantities in automobiles. Quite often, fleet vehicles have been used for testing (e.g., taxies, delivery vans, utility company trucks). This paves way for comparison with similar gasoline-fuelled vehicles, and simplifies fuelling of these vehicles.

The engines used for alternate fuels are modified engines which were originally designed for gasoline fuelling. They are, therefore, not the optimum design for the other fuels. Only when extensive research and development is done over a period of years, maximum performance and efficiency can be realized from these engines. However, the research and development is difficult to justify until the fuels are accepted as viable for large numbers of engines.

Some diesel engines have started appearing on the market. They use methanol or natural gas and a small amount of diesel fuel that is injected at the proper time to ignite both fuels. Most alternate fuels are very costly at present since the quantity used is very less. Many of these fuels will cost much less if the amount of their usage gets to the same order of magnitude as gasoline. The cost of manufacturing, distribution, and marketing would be less.

Another problem with alternate fuels is the lack of distribution points (service stations) where the fuel is available to the public. The public will be reluctant to purchase an automobile unless there is a large-scale network of service stations available where fuel for that automobile can be purchased. On the other hand, it is difficult to justify building a network of these service stations until there are enough automobiles to make them profitable. Some cities have started a few distribution points for some of these fuels, like propane, natural gas, LPG and methanol. The transfer from one major fuel type to another will be a slow, costly, and sometimes painful process. In the following sections we will discuss the various alternate fuels.

6.2 POSSIBLE ALTERNATIVES

Fuels are classified into three forms, viz. solid, liquid and gaseous. Present day automobiles use mainly liquid fuels of petroleum origin. However, some use gaseous fuels like CNG and LPG. It is interesting to note that during early days even solid fuels like coal, slurry and charcoal have been tried. In the following sections the various alternate fuels for IC engines are discussed in detail. Table 6.1 gives the properties of various fuels.

6.3 SOLID FUELS

Solid fuels are obsolete for IC engines. In order to have historical perspective, some of the earlier attempts are described in this section.

In the latter half of the 1800s, before petroleum-based fuels were perfected, many other fuels were tested and used in IC engines. When Rudolf Diesel was developing his engine, one of the fuels he used was a coal dust mixed with water. Fine particles of coal (carbon) were dispersed in water and injected and burned in early diesel engines. Although this never became a common fuel, a number of experimental engines using this fuel have been built over the last hundred years.

Even today, some work continues on this fuel technology. The major improvement in this type of fuel has been the reduction of the average coal particle size. In 1894 the average particle size was on the order of 100 μ ($1\ \mu = 1$ micron $= 10^{-6}$ m). This was reduced to about 70 μ in the 1940–1970 period and further reduced to about 10 μ by the early 1980s. The typical slurry is about 50% coal and 50% water by mass. One major problem with this fuel is the abrasiveness of the solid particles, which manifests itself in worn injectors and piston rings.

Coal is an attractive fuel because of the availability in large quantity. However, as an engine fuel, other methods of use seem more feasible. These include liquefaction or gasification of the coal.

In the late 1930s and early 1940s petroleum products became very scarce, especially in Europe, due to World War II. Just about all gasoline products were used by the German army, leaving no fuel for civilian automobile use.

Table 6.1 Data on fuel properties

Fuel	Formula (phase)	Molecular weight	Specific gravity (density†) (kg/m^3)	Heat of vaporization kJ/kg‡	Specific heat C_p Liquid kJ/kg K	Specific heat C_p Vapour kJ/kg K	Heating value Higher MJ/kg	Heating value Lower MJ/kg	LHV of stoich mixture, MJ/kg	$(A/F)_s$	Fuel cetane rating RON	Fuel cetane rating MON
Practical fuels												
Gasoline	$C_nH_{1.87n}(\ell)$	110	0.72-0.78	305	2.4	1.7	47.3	44.0	2.83	14.6	92-98	80-90
Light diesel	$C_nH_{1.8n}(\ell)$	170	0.84-0.88	270	2.2	1.7	44.8	42.5	2.74	14.5	-	-
Heavy diesel	$C_nH_{1.7n}(\ell)$	200	0.82-0.95	230	1.9	1.7	43.8	41.4	2.76	14.4	-	-
Natural gas*	$C_nH_{3.8n}N_{0.10n}(g)$	18	(0.79†)	-	-	2	50	45	2.9	14.5	-	-
Pure hydrocarbons												
Methane	$CH_4(g)$	16.04	(0.72†)	509	0.63	2.2	55.5	50.0	2.72	17.23	120	120
Propane	$C_3H_8(g)$	44.10	0.51(2.0†)	426	2.5	1.6	50.4	46.4	2.75	15.67	112	97
Isooctane	$C_8H_{18}(\ell)$	114.23	0.692	308	2.1	1.63	47.8	44.3	2.75	15.13	100	100
Cetane	$C_{16}H_{34}(\ell)$	226.44	0.773	358		1.6	47.3	44.0	2.78	14.82	-	-
Benzene	$C_6H_6(\ell)$	78.11	0.879	433	1.72	1.1	41.9	40.2	2.82	13.27	-	115
Toluene	$C_7H_8(\ell)$	92.14	0.867	412	1.68	1.1	42.5	40.6	2.79	13.50	120	109
Alcohols												
Methanol	$CH_4O(\ell)$	32.04	0.792	1103	2.6	1.72	22.7	20.0	2.68	6.47	106	92
Ethanol	$C_2H_6O(\ell)$	46.07	0.785	840	2.5	1.93	29.7	26.9	2.69	9.00	107	89
Other fuels												
Carbon	C(s)	12.01	2*	-	-	-	33.8	33.8	2.70	11.51		
Carbon monoxide	CO(g)	28.01	(1.25†)	-	-	1.05	10.1	10.1	2.91	2.467		
Hydrogen	$H_2(g)$	2.015	(0.090†)	-	-	1.44	142.0	120.0	3.40	34.3		

(ℓ) liquid phase; (g) gaseous phase; (s) solid phase. † Density in kg/m^3 at 0 °C and 1 atm. ‡ At 1 atm and 25 °C for liquid fuels: at 1 atm and boiling temperature for gaseous fuels. * Typical values. RON, research octane number; MON, motor octane number.

Although this was an inconvenience for the civilian population, it did not stop them from using their beloved automobiles. Enterprising people in several countries, mainly Sweden and Germany, developed a way to operate their automobiles using solid fuels like charcoal, wood, or coal.

6.4 LIQUID FUELS

Liquid fuels are preferred for IC engines because they are easy to store and have reasonably good calorific value. In the liquid fuel category the main alternative is the alcohol.

6.4.1 Alcohol

Alcohols are an attractive alternate fuel because they can be obtained from both natural and manufactured sources. Methanol (methyl alcohol) and ethanol (ethyl alcohol) are two kinds of alcohols that seem most promising. The advantages of alcohol as a fuel are:

(i) It can be obtained from a number of sources, both natural and manufactured.

(ii) It is a high octane fuel with anti-knock index numbers (octane number) of over 100. Engines using high-octane fuel can run more efficiently by using higher compression ratios. Alcohols have higher flame speed.

(iii) It produces less overall emissions compared to gasoline.

(iv) When alcohols are burned, it forms more moles of exhaust gases, which gives higher pressure and more power in the expansion stroke.

(v) It has high latent heat of vapourization (h_{fg}) which results in a cooler intake process. This raises the volumetric efficiency of the engine and reduces the required work input in the compression stroke.

(vi) Alcohols have low sulphur content in the fuel.

The disadvantages of alcohol as a fuel are:

(i) Alcohols have a low energy content or in other words the calorific value of the fuel is almost half. This means that almost twice as much alcohol as gasoline must be burned to give the same energy input to the engine. With equal thermal efficiency and similar engine output usage, twice as much fuel would have to be purchased, and the distance which could be driven with a given fuel tank volume would be cut in half. Automobiles as well as distribution stations would require twice as much storage capacity, twice the number of storage facilities, twice the volume of storage at the service station, twice as many tank trucks and pipelines, etc. Even with the lower energy content of alcohol, engine power for a given displacement would be about the same. This is because of the lower air-fuel ratio needed by alcohol. Alcohol contains oxygen and thus requires less air for stoichiometric combustion. More fuel can be burned with the same amount of air.

(ii) Combustion of alcohols produces more aldehydes in the exhaust. If as much alcohol fuel was consumed as gasoline, aldehyde emissions would be a serious exhaust pollution problem.

(iii) Alcohol is much more corrosive than gasoline on copper, brass, aluminum, rubber, and many plastics. This puts some restrictions on the design and manufacturing of engines to be used with this fuel. Fuel lines and tanks, gaskets, and even metal engine parts can deteriorate with long-term alcohol use (resulting in cracked fuel lines, the need for special fuel tank, etc). Methanol is very corrosive on metals.

(iv) It has poor cold weather starting characteristics due to low vapor pressure and evaporation. Alcohol-fuelled engines generally have difficulty in starting at temperatures below 10 °C. Often a small amount of gasoline is added to alcohol fuel, which greatly improves cold-weather starting. However, the need to do this greatly reduces the attractiveness of any alternate fuel.

(v) Alcohols have poor ignition characteristics in general.

(vi) Alcohols have almost invisible flames, which is considered dangerous when handling fuel. A small amount of gasoline removes this danger.

(vii) There is the danger of storage tank flammability due to low vapor pressure. Air can leak into storage tanks and create a combustible mixture.

(viii) There will be less NO_x emissions because of low flame temperatures. However, the resulting lower exhaust temperatures take longer time to heat the catalytic converter to an efficient operating temperature.

(ix) Many people find the strong odor of alcohol very offensive. Headaches and dizziness have been experienced when refueling an automobile.

(x) There is a possibility of vapor lock in fuel delivery systems.

6.4.2 Methanol

Of all the fuels being considered as an alternate to gasoline, methanol is one of the most promising and has experienced major research and development. Pure methanol and mixtures of methanol and gasoline in various percentages have been extensively tested in engines and vehicles for a number of years. The most common mixtures are M85 (85% methanol and 15% gasoline) and M10 (10% methanol and 90% gasoline). The data of these tests which include performance and emission levels are compared with pure gasoline (M0) and pure methanol (M100). Some smart flexible fuel (or variable fuel) engines are capable of using any random mixture combination of methanol and gasoline ranging from pure methanol to pure gasoline. Two fuel tanks are used and various flow rates of the two fuels can be pumped to the engine, passing through a mixing chamber. Using information from sensors in the intake and exhaust, the electronic monitoring system (EMS) adjusts to the proper air-fuel ratio, ignition timing, injection timing, and valve timing (where possible) for the fuel mixture being used.

One problem with gasoline-alcohol mixtures as a fuel is the tendency for alcohol to combine with any water present. When this happens the alcohol separates locally from the gasoline, resulting in a non-homogeneous mixture. This causes the engine to run erratically due to the large air-fuel ratio differences between the two fuels.

Methanol can be obtained from many sources, both fossil and renewable. These include coal, petroleum, natural gas, biomass, wood, landfills, and even the ocean. However, any source that requires extensive manufacturing or processing raises the price of the fuel.

Emissions from an engine using M10 fuel are about the same as those using gasoline. The advantage (and disadvantage) of using this fuel is mainly the 10% decrease in gasoline use. With M85 fuel there is a measurable decrease in HC and CO exhaust emissions. However, there is an increase in NO_x and a large ($\approx$ 500%) increase in formaldehyde emissions.

Methanol is used in some dual-fuel CI engines. Methanol by itself is not a good CI engine fuel because of its high octane number, but if a small amount of diesel oil is used for ignition, it can be used with good results. This is very attractive for developing countries, because methanol can often be obtained from much cheaper source than diesel oil.

6.4.3 Ethanol

Ethanol has been used as automobile fuel for many years in various countries of the world. Brazil is probably the leading user, where in the early 1990s. About 5 million vehicles operated on fuels that were 93% ethanol. For a number of years gasohol (gasoline + alcohol) has been available at service stations in the United States. Gasohol is a mixture of 90% gasoline and 10% ethanol. As with methanol, the development of systems using mixtures of gasoline and ethanol continues. Two mixture combinations that are important are E85 (85% ethanol) and E10 (gasohol). E85 is basically an alcohol fuel with 15% gasoline added to eliminate some of the problems of pure alcohol (i.e., cold starting, tank flammability, etc.). E10 reduces the use of gasoline with no modification needed to the automobile engine. Flexible-fuel engines are being tested which can operate on any ratio of ethanol-gasoline. Ethanol can be made from ethylene or from fermentation of grains and sugar. Much of it is made from corn, sugar beets, sugar cane, and even cellulose (wood and paper). The present cost of ethanol is high due to the manufacturing and processing required. This would be reduced if larger amounts of this fuel were used. However, very high production would create a food-fuel competition, with resulting higher costs for both. Some studies show that at present in the United States, crops grown for the production of ethanol consume more energy in ploughing, planting, harvesting, fermenting, and delivery than what is in the final product. This defeats one major reason for using an alternate fuel. Ethanol has less HC emissions than gasoline but more than methanol.

6.4.4 Alcohol for SI Engines

Alcohols have higher antiknock characteristic compared to gasoline. As such with an alcohol fuel, engine compression ratios between 11:1 and 13:1 are usual. Today's gasoline engines use a compression ratio of around 7:1 or 9:1, much too low for pure alcohol.

In a properly designed engine and fuel system, alcohol produces fewer harmful exhaust emissions. Alcohol contains about half the heat energy of gasoline per litre. The stoichiometric air fuel ratio is lesser for alcohol than for gasoline. To provide a proper fuel air mixture, a carburetor or fuel injector fuel passages should be doubled in area to allow extra fuel flow.

Alcohol does not vapourize as easily as gasoline. Its latent heat of vapourization is much greater. This affects cold weather starting. If the alcohol liquefies in the engine then it will not burn properly. Thus, the engine may be difficult or even impossible to start in extremely cold climate. To overcome this, gasoline is introduced in the engine until the engine starts and warms up. Once the engine warms, alcohol when introduced will vapourize quickly and completely and burn normally. Even during normal operation, additional heat may have to be supplied to completely vapourize alcohol. Alcohol burns at about half the speed of gasoline. As such, ignition timing must be changed, so that more spark advance is provided. This will give the slow burning alcohol more time to develop the pressure and power in the cylinder. Moreover, corrosion resistant materials are required for fuel system since alcohols are corrosive in nature.

6.4.5 Reformulated Gasoline for SI Engine

Reformulated gasoline is normal-type of gasoline with a slightly modified formulation and additives to help reduce engine emissions. Additives in the fuel include oxidation inhibitors, corrosion inhibitors, metal deactivators, detergents, and deposit control additives. Oxygenates such as methyl tertiary-butyl ether (MTBE) and alcohols are mixed, such that there is 1-3% oxygen by weight. This is to help in reducing CO in the exhaust. Levels of benzene, aromatic, and high boiling components are reduced, as is the vapor pressure. Recognizing that engine deposits contribute to emissions, cleaning additives are included. Some additives clean carburetors, some clean fuel injectors, and some clean intake valves, each of which often does not clean other components.

On the positive side is that all gasoline-fuelled engines, old and new, can use this fuel without modification. On the negative side is that only moderate emission reduction is realized, cost is increased, and the use of petroleum products is not considerably reduced.

6.4.6 Water-Gasoline Mixture for SI Engines

The development of the spark-ignition engine has been accompanied by the desire to raise the compression ratio for increased efficiency and fuel economy. One obstacle to this gain in economy at times has been the octane quality of the available gasoline. To circumvent this limitation, water was proposed as an antiknock additive.

Water addition to gasoline slows down the burning rate and reduces the gas temperature in the cylinder which probably suppresses detonation. Engine combustion chamber deposit reductions have also been reported when water was added to the intake charge. With respect to nitric oxide emissions, dramatic reductions were reported. Conversely, water addition probably increases hydrocarbon emissions. Finally, with respect to carbon monoxide emissions, water addition seems to have minimal effect. Only a very limited work has been carried out with the addition of water via an emulsion with the fuel rather than independently. Emulsion could eliminate the need for a separate tank, provide improved atomization and increase fuel safety. However, a water-fuel separation problem may exist.

6.4.7 Alcohol for CI Engines

Techniques of using alcohol in diesel engines are

(i) Alcohol/diesel fuel solutions

(ii) Alcohol diesel emulsions.

(iii) Alcohol fumigation

(iv) Dual fuel injection

(v) Surface ignition of alcohols.

(vi) Spark ignition of alcohols

(vii) Alcohols containing ignition improving additives.

Both ethyl and methyl alcohols have high self ignition temperatures. Hence, very high compression ratios (25-27) will be required to self ignite them. Since this would make the engine extremely heavy and expensive, the better method is to utilize them in dual fuel operation.

In the dual fuel engine, alcohol is carburetted or injected into the inducted air. Due to high self ignition temperature of alcohols there will be no combustion with the usual diesel compression ratios of 16 to 18. A little before the end of compression stroke, a small quantity of diesel oil is injected into the combustion chamber through the normal diesel pump and spray nozzle. The diesel oil readily ignites and this initiates combustion in the alcohol air mixture also.

Several methods are adopted for induction of alcohol into the intake manifold. They are microfog unit, pneumatic spray nozzle, vapourizer, carburetor and fuel injector. The degree of fineness in mixing of fuel and air are different for the above methods.

Another method tried is to inject alcohol into the combustion chamber after the diesel fuel injection. This way of alcohol injection avoids the alcohol cooling the charge in the cylinder to a degree which will jeopardize the ignition of the diesel fuel. However, this design calls for two complete and separate fuel systems with tank, fuel pump, injection pump and injectors.

In the dual fuel engines mentioned above, major portion of the heat release is by the alcohol supplied and this alcohol is ignited by a pilot spray of diesel oil injection. The performance of the dual fuel engine is influenced by the following properties of alcohols:

The calorific value of alcohols is lower than diesel oil and hence, a larger quantity of alcohol has to be used for producing the same amount of power output. However, their air requirement for combustion is lower, and hence, the energy content of the mixture is roughly the same. Since their latent heat of vapourization is very high, the temperature and pressure at the end of compression come down due to their evaporation. Hence, if the alcohol induction rate exceeds a limit, the injected diesel will not be able to ignite and hence, the engine will fail to function.

All the dual fuel systems described above have the basic disadvantage of requiring two different fuels and associated components. Since alcohols have a high tendency to pre-ignite in SI engines, recently, this property was made use of in a compression ignition engine by using a hot surface to initiate ignition.

6.5 SURFACE-IGNITION ALCOHOL CI ENGINE

The surface-ignition plug mounted on an alcohol fueled direct injection diesel engine can be seen in Fig.6.1.The basic concept of the system is as follows:

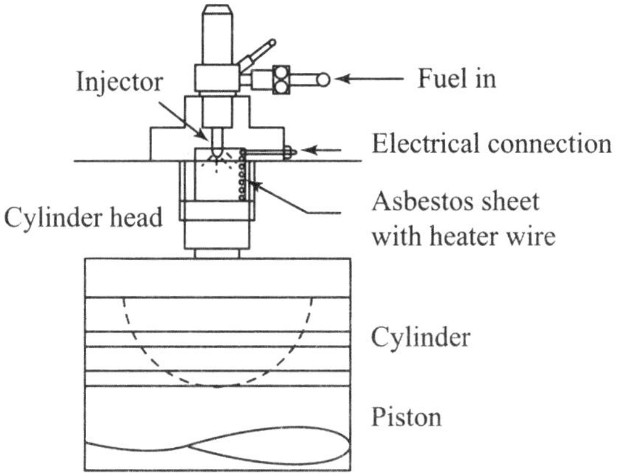

Fig. 6.1 Alcohol surface-ignition engine

A slab of insulator material, wound with a few strands of heating wire (kanthal heating element wire) is fixed on the combustion chamber with the wire running on the face exposed to the gases. The fuel injector is located such that a part of the spray impinges head on this surface. Ignition is thus initiated. The combustion chamber, which is in the cylinder head, is made relatively narrow so that the combustion spreads quickly to the rest of the space. Since a part of the fuel burns on the insulator surface and the heat losses from the plate are low, the surface after some minutes of operation reaches a temperature sufficient to initiate ignition without the aid of external electrical supply. The power consumption of the coil is about 50 W at 6 volts. The engine lends itself easily to the use of wide variety of fuels, including methanol, ethanol and gasoline. The engine was found to run smoothly on methanol with a performance comparable to diesel operation. The engine operates more smoothly at lower speeds than at higher speeds.

6.6 SPARK-ASSISTED DIESEL

In the future, it is predicted that broad cut fuel will appear as petroleum fuel. Alcohols and coal derived fuel will also penetrate as alternate fuels. One of the noted characteristics of these fuels is their low cetane value (cetane number of diesel : 55, gasoline : 13, ethanol : 8, methanol : 5). Hence, the appearance of these fuels might threaten the existence of diesel engine because the engine characteristics depend deeply upon high cetane value of fuel. Diesel engines have lot of advantages in its performance, especially in its high thermal efficiency. This advantage is very important in the future from the view point of energy saving. Keeping this in mind, a leading industry in Japan has developed a spark assisted diesel engine which can operate with future low cetane fuel without losing the characteristics of diesel engine. They have modified the conventional precombustion chamber type diesel engine, which has a compression ratio of 19:1 by installing a spark plug in its precombustion chamber. The igniter used is the commercial CDI, multistrike type.

California Energy commission has conducted experiments on two transit buses which are spark-assisted type. Both buses were tested in parallel with diesel powered counterparts. In comparing diesel with methanol fuel, road performance was nearly identical for each pair of buses. The methanol buses have a cleaner exhaust with smoke and odour eliminated. Oxides of nitrogen and particulates are also considerably lower with methanol.

6.7 VEGETABLE OIL

Vegetable oil is considered as one of the alternative fuels for diesel engines However, the viscosity of vegetable oil is higher compared to diesel. Therefore, it must be lowered to allow for proper atomization in engines designed to burn diesel fuel. Otherwise, incomplete combustion and carbon build up will ultimately damage the engine. Some literatures classify vegetable oil as Waste Vegetable Oil (WVO) and Straight Vegetable Oil (SVO) or Pure Plant Oil (PPO) to distinguish it from biodiesel. Free fatty acids in WVO have a detrimental effect on metals. Copper and its alloys, such as brass, are affected by WVO. Zinc and zinc-plating are stripped by FFA's and tin, lead, iron, and steel are affected too. Stainless steel and aluminum are generally unaffected.

As of 2010, the United States was producing in excess of 12 billion liters of waste vegetable oil annually, mainly from industrial deep fryers in potato processing plants, snack food factories and fast food restaurants. If all those 12 billion liters could be collected and used to replace the energy equivalent amount of petroleum almost 1% of US oil consumption could be offset. It is to be noted that use of waste vegetable oil as a fuel, competes with some other uses of the commodity. This has effects on its price as a fuel and increases its cost as an input to the other uses as well.

The main form of SVO/PPO used in various countries is rapeseed oil which has a freezing point of −10°C. Use of sunflower oil, which gels at around −12°C, is currently being investigated as a means of improving cold weather starting. Unfortunately oils with lower gelling points tend to be less saturated and polymerize more easily in the presence of atmospheric oxygen. Most diesel engines are suitable for the use of SVO/ PPO, with minor modifications. The relatively high kinematic viscosity of vegetable oils must be reduced to make them compatible with conventional C I engines fuel systems. It can be achieved either by co-solvent blending or can be reduced by preheating it using waste heat from the engine or using electricity. However, it is to be kept in mind that higher rates of wear and failure in fuel pumps and piston rings may occur and it should be appropriately tackled.

One common solution is to add a heat exchanger, and an additional fuel tank for "normal" diesel fuel (petrodiesel or biodiesel) and a three way valve to switch between this additional tank and the main tank of SVO/PPO. Engine reliability would depend on the condition of the engine. Attention to maintenance of the engine, particularly of the fuel injectors, cooling system and glow plugs will increase the life of the engine. Pure plant oil in contrast to waste vegetable oil, is not a byproduct of other industries, and thus its prospects for use as fuel are not limited by the capacities of other industries. Production of vegetable oils for use as fuels is theoretically limited only by the agricultural capacity of a given economy. However, doing so detracts from the supply of other uses of pure vegetable oil.

6.8 BIODIESEL

Biodiesel refers to a vegetable oil- or animal fat-based diesel engine fuel consisting of long-chain alkyl (ethyl, methyl, or propyl) esters. Biodiesel is typically produced by chemically reacting lipids (e.g., vegetable oil, animal fat) with an alcohol.

Biodiesel is meant to be used in standard diesel engines. It is distinct from the vegetable and waste oils used in fuel converted diesel engines. Biodiesel can be used alone, or blended with petro-diesel. Biodiesel can also be used as a low carbon alternative to heating oil. Blends of biodiesel and conventional hydrocarbon-based diesel are products most commonly distributed for use in the retail diesel fuel marketplace. Much of the world uses a system known as the "B" factor to state the amount of biodiesel in any fuel mix.

(i) 100% biodiesel, 0% petro-diesel is labeled B100,

(ii) 20% biodiesel, 80% petro-diesel is labeled B20,

(iii) 5% biodiesel, 95% petro-diesel is labeled B5,

(iv) 2% biodiesel, 98% petro-diesel is labeled B2.

Blends, less than 20% biodiesel can be used in diesel engines without any or with very minor modifications of the engine. Biodiesel can also be used in its pure form (B100), but may require certain engine modifications to avoid maintenance and performance problems.

Biodiesel can be blended with petro-diesel at any concentration in most diesel engine injection pump. Biodiesel has been known to break down deposits of residue in the fuel lines where petro-diesel has been used. As a result, fuel filters may get clogged with particulates if a quick transition to pure biodiesel is made. Therefore, it is recommended to change the fuel filters on engines and heaters shortly after first switching to a biodiesel blend. From the year 2005, biodiesel use has been increasing all over the world.

6.8.1 Production

Biodiesel is commonly produced by the transesterification of the vegetable oil or animal fat feedstock. The following methods are usually adopted for carrying out this transesterification reaction:

(i) common batch process,

(ii) supercritical processes,

(iii) ultrasonic methods, and

(iv) microwave methods.

Chemically, transesterified biodiesel comprises a mix of mono-alkyl esters of long chain fatty acids. The most common form uses methanol (converted to sodium methoxide) to produce methyl esters. These are commonly referred to as Fatty Acid Methyl Ester - FAME. It is the cheapest alcohol available, though ethanol can be used to produce an ethyl ester. It is commonly referred to as Fatty Acid Ethyl Ester - FAEE. Higher alcohols such as isopropanol and butanol have also been used. Higher molecular weight alcohols improve the cold flow properties of the resulting ester. However, it is at the cost of a less efficient transesterification reaction. A lipid transesterification production process is used to convert the base oil to the desired esters. Any free fatty acids (FFAs) in the base oil are either converted to soap and removed from the process, or they are esterified (yielding more biodiesel) using an acidic catalyst. After this processing, unlike straight vegetable oil, biodiesel has combustion properties very similar to those of petroleum diesel, and can replace it in most current uses.

A by-product of the transesterification process is the production of glycerol Research is being conducted globally to use this glycerol as a chemical building block. Usually this crude glycerol has to be purified, typically by performing vacuum distillation. This is rather energy intensive. The refined glycerol (98%+ purity) can then be utilized directly, or converted into other products. A variety of oils can be used to produce biodiesel. These include:

Virgin oil feedstock: At present rapeseed and soybean oils are most commonly used. It also can be obtained from field pennycress and jatropha and other crops such as mustard, flax, sunflower, palm oil, coconut, hemp etc.

Pure plant oil or straight vegetable oil: Production of vegetable oils for use as fuels is theoretically limited only by the agricultural capacity of a given economy. However, doing so detracts from the supply of other uses of pure vegetable oil.

Animal fats: These include tallow, lard, yellow grease, chicken fat, and the by-products of the production of Omega-3 fatty acids from fish oil. Animal fats are a by-product of meat production. Although it would not be efficient to raise animals (or catch fish) simply for their fat However, producing biodiesel with animal fat that would have otherwise been discarded could replace a small percentage of petro-diesel usage.

Algae: This can be grown using waste materials such as sewage and without displacing land currently used for food production.

Many believe that waste vegetable oil is the best source of oil to produce biodiesel, but since the available supply is very much less than the amount of petroleum-based fuel that is burned for transportation and home heating it may not be a viable proposition in the near future.

6.8.2 Properties

Biodiesel has better lubricating properties and much higher cetane ratings than today's lower sulphur petro-diesel fuels. Unlike SVO/PPO biodiesel addition reduces fuel system wear, and increases the life of high pressure fuel injection system equipment that relies on the fuel for its lubrication. The calorific value of biodiesel is lower than the petro-diesel which is about 37.27 MJ/kg. This is 9% lower than regular petrodiesel. Variation in biodiesel energy density is more dependent on the feedstock used than the production process. Still these variations are less than for petrodiesel. It has been claimed that biodiesel gives better lubricity and more complete combustion thus increasing the engine energy output and partially compensating for the higher energy density of petrodiesel.

Biodiesel is a liquid which varies in color between golden and dark brown depending on the production feedstock. It is immiscible with water, has a high boiling point and low vapor pressure. The flash point of biodiesel ($> 130°C$) is significantly higher than that of petroleum diesel (64°C) or gasoline (−45°C). Biodiesel has a density of 0.88 g/cc higher than petrodiesel ($\approx$0.85 g/cc)

Biodiesel has virtually no sulphur content, and it is often used as an additive to Ultra-Low Sulphur Diesel (ULSD) fuel to aid with lubrication, as the sulphur compounds in petrodiesel provide much of the lubricity.

6.8.3 Environmental Effects

The surge of interest in biodiesels has highlighted a number of environmental effects associated with its use. These potentially include reductions in greenhouse gas emissions, deforestation, pollution and the rate of biodegradation. According to the EPA's Renewable Fuel Standards Program Regulatory Impact Analysis, released in February 2010, biodiesel from soy oil results, on average, in a 57% reduction in greenhouse gases compared to fossil diesel, and biodiesel produced from waste grease results in an 86% reduction.

6.8.4 Current Research

There is ongoing research into finding more suitable crops and improving oil yield. Using the current yields, vast amounts of land and fresh water would be needed to produce enough oil to completely replace fossil fuel usage. It would require twice the land area of the US to be devoted to soybean production, or two-thirds to be devoted to rapeseed production, to meet current

US heating and transportation needs. Specially bred mustard varieties can produce reasonably high oil yields and are very useful in crop rotation with cereals, and have the added benefit that the meal leftover after the oil has been pressed out can act as an effective and biodegradable pesticide.

6.9 GASEOUS FUELS

Gaseous fuels are best suited for IC engines since physical delay is almost zero. However, as fuel displaces equal amount of air the engines may have poor volumetric efficiency. There are quite few gaseous fuels that can be used as alternate fuels. We will discuss them in details in the following sections.

6.9.1 Hydrogen

A number of automobile manufacturers have built with prototype or modified engines which operate on hydrogen fuel. The advantages of hydrogen as an IC engine fuel include:

- Low emissions. Essentially no CO or HC in the exhaust as there is no carbon in the fuel. Most exhaust would be H_2O and N_2 and NO_x.
- Fuel availability. There are a number of different ways of making hydrogen, including electrolysis of water.
- Fuel leakage to environment is not a pollutant.
- High energy content per volume when stored as a liquid. This would give a large vehicle range for a given fuel tank capacity, but see the following.

The disadvantages of using hydrogen as a fuel include:

- Requirement of heavy, bulky fuel storage both in vehicle and at the service stations. Hydrogen can be stored either as a cryogenic liquid or as a compressed gas. If stored as a liquid, it would have to be kept under pressure at a very low temperature requiring a thermally super-insulated fuel tank. Storing in a gas phase would require a high pressure vessel with limited capacity.
- Difficult to refuel and the possibility of detonation.
- Poor engine volumetric efficiency. Any time a gaseous fuel is used in an engine, the fuel will displace some of the inlet air and poorer volumetric efficiency will result.
- Fuel cost would be high at present-day technology and availability.
- High NO_x emissions because of high flame temperature.

The automobile company, Mazda, has adapted a rotary Wankel engine to run on hydrogen fuel. Hydrogen fuel ignites very easily and therefore design of fuel intake was done with at most care. This experimental car uses a metal-hydride fuel storage system.

6.10 HYDROGEN ENGINES

Hydrogen is another alternate fuel tried for IC engines. Investigations were carried out extensively in many countries. The most attractive features of hydrogen as an IC engine fuel are that it can be produced from a potentially available raw material, water, and the main product of its combustion again is water.

Hydrogen has very low density both as gas and as liquid. Hence, in spite of its high calorific value on mass basis its energy density as a liquid is only one fourth that of gasoline. As a gas it has less than one tenth the density of air and its heating value per unit volume is less than one third that of methane. This is one of its chief disadvantages. Hydrogen has to be stored as compressed gas, as liquid (in cryogenic containers) or in absorbed form (as metal hydrides), none of which is as convenient as gasoline storage.

Hydrogen has extremely wide ignition limits. This allows a spark ignition engine to operate on hydrogen with very little throttling, a decided advantage. Stoichiometric hydrogen air mixture burns seven times as fast as the corresponding gasoline air mixture. This too is a great advantage in IC engines, leading to higher engine speeds and greater thermal efficiency. Hydrogen has a high self-ignition temperature but requires very little energy to ignite it. Hence, it is highly prone to preignition and backflash in SI engines.

Adiabatic flame temperature for hydrogen is a little lower than for gasoline but the rapid combustion allows very little heat loss to the surroundings and hence, high, instantaneous, local temperatures are produced. This leads to high nitric oxide formation.

Hydrogen can be used in SI engines by three methods:

(i) By manifold induction

(ii) By direct introduction of hydrogen into the cylinder.

(iii) By supplementing gasoline.

In the manifold introduction of hydrogen, cold hydrogen is introduced through a valve controlled passage into the manifold. This helps to reduce the risk of back flash. The power output of the engine is limited by two factors, preignition and back flash. Also the energy content of air hydrogen mixture is lower than that of liquid hydrocarbon fuels.

In the direct introduction of hydrogen into the cylinder, hydrogen is stored in the liquid form in a cryogenic cylinder. A pump, pumps this liquid through a small heat exchanger where it is converted into cold hydrogen gas. The metering of the hydrogen is also done in this unit. The cold hydrogen helps to prevent preignition and also reduces NO_x formation.

Hydrogen can also be used as a supplementary fuel to gasoline in SI engines. In this system, hydrogen is inducted along with gasoline, compressed and ignited by a spark. The arrangements of liquid hydrogen storage and details of hydrogen induction into the SI engine cylinder can be seen in Figs.6.2 and 6.3 respectively.

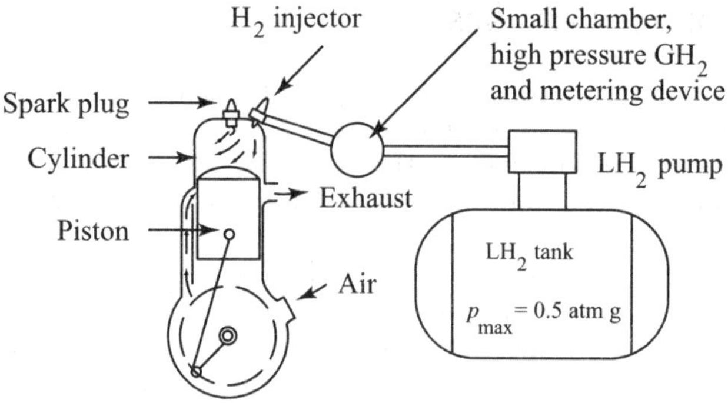

Fig. 6.2 Liquid hydrogen storage and gaseous hydrogen injection system

There are two methods by which hydrogen can be used in diesel engines.

(i) By introducing hydrogen with air and using a spray of diesel oil to ignite the mixture that is by the dual fuel mode. The limiting conditions are when the diesel quantity is too small to produce effective ignition, that is failure of ignition and when the hydrogen air mixture is so rich that the combustion becomes unacceptably violent. In between these limits, a wide range of diesel to hydrogen proportion can be tolerated. Investigations show that beyond a certain range (30 to 50% substitution of diesel fuel by hydrogen),leads to violent pressure rise.

(ii) By introducing hydrogen directly into the cylinder at the end of compression. Since the self ignition temperature of hydrogen is very high, the gas spray is made to impinge on a hot glow plug in the combustion chamber i.e. by surface ignition. It is also possible to feed a very lean hydrogen air mixture during the intake into an engine and then inject the bulk of the hydrogen towards the end of the compression stroke.

Since, hydrogen is a highly reactive fuel it requires great care in handling. Flash black arresters have to be provided between the engine and the storage tank to prevent flash back from going to the tank.

6.10.1 Natural Gas

Natural gas is found in various localities in oil and gas bearing sand strata located at various depths below the earth surface. The gas is usually under considerable pressure, and flows out naturally from the oil well. If the gas is used in an engine located near the well any entrained sand must be separated from the gas before its use. Natural gas obtained from oil wells is called casing head gas. It is usually treated for the recovery of gasoline. After this, it is called dry gas. It is delivered into the pipeline systems to be used as fuel. Natural gas can be used in the production of natural gasoline. Natural gas is a mixture of components, consisting mainly of methane (60–95%) with small amounts of other hydrocarbon fuel components. The composition varies considerably from place to place and from time to time. But usually contain

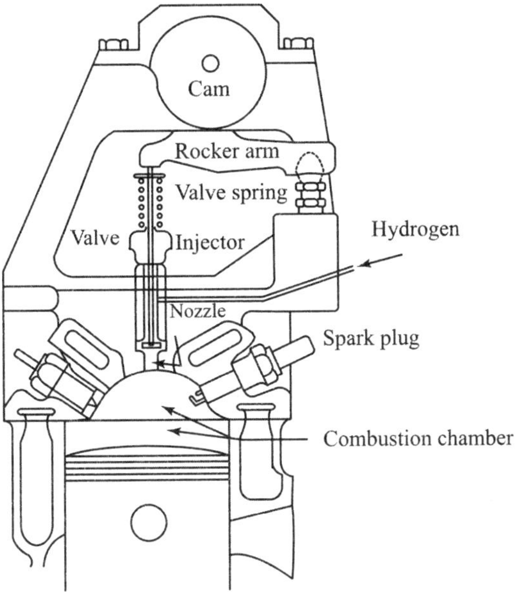

Fig. 6.3 Hydrogen induction in spark-ignition engine

a large amount of methane (CH_4) and small amount of ethane C_2H_5. In addition, it contains various amounts of N_2, CO_2, He, and traces of other gases. Its sulphur content ranges from very little (sweet) to larger amounts (sour). It is stored as compressed natural gas (CNG) at pressures of 16 to 25 bar, or as liquid natural gas (LNG) at pressures of 70 to 210 bar and a temperature around −160°C. As a fuel, it works best in an engine system with a single-throttle body fuel injector. This gives a longer mixing time, which is needed by this fuel. Tests using CNG in various sized vehicles continue to be conducted by government agencies and private industry.

6.10.2 Advantages of Natural Gas

Advantages of natural gas as a fuel include:

(i) Octane number is around 110, which makes it a very good SI engine fuel. Because of this high octane number the flame speed is higher and engines can operate with a high compression ratio.

(ii) Low engine emissions. Less aldehydes than with methanol.

(iii) Fuel is fairly abundant worldwide. It can be made from coal but the process of making is very costly.

6.10.3 Disadvantages of Natural Gas

Disadvantages of natural gas as an engine fuel:

(i) Low energy density resulting in low engine performance.

(ii) Low engine volumetric efficiency because it is a gaseous fuel.

(iii) Need for large pressurized fuel storage tank. There is some safety concern with a pressurized fuel tank.

(iv) Inconsistent fuel properties.

(v) Refueling is a slow process.

Some very large stationary CI engines operate on a fuel combination of methane and diesel fuel. Methane is the major fuel, amounting to more than 90% of the total. It is supplied to the engine as a gas through high-pressure pipes. A small amount of high grade, low sulphur diesel fuel is used for ignition purposes. The net result is very clean running engines. These engines would also be good power plants for large ships, except that high-pressure gas pipes are undesirable on ships.

6.10.4 Compressed Natural Gas (CNG)

Petroleum and natural gas are obtained by the process of drilling wells. As already known crude petroleum is composed of hydrocarbons. It contains some amount of water, sulphur and other impurities. Petroleum when mixed with natural gas produces a highly volatile liquid. This liquid is known as natural gasoline. When this petroleum-natural gas mixture is cooled, the gasoline condenses.

The natural gas can be compressed and then it is called Compressed Natural Gas (CNG). CNG is used to run an automobile vehicle just like LPG. The CNG fuel feed system is similar to the LPG fuel feed system. CNG conversion kits are used to convert petrol-driven cars into CNG-driven cars. These kits contain auxiliary parts like the converter, mixer and other essential parts required for conversion. Emission levels and a comparison between CNG-driven vehicles and petrol-driven vehicles are given in Table 6.2.

Table 6.2 Emission levels and comparison between CNG-driven vehicles and petrol-driven vehicles

Pollutants	Emission levels		
	Emission norms 1977	Petrol with catalytic converter	CNG with catalytic converter
CO (g/km)	5.60	0.92	0.05
HC (g/km)	–	0.36	0.24
NO_x (g/km)	1.92	0.25	0.93

6.10.5 Liquefied Petroleum Gas (LPG)

Propane and butane are obtained from oil and gas wells. They are also the products of the petroleum refining process. For automobile engines, two types of LPG are used. One is propane and the other is butane. Sometimes, a mixture of propane and butane is used as liquid petroleum gas in automobile engines. Liquid petroleum gases serve as fuel in place of petrol. They are used widely in buses, cars and trucks. Liquid petroleum gases are compressed and cooled to form liquid. This liquid is kept in pressure tanks which are sealed. Table 6.3 gives the comparison of petrol with LPG.

6.10.6 Advantages and Disadvantages of LPG

Liquefied petroleum gas has higher potential as an alternate fuel for IC engines. The advantages and disadvantages of using LPG are

Advantages :

(i) LPG contains less carbon than petrol. LPG powered vehicle produces 50 per cent less carbon monoxide per kilometre, though only slightly less nitrogen compounds. Therefore emission is much reduced by the use of LPG.

(ii) LPG mixes with air at all temperatures.

(iii) In multi-cylinder engines a uniform mixture can be supplied to all cylinders.

(iv) Since the fuel is in the form of vapour, there is no crankcase dilution.

(v) Automobile engines can use propane, if they have high compression ratios (10:1).

(vi) LPG has high antiknock characteristics.

(vii) Its heat energy is about 80 per cent of gasoline, but its high octane value compensates the thermal efficiency of the engine.

(viii) Running on LPG translates into a cost saving of about 50%.

(ix) The engine may have a 50 per cent longer life.

Disadvantages :

(i) Engines are normally designed to take in a fixed volume of the mixture of fuel and air. Therefore LPG will produce 10 per cent less horse power for a given engine, at full throttle.

(ii) The ignition temperature of LPG is somewhat higher than petrol. Therefore running on LPG could lead to a five per cent reduction in valve life.

(iii) A good cooling system is quite necessary, because LPG vaporizer uses engine coolant to provide the heat to convert the liquid LPG to gas.

(iv) The vehicle weight is increased due to the use of heavy pressure cylinders for storing LPG .

(v) A special fuel feed system is required for liquid petroleum gas.

Table 6.3 Comparison of petrol and LPG

Petrol	Liquefied Petroleum Gas (LPG)
Fuel consumption in petrol engine is less when compared to LPG.	Compared to petrol, running the engine on LPG results in around a 10% increase in consumption.
Petrol has odour	LPG is odourless
Octane rating of petrol is 81	Octane rating of LPG is 110
Petrol engine is not as smooth as LPG engine	Due to higher octane rating, the combustion of LPG is smoother and knocking is eliminated and the engine runs smoothly.
In order to increase octane number petrol required lead additives.	LPG is lead-free with high octane number
The mixture of petrol and air always leaks past the piston rings and washes away the lubricating oil from the upper cylinder wall surfaces in the process. This results in lack of lubricant which causes more wear. It also carries with it unburnt fuel components (black carbon) and falls into the engine oil. Thus the life of petrol engine is shorter.	When LPG leaks past the rings into the crankcase, it does not wash oil from cylinder walls and does not generate black carbon. Hence, the lubricating layer is not washed away. Thereby, the engine life is increased by 50%
Due to formation of carbon deposits on the spark plugs, the life of the spark plugs is shortened.	Due to absence of carbon deposits on the electrodes of the spark plugs, the life of the spark plugs is increased.
Carburetor supplies the mixture of petrol and air in the proper ratio to the engine cylinders for combustion.	The vaporizer functions as the carburetor when the engine runs on LPG. It is a control device that reduces LPG pressure, vaporizes it and supplies to the engine with a regular flow of gas as per the engine requirement.

6.10.7 Future Scenario for LPG Vehicles

Cost saving, longer life of the engine and less emission will attract the public for making use of LPG run vehicles. Future of LPG Vehicles is bright, provided the following improvements in the system are made.

(i) At present, in many countries LPG cylinders are used in the vehicles. The weight of the cylinders is a disadvantage. Some amount of power is wasted in carrying these cylinders along with the vehicles. However, in developed countries most LPG cars use LPG tanks. The tank is usually the same size as the spare wheel and fits snugly into the space for the spare wheel. Such LPG tanks instead of cylinders, should be used in cars running on LPG.

(ii) Effort must be made to have more LPG filling stations at convenient locations, so that LPG tanks can be filled up easily.

(iii) Safety devices are to be introduced to prevent accident due to explosion of gas cylinders or leakage in the gas pipes.

6.10.8 LPG (Propane) Fuel Feed System

Propane has been tested in fleet vehicles for a number of years. It is a good high octane SI engine fuel and produces less emissions than gasoline: about 60% less CO, 30% less HC, and 20% less NO_x. Propane is stored as a liquid under pressure and delivered through a high pressure line to the engine, where it is vaporized. Hence, proper and sufficient precautions are to be taken before fitting the vehicle with the fuel feed system. Otherwise, there is every possibility for gas leakage causing fire hazards. Being a gaseous fuel, it has the disadvantage of lower engine volumetric efficiency.

LPG (Propane) fuel feed system is shown in Fig.6.4. This fuel feed system has a storage tank placed in the rear portion of the vehicle. Vacuum filter fuel lock, the converter-regulator and the LPG propane carburetor are in front side of the system. In the fuel feed system, liquid LPG is pushed through the fuel pipe line to the converter. The liquid is converted into vapour by the converter. A large temperature drop occurs, as LPG changes from liquid to vapour. LPG should be prevented from freezing within the converter. For this purpose, the engine cooling water is passed close to the converter which prevents the gas from freezing. LPG vapours move to the LPG propane carburetor. This carburetor supplies the air-fuel mixture to the engine for combustion. At present, LPG auto conversion kits are available for converting petrol run cars into LPG gas run cars. These kits contain auxiliaries like the converter or pressure regulator, LPG vapour/air mixing unit known as the mixer and other units which are essential for conversion from petrol-driven vehicles to LPG-driven vehicles.

6.11 DUAL FUEL OPERATION

Automobiles can be made to run either on petrol or LPG. This dual fuel operation (refer Chapter 20) enables the user to change from LPG to petrol

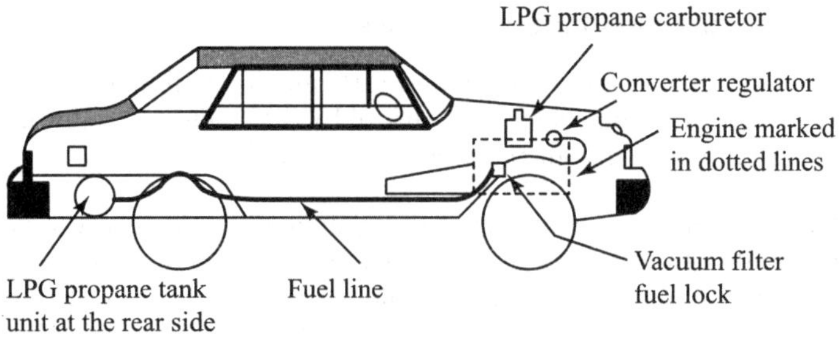

Fig. 6.4 Typical LPG propane fuel feed system of an automobile vehicle

or from petrol to LPG at his convenience by merely pressing a button. On the petrol line, there is an electro-mechanical solenoid. This device closes the flow of petrol during the operation of LPG and opens the petrol line when the engine is running on petrol.

6.12 OTHER POSSIBLE FUELS

Attempts to use many other types of fuel have been tried throughout the history of IC engines. Often, this was done out of necessity or to promote financial gain by some group. At present, a number of biomass fuels are being evaluated, mainly in Europe. These include fuel oil made from wood, barley, soya beans, rape seed, and even beef tallow. Advantages of these fuels generally include availability and low cost, low sulphur, and low emissions. Disadvantages include low energy content (heating value) and corresponding high specific fuel consumption. Using technology first researched 20 years earlier, many enthusiasts converted their vehicles by building a combustion chamber in the trunk of the car or on a small trailer pulled by the car. In this combustion chamber, the coal, wood, or other solid or waste fuel was burned with a restricted supply of oxygen (air). This generated a supply of carbon monoxide, which was then piped to the engine and used to fuel the engine.

Obviously the carburetor on the engine had to be modified and adjusted to supply the gaseous fuel and to give the correct air-fuel ratio. When this was done, the automobile could be operated, but with much less power and longevity. Impurities from the CO generator very quickly dirtied up the combustion chambers of the engine, even when extensive filtering was done. Another problem was with leakage of CO, which is a poisonous, odorless, colorless gas. When this occurred and CO got into the passenger compartment, the driver and other occupants were in danger of sickness and death. Drivers subjected to CO would react as if intoxicated in much the same way as a drunk driver, with the same results of erratic driving, accidents, and even death. As late as the 1970, Sweden was still working on the development of this method of using solid fuel to power automobiles.

6.12.1 Biogas

Biogas is another alternate fuel tried in diesels. Biogas can be produced by anaerobic digestion of organic matter. Potential raw materials available on a large scale are cow dung, municipal wastes, and plants specially grown for this purpose like water hyacinth, algae, certain types of grasses. The main advantage of bio-gas is that it can be produced in rural areas from readily available materials. Bio gas consists mainly of methane and carbon dioxide. Its calorific value is low but its knock resistance (octane number) is high and ignition quality (cetane number) is low. In dual fuel type diesel engine, the gas is mixed with the incoming air and ignited by pilot diesel fuel injection. Similar to the behaviour of alcohol diesel oil dual fuel engines, this gas engine also suffers a fall in efficiency at part loads, compared to the diesel engine, but has good efficiency at full power output.

6.12.2 Producer Gas

Producer gas is made by flowing air and steam through a thick coal or coke bed which ranges in temperature from red hot to low temperature. The oxygen in the air burns the carbon to CO_2. This CO_2 gets reduced to CO by contacting with carbon above the combustion zone. Steam gets dissociated, which introduces H_2 and the freed O_2 combines with the carbon. Producer gas has a high percentage of N_2, since air is used. Thus, it has a low heat value.

6.12.3 Blast Furnace Gas

Blast furnace gas is a byproduct of melting iron ore in steel plants. Its analysis varies considerably with the fuel used and the method of operating the blast furnace. It consists principally CO and N_2. It is similar to producer gas and has a low heat value. It contains lot of dust particles and therefore should be cleaned thoroughly.

6.12.4 Coke Oven Gas

Coke oven gas is obtained as a byproduct when making coke. Its analysis depends upon the coal used and also upon the method of operating the oven. The volatile portion of coal is driven off by the application of heat, and the heavier hydrocarbons are cracked, which results in a gas high in H_2 and CH_4. Its heat value per cubic meter is only about one half that of natural gas.

6.12.5 Benzol

Benzol is a coal tar distillate that consists of about 70% benzene (C_6H_6), 20 percent toluene (C_7H_8) and 10% xylene (C_8H_{10}) and trace amounts of sulphur burning compounds. It has high antiknock characteristic. It has a freezing point of 6 °C, which eliminates it as a fuel in cold climates. Its specific gravity is 0.88, specific heat 0.4, latent heat of vapourisation about (440 kJ/kg) and viscosity about 20 SSU. It is considerably less detonating than gasoline. As such compression ratio upto 6.9 can be used. When added to gasoline it improves the antiknock effect. About 20% of benzol addition is found to stop knocking in most gasoline engines.

6.12.6 Acetone

Acetone (C_3H_{60}) is more volatile than methanol. This may be used as a fuel without blending with other volatile fuels. Its antiknock quality is higher than that of butanol. Hence, it is a desirable fuel to blend with butanol.

6.12.7 Diethyl Ether

Diethyl ether ($C_4H_{10}O$) is a very volatile fuel. It is used with other fuels to increase the volatility of the blend. In summary it may be stated that with increasing air pollution problems and a petroleum shortage looming on the horizon, major research and development programs are being conducted throughout the world to find suitable alternate fuels to supply engine needs for the coming decades.

Review Questions

6.1 Explain the reasons for looking for alternate fuels for IC engines.

6.2 Can one use solid fuels for IC engines? If so how?

6.3 Explain alcohols as alternate fuels for IC engines bringing out their merits and demerits.

6.4 Explain the possibility of using reformulated gasoline and water-gasoline mixture as alternate fuel.

6.5 Can alcohol be used for CI engines? Explain.

6.6 Explain with a neat sketch the surface-ignition alcohol engine.

6.7 What are the advantages and disadvantages of using hydrogen in SI engine?

6.8 Explain the two methods by which hydrogen can be used in CI engine.

6.9 What is natural gas? What are the advantages and disadvantages of using natural gas as alternate fuels?

6.10 Give a brief account of LPG being used as an alternate fuel in SI engine.

6.11 What are the advantages and disadvantages of using LPG in SI engines?

6.12 Compare LPG and petrol as fuel for SI engines.

6.13 Explain the possibilities of using dual-fuel systems in engines.

6.14 With a sketch explain LPG (propane) fuel feed system.

6.15 What all other possible fuels for engines? Explain.

Multiple Choice Questions (choose the most appropriate answer)

1. Which of the following statements is not correct with respect to alcohols as alternate fuels in IC engines
   (a) anti-knock characteristics of alcohol is poor
   (b) alcohol contains about half the heat energy of gasoline/litre
   (c) alcohol does not vaporize as easily as gasoline
   (d) alcohols are corrosive in nature

2. Gasohol is a mixture of
   (a) 90% ethanol + 10% gasoline
   (b) 10% ethanol + 90% gasoline
   (c) 40% ethanol + 60% gasoline
   (d) 50% ethanol + 50% gasoline

3. Stoichiometric air-fuel ratio of alcohol when compared to gasoline is
   (a) higher
   (b) lower
   (c) equal
   (d) none of the above

4. Small amount of gasoline is often added to alcohol to
   (a) reduce the emission
   (b) to increase the power output
   (c) to increase the efficiency
   (d) to improve cold weather starting

5. Methanol by itself is not a good CI engine fuel because
   (a) its octane number is high
   (b) its cetane number is low
   (c) both (a) and (b)
   (d) none of the above

6. Anti-knock characteristics of alcohol when compared to gasoline is
   (a) higher
   (b) lower
   (c) equal
   (d) none of the above

7. Alcohols alone cannot be used in CI engines as
   (a) their self ignition temperature is high
   (b) latent heat of vaporization is low
   (c) both (a) and (b)
   (d) none of the above

8. Advantage of hydrogen as an IC engine fuel
   (a) high volumetric efficiency
   (b) low fuel cost
   (c) No HC and CO emissions
   (d) relatively safe

9. Disadvantage of hydrogen as a fuel in IC engine
   (a) storage is easy
   (b) low NO_x emissions
   (c) detonating tendency
   (d) easy handling

10. Major constituent of natural gas is
    (a) ethane
    (b) methane
    (c) propane
    (d) butane

11. Octane number of natural gas is
    (a) 60–80
    (b) 80–100
    (c) >100
    (d) <60

12. Major disadvantage of LPG as a fuel in automobile is
    (a) reduction in life of the engine
    (b) less power compared to gasoline
    (c) both (a) and (b)
    (d) knocking tendency

Ans: 1. – (a) 2. – (b) 3. – (b) 4. – (d) 5. – (c)
6. – (a) 7. – (c) 8. – (c) 9. – (c) 10. – (b)
11. – (c) 12. – (c)

7

CARBURETION

7.1 INTRODUCTION

Spark-ignition engines normally use volatile liquid fuels. Preparation of fuel-air mixture is done outside the engine cylinder and formation of a homogeneous mixture is normally not completed in the inlet manifold. Fuel droplets which remain in suspension continue to evaporate and mix with air even during suction and compression processes. The process of mixture preparation is extremely important for spark-ignition engines. The purpose of carburetion is to provide a combustible mixture of fuel and air in the required quantity and quality for efficient operation of the engine under all conditions.

7.2 DEFINITION OF CARBURETION

The process of formation of a combustible fuel-air mixture by mixing the proper amount of fuel with air before admission to engine cylinder is called carburetion and the device which does this job is called a carburetor.

7.3 FACTORS AFFECTING CARBURETION

Of the various factors, the process of carburetion is influenced by

(i) the engine speed

(ii) the vapourization characteristics of the fuel

(iii) the temperature of the incoming air and

(iv) the design of the carburetor

Since modern engines are of high speed type, the time available for mixture formation is very limited. For example, an engine running at 3000 rpm has only about 10 milliseconds (ms) for mixture induction during intake stroke. When the speed becomes 6000 rpm the time available is only 5 ms. Therefore, in order to have high quality carburetion (that is mixture with high vapour content) the velocity of the air stream at the point where the fuel is injected has to be increased. This is achieved by introducing a venturi section in the path of the air. The fuel is discharged from the main metering jet at the minimum cross section of the venturi (called throat).

Other factors which ensure high quality carburetion within a short period are the presence of highly volatile hydrocarbons in the fuel. Therefore, suitable evaporation characteristics of the fuel, indicated by its distillation curve, are necessary for efficient carburetion especially at high engine speeds.

The temperature and pressure of surrounding air has a large influence on efficient carburetion. Higher atmospheric air temperature increases the vaporization of fuel (percentage of fuel vapour increases with increase in mixture temperature) and produces a more homogeneous mixture. An increase in atmospheric temperature, however, leads to a decrease in power output of the engine when the air-fuel ratio is constant due to reduced mass flow into the cylinder or, in other words, reduced volumetric efficiency.

The design of the carburetor, the intake system and the combustion chamber have considerable influence on uniform distribution of mixture to the various cylinders of the engine. Proper design of carburetor elements alone ensures the supply of desired composition of the mixture under different operating conditions of the engine.

7.4 AIR–FUEL MIXTURES

An engine is generally operated at different loads and speeds. For this, proper air-fuel mixture should be supplied to the engine cylinder. Fuel and air are mixed to form three different types of mixtures.

(i) chemically correct mixture

(ii) rich mixture and

(iii) lean mixture

Chemically correct or stoichiometric mixture is one in which there is just enough air for complete combustion of the fuel. For example, to burn one kg of octane (C_8H_{18}) completely 15.12 kg of air is required. Hence chemically correct A/F ratio for C_8H_{18} is 15.12:1; usually approximated to 15:1. This chemically correct mixture will vary only slightly in numerical value between different hydrocarbon fuels. It is always computed from the chemical equation for complete combustion for a particular fuel. *Complete combustion* means all carbon in the fuel is converted to CO_2 and all hydrogen to H_2O.

A mixture which contains less air than the stoichiometric requirement is called a rich mixture (example, A/F ratio of 12:1, 10:1 etc.).

A mixture which contains more air than the stoichiometric requirement is called a lean mixture (example, A/F ratio of 17:1, 20:1 etc.).

There is, however, a limited range of A/F ratios in a homogeneous mixture, only within which combustion in an SI engine will occur. Outside this range, the ratio is either too rich or too lean to sustain flame propagation. This range of useful A/F ratio runs from approximately 9:1 (rich) to 19:1 (lean) as indicated in Fig.7.1

The carburetor should provide an A/F ratio in accordance with engine operating requirements and this ratio must be within the combustible range.

7.5 MIXTURE REQUIREMENTS AT DIFFERENT LOADS AND SPEEDS

The air-fuel ratio at which an engine operates has a considerable influence on its performance. Consider an engine operating at full throttle and constant

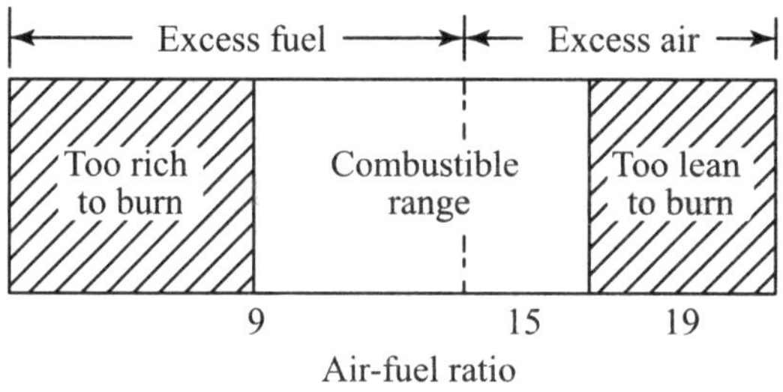

Fig. 7.1 Useful air-fuel mixture range of gasoline

speed with varying A/F ratio. Under these conditions, the A/F ratio will affect both the power output and the brake specific fuel consumption, as indicated by the typical curves shown in Fig.7.2. The mixture corresponding to the maximum output on the curve is called the *best power mixture* with an A/F ratio of approximately 12:1. The mixture corresponding to the minimum point on the $bsfc$ curve is called the *best economy mixture*. The A/F ratio is approximately 16:1. It may be noted that the best power mixture is much richer than the chemically correct mixture and the best economy mixture is slightly leaner than the chemically correct.

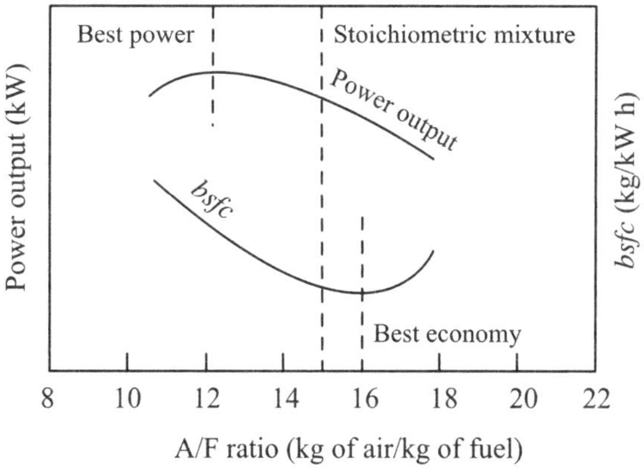

Fig. 7.2 Variation of power output and $bsfc$ with air-fuel ratio for an SI engine

Figure 7.2 is based on full throttle operation. The A/F ratios for the best power and best economy at part throttle are not strictly the same as at full throttle. If the A/F ratios for best power and best economy are constant over the full range of throttle operation and if the influence of other factors is disregarded, the ideal fuel metering device would be merely a two position carburetor. Such a carburetor could be set for the best power mixture when maximum performance is desired and for the best economy mixture when the primary consideration is the fuel economy. These two settings are indicated in Fig.7.3 by the solid horizontal lines X–X′ and Z–Z′, respectively. Actual engine requirements, however, again preclude the use of such a simple and convenient arrangement. These requirements are discussed in the succeeding section.

Under normal conditions it is desirable to run the engine on the maximum economy mixture, viz., around 16:1 air-fuel ratio. For quick acceleration and for maximum power, rich mixture, viz., 12:1 air-fuel ratio is required.

7.6 AUTOMOTIVE ENGINE AIR–FUEL MIXTURE REQUIREMENTS

Actual air-fuel mixture requirements in an automotive engine vary considerably from the ideal conditions discussed in the previous section. For successful operation of the engine, the carburetor has to provide mixtures which follow the general shape of the curve ABCD (single cylinder) and A′B′C′D′ (multi-cylinder) in Fig.7.3 which represents a typical automotive engine requirement. The carburetor must be suitably designed to meet the various engine requirements.

As indicated in Fig.7.3 there are three general ranges of throttle operation. In each of these, the automotive engine requirements differ. As a result, the carburetor must be able to supply the required air-fuel ratio to satisfy these demands. These ranges are:

(i) Idling (mixture must be enriched)

(ii) Cruising (mixture must be leaned)

(iii) High Power (mixture must be enriched)

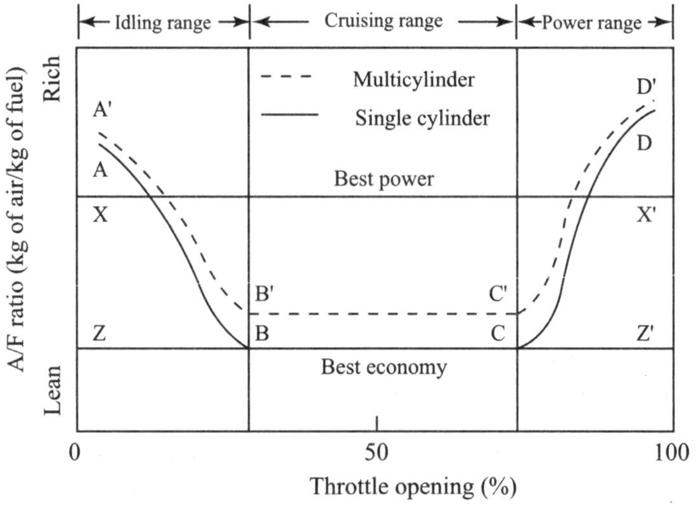

Fig. 7.3 Anticipated carburetor performance to fulfill engine requirements

7.6.1 Idling Range

An idling engine is one which operates at no load and with nearly closed throttle. Under idling conditions, the engine requires a rich mixture, as indicated by point A in Fig.7.3. This is due to the existing pressure conditions within the combustion chamber and the intake manifold which cause exhaust gas dilution of the fresh charge. The pressures indicated in Fig.7.4 are representative values which exist during idling. The exhaust gas pressure at the end of the exhaust stroke does not vary greatly from the value indicated in Fig.7.4, regardless of the throttle position. Since, the clearance volume is constant, the mass of exhaust gas in the cylinder at the end of the exhaust stroke tends to remain fairly constant throughout the idling range. The amount of fresh charge brought in during idling, however, is much less than that during full throttle operation, due to very small opening of the throttle (Fig.7.4). This results in a much larger proportion of exhaust gas being mixed with the fresh charge under idling conditions.

Further, with nearly closed throttle the pressure in the intake manifold is considerably below atmospheric due to restriction to the air flow. When the intake valve opens, the pressure differential between the combustion chamber and the intake manifold results in initial *backward* flow of exhaust gases into the intake manifold. As the piston proceeds down on the intake stroke, these exhaust gases are drawn back into the cylinder, along with the fresh charge. As a result, the final mixture of fuel and air in the combustion chamber is diluted more by exhaust gas. The presence of this exhaust gas tends to obstruct the contact of fuel and air particles — a requirement necessary for combustion. This results in poor combustion and, as a result, in loss of power. It is, therefore, necessary to provide more fuel particles by richening the air-fuel mixture. This richening increases the probability of contact between fuel and air particles and thus improves combustion.

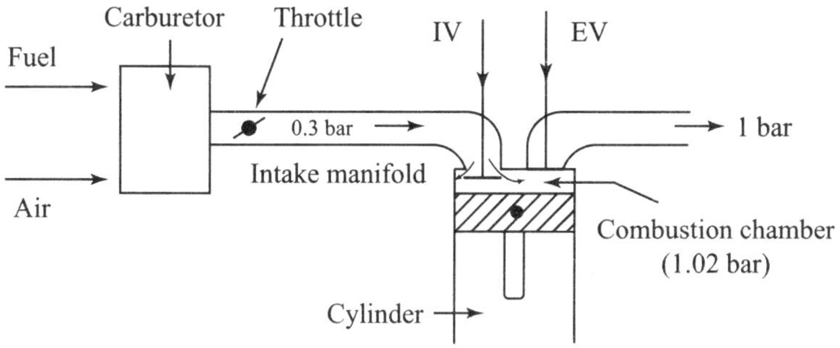

Fig. 7.4 Schematic diagram of combustion chamber and induction system at the start of intake stroke

As the throttle is gradually opened from A to B, (Fig.7.3), the pressure differential between the inlet manifold and the cylinder becomes smaller and the exhaust gas dilution of the fresh charge diminishes. Mixture requirements then proceed along line AB (Fig.7.3) to a leaner A/F ratio required for the cruising operation.

7.6.2 Cruising Range

In the cruising range from B to C (Fig.7.3), the exhaust gas dilution problem is relatively insignificant. The primary interest lies in obtaining the maximum fuel economy. Consequently, in this range, it is desirable that the carburetor provides the engine with the best economy mixture.

7.6.3 Power Range

During peak power operation the engine requires a richer mixture, as indicated by the line CD (Fig.7.3), for the following reasons

(i) *To provide best power*: Since high power is desired, it is logical to transfer the economy settings of the cruising range to that mixture which will produce the maximum power, or a setting in the vicinity of the best power mixture, usually in the range of 12:1.

(ii) *To prevent overheating of exhaust valve and the area near it*: At high power, the increased mass of gas at higher temperatures passing through the cylinder results in the necessity of transferring greater quantities of heat away from critical areas such as those around the exhaust valve. Enrichening the mixture reduces the flame temperature and the cylinder temperature. This reduces the cooling problem and also reduces the tendency to damage exhaust valves at high power. In the cruising range, the mass of charge is smaller and the tendency to burn the exhaust valve is not as high.

In an automobile engine, indication of knocking is available in the form of an audible sound and the operator can make the engine operating conditions less stringent by releasing the throttle or by shifting to a lower gear. Furthermore, automobile engines generally operate well below full power and a complicated and expensive system for enrichment for this purpose is not economically feasible, although some means of richening at high power is usually incorporated. For aircraft engine installations, the complication and expense is justified because of the necessity to increase power during takeoff.

Figure 7.3, then, is better representative of a typical engine requirements for the carburetor. Automobile engine requirements are similar in the idling and cruising ranges but tend to be relatively lower or less rich, in the power range (C to D in Fig.7.5). A more representative engine requirement curve for automobiles is shown in Fig.7.5. The portion of the curve from D to E indicates the requirements after the throttle is wide open and the load is further increased.

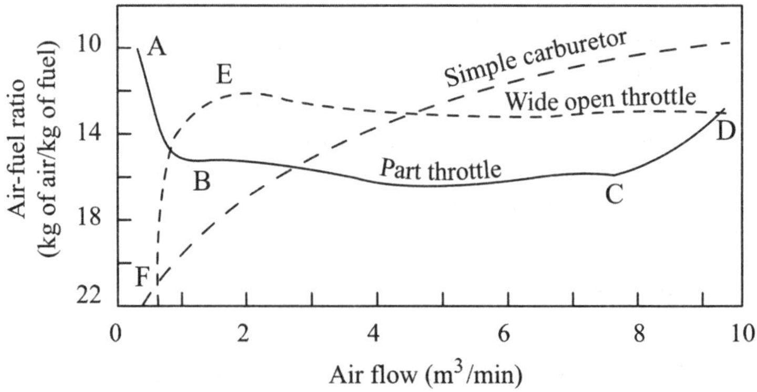

Fig. 7.5 Performance curve of an automobile carburetor

7.7 PRINCIPLE OF CARBURETION

Both air and gasoline are drawn through the carburetor and into the engine cylinders by the suction created by the downward movement of the piston. This suction is due to an increase in the volume of the cylinder and a consequent decrease in the gas pressure in this chamber. It is the difference in pressure between the atmosphere and cylinder that causes the air to flow into the chamber. In the carburetor, air passing into the combustion chamber picks up fuel discharged from a tube. This tube has a fine orifice called carburetor jet which is exposed to the air path. The rate at which fuel is discharged into the air depends on the pressure difference or pressure head between the float chamber and the throat of the venturi and on the area of the outlet of the tube. In order that the fuel drawn from the nozzle may be thoroughly atomized, the suction effect must be strong and the nozzle outlet comparatively small. In order to produce a strong suction, the pipe in the carburetor carrying air to the engine is made to have a restriction. At this restriction called throat due to increase in velocity of flow, a suction effect is created. The restriction is made in the form of a venturi as shown in Fig.7.6 to minimize throttling losses. The end of the fuel jet is located at the venturi or throat of the carburetor.

The geometry of venturi tube is as shown in Fig.7.6. It has a narrower path at the centre so that the flow area through which the air must pass is considerably reduced. As the same amount of air must pass through every point in the tube, its velocity will be greatest at the narrowest point. The smaller the area, the greater will be the velocity of the air, and thereby the suction is proportionately increased (see the manometer in the Fig.7.6).

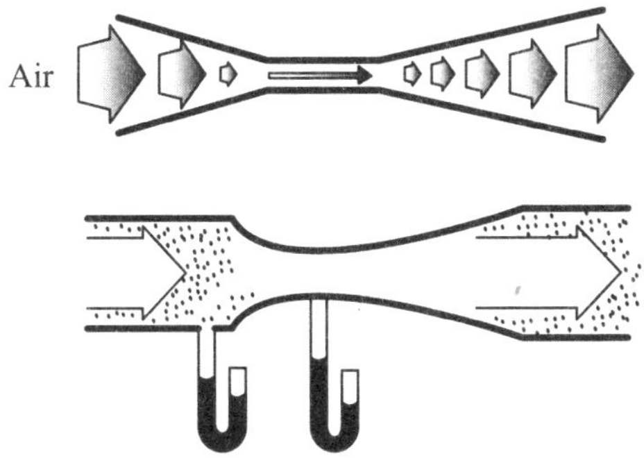

Fig. 7.6 Operation of the venturi tube

As mentioned earlier, the opening of the fuel discharge jet is usually located where the suction is maximum. Normally, this is just below the narrowest section of the venturi tube. The spray of gasoline from the nozzle and the air entering through the venturi tube are mixed together in this region and a combustible mixture is formed which passes through the intake manifold into the cylinders. Most of the fuel gets atomized and simultaneously a small part will be vapourized. Increased air velocity at the throat of the venturi helps the rate of evaporation of fuel. The difficulty of obtaining a mixture of sufficiently high fuel vapour-air ratio for efficient starting of the engine and for uniform fuel-air ratio in different cylinders (in case of multicylinder engine) cannot be fully met by the increased air velocity alone at the venturi throat.

7.8 THE SIMPLE CARBURETOR

Carburetors are highly complex. Let us first understand the working principle of a simple or elementary carburetor which provides an air-fuel mixture for cruising or normal range at a single speed. Later, other mechanisms to provide for the various special requirements like starting, idling, variable load and speed operation and acceleration will be included. Figure 7.7 shows the details of a simple carburetor. The simple carburetor mainly consists of a float cham-

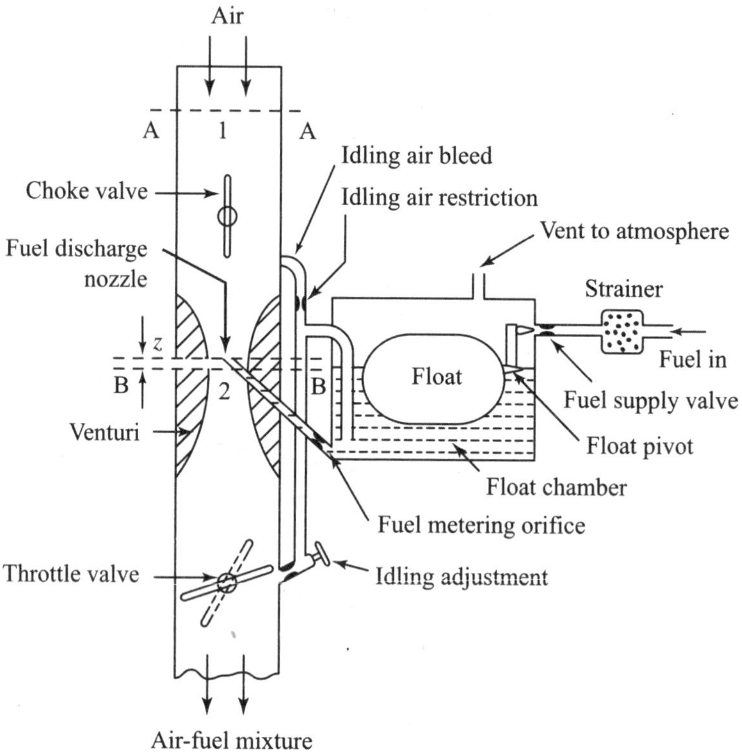

Fig. 7.7 Simple carburetor

ber, fuel discharge nozzle and a metering orifice, a venturi, a throttle valve and a choke. The float and a needle valve system maintains a constant level of gasoline in the float chamber. If the amount of fuel in the float chamber falls below the designed level, the float goes down, thereby opening the fuel supply valve and admitting fuel. When the designed level has been reached, the float closes the fuel supply valve thus stopping additional fuel flow from the supply system. Float chamber is vented either to the atmosphere or to the upstream side of the venturi.

During suction stroke air is drawn through the venturi. As already described, venturi is a tube of decreasing cross-section with a minimum area at the throat. Venturi tube is also known as the choke tube and is so shaped that it offers minimum resistance to the air flow. As the air passes through the venturi the velocity increases reaching a maximum at the venturi throat. Correspondingly, the pressure decreases reaching a minimum. From the float chamber, the fuel is fed to a discharge jet, the tip of which is located in the throat of the venturi. Because of the differential pressure between the float chamber and the throat of the venturi, known as *carburetor depression*, fuel is discharged into the air stream. The fuel discharge is affected by the size of the discharge jet and it is chosen to give the required air-fuel ratio. The pressure at the throat at the fully open throttle condition lies between 4 to 5 cm of Hg, below atmospheric and seldom exceeds 8 cm Hg below atmospheric. To avoid overflow of fuel through the jet, the level of the liquid in the float chamber is maintained at a level slightly below the tip of the discharge jet. This is called the tip of the nozzle. The difference in the height between the top of the nozzle and the float chamber level is marked h in Fig.7.7.

The gasoline engine is *quantity governed*, which means that when power output is to be varied at a particular speed, the amount of charge delivered to the cylinder is varied. This is achieved by means of a throttle valve usually of the butterfly type which is situated after the venturi tube. As the throttle is closed less air flows through the venturi tube and less is the quantity of air-fuel mixture delivered to the cylinder and hence power output is reduced. As the throttle is opened, more air flows through the choke tube resulting in increased quantity of mixture being delivered to the engine. This increases the engine power output.

A simple carburetor of the type described above suffers from a fundamental drawback in that it provides the required A/F ratio only at one throttle position. At the other throttle positions the mixture is either leaner or richer depending on whether the throttle is opened less or more. As the throttle opening is varied, the air flow varies and creates a certain pressure differential between the float chamber and the venturi throat. The same pressure differential regulates the flow of fuel through the nozzle. Therefore, the velocity of flow of air and fuel vary in a similar manner. At the same time, the density of air decreases as the pressure at the venturi throat decreases with increasing air flow whereas that of the fuel remains unchanged. This results in a simple carburetor producing a progressively rich mixture with increasing throttle opening. The mathematical analysis of the performance of a simple carburetor is given in the next section.

7.9 CALCULATION OF THE AIR–FUEL RATIO

A simple carburetor with the tip of the fuel nozzle h metres above the fuel level in the float chamber is shown in Fig.7.7. It may be noted that the density of air is not the same at the inlet to the carburetor (section A–A, point 1) and the venturi throat (section B–B, point 2). The calculation of exact air mass flow involves taking this change in density or compressibility of air into account.

Applying the steady flow energy equation to sections AA and B–B and assuming unit mass flow of air, we have,

$$q - w = (h_2 - h_1) + \frac{1}{2}(C_2^2 - C_1^2) \tag{7.1}$$

Here q, w are the heat and work transfers from entrance to throat and h and C stand for enthalpy and velocity respectively.

Assuming an adiabatic flow, we get $q = 0$, $w = 0$ and $C_1 \approx 0$,

$$C_2 = \sqrt{2(h_1 - h_2)} \tag{7.2}$$

Assuming air to behave like ideal gas, we get $h = C_pT$. Hence, Eq.7.2 can be written as,

$$C_2 = \sqrt{2C_p(T_1 - T_2)} \tag{7.3}$$

As the flow process from inlet to the venturi throat can be considered to be isentropic, we have

$$\frac{T_2}{T_1} = \left(\frac{p_2}{p_1}\right)^{\left(\frac{\gamma-1}{\gamma}\right)} \tag{7.4}$$

$$T_1 - T_2 = T_1\left[1 - \left(\frac{p_2}{p_1}\right)^{\left(\frac{\gamma-1}{\gamma}\right)}\right] \tag{7.5}$$

Substituting Eq.7.5 in Eq.7.3, we get

$$C_2 = \sqrt{2C_pT_1\left[1 - \left(\frac{p_2}{p_1}\right)^{\left(\frac{\gamma-1}{\gamma}\right)}\right]} \tag{7.6}$$

Now, mass flow of air,

$$\dot{m}_a = \rho_1 A_1 C_1 = \rho_2 A_2 C_2 \tag{7.7}$$

where A_1 and A_2 are the cross-sectional area at the air inlet (point 1) and venturi throat (point 2).

To calculate the mass flow rate of air at venturi throat, we have

$$p_1/\rho_1^\gamma = p_2/\rho_2^\gamma \tag{7.8}$$

$$\rho_2 = (p_2/p_1)^{1/\gamma}\rho_1$$

$$\dot{m}_a = \left(\frac{p_2}{p_1}\right)^{1/\gamma}\rho_1 A_2\sqrt{2C_pT_1\left[\left(1 - \frac{p_2}{p_1}\right)^{\frac{\gamma-1}{\gamma}}\right]} \tag{7.9}$$

$$= \left(\frac{p_2}{p_1}\right)^{1/\gamma}\frac{p_1}{RT_1}A_2\sqrt{2C_pT_1\left[1 - \left(\frac{p_2}{p_1}\right)^{\frac{\gamma-1}{\gamma}}\right]}$$

$$= \frac{A_2 p_1}{R\sqrt{T_1}} \sqrt{2C_p \left[\left(\frac{p_2}{p_1}\right)^{\frac{2}{\gamma}} - \left(\frac{p_2}{p_1}\right)^{\frac{\gamma+1}{\gamma}} \right]} \tag{7.10}$$

Substituting $C_p = 1005$ J/kg K, $\gamma = 1.4$ and $R = 287$ J/kg K for air,

$$\dot{m}_a = 0.1562 \frac{A_2 p_1}{\sqrt{T_1}} \sqrt{\left(\frac{p_2}{p_1}\right)^{1.43} - \left(\frac{p_2}{p_1}\right)^{1.71}}$$

$$= 0.1562 \frac{A_2 p_1}{\sqrt{T_1}} \phi \quad \text{kg/s} \tag{7.11}$$

where

$$\phi = \sqrt{\left(\frac{p_2}{p_1}\right)^{1.43} - \left(\frac{p_2}{p_1}\right)^{1.71}} \tag{7.12}$$

Here, p is in N/m^2, A is in m^2 and T is in K.

Equation 7.11 gives the theoretical mass flow rate. To get the actual mass flow rate, the above equation should be multiplied by the co-efficient of discharge for the venturi, C_{da}.

$$\dot{m}_{a_{actual}} = 0.1562 C_{da} \frac{A_2 p_1}{\sqrt{T_1}} \phi \tag{7.13}$$

Since C_{da} and A_2 are constants for a given venturi,

$$\dot{m}_{a_{actual}} \propto \frac{p_1}{\sqrt{T_1}} \phi \tag{7.14}$$

In order to calculate the air-fuel ratio, fuel flow rate is to be calculated. As the fuel is incompressible, applying Bernoulli's Theorem we get

$$\frac{p_1}{\rho_f} - \frac{p_2}{\rho_f} = \frac{C_f^2}{2} + gz \tag{7.15}$$

where ρ_f is the density of fuel, C_f is the fuel velocity at the nozzle exit and z is the height of the nozzle exit above the level of fuel in the float bowl

$$C_f = \sqrt{2\left[\frac{p_1 - p_2}{\rho_f} - gz\right]}$$

Mass flow rate of fuel,

$$\dot{m}_f = A_f C_f \rho_f \tag{7.16}$$

$$= A_f \sqrt{2\rho_f (p_1 - p_2 - gz\rho_f)} \tag{7.17}$$

where A_f is the area of cross-section of the nozzle and ρ_f is the density of the fuel

$$\dot{m}_{f_{actual}} = C_{df} A_f \sqrt{2\rho_f (p_1 - p_2 - gz\rho_f)} \tag{7.18}$$

where C_{df} is the coefficient of discharge for fuel nozzle

$$A/F \text{ ratio} = \frac{\dot{m}_{a_{actual}}}{\dot{m}_{f_{actual}}}$$

$$\frac{A}{F} = 0.1562 \frac{C_{da}}{C_{df}} \frac{A_2}{A_f} \frac{p_1 \phi}{\sqrt{2T_1 \rho_f (p_1 - p_2 - gz\rho_f)}} \tag{7.19}$$

7.9.1 Air–Fuel Ratio Neglecting Compressibility of Air

When air is considered as incompressible, Bernoulli's theorem is applicable to air flow also. Hence, assuming $U_1 \approx 0$

$$\frac{p_1}{\rho_a} - \frac{p_2}{\rho_a} = \frac{C_2^2}{2} \tag{7.20}$$

$$C_2 = \sqrt{2\left[\frac{p_1 - p_2}{\rho_a}\right]} \tag{7.21}$$

$$\dot{m}_a = A_2 C_2 \rho_a = A_2 \sqrt{2\rho_a (p_1 - p_2)} \tag{7.22}$$

$$\dot{m}_{a_{actual}} = C_{da} A_2 \sqrt{2\rho_a (p_1 - p_2)} \tag{7.23}$$

$$A/F \text{ ratio} = \frac{\dot{m}_a}{\dot{m}_f}$$

$$= \frac{C_{da}}{C_{df}} \frac{A_2}{A_f} \sqrt{\frac{\rho_a (p_1 - p_2)}{\rho_f (p_1 - p_2 - gz\rho_f)}} \tag{7.24}$$

If $z = 0$

$$\frac{\dot{m}_a}{\dot{m}_f} = \frac{C_{da}}{C_{df}} \frac{A_2}{A_f} \sqrt{\frac{\rho_a}{\rho_f}} \tag{7.25}$$

7.9.2 Air–Fuel Ratio Provided by a Simple Carburetor

(i) It is clear from expression for $\dot{m}_f$ (Eq.7.17) that if $(p_1 - p_2)$ is less than $gz\rho_f$ there is no fuel flow and this can happen at very low air flow. As the air flow increases, $(p_1 - p_2)$ increases and when $(p_1 - p_2) > gz\rho_f$ the fuel flow begins and increases with increase in the differential pressure.

(ii) At high air flows where $(p_1 - p_2)$ is large compared to $gz\rho_f$ the fraction $gz\rho_f/(p_1 - p_2)$ becomes negligible and the air-fuel ratio approaches

$$\frac{C_{d_a}}{C_{d_f}} \frac{A_2}{A_f} \sqrt{\frac{\rho_a}{\rho_f}}$$

(iii) A decrease in the density of air reduces the value of air-fuel ratio (i.e., mixture becomes richer). It happens at

(a) high air flow rates where $(p_1 - p_2)$ becomes large and ρ_2 decreases.

(b) high altitudes where the density of air is low.

7.9.3 Size of the Carburetor

The size of a carburetor is generally given in terms of the diameter of the venturi tube in mm and the jet size in hundredths of a millimeter. The calibrated jets have a stamped number which gives the flow in ml/min under a head of 500 mm of pure benzol.

For a venturi of 30 to 35 mm size (having a jet size which is one sixteenth of venturi size) the pressure difference $(p_1 - p_2)$ is about 50 mm of Hg. The velocity at throat is about 90 - 100 m/s and the coefficient of discharge for venturi C_{da} is usually 0.85.

7.10 ESSENTIAL PARTS OF A CARBURETOR

A carburetor consists essentially of the following parts, viz.

(i) fuel strainer

(ii) float chamber

(iii) main fuel metering and idling nozzles

(iv) choke and throttle

Various parts mentioned above are discussed briefly in the following sections.

7.10.1 The Fuel Strainer

As the gasoline has to pass through a narrow nozzle exit there is every possibility that the nozzle may get clogged during prolonged operation of the engine. To prevent possible blockage of the nozzle by dust particles, the gasoline is filtered by installing a fuel strainer at the inlet to the float chamber (Fig.7.8). The strainer consists of a fine wire mesh or other type of filtering device, cone shaped or cylindrical shaped. The strainer is usually removable so that it can be taken out and cleaned thoroughly. It is retained in its seat by a strainer plug or a compression spring.

7.10.2 The Float Chamber

The function of a float chamber in a carburetor is to supply the fuel to the nozzle at a constant pressure head. This is possible by maintaining a constant level of the fuel in the float bowl. The float in a carburetor is designed to control the level of fuel in the float chamber. This fuel level must be maintained slightly below the discharge nozzle outlet holes in order to provide the correct amount of fuel flow and to prevent leakage of fuel from the nozzle when the engine is not operating. The arrangement of a float mechanism in

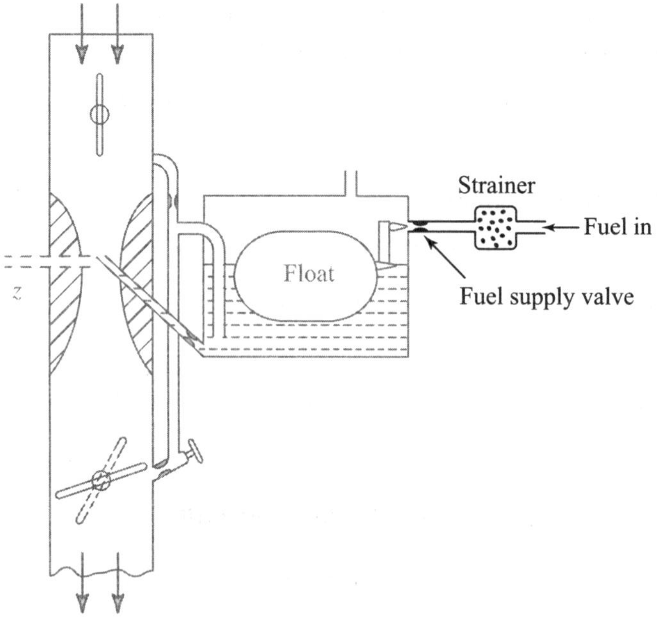

Fig. 7.8 Strainer

relation to the discharge nozzle is shown in Fig.7.9. When the float rises with the fuel coming in, the fuel supply valve closes and stops the flow of fuel into the chamber. At this point, the level of the fuel is correct for proper operation of the carburetor.

As shown in Fig.7.9, the float valve mechanism includes a fuel supply valve and a pivot. During the operation of the carburetor, the float assumes a position slightly below its highest level to allow a valve opening sufficient for replacement of the fuel as it is drawn out through the discharge nozzle.

7.10.3 The Main Metering and Idling System

The main metering system of the carburetor controls the fuel feed for cruising and full throttle operations (Fig.7.10). It consists of three principal units:

(i) the fuel metering orifice through which fuel is drawn from the float chamber

(ii) the main discharge nozzle

(iii) the passage leading to the idling system

The three functions of the main metering system are

(i) to proportion the fuel-air mixture

(ii) to decrease the pressure at the discharge nozzle exit

(iii) to limit the air flow at full throttle

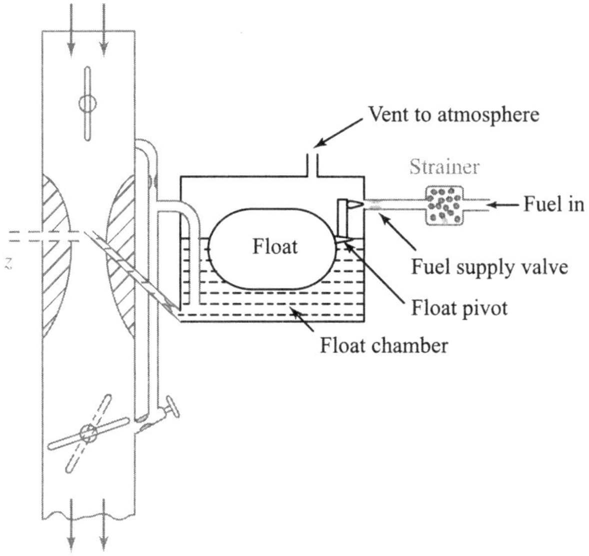

Fig. 7.9 Float chamber

The automobiles fitted with SI engine requires a rich mixture for idling and low speed operation (Fig.7.3). Figure 7.10 shows a schematic diagram of a carburetor highlighting the main metering and idling system. Usually air-fuel ratio of about 12:1 is required for idling. In order to provide such rich mixture, during idling, most of the modern carburetors incorporate special idling system is their construction. This consists of idling fuel passage and idling ports as shown in Fig.7.10. This system gets operational at starting, idling and very low speed running of the vehicle engine and is non-operational when throttle is opened beyond 15% to 20%. When the throttle is practically closed or marginally open, the very small quantity of air creates very little depression at the throat of the venturi, and that is not enough to suck any fuel from the nozzle. But very low pressure caused on the downstream side of the throttle due to suction stroke of the piston makes the fuel rise in the idling tube and the same is discharged through the idling discharge port, directly into the engine intake manifold. Due to the low pressure through idling air-bleed a small amount of air also is sucked. The idling air-bleed mixes air with gasoline drawn from float chamber and helps it to vapourize and atomize it and pass on through the idle passage. The air bleed also prevents the gasoline in the float chamber getting drained off through the idling passage due to syphon action, when the engine is not in operation.

With the opening of throttle and the engine passing through the idling range of operation, the suction pressure at the idle discharge port is not sufficient to draw the gasoline through the idling passage. And the idling system goes out of action. There after main air flow increases and the cruising range of operation is established. The desired fuel-air ratio for idling can be regulated by idling adjustment shown in Fig.7.10.

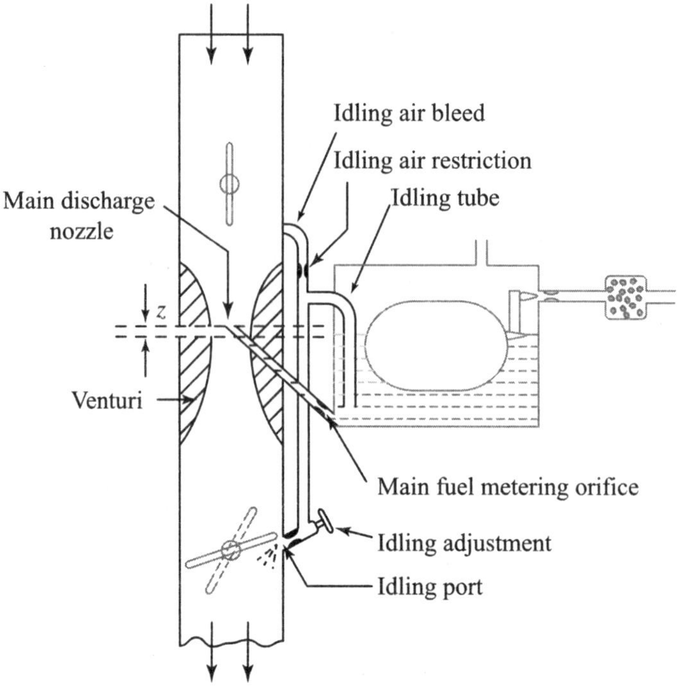

Fig. 7.10 Main metering and idling system

Hot Idling Compensator: Some modern automobiles have this system in the carburetor unit. Under certain extremely hot operating conditions (with increased engine room temperature and also a high carburetor body temperature) there is a tendency for the idling mixture to become too rich. This causes idling instability. The hot idling compensator system (HIC) incorporates bi-metallic valve which admits air directly into the manifold in correct quantity when needed. Thus the mixture richness is adjusted and stable idling is ensured.

7.10.4 The Choke and the Throttle

When the vehicle is kept stationary for a long period during cool winter seasons, may be overnight, starting becomes more difficult. As already explained, at low cranking speeds and intake temperatures a very rich mixture is required to initiate combustion. Sometimes air-fuel ratio as rich as 9:1 is required. The main reason is that very large fraction of the fuel may remain as liquid suspended in air even in the cylinder. For initiating combustion, fuel-vapour and air in the form of mixture at a ratio that can sustain combustion is required. It may be noted that at very low temperature vapour fraction of the fuel is also very small and this forms combustible mixture to initiate combustion. Hence, a very rick mixture must be supplied. The most popular method of providing such mixture is by the use of choke valve. This is simple butterfly valve located between the entrance to the carburetor and the venturi throat as shown in Fig.7.11. When the choke is partly closed, large pressure drop occurs at the venturi throat that would normally result from the quantity of air passing through the venturi throat. The very large depression at the throat inducts large amount of fuel from the main nozzle and provides a very rich mixture so that the ratio of the evaporated fuel to air in the cylinder is within the combustible limits. Sometimes, the choke valves are spring loaded to ensure that large carburetor depression and excessive choking does not persist after the engine has started, and reached a desired speed. This choke can be made to operate automatically by means of a thermostat so that the choke is closed when engine is cold and goes out of operation when engine warms up after starting. The speed and the output of an engine is controlled

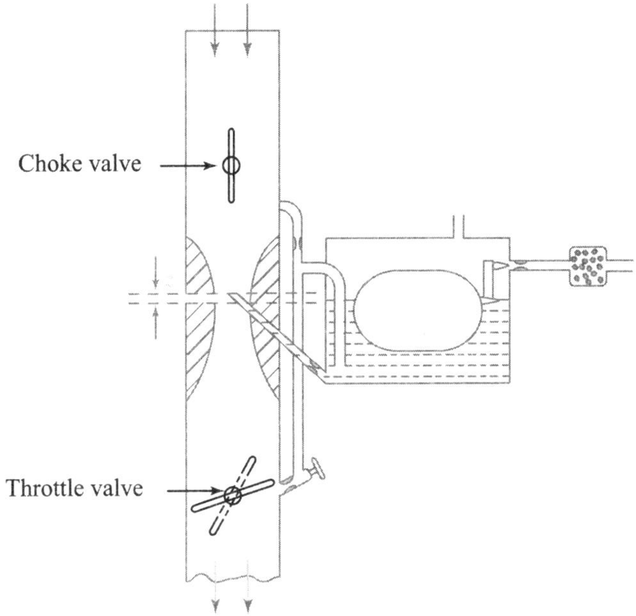

Fig. 7.11 Choke and the throttle

by the use of the throttle valve, which is located on the downstream side of the venturi. The more the throttle is closed the greater is the obstruction to the flow of the mixture placed in the passage and the less is the quantity of mixture delivered to the cylinders. The decreased quantity of mixture gives a less powerful impulse to the pistons and the output of the engine is reduced accordingly. As the throttle is opened, the output of the engine increases. Opening the throttle usually increases the speed of the engine. But this is not always the case as the load on the engine is also a factor. For example, opening the throttle when the motor vehicle is starting to climb a hill may or may not increase the vehicle speed, depending upon the steepness of the hill and the extent of throttle opening. In short, the throttle is simply a means to regulate the output of the engine by varying the quantity of charge going into the cylinder (Fig.7.11).

7.11 COMPENSATING DEVICES

An automobile on road has to run on different loads and speeds. The road conditions play a vital role. Especially on city roads, one may be able to operate the vehicle between 25 to 60% of the throttle only. During such conditions the carburetor must be able to supply nearly constant air-fuel ratio mixture which is economical (16:1). However, the tendency of a simple carburetor is to progressively richen the mixture as the throttle starts opening. The main metering system alone will not be sufficient to take care of the needs of the engine. Therefore, certain compensating devices are usually added in the carburetor along with the main metering system so as to supply a mixture with the required air-fuel ratio. A number of compensating devices are in use. The important ones are

(i) air-bleed jet

(ii) compensating jet

(iii) emulsion tube

(iv) back suction control mechanism

(v) auxiliary air valve

(vi) auxiliary air port

As already mentioned, in modern carburetors automatic compensating devices are provided to maintain the desired mixture proportions at the higher speeds. The type of compensation mechanism used determines the metering system of the carburetor. The principle of operation of various compensating devices are discussed briefly in the following sections.

7.11.1 Air-bleed jet

Figure 7.12 illustrates a principle of an air-bleed system in a typical modern down-draught carburetor. As could be seen it contains an air-bleed into the main nozzle. The flow of air through this bleed is restricted by an orifice and therefore it is called restricted air-bleed jet which is very popular. When the engine is not operating the main jet and the air bleed jet will be filled with fuel. When the engine starts, initially the fuel starts coming through the main as well as the air bleed jet (A). As the engine picks up, only air starts coming through the air bleed and mixes with fuel at B making a air-fuel emulsion. Thus the fluid stream which has become an emulsion of air and liquid has negligible viscosity and surface tension. Thus the flow rate of fuel is augmented and more fuel is sucked at low suctions. By proper design of hole size at B compatible with the entry hole at A, it is possible to maintain a fairly uniform mixture ratio for the entire power range of the operation of an engine. If the fuel flow nozzle of the air-bleed system is placed in the centre of the venturi, both the air-bleed nozzle and the venturi are subjected to same engine suction resulting approximately same fuel-air mixture for the entire power range of operation.

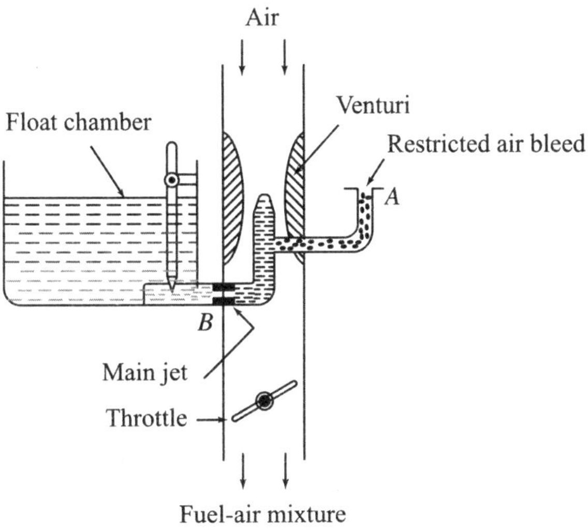

Fig. 7.12 Air-bleed principle in a typical modern carburetor

7.11.2 Compensating Jet

The principle of compensating jet device is to make the mixture leaner as the throttle opens progressively. In this method, as can be seen from Fig.7.13 in addition to the main jet, a compensating jet is incorporated. The compensating jet is connected to the compensation well. The compensating well is also vented to atmosphere like the main float chamber. The compensating well is supplied with fuel from the main float chamber through a restricting orifice. With the increase in air flow rate, there is decrease of fuel level in the compensating well, with the result that fuel supply through the compensating jet decreases. The compensating jet thus progressively makes the mixture leaner as the main jet progressively makes the mixture richer. The sum of the two tends to keep the fuel-air mixture more or less constant as shown in Fig.7.14. The main jet curve and the compensating jet curve are more or less reciprocals of each other.

7.11.3 Emulsion Tube

The mixture correction is attempted by air bleeding in modern carburetor. In one such arrangement as shown in Fig.7.15, the main metering jet is kept at a level of about 25 mm below the fuel level in the float chamber. Therefore, it is also called submerged jet. The jet is located at the bottom of a well. The sides of the well have holes. As can be seen from the figure these holes are in communication with the atmosphere. In the beginning the level of petrol in the float chamber and the well is the same. When the throttle is opened the pressure at the venturi throat decreases and petrol is drawn into the air stream. This results in progressively uncovering the holes in the central tube leading to increasing air-fuel ratios or decreasing richness of mixture when all holes have been uncovered. Normal flow takes place from the main jet. The air is drawn through these holes in the well, and the fuel is emulsified and the

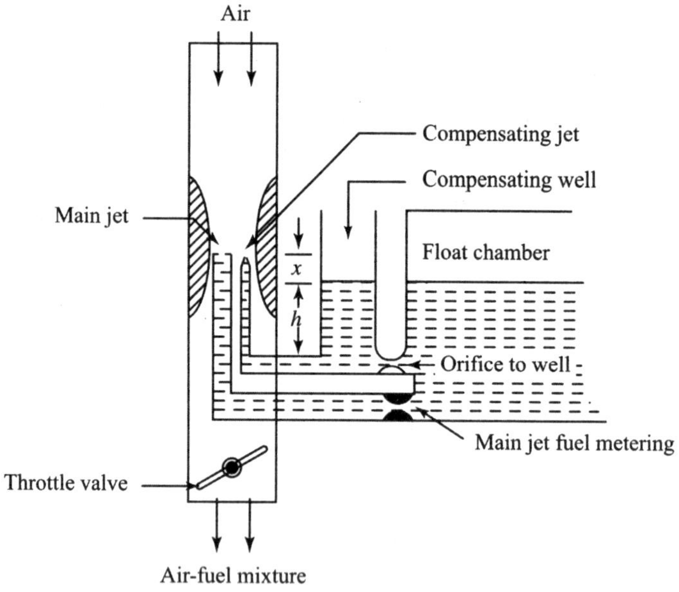

Fig. 7.13 Compensating jet device

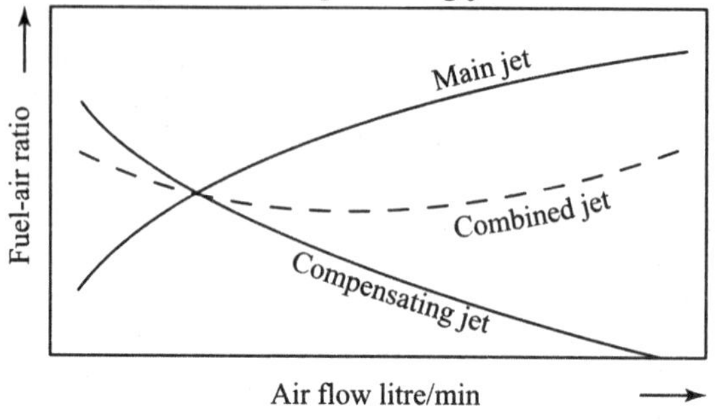

Fig. 7.14 Effect of compensating device on fuel-air ratio

pressure differential across the column of fuel is not as high as that in simple carburetor.

7.11.4 Back Suction Control Mechanism

Figure 7.16 gives the details of back suction control device. In this device, the top of the fuel float chamber is connected to air entry by means of a large vent line fitted with a control valve. Another line with a small orifice connects the top of the fuel float chamber with the venturi throat. When the control valve is completely open, the vent line is unrestricted and the pressure (p_1) in the float chamber is atmospheric and the throat pressure will be p_2. So the pressure differential acting on the orifice is $(p_1 - p_2)$. If the valve is closed, the float chamber pressure will equalize with the pressure at the venturi throat and no fuel can flow. By proper adjustment of the control valve, the required pressure differential can be obtained in the float chamber. Thus altering the

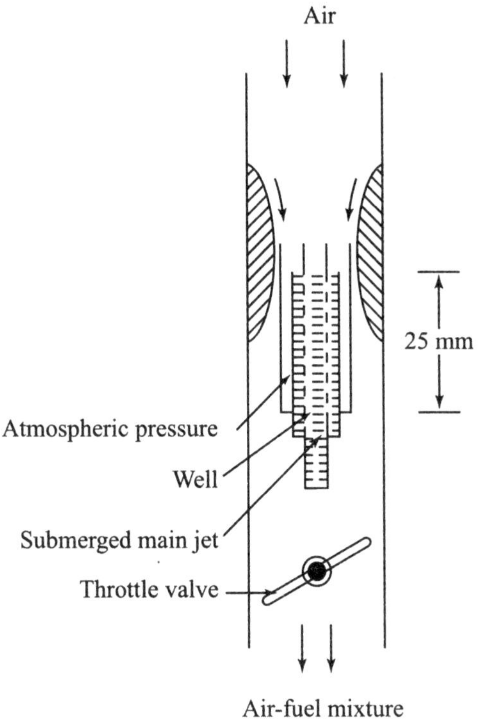

Fig. 7.15 Emulsion tube

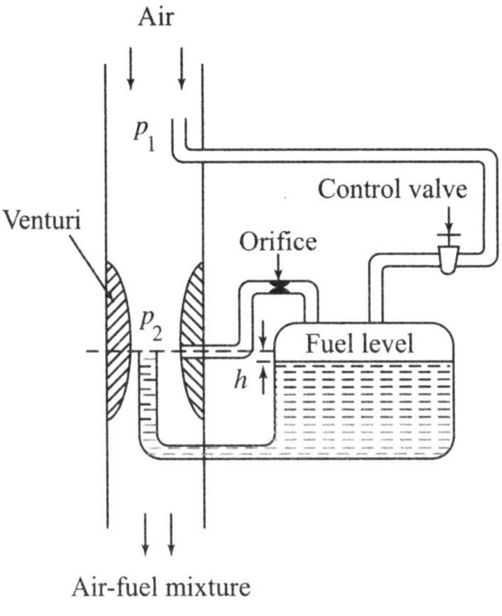

Fig. 7.16 Back suction control or pressure reduction method

quantity of fuel discharged from the nozzle the required air-fuel ratio mixture can be achieved. This method is employed only in large carburetors.

7.11.5 Auxiliary Valve

Figure 7.17 shows a simplified picture of an auxiliary valve device for understanding the principle. When the engine is not operating the pressure, p_1 acting on the top of the auxiliary valve is atmospheric. The vacuum at the venturi throat increases (the throat pressure, p_2 decreases) with increase in load. This pressure differential $(p_1 - p_2)$ lifts the valve against the tension of the spring. And as a result, more air is admitted and the mixture is prevented from becoming rich.

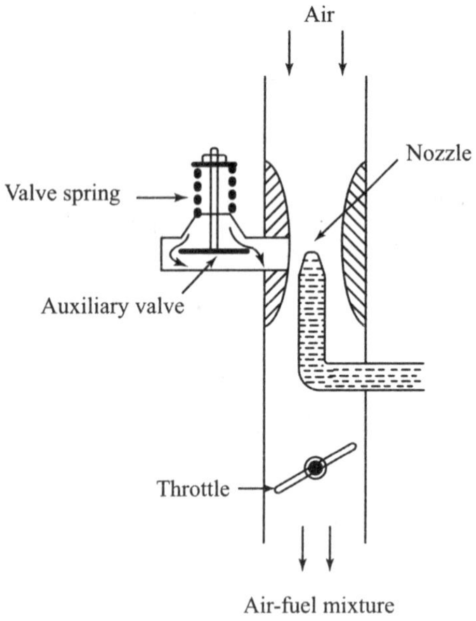

Fig. 7.17 Auxiliary valve

7.11.6 Auxiliary Port

Figure 7.18 shows an auxiliary port employed in a downdraught carburetor. If the butterfly valve is opened, additional air passes through this port reducing the flow of air through the venturi. This means that Δp will be comparatively smaller. As a result fuel drawn is reduced. This method was popular for aircraft carburetors to compensate for the loss in density of air at high altitudes.

7.12 ADDITIONAL SYSTEMS IN MODERN CARBURETORS

Apart from the above compensating devices there are few other systems normally used in modern carburetors for meeting the requirement of vehicles. The details of the various systems are explained in the following sections.

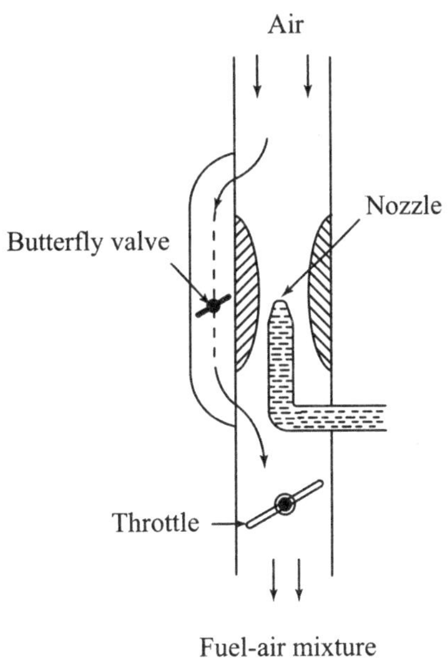

Fig. 7.18 Auxiliary port

7.12.1 Anti-dieseling System

An SI engine sometimes continuous to run for a very small period even after the ignition is switched off. This phenomenon is called dieseling (after running or run-on). Dieseling may take place due to one or more of the following:

(i) Engine idling speed set to high.

(ii) Increase in compression ratio due to carbon deposits.

(iii) Inadequate or low octane rating.

(iv) Engine overheating.

(v) Too high spark plug heat range.

(vi) Incorrect adjustment of idle fuel-air mixture (usually toulene).

(vii) Sticking of throttle.

(viii) Requirement of tune up of engine.

(ix) Oil entry into the cylinder.

Some modern automobiles use antidieseling system to prevent dieseling system. This system has a solenoid valve operated idling circuit. With ignition key turned on current flows in the solenoid coil of the solenoid valve generating a force. This force pulls the needle valve and opens the passage for slow mixture. When the ignition key is turned off the magnetic force disappears.

Then the needle valve is brought to the original (closed position) by the action of the spring in the solenoid valve. By this way the slow mixture passage is cut-off and hence the engine stops. This reduces hydrocarbon emissions.

7.12.2 Richer Coasting System

The richer coasting system is incorporated in some modern cars. When the car is travelling at high speed and when the accelerator pedal is suddenly released, the wheel will motor the engine at a high speed. Consequently, the vacuum in the inlet manifold and the combustion chamber increases too much and causes incomplete combustion. The richer coaster system is designed to overcome this problem by supplying a proper mixture to the intake manifold for proper combustion. This system has a chamber connected to the intake manifold for stable combustion. When the throttle valve is closed to decelerate the vacuum of the intake manifold increases. As this happens the vacuum applied to the chamber pulls the membrane and causes the coasting valve to open. Then the fuel in the float chamber is metered at the coasting fuel jet and mixed with air and sucked into the intake manifold.

7.12.3 Acceleration Pump System

Acceleration is a transient phenomenon. In order to accelerate the vehicle and consequently its engine, the mixture required is very rich and the richness of the mixture has to be obtained quickly and very rapidly. In automobile engines situations arise when it is necessary to accelerate the vehicle. This requires an increased output from the engine in a very short time. If the throttle is suddenly opened there is a corresponding increase in the air flow. However, because of the inertia of the liquid fuel, the fuel flow does not increase in proportion to the increase in air flow. This results in a *temporary lean mixture* causing the engine to misfire and a temporary reduction in power output. To prevent this condition, all modern carburetors are equipped with an accelerating system. Figure 7.19 illustrates simplified sketch of one such device. The pump comprises of a spring loaded plunger which takes care of the situation with the rapid opening of the throttle valve. The plunger moves into the cylinder and forces an additional jet of fuel at the venturi throat. When the throttle is partly open, the spring sets the plunger back. There is also an arrangement which ensures that fuel in the pump cylinder is not forced through the jet when valve is slowly opened or leaks past the plunger or some holes into the float chamber.

Mechanical linkage system, in some carburetor, is substituted by an arrangement whereby the pump plunger is held up by manifold vacuum. When this vacuum is decreased by rapid opening of the throttle, a spring forces the plunger down pumping the fuel through the jet.

7.12.4 Economizer or Power Enrichment System

At the maximum power range of operation from 80% to 100% load, richer air-fuel ratio of about 12 to 14 is required and at the maximum power, an air-fuel ratio of approximately 12 i.e. expected. An economizer is a valve which remains closed at normal cruise operation and gets opened to supply

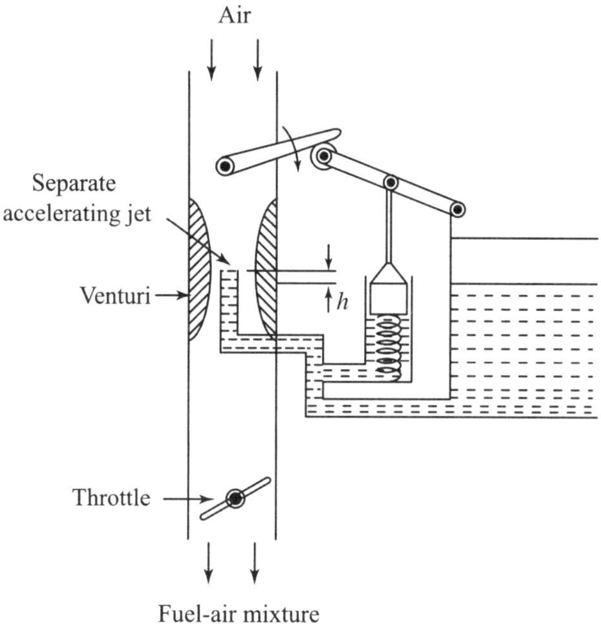

Fig. 7.19 Acceleration pump system

rich mixture at full throttle operation. It regulates the additional fuel supply during the full throttle operation. The term economizer is rather misleading. Probably as it does not interfere during cruising operation where an economy mixture is supplied it is called economizer! It should more appropriately be called power enrichment system. Figure 7.20 shows the skeleton outline of a metering rod economizer system. It allows a large opening to the main jet only when the throttle is opened beyond a specified limit. The metering rod may be tapered or stepped.

7.13 TYPES OF CARBURETORS

There are three general types of carburetors depending on the direction of flow of air. The first is the *updraught* type shown in Fig.7.21(a) in which the air enters at the bottom and leaves at the top so that the direction of its flow is upwards. The disadvantage of the updraught carburetor is that it must lift the sprayed fuel droplet by air friction. Hence, it must be designed for relatively small mixing tube and throat so that even at low engine speeds the air velocity is sufficient to lift and carry the fuel particles along. Otherwise, the fuel droplets tend to separate out providing only a lean mixture to the engine. On the other hand, the mixing tube is finite and small then it cannot supply mixture to the engine at a sufficiently rapid rate at high speeds. In order to overcome this drawback the *downdraught* carburetor [Fig.7.21(b)] is adopted. It is placed at a level higher than the inlet manifold and in which the air and mixture generally follow a downward course. Here the fuel does not have to be lifted by air friction as in the updraught carburetors but move

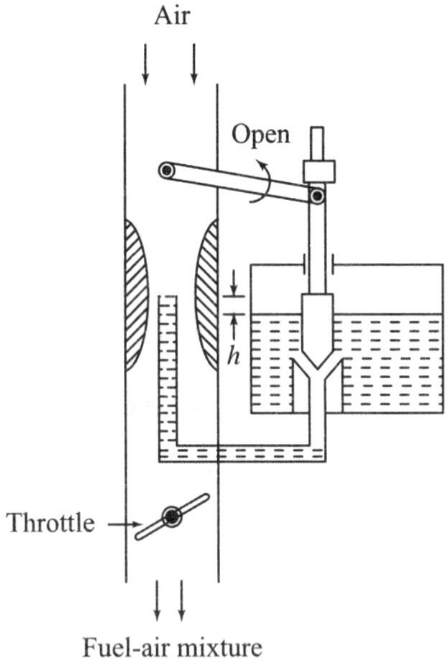

Fig. 7.20 Economizer or power enrichment system

into the cylinders by gravity even if the air velocity is low. Hence, the mixing tube and throat can be made large which makes high engine speeds and high specific outputs possible. A *cross-draught* carburetor consists of a horizontal mixing tube with a float chamber on one side of it [Fig.7.21(c)]. By using a cross-draught carburetor in engines, one right-angled turn in the inlet passage is eliminated and the resistance to flow is reduced.

7.13.1 Constant Choke Carburetor

In the constant choke carburetor, the air and fuel flow areas are always maintained to be constant. But the pressure difference or depression which causes the flow of fuel and air are being varied as per the demand on the engine. Solex and Zenith carburetors belong to this class.

7.13.2 Constant Vacuum Carburetor

In the constant vacuum carburetor, (sometimes called variable choke carburetor) air and fuel flow areas are being varied as per the demand on the engine, while the vacuum is maintained to be always same. The S.U. and Carter carburetors belong to this class.

7.13.3 Multiple Venturi Carburetor

Multiple venturi system uses double [Fig.7.22(a)] or triple [Fig.7.22(b)] venturi. The boost venturi is located concentrically within the main venturi. The discharge edge of the boost venturi is located at the throat of the main venturi. The boost venturi is positioned upstream of the throat of the larger main venturi. Only a fraction of the total air flows though the boost venturi.

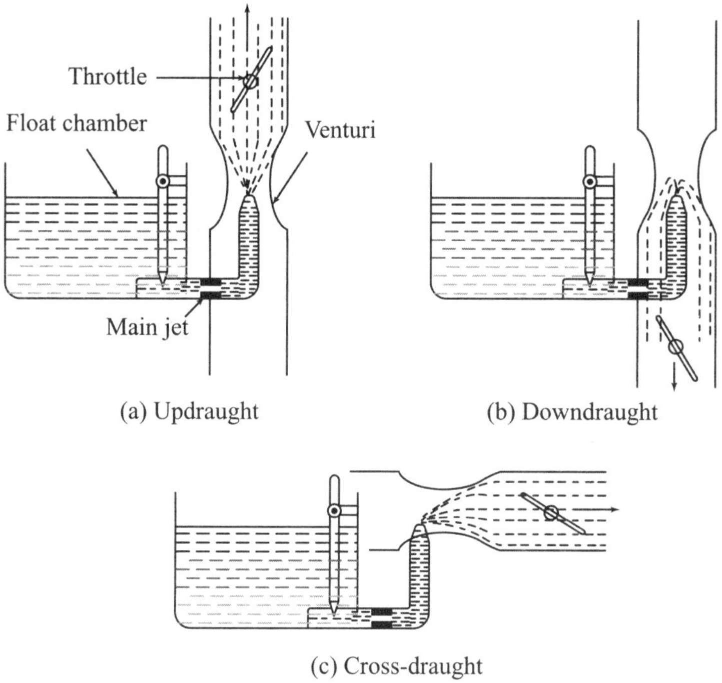

Fig. 7.21 Types of carburetors

Now the pressure at the boost venturi exit equals the pressure at the main venturi throat. The fuel nozzle is located at the throat of the boost venturi. This arrangement results in the following:

(i) High depression is created in the region of the fuel nozzle. Hence, better control over the fuel flow and improved atomization are possible. At the boost venturi throat, velocity of air is as high as 200 m/s.

(ii) An annular blanket of air is formed. This blanket keeps the fuel (droplets of fuel) off the walls of the induction tract.

(iii) Excellent low speed full throttle operation is possible.

(iv) More efficient mixing of the air and fuel is obtained without incurring an acceptable reduction in volumetric efficiency. Volumetric efficiency reduces only slightly since only the portion of the incoming air is subjected to the increased pressure drop.

Instead of two, three venturies arranged in series, are used in certain carburetors. Figure 7.22(b) shows a triple venturi carburetor. There are three venturi namely, the primary venturi, the secondary venturi and the main venturi. The outlet of the primary venturi is placed in the throat of the secondary venturi. The outlet of the secondary venturi is situated in the throat of the main venturi.

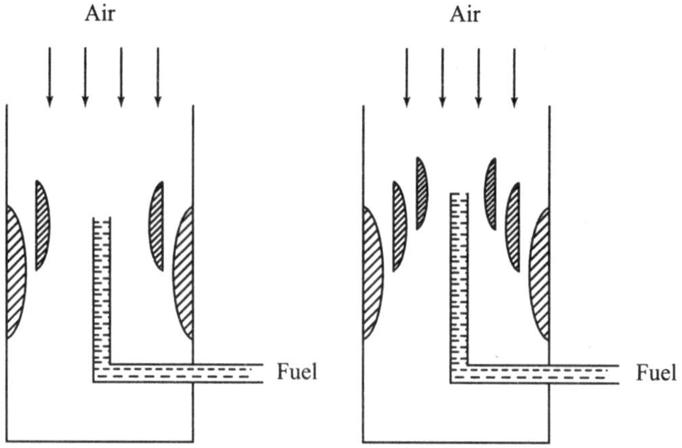

(a) Double venturi (b) Triple venturi

Fig. 7.22 Double and triple venturi carburetors

7.13.4 Advantages of a Multiple Venturi System

(i) *Reducing condensation of the fuel*: In a multiple venturi system, the main jet discharges the fuel in upward direction into the primary venturi against the downward air stream. The fuel is atomized by the air stream. The fuel thus atomized in the primary venturi is kept centrally located in the air stream by the primary venturi.

Besides, a blanket of air surrounding the primary venturi and passing into the secondary venturi, keeps the atomized fuel centrally located in the air stream. By this process, the carburetor walls are protected from coming into contact with the fuel for some distance, thereby reducing condensation.

(ii) *High speed system*: When the speed is to be increased from low to high, the throttle valve is opened sufficiently. When the throttle valve is opened wider, the air flows faster through the primary venturi. This air flow produces a vacuum in the portion of the jet orifice. Due to this increase in vacuum, additional fuel will be discharged from the main jet. A nearly constant air-fuel ratio is maintained by the high speed system.

7.13.5 Multijet Carburetors

A single barrel carburetor has only one barrel, whereas a dual carburetor has two barrels. Each of these two barrels in a dual carburetor contains a fuel jet, a venturi tube, an idling system, a choke and a throttle. The float chamber and the accelerating pump are common to both the barrels.

Passenger cars with six or more cylinders, are provided with dual carburetors. Each venturi supplies the air-fuel mixture to half the cylinders.

Certain advantages of a dual carburetor over a single barrel carburetor are:

(i) The dual carburetor supplies a charge of the mixture to the cylinders which is uniform in quality.

(ii) Volumetric efficiency is higher in case of a dual carburetor.

(iii) The charge of the air-fuel mixture is distributed to each cylinder in a better manner.

(iv) The dual carburetor is compact in its design.

7.13.6 Multi-barrel Venturi Carburetor

Most of the automotive engines are fitted with single barrel carburetors. A single barrel carburetor has one outlet connected to the intake manifold of the engine. This type of carburetor is used extensively on engines of six and less number of cylinders.

Carburetor with two outlets connected to two intake manifolds are known as two barrel or two throat carburetors. Such a unit is basically one with two carburetors. As such, it has two numbers of idling, high speed, power and accelerating systems, two throttles, two chokes but with alternate cylinders in the firing order (i.e. in the case of a six cylinder engine, one barrel supplies cylinders 1, 3 and 2 while the other barrel supplies cylinders 5, 6 and 4. A four barrel carburetor is used on V8 engine. It has four openings connected to the intake manifold. Float system is common to all the four barrels.

In some designs, half of the multibarrel carburetor operates as a unit during light load and cruising speeds. This usually occurs upto 50° throttle plate opening. The other half of the carburetor acts as a supplementary unit during top speed and full throttle operation. That portion of the carburetor which takes care of light loads is called primary side and the other portion is called secondary side. The throttle of the secondary unit remains closed at lower engine speeds. It starts to open when the air flow exceeds about 50% of the maximum engine air flow. It is opened either mechanically or automatically by a vacuum operated diaphragm. The primary carburetor has all the carburetor systems. The secondary carburetor do not contain idle, part throttle or choke systems. The secondary barrel is usually of larger cross sectional area.

The MIKUNI DIDS carburetor used in popular automobiles is a twin barrel, down draught, progressive carburetor of modern design. Such a design ensures satisfactory low end flexibility at the same time achieving maximum top end power. During low speed road driving conditions, when the air quantities inhaled by the engine are small, only the primary barrel works. This ensures high venturi air velocity for proper atomization of the fuel. Beyond certain predetermined operating conditions, when the air quantity increases, the throttle in the secondary barrel is opened by the pneumatic compounding device. At high speed, full load conditions, both barrels are open, and this provides adequate passage for the air flow. Multiple venturi devices are there in both the primary and secondary barrels of the carburetor. The secondary inner venturi helps to achieve a stronger depression at the mainjet/emulsion system thereby ensuring better atomization of the fuel.

7.14 AUTOMOBILE CARBURETORS

The details of various devices for carburetors to satisfy the demand of an automobile engine under different conditions have been discussed in the previous sections. Some of the popular brands of carburetors in use are (i) Solex, (ii) Carter, and (iii) S.U. carburetor Before going into the details of these carburetors let us see the important requirements of an automobile carburetors.

(i) Ease of starting the engine, particularly under low ambient conditions.

(ii) Ability to give full power quickly after starting the engine.

(iii) Equally good and smooth engine operation at various loads.

(iv) Good and quick acceleration of the engine.

(v) Developing sufficient power at high engine speeds.

(vi) Simple and compact in construction.

(vii) Good fuel economy.

(viii) Absence of racing of the engine under idling conditions.

(ix) Ensuring full torque at low speeds.

The operation of a SI engine depends primarily on the quality (air-fuel ratio) and the quantity of the air-fuel mixture delivered to the engine cylinder. A good carburetor must produce the desired air-fuel mixture ratio and supply the mixture to the engine at all speeds and loads and must do the same automatically.

7.14.1 Solex Carburetors

The solex carburetor is famous for its ease of starting, good performance and reliability. It is made in various models and is used in many automobile engines. The solex carburetor as shown in Fig.7.23 is a downdraught carburetor. This has the provision to supply richer mixture required for starting, and weaker mixture to cruise the vehicle. It consists of various fuel circuits such as starting, idling or low speed operation, normal running, acceleration etc.

Figure 7.23 gives the line sketch of a solex carburetor. It incorporates a device called bi-starter which is unique for this carburetor. This device is very useful for cold starting of the engine. The various components and the circuits for air and fuel are explained below for various ranges of operation.

Normal Running: A float (1) with a tapered needle valve at the top face of the float is fixed in the float chamber. This tapered valve takes care of the level of fuel in the float chamber. The main metering jet (2) supplies fuel and the air comes through the venturi (3). The fuel from the main jet goes into the well of the air-bleed emulsion system. The emulsion tube has lateral holes (4) as shown in the figure. Air correction jet (5), calibrates the air entering through it and ensures automatically the correct-balance of air and fuel. The metered emulsion of fuel and air is supplied through the spraying orifice or nozzles (6). These nozzles are drilled horizontally in the vertical stand pipe in the middle of the choke tube or the venturi. The conventional butterfly valve throttle valve is shown by (7).

Cold Starting and Warming: The uniqueness of solex carburetor is the incorporation of a Bi-Starter or a progressive starter. The starter valve is in the form of a flat disc (8) with holes of different sizes. These holes connect the starter gasoline jet (9) and, starter air jet sides, to the passage which opens into a hole just below the throttle valve at (10). Smaller or bigger size holes come opposite the passage depending upon the position of the starter lever (11). The starter lever is operated by flexible cable from the dash board control. Initially, for starting richer mixture is required and after the engine starts, the mixture has to be progressively leaned. In the start position bigger holes are in operation. The throttle valve being in the closed position, whole of the engine suction is applied to the starting passage (12), inducting gasoline from jet (9) and air from jet 10). The jets and passages are so shaped that the mixture provided to the carburetor is rich enough for starting.

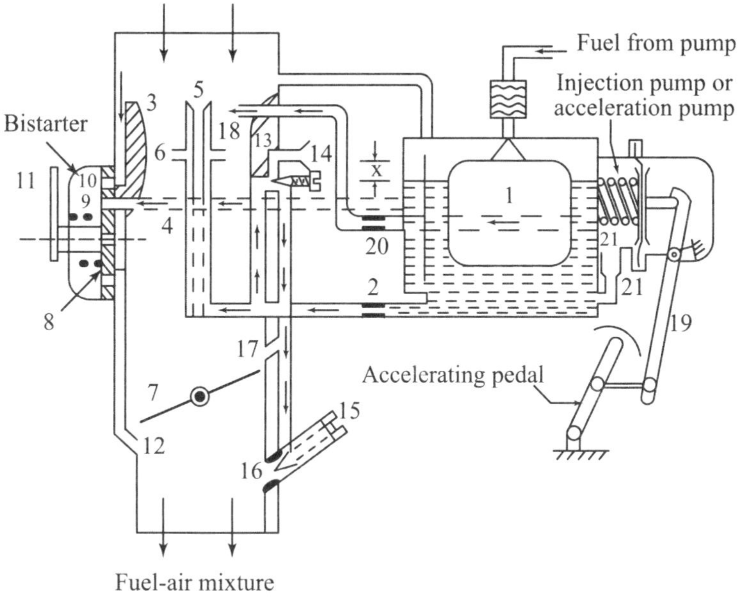

Fig. 7.23 Solex carburetor

Idling and Slow Running: From the well of the emulsion system a hole leads to the pilot jet (13). During idling, the throttle is practically closed and therefore the suction created by the engine on suction stroke gets communicated to the pilot jet (13). Fuel is inducted from there and mixed with little quantity of air coming from the small pilot air-bleed orifice (14). This form an emulsion which is sent down the vertical tube to below the throttle valve, but through the idling volume control screw (15). The idle running adjustment is done by the idle adjustment screw (15). The idling speed can be thus varied and set to a desired value.

In order to change over smoothly from the idle and low speed operation to the main jet operation without a flat spot, there is a by-pass orifice (17) on the venturi side of the throttle valve. As the throttle is opened, the suction at idle port (16) is reduced. But the suction pressure is exerted at a slow speed opening (17). This off sets the reduction of suction at the idle port (16). Thus flat spot is averted.

Acceleration: In order to avert flat spot during acceleration a diaphragm type acceleration pump is incorporated. This pump supplies extra fuel needed for acceleration through pump injector (18). Pump lever (19) is connected to the accelerator. When the pedal is pressed by foot the lever moves towards left and presses the pump diaphragm towards left. This forces the gasoline through pump jet (20) and injector (18). On releasing the pressure on the pedal, the lever moves the diaphragm back towards right and in so doing, creates vacuum towards left. The vacuum so created opens the pump inlet valve (21), and gasoline from float chamber enters the pump.

7.14.2 Carter Carburetor

Carter carburetor is normally used in Jeeps. It is a multiple jet, plain tube type of carburetor with only one adjustment which is for idling or low speed operation. A combination of gasoline and air is drawn into the nozzle chamber through the jets on side of nozzle forming a time spray which is carried by the stand pipe to the venturi or main air passage, where it is absorbed by incoming air forming mixture on which engine operates.

Jets on the side of the nozzle come into operation in direct proportion to throttle position. More and more the throttle is opened, the more jets are in operation. At wide-open-throttle (WOT) all jets are working and engine is getting maximum supply.

Low-speed jet assembly supplies gasoline to the engine at idle engine speed and up to approximately 20 km/h, gasoline flowing through a drilled passage connecting low speed jet chamber with carburetor well.

At idling gasoline is drawn through low speed jet and idling port at the edge of the throttle valve. With the idling screw, the mixture for idle running can be enriched or made leaner as required.

Figure 7.24 shows the down draught carter carburetor. The brief description of the components and air and fuel circuits is given. The gasoline enters the float chamber (1) which is a conventional type. Air enters the choke tube of the carburetor from the top. Carter carburetor is down-draught carburetor. A choke valve (2) in the air passage is always fully open during normal operation. Carter carburetor comprises three venturi diffusing type of choke tube. The smallest of the these venturi (3) is above the fuel level in the float chamber, and the remaining two venturi (6) and (5) are below the fuel level in the float chamber one below the other.

At low speed, the suction in the venturi (3) is sufficient to induct the fuel. Nozzle (4) enters the venturi (3) and throws the fuel up against the air stream evenly, thereby providing finely atomized fuel. The mixture from venturi (3)

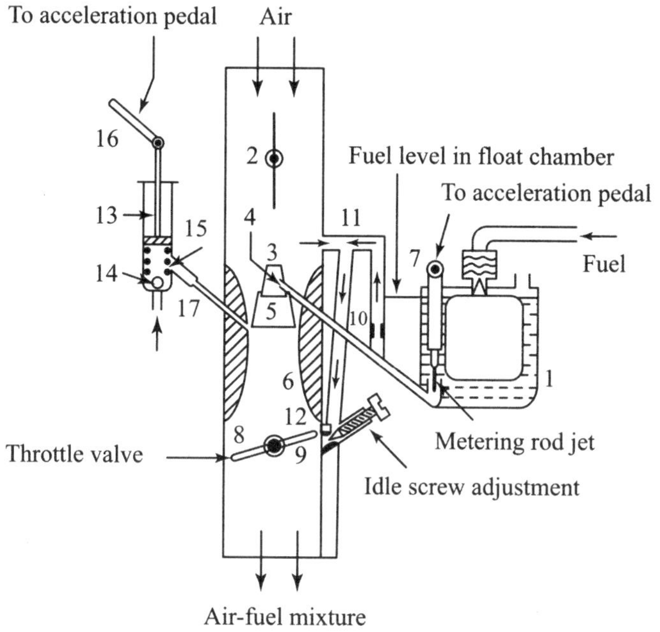

Fig. 7.24 Down draught carter carburetor

flows centrally through the second venturi (5), where it is surrounded by air steam and finally goes to the third main venturi (6), where also the fresh air supply insulates the stream from venturi (5). The fuel-air mixtures enters the engine in a well mixed and atomized state. The multiple venturi gives more homogeneous and better mixture at very low speeds resulting in steady and smooth operation at low speeds. This arrangement also ensures required quantity formed mixture at high speeds.

The metering system employed is mechanical. In the fuel circuit, a metering rod (7), stepped rod, is provided and the same is actuated by a linkage mechanism connected to the main throttle valve. The metering rod being stepped, provides the varying area for gasoline supply to the jet. Thus metering rod governs the quantity of gasoline inducted into the engine.

Starting Circuit: In order to start the engine, the choke (2) is incorporated in the air circuit. Choke valve is butterfly type of valve, one half of it is spring controlled. The valve is pivoted at the centre. When the engine is choked, the whole of the suction created by the piston on induction stroke, is exerted at the main nozzle which then provides fuel. Since the air flow is quite little, very rich fuel-air ratio mixture is provided. When the engine starts, the spring controlled half of the choke is sucked open to allow correct quantity of air during the period of warm up.

Idle and Low Speed Circuit: Rich mixture in small quantity is needed for idling. The throttle valve (8) practically closed, the entire suction pressure created by piston in the engine on suction stroke is exerted at the idle port (9). As a result the gasoline is inducted through the idle feed jet (9) and the air is inducted through first-by-pass (11)and a rich mixture is provided. This fuel-air ratio can be varied to get optimum idling speed by the idle screw adjustment. For low speed operation, the throttle valve is opened further and the main nozzle also begins to supply the fuel. For some duration, during the low speed operation, fuel is supplied by both main venturi and low speed port (12), through the idle passage.

Accelerating Pump Circuit: The purpose of acceleration pump is to avert flat spot in acceleration. The pump comprises of a plunger (13), operating inside a cylinder consisting non-return of inlet check valve (14) and the outlet check valve (15). The plunger of the pump to connected to the acceleration pedal by throttle control rod (16). On rapidly opening the throttle by pressing the accelerator pedal, the pump is actuated and a small amount of gasoline spurts into the choke tube by jet (17). Releasing the accelerator pedal takes the plunger back by spring force and in the process sucks gasoline from the float chamber for the next operation via the non-return value (14). The gasoline is delivered through jet (17) via checkout value (15). The main and sole purpose of the acceleration pump is to provide extra spurt of little quantity of fuel during acceleration to avert a flat spot. This pump does not supply any fuel during other situation of idling running, cruising and over loads.

7.14.3 S.U. Carburetor

Carburetors in general are constant choke type. Zenith, Solex and Carter carburetors are examples of this type. S.U. carburetors differs completely from them being *constant vacuum or constant depression* type with automatic variable choke.

A simplified sketch of this carburetor is shown in Fig.7.25. It consists of a sliding piston. The lower end of the piston is provided with a taper needle which is inserted into the main jet. When the piston is moved up and down the needle also moves up and down with the main jet. The upper end of the piston is given a flat form which is known as suction disc. The up and down movement of the piston and the suction disc is guided by means of piston rod and piston rod guide as shown in Fig.7.25.

The piston always remains loaded by a helical spring. The movement of the piston controls the air passage. The portion above the disc is called suction chamber which connects the air passage by means of a slot provided in the piston. The main jet of the carburetor can be moved up and down along the taper needle by operating a lever from the dash board. This movement is required to adjust the mixture strength throughout the operating range of the carburetor. The carburetor consists of an ordinary butterfly type throttle valve. The lower portion of the suction disc is connected to the atmosphere by means of an air rectifier hole and the upper portion to the throttle air passage. The system does not have any separate idling slow running and accelerating system.

The weight of the piston is constant and always acts down. The vacuum in the suction chamber always tends to move the piston upwards. Therefore, at a particular instant the position of the piston is balanced by the weight and

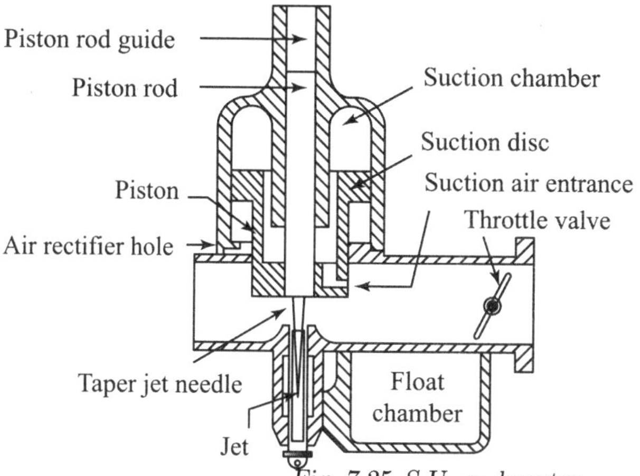

Fig. 7.25 S.U. carburetor

constant vacuum produced above the piston. In starting, a rich mixture is needed by the engine which can be obtained by pulling the jet downwards with the help of the lever attached to it. Therefore, as the throttle is opened more air is allowed to pass through the inlet due to upward movement of the piston. The upward movement of the taper needle also ensures more flow of fuel from the main jet. Thus the air and fuel passage are varied with different engine speeds and velocities of the fuel and air remains constant in this system.

7.15 ALTITUDE COMPENSATION

An inherent characteristic of the conventional float-type carburetor is to meter air and fuel by volume and not by weight as the basis of calculating combustible air-fuel ratio. The weight of one cubic meter of air decreases as altitude increases. Most automobile carburetors are calibrated at altitudes near sea level and similarly production carburetors are flow tested and adjusted in a controlled environment. When the atmospheric conditions are different from those at which the carburetor was calibrated, the air-fuel ratio changes. If the vehicle is operated at an altitude lower than the calibration altitude a lean mixture is obtained which results in poor drivability. At altitudes higher than the calibration altitude a rich mixture is supplied which causes incomplete combustion and emit hydrocarbon and carbon monoxide. The enrichment, E, due to variation of air density follows the relationship

$$E + 1 = \sqrt{\frac{\rho_0}{\rho}} = \sqrt{\frac{p_0 T}{p T_0}} \qquad (7.26)$$

where subscript '0' refers to the calibration conditions. Thus if the density ratio is (say) 0.84, then the enrichment E is given by

$$E + 1 = \sqrt{\frac{1}{0.84}} = 1.091$$

$$E = 0.091 = 9.1\% \qquad (7.27)$$

This is the enrichment of the charge over the basic calibrated air-fuel ratio in an uncompensated carburetor. Figure 7.26 shows the flow characteristic of a typical carburetor at various altitude levels. It also illustrates the early enrichments caused by the effect of low manifold vacuum on the power enrichment system.

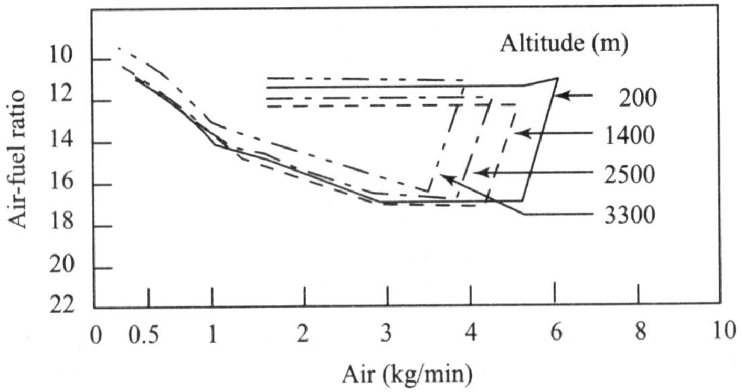

Fig. 7.26 Flow characteristics of a typical carburetor

7.15.1 Altitude Compensation Devices

The problem of mixture enrichment is quite acute in aircraft carburetors. At higher altitudes, density of air is less and therefore the mass of the air taken into engine decreases and the power is reduced in approximately the same proportion. Since, the quantity of oxygen taken into the engine decreases, the fuel-air mixture becomes too rich for normal operation. The mixture strength delivered by the carburetor becomes richer at a rate inversely proportional to the square root of the density ratio as given by the Eq.7.26 If the pressure remains constant, the density of the air will vary according to temperature, increasing as the temperature drops. This will cause a leaning of the fuel-air mixture in the carburetor because the denser air contains more oxygen. The change in air pressure due to altitude is considerably more of a problem than the change in density due to temperature changes. At 6,000 m altitude, the air pressure is approximately one-half the pressure at sea level. Hence, in order to provide a correct mixture, the fuel flow would have to be reduced to almost one-half what it would be at sea level. The adjustment of fuel flow to compensate for changes in air pressure and temperature is a principal function of the mixture control.

Briefly, the *mixture-control system* can be described as a mechanism or device by means of which the richness of the mixture entering the engine during flight can be controlled to a reasonable extent. This control should exist through all normal altitudes of operation to prevent the mixture from becoming too rich at high altitudes and to economize on fuel during engine operation in the low-power range where cylinder temperature will not become excessive with the use of the leaner mixture.

Mixture-control systems may be classified according to their principles of operation as

(i) *back suction type*, which reduces the effective suction on the metering system

(ii) *needle type*, which restricts the flow of fuel through the metering system; and

(iii) the *air-port type*, which allows additional air to enter the carburetor between the main discharge nozzle and the throttle valve.

It may be noted that piston engines have become obsolete in aircraft. Hence, the details of the altitude compensating mechanisms are not discussed.

Worked out Examples

7.1 A simple jet carburetor is required to supply 5 kg of air and 0.5 kg of fuel per minute. The fuel specific gravity is 0.75. The air is initially at 1 bar and 300 K. Calculate the throat diameter of the choke for a flow velocity of 100 m/s. Velocity coefficient is 0.8. If the pressure drop across the fuel metering orifice is 0.80 of that of the choke, calculate orifice diameter assuming, $C_{df} = 0.60$ and $\gamma = 1.4$.

Solution

Velocity at throat, C_2

$$C_2 = V_c\sqrt{2C_pT_1\left[1-\left(\frac{p_2}{p_1}\right)^{\frac{\gamma-1}{\gamma}}\right]}$$

$$100 = 0.8 \times \sqrt{2 \times 1005 \times 300 \times \left[1-\left(\frac{p_2}{p_1}\right)^{0.286}\right]}$$

$$\left(\frac{p_2}{p_1}\right)^{0.286} = 1-\left(\frac{100}{0.8}\right)^2 \times \frac{1}{2 \times 1005 \times 300} = 0.974$$

$$\frac{p_2}{p_1} = (0.974)^{1/0.286} = 0.912$$

$$p_2 = 0.912 \text{ bar}$$

$$v_1 = \frac{RT_1}{p_1} = \frac{0.287 \times 300}{10^5} \times 1000 = 0.861 \text{ m}^3$$

$$p_1v_1^\gamma = p_2v_2^\gamma$$

$$v_2 = v_1\left(\frac{p_1}{p_2}\right)^{\frac{1}{\gamma}} = 0.861 \times \left(\frac{1}{0.912}\right)^{0.714} = 0.919 \text{ m}^3/\text{kg}$$

$$\text{Throat area, } A_2 = \frac{\dot{m}_a \times v_2}{C_2} = \frac{5}{60} \times \frac{0.919}{100} \times 10^4 = 7.658 \text{ cm}^2$$

$$d_2 = \sqrt{7.658 \times \frac{4}{\pi}} = 3.12 \text{ cm}$$

$$\Delta p_a = 1 - 0.912 = 0.088$$

$$\Delta p_f = 0.80 \times 0.088 = 0.07 \text{ bar}$$

$$\dot{m}_f = A_f C_f \sqrt{2\rho_f \Delta p_f}$$

$$\frac{0.5}{60} = A_f \times 0.6 \times \sqrt{2 \times 750 \times 0.07 \times 10^5}$$

$$A_f = \frac{0.5 \times 10^4}{60 \times 0.6 \times 3.24 \times 10^3} = 0.0428 \text{ cm}^2$$

$$d_f = \mathbf{2.34 \text{ mm}}$$ Ans

7.2 A four-cylinder, four-stroke square engine running at 40 rev/s has a carburetor venturi with a 3 cm throat. Assuming the bore to be 10 cm, volumetric efficiency of 75%, the density of air to be 1.15 and coefficient of air flow to be 0.75. Calculate the suction at the throat.

Solution

$$\text{Swept volume, } V_s = \frac{\pi}{4} \times 10^2 \times 10 \times 10^{-6} \times 4$$

$$= 0.00314 \text{ m}^3$$

$$\textit{Volume sucked/s} = \eta_v \times V_s \times n$$

$$= 0.75 \times 0.00314 \times \frac{40}{2} = 0.047 \text{ m}^3/\text{s}$$

$$\dot{m}_a = 0.047 \times 1.15 = 0.054 \text{ kg/s}$$

Since the initial temperature and pressure is not given, the problem is solved by neglecting compressibility of the air

$$\dot{m}_a = C_d A_2 \sqrt{2\rho_a \Delta p_a}$$

$$\Delta p_a = \left(\frac{\dot{m}_a}{C_d A_2}\right)^2 \frac{1}{2\rho_a}$$

$$= \left(\frac{0.054}{0.75 \times \frac{\pi}{4} \times (0.03)^2}\right)^2 \times \frac{1}{2 \times 1.15}$$

$$= 4510.99 \text{ N/m}^2$$

$$= \mathbf{0.0451 \text{ bar}}$$ Ans

7.3 An experimental four-stroke gasoline engine of 1.7 litre capacity is to develop maximum power at 5000 revolutions per minute. The volumetric efficiency is 75% and the air-fuel ratio is 14:1. Two carburetors are to be fitted and it is expected that at maximum power the air speed at the choke is 100 m/s. The coefficient of discharge for the venturi is assumed to be 0.80 and that of main jet is 0.65. An allowance should be made for emulsion tube, the diameter of which can be taken as 1/3 of choke diameter. The gasoline surface is 6 mm below the choke at this engine condition. Calculate the sizes of a suitable choke and main jet. The specific gravity of the gasoline is 0.75. p_a and T_a are 1 bar and 300 K respectively.

Solution

Actual volume of air sucked per second

$$= \eta_v \times V_{cyl} \times \frac{rpm}{2} \times \frac{1}{60}$$

$$= 0.75 \times 1.7 \times 10^{-3} \times \frac{5000}{2} \times \frac{1}{60}$$

$$= 0.053125 \text{ m}^3/\text{s}$$

Air flow through each carburetor at atmospheric conditions, V_1,

$$V_1 = \frac{0.053125}{2} = 0.0265 \text{ m}^3/\text{s}$$

$$\rho_a = \frac{p_a}{RT_a} = \frac{1 \times 10^5}{0.287 \times 10^3 \times 300}$$

$$= 1.16 \text{ kg/m}^3$$

$$\dot{m}_a = \rho_a V_1 = 1.16 \times 0.0265$$

$$= 0.0308 \text{ kg/s}$$

The velocity of air at throat, C_2

$$C_2 = \sqrt{2C_pT_1\left[1 - \left(\frac{p_2}{p_1}\right)^{\frac{\gamma-1}{\gamma}}\right]}$$

$$100^2 = 2 \times 1005 \times 300 \times \left[1 - \left(\frac{p_2}{p_1}\right)^{0.286}\right]$$

$$1 - \left(\frac{p_2}{p_1}\right)^{0.286} = 0.0166$$

$$\frac{p_2}{p_1} = (1 - 0.0166)^{1/0.286} = 0.943$$

$$\textit{Pressure at throat} = 0.943 \text{ bar}$$

$$\text{Volume flow at choke, } V_2 = V_1\left(\frac{p_1}{p_2}\right)^{1/\gamma}$$

$$= 0.0265 \times \left(\frac{1}{0.943}\right)^{1/1.4} = 0.0276 \text{ m}^3/\text{s}$$

If compressibility is neglected, $V_1 = V_2$

$$\text{Nominal choke area, } A_2 = \frac{V_2}{C_2 \times C_{da}}$$

$$= \frac{0.0276}{100 \times 0.80} \times 10^4 = 3.45 \text{ cm}^2$$

If D is the diameter of choke tube and d is the diameter of the emulsion tube

$$A_2 = \frac{\pi}{4}(D^2 - d^2)$$

since $d = \frac{D}{3}$, we have

$$\frac{\pi}{4}\left[D^2 - \left(\frac{D}{3}\right)^2\right] = \frac{\pi}{4} \times \frac{8D^2}{9} = 3.45$$

$$D = \mathbf{2.22 \text{ cm}}$$ Ans

$$\dot{m}_f = \frac{\dot{m}_a}{14} = \frac{0.0308}{14} = 0.0022 \text{ kg/s}$$

$$\dot{m}_f = C_{df} A_f \rho_f \sqrt{\frac{2\Delta p_f}{\rho_f}}$$

$$= C_{df} A_f \sqrt{2\rho_f \Delta p_f}$$

For gasoline the pressure difference across the main jet is given by

$$\Delta p_f = p_a - p_f - gh\rho_f$$

$$\dot{m}_f = C_{df} A_f \sqrt{2\rho_f(p_a - p_2 - gh\rho_f)}$$

$$0.0022 = 0.65 \times A_f \sqrt{2 \times 750\left[10^5(1 - 0.943) - 9.81 \times \frac{6}{10^3} \times 750\right]}$$

$$A_f = 1.162 \times 10^{-6} \text{ m}^2 = 0.01162 \text{ cm}^2$$

$$d = 0.122 \text{ cm} = \mathbf{1.22 \text{ mm}}$$ Ans

7.4 Determine the change of air-fuel ratio in an airplane-engine carburetor when it takes off from sea level to a height of 5000 m. Carburetor is adjusted for 15:1 ratio at sea level where air temperature is 27°C and pressure 1 bar.
Assume the variation of temperature of air with altitude at $t = t_s - 0.0065\ h$ where h is in m and t is in °C. The air pressure decreases with altitude as per the relation $h = 19200 \log_{10}(1/p)$, where p is in bar. Evaluate the variation of air-fuel ratio with respect to altitude in steps of 1000 m on the trend. Show the variation on a graph and discuss.

Solution

We shall illustrate the calculation for 5000 m

Temperature at 5000 m

$$t = 300 - 0.0065 \text{ h}$$

$$= 300 - 0.0065 \times 5000 = 267.5 \text{ K}$$

$$h = 19200 \log_{10}\left(\frac{1}{p}\right)$$

$$10^{h/19200} = \frac{1}{p}$$

$$p = \frac{1}{10^{h/19200}} = 10^{-h/19200} = 0.549 \text{ bar}$$

$$\rho_{sl} = \frac{p_{sl}}{RT_{sl}} = \frac{1 \times 10^5}{287 \times 300} = 1.161$$

$$\rho_{al} = \frac{p_{al}}{RT_{al}} = \frac{0.5490 \times 10^5}{0.287 \times 1000 \times 267.5} = 0.715$$

$$A/F_{al} = A/F_{sl} \times \sqrt{\frac{\rho_{al}}{\rho_{sl}}} = 15 \times \sqrt{\frac{0.715}{1.16}}$$

$$= \mathbf{11.77}$$

Ans ⟸

Similarly we can calculate A/F for various altitudes. The results are given in the table. The variation is shown in the following graph.

h	0	1000	2000	3000	4000	5000
A/F	15	14.283	13.603	12.959	12.348	11.77

It is seen from the graph that with increase in altitude the mixture becomes richer and richer. Therefore some altitude compensating device should be incorporated. Otherwise proper combustion will not take place.

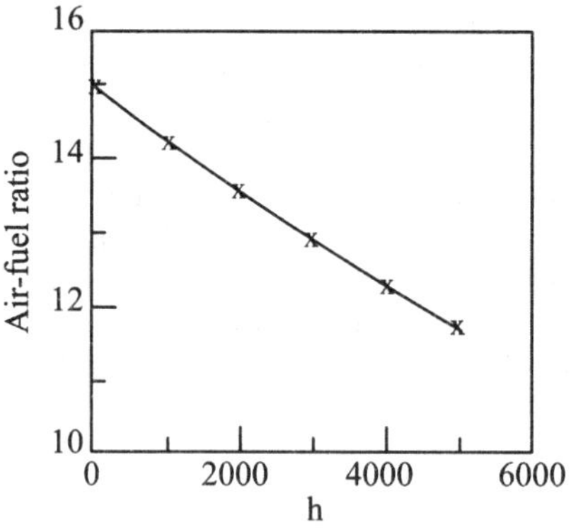

7.5 The venturi of a simple carburetor has a throat diameter of 20 mm and the coefficient of flow is 0.8. The fuel orifice has a diameter of 1.14 mm and the coefficient of fuel flow is 0.65. The gasoline surface is 5 mm below the throat, calculate

(i) the air-fuel ratio for a pressure drop of 0.08 bar when the nozzle tip is neglected

(ii) the air-fuel ratio when the nozzle tip is taken into account

(iii) the minimum velocity of air or critical air velocity required to start the fuel flow when the nozzle tip is provided.

Assume the density of air and fuel as 1.20 and 750 kg/m^3 respectively.

Solution

(i) When the nozzle tip is neglected

$$\dot{m}_a = C_{da} A_a \sqrt{2\rho_a \Delta p}$$

$$\dot{m}_f = C_{df} A_f \sqrt{2\rho_f \Delta p}$$

$$A/F = \frac{C_{da}}{C_{df}} \frac{A_a}{A_f} \sqrt{\frac{\rho_a}{\rho_f}} = \frac{0.80}{0.65} \times \left(\frac{20}{1.14}\right)^2 \times \sqrt{\frac{1.20}{750}}$$

$$= \mathbf{15.15}$$

Ans ⟸

(ii) When the nozzle tip is taken into account, $\dot{m}_a$ will remain the same, But

$$\dot{m}_f = C_{df} A_F \sqrt{2\rho_f(\Delta p - \rho_f g h_f)}$$

$$\rho_f g h_f = \frac{5}{1000} \times 9.81 \times 750 = 36.79 \text{ N/m}^2$$

$$= 36.79 \times 10^{-5} = 0.00037 \text{ bar}$$

$$\Delta p - \rho_f g h_f \quad = \quad 0.08 - 0.00037 \quad = \quad 0.0796 \text{ bar}$$

$$A/F \quad = \quad \frac{C_{da}}{C_{df}} \frac{A_a}{A_f} \sqrt{\frac{\rho_a}{\rho_f}} \sqrt{\frac{\Delta p}{\Delta p - \rho_f g h_f}}$$

$$= \quad \frac{0.8}{0.65} \times \left(\frac{20}{1.14}\right)^2 \times \sqrt{\frac{1.2}{750}} \times \sqrt{\frac{0.08}{0.0796}}$$

$$= \quad \mathbf{15.19}$$

Ans ⇐

When there is a nozzle tip, the fuel flow will start only when there is minimum velocity of air required to create the requisite pressure difference for the flow of fuel to overcome nozzle tip effect. The pressure difference Δp must be equal to $\rho_f g h_f$. Assuming velocity at the entrance of venturi $C_1 = 0$, we have

$$\frac{p_1}{\rho_a} \quad = \quad \frac{p_2}{\rho_a} + \frac{C_2^2}{2}$$

$$\frac{\Delta p}{\rho_a} \quad = \quad \frac{C_2^2}{2} \quad = \quad \frac{\rho_f g h_f}{\rho_a}$$

$$C_{min} \quad = \quad \sqrt{2 g h_f \frac{\rho_f}{\rho_a}}$$

$$= \quad \sqrt{2 \times 9.81 \times \frac{5}{1000} \times \frac{750}{1.2}}$$

$$= \quad \mathbf{7.83 \ m/s}$$

Ans ⇐

The nozzle tip is the height of fuel nozzle in the throat above the gasoline surface in the carburetor. This is provided to avoid spilling of fuel due to vibration or slight inclination position of the carburetor. This would avoid wastage of fuel.

7.6 A carburetor, tested in the laboratory has its float chamber vented to atmosphere. The main metering system is adjusted to give an air-fuel ratio of 15:1 at sea level conditions. The pressure at the venturi throat is 0.8 bar. The atmospheric pressure is 1 bar. The same carburetor is tested again when an air cleaner is fitted at the inlet to the carburetor. The pressure drop to air cleaner is found to be 30 mm of Hg when air flow at sea level condition is 240 kg/h. Assuming zero tip and constant coefficient of flow, calculate (i) the throat pressure when the air cleaner is fitted and (ii) air-fuel ratio when the air cleaner is fitted.

Solution

$$\dot{m}_a \quad = \quad C_{da} A \sqrt{2 \rho_a \Delta p_a}$$

$$\Delta p_a \quad = \quad 1 - 0.8 \quad = \quad 0.2 \text{ bar}$$

when air cleaner is fitted, let p'_t be the throat pressure, then

$$\Delta p'_a = (1 - 0.04 - p'_t) = 0.96 - p'_t$$

For the same air flow and constant coefficients

$$\Delta p_a = \Delta p'_a$$

$$0.2 = 0.96 - p'_t$$

$$p'_t = 0.96 - 0.2 = \mathbf{0.76\ bar}$$ Ans ⟸

Without air cleaner

$$\Delta p_a = 0.20 \text{ bar}$$

With air cleaner fitted with float chamber still vented to atmosphere

$$\Delta p_f = 1 - 0.76 = 0.24$$

Since Δp_f has increased more fuel will flow through, making the mixture richer

$$\text{New } A/F = 15 \times \sqrt{\frac{0.2}{0.24}} = \mathbf{13.7}$$ Ans ⟸

7.7 A four-cylinder, four-stroke SI engine, having a bore of 10 cm and stroke 9 cm runs at 4000 rpm. The fuel used has a carbon content of 84.50 per cent and hydrogen content of 15.50 per cent by weight. The volumetric efficiency of the engine at 75% of full throttle and at 4000 rpm is 0.85 referred to 300 K and 1 bar. The engine is to be supplied with a mixture of air coefficient 0.95 when running at 75% of full throttle. Calculate the throat diameter of the venturi if the air velocity at throat is not to exceed 200 m/s under the above operating conditions. Also calculate the rate of fuel flow in kg/s at the pressure drop at venturi throat. Discharge coefficient for the venturi is 0.8 and the area ratio of the venturi is 0.8. Take R for air as 0.287 kJ/kg K and for fuel vapour is 0.09 kJ/kg K.

Solution

Volume flow rate of mixture/second

$$= \frac{\pi}{4} \times 10^2 \times 9 \times 10^{-6} \times \frac{4000}{2 \times 60} \times 4 \times 0.85$$

$$= 0.08 \text{ m}^3/\text{s}$$

Air required for the stoichiometric mixture with 1 kg of fuel

$$= \left(\frac{0.845}{12} \times 32 + \frac{0.155}{2} \times 16\right) \times \frac{100}{23.3}$$

$$= (2.25 + 1.24) \times \frac{100}{23.3} = 14.98 \text{ kg/kg fuel}$$

$$\dot{m}_a = 0.95 \times 14.98 = 14.23 \text{ kg/kg of fuel}$$

$$F/A = \frac{1}{14.23} = 0.07$$

$$v_a = \frac{287 \times 300}{1 \times 10^5} = 0.861 \text{ m}^3/\text{kg}$$

$$v_f = \frac{90 \times 300}{1 \times 10^5} = 0.27 \text{ m}^3/\text{kg}$$

Volume flow rate of air + Volume flow rate of fuel = Volume flow rate of mixture

Since A/F ratio is 14.23, we have

$$\dot{m}_a v_a + \dot{m}_f v_f = 0.08$$

$$\dot{m}_f = \frac{0.08}{14.23 \times 0.861 + 0.27}$$

$$= \mathbf{0.00639 \text{ kg/s}}$$ Ans ⟸

Density of air at inlet, ρ_1

$$\rho_1 = \frac{1 \times 10^5}{0.287 \times 300 \times 1000} = 1.16 \text{ kg/m}^3$$

Pressure drop between inlet and venturi,

$$\Delta p = \frac{\rho_1}{2} C^2 \left[1 - \left(\frac{A_2}{A_1}\right)^2\right]$$

$$= \frac{1.16}{2} \times 200^2 \times (1 - 0.8^2) \times 10^{-5} = 0.0835 \text{ bar}$$

$$C_2 = \frac{\dot{m}_a}{A_2 C_{da} \rho_1}$$

$$200 = \frac{0.00639 \times 14.23}{A_2 \times 0.8 \times 1.16} = \frac{0.098}{A_2}$$

$$A_2 = \frac{0.098}{200} = 4.9 \times 10^{-4} \text{ m}^2 = 4.9 \text{ cm}^2$$

$$D_2 = \sqrt{\frac{4.9 \times 4}{\pi}} = \mathbf{2.50 \text{ cm}}$$ Ans ⟸

Review Questions

7.1 *Define carburetion.*

7.2 *Explain the factors that affect the process of carburetion.*

7.3 *What are different air-fuel mixture on which an engine can be operated?*

7.4 *Explain the following: (i) rich mixture, (ii) stoichiometric mixture, and (iii) lean mixture.*

7.5 *How the power and efficiency of the SI engine vary with air-fuel ratio for different load and speed conditions?*

7.6 *By means of a suitable graph explain the necessary carburetor performance to fulfill engine requirements.*

7.7 *Briefly discuss the air-fuel ratio requirements of a petrol engine from no load to full load.*

7.8 *Explain why a rich mixture is required for the following: (i) idling, (ii) maximum power, and sudden acceleration.*

7.9 *Explain the principle of carburetion.*

7.10 *With a neat sketch explain the working principle of a simple carburetor.*

7.11 *Derive an expression for air-fuel ratio of a simple carburetor.*

7.12 *Develop an expression for air-fuel ratio neglecting compressibility for a simple carburetor.*

7.13 *Explain why a simple carburetor cannot meet the various engine requirements.*

7.14 *Describe the essential parts of a modern carburetor.*

7.15 *Describe with suitable sketches the following system of a modern carburetor:*

(i) *main metering system*
(ii) *idling system*
(iii) *economizer system*
(iv) *acceleration pump system*
(v) *choke*

7.16 *What are the three basic types of carburetors? Explain.*

7.17 *With suitable sketches explain the various modern automobile carburetors.*

7.18 *With a suitable sketch explain the starting circuit of a Solex carburetor.*

7.19 Draw the sketch of a carter downdraught carburetor. How do the idle and low speed circuit work in this carburetor?

7.20 What are the special requirements of an air craft carburetor? What do you understand by altitude compensation? Explain.

Exercise

7.1 The fuel consumption of a gasoline engine is 6 litres/hour. Carburetor provides an air-fuel ratio of 15:1. The venturi diameter is 15 mm. Determine the diameter of the main metering jet if the tip of the jet is 2.5 mm above the fuel level in the float chamber. The barometric reading is 750 mm of Hg and the atmospheric temperature is 27 °C. Assume $C_a = 0.85$ and $C_f = 0.7$. Take specific gravity of fuel as 0.7, and 1 atmosphere = 760 mm of Hg = 1 bar. Neglect compressibility effect. *Ans:* 0.86 mm

7.2 A simple carburetor is designed to supply 6 kg of air per minute and 0.4 kg of fuel per minute. The density of the fuel is 770 kg/m^3. The air is initially at 1 bar and 17 °C. Calculate the venturi throat diameter if the velocity of air at throat is 100 m/s. Assume $C_{da} = 0.84$, $C_{df} = 0.65$ and $\gamma = 1.4$. If the drop across the fuel metering orifice is 0.85 of the pressure at the throat. *Ans:* 2.09 mm

7.3 An engine fitted with a single jet carburetor having a jet diameter of 1.25 mm has a fuel consumption of 6 kg/h. The specific gravity of fuel is 0.7. The level of fuel in the float chamber is 5 mm below the top of the jet when the engine is not running. Ambient conditions are 1 bar and 17 °C. The fuel jet diameter is 0.6 mm. The discharge coefficient of air is 0.85. Air-fuel ratio is 15. Determine the critical velocity of flow at throat and the throat diameter. Express the pressure at throat in mm of water column. Neglect compressibility effect. *Ans:* (i) 6.43 m/s (ii) 20 mm (iii) 360 mm of water

7.4 A six cylinder four-stroke engine with bore and stroke 10 cm each, uses gasoline with the following composition: C = 85% and H_2 = 15%. The throat diameter of the venturi is 50 mm. The volumetric efficiency at 4000 rpm is 0.75 referred to 17°C and 1 bar. The pressure differential at venturi is 0.12 bar. The temperature at throat is 27 °C. If chemically correct air-fuel ratio is supplied by the carburetor determine

(i) fuel consumption in kg/h and

(ii) the air velocity at throat

Assume R for air = 287 J/kg K and for fuel 97 J/kg K. *Ans:* (i) 33 kg/h (ii) 69.1 m/s

7.5 A carburetor with float chamber vented to atmosphere is tested in a laboratory without air cleaner. The engine is run on economy mode with an air-fuel ratio of 16 at 1 bar. The throat pressure measured is

0.82 bar. The same carburetor is once again test with air cleaner fitted on to it. The additional pressure drop due to air cleaner is 0.04 bar. With air flow at the atmospheric conditions to remain unchanged at 250kg/h. Assuming same air flow in both cases and constant coefficient of flow determine

(i) throat pressure with air cleaner fitted

(ii) the air fuel ratio with air cleaner fitted

Ans: (i) 0.78 bar (ii) 14.47

7.6 A four-stroke engine carburetor is set for a 10% lean operation at sea level where the temperature and pressure are 27 °C and 1 bar. The same engine was tested at 3 km altitude. Determine the percentage richness the carburetor will provide at 3 km if the temperature and pressure at altitude varies according to the following equations.

$$t = t_s - 0.008H$$

$$H = 8400\ln\left(\frac{1}{p}\right)$$

where t_s is the temperature at sea level ($°C$), H is the height in meters, p is the pressure at altitude in bar. *Ans:* 6.66%

7.7 A 1.6 litre cubic capacity four-stroke SI engine has a volumetric efficiency of 75% at a speed of 5000 rpm. The carburetor gives an air-fuel ratio of 14. The air velocity at the throat is 100 m/s. Take C_{da} = 0.9 and C_{df} = 0.7. Lip height h = 5mm, specific gravity of fuel = 0.8. Atmospheric pressure and temperature are 1 bar and 27 °C. An allowance must be made for the emulsion tube. The diameter of the tube may be assumed $\frac{1}{25}$ of the choke diameter. C_p of air 1.005 kJ/kg K. Determine the size of the venturi throat and main jet diameter. *Ans:* (i) 29.62 mm (ii) 1.58 mm

7.8 The cubic capacity of a four-stroke SI engine is 50 cc. It runs at 6000 rpm with an air-fuel ratio of 15:1. The ratio of venturi throat diameter to the fuel jet diameter is 10. The engine works with a volumetric efficiency of 75%. The venturi throat diameter is 10 mm with a discharge coefficient of 0.85. The discharge coefficient of fuel nozzle is 0.65. Specific gravity of the fuel is 0.75. Calculate the lip height of the fuel nozzle. Take atmospheric conditions as 1 bar and 300 K. Neglect compressibility effect. *Ans:* 3.89 mm

7.9 Determine the air-fuel ratio supplied at 4000 m altitude by a carburetor which is adjusted to give a stoichiometric air-fuel ratio at sea level where air temperature is 300 K and pressure is 1 bar. Assume that the temperature of air decreases with altitude given by

$$t = t_s - 0.00675h$$

where h is height in metres and t_s is sea level temperature in °C. The air pressure decreases with altitude as per the relation

$$h = 19000 \log_{10}\left(\frac{1}{p}\right)$$

where p is in bar. State any assumption made.

Ans: A/F at 4000 m = 12.35

7.10 Determine the size of fuel orifice to give a 13.5:1 air-fuel ratio, if the venturi throat has 3 cm diameter and the pressure drop in the venturi is 6.5 cm Hg. The air temperature and pressure at carburetor entrance are 1 bar and 27 °C respectively. The fuel orifice is at the same level as that of the float chamber. Take density of gasoline as 740 kg/m^3 and discharge coefficient as unity. Assume atmospheric pressure to be 76 cm of Hg. *Ans:* Orifice diameter = 1.62 mm

7.11 A four-stroke gasoline engine with a swept volume of 5 litres has a volumetric efficiency of 75% when running at 3000 rpm. The engine is fitted with a carburetor which has a choke diameter of 35 mm. Assuming the conditions of a simple carburetor and neglecting the effects of compressibility, calculate the pressure and the air velocity at the choke. Take the coefficient of discharge at the throat as 0.85 and take the atmospheric conditions as 1bar and 27 °C.

Ans: (i) Air velocity at the choke = 114.6 m/s
(ii) Pressure at the choke = 0.925 bar

7.12 A single jet carburetor is to supply 6 kg/min of air and 0.44 kg/min of petrol of specific gravity 0.74. The air is initially at 1 bar and 27 °C. Assuming an isentropic coefficient of 1.35 for air, determine (i) the diameter of the venturi if the air speed is 90 m/s and the velocity coefficient for venturi is 0.85 (ii) the diameter of the jet if the pressure drop at the jet is 0.8 times the pressure drop at the venturi, and the coefficient of discharge for the jet is 0.66. *Ans:* (i) Diameter of the venturi = 3.58 cm
(ii) Diameter of the jet = 2.2 mm

7.13 A 8.255 cm × 8.9 cm four-cylinder, four-stroke cycle SI engine is to have a maximum speed of 3000 rpm and a volumetric efficiency of 80 per cent. If the maximum venturi depression is to be 0.1 bar (i) what must be the size of the venturi? (ii) Determine the size of fuel orifice if an air-fuel ratio of 12 to 1 is desired. Assume $\rho_a = 1.2$ kg/m^3, $\rho_f = 740$ kg/m^3, $C_{da} = 0.8$ $C_{df} = 0.6$. *Ans:* (i) Diameter of the venturi = 2.16 cm
(ii) Diameter of the jet = 1.45 mm

7.14 A six-cylinder, four-stroke cycle engine has a bore of 8 cm and a stroke of 11 cm and operates at a speed of 2000 rpm with volumetric efficiency of 80 per cent. If the diameter of the venturi section is 2.5 cm, what should be the diameter of the fuel orifice to obtain an A/F ratio of 12 to 1? Assume air density as 1.16 kg/m^3.

Ans: Diameter of the fuel orifice = 1.66 mm

7.15 An automobile carburetor having its float chamber vented to the atmosphere is tested in the factory without an air cleaner at sea-level conditions, the main metering system of this carburetor is found to yield a fuel-air ratio of 0.065. The venturi throat pressure is 0.84 bar. This carburetor is now installed in an automobile and an air cleaner is placed on the inlet to the carburetor. With the engine operating at 230 kg/h air consumption and at sea-level conditions, there is found to be a pressure drop through the air filter of 0.035 bar. Assuming $z = 0$ and orifice coefficients constant, calculate

(i) the venturi throat pressure with air cleaner

(ii) fuel-air ratio with air cleaner

Assume that the flow through the carburetor is incompressible.

Ans: (i) Venturi throat pressure with air cleaner=0.805 bar
(ii) Fuel-air ratio with air cleaner = 0.0717

Multiple Choice Questions (choose the most appropriate answer)

1. Stoichiometric air-fuel ratio of petrol is roughly

   (a) 50:1
   (b) 25:1
   (c) 15:1
   (d) 1:1

2. Venturi in the carburetor results in

   (a) decrease of air velocity
   (b) increase of air velocity
   (c) decrease of fuel flow
   (d) increase of manifold vacuum

3. The choke is closed when the engine is

   (a) accelerating
   (b) hot
   (c) cold
   (d) idling

4. Lean air mixture is required during

   (a) idling
   (b) starting
   (c) accelerating
   (d) cruising

5. The limits of air-fuel for SI engine are
   (a) 8/1 to 18/1
   (b) 8/1 to 50/1
   (c) 25/1 to 50/1
   (d) 50/1 to 100/1

6. In a SI engine for maximum power, the relative fuel-air ratio is
   (a) 1.5
   (b) 1.2
   (c) 0.8
   (d) 0.6

7. For maximum thermal efficiency, the fuel-air mixture in SI engines should be
   (a) lean
   (b) rich
   (c) stoichiometric
   (d) may be rich or lean

8. During starting petrol engines require
   (a) stoichiometric mixture
   (b) lean mixture
   (c) rich mixture
   (d) any air-fuel ratio is alright

9. For petrol engines the method of governing is
   (a) hit and miss governing
   (b) quality governing
   (c) quantity governing
   (d) none of the above

10. Economizer is used to provide enriched mixture during
   (a) starting
   (b) idling
   (c) cruising
   (d) full throttle operation

11. When the throttle is suddenly opened, the mixture from the simple carburetor tends to become

    (a) rich
    (b) lean
    (c) stoichiometric
    (d) not affected

12. Precise petrol injection system is

    (a) direct injection
    (b) sequential injection
    (c) throttle body injection
    (d) port injection

13. The choke in an automobile meant for supplying

    (a) lean mixture
    (b) rich mixture
    (c) stoichiometric mixture
    (d) weak mixture

14. Modern carburettors provide the correct quality of air-fuel mixture during

    (a) starting
    (b) idling
    (c) cruising
    (d) all conditions

15. A simple carburettor supplies rich mixture during

    (a) starting
    (b) idling
    (c) cruising
    (d) accelerating

Ans:					
	1. – (c)	2. – (b)	3. – (c)	4. – (d)	5. – (a)
	6. – (b)	7. – (a)	8. – (c)	9. – (c)	10. – (d)
	11. – (b)	12. – (c)	13. – (b)	14. – (d)	15. – (d)

8

MECHANICAL INJECTION SYSTEMS

8.1 INTRODUCTION

The fuel-injection system is the most vital component in the working of CI engines. The engine performance viz., power output, economy etc. is greatly dependent on the effectiveness of the fuel-injection system. The injection system has to perform the important duty of initiating and controlling the combustion process.

Basically, the purpose of carburetion and fuel-injection is the same viz., preparation of the combustible charge. But in case of carburetion fuel is atomized by processes relying on the air speed greater than fuel speed at the fuel nozzle, whereas, in fuel-injection the fuel speed at the point of delivery is greater than the air speed to atomize the fuel. In carburetors, as explained in Chapter 7, air flowing through a venturi picks up fuel from a nozzle located there. The amount of fuel drawn into the engine depends upon the air velocity in the venturi. In a fuel-injection system, the amount of fuel delivered into the air stream going to the engine is controlled by a pump which forces the fuel under pressure.

When the fuel is injected into the combustion chamber towards the end of compression stroke, it is atomized into very fine droplets. These droplets vaporize due to heat transfer from the compressed air and form a fuel-air mixture. Due to continued heat transfer from hot air to the fuel, the temperature reaches a value higher than its self-ignition temperature. This causes the fuel to ignite spontaneously initiating the combustion process.

8.2 FUNCTIONAL REQUIREMENTS OF AN INJECTION SYSTEM

For a proper running and good performance from the engine, the following requirements must be met by the injection system:

(i) Accurate metering of the fuel injected per cycle. This is very critical due to the fact that very small quantities of fuel being handled. Metering errors may cause drastic variation from the desired output. The quantity of the fuel metered should vary to meet changing speed and load requirements of the engine.

(ii) Timing the injection of the fuel correctly in the cycle so that maximum power is obtained ensuring fuel economy and clean burning.

(iii) Proper control of rate of injection so that the desired heat-release pattern is achieved during combustion.

(iv) Proper atomization of fuel into very fine droplets.

(v) Proper spray pattern to ensure rapid mixing of fuel and air.

(vi) Uniform distribution of fuel droplets in the combustion chamber.

(vii) To supply equal quantities of metered fuel to all cylinders in case of multi cylinder engines.

(viii) No lag during beginning and end of injection i.e., to eliminate dribbling of fuel droplets into the cylinder.

8.3 CLASSIFICATION OF INJECTION SYSTEMS

In a constant-pressure cycle or diesel engine, only air is compressed in the cylinder and then fuel is injected into the cylinder by means of a fuel-injection system. For producing the required pressure for atomizing the fuel either air or a mechanical means is used. Accordingly the injection systems can be classified as:

(i) Air injection systems

(ii) Solid injection systems

8.3.1 Air Injection System

In this system, fuel is forced into the cylinder by means of compressed air. This system is little used nowadays, because it requires a bulky multi-stage air compressor. This causes an increase in engine weight and reduces the brake power output further. One advantage that is claimed for the air injection system is good mixing of fuel with the air with resultant higher mean effective pressure. Another is the ability to utilize fuels of high viscosity which are less expensive than those used by the engines with solid injection systems. These advantages are off-set by the requirement of a multistage compressor thereby making the air-injection system obsolete.

8.3.2 Solid Injection System

In this system the liquid fuel is injected directly into the combustion chamber without the aid of compressed air. Hence, it is also called *airless mechanical injection* or *solid injection system*. Solid injection systems can be classified as:

(i) Individual pump and nozzle system

(ii) Unit injector system

(iii) Common rail system

(iv) Distributor system

All the above systems comprise mainly of the following components.

(i) fuel tank,

(ii) fuel feed pump to supply fuel from the main fuel tank to the injection system,

(iii) injection pump to meter and pressurize the fuel for injection,

(iv) governor to ensure that the amount of fuel injected is in accordance with variation in load,

(v) injector to take the fuel from the pump and distribute it in the combustion chamber by atomizing it into fine droplets,

(vi) fuel filters to prevent dust and abrasive particles from entering the pump and injectors thereby minimizing the wear and tear of the components.

A typical arrangement of various components for the solid injection system used in a CI engine is shown in Fig.8.1. Fuel from the fuel tank first enters the coarse filter from which is drawn into the plunger feed pump where the pressure is raised very slightly. Then the fuel enters the fine filter where all the dust and dirt particles are removed. From the fine filter the fuel enters the fuel pump where it is pressurized to about 200 bar and injected into the engine cylinder by means of the injector. Any spill over in the injector is returned to the fine filter. A pressure relief valve is also provided for the safety of the system. The above functions are achieved with the components listed above. The types of solid injection system described in the following sections differ only in the manner of operation and control of the components mentioned above.

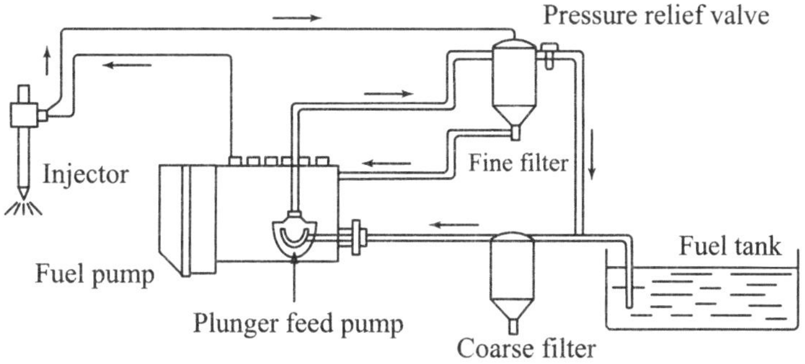

Fig. 8.1 Typical fuel feed system for a CI engine

8.3.3 Individual Pump and Nozzle System

The details of the individual pump and nozzle system are shown in Fig.8.2(a) and (b). In this system, each cylinder is provided with one pump and one injector. In this arrangement a separate metering and compression pump is provided for each cylinder. The pump may be placed close to the cylinder as shown in Fig.8.2(a) or they may be arranged in a cluster as shown in

Fig.8.2(b). The high pressure pump plunger is actuated by a cam, and produces the fuel pressure necessary to open the injector valve at the correct time. The amount of fuel injected depends on the effective stroke of the plunger.

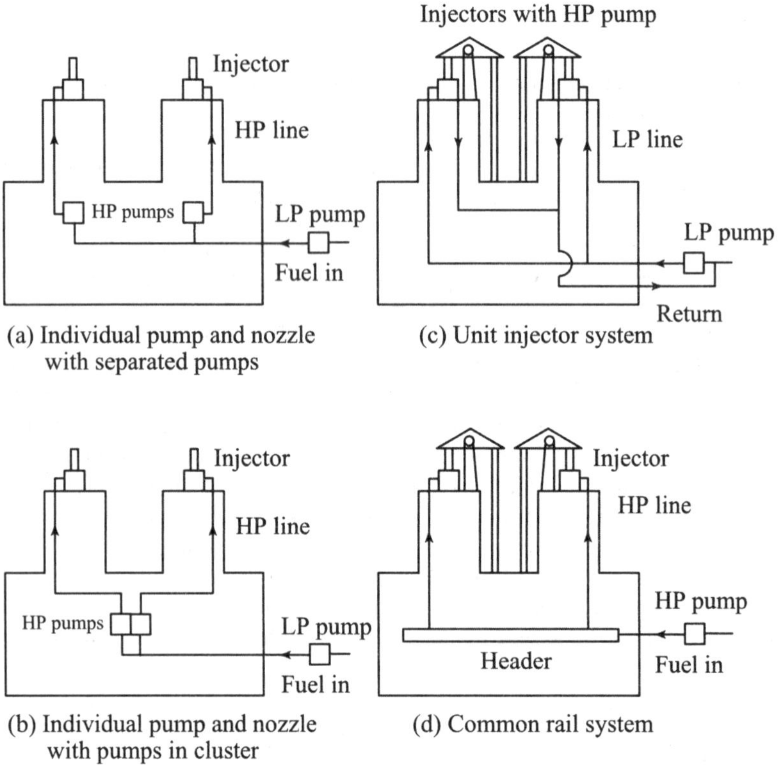

Fig. 8.2 Injection systems with pump and nozzle arrangements used in CI engines

8.3.4 Unit Injector System

The unit injector system, Fig.8.2(c), is one in which the pump and the injector nozzle are combined in one housing. Each cylinder is provided with one of these unit injectors. Fuel is brought up to the injector by a low pressure pump, where at the proper time, a rocker arm actuates the plunger and thus injects the fuel into the cylinder. The amount of fuel injected is regulated by the effective stroke of the plunger. The pump and the injector can be integrated in one unit as shown in Fig.8.2(c).

8.3.5 Common Rail System

In the common rail system, Fig.8.2(d), a HP pump supplies fuel, under high pressure, to a fuel header. High pressure in the header forces the fuel to each of the nozzles located in the cylinders. At the proper time, a mechanically

Table 8.1 Comparison of Various Fuel-Injection Systems

Job	Air injection system	Solid injection system		
		Individual pump	Common rail	Distributor
Metering	Pump	Pump	Injection valve	Pump
Timing	Fuel cam	Pump cam	Fuel cam	Fuel cam
Injection rate	Spray valve	Pump cam	Spray valve	Fuel cam
Atomization	Spray valve	Spray tip	Spray tip	Spray tip
Distribution	Spray valve	Spray tip	Spray tip	Spray tip

operated (by means of a push rod and rocker arm) valve allows the fuel to enter the proper cylinder through the nozzle. The pressure in the fuel header must be that, for which the injector system was designed, i.e., it must enable to penetrate and disperse the fuel in the combustion chamber. The amount of fuel entering the cylinder is regulated by varying the length of the push rod stroke. A high pressure pump is used for supplying fuel to a header, from where the fuel is metered by injectors (assigned one per cylinder). The details of the system are illustrated in Fig.8.2(d).

8.3.6 Distributor System

Figure 8.3 shows a schematic diagram of a distributor system. In this system the pump which pressurizes the fuel also meters and times it. The fuel pump after metering the required amount of fuel supplies it to a rotating distributor at the correct time for supply to each cylinder. The number of injection strokes per cycle for the pump is equal to the number of cylinders. The details of the system are given in Fig.8.3. Since there is one metering element in each pump, a uniform distribution is automatically ensured. Not only that, the cost of the fuel-injection system also reduces to a value less than two-thirds of that for individual pump system. A comparison of various fuel-injection systems is given in Table 8.1.

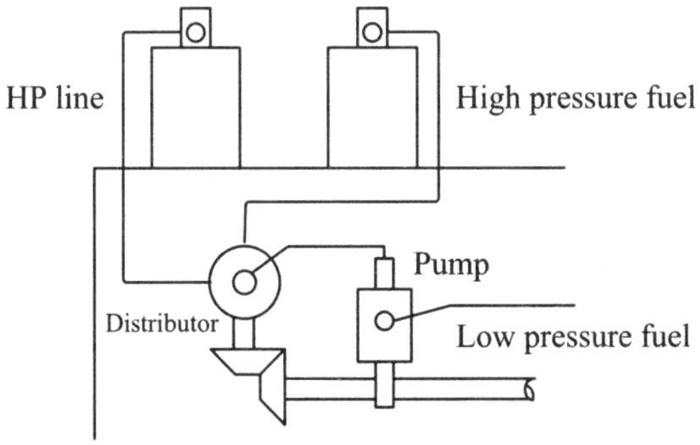

Fig. 8.3 Schematic diagram of distributor system

8.4 FUEL FEED PUMP

A schematic sketch of fuel feed pump is shown in Fig.8.4. It is of spring loaded plunger type. The plunger is actuated through a push rod from the cam shaft. At the minimum lift position of the cam the spring force on the plunger creates

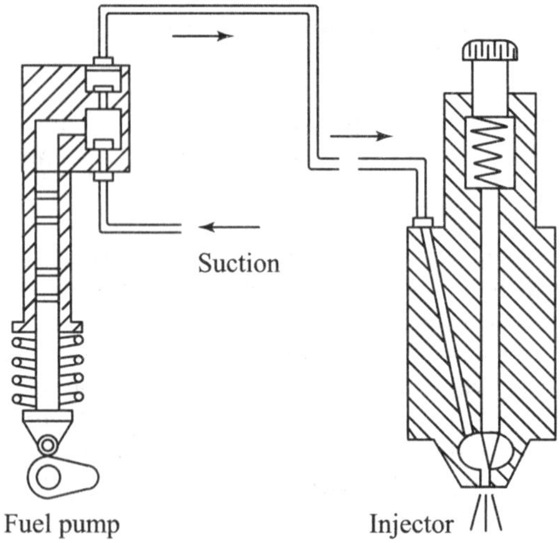

Fig. 8.4 Schematic diagram of fuel feed pump

a suction which causes fuel flow from the main tank into the pump. When the cam is turned to its maximum lift position, the plunger is lifted upwards. At the same time the inlet valve is closed and the fuel is forced through the outlet valve. When the operating pressure gets released, the plunger return spring ceases to function resulting in varying of the pumping stroke under varying engine loads according to the quantity of fuel required by the injection pump.

8.5 INJECTION PUMP

The main objectives of fuel-injection pump is to deliver accurately metered quantity of fuel under high pressure (in the range from 120 to 200 bar) at the correct instant to the injector fitted on each cylinder. Injection pumps are of two types, viz. (i) Jerk type pumps (ii) Distributor type pumps

8.5.1 Jerk Type Pump

It consists of a reciprocating plunger inside a barrel. The plunger is driven by a camshaft. The working principle of jerk pump is illustrated in Fig.8.5.

(a) A sketch of a typical plunger is shown.

(b) A schematic diagram of the plunger within the barrel is shown. Near the port A, fuel is always available under relatively low pressure. While the axial movement of the plunger is through cam shaft, its rotational

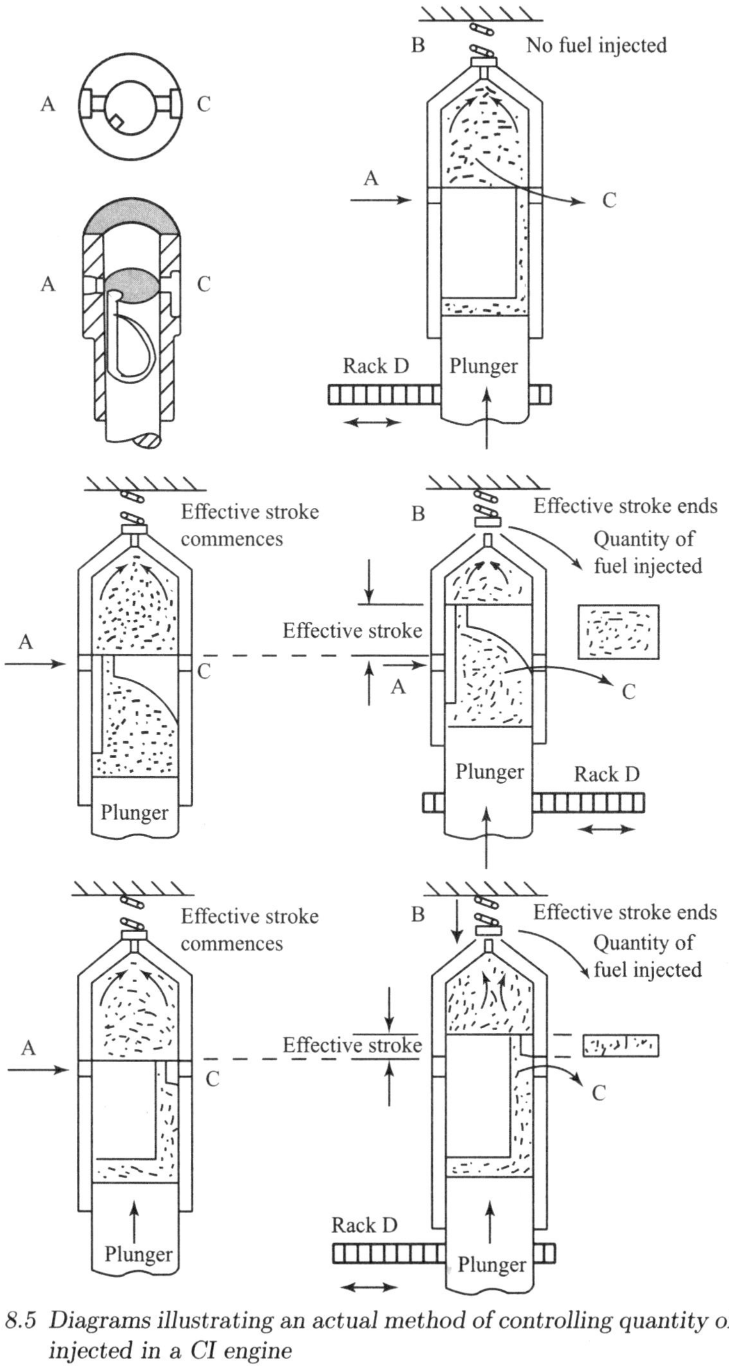

Fig. 8.5 Diagrams illustrating an actual method of controlling quantity of fuel injected in a CI engine

movement about its axis by means of rack D. Port B is the orifice through which fuel is delivered to the injector. At this stage it is closed by means of a spring loaded check valve.

When the plunger is below port A, the fuel gets filled in the barrel above it. As the plunger rises and closes the port A the fuel will flow out through port C. This is because it has to overcome the spring force of the check valve in order to flow through port B. Hence it takes the easier way out via port C.

(c) At this stage rack rotates the plunger and as a result port C also closes. The only escape route for the fuel is past the check valve through orifice B to the injector. This is the beginning of injection and also the effective stroke of the plunger.

(d) The injection continues till the helical indentation on the plunger uncovers port C. Now the fuel will take the easy way out through C and the check valve will close the orifice B. The fuel-injection stops and the effective stroke ends. Hence the effective stroke of the plunger is the axial distance traversed between the time port A is closed off and the time port A is uncovered.

(e) & (f) The plunger is rotated to the position shown. The same sequence of events occur. But in this case port C is uncovered sooner. Hence the effective stroke is shortened.

It is important to remember here that though the axial distance traversed by the plunger is same for every stroke, the rotation of the plunger by the rack determining the length of the effective stroke and thus the quantity of fuel injected. A typical example of this type of pump is the Bosch fuel-injection pump shown in Fig.8.6.

8.5.2 Distributor Type Pump

This pump has only a single pumping element and the fuel is distributed to each cylinder by means of a rotor (Fig.8.7). There is a central longitudinal passage in the rotor and also two sets of radial holes (each equal to the number of engine cylinders) located at different heights. One set is connected to pump inlet via central passage whereas the second set is connected to delivery lines leading to injectors of the various cylinders. The fuel is drawn into the central rotor passage from the inlet port when the pump plunger move away from each other. Wherever, the radial delivery passage in the rotor coincides with the delivery port for any cylinder the fuel is delivered to each cylinder in turn. Main advantages of this type of pump lies in its small size and its light weight. A schematic diagram of Roosa Master distributor pump is shown in Fig.8.8.

8.6 INJECTION PUMP GOVERNOR

In a CI Engine the fuel delivered is independent of the injection pump characteristic and the air intake. Fuel delivered by a pump increases with speed whereas the opposite is true about the air intake. This results in over fueling

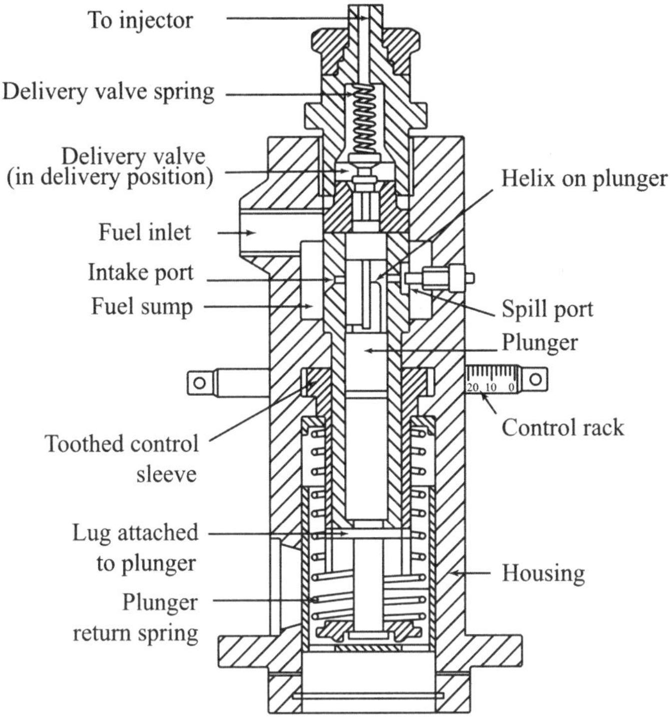

Fig. 8.6 Single cylinder jerk pump type fuel-injection system

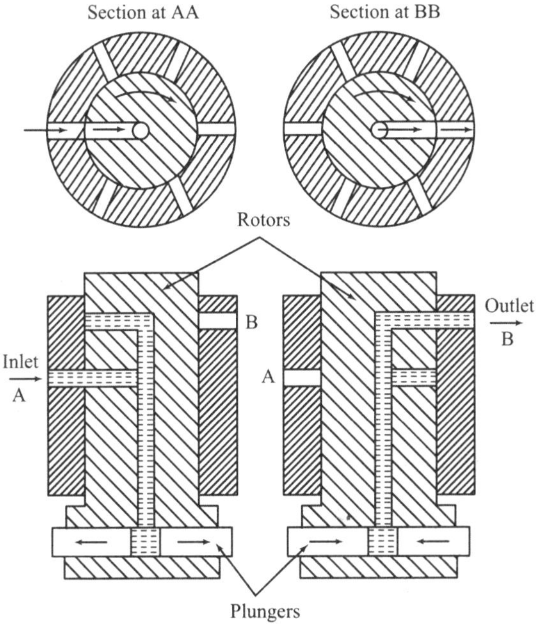

Fig. 8.7 Principle of working of distributor type fuel-injection pump

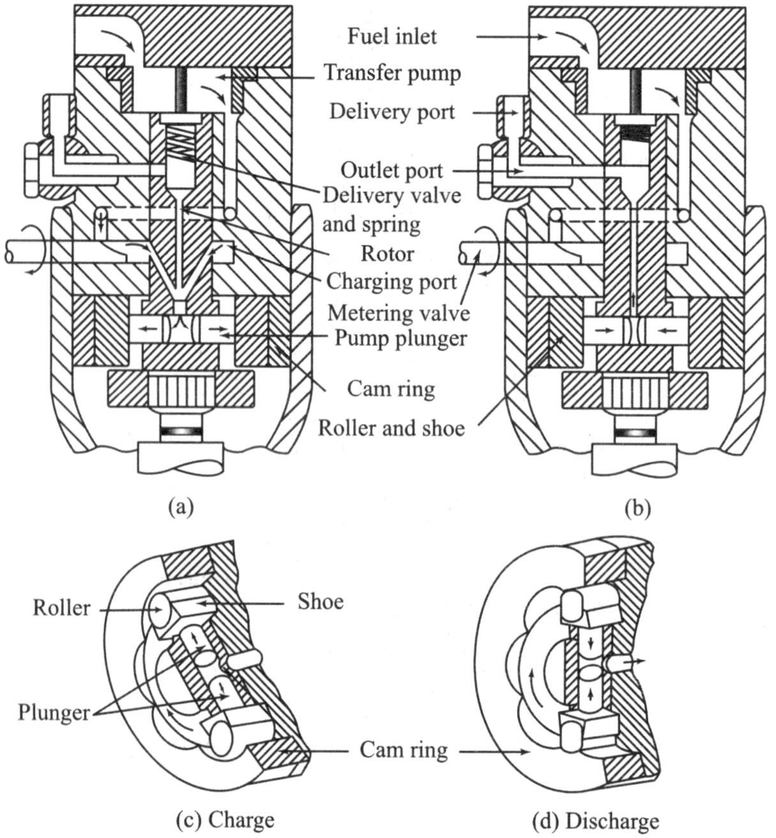

Fig. 8.8 Schematic of Roosa Master distributor pump

at higher speeds, and at idling speeds (low speeds) the engine tends to stall due to insufficiency of fuel.

Quantity of fuel delivered increases with load causing excessive carbon deposits and high exhaust temperature. Drastic reduction in load will cause over speeding to dangerous values. It is the duty of an injection pump governor to take care of the above limitations. Governors are generally of two types,

(i) mechanical governor, and

(ii) pneumatic governor.

8.7 MECHANICAL GOVERNOR

The working principle of mechanical governor is illustrated in Fig.8.9. When the engine speed tends to exceed the limit the weights fly apart. This causes the bell crank levers to raise the sleeve and operate the control lever in downward direction. This actuates the control rack on the fuel-injection pump in a direction which reduces the amount of fuel delivered. Lesser fuel causes the engine speed to decrease. The reverse happens when engine speed tends to decrease.

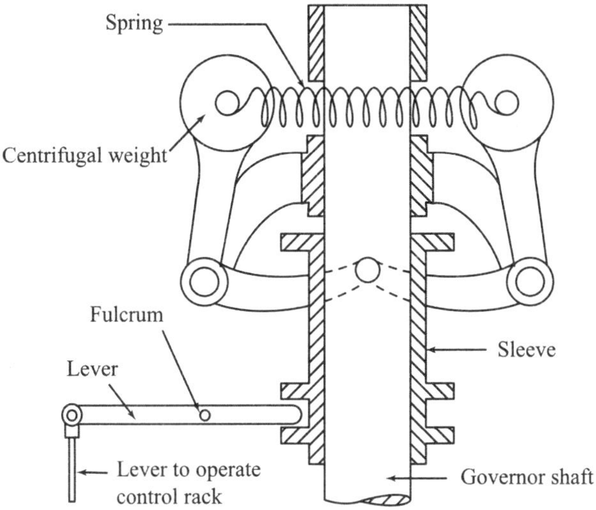

Fig. 8.9 Principle of mechanical governor

8.8 PNEUMATIC GOVERNOR

The details of a pneumatic governor is shown in Fig.8.10. The amount of vacuum applied to the diaphragm is controlled by the accelerator pedal through the position of the butterfly valve in the venturi unit. A diaphragm is connected to the fuel pump control rack. Therefore, position of the accelerator pedal also determines the position of the pump control rack and hence the amount of fuel injected.

8.9 FUEL INJECTOR

Quick and complete combustion is ensured by a well designed fuel injector. By atomizing the fuel into very fine droplets, it increases the surface area of the fuel droplets resulting in better mixing and subsequent combustion. Atomization is done by forcing the fuel through a small orifice under high pressure. The injector assembly consists of

(i) a needle valve

(ii) a compression spring

(iii) a nozzle

(iv) an injector body

A cross sectional view of a typical Bosch fuel injector is shown in Fig.8.11. When the fuel is supplied by the injection pump it exerts sufficient force

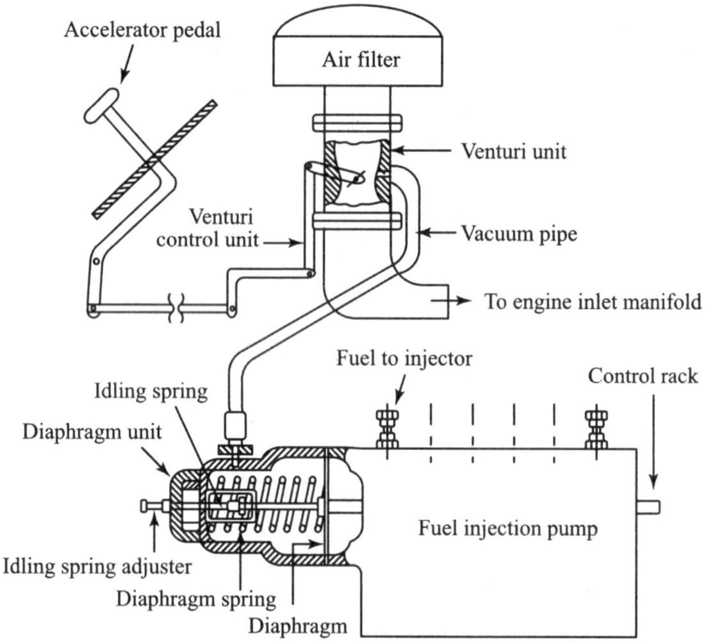

Fig. 8.10 Principle of pneumatic governor

against the spring to lift the nozzle valve, fuel is sprayed into the combustion chamber in a finely atomized particles. After, fuel from the delivery pump gets exhausted, the spring pressure pushes the nozzle valve back on its seat. For proper lubrication between nozzle valve and its guide a small quantity of fuel is allowed to leak through the clearance between them and then drained back to fuel tank through leak off connection. The spring tension and hence the valve opening pressure is controlled by adjusting the screw provided at the top.

8.10 NOZZLE

Nozzle is that part of an injector through which the liquid fuel is sprayed into the combustion chamber.

The nozzle should fulfill the following functions:

(i) *Atomization* : This is a very important function since it is the first phase in obtaining proper mixing of the fuel and air in the combustion chamber.

(ii) *Distribution of fuel* : Distribution of fuel to the required areas within the combustion chamber. Factors affecting this are:

(a) *Injection pressure* : Higher the injection pressure better the dispersion and penetration of the fuel into all the desired locations in combustion chamber.

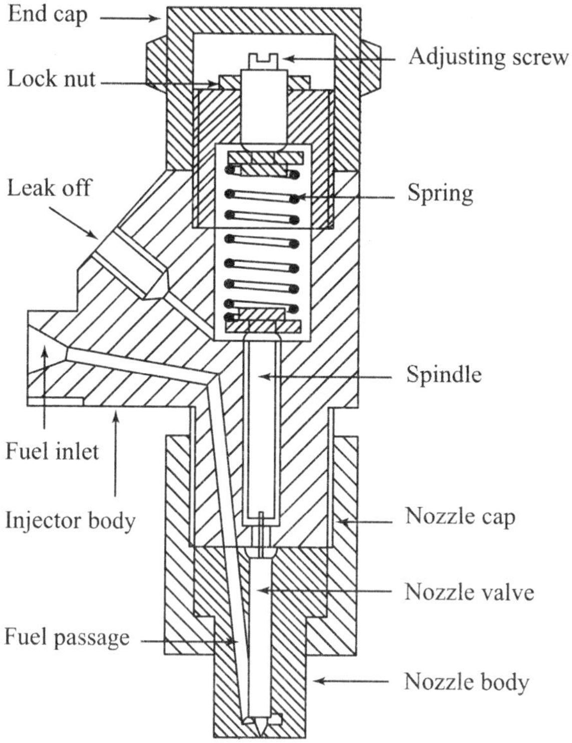

Fig. 8.11 Fuel injector (Bosch)

(b) *Density of air in the cylinder* : If the density of compressed air in the combustion chamber is high then the resistance to the movement of the droplets is higher and dispersion of the fuel is better.

(c) *Physical properties of fuel* : The properties like self-ignition temperature, vapour pressure, viscosity, etc. play an important role in the distribution of fuel.

(iii) *Prevention of impingement on walls* : Prevention of the fuel from impinging directly on the walls of combustion chamber or piston. This is necessary because fuel striking the walls decomposes and produces carbon deposits. This causes smoky exhaust as well as increase in fuel consumption.

(iv) *Mixing* : Mixing the fuel and air in case of non-turbulent type of combustion chamber should be taken care of by the nozzle.

8.10.1 Types of Nozzle

The design of the nozzle must be such that the liquid fuel forced through the nozzle will be broken up into fine droplets, or atomized, as it passes into the combustion chamber. This is the first phase in obtaining proper mixing of the fuel and air in the combustion chamber.

The fuel must then be properly distributed, or dispersed, in the desired areas of the chamber. In this phase, the injection pressure, the density of the air in the cylinder and the physical qualities of the fuel in use, as well as the nozzle design, become important factors. Higher injection pressure results in better dispersion as well as greater penetration of the fuel into all locations in the chamber where is presence is desired. It also produces finer droplets which tend to mix more readily with the air. The greater the density of the compressed air in the combustion chamber, the greater the resistance offered to the travel of the fuel droplets across the chamber, with resultant better dispersion of the fuel. The physical qualities of the fuel itself, such as viscosity, surface tension, etc. also enter into the dispersion of the fuel.

The nozzle must spray the fuel into the chamber in such a manner as to minimize the quantity of fuel reaching the surrounding walls. Any fuel striking the walls tends to decompose, producing carbon deposits, unpleasant odour and a smoky exhaust, as well as an increase in fuel consumption.

The design of the nozzle is closely interrelated to the type of combustion chamber used. It is sufficient to state here that the *turbulent* type of combustion chamber depends upon chamber turbulence to produce the required mixing of the fuel and air. The *non-turbulent* type of combustion chamber, on the other hand, depends almost entirely on both the nozzle design and injection pressure to secure the desired *mixing* in the combustion chamber; consequently, with this type of chamber, the nozzle must accomplish the additional function of *mixing* the fuel and air.

Various types of nozzles are used in CI engines. These types are shown in Fig.8.12. The most common types are:

(i)	the pintle nozzle,	(ii)	the single hole nozzle
(iii)	the multi-hole nozzle,	(iv)	pintaux nozzle

(i) *Pintle Nozzle :* The stem of the nozzle valve is extended to form a pin or pintle which protrudes through the mouth of the nozzle [Fig.8.12(a)]. The size and shape of the pintle can be varied according to the requirement. It provides a spray operating at low injection pressures of 8-10 MPa. The spray cone angle is generally 60°. Advantage of this nozzle is that it avoids weak injection and dribbling. It prevents the carbon deposition on the nozzle hole.

(ii) *Single Hole Nozzle :* At the centre of the nozzle body there is a single hole which is closed by the nozzle valve [Fig.8.12(b)]. The size of the hole is usually of the order of 0.2 mm. Injection pressure is of order of 8-10 MPa and spray cone angle is about 15°. Major disadvantage with such nozzle is that they tend to dribble. Besides, their spray angle is too narrow to facilitate good mixing unless higher velocities are used.

(iii) *Multi-hole Nozzle :* It consists of a number of holes bored in the tip of the nozzle [Fig.8.12(c)]. The number of holes varies from 4 to 18 and the size from 35 to 200 μm. The hole angle may be from 20° upwards. These nozzles operate at high injection pressures of the order of 18 MPa. Their advantage lies in the ability to distribute the fuel properly even with lower air motion available in open combustion chambers.

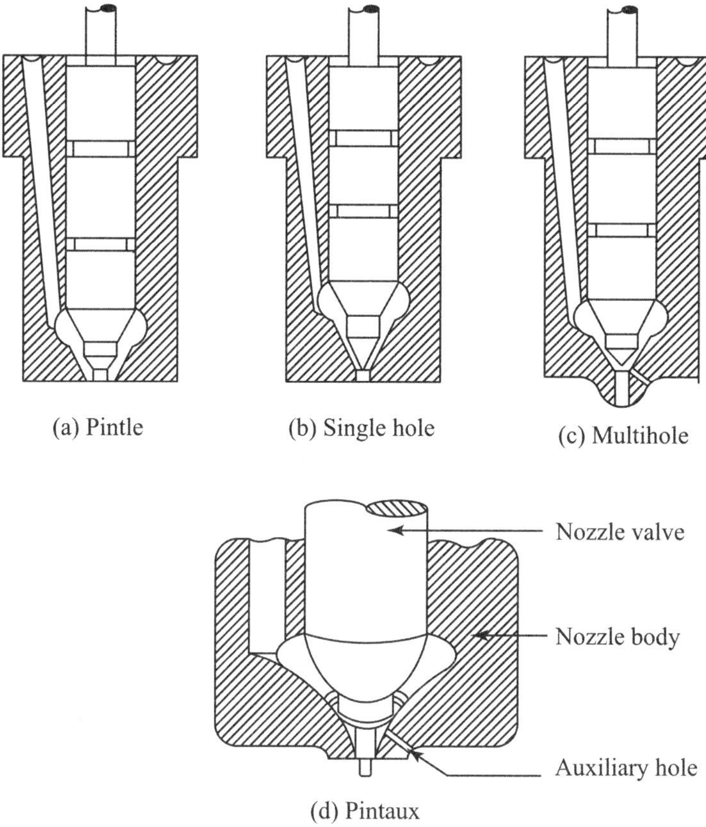

Fig. 8.12 Types of nozzles

(iv) *Pintaux Nozzle :* It is a type of pintle nozzle which has an auxiliary hole drilled in the nozzle body [Fig.8.12(d)]. It injects a small amount of fuel through this additional hole which is called pilot injection in the upstream direction slightly before the main injection. The needle valve does not lift fully at low speeds and most of the fuel is injected through the auxiliary hole. Main advantage of this nozzle is better cold starting performance. (20 to 25 °C lower than multi hole design). A major drawback of this nozzle is that its injection characteristics are poorer than the multihole nozzle.

8.10.2 Spray Formation

The various phases of spray formation as the fuel is injected through the nozzle are shown in Fig.8.13. At the start of the fuel-injection the pressure difference across the orifice is low. Therefore single droplets are formed as in Fig.8.13(a). As the pressure difference increases the following process occur one after the other.

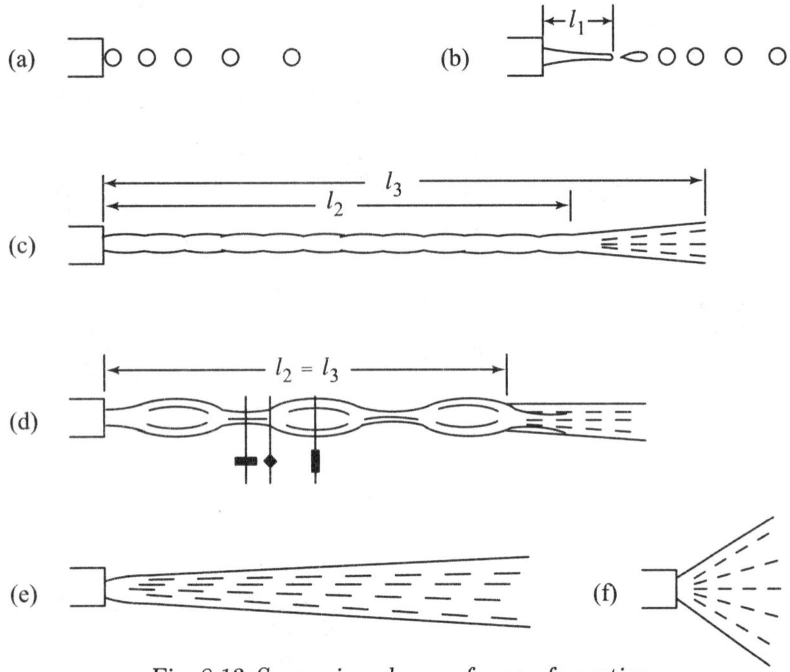

Fig. 8.13 Successive phases of spray formation

(i) A stream of fuel emerges from the nozzle, [Fig.8.13(b)].

(ii) The stream encounters aerodynamic resistance from the dense air present in the combustion chamber (12 to 14 times the ambient pressure) and breaks into a spray, say at a distance of l_3, [Fig.8.13(c)]. The distance of this point where this event occurs from the orifice is called the *break-up distance.*

(iii) With further and further increase in the pressure difference, the break-up distance decreases and the cone angle increases until the apex of the cone practically coincides with the orifice [Fig.8.13(d), (e) and (f)].

At the exit of the orifice the fuel jet velocity, V_f, is of the order of 400 m/s. It is given by the following equation

$$V_f = C_d\sqrt{\frac{2\,(p_{inj} - p_{cyl})}{\rho_f}}$$

where C_d = coefficient of discharge for the orifice
p_{inj} = fuel pressure at the inlet to injector, N/m^2
p_{cyl} = pressure of charge inside the cylinder, N/m^2
ρ_f = fuel density, kg/m^3

The spray from a circular orifice has a denser and compact core, surrounded by a cone of fuel droplets of various sizes and vaporized liquid. Larger droplets provide a higher penetration into the chamber but smaller droplets are required for quick mixing and evaporation of the fuel. The diameter of most of the droplets in a fuel spray is less than 5 microns. The droplet sizes depends on various factors which are listed below:

(i) Mean droplet size decreases with increase in injection pressure.

(ii) Mean droplet size decreases with increase in air density.

(iii) Mean droplet size increases with increase in fuel viscosity.

(iv) Size of droplets increases with increase in the size of the orifice.

8.10.3 Quantity of Fuel and the Size of Nozzle Orifice

The quantity of the fuel injected per cycle depends to a great extent upon the power output of the engine. As already mentioned the fuel is supplied into the combustion chamber through the nozzle holes and the velocity of the fuel for good atomization is of the order of 400 m/s. The velocity of the fuel through nozzle orifice in terms of h can be given by

$$V_f = C_d\sqrt{2gh}$$

where h is the pressure difference between injection and cylinder pressure, measured in m of fuel column.

The volume of the fuel injected per second, Q, is given by

$$\begin{aligned} Q = {} & \text{Area of all orifices} \times \text{fuel jet velocity} \times \\ & \text{time of one injection} \times \text{number of injections} \\ & \text{per second for one orifice} \end{aligned}$$

$$Q = \left(\frac{\pi}{4}d^2 \times n\right) \times V_f \times \left(\frac{\theta}{360} \times \frac{60}{N}\right) \times \left(\frac{N_i}{60}\right)$$

where N_i for four-stroke engine is rpm/2 and for a two-stroke engine N_i is rpm itself and d is the diameter of one orifice in m, n is the number of orifices, θ is the duration of injection in crank angle degrees and N_i is the number of injections per minute. Usually the rate of fuel-injection is expressed in mm^3/degree crank angle/litre cylinder displacement volume to normalize the effect of engine size.

The rate of fuel injected/degree of crankshaft rotation is a function of injector camshaft velocity, the diameter of the injector plunger, and flow area of the tip orifices. Increasing the rate of injection decreases the duration of injection for a given fuel input and subsequently introduces a change in injection timing. A higher rate of injection may permit injection timing to be retarded from optimum value. This helps in maintaining fuel economy without excessive smoke emission. However, an increase in injection rate requires an increased injection pressure and increases the load on the injector push rod and the cam. This may affect the durability of the engine.

8.11 INJECTION IN SI ENGINE

Fuel-injection systems are commonly used in CI engines. Presently gasoline injection system is coming into vogue in SI engines because of the following drawbacks of the carburetion.

(i) Non uniform distribution of mixture in multicylinder engines.

(ii) Loss of volumetric efficiency due to restrictions for the mixture flow and the possibility of back firing.

A gasoline injection system eliminates all these drawbacks. The injection of fuel into an SI engine can be done by employing any of the following methods which are shown in Fig.8.14.

(a) direct injection of fuel into the cylinder

(b) injection of fuel close to the inlet valve

(c) injection of fuel into the inlet manifold

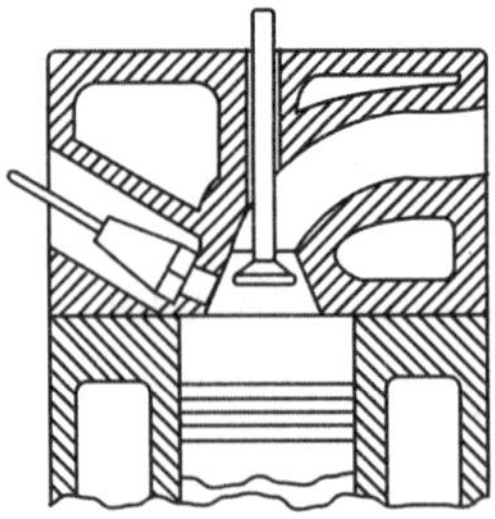

(a) Direct injection into the cylinder

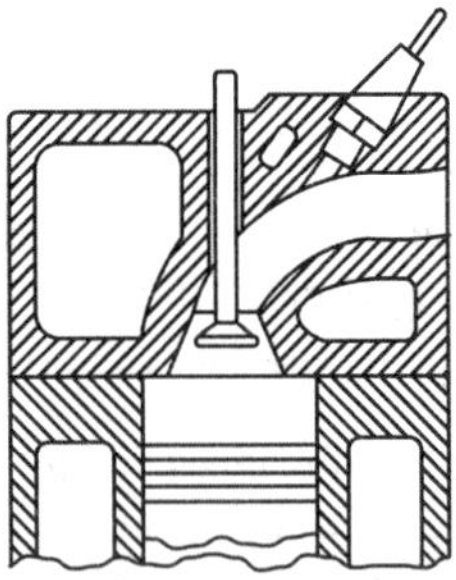

(b) Injection upstream of inlet valve

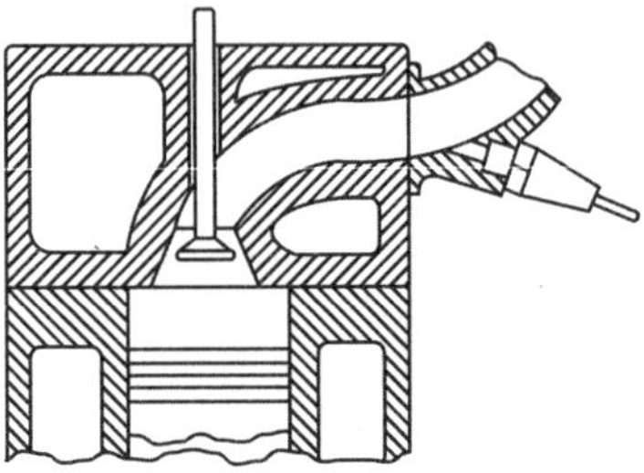

(c) Injection into the inlet manifold

Fig. 8.14 Location of injection nozzle

There are two types of gasoline injection systems, viz.,

(i) *Continuous Injection :* Fuel is continuously injected. It is adopted when manifold injection is contemplated.

(ii) *Timed Injection :* Fuel is injected only during induction stroke over a limited period. Injection timing is not a critical factor in SI engines.

Major advantages of fuel-injection in an SI engine are:

(i) Increased volumetric efficiency

(ii) Better thermal efficiency

(iii) Lower exhaust emissions

(iv) High quality fuel distribution

The use of petrol injection is limited by its high initial cost, complex design and increased maintenance requirements. It is believed that the petrol injection has a promising future compared to carburetion and may replace carburetor in the near future.

Worked out Examples

8.1 A six cylinder, four-stroke diesel engine develops 125 kW at 3000 rpm. Its brake specific fuel consumption is 200 gm/kW h. Calculate the quantity of fuel to be injected per cycle per cylinder. Specific gravity of the fuel may be taken as 0.85.

Solution

$$\textit{Fuel consumed/hour} = bsfc \times \textit{Power output}$$

$$= 200 \times 10^{-3} \times 125 = 25 \text{ kg}$$

$$\textit{Fuel consumption/cylinder} = \frac{25}{6} = 4.17 \text{ kg/h}$$

$$\textit{Fuel consumption/cycle} = \frac{\textit{Fuel consumption/minute}}{n}$$

where $n = N/2$ for four-stroke cycle engines

$$= \frac{4.17/60}{3000/2} = 4.63 \times 10^{-5} \text{ kg}$$

$$= 0.0463 \text{ gm}$$

$$\textit{Volume of fuel injected} = \frac{0.0463}{0.85}$$

$$= \mathbf{0.0545\ cc/cycle}$$

Ans ⟸

8.2 Calculate the diameter of the fuel orifice of a four-stroke engine which develops 25 kW per cylinder at 2500 rpm. The specific fuel consumption is 0.3 kg/kW h fuel with 30°API. The fuel is injected at a pressure of 150 bar over a crank travel of 25°. The pressure in the combustion chamber is 40 bar. Coefficient of velocity is 0.875 and specific gravity is given by

$$S.G. = \frac{141.5}{131.5 + {}^{\circ}API}$$

Solution

$$\text{Duration of injection} = \frac{25}{360 \times 2500/60} = 1.667 \times 10^{-3} \text{ s}$$

$$S.G. = \frac{141.5}{131.5 + 30^{\circ}} = 0.8762$$

$$\text{Velocity of injection}, V_{inj} = C_d \sqrt{\frac{2(p_{inj} - p_{cyl})}{\rho_f}}$$

$$= 0.875 \times \sqrt{\frac{2 \times (150 - 40) \times 10^5}{876.2}}$$

$$= 138.65 \text{ m/s}$$

$$\text{Vol. of fuel injected/cycle} = \frac{(bsfc/60) \times output}{(rpm/2) \times \rho_{fuel}}$$

$$= \frac{(0.3/60) \times 25}{(2500/2) \times 876.2}$$

$$= 0.114 \times 10^{-6} \text{ m}^3/\text{cycle}$$

$$\text{Nozzle orifice area}, A_f = \frac{\text{Volume of fuel injected/cycle}}{\text{Inj. velocity} \times \text{Inj. time}}$$

$$= \frac{0.114 \times 10^{-6}}{138.65 \times 1.667 \times 10^{-3}}$$

$$= 0.4932 \times 10^{-6} \text{ m}^2$$

$$\text{Area of the orifice} = \frac{\pi}{4} \times d^2 = 0.4932 \times 10^{-6}$$

$$d = \sqrt{\frac{4 \times 0.4932 \times 10^{-6}}{\pi}}$$

$$= 0.792 \times 10^{-3} \text{ m} = \mathbf{0.792 \text{ mm}}$$ Ans ⟸

8.3 A four-cylinder, four-stroke diesel engine develops a power of 180 kW at 1500 rpm. The $bsfc$ is 0.2 kg/kW h. At the beginning of injection pressure is 30 bar and the maximum cylinder pressure is 50 bar. The injection is expected to be at 200 bar and maximum pressure at the injector is set to be about 500 bar. Assuming the following:

C_d for injector	=	0.7
S.G. of fuel	=	0.875
Atmospheric pressure	=	1 bar
Effective pressure difference	=	Average pressure difference over the injection period

Determine the total orifice area required per injector if the injection takes place over 15° crank angles.

Solution

$$\text{Power output/cylinder} = \frac{180}{4} = 45 \text{ kW}$$

$$\text{Fuel consumption/cylinder} = 45 \times bsfc$$

$$= 45 \times 0.2 = 9 \text{ kg/h}$$

$$= 0.15 \text{ kg/min}$$

$$\text{Fuel injected/cycle} = \frac{0.15}{(rpm/2)} = \frac{0.15}{(1500/2)}$$

$$= 2 \times 10^{-4} \text{ kg}$$

$$\text{Time for injection} = \frac{\theta}{360 \times rpm/60}$$

$$= \frac{15 \times 60}{360 \times 1500}$$

$$= 1.667 \times 10^{-3} \text{ s}$$

$$\text{Pressure difference at beginning} = 200 - 30 = 170 \text{ bar}$$

$$\text{Pressure difference at end} = 500 - 50 = 450 \text{ bar}$$

$$\text{Average pressure difference} = \frac{450 + 170}{2} = 310 \text{ bar}$$

$$\text{Velocity of injection}, V_{inj} = C_d \sqrt{\frac{2(p_{inj} - p_{cyl})}{\rho_f}}$$

$$= 0.7 \times \sqrt{\frac{2 \times 310 \times 10^5}{875}}$$

$$= 186.33 \text{ m/s}$$

$$\text{Volume of fuel injected/cycle} = \frac{2 \times 10^{-4}}{875}$$

$$= 0.2286 \times 10^{-6} \text{ m}^3/\text{cycle}$$

$$A_f = \frac{0.2286 \times 10^{-6}}{186.33 \times 1.667 \times 10^{-3}}$$

$$= \mathbf{0.736 \times 10^{-6} \text{ m}^2} \quad \stackrel{\text{Ans}}{\Longleftarrow}$$

8.4 A closed type injector has a nozzle orifice diameter of 0.949 mm and the maximum cross sectional area of the passage between the needle cone and the seat is 1.75 mm^2. The discharge coefficient for the orifice is 0.85 and for the passage is 0.80. The injection pressure is 175 bar and the average pressure of charge during injection is 25 bar, when the needle cone is fully lifted up. Calculate the volume rate of flow per second of fuel through the injector and the velocity of jet at that instant. Density of fuel is 850 kg/m^3.

Solution

$$p_{inj} - p = \frac{\dot{V}_f^2 \times \rho_f}{2 \times 10^5} \frac{1}{(C_d A)^2} \text{ bar}$$

Now we have two equations

$$175 - p = \frac{\dot{V}_f^2 \times 850}{2 \times 10^5} \times \frac{1}{(0.8 \times 1.75 \times 10^{-6})^2} \text{ bar}$$

$$= 2.1684 \times 10^9 \times \dot{V}_f^2 \qquad (1)$$

$$p - 25 = \frac{V_f^2 \times 850}{2 \times 10^5} \times \frac{1}{(0.85 \times 0.7854 \times 0.949^2 \times 10^{-6})^2}$$

$$= 12.6261 \times 10^9 \times \dot{V}_f^2 \text{ bar} \qquad (2)$$

Adding (1) and (2), we get

$$150 = \dot{V}_f^2 \times (2.1684 + 12.6261) \times 10^9$$

$$= 14.7945 \times 10^9 \times V_f^2$$

$$\dot{V}_f = \sqrt{\frac{150}{14.7945 \times 10^9}} = 1.007 \times 10^{-4} \text{ m}^3/\text{s}$$

$$= \mathbf{100.7\ cc/s} \qquad \text{Ans}$$

Now, from Eq.1,

$$p = 175 - 2.1684 \times 10^9 \times (1.007 \times 10^{-4})^2$$

$$= 153.01 \text{ bar}$$

Velocity of fuel through orifice

$$= \sqrt{\frac{2 \times (153.01 - 25)}{850} \times 10^5}$$

$$= \mathbf{173.55\ m/s} \qquad \text{Ans}$$

8.5 At injection pressure of 150 bar a spray penetration of 25 cm in 20 milliseconds is obtained. If an injection pressure of 250 bar had been used, what would have been the time taken to penetrate the same distance. Assume the same orifice and combustion chamber density. The combustion chamber pressure is 25 bar.

Use the relation

$$S \quad \propto \quad t\sqrt{\Delta p}$$

where S is penetration in cm
t is time in millisecond
Δp is the pressure difference between injection pressure and combustion chamber pressure

Solution

$$\frac{S_1}{S_2} = \frac{t_1\sqrt{\Delta p_1}}{t_2\sqrt{\Delta p_2}}$$

$$\Delta p_1 = p_{inj,1} - p_{cyl} = 150 - 25$$

$$\Delta p_2 = p_{inj,2} - p_{cyl} = 250 - 25$$

$$t_2 = \frac{S_2}{S_1} t_1 \frac{\sqrt{\Delta p_1}}{\sqrt{\Delta p_2}}$$

$$= 1 \times 20 \times \sqrt{\frac{125}{225}} = \mathbf{14.91\ ms}$$ Ans ⟸

8.6 A six cylinder diesel engine produces 100 kW at 1500 rpm. The specific fuel consumption of the engine is 0.3 kg/kW h. Each cylinder has a separate fuel pump, injector and pipe line. At the beginning of effective plunger stroke of one fuel pump, the fuel in the pump barrel is 4 cc, fuel inside the injector is 2 cc and fuel in the pipe line is 3 cc. If the average injector pressure is 300 bar and average pressure of charge during injection is 40 bar, calculate the displacement volume of one plunger per cycle and power lost in pumping fuel to the engine (for all cylinders). Specific gravity of fuel is 0.9 and the fuel enter the pump barrel at 1 bar. Coefficient of compressibility of fuel may be taken as 80×10^{-6} per bar.

Solution

$$\textit{Fuel consumed} = \frac{100}{6} \times 0.3 \times \frac{1}{3600}$$

$$= 1.3888 \times 10^{-3}\ \text{kg/s}$$

$$\dot{V}_f = \frac{1.3888 \times 10^{-3}}{\left(\frac{1500}{2\times 60}\right)} \times \frac{1}{0.9 \times 10^3}$$

$$= 0.12345 \times 10^{-6} \text{ m}^3/\text{s}$$

$$= 0.12345 \text{ cc/s}$$

Coefficient of compressibility is defined as

$$K_{comp} = \frac{\textit{Change in volume/unit volume}}{\textit{Difference in pressure causing the compression}}$$

$$= \frac{(V_1 - V_2)/V_1}{(p_2 - p_1)}$$

Here,

$$K_{comp} = 80 \times 10^{-6} \textit{ per bar}$$

$$V_1 = \textit{Fuel in pump barrel} + \textit{Fuel inside the injector} + \textit{Fuel in pipe line}$$

$$= 4 + 2 + 3 = 9 \textit{ cc}$$

$$V_1 - V_2 = K_{comp} \times V_1 \times (p_2 - p_1)$$

$$= 80 \times 10^{-6} \times 9 \times (300 - 1) = 0.21528 \textit{ cc}$$

Plunger/displacement volume

$$= 0.12345 + 0.21528$$

$$= \mathbf{0.339 \text{ cc}}$$ Ans

$$\text{Pump work, } W_P = \frac{1}{2}(p_{inj} - p_\circ)(V_1 - V_2) + (p_{inj} - p_{cyl})V_f$$

$$= \frac{1}{2}(300 - 1) \times 10^5 \times 0.2153 \times 10^{-6} + (300 - 40) \times 10^5 \times 0.12345 \times 10^{-6}$$

$$= 3.22 + 3.21$$

$$= 6.43 \; J$$

Power lost for pumping the fuel

$$= \frac{6.43}{1000} \times \frac{1500}{2 \times 60}$$

$$= \mathbf{0.08 \text{ kW}}$$ Ans

8.7 Before commencement of the effective stroke, fuel in the pump barrel of a diesel fuel injection system is 6 cc. The diameter and the length of the fuel line from pump to injector is 2.5 mm and 600 mm respectively. The fuel in the injection valve is 2 cc.

(i) To deliver 0.10 cc of fuel at a pressure of 150 bar, how much displacement the plunger undergoes. Assume a pump inlet pressure of 1 bar.

(ii) What is the effective stroke of the plunger if its diameter is 7 mm.

Assume coefficient of compressibility of oil as 75×10^{-6} per bar at atmospheric pressure.

Solution

$$K = \frac{(V_1 - V_2)}{V_1(p_2 - p_1)}$$

Change in volume due to compression,

$$\begin{aligned} V_1 &= \textit{Total initial fuel volume} \\ &= \textit{Volume of fuel in barrel} + \\ &\quad \textit{Volume of fuel in delivery line} + \\ &\quad \textit{Volume of fuel in injection valve} \\ &= 6 + \frac{\pi}{4} \times (0.25)^2 \times \frac{600}{10} + 2 = 10.95 \text{ cc} \end{aligned}$$

$$\begin{aligned} V_1 - V_2 &= K \times V_1 \times (p_2 - p_1) \\ &= 75 \times 10^{-6} \times 10.95 \times (150 - 1) = 0.122 \text{ cc} \end{aligned}$$

Total displacement of plunger

$$\begin{aligned} &= (V_1 - V_2) + 0.10 = 0.122 + 0.10 \\ &= \mathbf{0.222\ cc} \qquad \text{Ans} \Leftarrow \end{aligned}$$

$$\frac{\pi}{4} d^2 \times l = 0.222$$

Effective stroke of plunger

$$\begin{aligned} &= 0.222 \times \frac{4}{\pi} \times \frac{1}{(0.7)^2} \\ &= 0.577 \text{ cm} \\ &= \mathbf{5.77\ mm} \qquad \text{Ans} \Leftarrow \end{aligned}$$

Review Questions

8.1 What are the functional requirements of an injection system?

8.2 How are the injection system classified? Describe them briefly. Why the air injection system is not used nowadays?

8.3 How is the solid injection further classified? With a neat sketch explain the various components of a fuel feed system of a CI engine.

8.4 Explain

(i) individual pump and nozzle system

(ii) unit injector system

(iii) common rail system

(iv) distributor system.

8.5 Draw a schematic diagram of fuel feed pump and explain its working principle.

8.6 What are the main functions of an injection pump? What are two types of injection pump that are commonly used?

8.7 With a neat sketch explain the jerk pump type injection system.

8.8 With a neat sketch explain the working principle of a distributor type fuel-injection pump.

8.9 What is the purpose of using a governor in CI engines? What are the two major type of governors?

8.10 Explain with a neat sketch the working principle of a mechanical governor.

8.11 With a neat diagram bring out clearly the working principle of a pneumatic governor.

8.12 What is the purpose of a fuel injector? Mention the various parts of a injector assembly.

8.13 What are the functions of a nozzle? With sketches explain the various types of nozzles.

8.14 Give a brief account of the injection in SI engine.

8.15 With sketches explain the possible locations of the injection nozzles in SI engines.

8.16 Draw a sketch of pintaux nozzle and discuss it merits and demerits.

8.17 Derive an expression for the velocity of injection.

8.18 Develop an equation for the amount of fuel injected per cycle in terms of brake horse power and speed of a four-stroke CI engine.

Exercise

8.1 A four-cylinder, four-stroke diesel engine develops 100 kW at 3500 rpm. Its brake specific fuel consumption is 180 gm per kW h. Calculate the quantity of fuel to be injected per cycle per cylinder. Specific gravity of the fuel may be taken as 0.88.

Ans: Volume of the fuel injected = 0.0487 cc

8.2 Calculate the diameter of the fuel orifice of a four-stroke engine which develops 20 kW per cylinder at 2000 rpm. The specific fuel consumption is 0.25 kg/kW h of fuel with 30°API. The fuel is injected at a pressure of 180 bar over a crank travel of 25°. The pressure in the combustion chamber is 38 bar. Coefficient of velocity is 0.85 and specific gravity is given by

$$S.G. \quad = \quad \frac{141.5}{131.5 + {}^\circ API}$$

Ans: Diameter of fuel orifice = 0.754 mm

8.3 A six-cylinder, four-stroke diesel engine develops a power of 200 kW at 2000 rpm. The $bsfc$ is 0.2 kg/kW h. At the beginning of injection, pressure is 35 bar and the maximum cylinder pressure is 55 bar. The injection is expected to be at 180 bar and maximum pressure at the injector is set to be about 520 bar. Assuming the following:

C_d for injector	=	0.75
S.G. of fuel	=	0.85
Atmospheric pressure	=	1 bar
Effective pressure difference	=	Average pressure difference over the injection period

(i) Determine the total orifice area required per injector if the injection takes place over 16° crank angles.

Ans: Orifice area = 0.4876×10^{-6} m^2

8.4 A closed type injector has a nozzle orifice diameter of 1.0 mm and the maximum cross sectional area of the passage between the needle cone and the seat is 2.0 mm^2. The discharge coefficient for the orifice is 0.85 and for the passage is 0.80. The injection pressure is 200 bar and the average pressure of charge during injection is 25 bar, when the needle cone is fully lifted up. Calculate the volume rate of flow per second of fuel through the injector and the velocity of jet at that instant. Specific gravity of fuel is 0.85. *Ans:* (i) Volume rate of flow of fuel = 125 cc/s
(ii) Velocity of jet = 187.27 m/s

8.5 At injection pressure of 180 bar a spray penetration of 30 cm in 22 milliseconds is obtained. If an injection pressure of 240 bar had been used, what would have been the time taken to penetrate the same distance. Assume the same orifice and combustion chamber density. The combustion chamber pressure is 30 bar. Use the relation:

$$S \quad \propto \quad t\sqrt{\Delta p}$$

where S is penetration in cm
t is time in millisecond
Δp is the pressure difference between injection pressure and combustion chamber pressure

Ans: (i) Time taken for penetration = 18.593 milliseconds

8.6 A four-cylinder diesel engine produces 100 kW at 1500 rpm. The specific fuel consumption of the engine is 0.28 kg/kW h. Each cylinder has a separate fuel pump, injector and pipe line. At the beginning of effective plunger stroke of one fuel pump, the fuel in the pump barrel is 4 cc, fuel inside the injector is 2 cc and fuel in the pipe line is 4 cc. If the average injector pressure is 200 bar and average pressure of charge during injection is 30 bar, calculate the displacement volume of one plunger per cycle and power lost in pumping fuel to the engine (for all cylinders). Specific gravity of fuel is 0.85 and the fuel enter the pump barrel at 1 bar. Coefficient of compressibility of fuel is 80×10^{-6} per bar.

Ans: (i) Disp. volume of each plunger/cycle = 0.3422 cc
(ii) Power lost in pumping = 0.058 kW

8.7 Before commencement of the effective stroke the fuel in the pump barrel of a diesel fuel injection pump is 7 cc. The diameter of the fuel line from pump to injector is 3 mm and is 600 mm long. The fuel in the injection valve is 3 cc.

(i) To deliver 0.10 cc of fuel at a pressure of 150 bar, how much displacement the plunger undergoes? Assume a pump inlet pressure of 1 bar.

(ii) What is the effective stroke of the plunger if its diameter is 6 mm?

(iii) Assume coefficient of compressibility of oil as 78×10^{-6} at atmospheric pressure.

Ans: (i) Plunger displacement = 0.2655 cc
(ii) Effective stroke of plunger = 9.39 mm

Multiple Choice Questions (choose the most appropriate answer)

1. Fuel injector is used for

   (a) gas engines
   (b) CI engines
   (c) SI engines
   (d) none of the above

2. Advantage of air injection system is

   (a) cheaper fuels can be used
   (b) mep is high

(c) fine atomization and distribution of the fuel
(d) all of the above

3. Commonly used injection system in automobiles is

(a) air injection
(b) solid injection
(c) combination of (a) and (b)
(d) none of the above

4. Fuel injection pressure in solid injection system is around

(a) <10 bar
(b) 10–20 bar
(c) 30–50 bar
(d) 200–250 bar

5. Fuel filters do not use generally

(a) oil
(b) paper
(c) cloth
(d) felt

6. Fuel is injected in a four-stroke CI engine

(a) at the end of suction stroke
(b) at the end of expansion stroke
(c) at the end of compression stroke
(d) at the end of exhaust stroke

7. Injection system in which the pump and the injector nozzle is combined in one housing is known as

(a) common rail system
(b) distributor system
(c) unit injector system
(d) individual pump and nozzle system

8. Main advantage of pintaux nozzle is

(a) better cold starting performance
(b) ability to distribute the fuel

(c) good penetration
(d) good atomization

9. The most accurate gasoline injection system is

(a) direct injection
(b) port injection
(c) throttle body injection
(d) manifold injection

10. Advantage of fuel injection in SI engine is

(a) low initial cost
(b) low maintenance requirements
(c) increased volumetric efficiency
(d) none of the above

Ans: 1. – (b) 2. – (d) 3. – (b) 4. – (d) 5. – (b)
6. – (c) 7. – (c) 8. – (a) 9. – (b) 10. – (c)

9

ELECTRONIC INJECTION SYSTEMS

9.1 INTRODUCTION

The year 1903 is a memorable year in the history of IC engine development. It is in that year the Wright Brothers made the maiden SI engine powered flight which had a gear pump that injected fuel into the intake ports. Soon after, in 1906 the Brazilian Santos Dumont made his first flight in Europe with plunger pump. The famous Grade Enddecker who in 1909 flew 13 kilometers, also did it with injection in gasoline engine: a two-stroke engine in which each cylinder's crankcase pressure was utilized as injection pressure for the fuel. Therefore, the injection system for gasoline engines is not a new proposition.

In case of automotive engines a continuous metered quantity of the gasoline-air mixture must be ensured to make the engine run smoothly. In a gasoline injection system, the fuel is injected into the intake manifold or near the intake port through an injector. The gasoline is received by the injector from the pump and is sprayed into the air stream in a finely atomized form. Compared to carburetion the mixing of gasoline with the air stream is better in this case.

It may be observed that in both the carburettor and the gasoline injection system, the position of the throttle valve controls the flow of the mixture into the intake manifold. Nowadays, gasoline injection is employed in a number of automobiles. Well established manufacturers like Ford, Daewoo, Fiat, Mitsubishi, Honda etc. have come out with gasoline injection system in their models.

9.2 WHY GASOLINE INJECTION?

In a carburettor engine, uniformity of mixture strength is difficult to realize in each cylinder of a multicylinder engine. Figure 9.1 shows a typical pattern of mixture distribution in an intake manifold of a multicylinder engine. As may be noticed that the intake valve is open in cylinder 2. As can also be observed the gasoline moves to the end of the manifold and accumulates there. This enriches the mixture going to the end cylinders. However, the central cylinders, which are very close to the carburettor, get the leanest mixture. Thus the various cylinders receive the air-gasoline mixture in varying quantities and richness. This problem is called the maldistribution and can be solved by the port injection system by having the same amount of gasoline injected at each intake manifold. Therefore, there is an urgent need to develop injection systems for gasoline engines. By adopting gasoline injection each cylinder can get the same richness of the air-gasoline mixture and the maldistribution can be avoided to a great extent.

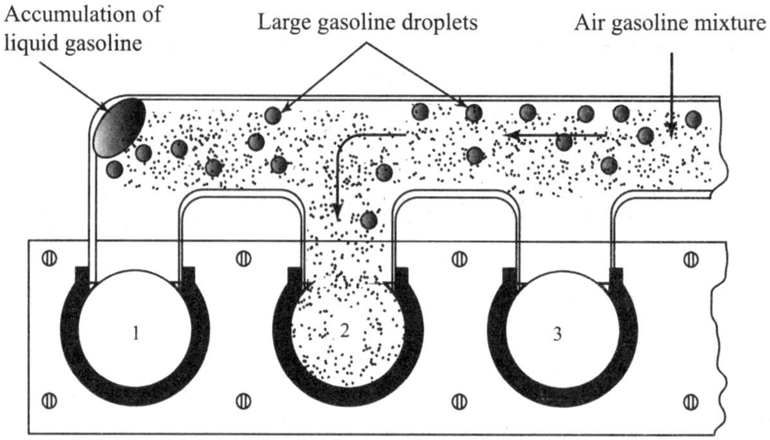

Fig. 9.1 Typical pattern of mixture distribution in a multi-cylinder engine

As already mentioned, some of the recent automotive engines are equipped with gasoline injection system, instead of a carburetion for one or more of the following reasons:

(i) To have uniform distribution of fuel in a multicylinder engine.

(ii) To improve breathing capacity i.e. volumetric efficiency.

(iii) To reduce or eliminate detonation.

(iv) To prevent fuel loss during scavenging in case of two-stroke engines.

9.2.1 Types of Injection Systems

The fuel injection system can be classified as:

(i) Gasoline direct injection into the cylinder (GDI)

(ii) Port injection

(a) Timed, and (b) Continuous

(iii) Manifold injection

The above fuel injection systems can be grouped under two heads, viz., single-point and multi-point injection. In the single point injection system, one or two injectors are mounted inside the throttle body assembly. Fuel sprays are directed at one point or at the center of the intake manifold. Another name of the single point injection is throttle body injection. Multipoint injection has one injector for each engine cylinder. In this system, fuel is injected in more than one location. This is more common and is often called port injection system.

As already mentioned the gasoline fuel injection system used in a spark-ignition engine can be either of continuous injection or timed injection.

(i) *Continuous injection systems:* This system usually has a rotary pump. The pump maintains a fuel line gauge pressure of about 0.75 to 1.5 bar. The system injects the fuel through a nozzle located in the manifold immediately downstream of the throttle plate. In a supercharged engine, fuel is injected at the entrance of the supercharger. The timing and duration of the fuel injection is determined by Electronic Control Unit (ECU) depending upon the load and speed.

(ii) *Timed fuel injection system:* This system has a fuel supply pump which sends fuel at a low pressure of about 2 bar when the engine is running at maximum speed. A fuel metering or injection pump and a nozzle are the other parts of the system. The nozzle injects the fuel in the manifold or the cylinder head port at about 6.5 bar or into the combustion chamber at pressures that range from 16 to 35 bar. Timed injection system injects fuel usually during the early part of the suction stroke. During maximum power operation injection begins after the closure of the exhaust valve and ends usually after BDC. Direct in-cylinder injection is superior and always desirable and better compared to manifold injection. In this case both low and high volatile fuels can be used and higher volumetric efficiencies can be achieved. However, it was noticed that direct injection caused oil dilution in the frequent warm up phases if the car is used for daily transportation.

Typical fuel injection methods used in four stroke and two stroke gasoline engines are shown in Fig.9.2(a) and Fig.9.2(b) respectively .

9.2.2 Components of Injection System

The objectives of the fuel injection system are to meter, atomize and uniformly distribute the fuel throughout the air mass in the cylinder. At the same time it must maintain the required air-fuel ratio as per the load and speed requirement of the engine. To achieve all the above tasks, a number of components are required in the fuel injection system, the functions of which are mentioned below.

(i) *Pumping element* – moves the fuel from the fuel tank to the injector. This includes necessary piping, filter etc.

(ii) *Metering element* – measures and supplies the fuel at the rate demanded by load and speed conditions of the engine.

(iii) *Mixing element* – atomizes the fuel and mixes it with air to form a homogenous mixture.

(iv) *Metering control* – adjusts the rate of metering in accordance with load and speed of the engine.

(v) *Mixture control* – adjusts fuel-air ratio as demanded by the load and speed.

(vi) *Distributing element* – divides the metered fuel equally among the cylinders.

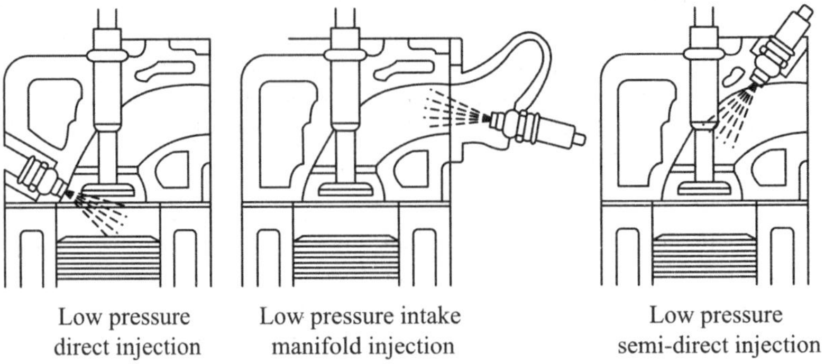

(a) Gasoline injection in four-stroke engines

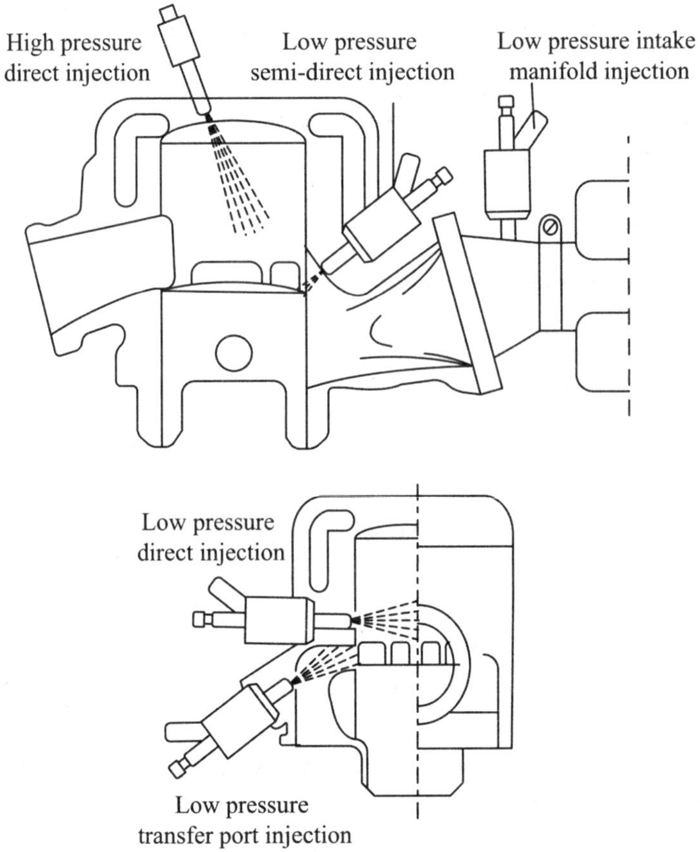

(b) Fuel injection in two-stroke engines

Fig. 9.2 Different methods of fuel injection

(vii) *Timing control* – fixes the start and stop of the fuel-air mixing process.

(viii) *Ambient control* – compensates for changes in temperature and pressure of either air or fuel that may affect the various elements of the system.

9.3 ELECTRONIC FUEL INJECTION SYSTEM

Modern gasoline injection systems use engine sensors, a computer, and solenoid operated fuel injectors to meter and inject the right amount of fuel into the engine cylinders. These systems called electronic fuel injection (EFI) use electrical and electronic devices to monitor and control engine-operation.

An electronic control unit (ECU) or the computer receives electrical signals in the form of current or voltage from various sensors. It then uses the stored data to operate the injectors, ignition system and other engine related devices. As a result, less unburned fuel leaves the engine as emissions, and the vehicle gives better mileage. Typical sensors for an electronic fuel injection system includes the following:

(i) *Exhaust gas or oxygen sensor* – senses the amount of oxygen in the engine exhaust and calculates air-fuel ratio. Sensor output voltage changes in proportion to air-fuel ratio.

(ii) *Engine temperature sensor* – senses the temperature of the engine coolant, and from this data the computer adjusts the mixture strength to rich side for cold starting.

(iii) *Air flow sensor* – monitors mass or volume of air flowing into the intake manifold for adjusting the quantity of fuel.

(iv) *Air inlet temperature sensor* – checks the temperature of the ambient air entering the engine for fine tuning the mixture strength.

(v) *Throttle position sensor* – senses the movement of the throttle plate so that the mixture flow can be adjusted for engine speed and acceleration.

(vi) *Manifold pressure sensor* – monitors vacuum in the engine intake manifold so that the mixture strength can be adjusted with changes in engine load.

(vii) *Camshaft position sensor* – senses rotation of engine camshaft/crankshaft for speed and timing of injection.

(viii) *Knock sensor* – microphone type sensor that detects ping or preignition noise so that the ignition timing can be retarded.

The fuel injector in an EFI is nothing but a fuel valve. When it is not energized, spring pressure makes the injector to remain closed and no fuel will enter the engine. When the computer sends the signal through the injector coil, the magnetic field attracts the injector armature. Fuel then spurts into the intake manifold.

The injector pulse width is an indication of the period for which each injector is energized and kept open. The computer decides and controls the injector pulse width based on the signals received from the various sensors.

Under full load, the computer will sense a wide open throttle, high intake manifold pressure, and high inlet air flow. The ECU will then increase the injector pulse width to enrich the mixture which will enable the engine to produce higher power.

Under low load and idling conditions, the ECU will shorten the pulse width by which the injectors are kept in the closed position over a longer period of time. Because of this, air-fuel mixture will become leaner and will result in better fuel economy.

Electronic fuel injection system has a cold start injector too. This is an extra injector that sprays fuel into the center of the engine intake manifold, when the engine is cold. It serves the same purpose as the carburettor choke. The cold start injector ensures easy engine startup in very cold weather.

9.3.1 Merits of EFI System

The spark ignition engine with an EFI system compared with a carburettor unit have the following favourable points:

(i) Improvement in the volumetric efficiency due to comparatively less resistance in the intake manifolds which will cause less pressure losses. It eliminates majority of carburettor pressure losses and almost eliminates the requirement of manifold heating.

(ii) Manifold wetting is eliminated due to the fuel being injected into or close to the cylinder and need not flow through the manifold.

(iii) Atomization of fuel is independent of cranking speed and therefore starting will be easier.

(iv) Better atomization and vapourization will make the engine less knock prone.

(v) Formation of ice on the throttle plate is eliminated.

(vi) Distribution of fuel being independent of vapourization, less volatile fuel can be used.

(vii) Variation of air-fuel ratio is almost negligible even when the vehicle takes different positions like turning, moving on gradients, uneven roads etc.

(viii) Position of the injection unit is not so critical and thereby the height of the engine (and hood) can be less.

9.3.2 Demerits of EFI System

Some of the disadvantages of EFI system are:

(i) high maintenance cost,

(ii) difficulty in servicing, and

(iii) possibility of malfunction of some sensors.

9.4 MULTI-POINT FUEL INJECTION (MPFI) SYSTEM

The main purpose of the Multi-Point Fuel Injection (MPFI) system is to supply a proper ratio of gasoline and air to the cylinders. These systems function under two basic arrangements, namely

(i) Port injection

(ii) Throttle body injection

9.4.1 Port Injection

In the port injection arrangement, the injector is placed on the side of the intake manifold near the intake port (Fig.9.3), The injector sprays gasoline into the air, inside the intake manifold. The gasoline mixes with the air in a reasonably uniform manner. This mixture of gasoline and air then passes through the intake valve and enters into the cylinder.

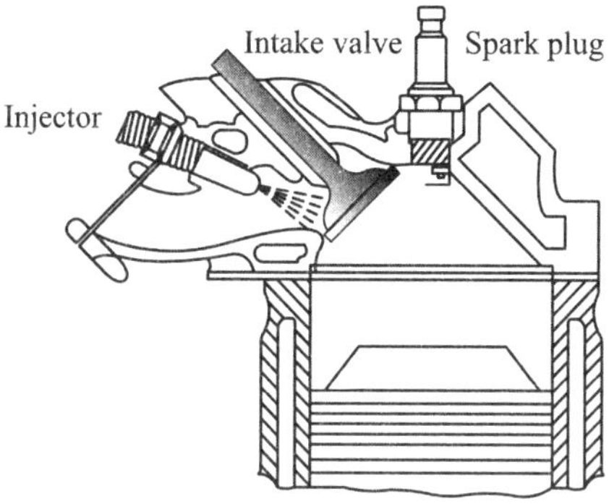

Fig. 9.3 Port injection

Every cylinder is provided with an injector in its intake manifold. If there are six cylinders, there will be six injectors. Figure 9.4 shows a simplified view of a port or multi point fuel injection (MPFI) system.

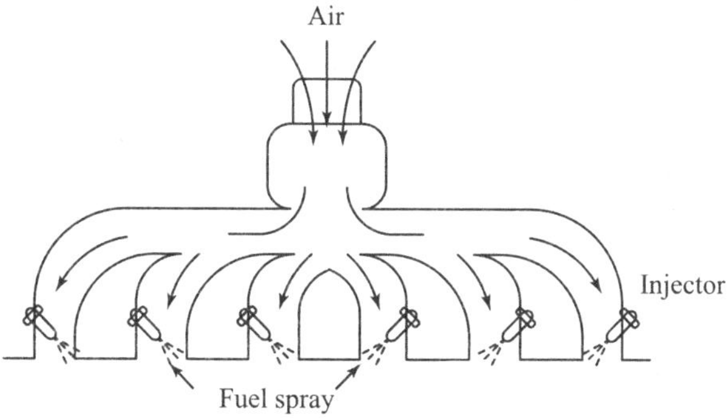

Fig. 9.4 Multi-point fuel injection (MPFI) near port

9.4.2 Throttle Body Injection System

Figure 9.5 illustrates the simplified sketch of throttle body injection system (Single point injection). This throttle body is similar to the carburettor throttle body, with the throttle valve controlling the amount of air entering the intake manifold.

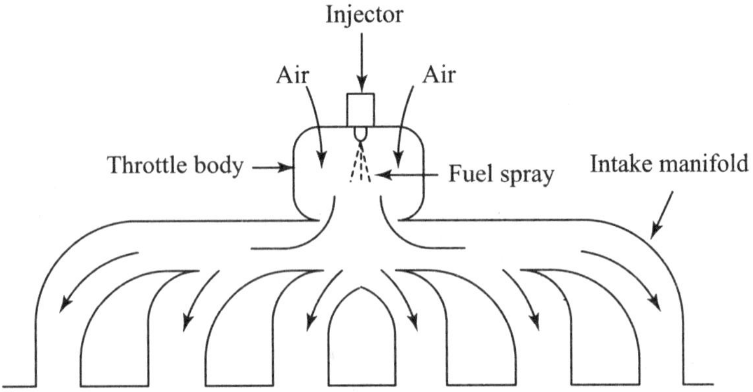

Fig. 9.5 Throttle body injection (single point)

An injector is placed slightly above the throat of the throttle body. The injector sprays gasoline into the air in the intake manifold where the gasoline mixes with air. This mixture then passes through the throttle valve and enters into the intake manifold.

As already mentioned, fuel-injection systems can be either timed or continuous. In the timed injection system, gasoline is sprayed from the injectors in pulses. In the continuous injection system, gasoline is sprayed continuously from the injectors. The port injection system and the throttle-body injection system may be either pulsed systems or continuous systems. In both systems, the amount of gasoline injected depends upon the engine speed and power demands. In some literature MPFI systems are classified into two types: D-MPFI and L-MPFI.

9.4.3 D-MPFI System

The D-MPFI system is the manifold fuel injection system. In this type, the vacuum in the intake manifold is first sensed. In addition, it senses the volume of air by its density. Figure 9.6 gives the block diagram regarding the functioning of the D-MPFI system. As air enters into the intake manifold, the manifold pressure sensor detects the intake manifold vacuum and sends the information to the ECU. The speed sensor also sends information about the rpm of the engine to the ECU. The ECU in turn sends commands to the injector to regulate the amount of gasoline supply for injection. When the injector sprays fuel in the intake manifold the gasoline mixes with the air and the mixture enters the cylinder.

9.4.4 L-MPFI System

The L-MPFI system is a port fuel-injection system. In this type the fuel metering is regulated by the engine speed and the amount of air that actually enters the engine. This is called *air-mass metering* or *air-flow metering.* The block diagram of an L-MPFI system is shown in Fig.9.7. As air enters into the intake manifold, the air flow sensor measures the amount of air and sends information to the ECU. Similarly, the speed sensor sends information about the speed of the engine to the ECU. The ECU processes the information received and sends appropriate commands to the injector, in order to regulate the amount of gasoline supply for injection. When injection takes place, the gasoline mixes with the air and the mixture enters the cylinder.

9.5 FUNCTIONAL DIVISIONS OF MPFI SYSTEM

The MPFI system can be functionally divided into

(i) electronic control system,

(ii) fuel system, and

(iii) air induction system.

These functional divisions are described in the following sections.

9.5.1 MPFI-Electronic Control System

The MPFI-electronic control system is shown in the form of block diagram in Fig.9.8. The sensors that monitor intake air temperature, the oxygen, the water temperature, the starter signal and the throttle position send signals to the ECU. The air-flow sensor sends signals to the ECU regarding the intake air volume. The ignition sensor sends information about the engine speed.

The ECU processes all these signals and sends appropriate commands to the injectors, to control the volume of the fuel for injection. When necessary the cold-start injector timing switch off the ECU operates the cold start injector which is a part of the fuel system.

9.5.2 MPFI-Fuel System

The MPFI-fuel system is shown in the form of block diagrams in Fig.9.9. In this system, fuel is supplied by the fuel pump. At the time of starting, the cold start injector is operated by the cold start injector time switch. The cold start injector injects fuel into the air intake chamber, thus enriching the air-fuel mixture. The pressure regulator regulates the pressure of the fuel. The injectors receive signals from the ECU and inject the fuel into the intake manifold.

9.5.3 MPFI-Air Induction System

The MPFI-air induction system is shown in the block diagram in Fig.9.10. The air cleaner, the air-flow meter, the throttle body and the air valve supply a proper amount of air to the air intake chamber and intake manifold. The quantity of air supplied is just what is necessary for complete combustion.

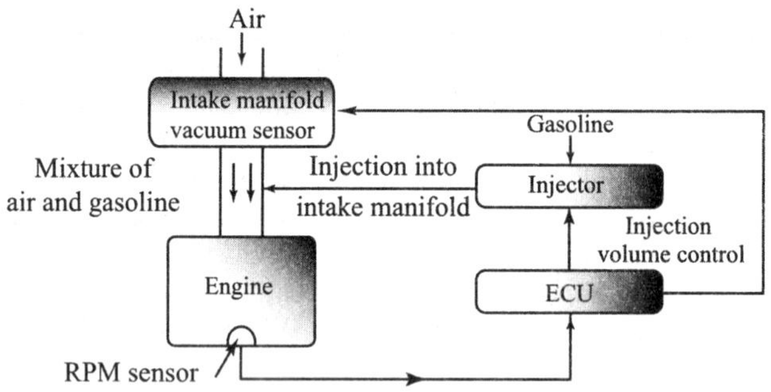

Fig. 9.6 D-MPFI gasoline injection system

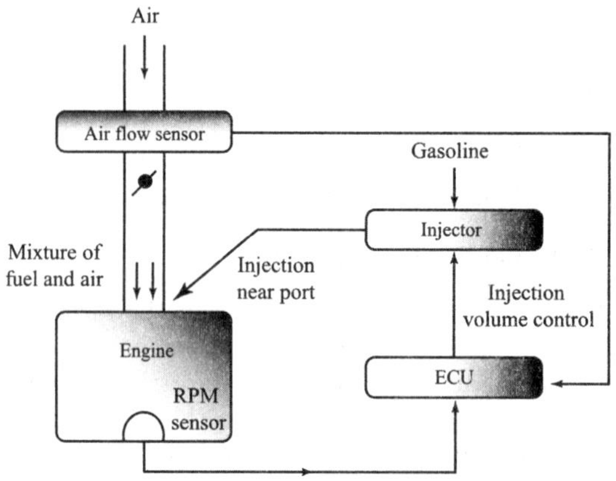

Fig. 9.7 L-MPFI gasoline injection system

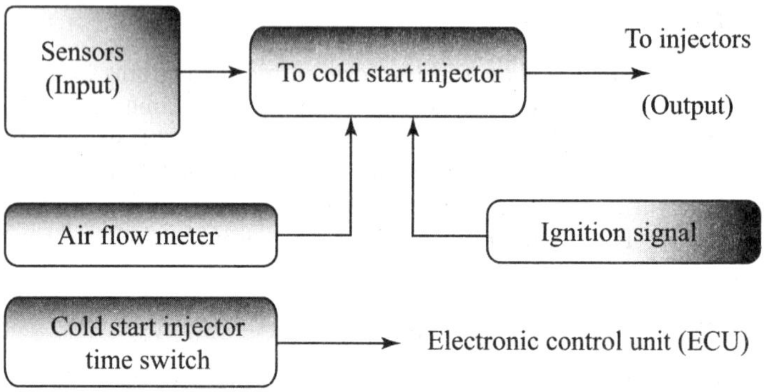

Fig. 9.8 MPFI-electronic control system

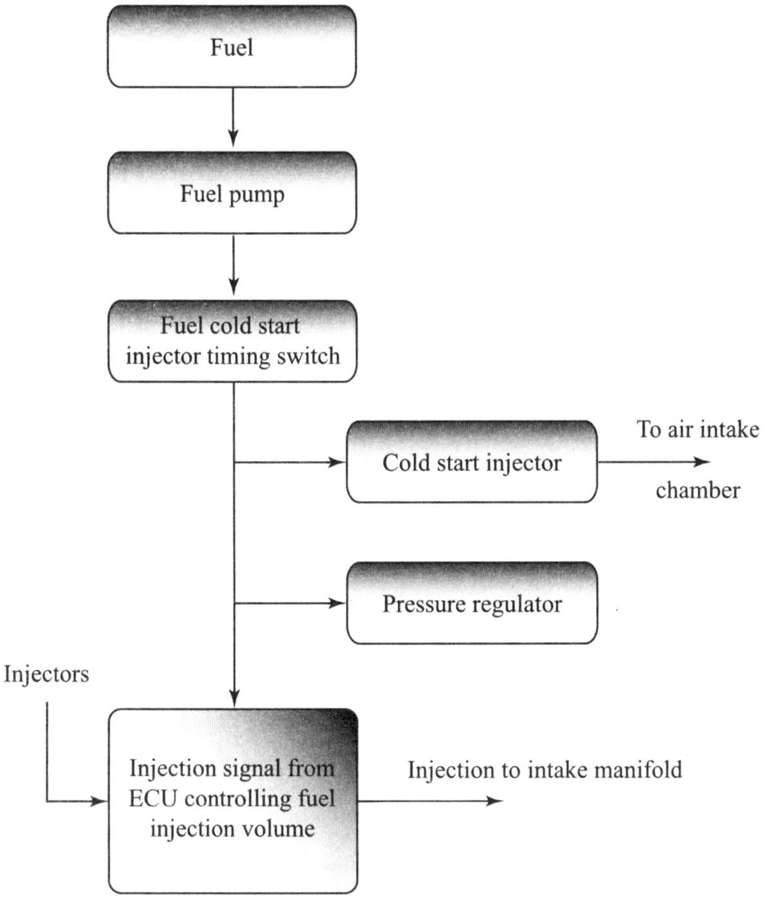

Fig. 9.9 MPFI-fuel system

9.6 ELECTRONIC CONTROL SYSTEM

The electronic control system consists of mainly the Electronic Control Unit (ECU), which determines the duration of operation of the injectors. In addition to this, there is a starter timing switch, which controls the operation of the cold start injector during engine starting. There is a circuit opening relay to control fuel pump operation. There is also a resistor, which stabilizes the injector operation.

9.6.1 Electronic Control Unit (ECU)

The ECU in the electronic control system, receives signals from the sensors and determines the opening time for the injector's land which also controls the injection volume.

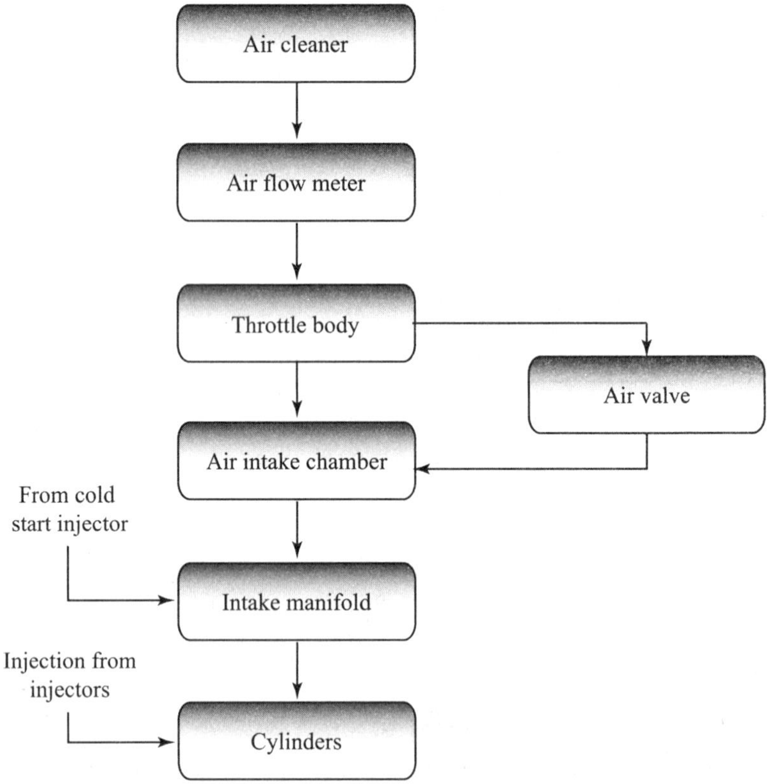

Fig. 9.10 MPFI-air induction system

9.6.2 Cold Start Injector

When the engine is cold, the starting of the engine is usually not easy. When a cold engine is started, it requires a richer mixture. The cold start injector serves the purpose of supplying more fuel at the time of starting. In Fig.9.11, the cold start injector, the main injector and the air valve are shown. The cold start injector is a type of solenoid valve to which power is supplied from a battery for the opening and closing of the valve inside, thus for injecting the fuel. The fuel injected should not be excessive. Therefore the duration of injection time is controlled by a timing switch. The timing switch is composed of a bimetal element and an electric heater coil.

When the engine is cold, the starter motor cranks the engine. At this time, the cold start injector injects fuel to enrich the mixture. The main injector also injects fuel during the same time. The injection by both the injectors is shown in Fig.9.11. When the engine is hot, the cold start injector will stop injection and only the main injector will inject the fuel to the cylinder.

9.6.3 Air Valve

The position of the air valve is shown in the Fig.9.11 for the cold engine. As the temperature is low, the air valve speeds up the engine idle speed to

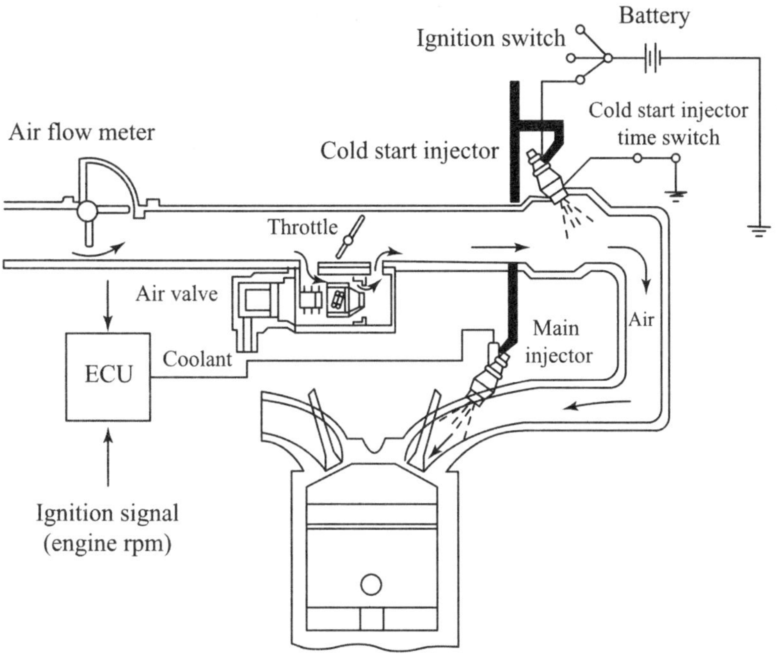

Fig. 9.11 Operation of cold start injector in MPFI system

fast idling. When the engine is cold, the throttle plate will be in the closed position. As can be seen in Fig.9.11 the engine sucks air through the air valve.

When the temperature is low, the air valve opens completely. Thus a large volume of air passes through the air valve to the intake manifold. As the temperature rises, the air valve closes gradually. When the engine reaches the normal operating temperature, the valve closes completely and the air flow is cut-off from the air valve. A thermo wax valve operates depending on the temperature of the engine coolant. This valve controls the opening and closing of the air valve.

9.7 INJECTION TIMING

Consider a cylinder of a four cylinder engine. The fuel is injected into the inlet manifold of each cylinder at different timings. The timing at which the injection of the fuel takes place inside the inlet manifold is called injection timing.

The injection timing for one cylinder of this four cylinder engine is described below.

In one cylinder, the piston moves up from BDC (Bottom Dead Centre) to TDC (Top Dead Centre) during the exhaust stroke. Just before the piston reaches TDC during this exhaust stroke, injection of the fuel takes place into the inlet manifold of this cylinder at about 60° crankangle before TDC. This injected fuel mixes with the air in the air intake chamber. Thus the air-fuel mixture is obtained. At the beginning of the suction stroke, intake valve opens and the air-fuel mixture is sucked into the cylinder during the suction stroke.

According to the firing order, the injection of the fuel takes place inside the inlet manifolds of the other three cylinders at various timings.

In this four cylinder engine, the ECU calculates the appropriate injection timing for each cylinder and the air fuel-mixture is made available at each suction stroke.

In order to meet the operating conditions, the injection valve is kept open for a longer time by ECU. For example, if the vehicle is accelerating, the injection valve will be opened for longer time, in order to supply additional fuel to the engine.

9.8 GROUP GASOLINE INJECTION SYSTEM

In an engine having group gasoline injection system, the injectors are not activated individually, but are activated in groups. In a four-cylinder engine also there are two groups, each group having two injectors. In a six-cylinder engine, there are two groups, each group having 3 injectors.

Figure 9.12 shows a block diagram with sensors and the Electronic Control Unit (ECU), for a group injection system. Sensors for detecting pressure in the manifold, engine speed in rpm, throttle position, intake manifold air temperature and the coolant temperature send information to the ECU. With this information, the ECU computes the amount of gasoline that the engine needs. The ECU then sends signals to the injectors and other parts of the system. The timing of the injectors is decided by the engine-speed sensor.

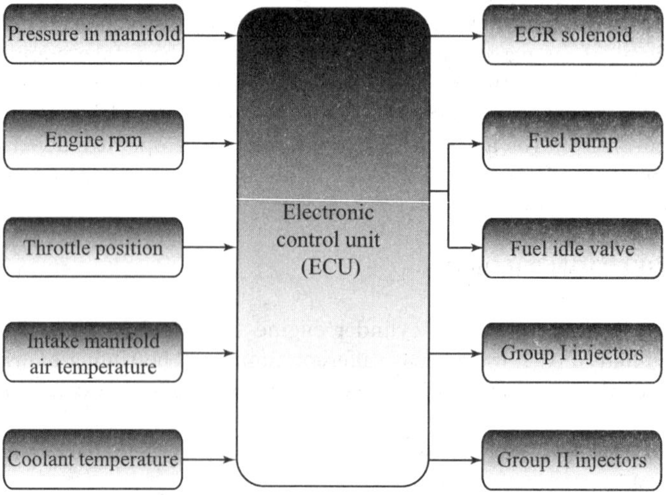

Fig. 9.12 Block diagram showing the sensors and ECU for group injection system

The injectors are divided into two groups. Based on the signals from the speed sensor, the ECU activates one group of injectors. Subsequently,

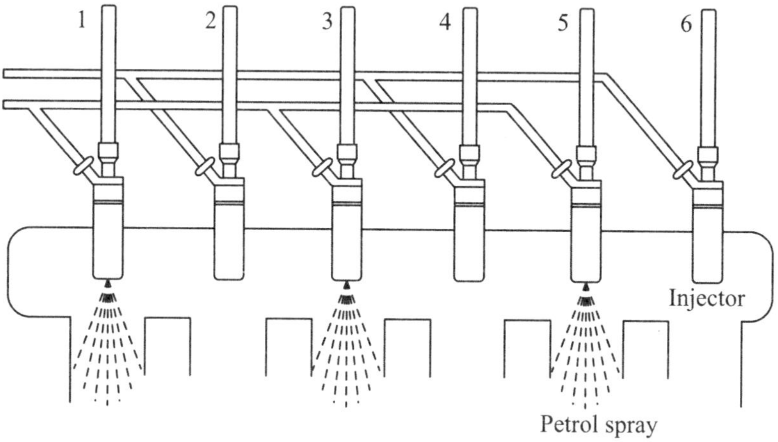

Fig. 9.13 Injectors grouping in a six-cylinder engine

the ECU activates the other group of injectors. For example, the injector grouping for a six-cylinder engine is shown in Fig.9.13. Injectors for cylinders 1, 3 and 5 open at the same time and inject gasoline into the intake manifold. After these injectors close, the injectors for the cylinders 2, 4 and 6 open and inject gasoline.

Figure 9.14 shows a port injection using the electronic group fuel-injection system for an eight-cylinder engine. Eight injectors are connected to a fuel system and are divided into two groups, each group having four injectors. Each group of injectors is alternately turned on by the ECU. When the crankshaft makes two revolutions, the injectors are turned on once. Thus it is seen that the modern engines are controlled more and more by electronics and the days are not far off when electronics may completely take over leaving bare minimum room for any mechanical or manual control.

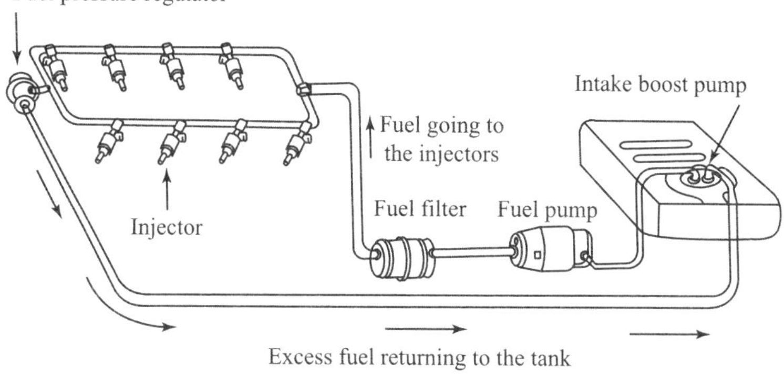

Fig. 9.14 Injector grouping in a eight-cylinder engine

9.9 ELECTRONIC DIESEL INJECTION SYSTEM

It may be noted that meeting future emission and other norms puts a large stress on the fuel injection system of a diesel engine. A conventional fuel injection pump with variable delivery capability is already seen in Fig.8.7. All parameters related to the injection process like, timing, rate of injection, end of injection, quantity of injected fuel etc. have to be precisely controlled if the engine has to operate with a high efficiency and low emission levels. Such a control is difficult with conventional mechanical systems. Mechanical systems only sense a few parameters and meter the fuel quantity or adjust the injection timing. They seldom change the injection rate or the injection pressure.

Use of pilot injection systems can lead to significant advantages. Here, a small quantity of fuel is first injected and allowed to undergo the ignition delay and burn. Subsequently the main injection takes place into gases, which are already hot. Thus the amount of fuel taking part in the premixed or the uncontrolled combustion phase is minimized and this leads to a reduction in noise and NO_x levels. Such a system will need an injection rate variation with time which is rather difficult to achieve precisely in mechanical systems. Hence, different types of injection systems with electronic controls have been developed.

By means of EFI systems one can achieve the precise control of:

(i) Injection timing,

(ii) Fuel injection quantity,

(iii) Injection rate during various stages of injection,

(iv) Injection pressure during injection,

(v) Nozzle opening speed and

(vi) Pilot injection timing and its quantity,

The following are easy to obtain with such systems:

(i) Very high injection pressure,

(ii) Sharp start and stop of injection,

(iii) Cylinder cut off,

(iv) Diagnostic capability,

(v) Turbocharger control and

(vi) Two stage injection

9.10 ELECTRONIC DIESEL INJECTION CONTROL

There are various versions of electronically controlled diesel injection systems. Some of the important ones are discussed below:

(i) Electronically controlled injection pumps (inline and distributor type)

(ii) Electronically controlled unit injectors

(iii) Common rail fuel injection system

Electronically controlled diesel fuel injection systems may use the following as inputs:

(i) Engine speed

(ii) Crank shaft position

(iii) Accelerator pedal position

(iv) Intake air temperature

(v) Lubricating oil temperature

(vi) Ambient air temperature and

(vii) Turbocharger boost pressure

(viii) Intake air mass flow rate

These are parameters, which can significantly affect the performance of the engine. The frequency of injection depends on the engine speed and number of cylinders. The timing of injection has to be advanced as the speed increases. The accelerator pedal position indicates the load on the engine. Intake air temperature and pressure indicate atmospheric conditions based on which the injection quantity and timing may have to be altered. The lubricating oil and coolant temperatures indicate the engine condition. This input can be used to detect cold start and warm up conditions, which will need the injection timing to be retarded and the fuel quantity to be momentarily increased. The turbocharger boost pressure can be used to detect the mass flow rate of air, which can be used to decide the fuel injection quantity. Alternatively a hot wire sensor can measure the mass flow rate of air. Various electronically controlled injection systems are discussed below in some detail.

9.10.1 Electronically Controlled Unit Injectors

The schematic layout of the entire system is indicated in Fig.9.15. Unit injectors can be combination of high-pressure pumps and injectors in one unit. They do not have high-pressure lines and hence the injection lag is low. The main high-pressure pump is situated above the injector. Fuel is fed into the high-pressure pump by a supply gear pump at low pressure. The plunger of the high-pressure pump is pushed down at the appropriate time by a cam, and rocker mechanism. A simplified cross section of the unit injector and phases of injection are shown in Fig.9.16. The fuel pushed down by the injector just bypasses the injection nozzle till the solenoid controlled spill valve closes the spill port. The closure of the spill port initiates the injection process. The injection stops when the solenoid valve opens the spill port. The timing and duration of the square pulse given to the solenoid can thus control the fuel timing and injection quantity. The solenoid can also be opened and closed more than once to have a pilot injection spray followed by the main spray. The pressure of injection is however controlled by the rate of displacement of the fuel and the size of the hole in the nozzle. The ECU generates the pulses to operate the solenoid controlled spill valve.

9.10.2 Electronically Controlled Injection Pumps (Inline and Distributor Type)

Diesel engines use inline and distributor pumps. The start of injection in the conventional inline element is determined by the instant when the top of the plunger covers the bypass or the spill ports. The end of delivery occurs when the helical slot or groove on the plunger uncovers these ports. The start of delivery is fixed but the end of delivery depends on the amount of fuel to be delivered.

In the case of the electronically controlled system there will be a control sleeve which can be moved up and down by an actuator which is controlled by the ECU (Electronic Control Unit). The ECU determines the amount of fuel to be injected depending on the throttle position, engine speed, and other parameters. Once this is obtained the control sleeve is positioned so that the required quantity of fuel can be injected. The timing of injection is still done mechanically.

Distributor pumps use control sleeves for metering the injected quantity. Thus they can be easily be made to work with an electronically controlled solenoid actuator. The principle of operation is similar to the one explained above.

Inline pump governors in mechanical systems are quite complex. These basically alter the injected fuel quantity of the pump so that the engine speed can be maintained. A mechanical governor is used, which senses the engine speed through the use of flyweights. In addition to the speed the governor also puts a limit on the maximum fuel delivery depending on engine operating and ambient conditions. It also has to supply excess fuel just for starting. The fuel delivery has to be controlled based on the turbocharger outlet conditions. The governor has to also limit the maximum speed and ensure stable idling operation.

The schematic of an electronically controlled inline fuel injection system is given in the Fig.9.17 as a block diagram. The various inputs are as shown in the figure. The ECU determines the correct quantity of the fuel to be injected based on the inputs and the data in the look up table. The fuel input depends on the rack position and thus the ECU controls the rack position using a solenoid. The position of the rack is measured and used for feedback. The accelerator pedal position is the input from the driver and a potentiometer is used to sense it. The system can maintain the vehicle speed at any set

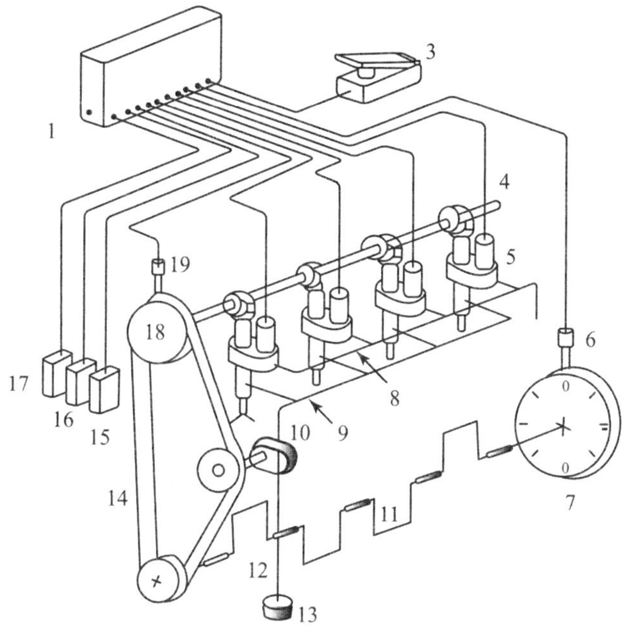

1 Battery supply (12 V or 24 V)
2 Electronic control unit (ECU)
3 Driver command (Accelerator pedal)
4 Injector camshaft
5 Injector unit
6 Magnetic transducer monitors engine speed and crankshaft position
7 Sixty tooth flywheel
8 Fuel return gallery
9 Fuel supply gallery
10 Fuel gear pump
11 Crankshaft
12 Fuel pickup
13 Gauze strainer
14 Timing belt
15 Boost sensor connection
16 Coolant temperature connection
17 Other sensor connection
18 Camshaft four-toothed gear wheel
19 Magnetic transducer firing order sensor

Fig. 9.15 A typical electronically controlled diesel injection system

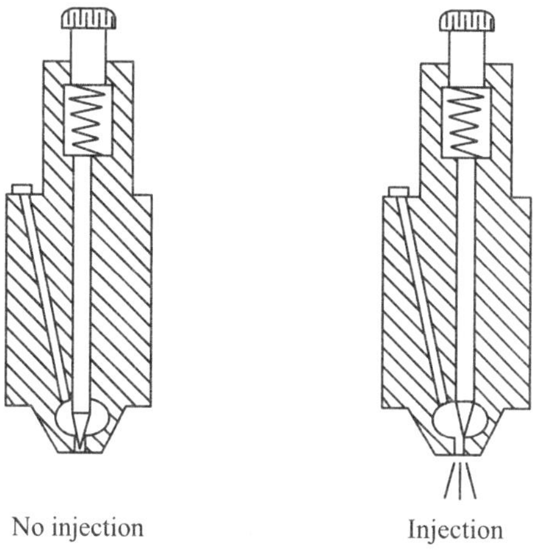

Fig. 9.16 Unit injectors

value. The ECU can also regulate the fuel quantity depending on other conditions like braking. The ECU also protects the engine against overheating by regulating the maximum quantity of fuel delivered.

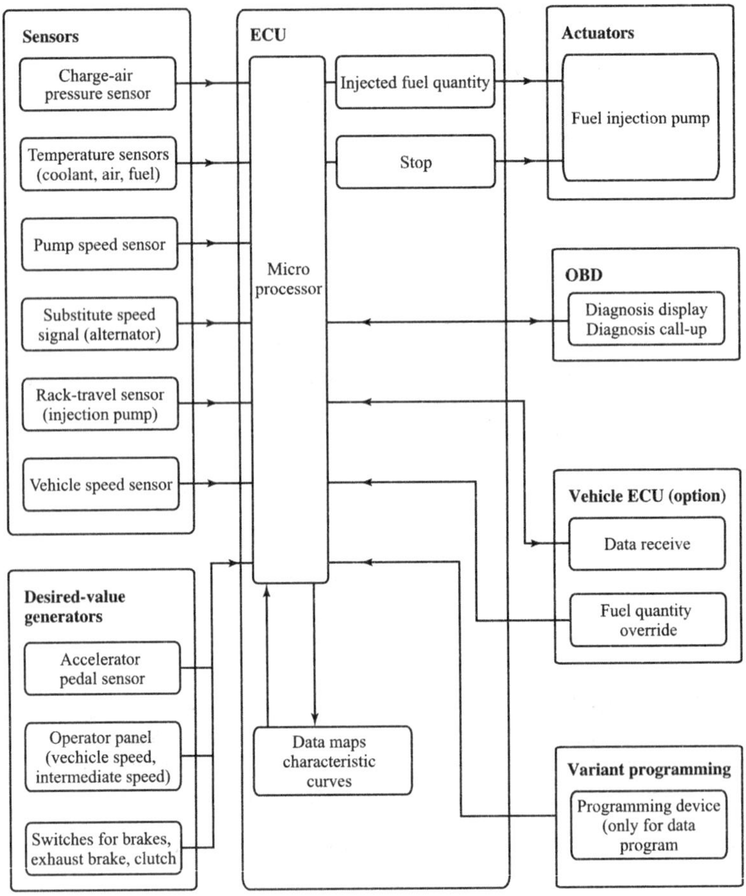

Fig. 9.17 System blocks for electronic diesel control (EDC)

9.10.3 Common-Rail Fuel Injection System

The common rail fuel injection system is finding increasing use in diesel engines as it has the potential to drastically cut emissions and fuel consumption. This system provides control of many important parameters linked to the injection system (refer Chapter 20). It has a wide range of application, from small to heavy duty engines. Some important features are:

(i) Very high injection pressures of the order of 1500 bar.

(ii) Complete control over start, and end of injection

(iii) Injection pressure is independent of engine speed

(iv) Ability to have pilot, main and post injection

(v) Variable injection pressure.

The common rail injection system has a high pressure pump which operates continuously and charges a high pressure rail or reservoir or accumulator. Fuel is led from this rail to the injector mounted on the cylinder head through lines. The injector is solenoid operated. It received pulses from the ECU to open the same.

The engine directly drives the pump of the common rail system. It is generally of the multi-cylinder radial piston type. The generated pressure is independent of the injection process unlike conventional injection systems. The rail pressure pump is generally much smaller than conventional pumps and also is subjected to lesser pressure pulsations. The injection occurs when the solenoid is energized. The quantity of fuel injected is directly dependent on the duration of the pulse when the injection pressure is constant. Sensors on the crankshaft indicate its position and speed and so the timing of injection and its frequency can be controlled. A typical layout of the common rail fuel injection system is indicated in Fig.9.18.

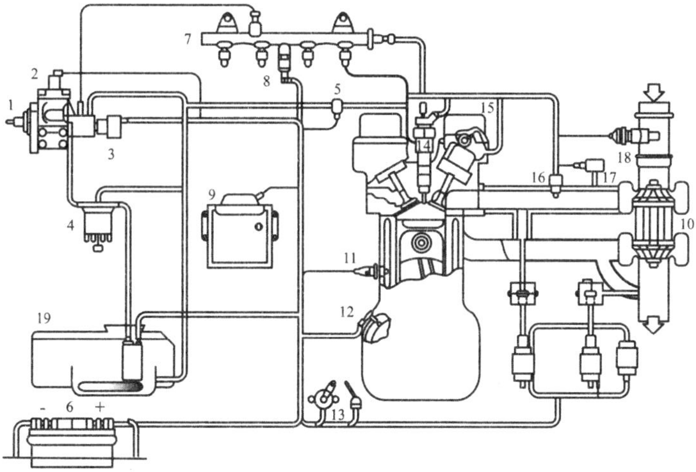

1	High pressure pump	7	High pressure accumulator	13	Accelerator pedal sensor
2	Element shutoff valve	8	Rail pressure sensor	14	Injector
3	Pressure control valve	9	ECU	15	Camshaft speed sensor
4	Fuel filter	10	Turbocharger	16	Intake air temperature sensor
5	Fuel temperature sensor	11	Coolant temperature sensor	17	Boost pressure sensor
6	Battery	12	Crankshaft speed	18	Air mass meter

19 Fuel tank with prefilter and presupply pump

Fig. 9.18 Sensors of a common rail injection system, together with various system components

Fuel from the tank is lifted by a low pressure pump and passed through a filter. The pump is generally run by an electric motor independent of the engine speed. The main pumping element can be a conventional gear pump or of the roller cell type. The roller cell pump has a rotor with radial slots. These slots house rollers which are always in contact with the inner surface of the housing due to fuel pressure and centrifugal forces. The space between the rotor and the housing varies as the rotor turns and this is responsible for the suction and delivery.

Lucas diesel systems is of a high pressure pump which is seen in Fig.9.19. This pump has a cam which is stationary and a rotating hydraulic head which houses two plungers. These plungers touch the cam and are pushed in four times a rotation. Thus fuel is pumped four times per rotation. A non return valve is used to send the fuel to the rail. The inlet of the pump is controlled to maintain the needed delivery. It may be noted that any excess delivery is ultimately returned back from the rail pressure regulator after it is throttled down to tank pressure. This amounts to fuel heating and also loss of work takes place to pump the fuel. Hence, controlling the delivery at the pump is a good idea. A high pressure regulator is also used. Both these valves are solenoid operated and are controlled by the ECU.

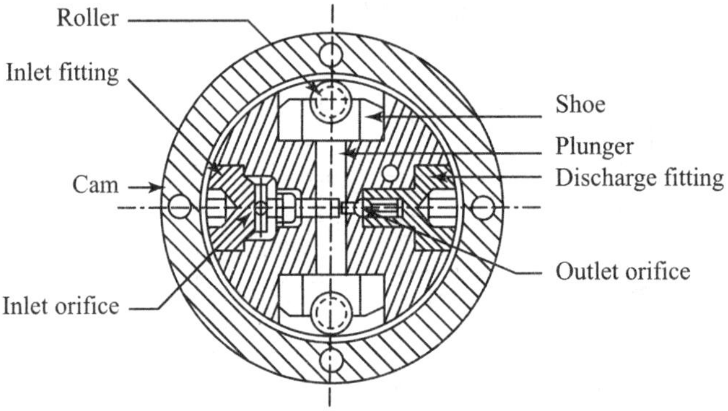

Fig. 9.19 LDCR high pressure pump

In the rail-pressure regulator the spring force and the electromagnetic force generated by the coil regulate the pressure. The pressure is controlled by the ECU. The electromagnet receives a pulse at a frequency of 1 kHz whose width is modulated to change the effective current through the electromagnet. The common rail system also has a pressure sensor and a pressure limiter attached to the rail. There is also a flow limiter to prevent continuous injection if one of the injectors mal functions. Thus, it is seen that engine management is gradually turning into electronic control thereby better combustion and economy as well as low emissions can be achieved.

Review Questions

9.1 What is the necessity for gasoline injection? Explain with suitable sketch.

9.2 Mention the various types of gasoline injection systems.

9.3 Enumerate various components of a electronic injection system and mention their functions.

9.4 What are the various sensors used in electronic fuel injection system?

9.5 Explain the merits and demerits of a EFI system.

9.6 Describe briefly the MPFI system with a neat sketch.

9.7 Explain port injection and throttle body injection system.

9.8 Describe D-MPFI and L-MPFI injection system.

9.9 With a neat sketch explain the functions of MPFI system.

9.10 Explain the functions of electronic control systems.

9.11 What do you understand by group gasoline injection system? Explain.

9.12 Briefly explain the electronic diesel injection system with necessary controls.

9.13 Explain with a layout electronically controlled injection pump system.

9.14 What is a common rail system? Explain.

9.15 With a neat sketch explain LDCR high pressure pump.

Multiple Choice Questions (choose the most appropriate answer)

1. Multi-point fuel injection system uses

   (a) manifold injection
   (b) direct injection
   (c) port injection
   (d) throttle body injection
   (e) both (c) and (d)

2. L-MPFI system uses

   (a) port injection
   (b) direct injection
   (c) manifold injection
   (d) throttle body injection

3. D-MPFI system uses

   (a) port injection
   (b) manifold injection
   (c) direct injection
   (d) throttle body injection

4. Common rail injection system uses injection pressures of the order
   (a) 100–200 bar
   (b) 200–400 bar
   (c) 400–600 bar
   (d) 1500 bar
5. Continuous injection system usually has
   (a) plunger pump
   (b) rotary pump
   (c) gear pump
   (d) vane pump
6. The cold start injector
   (a) maintain stoichiometric air-fuel ratio
   (b) provides lean air-fuel ratio
   (c) gives rich air-fuel ratio
   (d) is not used for any of the above functions
7. ECU is an electronic injection system used for
   (a) calculating the appropriate injection timing
   (b) meeting only certain operating conditions
   (c) closing the injection valve only
   (d) none of the above
8. With EFI of diesel engines
   (a) sharp start and stop is not possible
   (b) very high injection pressure can be obtained
   (c) sudden cylinder cut-off is impossible
   (d) diagnostic properties are poor
9. EFI system can achieve
   (a) proper injection timing
   (b) proper injection quantity
   (c) proper injection pressure
   (d) all of the above

Ans: 1. – (e) 2. – (a) 3. – (b) 4. – (d) 5. – (b)
6. – (c) 7. – (a) 8. – (b) 9. – (d)

10
IGNITION

10.1 INTRODUCTION

In spark-ignition engines, as compression ratio is lower, and the self-ignition temperature of gasoline is higher, for igniting the mixture for the initiation of combustion an ignition system is a must.

The electrical discharge produced between the two electrodes of a spark plug by the ignition system starts the combustion process in a spark-ignition engine. This takes place close to the end of the compression stroke. The high temperature plasma kernel created by the spark, develops into a self sustaining and propagating flame front. In this thin reaction sheet certain exothermic chemical reactions occur. The function of the ignition system is to initiate this flame propagation process. It must be noted that the spark is to be produced in a repeatable manner viz., cycle-by-cycle, over the full range of load and speed of the engine at the appropriate moment in the engine cycle.

By implication, ignition is merely a prerequisite for combustion. Therefore, the study of ignition is a must to understand the phenomenon of combustion so that a criterion may be established to decide whether ignition has occurred. Although the ignition process is intimately connected with the initiation of combustion, it is not associated with the gross behaviour of combustion. Instead, it is a local small-scale phenomenon that takes place within a small zone in the combustion chamber.

In terms of its simplest definition, ignition has no degree, intensively or extensively. Either the combustion of the medium is initiated or it is not. Therefore, it is reasonable to consider ignition from the standpoint of the beginning of the combustion process that it initiates.

10.2 ENERGY REQUIREMENTS FOR IGNITION

The total enthalpy required to cause the flame to be self sustaining and promote ignition, is given by the product of the surface area of the spherical flame and the enthalpy per unit area. It is reasonable to assume that the basic requirement of the ignition system is that it should supply this energy within a small volume. Further, ignition should occur in a time interval sufficiently short to ensure that only a negligible amount of energy is lost other than to establish the flame. In view of this last mentioned condition, it is apparent that the rate of supply of energy is as important a factor as the total energy supplied.

A small electric spark of short duration would appear to meet most of the requirements for ignition. A spark can be caused by applying a sufficiently high voltage between two electrodes separated by a gap, and there is a critical voltage below which no sparking occurs. This critical voltage is a function of the dimension of the gap between the electrodes, the fuel-air ratio and the pressure of the gas. Additionally, the manner in which the voltage is raised to the critical value and the configuration and the condition of the electrodes are important in respect of the energy required.

An ignition process obeys the law of conservation of energy. Hence, it can be treated as a balance of energy between:

(i) that provided by an external source

(ii) that released by chemical reaction and

(iii) that dissipated to the surroundings by means of thermal conduction, convection and radiation

10.3 THE SPARK ENERGY AND DURATION

With a homogeneous mixture in the cylinder, spark energy of the order of 1 mJ and a duration of a few micro-seconds would suffice to initiate the combustion process. However, in practice, circumstances are less than the ideal. The pressure, temperature and density of the mixture between the spark plug electrodes have a considerable influence on the voltage required to produce a spark. Therefore, the spark energy and duration are to be of sufficient order to initiate combustion under the most unfavourable conditions expected in the vicinity of the spark plug over the complete range of engine operation. Usually, if the spark energy exceeds 40 mJ and the duration is longer than 0.5 ms, reliable ignition is obtained. If the resistance of the deposits on the spark plug electrodes is sufficiently high, the loss of electrical energy through these deposits may prevent the spark discharge.

10.4 IGNITION SYSTEM

In principle, a conventional ignition system should provide sufficiently large voltage across the spark plug electrodes to affect the spark discharge. Further, it should supply the required energy for the spark to ignite the combustible mixture adjacent to the plug electrodes under all operating conditions. It may be noted that for a given engine design, the optimum spark timing varies with engine speed, inlet manifold pressure and mixture composition. The design of a conventional ignition system should take these factors into account to provide the spark of proper energy and duration at the appropriate time.

As air is a poor conductor of electricity an air gap in an electric circuit acts as a high resistance. But when a high voltage is applied across the electrodes of a spark plug it produces a spark across the gap. When such a spark is produced to ignite a homogeneous air-fuel mixture in the combustion chamber of an engine it is called the spark-ignition system. The ignition systems are classified depending upon how the primary energy for operating the circuit is made available as:

(i) battery ignition systems

(ii) magneto ignition systems

10.5 REQUIREMENTS OF AN IGNITION SYSTEM

A smooth and reliable functioning of an ignition system is essential for reliable working of an engine. The requirements of such an ignition system are:

(i) It should provide a good spark between the electrodes of the plugs at the correct timing.

(ii) It should function efficiently over the entire range of engine speed.

(iii) It should be light, effective and reliable in service.

(iv) It should be compact and easy to maintain.

(v) It should be cheap and convenient to handle.

(vi) The interference from the high voltage source should not affect the functioning of the radio and television receivers inside an automobile.

10.6 BATTERY IGNITION SYSTEM

Most of the modern spark-ignition engines use battery ignition system. In this system, the energy required for producing spark is obtained from a 6 or 12 volt battery. The construction of a battery ignition system is extremely varied. It depends on the type of ignition energy storage as well as on the ignition performance which is required by the particular engine. The reason for this is that an ignition system is not an autonomous machine, that is, it does not operate completely by itself, but instead it is but one part of the internal combustion engine, the *heart of the engine*. It is therefore extremely important that the ignition system be matched sufficiently well to its engine.

Passenger cars, light trucks, some motorcycles and large stationary engines are fitted with battery ignition systems. The details of the battery ignition system of a six-cylinder engine are shown in Fig.10.1.

The essential components of the system are:

(i) battery

(ii) ignition switch

(iii) ballast resistor

(iv) ignition coil

(v) contact breaker

(vi) capacitor

(vii) distributor

(viii) spark plug

In the above list the first three components are housed in the primary side of the ignition coil whereas the last four are in the secondary side. The details of the various components are described briefly in the following sections.

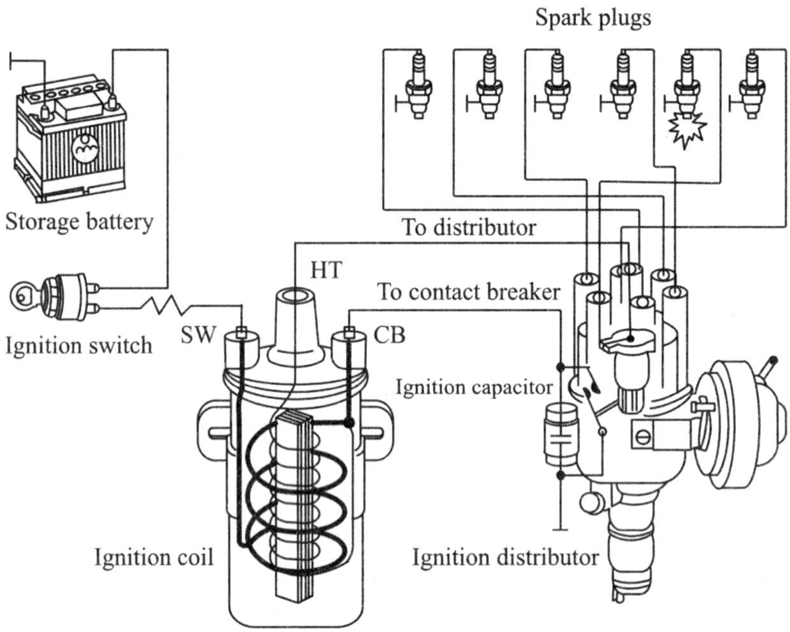

Fig. 10.1 Battery ignition system for a six-cylinder engine

10.6.1 Battery

To provide electrical energy for ignition, a storage battery is used. It is charged by a dynamo driven by the engine. Owing to the electro-chemical reactions, it is able to convert the chemical energy into electrical energy. The battery must be mechanically strong to withstand the strains to which it is constantly subjected to. Given reasonable care and attention two years or more trouble-free life may be obtained from a battery.

A lead acid battery consists of a number of cells connected together in series and each having a nominal potential of 2 volts when fully charged. A six volt battery has three such cells and a 12 volt battery has six. Figure 10.2 illustrates how six cells are coupled together to form a 12 volt battery and shows that for this coupling in series the positive of one cell is connected to the negative of the next.

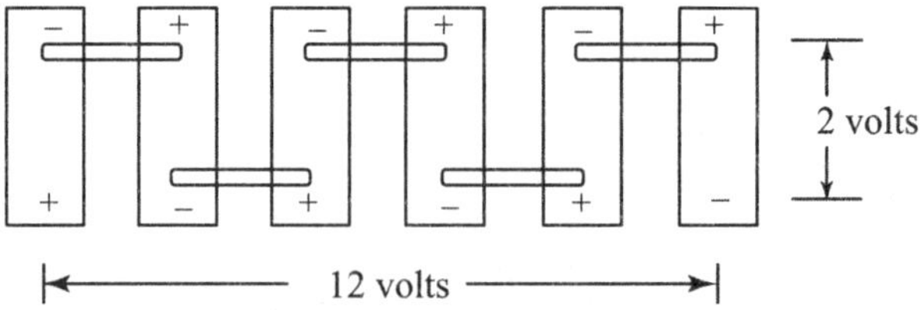

Fig. 10.2 Cell connections for 12 volt battery

Two types of batteries are used for spark-ignition engines, the lead acid battery and the alkaline battery. The former is used in light duty commercial vehicles and the later on heavy duty commercial vehicles.

10.6.2 Ignition Switch

Battery is connected to the primary winding of the ignition coil through an ignition switch and ballast resistor. With the help of the ignition switch the ignition system can be turned on or off.

10.6.3 Ballast Resistor

A ballast resistor is provided in series with the primary winding to regulate the primary current. The object of this is to prevent injury to the spark coil by overheating if the engine should be operated for a long time at low speed, or should be stalled with the breaker in the *closed* position. This coil is made of iron wire, and iron has the property that its electrical resistance increases very rapidly if a certain temperature is exceeded. The coil is therefore made of wire of such size that if the primary current flows nearly continuously, the ballast coil reaches a temperature above that where this rapid increase in resistance occurs. This additional resistance in the primary circuit holds the primary current down to a safe value. For starting from cold this resistor is by-passed to allow more current to flow in the primary circuit.

10.6.4 Ignition Coil

Ignition coil is the source of ignition energy in the conventional ignition system. This coil stores the energy in its magnetic field and delivers it at the appropriate time in the form of a ignition pulse through the high-tension ignition cables to the respective spark plug. The purpose of the ignition coil is to step up the 6 or 12 volts of the battery to a high voltage, sufficient to induce an electric spark across the electrodes of the spark plug. The ignition coil consists of a magnetic core of soft iron wire or sheet and two insulated conducting coils, called primary and the secondary windings. A typical ignition coil is shown in Fig.10.3.

The secondary coil consists of about 21,000 turns of 38-40 gauge enameled copper wire sufficiently insulated to withstand the high voltage. It is wound close to the core with one end connected to the secondary terminal and the other end grounded either to the metal case or the primary coil.

The primary winding, located outside the secondary coil is generally formed of 200-300 turns of 20 gauge wire to produce a resistance of about 1.15Ω. The ends are connected to exterior terminals. More heat is generated in the primary than in the secondary and with the primary coil wound over the secondary coil, it is easier to dissipate the heat. The entire unit when assembled, is enclosed in a metal container and forms a neat and compact unit. On the top of the coil assembly is the heavily insulated terminal block, which supports three terminals. To the two smaller terminals (Fig.10.3), usually marked SW (switch wire) and CB (contact breaker) the two ends of the primary are connected.

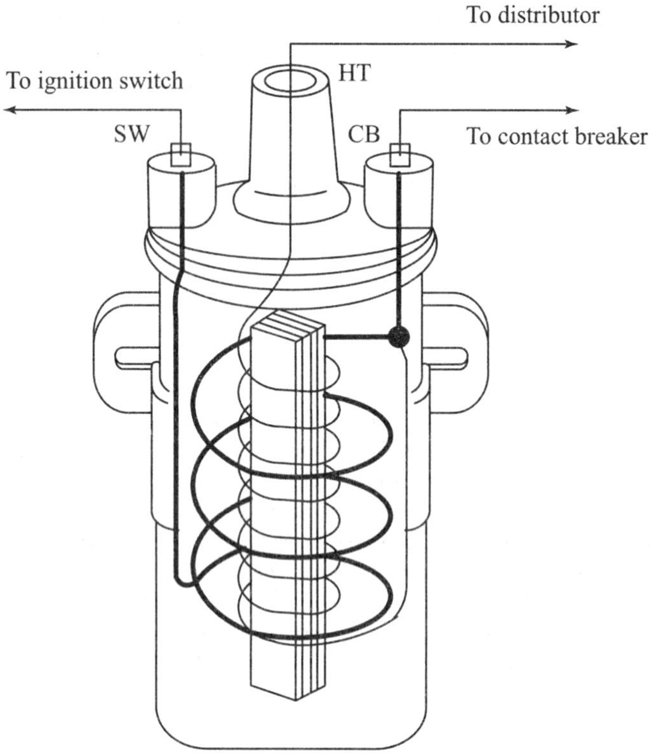

Fig. 10.3 Ignition coil

As can be seen in Fig.10.3, one end of the secondary winding is connected to the central high-tension terminal in the moulded cover of the distributor. The other end is connected to the primary. An external high tension wire connects this central terminal to the central terminal of the distributor.

10.6.5 Contact Breaker

This is a mechanical device for making [Fig.10.4(a)] and breaking [Fig.10.4(b)] the primary circuit of the ignition coil. It consists essentially of a fixed metal point against which, another metal point bears which is being on a spring loaded pivoted arm. The metal used is invariably one of the hardest metals, usually tungsten and each point has a circular flat face of about 3 mm diameter. The fixed contact point is earthed by mounting it on the base of the contact breaker assembly whereas the arm to which the movable contact point is attached, is electrically insulated. When the points are closed the current flows and when they are open, the circuit is broken and the flow of current stops. The pivoted arm has, generally, a heel or a rounded part of some hard plastic material attached in the middle and this heel bears on the cam which is driven by the engine. Consequently, every time the cam passes under the heel, the points are forced apart and the circuit is broken. The pivoted arm is

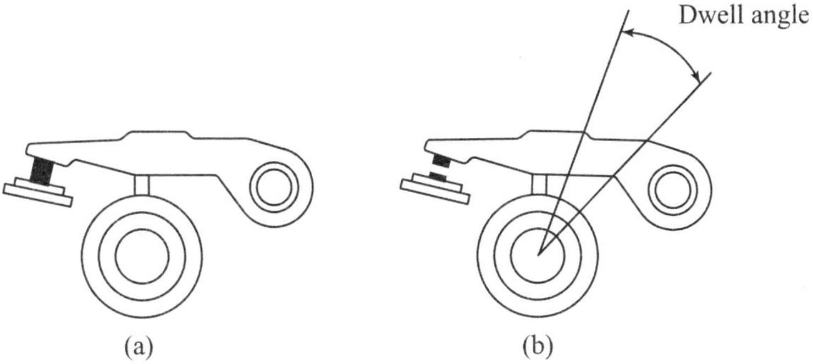

Fig. 10.4 Contact breaker

spring loaded, so that when the points are not separated by the action of the cam, they are held together by the pressure of the spring thereby closing the primary circuit. The condition and adjustment of the contact breaker points are important. The points are subjected to a very severe hammering during their period of service. Uneven wear of the points may require a refacing or replacing depending upon the condition of the points.

An eight cylinder engine running at 3000 rpm requires 12000 sparks per minute, i.e. 200 sparks per second. If the breaker is to operate satisfactorily at this speed, the travel of the breaker arm must be held down to the minimum to ensure a positive spark and the breaker arm must be made very light.

10.6.6 Capacitor

The principle of construction of the ignition capacitor is the same as that of every electrical capacitor, which is very simple: two metal plates – separated by an insulating material – are placed face to face. The insulation is often only air (for example, in the case of air capacitors), but in most cases it consists of some high-quality insulating material suitable for the particular technical requirements, material which because of space limitation must be as thin as possible but nevertheless capable of withstanding electrostatic stresses without suffering damage. The metal plates themselves are usually replaced by metal foil or by metallic layers deposited by evaporation on the insulating material itself. In order to save space, these thin strips, for example, consisting of two strips of aluminium foil and several layers of special capacitor paper, are rolled up in a solid roll. Contacts are attached to the two metal strips and the entire roll is first impregnated in an oily or waxy material to improve the insulating properties of the paper, and then the roll is inserted into a metal shell for protection against moisture, external physical contact and damage.

10.6.7 Distributor

The function of the distributor is to distribute the ignition surges to the individual spark plugs in the correct sequence and at the correct instants in time. Depending on whether a particular engine has 4, 6 or 8 cylinders, there are 4, 6 or 8 ignition pulses (surges) generated for every rotation of the distributor shaft. The use of a distributor represents a considerable simplification in a battery ignition system because in most cases we want to use only a single ignition circuit. The contact breaker and the spark advance mechanism are combined with the distributor in a single unit because of the absolute necessity that the distributor operate in synchronism with the crankshaft.

There are two types of distributors, the brush type and the gap type. In the former, carbon brush carried by the rotor arm slides over metallic segments embedded in the distributor cap of molded insulating material, thus establishing electrical connection between the secondary winding of the coil and the spark plug, while in the latter the electrode of the rotor arm pass close to, but does not actually contact the segments in the distributor cap. With the latter type of distributor, there will not be any appreciable wear of the electrodes.

The distributor unit also consists of several other auxiliary units. In the lower part of the housing there is a speed sensitive device or governor, whose function is to advance the spark with increase in engine speed. Above this unit is the contact breaker assembly which can be rotated to adjust the timing of spark. In the upper part of the housing is located the high tension distributor. It also carries the vacuum ignition governor, which serves to retard the spark as the load on the engine increases. Each of the segments of the distributor is connected to a sparking plug and as the rotor presses it, the contact breaker opens, the high tension current is passed through the rotor and brass segment through the high tension wiring to the appropriate spark plug. Obviously, the order in which the sparking plugs are connected to the distributor head will depend on the firing order of the engine.

10.6.8 Spark Plug

The spark plug provides the two electrodes with a proper gap across which the high potential discharges to generate a spark and ignite the combustible mixture within the combustion chamber. A sectional view of a spark plug is shown in Fig.10.5.

A spark plug consists essentially of a steel shell, an insulator and two electrodes. The central electrode to which the high tension supply from the ignition coil is connected, is well insulated with porcelain or other ceramic materials. The other electrode is welded to the steel shell of the plug and thereby is automatically grounded when the plug is installed on the cylinder head of the engine. The electrodes are usually made of high nickel alloy to withstand the severe erosion and corrosion to which they are subjected in use.

The tips of the central electrode and the insulator are exposed to the combustion gases. This results in the insulators having a tendency to crack from the high thermal and mechanical stresses. Some insulators are also seriously affected by moisture and by abnormal surface deposits. Since, the central electrode and the insulator are subjected to the high temperature of the combustion gases, the heat must flow from the insulator to the steel shell which is in contact with the relatively cool cylinder head in order to cool the electrodes and thereby prevent preignition.

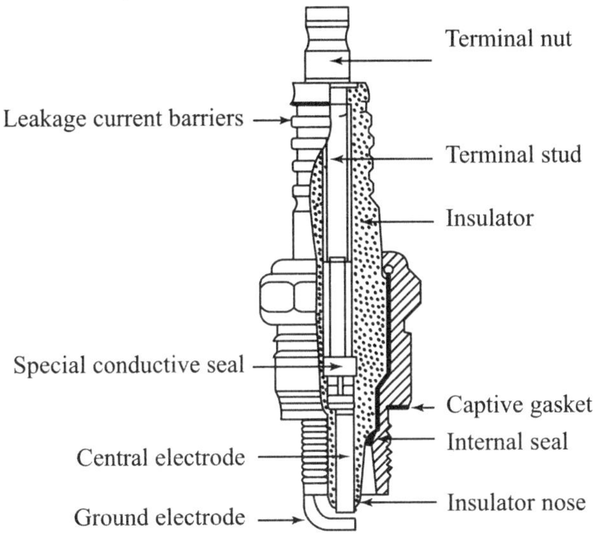

Fig. 10.5 Schematic of a typical spark plug

Spark plugs are usually classified as *hot plugs or cold plugs* depending upon the relative operating temperature range of the tip of the high tension electrode. The operating temperature is governed by the amount of heat transferred which in turn depends on the length of the heat transfer path from the tip to the cylinder head and on the amount of surface area exposed to the combustion gases. A *cold plug* has a short heat transfer path and a small area exposed to the combustion gases as compared to a hot plug as shown in Fig.10.6.

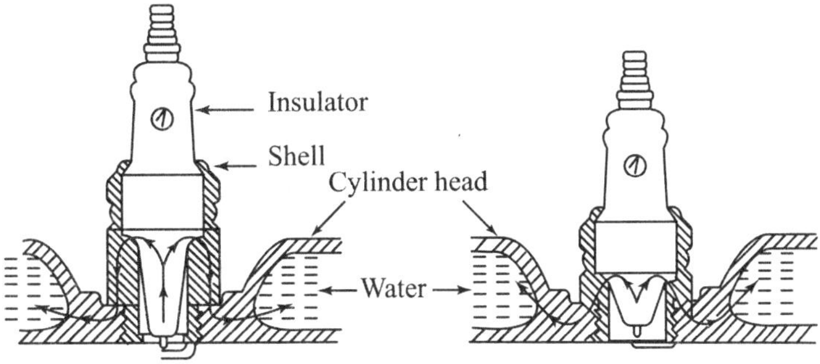

Fig. 10.6 Heat transfer path of hot and cold spark plugs

The type of spark plug used in an engine depends on the particular engine requirements. Every engine manufacturer determines the type of plug, cold or hot, that is best suited to his engine. A spark plug which runs at a satisfactory temperature at cruising speeds may run so cool at idling speed that abnormal deposits are likely to foul the electrodes. These deposits may be of soft dull carbon from incomplete combustion or of hard shiny carbon from excess lubricating oil that passes the piston rings and enters the combustion chamber. The carbon deposits from incomplete combustion will burn off at temperatures above 340 °C while the excess oil carbon deposits from lubricating oil require a temperature above 540 °C to burn. If a spark plug runs hot enough at idling speeds to prevent carbon deposits, it may run too hot at high speeds and cause preignition. If a spark plug runs at a temperature above 800 °C preignition usually results. A compromise must be made in order to obtain a proper spark plug which would operate satisfactorily throughout the entire engine operating range. An improper spark plug is always a major source of engine trouble such as misfiring and preignition.

10.7 OPERATION OF A BATTERY IGNITION SYSTEM

The source of the ignition energy in the battery ignition system is the ignition coil. This coil stores the energy in its magnetic field and delivers it at the instant of ignition (firing point) in the form of a surge of high voltage current (ignition pulse) through the high tension ignition cables to the correct spark plug. Storage of energy in the magnetic field is based on an inductive process, as a result of which we also designate the ignition coil as an *inductive storage device*. The schematic diagram of a conventional battery ignition system for a four-cylinder engine is shown in Fig.10.7.

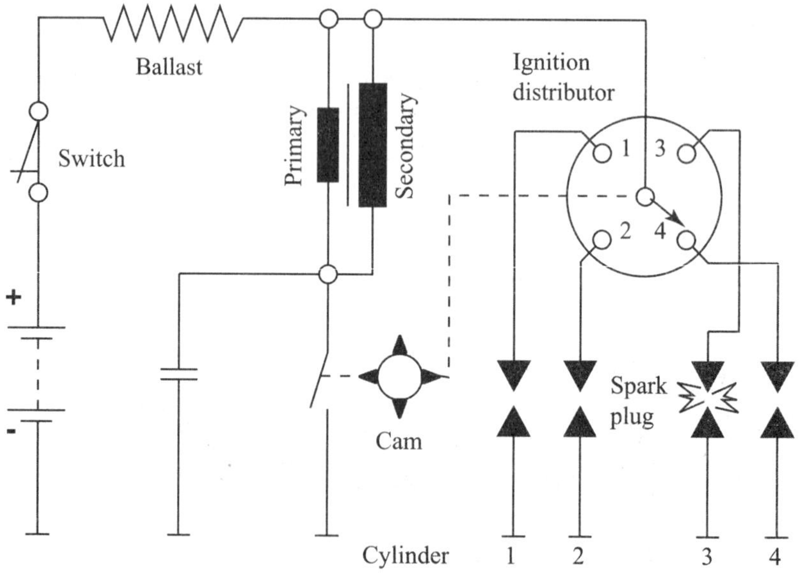

Fig. 10.7 Conventional coil ignition system for four-cylinder engines – schematic diagram

As already explained the ignition coil consists of two coils of wire, one wound around the other, insulated from each other; the primary winding,

L_1 with few turns of heavy copper wire and the secondary winding, L_2 with many turns of fine copper wire. The primary and secondary winding are wound around a laminated iron core which has the effect of increasing the strength of the magnetic field and thus of the amount of energy stored.

One end of the primary winding is connected through the ignition switch to the positive terminal post of the storage battery, and the other end is grounded through the contact breaker. The ignition capacitor is connected in parallel with the contact breaker. One end of the secondary winding is also grounded through the contact breaker, and the other end is connected through the distributor and the high-tension ignition cables to the center electrode of the spark plug.

When the ignition switch is closed, the primary winding of the coil is connected to the positive terminal post of the storage battery. If the primary circuit is closed through the breaker contacts, a current flows, the so called *primary current.*

This current, flowing through the primary coil, which is wound on a soft iron core, produces a magnetic field in the core. A cam driven by the engine shaft, is arranged to open the breaker points whenever an ignition discharge is required. When the breaker points open, the current which had been flowing through the points now flows into the condenser, which is connected across the points. As the condenser becomes charged, the primary current falls and the magnetic field collapses. The collapse of the field induces a voltage in the primary winding, which charges the condenser to a voltage much higher than battery voltage. The condenser then discharges into the battery, reversing the direction of both the primary current and the magnetic field. The rapid collapse and reversal of the magnetic field in the core induce a very high voltage in the secondary winding of the ignition coil. The secondary winding consists of a large number of turns of very fine wire wound on the same core with the primary. The high secondary voltage is led to the proper spark plug by means of a rotating switch called the distributor, which is located in the secondary or high tension circuit of the ignition system.

If a condenser were not used in the primary circuit, the high primary voltage caused by the collapse of the magnetic field around the primary winding would cause an arc across the breaker points. The arc would burn and destroy the points and would also prevent the rapid drop in primary current and magnetic field which is necessary for the production of the high secondary voltage.

Note that the spark timing is controlled by the crank angle at which the breaker points open, while the distributor merely determines the firing sequence of the spark plugs. Changes in ignition timing may be affected by rotating the plate which holds the breaker points, relative to the cam. Because of this ignition will be delayed if the plate is displaced in the direction in which the camshaft rotates.

10.8 LIMITATIONS

(i) The primary voltage decreases as the engine speed increases due to the limitations in the current switching capability of the breaker system.

(ii) Time available for build-up of the current in the primary coil and the stored energy decrease as the engine speed increases due to the dwell period becoming shorter.

(iii) Because of the high source impedance (about 500 kΩ) the system is sensitive to side-tracking across the spark plug insulator.

(iv) The breaker points are continuously subjected to electrical as well as mechanical wear which results in short maintenance intervals. Increased currents cause a rapid reduction in breaker point life and system reliability. Acceptable life for these systems is obtained with a primary current limited to about 4 amperes.

10.9 DWELL ANGLE

The period, measured in degree of cam rotation, during which the contact points remain *closed* is called the *dwell angle* or the *cam angle*. This is illustrated in Fig.10.8. The dwell angle must be sufficiently large to allow magnetic saturation of the primary coil. Too small a dwell angle will result in lower secondary voltage and hence poor sparks or even misfiring. Too large a dwell angle will lead to burning of condenser and the contact points due to over-saturation of windings.

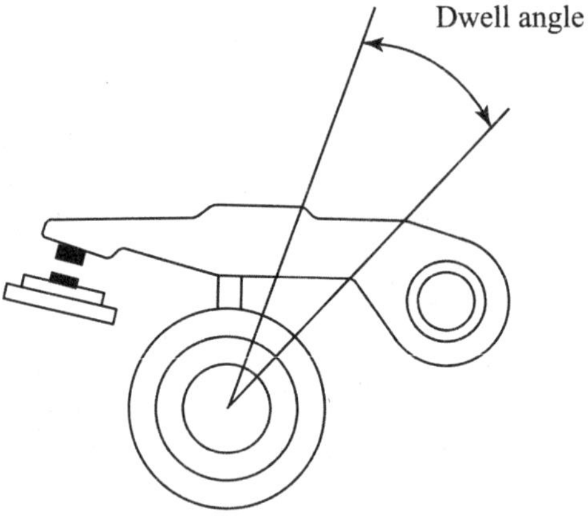

Fig. 10.8 Dwell angle

The magnitude of the dwell angle depends upon the gap between the points and also the angle between the cam lobes. The gap between the points is generally of the order of 0.35 mm to 0.55 mm. The angle between the cam lobes depends upon the number of engine cylinders. If a single contact breaker is used the number of lobes on the cam is the same as the number of cylinders. This means that at any given engine speed the time available to supply energy to the primary winding decreases as the number of cylinders increases, thereby imposing a high-speed limit on an engine having large number of cylinders. The effects of inertia and spring lag further worsen the situation.

As the number of cylinders is increased, the dwell angle must be reduced because more and more closing and opening operations must be accommodated during every rotation of the distributor camshaft; in the four-cylinder engine the dwell angle is about 50°, in the six-cylinder engine it is about 38°, and in the eight-cylinder engine it is about 33°. The following formula shows the way in which the dwell period can be expressed as a function of the dwell angle and the engine speed (in rev/min).

$$\text{Dwell period (milliseconds)} = \frac{1000 \times \text{ dwell angle (degrees)}}{6 \times \text{ engine speed (rev/min)}}$$

The smaller the gap between the contact points when they are fully open, the larger the dwell angle, and vice versa. This has led to the use of twin contact breakers connected in parallel between the primary winding and earth and a cam having number of lobes half that of the number of cylinders, to increase the dwell angle and thereby allow sufficient build-up of primary coil energy. Six cylinder engine will, thus have a 60° lobe angle with a twin contact breaker. Such an arrangement however, requires accurate synchronization of the arms of the contact breaker which very often causes problems in service. To avoid this, nowadays a cam having the same number of lobes as there are engine cylinders is used in conjunction with two contact breakers arranged in parallel. One contact breaker always opens the points while the other always closes the points, i.e., the dwell angle is doubled.

10.10 ADVANTAGE OF A 12 V IGNITION SYSTEM

Until about 1950 all car engines had 6-volt ignition systems. The chief advantage of the 6-volt system is that it uses the three cell storage battery which is cheaper, lighter and less bulky than a six-cell battery of the same watt-hour capacity. With the relatively low compression ratios used in those days the 6-volt system gave satisfactory results. As the compression ratios and the engine speeds increased, the voltage required to break down the spark gap rose. Hence, the 12-volt system came to be preferred as considerably higher secondary voltages are obtainable with it.

The other advantages are as follows:

(i) for transmitting equal power without excessive voltage drop, the cables in a 6-volt system need theoretically to be twice the thickness of 12-volt cables.

(ii) starting, in particular, is much improved by the 12-volt system since almost twice the power is available for ignition coil during the starting surge.

(iii) the 12-volt system has adequate electric power to supply the increasing number of electrical accessories used.

10.11 MAGNETO IGNITION SYSTEM

Magneto is a special type of ignition system with its own electric generator to provide the necessary energy for the system. It is mounted on the engine and replaces all the components of the coil ignition system except the spark plug. A magneto when rotated by the engine is capable of producing a very high voltage and does not need a battery as a source of external energy.

A schematic diagram of a high tension magneto ignition system is shown in Fig.10.9. The high tension magneto incorporates the windings to generate the primary voltage as well as to step up the voltage and thus does not require a separate coil to boost up the voltage required to operate the spark plug.

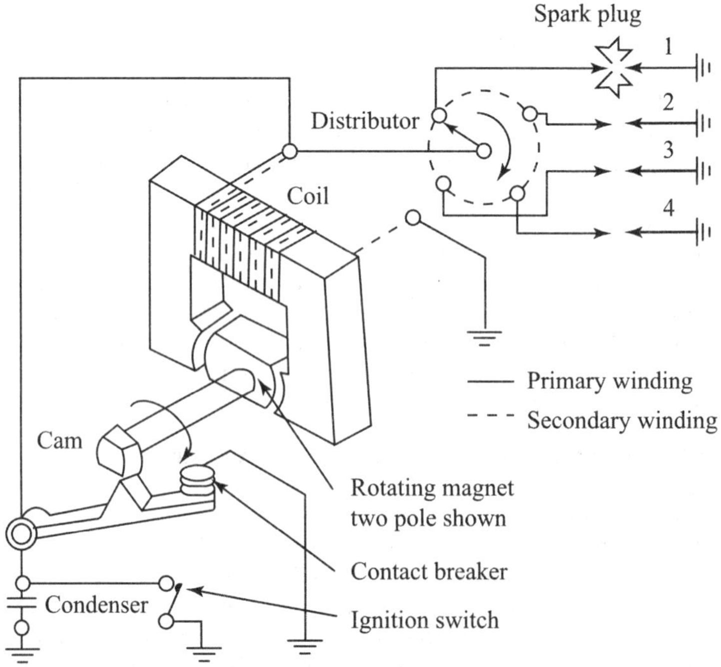

Fig. 10.9 High tension magneto ignition system

Magneto can be either *rotating armature type* or *rotating magnet type*. In the first type, the armature consisting of the primary and secondary windings all rotate between the poles of a stationary magnet, whilst, in the second type the magnet revolves and the windings are kept stationary. A third type of magneto called the *polar inductor type* is also in use. In the polar inductor type *magneto* both the magnet and the windings remain stationary but the voltage is generated by reversing the flux field with the help of soft iron polar projections, called inductors.

The working principle of the magneto ignition system is exactly the same as that of the coil ignition system. With the help of a cam, the primary circuit flux is changed and a high voltage is produced in the secondary circuit.

The variation of the breaker current with speed for the coil ignition system and the magneto ignition system is shown in Fig.10.10. It can be seen that since the cranking speed at start is low the current generated by the magneto is quite small. As the engine speed increases the flow of current also increases.

Thus, with magneto there is always a starting difficulty and sometimes a separate battery is needed for starting. The magneto is best at high speeds and therefore is widely used for sports and racing cars, aircraft engines etc.

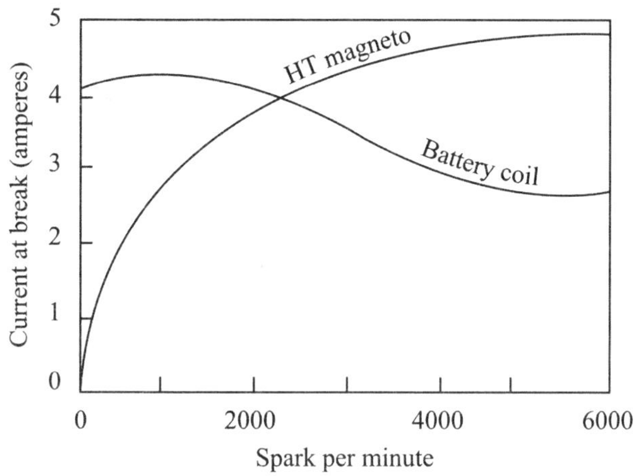

Fig. 10.10 Breaker current versus speed in coil and magneto ignition systems

In comparison, the battery ignition system is more expensive but highly reliable. Because of the poor starting characteristics of the magneto system invariably the battery ignition system is preferred to the magneto system in automobile engines. However, in two wheelers magneto ignition system is favoured due to light weight and less maintenance.

The main disadvantage of the high tension magneto ignition system lies in the fact that the wirings carry a very high voltage and thus there is a strong possibility of causing engine misfire due to leakage. To avoid this the high tension wires must be suitably shielded. The development of the low tension magneto system is an attempt to avoid this trouble. In the low tension magneto system the secondary winding is changed to limit the secondary voltage to a value of about 400 volts and the distributor is replaced by a brush contact. The high voltage is obtained with the help of a step-up transformer. All these changes have the effect of limiting the high voltage current in the small portion of the ignition system wiring and thus avoid the possibilities of leakage etc. Table 10.1 gives the comparison of battery and magneto ignition systems.

10.12 MODERN IGNITION SYSTEMS

The major limitations of the breaker-operated ignition systems are the decrease in available voltage as the engine speed increases due to limitations in the current switching capability of the breaker system and the decreasing time available to build up the stored energy in the primary coil. A further disadvantage is that due to their high current load, the breaker points are subjected to electrical wear in addition to mechanical wear which results in

Table 10.1 Comparison between battery ignition and magneto ignition system

Battery Ignition System	Magneto Ignition System
Battery is necessary. Difficult to start the engine when battery is discharged.	No battery is needed and therefore there is no problem of battery discharge.
Maintenance problems are more due to battery.	Maintenance problems are less since there is no battery.
Current for primary circuit is obtained from the battery.	The required electric current is generated by the magneto.
A good spark is available at the spark plug even at low speed.	During starting, quality of spark is poor due to low speed.
Efficiency of the system decreases with the reduction in spark intensity as engine speed rises.	Efficiency of the system improves as the engine speed rises due to high intensity spark.
Occupies more space.	Occupies less space.
Commonly employed in cars and light commercial vehicles.	Mainly used in racing cars and two wheelers.

short maintenance intervals. The life of the breaker points is dependent on the current they are required to switch.

In order to overcome the above problems in the conventional ignition systems modern ignition systems use electronic circuits. The ability of a transistor to interrupt a circuit carrying a relatively high current makes it an ideal replacement for the breaker points and condenser. One of the pioneering versions was from Ford Motor Company in 1963 and many of the variations are available nowadays. In modern automobiles the following two types are in common use.

(i) Transistorized coil ignition system (TCI system)

(ii) Capacitive discharge ignition system (CDI system)

The details of these ignition systems are explained in the following sections.

10.12.1 Transistorized Coil Ignition (TCI) System

In automotive applications, the transistorized coil ignition systems which provide a higher output voltage and use electronic triggering to maintain the required timing are fast replacing the conventional ignition systems. These systems are also called high energy electronic ignition systems. These have the following advantages:

(i) reduced ignition system maintenance

(ii) reduced wear of the components

(iii) increased reliability

(iv) extended spark plug life

(v) improved ignition of lean mixtures

The circuit diagram of a transistorized coil ignition system is shown in Fig.10.11. The contact breaker and the cam assembly of the conventional ignition system are replaced by a magnetic pulse generating system which detects the distributor shaft position and sends electrical pulse to an electronic control module.

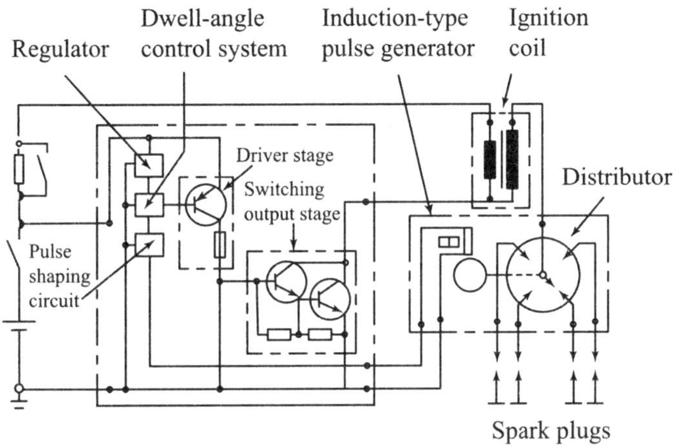

Fig. 10.11 Schematic diagram of transistorized coil ignition (TCI) system with induction pulse generator

The module switches off the flow of current to the primary coil inducing a high voltage in the secondary winding which is distributed to the spark plugs as in the conventional breaker system. The control module contains timing circuit which later closes the primary circuit so that the buildup of the primary circuit current can occur for the next cycle. There are many types of pulse generators that could trigger the electronic circuit of the ignition system.

A magnetic pulse generator where a gear shaped iron rotor driven by the distributor shaft rotates past the pole of a stationary magnetic pickup, is generally used. The number of teeth on the rotor is equal to the number of cylinders. The magnetic field is provided by a permanent magnet. As each rotor tooth passes the magnet pole it first increases and then decreases the magnetic field strength ψ linked with the pickup coil wound on the magnet, producing a voltage signal proportional to $\frac{d\psi}{dt}$. In response to this the electronic module switches off the primary circuit coil current to produce the spark as the rotor tooth passes through alignment and the pickup coil voltage abruptly reverses and passes through zero. The increasing portion of the voltage waveform, after this voltage reversal, is used by the electronic module to establish the point at which the primary coil current is switched on for the next ignition pulse.

10.12.2 Capacitive Discharge Ignition (CDI) System

The details of capacitive discharge ignition system are shown in Fig.10.12. In this system, a capacitor rather than an induction coil is used to store the ignition energy. The capacitance and charging voltage of the capacitor determine the amount of stored energy. Ignition transformer steps up the primary voltage generated at the time of spark by the discharge of the capacitor through the thyristor to the high voltage required at the spark plug. The CDI trigger

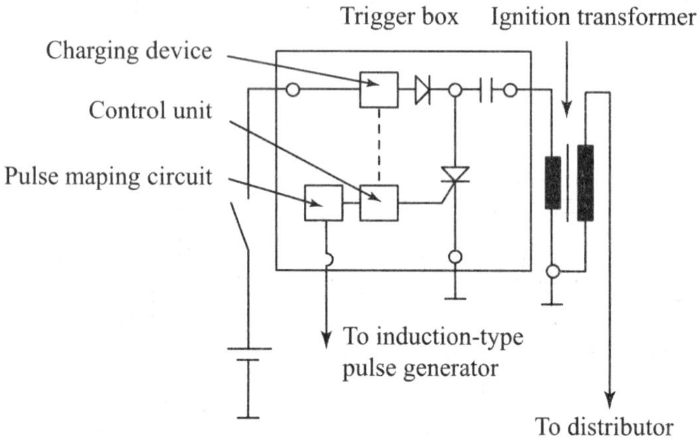

Fig. 10.12 Schematic of capacitive discharge ignition (CDI) system

box contains the capacitor, thyristor power switch, charging device (to convert battery voltage to charging voltage of 300 to 500 V by means of pulses via a voltage transformer), pulse shaping unit and control unit. The advantage of using this system is that it is insensitive to electrical shunts resulting from spark plug fouling. Because of the fast capacitive discharge, the spark is strong but short (0.1 to 0.3 ms) which leads to ignition failure during lean mixture operating conditions. This is the main disadvantage of the CDI system.

10.13 FIRING ORDER

Every engine cylinder must fire once in every cycle. This requires that for a four-stroke four-cylinder engine the ignition system must fire for every 180 degrees of crank rotation. For a six-cylinder engine the time available is only 120 degrees of crank rotation.

The order in which various cylinders of a multicylinder engine fire is called the *firing order*. The number of possibilities of firing order depends upon the number of cylinders and throws of the crankshaft. It is desirable to have the power impulses equally spaced and from the point of view of balancing this has led to certain conventional arrangements of crankshaft throws. Further, there are three factors which must be considered before deciding the optimum firing order of an engine. These are:

(i) engine vibrations

(ii) engine cooling and

(iii) development of back pressure

Consider that the cylinder number 1 of the four-cylinder engine, shown in Fig.10.13, is fired first. Pressure, p, generated in the cylinder number 1 will give rise to a force equal to $pA[b/(a+b)]$ and $pA[a/(a+b)]$ on the two bearings A and B respectively. The load on bearing A is much more than load on bearing B. If the next cylinder fired is cylinder number 2, this imbalance in load on the two bearings would further aggravate the problem of balancing of the crankshaft vibrations. If we fire cylinder number 3 after cylinder number 1, the load may be more or less evenly distributed.

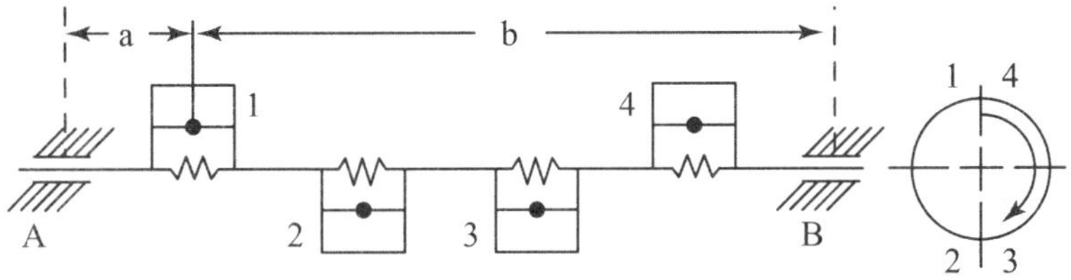

Fig. 10.13 Firing order

Further, consider the effect of firing sequence on engine cooling. When the first cylinder is fired its temperature increases. If the next cylinder that fires is number 2, the portion of the engine between the cylinder number 1 and 2 gets overheated. If then the third cylinder is fired, overheating is shifted to the portion between the cylinders 2 and 4. Thus we see that the task of the cooling system becomes very difficult because it is then, required to cool more at one place than at other places and this imposes great strain on the cooling system. If the third cylinder is fired after the first the overheating problem can be controlled to a greater extent.

Next, consider the flow of exhaust gases in the exhaust pipe. After firing the first cylinder, exhaust gases flow out to the exhaust pipe. If the next cylinder fired is the cylinder number 2, we find that before the gases exhausted by the first cylinder go out of the exhaust pipe the gases exhausted from the second cylinder try to overtake them. This would require that the exhaust pipe be made bigger. Otherwise the back pressure in it would increase and the possibility of back flow would arise. If instead of firing cylinder number 2, cylinder number 3 is fired then by the time the gases exhausted by the cylinder 3 come into the exhaust pipe, the gases from cylinder 1 would have sufficient time to travel the distance between cylinder 1 and cylinder 3 and thus, the development of a high back pressure is avoided.

It should be noted that to some extent all the above three requirements are conflicting and therefore a trade-off is necessary. For four-cylinder engines the possible firing orders are:

$$1-3-4-2 \quad \text{or} \quad 1-2-4-3$$

The former is more commonly used in the vertical configuration of cylinders. For a six-cylinder engine the firing orders can be:

$$1-5-3-6-2-4 \quad \text{or} \quad 1-5-4-6-2-3 \quad \text{or}$$
$$1-2-4-6-5-3 \quad \text{or} \quad 1-2-3-6-5-4$$

The first one is more commonly used.

10.14 IGNITION TIMING AND ENGINE PARAMETERS

In order to obtain maximum power from an engine, the compressed mixture must deliver its maximum pressure at a time when the piston is about to commence its downward stroke and is very close to TDC. Since, there is a time lag between occurrence of spark and the burning of the mixture the spark must take place before the piston reaches top dead centre on its compression stroke. Usually the spark should occur at about 15 degrees $bTDC$. If the spark occurs too early the combustion takes place before the compression stroke is completed and the pressure so developed would oppose the piston motion and thereby reduce the engine power. If the spark occurs too late, the piston would have already completed a certain part of the expansion stroke before the pressure rise occurs and a corresponding amount of engine power is lost.

The correct instant for the introduction of a spark is mainly determined by the ignition lag. The ignition lag depends on many factors, such as compression ratio, mixture strength, throttle opening, engine temperature, combustion chamber design and speed. Some of the important engine parameters affecting the ignition timings are discussed in the following sections.

10.14.1 Engine Speed

Suppose an engine has got ignition advance of d degrees and operating speed is N rpm. Then time available for combustion is

$$\frac{d}{360\ \text{N}}\ \text{min}$$

Now if the engine rpm is increased to $2N$, then in order to have the same time available for combustion an ignition advance of $2d$ degrees is required. Thus, if the combustion time for a given mixture strength, compression ratio and volumetric efficiency be assumed constant, then as the engine speed is increased it will be necessary to advance the ignition progressively in order to follow Upton's rule for optimum advance. The variation of ignition advance required at different speeds is shown in Fig.10.14.

Figure 10.15 shows indicator diagrams taken for a petrol engine running at 1000 and 2000 rpm respectively but with the ignition advance adjusted in each case to give the maximum pressure peak at about 12 degrees after top dead centre. It is seen that at the higher speed a spark advance of 20 degrees is necessary as against 10 degrees at the lower speed. Corresponding delay periods between the passage of the spark and commencement of pressure rise were 20 and 10 degrees respectively, i.e. proportional to the engine speeds.

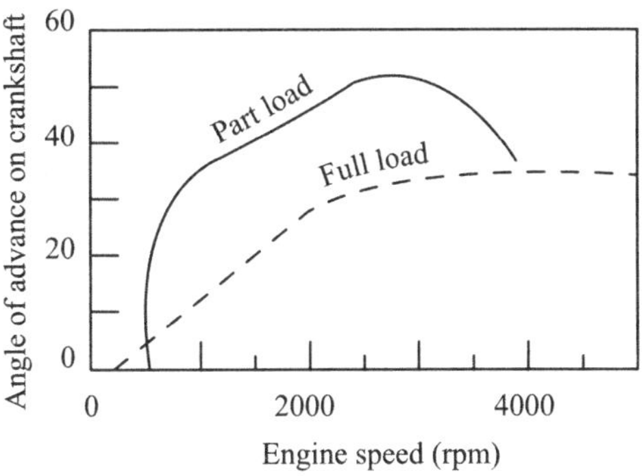

Fig. 10.14 Variation in ignition advance with speed

10.14.2 Mixture Strength

In general, rich mixtures burn faster. Hence, if the engine is operating with richer mixtures the optimum spark timing must be retarded, i.e., the number of degrees of crank angle before TDC at the time of ignition is decreased and the spark occurs closer to TDC.

10.14.3 Part Load Operation

Part load operation of a spark ignition engine is affected by throttling the incoming charge. Due to throttling a smaller amount of charge enters the cylinder and the dilution due to residual gases is also greater. This results in the combustion process being slower. In order to overcome the problem of exhaust gas dilution and the low charge density at part load operation the spark advance must be increased.

10.14.4 Type of Fuel

Ignition delay will depend upon the type of the fuel used in the engine. For maximum power and economy a slow burning fuel needs a higher spark advance than a fast burning fuel.

10.15 SPARK ADVANCE MECHANISM

It is obvious from the above discussion that the point in the cycle where the spark occurs must be regulated to ensure maximum power and economy at different speeds and loads and this must be done automatically. The purpose of the spark advance mechanism is to assure that under every condition of engine operation, ignition takes place at the most favourable instant in time, i.e., most favourable from a standpoint of engine power, fuel economy, and minimum exhaust dilution. By means of these mechanisms the advance angle is accurately set so that ignition occurs before the top dead-center point of the piston. The engine speed and the engine load are the control quantities required for the automatic adjustment of the ignition timing. Most of the engines are fitted with mechanisms which are integral with the distributor

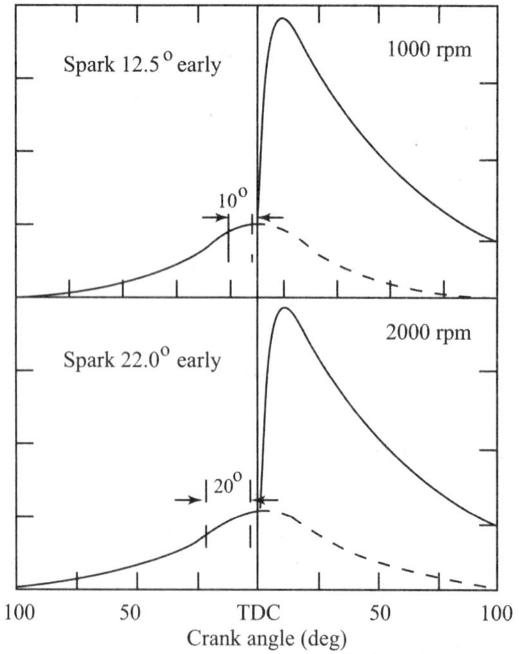

Fig. 10.15 Effect of spark advance on pressure-crank angle diagram

and automatically regulate the optimum spark advance to account for change of speed and load. The two mechanisms used are:

(i) Centrifugal advance mechanism

(ii) Vacuum advance mechanism

These mechanisms are discussed in greater details in the following sections.

10.15.1 Centrifugal Advance Mechanism

The centrifugal advance mechanism controls the ignition timing for full-load operation. The adjustment mechanism is designed so that its operation results in the desired advance of the spark. The cam is mounted, movably, on the distributor shaft so that as the speed increases, the flyweights which are swung farther and farther outward, shift the cam in the direction of shaft rotation. As a result, the cam lobes make contact with the breaker lever rubbing block somewhat earlier, thus shifting the ignition point in the *early* or advance direction. Depending on the speed of the engine, and therefore of the shaft, the weights are swung outward a greater or a lesser distance from the center. They are then held in the extended position, in a state of equilibrium corresponding to the shifted timing angle, by a retaining spring which exactly balances the centrifugal force. The weights shift the cam either on a rolling contact or sliding contact basis; for this reason we distinguish between the rolling contact type and the sliding contact type of centrifugal advance mechanism.

The beginning of the timing adjustment in the range of low engine speeds and the continued adjustment based on the full load curve are determined by the size of the weights, by the shape of the contact mechanisms (rolling or sliding contact type), and by the retaining springs, all of which can be widely differing designs. The centrifugal force controlled cam is fitted with a lower limit stop for purposes of setting the beginning of the adjustment, and also with an upper limit stop to restrict the greatest possible full-load adjustment. A typical sliding contact type centrifugal advance mechanism is shown in Fig.10.16(a) and (b).

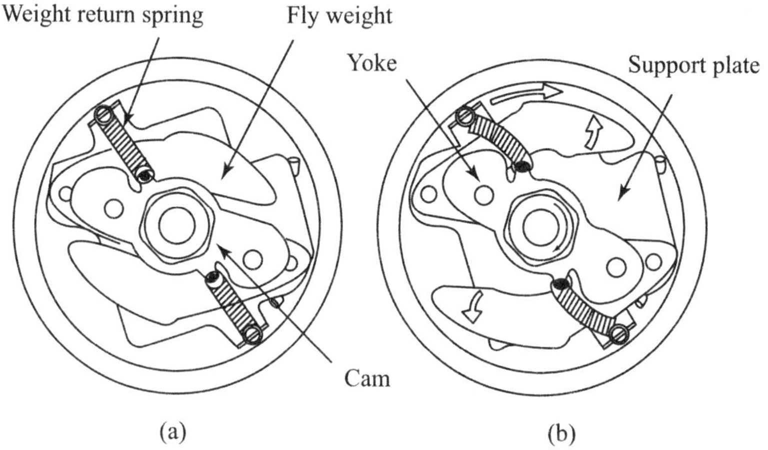

Fig. 10.16 Sliding contact type centrifugal advance mechanism

10.15.2 Vacuum Advance Mechanism

Vacuum advance mechanism shifts the ignition point under part load operation. The adjustment system is designed so that its operation results in the prescribed part-load advance curve. In this mechanism the adjustment control quantity is the static vacuum prevailing in the carburettor, a pressure which depends on the position of the throttle valve at any given time and which is at a maximum when this valve is about half open. This explains the vacuum maximum.

The diaphragm of a vacuum unit is moved by changes in gas pressure. The position of this diaphragm is determined by the pressure differential at any given moment between the prevailing vacuum and atmospheric pressure. The beginning of adjustment is set by the pre-established tension on a compression spring. The diaphragm area, the spring force, and the spring rigidity are all selected in accordance with the part-load advance curve which is to be followed and are all balanced with respect to each other. The diaphragm movement is transmitted through a vacuum advance arm connected to the movable breaker plate, and this movement shifts the breaker plate an additional amount under part-load conditions in a direction opposite to the direction of rotation of the distributor shaft. Limit stops on the vacuum advance arm in the base of the vacuum unit restrict the range of adjustment.

The vacuum advance mechanism operates independent of the centrifugal advance mechanism. The mechanical interplay between the two advance mechanisms, however, permits the total adjustment angle at any given time to be the result of the addition of the shifts provided by the two individual mechanisms. In other words, the vacuum advance mechanism operates in conjunction with the centrifugal advance mechanism to provide the total adjustment required when the engine is operating under part load. A typical vacuum advance mechanism is shown in Fig.10.17.

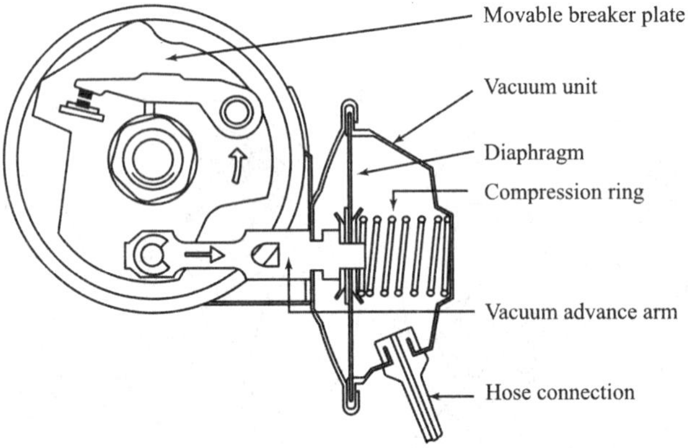

Fig. 10.17 Vacuum advance mechanism

10.16 IGNITION TIMING AND EXHAUST EMISSIONS

Idling, deceleration and running rich with closed throttle are some engine operating conditions which produce excessive unburnt hydrocarbons and carbon monoxide in exhaust. The emission quality is greatly affected by the ignition timing as shown in Fig.10.18.

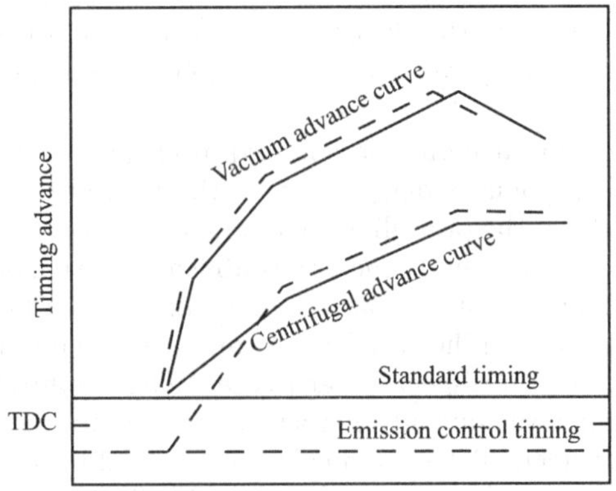

Fig. 10.18 Typical distributor advance curve for lower HC and CO exhaust emission

Retarding ignition timing at *idle* tends to reduce exhaust emission in two ways. With retarded timing, exhaust gas temperatures are higher (fuel economy is adversely affected), thereby promoting additional burning of the hydrocarbons in the exhaust manifold. Since engine efficiency is reduced, retarded timing requires a slightly larger throttle opening to maintain the same idle speed. The larger throttle opening means the possibility of better mixing and combustion during idling. This reduces exhaust emissions appreciably especially during deceleration.

Review Questions

10.1 What is meant by ignition? What is the interrelation between ignition and combustion?

10.2 What are various types of ignition system that are commonly used?

10.3 Explain the basic energy requirements for spark ignition.

10.4 What is capacitance spark and how is it produced?

10.5 With a neat sketch explain an induction coil.

10.6 How does gas movement affect spark-ignition?

10.7 Comment on the spark energy and its duration in the initiation of combustion.

10.8 What are the important requirements of the high voltage ignition source for the spark-ignition process?

10.9 What are the two conventional types of ignition systems that are normally used in automobiles?

10.10 Mention the various important qualities of a good ignition system.

10.11 With a neat sketch explain the battery ignition system.

10.12 Explain TCI ignition system with a sketch.

10.13 Explain CDI ignition system with a suitable diagram.

10.14 With a neat sketch explain the magneto ignition system.

10.15 What is the main function of a spark plug? Draw a neat sketch of a spark plug and explain its various parts.

10.16 Explain the details of firing order.

10.17 Briefly discuss the various factors which affect the ignition timing.

10.18 Why spark advance is required? Explain.

10.19 Briefly explain the centrifugal advance mechanism.

10.20 Explain with a neat sketch the vacuum advance mechanism.

Multiple Choice Questions (choose the most appropriate answer)

1. The secondary winding of ignition coil consists of

   (a) few turns of fine wire
   (b) few turns of thick wire
   (c) many turns of fine wire
   (d) many turns of thick wire

2. Dwell is the time

   (a) for which the points remain closed
   (b) for which the points remain open
   (c) time during which inlet and exhaust valves are open
   (d) none of the above

3. Dwell period

   (a) is directly proportional to engine speed
   (b) is inversely proportional to engine speed
   (c) does not depend on engine speed
   (d) none of the above

4. If the contact breaker gap is small, it results in

   (a) advanced timing
   (b) increased dwell
   (c) rapid burning of the pointer gaps
   (d) none of the above

5. For a four cylinder engine operating at N rpm, the contact breaker must make and break the circuit

   (a) N times
   (b) 2N times
   (c) $\frac{N}{2}$ times
   (d) none of the above

6. Contact breaker should be set

   (a) just before starting the engine
   (b) before adjustment of dwell angle
   (c) after adjustment of dwell angle
   (d) before setting spark plug gap

7. Dwell meter is used for

   (a) setting spark plug gap
   (b) contact breaker gap
   (c) setting the ignition advance
   (d) setting

8. For a four cylinder vertical engine, the commonly used firing order is

   (a) 1–2–3–4
   (b) 3–4–1–2
   (c) 1–3–4–2
   (d) 4–3–2–1

9. For engine operating with rich mixtures the optimum spark timing

   (a) must be advanced
   (b) must be retarded
   (c) must be at TDC
   (d) none of the above

10. For peak lead operation, the spark advance

    (a) must be decreased
    (b) must be increased
    (c) need not be altered
    (d) none of the above

11. Ignition timing is adjusted by

    (a) tachometer
    (b) stroboscopic light
    (c) stop watch
    (d) accurate clock

12. Vacuum advance mechanism shifts the ignition point under

    (a) no load operation
    (b) full load operation
    (c) part load operation
    (d) under sudden acceleration

13. Which of the following statement is wrong?

    (a) retarded timing causes exhaust gas temperature to be higher
    (b) retarded timing improves fuel economy
    (c) retarded timing requires slightly longer throttle opening
    (d) retarded timing causes burning of the hydrocarbons in the exhaust

14. Choose the correct statement from the following

    (a) maintenance problem in magneto-ignition system is more
    (b) magneto ignition system occupies more space
    (c) magneto ignition system is used in larger four wheelers
    (d) magneto ignition system has poor quality of spark during starting

15. Battery ignition system

    (a) occupies more space
    (b) has more maintenance problem
    (c) is commonly employed in four wheelers
    (d) all of the above

Ans:					
	1. – (c)	2. – (a)	3. – (b)	4. – (c)	5. – (b)
	6. – (c)	7. – (b)	8. – (c)	9. – (a)	10. – (b)
	11. – (b)	12. – (c)	13. – (b)	14. – (d)	15. – (d)

11 COMBUSTION AND COMBUSTION CHAMBERS

11.1 INTRODUCTION

Combustion is a chemical reaction in which certain elements of the fuel like hydrogen and carbon combine with oxygen liberating heat energy and causing an increase in temperature of the gases. The conditions necessary for combustion are the presence of combustible mixture and some means of initiating the process. The theory of combustion is a very complex subject and has been a topic of intensive research for many years. In spite of this, not much knowledge is available concerning the phenomenon of combustion.

The process of combustion in engines generally takes place either in a homogeneous or a heterogeneous fuel vapour-air mixture depending on the type of engine.

11.2 HOMOGENEOUS MIXTURE

In spark-ignition engines a nearly homogeneous mixture of air and fuel is formed in the carburettor. Homogeneous mixture is thus formed outside the engine cylinder and the combustion is initiated inside the cylinder at a particular instant towards the end of the compression stroke. The flame front spreads over a combustible mixture with a certain velocity. In a homogeneous gas mixture the fuel and oxygen molecules are more or less, uniformly distributed.

Once the fuel vapour-air mixture is ignited, a flame front appears and rapidly spreads through the mixture. The flame propagation is caused by heat transfer and diffusion of burning fuel molecules from the combustion zone to the adjacent layers of unburnt mixture. The flame front is a narrow zone separating the fresh mixture from the combustion products. The velocity with which the flame front moves, with respect to the unburned mixture in a direction normal to its surface is called the normal flame velocity.

In a homogeneous mixture with an equivalence ratio, ϕ, *(the ratio of the actual fuel-air ratio to the stoichiometric fuel-air ratio)* close to 1.0, the flame speed is normally of the order of 40 cm/s. However, in a spark-ignition engine the maximum flame speed is obtained when ϕ is between 1.1 and 1.2, i.e., when the mixture is slightly richer than stoichiometric.

If the equivalence ratio is outside this range the flame speed drops rapidly to a low value. When the flame speed drops to a very low value, the heat loss from the combustion zone becomes equal to the amount of heat-release due to combustion and the flame gets extinguished. Therefore, it is quite preferable to operate the engine within an equivalence ratio of 1.1 to 1.2 for proper combustion. However, by introducing turbulence and incorporating proper air movement, the flame speed can be increased in mixtures outside the above range.

11.3 HETEROGENEOUS MIXTURE

In a heterogeneous gas mixture, the rate of combustion is determined by the velocity of mutual diffusion of fuel vapours and air and the rate of chemical reaction is of minor importance. Self-ignition or spontaneous ignition of fuel-air mixture, at the high temperature developed due to higher compression ratios, is of primary importance in determining the combustion characteristics.

When the mixture is heterogeneous the combustion can take place in an overall lean mixture since, there are always local zones where ϕ varies between 1.0 and 1.2 corresponding to maximum rate of chemical reaction. Ignition starts in this zone and the flame produced helps to burn the fuel in the adjoining zones where the mixture is leaner. Similarly, in the zones where the mixture is rich the combustion occurs because of the high temperature produced due to combustion initiated in the zones where ϕ is 1.0 to 1.2.

A comprehensive study of combustion in both spark-ignition and compression-ignition engines is given in the following sections.

11.4 COMBUSTION IN SPARK–IGNITION ENGINES

As already mentioned, in a conventional spark-ignition engine, the fuel and air are homogeneously mixed together in the intake system, inducted through the intake valve into the cylinder where it mixes with residual gases and is then compressed. Under normal operating conditions, combustion is initiated towards the end of the compression stroke at the spark plug by an electric discharge. A turbulent flame develops following the ignition and propagates through this premixed charge of fuel and air, and also the residual gas in the clearance volume until it reaches the combustion chamber walls. Combustion in the SI engine may be broadly divided into two general types, viz., normal combustion and abnormal combustion.

11.5 STAGES OF COMBUSTION IN SI ENGINES

A typical theoretical pressure-crank angle diagram, during the process of compression (a→b), combustion (b→c) and expansion (c→d) in an ideal four-stroke spark-ignition engine is shown in Fig.11.1. In an ideal engine, as can be seen from the diagram, the entire pressure rise during combustion takes place at constant volume i.e., at TDC. However, in an actual engine this does not happen. The detailed process of combustion in an actual SI engine is described below.

Sir Ricardo, known as the father of engine research, describes the combustion process in a SI engine as consisting of three stages:

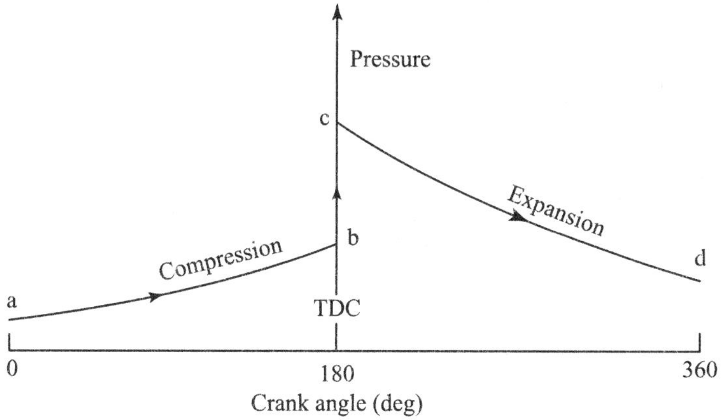

Fig. 11.1 Theoretical p-θ diagram

The pressure variation due to combustion in a practical engine is shown in Fig.11.2. In this figure, A is the point of passage of spark (say 20°$bTDC$), B is the point at which the beginning of pressure rise can be detected (say 8° $bTDC$) and C the attainment of peak pressure. Thus AB represents the first stage and BC the second stage and CD the third stage.

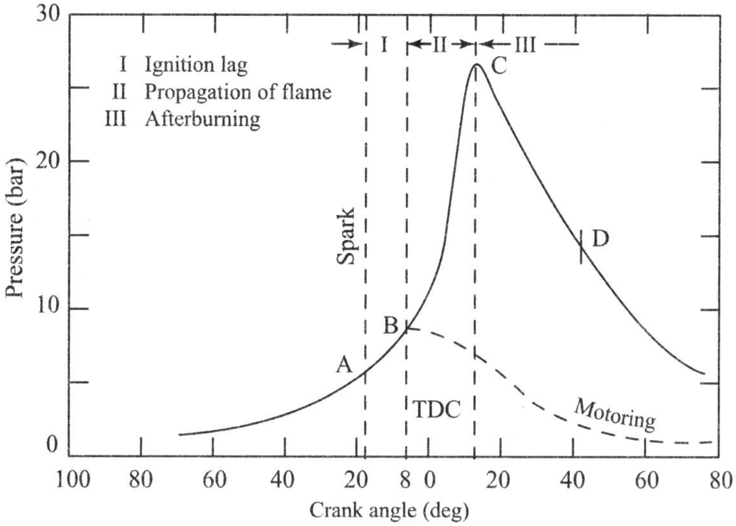

Fig. 11.2 Stages of combustion in an SI engine

The *first stage* (A→B) is referred to as the ignition lag or preparation phase in which growth and development of a self propagating nucleus of flame takes place. This is a chemical process depending upon both temperature and pressure, the nature of the fuel and the proportion of the exhaust residual gas. Further, it also depends upon the relationship between the temperature and the rate of reaction.

The *second stage* (B→C) is a physical one and it is concerned with the spread of the flame throughout the combustion chamber. The starting point of the second stage is where the first measurable rise of pressure is seen on the indicator diagram i.e., the point where the line of combustion departs from the compression line (point B). This can be seen from the deviation from the motoring curve.

During the second stage the flame propagates practically at a constant velocity. Heat transfer to the cylinder wall is low, because only a small part of the burning mixture comes in contact with the cylinder wall during this period. The rate of heat-release depends largely on the turbulence intensity and also on the reaction rate which is dependent on the mixture composition. The rate of pressure rise is proportional to the rate of heat-release because during this stage, the combustion chamber volume remains practically constant (since piston is near the top dead centre).

The starting point of the *third stage* is usually taken as the instant at which the maximum pressure is reached on the indicator diagram (point C). The flame velocity decreases during this stage. The rate of combustion becomes low due to lower flame velocity and reduced flame front surface. Since the expansion stroke starts before this stage of combustion, with the piston moving away from the top dead centre, there can be no pressure rise during this stage.

11.6 FLAME FRONT PROPAGATION

For efficient combustion the rate of propagation of the flame front within the cylinder is quite critical. The two important factors which determine the rate of movement of the flame front across the combustion chamber are the *reaction rate* and the *transposition rate.* The *reaction rate* is the result of a purely chemical combination process in which the flame *eats* its way into the unburned charge. The *transposition rate* is due to the physical movement of the flame front relative to the cylinder wall and is also the result of the pressure differential between the burning gases and the unburnt gases in the combustion chamber.

Figure 11.3 shows the rate of flame propagation. In area I, (A→B), the flame front progresses relatively slowly due to a low *transposition rate* and low turbulence. The transposition of the flame front is very little since there is a comparatively small mass of charge burned at the start. The low reaction rate plays a dominant role resulting in a slow advance of the flame. Also, since the spark plug is to be necessarily located in a quiescent layer of gas that is close to the cylinder wall, the lack of turbulence reduces the reaction rate and hence the flame speed. As the flame front leaves the quiescent zone and proceeds into more turbulent areas (area II) where it consumes a greater mass of mixture, it progresses more rapidly and at a constant rate (B→C) as shown in Fig.11.3.

The volume of unburned charge is very much less towards the end of flame travel and so the *transposition rate* again becomes negligible thereby reducing the flame speed. The reaction rate is also reduced again since the flame is entering a zone (area III) of relatively low turbulence (C→D) in Fig.11.3.

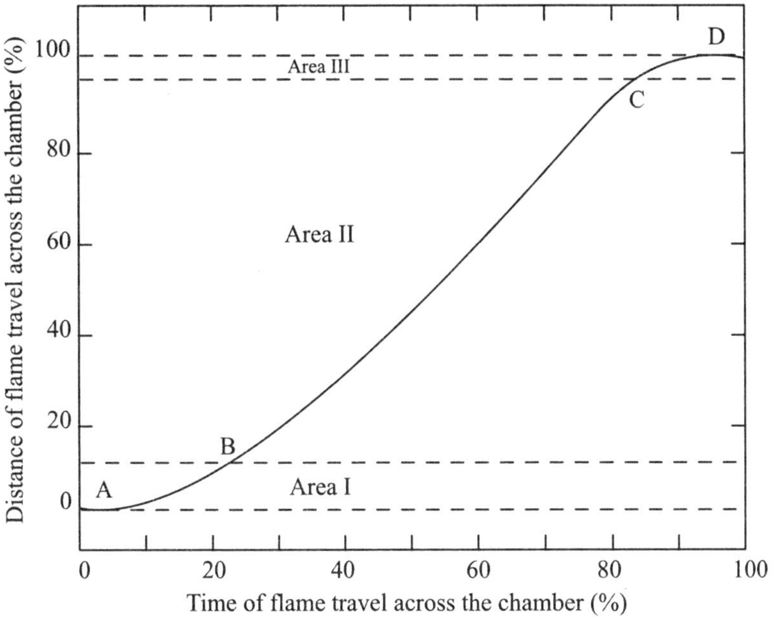

Fig. 11.3 Details of flame travel

11.7 FACTORS INFLUENCING THE FLAME SPEED

The study of factors which affect the velocity of flame propagation is important since the flame velocity influences the rate of pressure rise in the cylinder and it is related to certain types of abnormal combustion that occur in spark-ignition engines. There are several factors which affect the flame speed, to a varying degree, the most important being the turbulence and the fuel-air ratio. Details of various factors that affect the flame speed are discussed below.

Turbulence: The flame speed is quite low in non-turbulent mixtures and increases with increasing turbulence. This is mainly due to the additional physical intermingling of the burning and unburned particles at the flame front which expedites reaction by increasing the rate of contact. The turbulence in the incoming mixture is generated during the admission of fuel-air mixture through comparatively narrow sections of the intake pipe, valve openings etc., in the suction stroke. Turbulence which is supposed to consist of many minute swirls appears to increase the rate of reaction and produce a higher flame speed than that made up of larger and fewer swirls. A suitable design of the combustion chamber which involves the geometry of cylinder head and piston crown increases the turbulence during the compression stroke.

Generally, turbulence increases the heat flow to the cylinder wall. It also accelerates the chemical reaction by intimate mixing of fuel and oxygen so that spark advance may be reduced. This helps in burning lean mixtures also. The increase of flame speed due to turbulence reduces the combustion duration and hence minimizes the tendency of abnormal combustion. However, excessive turbulence may extinguish the flame resulting in rough and noisy operation of the engine.

Fuel-Air Ratio: The fuel-air ratio has a very significant influence on the flame speed. The highest flame velocities (minimum time for complete combustion) are obtained with somewhat richer mixture (point A) as shown in Fig.11.4 which shows the effect of mixture strength on the rate of burning as indicated by the time taken for complete burning in a given engine. When

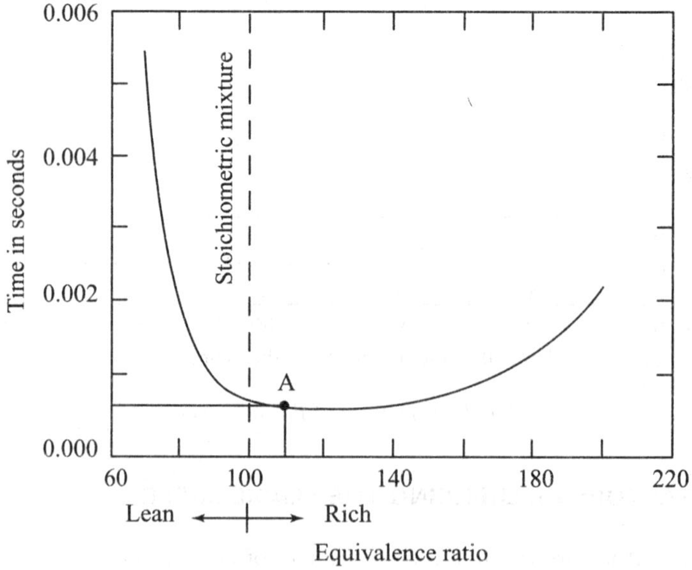

Fig. 11.4 Effect of mixture strength on the rate of burning

the mixture is made leaner or richer (see point A in Fig.11.4) the flame speed decreases. Less thermal energy is released in the case of lean mixtures resulting in lower flame temperature. Very rich mixtures lead to incomplete combustion which results again in the release of less thermal energy.

Temperature and Pressure: Flame speed increases with an increase in intake temperature and pressure. A higher initial pressure and temperature may help to form a better homogeneous air-vapour mixture which helps in increasing the flame speed. This is possible because of an overall increase in the density of the charge.

Compression Ratio: A higher compression ratio increases the pressure and temperature of the working mixture which reduce the initial *preparation phase* of combustion and hence less ignition advance is needed. High pressures and temperatures of the compressed mixture also speed up the second phase of combustion. Increased compression ratio reduces the clearance volume and therefore increases the density of the cylinder gases during burning. This increases the peak pressure and temperature and the total combustion duration is reduced. Thus engines having higher compression ratios have higher flame speeds.

Engine Output: The cycle pressure increases when the engine output is increased. With the increased throttle opening the cylinder gets filled to a higher density. This results in increased flame speed. When the output is decreased by throttling, the initial and final compression pressures decrease and the dilution of the working mixture increases. The smooth development of self-propagating nucleus of flame becomes unsteady and difficult. The main disadvantages of SI engines are the poor combustion at low loads and the necessity of mixture enrichment (ϕ between 1.2 to 1.3) which causes wastage of fuel and discharge of unburnt hydrocarbon and the products of incomplete combustion like carbon monoxide etc. in the atmosphere.

Engine Speed: The flame speed increases almost linearly with engine speed since the increase in engine speed increases the turbulence inside the cylinder. The time required for the flame to traverse the combustion space would be halved, if the engine speed is doubled. Double the engine speed and hence half the original time would give the same number of crank degrees for flame propagation. The crank angle required for the flame propagation during the entire phase of combustion, will remain nearly constant at all speeds.

Engine Size: The size of the engine does not have much effect on the rate of flame propagation. In large engines the time required for complete combustion is more because the flame has to travel a longer distance. This requires increased crank angle duration during the combustion. This is one of the reasons why large sized engines are designed to operate at low speeds.

11.8 RATE OF PRESSURE RISE

The rate of pressure rise in an engine combustion chamber exerts a considerable influence on the peak pressure developed, the power produced and the smoothness with which the forces are transmitted to the piston. The rate of pressure rise is mainly dependent upon the mass rate of combustion of mixture in the cylinder.

The relationship between the pressure and the crank angle for three different combustion rates is shown in Fig.11.5. Curve I is for a high, curve II for the normal and curve III for a low rate of combustion. It is clear from the figure that with lower rate of combustion longer time is required for the completion of combustion which necessitates the initiation of burning at an early point on the compression stroke. Also, it may be noted that higher rate of combustion results in higher rate of pressure rise producing higher peak pressures at a point closer to TDC. This generally is a desirable feature because higher peak pressures closer to TDC produce a greater force acting through a large part of the power stroke and hence, increase the power output of the engine. The higher rate of pressure rise causes rough running of the engine because of vibrations produced in the crankshaft rotation. It also tends to promote an undesirable occurrence known as knocking.

A compromise between these opposing factors is accomplished by designing and operating the engine in such a manner that approximately one-half of the maximum pressure is reached by the time the piston reaches TDC. This results in the peak pressure being reasonably close to the beginning of the power stroke, yet maintaining smooth engine operation.

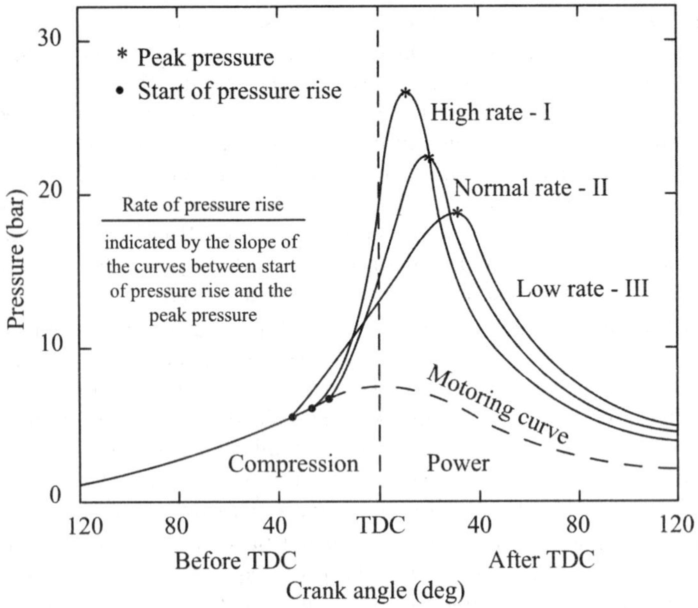

Fig. 11.5 Illustrations of various combustion rates

11.9 ABNORMAL COMBUSTION

In normal combustion, the flame initiated by the spark travels across the combustion chamber in a fairly uniform manner. Under certain operating conditions the combustion deviates from its normal course leading to loss of performance and possible damage to the engine. This type of combustion may be termed as an abnormal combustion or knocking combustion. The consequences of this abnormal combustion process are the loss of power, recurring preignition and mechanical damage to the engine.

11.10 THE PHENOMENON OF KNOCK IN SI ENGINES

In a spark-ignition engine combustion which is initiated between the spark plug electrodes spreads across the combustible mixture. A definite flame front which separates the fresh mixture from the products of combustion travels from the spark plug to the other end of the combustion chamber. Heat-release due to combustion increases the temperature and consequently the pressure, of the burned part of the mixture above those of the unburned mixture. In order to effect pressure equalization the burned part of the mixture will expand, and compress the unburned mixture adiabatically thereby increasing its pressure and temperature. This process continues as the flame front advances through the mixture and the temperature and pressure of the unburned mixture are increased further.

If the temperature of the unburnt mixture exceeds the self-ignition temperature of the fuel and remains at or above this temperature during the period of preflame reactions (ignition lag), spontaneous ignition or autoignition occurs at various pin-point locations. This phenomenon is called knocking. The process of autoignition leads towards engine knock.

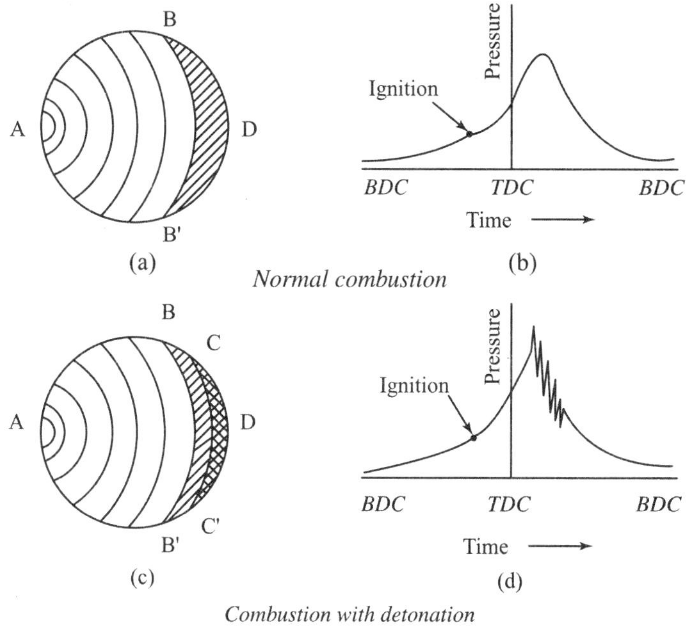

Fig. 11.6 Normal and abnormal combustion

The phenomenon of knock may be explained by referring to Fig.11.6(a) which shows the cross-section of the combustion chamber with flame advancing from the spark plug location A without knock whereas Fig.11.6(c) shows the combustion process with knock. In the normal combustion the flame travels across the combustion chamber from A towards D. The advancing flame front compresses the end charge BB′D farthest from the spark plug, thus raising its temperature. The temperature is also increased due to heat transfer from the hot advancing flame-front. Also some preflame oxidation may take place in the end charge leading to further increase in temperature. In spite of these factors if the temperature of the end charge had not reached its self-ignition temperature, the charge would not autoignite and the flame will advance further and consume the charge BB′D. This is the normal combustion process which is illustrated by means of the pressure-time diagram, Fig.11.6(b). However, if the end charge BB′D reaches its autoignition temperature and remains upto the time of preflame reactions the charge will autoignite, leading to knocking combustion. In Fig.11.6(c), it is assumed that when flame has reached the position BB′, the charge ahead of it has reached critical autoignition temperature. During the preflame reaction period if the flame front could move from BB′ to only CC′ then the charge ahead of CC′ would autoignite.

Because of the autoignition, another flame front starts traveling in the opposite direction to the main flame front. When the two flame fronts collide, a severe pressure pulse is generated. The gas in the chamber is subjected to compression and rarefaction along the pressure pulse until pressure equilibrium is restored. This disturbance can force the walls of the combustion chambers to vibrate at the same frequency as the gas. Gas vibration frequency in automobile engines is of the order of 5000 cps. The pressure-time trace of such a situation is shown in Fig.11.6(d).

It is to be noted that the onset of knocking is very much dependent on the properties of fuel. It is clear from the above description that if the unburned charge does not reach its autoignition temperature there will be no knocking. Further, if the initial phase i.e., ignition lag period, is longer than the time required for the flame front to burn through the unburned charge, there will be no knocking. But, if the critical temperature is reached and maintained, and the ignition lag is shorter than the time it takes for the flame front to burn through the unburned charge then the end charge will detonate. Hence, in order to avoid or inhibit detonation, a high autoignition temperature and a long ignition lag are the desirable qualities for SI engine fuels.

In summary, when autoignition occurs, two different types of vibration may be produced. In one case a large amount of mixture may autoignite giving rise to a very rapid increase in pressure throughout the combustion chamber and there will be a direct blow on the engine structure. The human ear can detect the resulting thudding sound and consequent noise from free vibrations of the engine parts. In the other case, large pressure differences may exist in the combustion chamber and the resulting gas vibrations can force the walls of the chamber to vibrate at the same frequency as the gas. An audible sound may be evident.

The impact of knock on the engine components and structure can cause engine failure and in addition the noise from engine vibration is always objectionable. The pressure differences in the combustion chamber cause the gas to vibrate and scrub the chamber walls causing increased loss of heat to the coolant. The presence or absence of knocking combustion in engines is often judged from a distinctly audible sound. A scientific method to detect the phenomenon of knocking is to use a pressure transducer. The output of this transducer is connected, usually, to a cathode ray oscilloscope. Typical pressure-time traces which can be obtained from a pressure transducer are given in Fig.11.6(b) for a normal combustion and in Fig.11.6(d) for knocking combustion.

11.10.1 Knock Limited Parameters

It should be the aim of the designer to reduce the tendency of knocking in the engine. In this connection, certain knock limited parameters are explained.

Knock Limited Compression Ratio: The knock limited compression ratio is obtained by increasing the compression ratio on a variable compression ratio engine until incipient knocking is observed. Any change in operating conditions such as fuel-air ratio or in the engine design that increases the knock limited compression ratio is said to reduce the tendency towards knocking.

Knock Limited Inlet Pressure: The inlet pressure can be increased by opening the throttle or increasing supercharger delivery pressure until incipient knock is observed. An increase in knock limited inlet pressure indicates a reduction in the knocking tendency.

Knock Limited Indicated Mean Effective Pressure: The indicated mean effective pressure measured at incipient knock is usually abbreviated as *Klimep*. This parameter and the corresponding fuel consumption are obviously of great practical interest.

An useful measure of knocking tendency called the performance number, has been developed from the concept of knock limited indicated mean effective pressure. This number is defined as the ratio of *Klimep* with the fuel in question to *Klimep* with iso-octane when the inlet pressure is kept constant. This performance number is related to octane number and one of the advantages of this is that it can be applied to fuels whose knocking characteristics are superior to that of iso-octane, i.e., it extends the octane scale beyond 100.

Further simplification on the use of performance number requirements is done by introducing the concept of relative performance number, *rpn*, which is defined as:

$$rpn = \frac{\text{Actual Performance number}}{\text{Performance number corresponding to the imep of 100}}$$

11.11 EFFECT OF ENGINE VARIABLES ON KNOCK

From the discussion on knock in the previous section, it may be seen that four major factors are involved in either producing or preventing knock. These are the temperature, pressure, density of the unburned charge and the time factors. Since, the effect of temperature, pressure and density are closely interrelated, these three are consolidated into one group and the time factors into another group.

11.11.1 Density Factors

Any factor in the design or operation of an engine which tends to reduce the temperature of the unburned charge should reduce the possibility of knocking by reducing the temperature of the end charge for autoignition. Similarly, any factor which reduces the density of the charge tends to reduce knocking by providing lower energy release. Further, the effect of the following parameters which are directly or indirectly connected with temperature, pressure and density factors on the possibility of knocking is discussed below.

Compression Ratio: Compression ratio of an engine is an important factor which determines both the pressure and temperature at the beginning of the combustion process. Increase in compression ratio increases the pressure and temperature of the gases at the end of the compression stroke. This decreases the ignition lag of the end gas and thereby increasing the tendency for knocking. The overall increase in the density of the charge due to higher compression ratio increases the preflame reactions in the end charge thereby increasing the knocking tendency of the engine. The increase in the knocking tendency of the engine with increasing compression ratio is the main reason for limiting the compression ratio to a lower value.

Mass of Inducted Charge: A reduction in the mass of the inducted charge into the cylinder of an engine by throttling or by reducing the amount of supercharging reduces both temperature and density of the charge at the time of ignition. This decreases the tendency of knocking.

Inlet Temperature of the Mixture: Increase in the inlet temperature of the mixture makes the compression temperature higher thereby, increasing the tendency of knocking. Further, volumetric efficiency will be lowered. Hence, a lower inlet temperature is always preferable to reduce knocking. It is important that the temperature should not be so low as to cause starting and vaporization problems in the engine.

Temperature of the Combustion Chamber Walls: Temperature of the combustion chamber walls play a predominant role in knocking. In order to prevent knocking the hot spots in the combustion chamber should be avoided. Since, the spark plug and exhaust valve are two hottest parts in the combustion chamber, the end gas should not be compressed against them.

Retarding the Spark Timing: By retarding the spark timing from the optimized timing, i.e., having the spark closer to TDC, the peak pressures are reached farther down on the power stroke and are thus of lower magnitude. This might reduce the knocking. However, the spark timing will be different from the MBT timing. This will affect the brake torque and power output of the engine.

Power Output of the Engine: A decrease in the output of the engine decreases the temperature of the cylinder and the combustion chamber walls and also the pressure of the charge thereby lowering mixture and end gas temperatures. This reduces the tendency to knock.

11.11.2 Time Factors

Increasing the flame speed or increasing the duration of the ignition lag or reducing the time of exposure of the unburned mixture to autoignition condition will tend to reduce knocking. The following factors, in most cases, reduce the possibility of knocking.

Turbulence: Turbulence depends on the design of the combustion chamber and on engine speed. Increasing turbulence increases the flame speed and reduces the time available for the end charge to attain autoignition conditions thereby decreasing the tendency to knock.

Engine Speed: An increase in engine speed increases the turbulence of the mixture considerably resulting in increased flame speed, and reduces the time available for preflame reactions. Hence knocking tendency is reduced at higher speeds.

Flame Travel Distance: The knocking tendency is reduced by shortening the time required for the flame front to traverse the combustion chamber. Engine size (combustion chamber size), and spark plug position are the three important factors governing the flame travel distance.

Engine Size: The flame requires a longer time to travel across the combustion chamber of a larger engine. Therefore, a larger engine has a greater tendency for knocking than a smaller engine since there is more time for the end gas to autoignite. Hence, a spark-ignition engine is generally limited to size of about 150 mm bore.

Combustion Chamber Shape: Generally, the more compact the combustion chamber is, the shorter is the flame travel and the combustion time and hence better antiknock characteristics. Therefore, the combustion chambers are made as spherical as possible to minimize the length of the flame travel for a given volume. If the turbulence in the combustion chamber is high, the combustion rate is high and consequently combustion time and knocking tendency are reduced. Hence, the combustion chamber is shaped in such a way as to promote turbulence.

Location of Spark Plug: In order to have a minimum flame travel, the spark plug is centrally located in the combustion chamber, resulting in minimum knocking tendency. The flame travel can also be reduced by using two or more spark plugs in case of large engines.

11.11.3 Composition Factors

Once the basic design of the engine is finalized, the fuel-air ratio and the properties of the fuel, particularly the octane rating, play a crucial role in controlling the knock.

Fuel-Air Ratio: The flame speeds are affected by fuel-air ratio. Also the flame temperature and reaction time are different for different fuel-air ratios. Maximum flame temperature is obtained when $\phi \approx 1.1$ to 1.2 whereas $\phi = 1$ gives minimum reaction time for autoignition.

Figure 11.7 shows the variation of knock limited compression ratio with respect to equivalence ratio for iso-octane. The maximum tendency to knock takes place for the fuel-air ratio which gives minimum reaction time as discussed earlier. Thus, the most predominant factor is the reaction time of the mixture in this case.

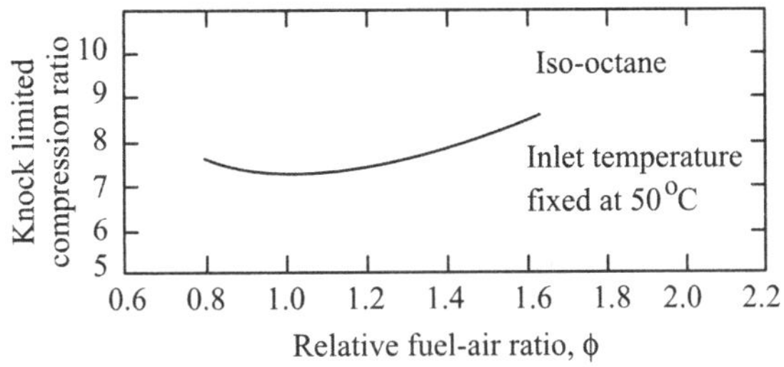

Fig. 11.7 Effect of equivalence ratio on knock limited compression ratio

In general except at rich end, the behaviour in the engine follows the same pattern as the fuel-air ratio versus reaction time discussed earlier. The drop in *Klimep* at very rich end is caused by large drop in thermal efficiency.

Octane Value of the Fuel: A higher self-ignition temperature of the fuel and a low preflame reactivity would reduce the tendency of knocking. In general, paraffin series of hydrocarbon have the maximum and aromatic series the minimum tendency to knock. The naphthene series comes in between the

Table 11.1 Summary of variables affecting knock in an SI engine

Increase in variable	**Major effect on unburned reduce charge**	**Action to be taken to knocking**	**Can operator usually control?**
Compression ratio	Increases temperature & pressure	Reduce	No
Mass of charge inducted	Increases pressure	Reduce	Yes
Inlet temperature	Increases temperature	Reduce	In some cases
Chamber wall temperature	Increases temperature	Reduce	Not ordinarily
Spark advance	Increases temperature & pressure	Retard	In some cases
A/F ratio	Increases temperature & pressure	Make very rich	In some cases
Turbulence	Decreases time factor	Increase	Somewhat (through engine speed)
Engine speed	Decreases time factor	Increase	Yes
Distance of flame travel	Increases time factor	Reduce	No

two. Usually, compounds with more compact molecular structure are less prone to knock. In aliphatic hydrocarbons, unsaturated compounds show lesser knocking tendency than saturated hydrocarbons, the exception being ethylene, acetylene and propylene.

Table 11.1 gives the general summary of variables affecting the knock in an SI engine and shows whether the various factors can be controlled by the operator.

11.12 COMBUSTION CHAMBERS FOR SI ENGINES

The design of the combustion chamber for an SI engine has an important influence on the engine performance and its knocking tendencies. The design involves the shape of the combustion chamber, the location of spark plug and the location of inlet and exhaust valves. Because of this importance, the combustion chamber design has been a subject of considerable amount of research and development in the last fifty years. It has resulted in the raising of the compression ratio of the engine from 4 before the first world war period to 11 in the present times with special combustion chamber designs and suitable antiknock fuels. The important requirements of an SI engine combustion chamber are to provide high power output with minimum octane requirement, high thermal efficiency and smooth engine operation.

Combustion chambers must be designed carefully, keeping in mind the following general objectives.

11.12.1 Smooth Engine Operation

The aim of any engine design is to have a smooth operation and a good economy. These can be achieved by the following:

Moderate Rate of Pressure Rise: The rate of pressure rise can be regulated such that the greatest force is applied to the piston as closely after TDC on the power stroke as possible, with a gradual decrease in the force on the piston during the power stroke. The forces must be applied to the piston smoothly, thus limiting the rate of pressure rise as well as the position of the peak pressure with respect to TDC.

Reducing the Possibility of Knocking: Reduction in the possibility of knocking in an engine can be achieved by,

(i) Reducing the distance of the flame travel by centrally locating the spark plug and also by avoiding pockets of stagnant charge.

(ii) Satisfactory cooling of the spark plug and of exhaust valve area which are the source of hot spots in the majority of the combustion chambers.

(iii) Reducing the temperature of the last portion of the charge, through application of a high surface to volume ratio in that part where the last portion of the charge burns. Heat transfer to the combustion chamber walls can be increased by using high surface to volume ratio thereby reducing the temperature.

11.12.2 High Power Output and Thermal Efficiency

The main objective of the design and development of an engine is to obtain high power as well as high thermal efficiency. This can be achieved by considering the following factors:

(i) A high degree of turbulence is needed to achieve a high flame front velocity. Turbulence is induced by inlet flow configuration or squish. Squish can be induced in spark-ignition engines by having a bowl in piston or with a dome shaped cylinder head. Squish is the rapid radial movement of the gas trapped in between the piston and the cylinder head into the bowl or the dome.

(ii) High volumetric efficiency, i.e., more charge during the suction stroke, results in an increased power output. This can be achieved by providing ample clearance around the valve heads, large diameter valves and straight passages with minimum pressure drop.

(iii) Any design of the combustion chamber that improves its antiknock characteristics permits the use of a higher compression ratio resulting in increased output and efficiency.

(iv) A compact combustion chamber reduces heat loss during combustion and increases the thermal efficiency. Different types of combustion chambers have been developed over a period of time. Some of them are shown in Fig.11.8. Brief description of these combustion chambers are given below.

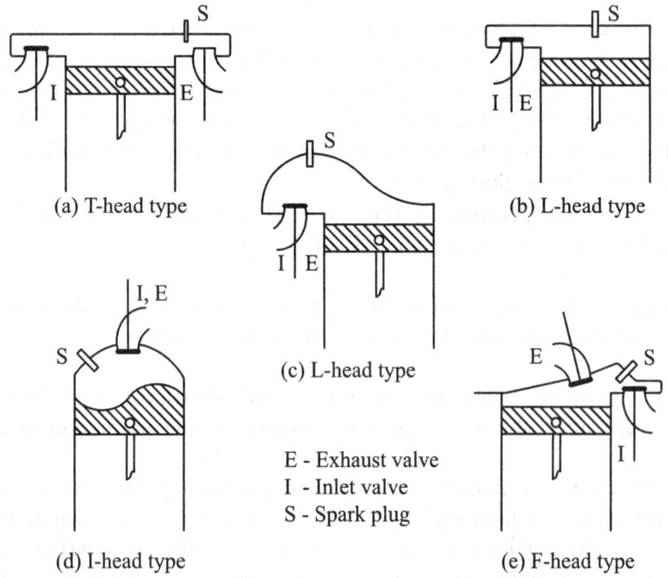

Fig. 11.8 Examples of typical combustion chamber

T-Head Type: The T-head combustion chambers [Fig.11.8(a)] were used in the early stage of engine development. Since the distance across the combustion chamber is very long, knocking tendency is high in this type of engines. This configuration provides two valves on either side of the cylinder, requiring two camshafts. From the manufacturing point of view, providing two camshafts is a disadvantage.

L-Head Type: A modification of the T-head type of combustion chamber is the L-head type which provides the two valves on the same side of the cylinder and the valves are operated by a single camshaft. Figures 11.8(b) and (c) show two types of this side valve engine. In these types, it is easy to lubricate the valve mechanism. With the detachable head it may be noted that the cylinder head can be removed without disturbing valve gear etc. In

Fig.11.8(b) the air flow has to take two right angle turns to enter the cylinder. This causes a loss of velocity head and a loss in turbulence level resulting in a slow combustion process.

The main objectives of the Ricardo's turbulent head design, Fig.11.8(c), are to obtain fast flame speed and reduced knock. The main body of the combustion chamber is concentrated over the valves leaving a slightly restricted passage communicating with the cylinder thereby creating additional turbulence during the compression stroke. This design reduces the knocking tendency by shortening the effective flame travel length by bringing that portion of the head which lay over the farther side of the piston into as close a contact as possible with the piston crown, forming a quench space. The thin layer of gas (entrapped between the relatively cool piston and also cooler head) loses its heat rapidly because of large enclosing surface thereby avoiding knocking. By placing the spark plug in the centre of the effective combustion space slightly towards the hot exhaust valve, the flame travel length is reduced.

I-Head Type or Overhead Valve: The I-head type is also called the overhead valve combustion chamber in which both the valves are located on the cylinder head. The overhead valve engine [Fig.11.8(d)] is superior to a side valve or an L-head engine at high compression ratios. Some of the important characteristics of this type of valve arrangement are:

(i) less surface to volume ratio and therefore less heat loss

(ii) less flame travel length and hence greater freedom from knock

(iii) higher volumetric efficiency from larger valves or valve lifts

(iv) confinement of thermal failures to cylinder head by keeping the hot exhaust valve in the head instead of the cylinder block.

F-Head Type: The F-head type of valve arrangement is a compromise between L-head and I-head types. Combustion chambers in which one valve is in the cylinder head and the other in the cylinder block are known as F-head combustion chambers [Fig.11.8(e)]. Modern F-head engines have exhaust valve in the head and inlet valve in the cylinder block. The main disadvantage of this type is that the inlet valve and the exhaust valve are separately actuated by two cams mounted on two camshafts driven by the crankshaft through gears.

11.13 COMBUSTION IN COMPRESSION-IGNITION ENGINES

There are certain basic differences existing between the combustion process in the SI and CI engines. In the SI engine, a homogeneous carburetted mixture of gasoline vapour and air, in a certain proportion, is compressed (compression ratio 6:1 to 10:1) and the mixture is ignited at one place before the end of the compression stroke by means of an electric spark. A single flame front progresses through the air-fuel mixture after ignition.

In the CI engine, only air is compressed through a high compression ratio (16:1 to 20:1) raising its temperature and pressure to a high value. Fuel is injected through one or more jets into this highly compressed air in the combustion chamber. Here, the fuel jet disintegrates into a core of fuel surrounded by a spray envelope of air and fuel particles [Fig.11.9(a)]. This spray envelope is created both by the atomization and vaporization of the fuel. The turbulence of the air in the combustion chamber passing across the jet tears the fuel particles from the core. A mixture of air and fuel forms at some location in the spray envelope and oxidation starts.

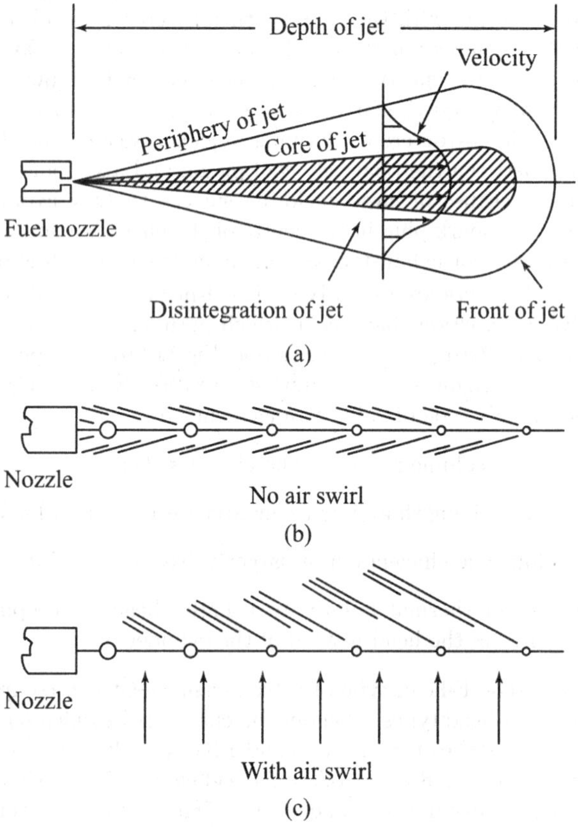

Fig. 11.9 Schematic representation of the disintegration of a fuel jet

The liquid fuel droplets evaporate by absorbing the latent heat of vaporization from the surrounding air which reduces the temperature of a thin layer of air surrounding the droplet and some time elapses before this temperature can be raised again by absorbing heat from the bulk of air. As soon as this vapour and the air reach the level of the autoignition temperature and if the local A/F ratio is within the combustible range, ignition takes place. Thus, it is obvious that at first there is a certain delay period before ignition takes place.

Since the fuel droplets cannot be injected and distributed uniformly throughout the combustion space, the fuel-air mixture is essentially heterogeneous. If the air within the cylinder were motionless under these conditions, there will not be enough oxygen in the burning zone and burning of the fuel would be either slow or totally fail as it would be surrounded by its own products of combustion [Fig.11.9(b)]. Hence, an orderly and controlled movement must be imparted to the air and the fuel so that a continuous flow of fresh air is brought to each burning droplet and the products of combustion are swept away. This air motion is called the air swirl and its effect is shown in Fig.11.9(c).

In an SI engine, the turbulence is a disorderly air motion with no general direction of flow. However, the swirl which is required in CI engines, is an orderly movement of the whole body of air with a particular direction of flow and it assists the breaking up of the fuel jet. Intermixing of the burned and unburned portions of the mixture also takes place due to this swirl. In the SI engine, the ignition occurs at one point with a slow rise in pressure whereas in the CI engine, the ignition occurs at many points simultaneously with consequent rapid rise in pressure. In contrast to the process of combustion in SI engines, there is no definite flame front in CI engines.

In an SI engine, the air-fuel ratio remains close to stoichiometric value from no load to full load. But in a CI engine, irrespective of load, at any given speed, an approximately constant supply of air enters the cylinder. With change in load, the quantity of fuel injected is changed, varying the air-fuel ratio. The overall air-fuel ratio thus varies from about 18:1 at full load to about 80:1 at no load. It is the main aim of the CI engine designer that the A/F ratio should be as close to stoichiometric as possible while operating at full load since the mean effective pressure and power output are maximum at that condition. Thermodynamic analysis of the engine cycles has clearly

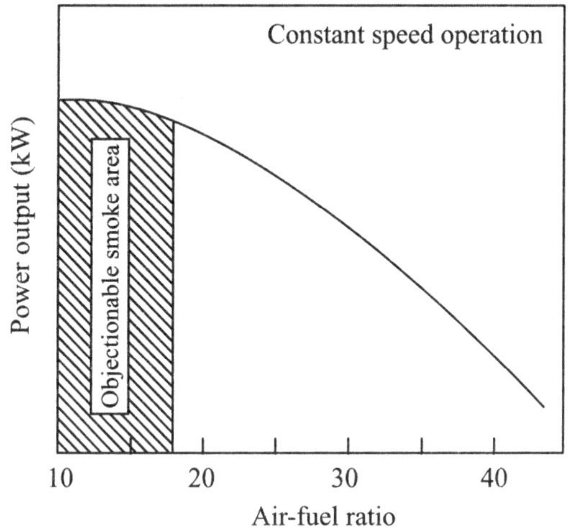

Fig. 11.10 Effect of A/F ratio on power output of a CI engine

established that operating an engine with a leaner air-fuel ratio always gives a better thermal efficiency but the mean effective pressure and the power output reduce. Therefore, the engine size becomes bigger for a given output if it is operated near the stoichiometric conditions, the A/F ratio in certain regions within the chamber is likely to be so rich that some of the fuel molecules will not be able to find the necessary oxygen for combustion and thus produce a noticeably black smoke. Hence the CI engine is always designed to operate with an excess air, of 15 to 40% depending upon the application. The power output curve for a typical CI engine operating at constant speed is shown in Fig.11.10. The approximate region of A/F ratios in which visible black smoke occurs is indicated by the shaded area.

11.14 STAGES OF COMBUSTION IN CI ENGINES

The combustion in a CI engine is considered to be taking place in four stages (Fig.11.11). It is divided into the ignition delay period, the period of rapid combustion, the period of controlled combustion and the period of after-burning. The details are explained below.

11.14.1 Ignition Delay Period

The ignition delay period is also called the preparatory phase during which some fuel has already been admitted but has not yet ignited. This period is counted from the start of injection to the point where the pressure-time curve separates from the motoring curve indicated as start of combustion in Fig.11.11.

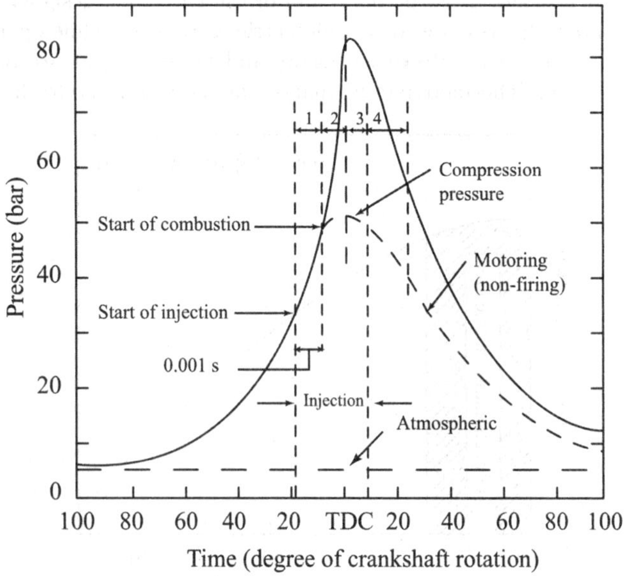

Fig. 11.11 Stages of combustion in a CI engine

The delay period in the CI engine exerts a very great influence on both engine design and performance. It is of extreme importance because of its effect on both the combustion rate and knocking and also its influence on engine starting ability and the presence of smoke in the exhaust. The fuel does not ignite immediately upon injection into the combustion chamber. There is a definite period of inactivity between the time when the first droplet of fuel hits the hot air in the combustion chamber and the time it starts through the actual burning phase. This period is known as the ignition delay period. In Fig.11.12 the delay period is shown on pressure crank angle (or time) diagram between points a and b. Point a represents the time of injection and point b represents the time at which the pressure curve (caused by combustion) first separates from the motoring curve. The ignition delay period can be divided into two parts, the physical delay and the chemical delay.

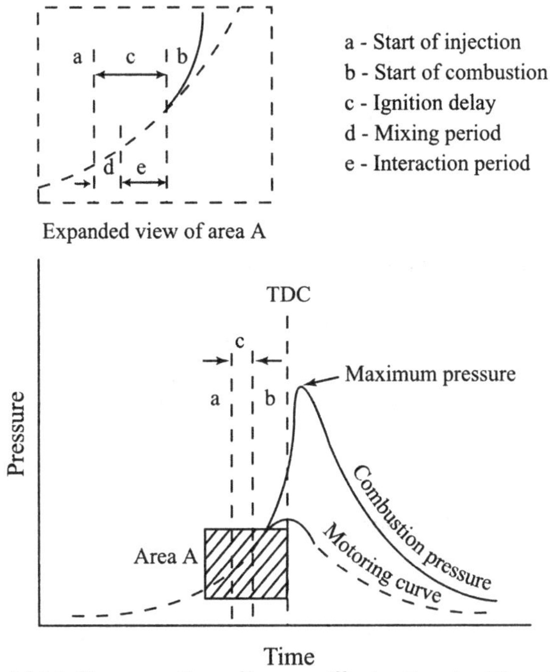

Fig. 11.12 Pressure-time diagram illustrating ignition delay

Physical Delay: The physical delay is the time between the beginning of injection and the attainment of chemical reaction conditions. During this period, the fuel is atomized, vaporized, mixed with air and raised to its self-ignition temperature. This physical delay depends on the type of fuel, i.e., for light fuel the physical delay is small while for heavy viscous fuels the physical delay is high. The physical delay is greatly reduced by using high injection pressures, higher combustion chamber temperatures and high turbulence to facilitate breakup of the jet and improving evaporation.

Chemical Delay: During the chemical delay, reactions start slowly and then accelerate until inflammation or ignition takes place. Generally, the chemical delay is larger than the physical delay. However, it depends on the temperature of the surroundings and at high temperatures, the chemical reactions are faster and the physical delay becomes longer than the chemical delay. It is clear that, the ignition lag in the SI engine is essentially equivalent to the chemical delay for the CI engine. In most CI engines the ignition lag is shorter than the duration of injection.

11.14.2 Period of Rapid Combustion

The period of rapid combustion also called the uncontrolled combustion, is that phase in which the pressure rise is rapid. During the delay period, the droplets have had time to spread over a wide area and fresh air is always available around the droplets. Most of the fuel admitted would have evaporated and formed a combustible mixture with air. By this time, the preflame reactions would have also been completed. The period of rapid combustion is counted from end of delay period or the beginning of the combustion to the point of maximum pressure on the indicator diagram. The rate of heat-release is maximum during this period. It may be noted that the pressure reached during the period of rapid combustion will depend on the duration of the delay period (the longer the delay the more rapid and higher is the pressure rise since more fuel would have accumulated in the cylinder during the delay period).

11.14.3 Period of Controlled Combustion

The rapid combustion period is followed by the third stage, the controlled combustion. The temperature and pressure in the second stage is already quite high. Hence the fuel droplets injected during the second stage burn faster with reduced ignition delay as soon as they find the necessary oxygen and any further pressure rise is controlled by the injection rate. The period of controlled combustion is assumed to end at maximum cycle temperature.

11.14.4 Period of After-Burning

Combustion does not cease with the completion of the injection process. The unburnt and partially burnt fuel particles left in the combustion chamber start burning as soon as they come into contact with the oxygen. This process continues for a certain duration called the after-burning period. Usually this period starts from the point of maximum cycle temperature and continues over a part of the expansion stroke. Rate of after-burning depends on the velocity of diffusion and turbulent mixing of unburnt and partially burnt fuel with the air. The duration of the after-burning phase may correspond to 70-80 degrees of crank travel from TDC.

The sequence of the events in the entire combustion process in a CI engine including the delay period is shown in Fig.11.13 by means of a block diagram.

11.15 FACTORS AFFECTING THE DELAY PERIOD

Many design and operating factors affect the delay period. The important ones are:

(i) compression ratio

(ii) engine speed

(iii) output

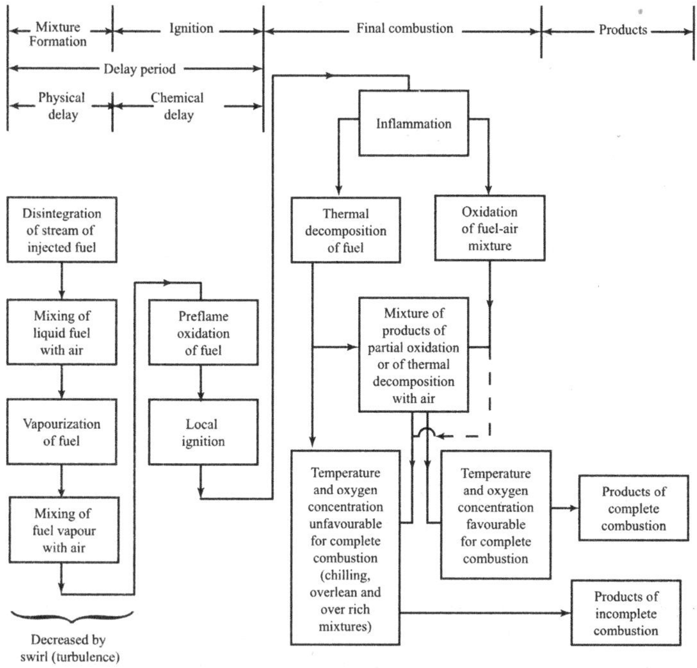

Fig. 11.13 Block diagram illustrating the combustion process in a CI engine

(iv) atomization of fuel and duration of injection

(v) injection timing

(vi) quality of the fuel

(vii) intake temperature

(viii) intake pressure

The effect of these factors on the delay period is discussed in detail in the following sections.

11.15.1 Compression Ratio

The increase in the compression temperature of the air with increase in compression ratio evaluated at the end of the compression stroke is shown in Fig.11.14. It is also seen from the same figure that the minimum autoignition temperature of a fuel decreases due to increased density of the compressed air. This results in a closer contact between the molecules of fuel and oxygen reducing the time of reaction. The increase in the compression temperature as well as the decrease in the minimum autoignition temperature decreases the delay period. The peak pressure during the combustion process is only marginally affected by the compression ratio (because delay period is shorter with higher compression ratio and hence the pressure rise is lower).

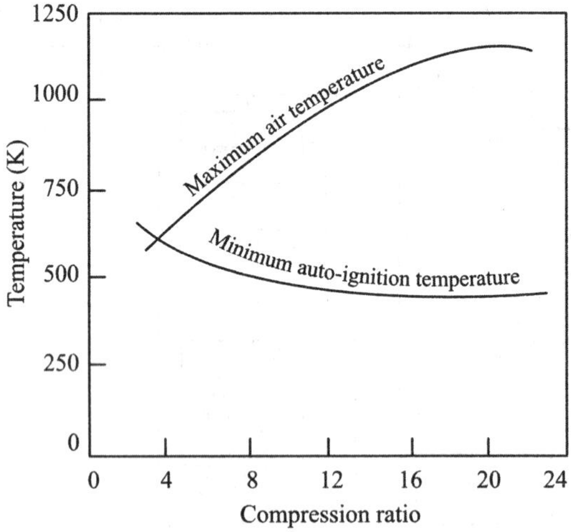

Fig. 11.14 Effect of compression ratio on maximum air temperature and minimum autoignition temperature

One of the practical disadvantages of using a very high compression ratio is that the mechanical efficiency tends to decrease due to increase in weight of the reciprocating parts. Therefore, in practice the engine designers always try to use a lower compression ratio which helps in easy cold starting and light load running at high speeds.

11.15.2 Engine Speed

The delay period could be given either in terms of absolute time (in milliseconds) or in terms of crank angle degrees. Fig.11.15 shows the decrease in delay period in terms of milliseconds with increase in engine speed in a variable speed operation with a given fuel.

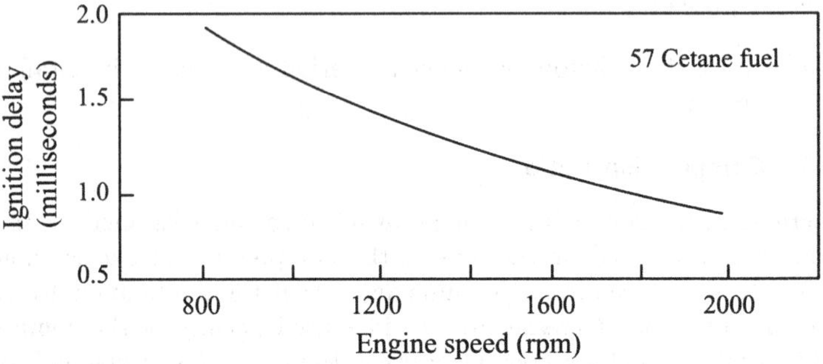

Fig. 11.15 Effect of speed on ignition delay in a diesel engine

With increase in engine speed, the loss of heat during compression decreases, resulting in the rise of both the temperature and pressure of the compressed air thus reducing the delay period in milliseconds. However, in degrees of crank travel the delay period increases as the engine operates at a higher rpm. The fuel pump is geared to the engine, and hence the amount of fuel injected during the delay period depends on crank degrees and not on absolute time. Hence, at high speeds, there will be more fuel present in the cylinder to take part in the second stage of uncontrolled combustion resulting in high rate of pressure rise.

11.15.3 Output

With an increase in engine output the air-fuel ratio decreases, operating temperatures increase and hence delay period decreases. The rate of pressure rise is unaffected but the peak pressure reached may be high.

11.15.4 Atomization and Duration of Injection

Higher fuel-injection pressures increase the degree of atomization. The fineness of atomization reduces ignition delay, due to higher surface volume ratio. Smaller droplet size will have low depth of penetration due to less momentum of the droplet and less velocity relative to air from where it has to find oxygen after vapourisation. Because of this air utilization factor will be reduced due to fuel spray path being shorter. Also with smaller droplets, the aggregate area of inflammation will increase after ignition, resulting in higher pressure rise during the second stage of combustion. Thus, lower injection pressure, giving larger droplet size may give lower pressure rise during the second stage of combustion and probably smoother running. Hence, an optimum group mean diameter of the droplet size should be attempted as a compromise. Also the fuel delivery law i.e., change in the quantity of fuel supplied with the crank angle travel will affect the rates of pressure rise during second stage of combustion though ignition delay remains unaffected by the same.

11.15.5 Injection Timing

The effect of injection advance on the pressure variation is shown in Fig.11.16 for three injection advance timings of 9°, 18°, and 27° before TDC. The injected quantity of fuel per cycle is constant. As the pressure and temperature at the beginning of injection are lower for higher ignition advance, the delay period increases with increase in injection advance. The optimum angle of injection advance depends on many factors but generally it is about $20° bTDC$.

11.15.6 Quality of Fuel

Self-ignition temperature is the most important property of the fuel which affects the delay period. A lower self-ignition temperature results in a lower delay period. Also, fuels with higher cetane number give lower delay period and smoother engine operation. Other properties of the fuel which affect the delay period are volatility, latent heat, viscosity and surface tension.

11.15.7 Intake Temperature

Increase in intake temperature increases the compressed air temperature resulting in reduced delay period. However, preheating of the charge for this

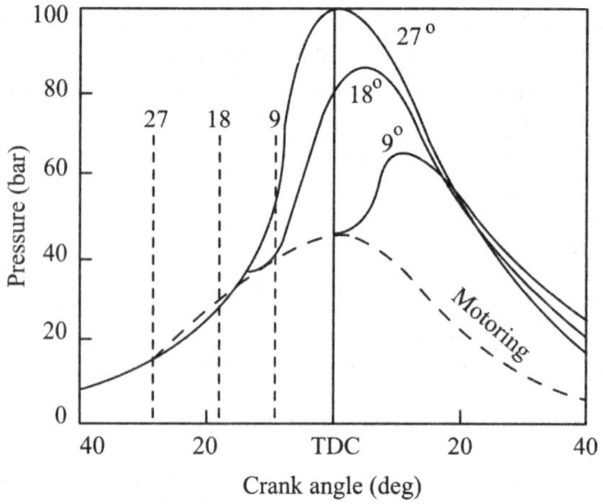

Fig. 11.16 Effect of injection timing on indicator diagram

purpose would be undesirable because it would reduce the density of air reducing the volumetric efficiency and power output.

11.15.8 Intake Pressure

Increase in intake pressure or supercharging reduces the autoignition temperature and hence reduces the delay period. The peak pressure will be higher since the compression pressure will increase with intake pressure. Table 11.2 gives the summary of the factors which influence the delay period in an engine.

11.16 THE PHENOMENON OF KNOCK IN CI ENGINES

In CI engines the injection process takes place over a definite interval of time. Consequently, as the first few droplets to be injected are passing through the ignition delay period, additional droplets are being injected into the chamber. If the ignition delay of the fuel being injected is short, the first few droplets will commence the *actual burning* phase in a relatively short time after injection and a relatively small amount of fuel will be accumulated in the chamber when *actual burning* commences. As a result, the mass rate of mixture burned will be such as to produce a rate of pressure rise that will exert a smooth force on the piston, as shown in Fig.11.17(a). If, on the other hand, the ignition delay is longer, the *actual burning* of the first few droplets is delayed and a greater quantity of fuel droplets gets accumulated in the chamber. When the *actual burning* commences, the additional fuel can cause too rapid a rate of pressure rise as shown in Fig.11.17(b), resulting in a *jamming* of forces against the piston and rough engine operation. If the ignition delay is quite long, so much fuel can accumulate that the rate of pressure rise is almost instantaneous, as shown in Fig.11.17(c). Such a situation produces the extreme pressure differentials and violent gas vibrations known as knocking and is evidenced by audible knock. The phenomenon is similar to that in the SI engine. However,

Table 11.2 Effect of Variables on the Delay Period

Increases in variable	Effect on Delay Period	Reason
Cetane number of fuel	Reduces	Reduces the self-ignition temperature
Injection pressure	Reduces	Reduces physical delay due to greater surface-volume ratio
Injection timing advance	Reduces	Reduced pressures and temperatures when the injection begins
Compression ratio	Reduces	Increases air temperature and pressure and reduces autoignition temperature
Intake temperature	Reduces	Increases air temperature
Jacket water temperature	Reduces	Increases wall and hence air temperature
Fuel temperature	Reduces	Increases chemical reaction due to better vaporization
Intake pressure (supercharging)	Reduces	Increases density and also reduces autoignition temperature
Speed	Increases in terms of crank angle. Reduces in terms of milliseconds	Reduces loss of heat
Load (fuel-air ratio)	Decreases	Increases the operating temperature
Engine size	Decreases in terms of crank angle. Little effect in terms of milliseconds	Larger engines operate normally at low speeds
Type of combustion chamber	Lower for engines with precombustion chamber	Due to compactness of the chamber

in the SI engine, knocking occurs near the end of combustion whereas in the CI engine, knocking occurs near the beginning of combustion.

In order to decrease the tendency of knock it is necessary to start the *actual burning* as early as possible after the injection begins. In other words, it is necessary to decrease the ignition delay and thus decrease the amount of fuel present when the *actual burning* of the first few droplets start.

11.17 COMPARISON OF KNOCK IN SI AND CI ENGINES

It may be interesting to note that knocking in spark-ignition engines and compression-ignition engines is fundamentally due to the autoignition of the fuel-air mixture. In both the cases, the knocking depends on the autoignition lag of the fuel-air mixture. But careful examination of the knocking phenomenon in spark-ignition and the compression-ignition engines reveals the following differences. A comparison of the knocking process in SI and CI engines is shown on the pressure-time diagrams of Fig.11.18.

(i) In spark-ignition engines, the autoignition of the end gas away from the spark plug, most likely near the end of the combustion causes knocking. But in compression-ignition engines the autoignition of the charge causing knocking is at the start of combustion. It is the first charge that autoignites and causes knocking in the compression-ignition engines. This is illustrated in Fig.11.18. It is clear from Fig.11.18 that explosive auto- ignition is more or less over before the peak pressure for the compression-ignition engines. But for spark-ignition engines, the condition for explosive autoignition of the end charge is more favourable after the peak pressure. In order to avoid knocking in spark-ignition engines, it is necessary to prevent autoignition of the end gas to take place at all. In compression-ignition engine, the earliest possible autoignition is necessary to avoid knocking.

(ii) In spark-ignition engine, the charge that autoignites is homogeneous and therefore intensity of knocking or the rate of pressure rise at explosive autoignition is likely to be more than that in compression-ignition engines where the fuel and air are not homogeneously mixed even when explosive autoignition of the charge occurs. Therefore, it is often called detonation in SI engines.

(iii) In compression-ignition engines, only air is compressed during the compression stroke and the ignition can take place only after fuel is injected just before the top dead centre. Thus there can be no preignition in compression-ignition engines as in spark-ignition engines.

(iv) It has already been pointed out that, the normal process of combustion in compression-ignition engines is by autoignition. And thus normal rate of pressure rise for the first part of the charge for compression-ignition are higher than those for spark-ignition engine, in terms of per degree crank rotation. And normally, audible knock is always present

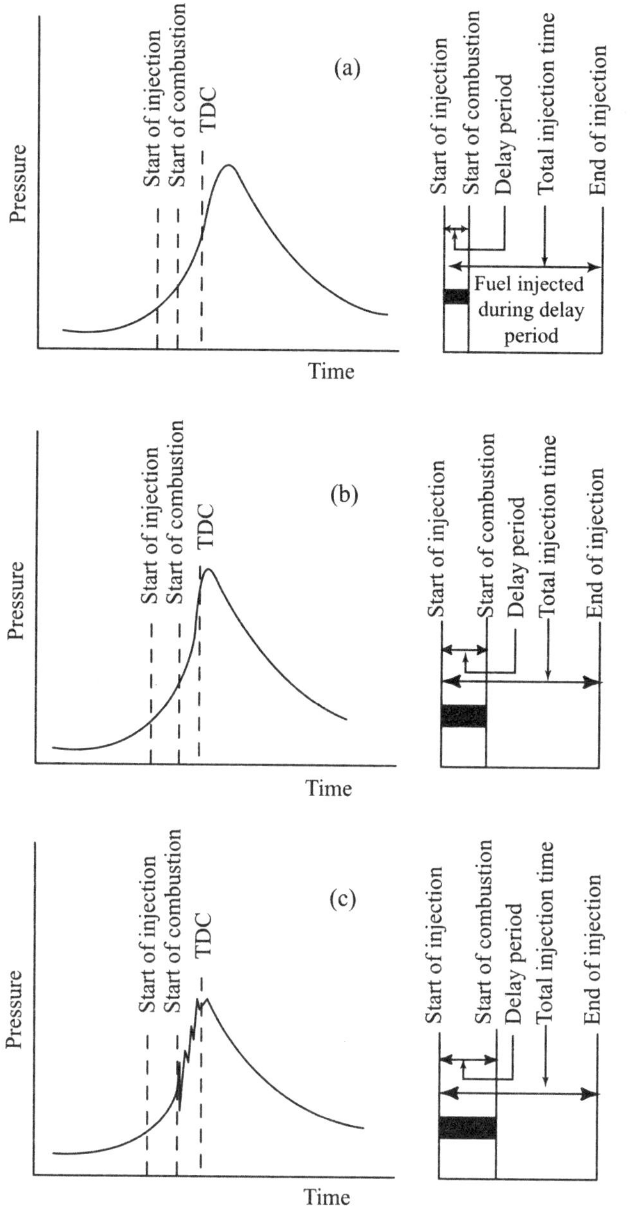

Fig. 11.17 Diagrams illustrating the effect of ignition delay on the rate of pressure rise in a CI engine

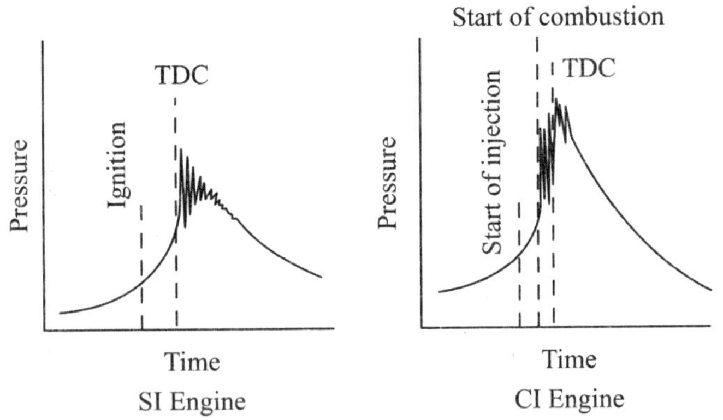

Fig. 11.18 Diagrams illustrating knocking combustion in SI and CI engines

in compression-ignition engine. Thus when the audible noise becomes severe and causes heavy vibrations in the engine, it is said that the engine is knocking. Therefore, it is also a matter of judgement. A definite demarcation between normal combustion and knocking combustion is very difficult. The rate of pressure rise may be as high as 10 bar per degree crank rotation in compression-ignition engines. The factors that tend to increase autoignition reaction time and prevent knock in SI engines promote knock in CI engines. Also, a good fuel for spark-ignition engine is a poor fuel for compression-ignition engine. The spark-ignition fuels have high octane rating 80 to 100 and low cetane rating of about 20, whereas diesel fuels have high cetane rating of about 45 to 65 and low octane rating of about 30.

Table 11.3 gives a comparative statement of various characteristics that reduce knocking in spark-ignition engines and compression-ignition engines.

11.18 COMBUSTION CHAMBERS FOR CI ENGINES

The most important function of the CI engine combustion chamber is to provide proper mixing of fuel and air in a short time. In order to achieve this, an organized air movement called the air swirl is provided to produce high relative velocity between the fuel droplets and the air. The effect of swirl has already been discussed in Section 11.13. The fuel is injected into the combustion chamber by an injector having a single or multihole orifices. The increase in the number of jets reduces the intensity of air swirl needed.

When the liquid fuel is injected into the combustion chamber, the spray cone gets disturbed due to the air motion and turbulence inside. The onset of combustion will cause an added turbulence that can be guided by the shape of the combustion chamber. Since the turbulence is necessary for better mixing, and the fact that it can be controlled by the shape of the combustion chamber, makes it necessary to study the combustion chamber design in detail.

CI engine combustion chambers are classified into two categories:

Table 11.3 Characteristics tending to reduce detonation or knock

S.No.	Characteristics	SI Engines	CI Engines
1.	Ignition temperature of fuel	High	Low
2.	Ignition delay	Long	Short
3.	Compression ratio	Low	High
4.	Inlet temperature	Low	High
5.	Inlet pressure	Low	High
6.	Combustion wall temperature	Low	High
7.	Speed, rpm	High	Low
8.	Cylinder size	Small	Large

(i) *Direct-Injection (DI) Type*: This type of combustion chamber is also called an open combustion chamber. In this type the entire volume of the combustion chamber is located in the main cylinder and the fuel is injected into this volume.

(ii) *Indirect-Injection (IDI) Type*: In this type of combustion chambers, the combustion space is divided into two parts, one part in the main cylinder and the other part in the cylinder head. The fuel-injection is affected usually into that part of the chamber located in the cylinder head. These chambers are classified further into:

   (a) Swirl chamber in which compression swirl is generated.

   (b) Precombustion chamber in which combustion swirl is induced.

   (c) Air cell chamber in which both compression and combustion swirl are induced.

11.18.1 Direct–Injection Chambers

An open combustion chamber is defined as one in which the combustion space is essentially a single cavity with little restriction from one part of the chamber to the other and hence with no large difference in pressure between parts of the chamber during the combustion process. There are many designs of open chamber some of which are shown in Fig.11.19.

In four-stroke engines with open combustion chambers, induction swirl is obtained either by careful formation of the air intake passages or by masking a portion of the circumference of the inlet valve whereas in two-stroke engines it is created by suitable form for the inlet ports. These chambers mainly consist of space formed between a flat cylinder head and a cavity in the piston crown in different shapes. The fuel is injected directly into this space. The injector

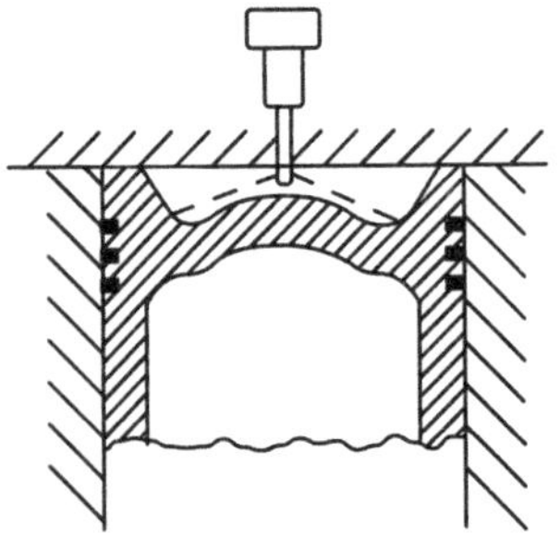

(a) Shallow depth chamber

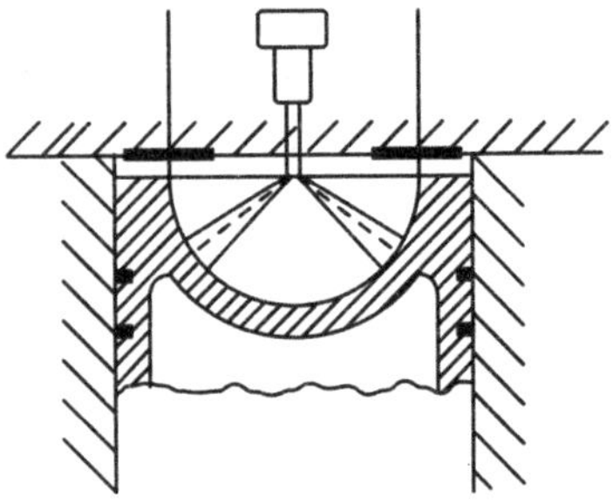

(b) Hemispherical chamber

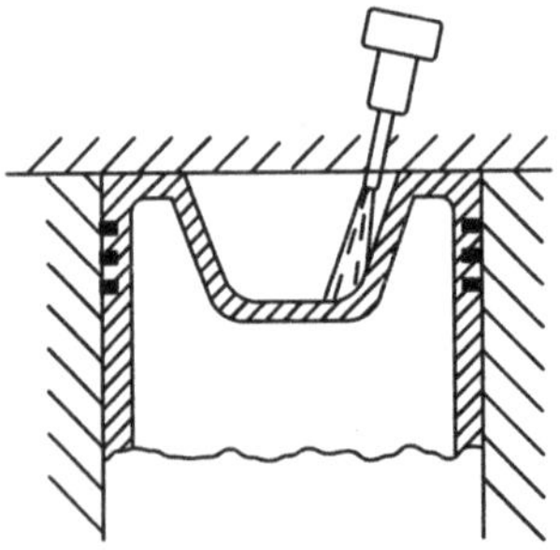

(c) Cylindrical chamber

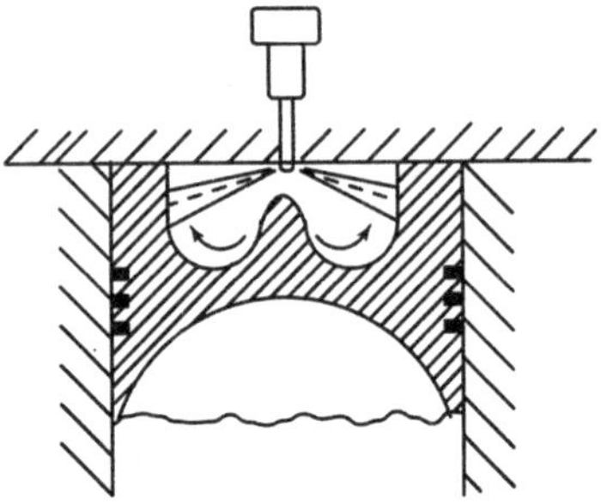

(d) Toroidal chamber

Fig. 11.19 Open combustion chambers

nozzles used for this type of chamber are generally of multihole type working at a relatively high pressure (about 200 bar). The main advantages of this type of chambers are:

(i) Minimum heat loss during compression because of lower surface area to volume ratio and hence, better efficiency.

(ii) No cold starting problems.

(iii) Fine atomization because of multihole nozzle.

The drawbacks of these combustion chambers are:

(i) High fuel-injection pressure required and hence complex design of fuel-injection pump.

(ii) Necessity of accurate metering of fuel by the injection system, particularly for small engines.

Shallow Depth Chamber: In shallow depth chamber the depth of the cavity provided in the piston is quite small. This chamber [Fig.11.19(a)] is usually adopted for large engines running at low speeds. Since the cavity diameter is very large, the squish is negligible.

Hemispherical Chamber: This chamber [Fig.11.19(b)] also gives small squish. However, the depth to diameter ratio for a cylindrical chamber can be varied to give any desired squish to give better performance.

Cylindrical Chamber: This design [Fig.11.19(c)] was attempted in recent diesel engines. This is a modification of the cylindrical chamber in the form of a truncated cone with base angle of 30°. The swirl was produced by masking the valve for nearly 180° of circumference. Squish can also be varied by varying the depth.

Toroidal Chamber: The idea behind this shape [Fig.11.19(d)] is to provide a powerful squish along with the air movement, similar to that of the familiar smoke ring, within the toroidal chamber. Due to powerful squish the mask needed on inlet valve is small and there is better utilization of oxygen. The cone angle of spray for this type of chamber is 150° to 160°.

11.18.2 Indirect–Injection Chambers

A divided combustion chamber is defined as one in which the combustion space is divided into two or more distinct compartments connected by restricted passages. This creates considerable pressure differences between them during the combustion process.

Swirl Chamber: Swirl chamber consists of a spherical-shaped chamber separated from the engine cylinder and located in the cylinder head (Fig.11.20). Into this chamber, about 50% of the air is transferred during the compression stroke. A throat connects the chamber to the cylinder which enters the chamber in a tangential direction so that the air coming into this chamber is given a strong rotary movement inside the swirl chamber and after combustion, the products rush back into the cylinder through the same throat at much higher velocity. This causes considerable heat loss to the walls of the passage which can be reduced by employing a heat-insulated chamber. However, in this type of combustion chambers even with a heat insulated passage, the heat loss is greater than that in an open combustion chamber which employs induction swirl.

This type of combustion chamber finds application where fuel quality is difficult to control, where reliability under adverse conditions is more important than fuel economy. The use of single hole of larger diameter for the fuel spray nozzle is often important consideration for the choice of swirl chamber engine.

Precombustion Chamber: A typical precombustion chamber (Fig.11.21) consists of an antichamber connected to the main chamber through a number of small holes (compared to a relatively large passage in the swirl chamber). The precombustion chamber is located in the cylinder head and its volume accounts for about 40% of the total combustion space. During the compression stroke the piston forces the air into the precombustion chamber. The fuel is injected into the prechamber and the combustion is initiated. The resulting pressure rise forces the flaming droplets together with some air and their combustion products to rush out into the main cylinder at high velocity through the small holes. Thus it creates both strong secondary turbulence and distributes the flaming fuel droplets throughout the air in the main com-

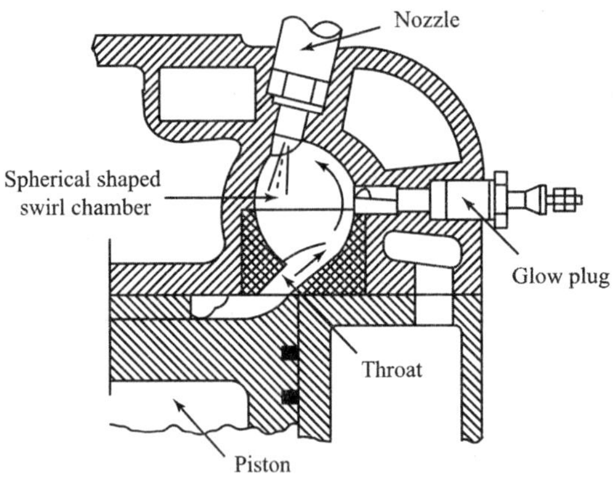

Fig. 11.20 Ricardo swirl chamber comet, Mark II

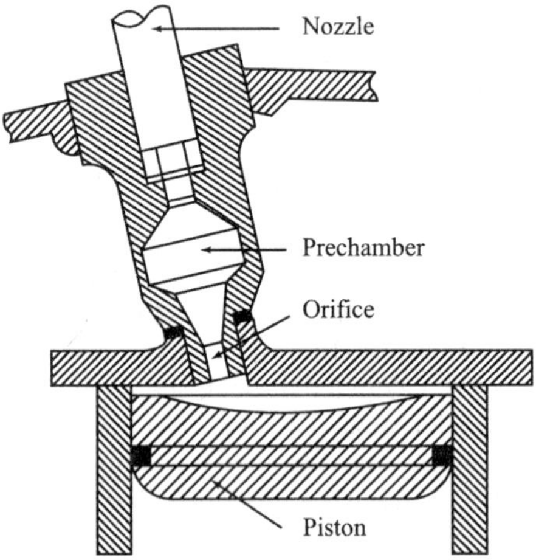

Fig. 11.21 Precombustion chamber

bustion chamber where bulk of combustion takes place. About 80% of energy is released in main combustion chamber.

The rate of pressure rise and the maximum pressure is lower compared to those of open type chamber. The initial shock of combustion is limited to precombustion chamber only. The precombustion chamber has multi-fuel capability without any modification in the injection system because of the temperature of prechamber. The variation in the optimum injection timing for petrol and diesel operations is only 2° for this chamber compared to 8° to 10° in the other designs.

Air-Cell Chamber: In this chamber (Fig.11.22), the clearance volume is divided into two parts, one in the main cylinder and the other called the energy cell. The energy cell is divided into two parts, major and minor, which are separated from each other and from the main chamber by narrow orifices. A pintle type of nozzle injects the fuel across the main combustion chamber

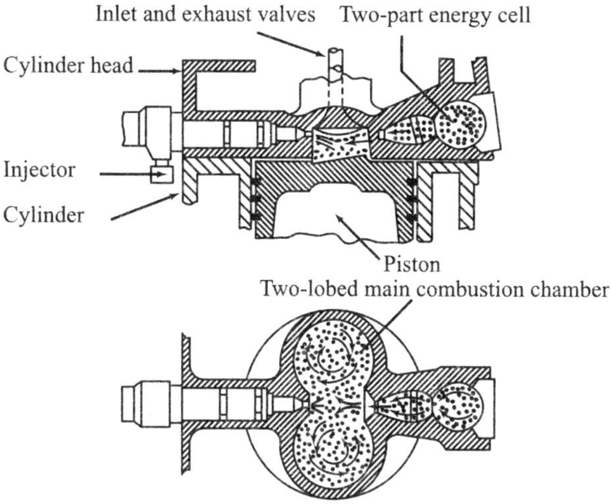

Fig. 11.22 Lanova air-cell combustion chamber

space towards the open neck of the air cell.

During compression, the pressure in the main chamber is higher than that inside the energy cell due to restricted passage area between the two. At the *TDC*, the difference in pressure will be high and air will be forced at high velocity through the opening into the energy cell and this moment the fuel-injection also begins. Combustion starts initially in the main chamber where the temperature is comparatively higher but the rate of burning is very slow due to absence of any air motion. In the energy cell, the fuel is well mixed with air and high pressure is developed due to heat-release and the hot burning gases blow out through the small passage into the main chamber. This high velocity jet produces swirling motion in the main chamber and thereby thoroughly mixes the fuel with air resulting in complete combustion. The design is not suitable for variable speed operation as the combustion induced swirl has no relationship to the speed of the engine. The energy cell is designed to run hot, to reduce ignition lag.

The main advantages of the indirect-injection combustion chambers are:

(i) injection pressure required is low

(ii) direction of spraying is not very important.

These chambers have the following serious drawbacks which have made its application limited.

(i) Poor cold starting performance requiring heater plugs.

(ii) Specific fuel consumption is high because there is a loss of pressure due to air motion through the duct and heat loss due to large heat transfer area.

Review Questions

11.1 *What are homogeneous and heterogeneous mixtures? In which engines these mixtures are used? Explain.*

11.2 *Briefly explain the stages of combustion in SI engines elaborating the flame front propagation.*

11.3 *Explain the various factors that influence the flame speed.*

11.4 *What is meant by abnormal combustion? Explain the phenomena of knock in SI engines.*

11.5 *Explain the effect of various engine variables on SI engine knock.*

11.6 *What are the various types of combustion chambers used in SI engines? Explain them briefly.*

11.7 *Bring out clearly the process of combustion in CI engines and also explain the various stages of combustion.*

11.8 *What is delay period and what are the factors that affect it?*

11.9 *Explain the phenomenon of knock in CI engines and compare it with SI engine knock.*

11.10 *Explain with figures the various types of combustion chambers used in CI engines.*

Multiple Choice Questions (choose the most appropriate answer)

1. In SI engines maximum flame speed is obtained when the equivalent ratio is between

   (a) 1.1 and 1.2
   (b) 1.0 and 1.1
   (c) 1.2 and 1.3
   (d) less than 1

2. In SI engines flame speed increases

   (a) with turbulence
   (b) with fuel-air ratio
   (c) both (a) and (b)
   (d) none of the above

3. With increase in compression ratio flame speed

   (a) increases
   (b) decreases
   (c) remains the same
   (d) none of the above

4. With increase in speed the crank angle required for flame propagation

   (a) increases
   (b) decreases
   (c) not affected
   (d) none of the above

5. Increasing the compression ratio in SI engines the knocking tendency

   (a) decreases
   (b) increases
   (c) not affected
   (d) none of the above

6. Decreasing the cooling water temperature in SI engines the knocking tendency

   (a) increases
   (b) decreases
   (c) not affected
   (d) none of the above

7. Detonation in SI engines occur due to

   (a) preignition of the charge before the spark
   (b) sudden ignition of the charge before the spark
   (c) autoignition of the charge after the spark in struck
   (d) none of the above

8. Desirable characteristics of the combustion chamber for SI engines to avoid knock is

   (a) small bore
   (b) short ratio of flame path to bore
   (c) absence of hot surfaces in the last region of the charge
   (d) all of the above

9. In CI engines with increase in compression ratio the delay period

   (a) increases
   (b) decreases
   (c) first increases and then decreases
   (d) not affected

10. Knocking takes place in CI engines
    (a) at the start of combustion
    (b) at the end of combustion
    (c) during combustion
    (d) none of the above
11. In CI engines knocking tendency increases with
    (a) increase in compression ratio
    (b) increasing inlet temperature of air
    (c) decrease in compression ratio
    (d) increasing coolant water temperature
12. In CI engines by increasing inlet air pressure the knocking tendency
    (a) increases
    (b) decreases
    (c) not affected
    (d) first decreases and then increases
13. Open combustion chambers in CI engines require
    (a) high injection pressures
    (b) accurate metering of fuel by the injection system
    (c) both (a) and (b)
    (d) none of the above
14. The advantages of the indirect injection combustion chambers are
    (a) low injection pressure
    (b) direction of spray is not critical
    (c) both (a) and (b)
    (d) good cold starting performance
15. In CI engines the delay period is affected by
    (a) compression ratio
    (b) engine speed
    (c) output
    (d) all of the above

Ans:					
	1. – (a)	2. – (c)	3. – (a)	4. – (c)	5. – (b)
	6. – (b)	7. – (c)	8. – (d)	9. – (b)	10. – (a)
	11. – (c)	12. – (b)	13. – (c)	14. – (c)	15. – (d)

12

ENGINE FRICTION AND LUBRICATION

12.1 INTRODUCTION

Friction generally refers to forces acting between surfaces in relative motion. In engines, frictional losses are mainly due to sliding as well as rotating parts. Normally, engine friction, in its broader sense, is taken as the difference between the indicated power, *ip*, and the brake power, *bp*. Usually engine friction is expressed in terms of frictional power, *fp*. Frictional loss is mainly attributed to the following mechanical losses.

(i) direct frictional losses

(ii) pumping losses

(iii) power loss to drive the components to charge and scavenge

(iv) power loss to drive other auxiliary components

A good engine design should not allow the total frictional losses to be more than 30% of the energy input in reciprocating engines. It should be the aim of a good designer to reduce friction and wear of the parts subjected to relative motion. This is achieved by proper lubrication. In this section the various losses associated with friction is enumerated.

12.1.1 Direct Frictional Losses

It is the power absorbed due to the relative motion of different bearing surfaces such as piston rings, main bearings, cam shaft bearings etc. Since, there are a number of moving parts, the frictional losses are comparatively higher in reciprocating engines.

12.1.2 Pumping Loss

In case of the four-stroke engines a considerable amount of energy is spent during intake and exhaust processes. The pumping loss is the net power spent by the engine (piston) on the working medium (gases) during intake and exhaust strokes. In the case of two-stroke engines this is negligible since the incoming fresh mixture is used to scavenge the exhaust gases.

12.1.3 Power Loss to Drive Components to Charge and Scavenge

In certain types of four-stroke engines the intake charge is supplied at a higher pressure than the naturally aspirated engines. For this purpose a mechanically driven compressor or a turbine driven compressor is used. Accordingly the engine is called the supercharged or turbocharged engine. In case of a supercharged engine, the engine itself supplies power to drive the compressor whereas in a turbocharged engine, the turbine is driven by the exhaust gases of the engine. These devices take away a part of the engine output. This loss is considered as negative frictional loss. In case of two-stroke engines with a scavenging pump, the power to drive the pump is supplied by the engine.

12.1.4 Power Loss to Drive the Auxiliaries

A good percentage of the generated power output is spent to drive auxiliaries such as water pump, lubricating oil pump, fuel pump, cooling fan, generator etc. This is considered a loss because the presence of each of these components reduces the net output of the engine.

12.2 MECHANICAL EFFICIENCY

The various losses described above can be clubbed into one heading, viz., the mechanical losses. The mechanical losses can be written in terms of mean effective pressure that is frictional torque divided by engine displacement volume per unit time. Therefore, frictional mean effective pressure, $fmep$, can be expressed as

$$fmep = mmep + pmep + amep + cmep$$

where
- $mmep$: mean effective pressure required to overcome mechanical friction
- $pmep$: Mean effective pressure required for charging and scavenging
- $amep$: mean effective pressure required to drive the auxiliary components
- $cmep$: mean effective pressure required to drive the compressor or scavenging pump

Because of the various mechanical losses in the engine the term mechanical efficiency is usually associated with the reciprocating internal combustion engine.

As already explained in Chapter 1, mechanical efficiency is defined as the ratio of bp to ip or $bmep$ to $imep$. It is written as

$$\eta_m = \frac{bp}{ip} = \frac{bmep}{imep}$$

Knowledge of engine friction is essential for calculating the mechanical efficiency of the engine. Mechanical efficiency indicates how good an engine is, in converting the indicated power to useful power. The value of mechanical efficiency varies widely with the design and operating conditions. It is evidently zero under idling conditions, i.e. all the indicated power developed by the engine is spent in overcoming friction. It should be the aim of any designer to increase the mechanical efficiency to the maximum by reducing the frictional losses to a minimum.

12.3 MECHANICAL FRICTION

As mentioned earlier, friction loss comes into picture in the bearing surfaces of the engine components due to their relative motion. Mechanical friction in engine may be divided into six classes which are discussed in the following sections.

12.3.1 Fluid-film or Hydrodynamic Friction

The hydrodynamic friction is associated with the phenomena when a complete film of lubricant exists between the two bearing surfaces. In this case the friction force entirely depends on the lubricant viscosity. This type of friction is the main mechanical friction loss in the engine.

12.3.2 Partial-film Friction

When rubbing (metal) surfaces are not sufficiently lubricated, there is a contact between the rubbing surfaces in some regions. During normal engine operation there is almost no metallic contact except between the compression (top) piston ring and cylinder walls. This is mainly at the end of each stroke where the piston velocity is nearly zero. During starting of the engine, the journal bearings operate in partial-film friction. Thus, partial-film friction contributes very little to total engine friction and hence, it may be neglected.

12.3.3 Rolling Friction

The rolling friction is due to rolling motion between the two surfaces. Ball and roller bearings and tappet rollers are subjected to rolling friction. Bearings of this type have a coefficient of friction which is nearly independent of load and speed. This friction is partly due to local rubbing from distortion under load and partly due to continuous *climbing* of roller. Rolling friction coefficient is lower than journal bearing friction coefficient during starting and initial running of engine. The reason is that the oil viscosity is high and moreover, partial friction exists in journal bearing during starting where engine uses plain journal bearings on the crankshaft. Rolling friction is negligible compared to total friction.

12.3.4 Dry Friction

Even when an engine is not operated for a long time there is little possibility for direct metal to metal contact. Always some lubricant exists between the rubbing surfaces even after long periods of disuse. One can take the dry friction to be non-existent and hence, this can be safely neglected while considering engine friction.

12.3.5 Journal Bearing Friction

A circular cylindrical shaft called journal rotates against a cylindrical surface called the bearing. Journal bearings are called partial when the bearing surface is less than full circumference. The rotary motion may be either continuous or oscillatory. Much theoretical and experimental work has been done to find the performance of journal bearing under various operating conditions. Engine journal bearing operates under load which varies in magnitude and direction with time. However, the same basic relations obtained for ordinary journal bearing apply to engine journal bearing but the coefficients of friction are usually different.

12.3.6 Friction due to Piston Motion

Friction due to the motion of piston can be divided into

(i) viscous friction due to piston

(ii) non-viscous friction due to piston ring

The non-viscous piston ring friction can be further subdivided into

(i) friction due to ring tension

(ii) friction due to gas pressure behind the ring

Tests show that the quantity of the lubricant between the piston and the cylinder wall is normally insufficient to fill the entire space between the piston and the cylinder wall. The oil film thickness between piston and the cylinder is also affected by the piston side-thrust and the resulting vibrations. Average oil film thickness between the piston and the cylinder wall varies with load and speed. Piston friction also depends upon the viscosity of the oil and the temperature at the various points on the piston.

Piston rings are categorized into compression rings and oil rings. Compression rings are on the top portion of the piston to seal against gas pressure. The pressure exerted by the compression ring on the cylinder wall is partly due to the elasticity of the ring and partly due to the gas pressure which leaks into the space between the ring and the piston. The gas pressure behind the top ring (compression ring) is nearly equal to the cylinder pressure, less than the cylinder pressure in the second ring groove and much less in the third.

Oil rings are designed to scrape some of the oil from the cylinder wall and allow it to return to the oil sump through radial passage in the ring. These grooves for the rings are vented by holes drilled into the piston interior and therefore no gas pressure can act behind it. In this case the pressure of the ring surface on the cylinder wall is entirely due to the elasticity (tension) of the rings. Piston rings press against the cylinder walls at all times because of their spring action. Therefore, the friction due to piston motion always exists.

12.4 BLOWBY LOSSES

It is the phenomenon of leakage of combustion products (gases) from the cylinder to the crankcase past the piston and piston rings. It depends on the compression ratio, inlet pressure and the condition of the piston rings. In case of worn out piston rings this loss is more. This loss is usually accounted in the overall frictional losses.

12.5 PUMPING LOSS

The work spent to charge the cylinder with fresh mixture during the suction stroke and to discharge the combustion products during the exhaust stroke is called the pumping loss. This pumping loss may be reduced by increasing the valve areas. However, this area cannot be greatly increased due to the practical limitation on the availability of space in the cylinder head. Further, engine speed also plays a role on the pumping loss. For four-stroke engines pumping loss may be divided into three parts as shown in the indicator diagram, Fig.12.1.

12.5.1 Exhaust Blowdown Loss

To reduce the work spent by the piston to drive out the exhaust gases the exhaust valve is made to open before piston reaches BDC on its expansion stroke. During this period the combustion gases rush out of cylinder due to pressure difference. Because of this there is a certain loss of power indicated by the area shown in Fig.12.1. This loss is called the blowdown loss. This mainly depends on the exhaust valve timing and its size. With large valve area and earlier exhaust valve opening the blowdown loss will be higher whereas with increase in speed this loss tends to be lower.

12.5.2 Exhaust Stroke Loss

The work required to force the products of combustion out of the cylinder after the blowdown process is the exhaust loss. During the starting of blowdown process the gas pressure inside the cylinder is more than three to four times the gas pressure inside the exhaust pipe, therefore, the gases flow out with high velocity. Due to inertia, the high velocity of exhaust gases tends to persist even during exhaust stroke and the cylinder pressure may momentarily drop below the gas pressure in the exhaust pipe. When the piston moves up again, pressure rises and gases are pushed into exhaust pipe. Thus, as mentioned earlier, the power required to drive the exhaust gases out is called the exhaust loss. This loss is shown in indicator diagram. This loss depends on valve size, valve timing and valve flow coefficient. Increase in valve size, early opening of valve and higher valve flow coefficient may tend to reduce exhaust stroke loss. Increase in speed increases the exhaust stroke loss. Thus factors like high speed, late opening of exhaust valve, reduced exhaust valve size which tend to increase the exhaust stroke loss may tend to reduce blowdown loss. The combination of the two losses should be minimal for getting better performance from the engine.

12.5.3 Intake Stroke Loss

Energy is supplied to the piston to produce a pressure difference across the inlet valve so that fresh charge could be drawn into the cylinder. This is

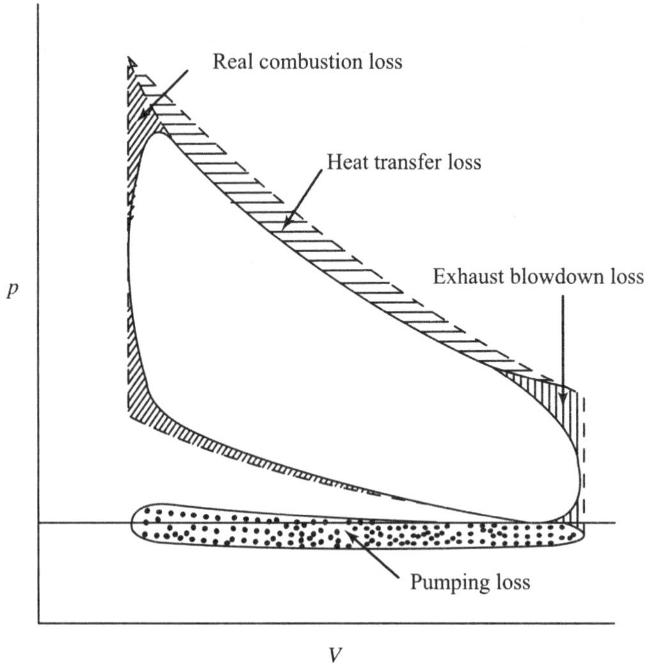

Fig. 12.1 Pumping and blowdown losses

done to overcome the friction and inertia of the gas in the intake system and the power spent by the piston for doing this is called the intake stroke loss. The combination of intake and exhaust stroke loss is called the pumping loss illustrated in the Fig.12.1.

12.6 FACTORS AFFECTING MECHANICAL FRICTION

Various factors affect the engine friction. In this section, the effect of some of these factors on mechanical friction is discussed.

12.6.1 Engine Design

The design parameters which influence the friction losses are:

(i) *Stroke-bore Ratio :* Lower stroke-bore ratio may tend to slightly decrease the $fmep$. It is mainly due to less frictional area in case of lower stroke to bore ratio.

(ii) *Effect of Engine Size :* Larger engines have more frictional surfaces. Hence, lubrication requirements are more in such engines.

(iii) *Piston Rings :* Reducing the number of piston rings and reducing the contacting surface of the ring with cylinder wall reduces the friction. Light ring pressure also reduces the friction.

(iv) *Compression Ratio :* The friction mean effective pressure increases with increase in compression ratio. But the mechanical efficiency either remains or may improve slightly because of the increase in the *imep*.

(v) *Journal Bearings :* Reducing journal diameter/diametrical clearance ratio in journal bearing reduces the *fmep*. Short pistons with reduced mass along the gudgeon pin axis will minimize inertia loads. This in turn will reduce the friction loss.

12.6.2 Engine Speed

Friction increases rapidly with increasing speed. At higher speeds mechanical efficiency starts deteriorating considerably. This is one of the reasons for restricting the speeds of engines.

12.6.3 Engine Load

Increasing the load increases the maximum pressure in the cylinder which results in slight increase in friction values. At the same time increases in load results in increase in temperature inside the cylinder and also temperature of the lubricating oil. The decrease in oil viscosity due to higher temperature slightly reduces the friction.

In gasoline engines the throttling losses reduce as the throttle is opened more so as to supply more fuel. Results of the above may tend to bring down the frictional losses in such engines (SI engine). However, for diesel engines the frictional losses due to engine load are more or less constant since there is no throttling effect.

12.6.4 Cooling Water Temperature

A rise in cooling water temperature slightly reduces engine friction by reducing oil viscosity. Friction losses are high during starting since temperature of water and oil are low and viscosity is high.

12.6.5 Oil Viscosity

Viscosity and friction loss are (directly) proportional to each other. The viscosity can be reduced by increasing the temperature of the oil. But beyond a certain value of oil temperature, failure of local oil film may occur resulting in partial fluid film friction or even metal to metal contact which is very harmful to the engine.

12.7 LUBRICATION

From the above discussion it can be understood that lubrication is essential to reduce friction and wear between the components in an engine. In the following sections the details of engine lubrication are discussed.

12.7.1 Function of Lubrication

Lubrication is an art of admitting a lubricant (oil, grease, etc.) between two surfaces that are in contact and in relative motion. The purpose of lubrication in an engine is to perform one or several of the following functions.

(i) To reduce friction and wear between the moving parts and thereby the energy loss and to increase the life of the engine.

(ii) To provide sealing action e.g. the lubricating oil helps the piston rings to maintain an effective seal against the high pressure gases in the cylinder from leaking out into the crankcase.

(iii) To cool the surfaces by carrying away the heat generated in engine components.

(iv) To clean the surfaces by washing away carbon and metal particles caused by wear.

Of all these functions, the first function is considered to be the most important one. In internal combustion engines, the problems of lubrication become more difficult because of the high temperatures experienced during the combustion process and by the wide range of temperatures encountered throughout the cycle. As stated earlier, the energy loss from the friction between different components of the engine can be minimized by providing proper lubrication.

Moreover, because of the variation in the gas force on the piston and the inertia force of the moving parts, the bearings are subjected to fluctuating loads where effective lubrication at all operating conditions is extremely difficult. The temperature extremes are emphasized to minimize starting problems during which the flow of lubricating oil is difficult. Therefore, the moving parts may suffer from inadequate supply of lubricating oil and metal to metal contact may result. The basic problems associated with the proper lubrication of the various types of bearings encountered in an internal combustion engine will be discussed in general in this chapter. In addition, the properties of lubricating oils, the effect of engine operation on these properties and the types of lubricating systems will also be discussed.

12.7.2 Mechanism of Lubrication

Consider two solid blocks which are in contact with each other. In order to move the upper block over the surface of the lower block, a constant tangential force must be applied. The force due to the weight of the upper block acting perpendicular to the surface is called the *normal force*. The ratio of the tangential force to the normal force is known as the *dynamic coefficient of friction or the coefficient of friction, f*.

$$\text{Coefficient of friction, } f = \frac{\text{Tangential force}}{\text{Normal force}}$$

To keep the block in motion, a constant tangential force is required to overcome the frictional resistance between the two surfaces. This frictional resistance arises because the moving surfaces are rough, and hence small irregularities will fit together at the contact area (interface) to give a mechanical lock to the motion. Also, if the moving surfaces are too smooth, the molecular attraction will be more in the interface and will resist the motion. Therefore, friction between dry surfaces may arise either from surface irregularities or from molecular attraction or from both.

The coefficient of friction between two dry surfaces tends to be constant and independent of the load (normal force), relative speed and contact areas of the surfaces but varies with the materials and the surface finish.

The resistance between moving surfaces can be reduced by the introduction of a small film of lubricant between the moving surfaces so that the two surfaces are not in physical contact. The lubricant film layer provides lesser resistance than that of the solid surface and hence less force is required to accomplish a relative motion. The friction due to surface irregularities and larger molecular attraction is also reduced. The solid friction is replaced with a definitely lesser fluid friction.

Consider the case of two parallel plates filled with viscous oil in between them, of which one is stationary and other is in motion with a constant velocity in the direction as shown in Fig.12.2. It is assumed that

(i) the width of the plates in the direction perpendicular to the motion is large so that the flow of lubricant in this direction is negligibly small

(ii) the fluid is incompressible

Let us imagine the film as composed of a series of horizontal layers and the force, F causing layers to deform or slide one over another, just like a deck of cards. The first layer clinging to the moving surface will move with the

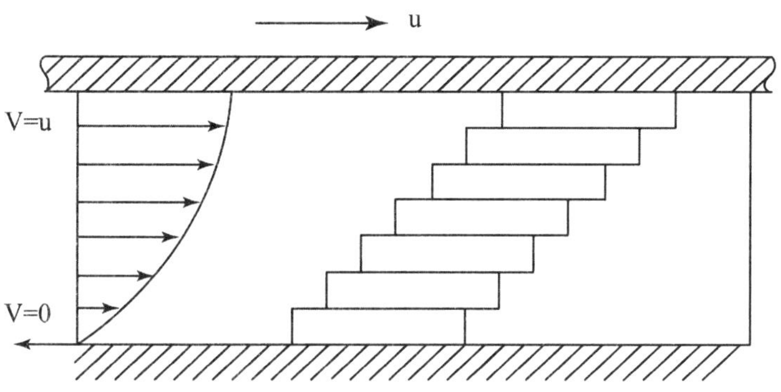

Fig. 12.2 Mechanism of lubrication in parallel surfaces

plate because of the adhesive force between the plate and the oil layer while the next layer is moving by at slower pace. The subsequent layers below keep moving at gradually reducing velocities. The layer clinging to the surface of the stationary plate will have zero velocity. The reason is that each layer of the oil is subjected to a shearing stress and the force required to overcome this stress is the fluid friction. Thus the velocity profile across the oil film varies from zero at the stationary plate to the velocity of the plate at the moving surface, as shown in Fig.12.2.

In the above example, the fluid or internal friction arose because of the resistance of the lubricant to shearing stress. A measure of the resistance to shear is a property called *dynamic viscosity or coefficient of viscosity.*

Now let us consider that the above mentioned plates are non-parallel and the upper one (A′B′) is moving while the lower one (AB) remains stationary. The cross section of the fluid at the leading edge is less than that of the trailing edge. This arrangement is shown in Fig.12.3. The discussion with regard to Fig.12.2 indicates that the velocity distributions across the oil film at the edges are expected to have the shape shown by dotted line in Fig.12.3. But as the fluid is incompressible, the actual volume of oil carried into the

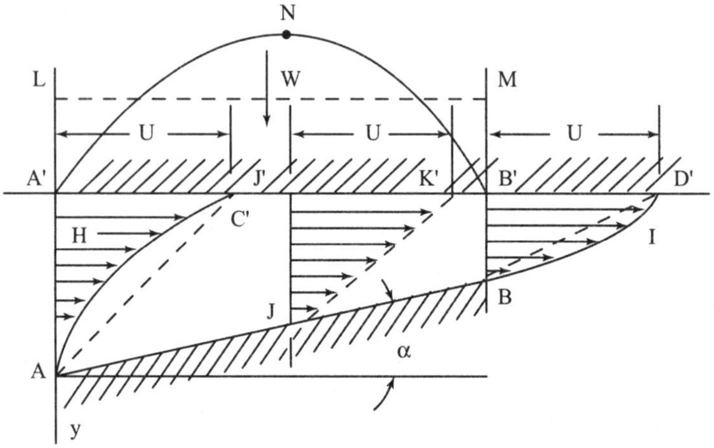

Fig. 12.3 Mechanism of lubrication on wedge shaped surfaces

space at the trailing edge must be equal to the volume discharged from this space at the leading edge. Therefore, the excess volume of oil carried into the space is squeezed out through either ends producing a constant pressure, which induces a flow through these sections. It is to be remembered that the width of the plates is assumed to be large so that there is no leakage along the side ends of the plate. In addition, the viscosity of the fluid also retards the escape of lubricant resulting from the squeezing action of the normal faces that tends to bring the surface together. This creates a pressure in the lubricant film. Therefore, the actual velocity distribution in the section at the edges is the result of the combined flow of lubricant due to pressure induced flow and due to viscous drag, which is indicated by continuous lines (curved lines) across the section at the edges. This oil film pressure enables to carry the load. This type of lubrication where a wedge shaped oil film is formed between two moving surface is called hydrodynamic lubrication. The important feature of this type of lubrication is that the load carrying capacity of the bearing increases with increase in relative speed of the moving surfaces. This is because at high speed, the available time for the oil to squeeze out is less and hence the pressure rise tends to be high.

It can be seen that with the above mentioned arrangement a positive pressure in the oil film is developed. This condition exists when the thickness of the film decreases in the direction of motion of surface. Such a film is known as convergent film.

If the motion of the upper plate is reversed, with the inclination of the lower plate unchanged, the volume of the lubricant that the moving surface tends to drag into the space becomes less than the volume which tends to discharge from the space and the pressure developed in the oil film tends to be negative (less than atmospheric pressure). The bearing will be unable to support any load by the film. Such a film is known as a diverging film.

12.7.3 Elastohydrodynamic Lubrication

Elastohydrodynamic lubrication is the phenomenon that occurs when the bearing material itself deforms elastically against the pressure built up of the oil film. This type of lubrication occurs between cams and followers, gear teeth and roller bearings where the contact pressures are extremely high. Hydrostatic lubrication is obtained by introducing the lubricant, which is sometimes air or water, into the load-bearing area at a pressure high enough to separate the surfaces with a relatively thick film of lubricant. So, unlike hydrodynamic lubrication, motion of one surface relative to another is not required.

Insufficient surface area, a drop in relative velocity of the moving surface during the period of starting and stopping, an inadequate quantity of lubricant, an increase in the bearing load, or a decrease in viscosity of the lubricant due to increase in temperature — anyone of these — may prevent the buildup of a film thick enough to full film lubrication. When this happens the highest asperities may be separated by lubricant films by a few micron thicknesses. This is called boundary lubrications. The change from hydrodynamic to boundary lubrication is not an abrupt change. It is probable that a mixed hydrodynamic and boundary type lubrication occurs first, and as the surfaces move closer together, the boundary type lubrication becomes predominant. The viscosity of the lubricant is not as much important with boundary lubrication as the chemical composition of the lubricant. This is illustrated in Fig.12.4.

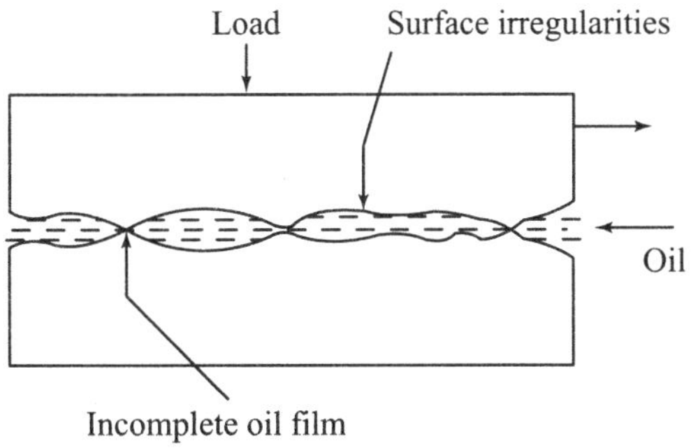

Fig. 12.4 Illustration of boundary lubrication

12.7.4 Journal Bearing Lubrication

Let us examine the formation of a lubricant film in a journal bearing. Fig.12.5 shows a full journal bearing, with the clearance greatly exaggerated. Assume that the space between the journal and bearing is filled with a fluid lubricant. In Fig.12.5(a), the journal loaded by a vertical load, W, is at rest.

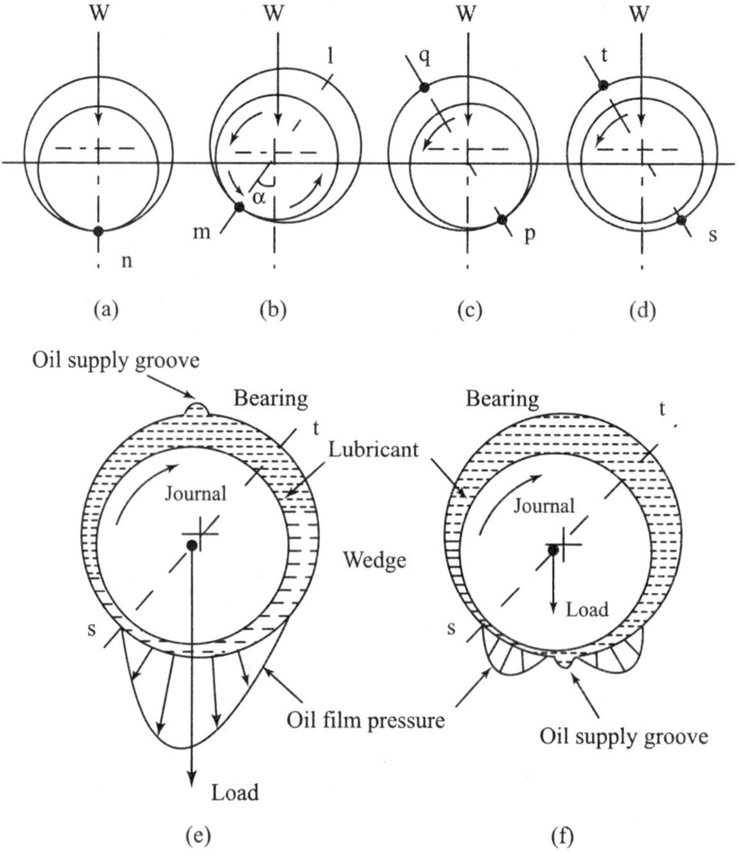

Fig. 12.5 Mechanism of lubrication of journal bearings

In this case the metal to metal contact between the surface of the journal and the bearing is at point n on the line of action of the load. If the journal is just beginning to rotate in an anti-clockwise direction, it tends to climb or roll up the left side of the bearing. Under these conditions, a dry bearing equilibrium is obtained when the friction force is balanced by the tangential component of the bearing load. Therefore, the point of contact will move into position m [Fig.12.5(b)].

It is easy to see that if the speed is quite low, the pressure built in the film can be neglected. The angle α is equal to the angle of sliding friction between the surfaces. With fluid lubricant present, the friction in this case corresponds to the conditions of boundary or extreme boundary conditions.

In this position, the continuous oil film consists of two parts, a convergent part above the line m-ℓ and a divergent part below this line. As explained previously, under such conditions a positive pressure is developed in the converging parts of the oil film. This pressure makes the journal to move to the right. Therefore, with an increase in journal speed, the pressure forces will overcome at the point of contact and will move the journal to the right as shown in Fig.12.5(c).

When the journal reaches a certain speed, the journal is lifted up as shown in Fig.12.5(d) because of the oil pressure. The centre of the journal has moved to such a position that the minimum film thickness is now at point s. From s to t in the direction of motion the oil film is diverging film and t to s it is a converging film and therefore is able to support the load.

An oil film pressure is developed as shown in Fig.12.5(e), the journal is thus operating in the thick film region and the load is carried by the wedge of oil, shown as the shaded area in Fig.12.5(e). To form and to maintain the fluid film, it is necessary to supply a sufficient quantity of lubricant to replace that lost due to end leakage from the bearing and to prevent rupture. This will enable a continuous film around the journal. The proper place where the lubricant must be introduced into the bearing is where the film pressure is low. The part of the film s to t in the direction of motion is diverging. From the foregoing discussion it is clear that no positive pressure can be developed in this region. On the contrary a negative pressure is expected in this region, which may cause a break in the film. This region can be utilized to supply the lubricant so that a continuous oil film can be maintained. If an oil supply groove is cut in the loaded region as in Fig.12.5(f) the oil film pressure is reduced, resulting in a large reduction in load carrying capacity.

As discussed earlier, if the surface velocity of the journal is high enough and if there is sufficient oil supply, enough oil pressure may be developed due to the creation of wedge film to raise the shaft off the bearing. The same wedge film can be created if either the journal is held stationary and the bearing rotates or both rotate. The reader should apply the same reasoning for the hydrodynamic pressure development for the journal rotation and stationary bearing as discussed previously. The relative velocity between journal and the bearing plays a vital role in the hydrodynamic pressure development and hence, the load carrying capacity. In addition, the load may also vary either in magnitude (fluctuating) or in direction (rotating) or both. For example, the bearings of the crankshafts of an internal combustion engine are subjected to a fluctuating and rotating load.

In some other cases, the bearing may still support a load even when the journal and bearing are held stationary but the load is rotating. Also from investigations, one interesting phenomenon noted is that the bearing will not support any load when it is stationary and the load rotates at one half of the speed and also in the same direction as the journal. As regard to the piston pins, the wedge action due to rotation is absent as neither the journal nor the bearing rotates. However, the loads on the piston pins are adequately supported and the piston pin bushings rarely fail in practice. The r on for the above is as discussed below.

Analysis on bearings reveals that a non rotating shaft can support a reciprocating load of considerable magnitude. Physically, it means that as the load is applied in one direction, the journal acts like piston in a hydraulic damping mechanism squeezing out the oil on one side and sucking in on the other side and thereby it can take the load. To explain this, the theory assumes that the journal will move just as slowly away from the bearing as towards it when they are in close proximity due to negative pressures developing in the oil film. Since, cavitations probably occur long before negative pressures of magnitude, comparable to the positive ones developed during the approach portion of the cycle are reached. The journal can always precede from the bearing wall on the near side much more quickly than it approaches it. In this way it is saved from actual metal to metal contact. Also the relative sliding speeds between the pin and its bushing are generally small and hence the heat generation due to fluid friction is also minimal. So, one would not expect severe damage in any case. Obviously the higher the frequency of the load cycle, the higher the load that can be carried by the bearing.

12.7.5 Stable Lubrication

As discussed earlier, with lower relative velocity of the moving surfaces, adequate pressure cannot be developed to support the load by the oil film. At this point of time boundary lubrication will exist. This will occur especially during starting and stopping of an engine. As the speed increases, a sufficient film pressure is developed and the load is supported by the oil film. The phenomenon of shift from boundary lubrication to hydrodynamic lubrication is shown in Fig.12.6 for the change in the coefficient of friction, f, versus the characteristic number, $\nu N/p$ of the bearing.

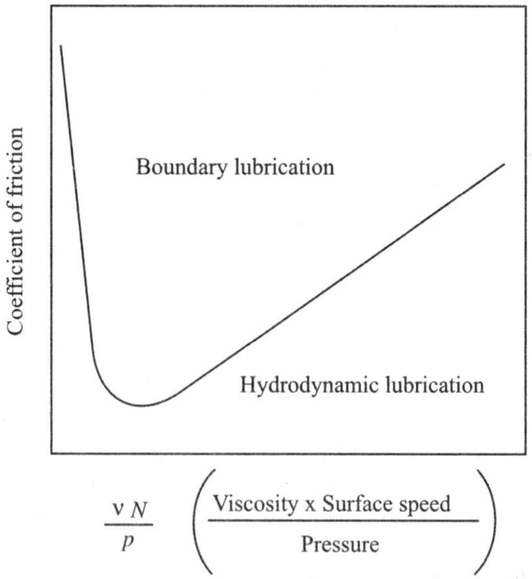

Fig. 12.6 Region of boundary and hydrodynamic lubrication

Here ν is the oil viscosity, p is the pressure and N is the speed. To the left of the point the hydrodynamic pressure developed by the film is too low to support the load and metal to metal contact occurs. This is the zone of boundary lubrication. Even a small reduction in $\nu N/p$ will increase the coefficient of friction drastically and will result in more heat generation which is undesirable for any hydrodynamic bearing.

The bearing operation to the right of this, minimum $\nu N/p$ point is stable. An increase in bearing temperature reduces the oil viscosity and hence, results in lower friction coefficient which gives rise to lower bearing temperature due to reduced heat generation, thereby stabilizing the bearing temperature.

12.8 LUBRICATION OF ENGINE COMPONENTS

In a reciprocating engine there are many surfaces in contact with each other and therefore they should be lubricated to reduce friction. The principal friction surfaces requiring lubrication in an internal combustion engine are

(i) piston and cylinders

(ii) crankshaft and their bearings

(iii) crankpin and their bearings

(iv) wristpin and their bearings

(v) valve gear

12.8.1 Piston

Since the piston and piston rings are exposed to high temperatures, the oil that is supplied to the cylinder walls must provide proper lubrication under extreme conditions. In addition, the lubricant on the cylinder walls must function as a seal to minimize the amount of the gases of combustion that pass the piston rings and enter the crankcase.

Pistons of high speed engines used in automobiles, usually do not need any special lubricating provisions. The oil which flows from the main bearings and crankpin is splashed by the crank webs and connecting rods and the oil mist which is formed in the enclosed crankcase by the fast moving parts furnish sufficient lubrication for the pistons. These conditions exist not only when the oil in the crankcase is kept at a certain level to allow its pick-up by the connecting rods but even when the oil level is low in the crankcase because of the state of constant ignition in the sump in the many vehicles.

Pistons of low and medium speed engines are lubricated by positive feed mechanical oilers. A positive feed mechanical oiler has a small plunger which discharges oil to the cylinder surface during its forward stroke. On its return stroke a check valve prevents the oil from being sucked back and oil is drawn in through another line.

Tests indicate that the piston rings and cylinders operate in the thin-film lubrication region a great deal of time. Thick-film lubrication would result in excessive oil consumption. In thin film region, oiliness and surface finish will play a vital role in reducing wear and scuffing. A smooth surface has flat spots with many small indentations interposed among them. These irregularities help the oil to maintain a film on the surface and act as individual oil reservoirs. Surface damage may be further reduced by adding sulphur and chlorine compounds in the lubricant. These compounds convert the material into sulphides and chlorides and prevent welding of stressed points. In high speed engines with higher specific power output an oil gallery is provided by which the lubricant helps to remove heat to a greater extent.

12.8.2 Crankshaft Bearings

In small stationary engines, the main bearings of the crankshaft are made with ring oilers. A ring oiler is nothing but a ring which is slipped over the shaft and runs over the journal. The diameter of the ring is bigger than the journal diameters which enable the ring to slip over the shaft when it is rotating. Because of the shaft rotation the ring will also tends to rotate. While rotating, the bottom portion of the ring picks up the oil from the reservoir and carries it to the top of the journal where it is able to flow into the bearing oil grooves and bearing clearance space, to be distributed to the entire bearing surface.

For large engines, with open or at least not very tight crankcase, as in the case of most horizontal engines, the main bearings are lubricated by positive feed lubricators. Engines with enclosed crankcases as in the case of the most vertical engines, are usually built with pressure lubrication. The oil is drawn by a gear pump and delivered it to the oil gallery in the crankcase which distributes it to the bearings. Oil coming out of the bearing goes to an oil sump where it is picked up by a scavenging pump. Then it is pumped through a filter to oil cooler and to a supply tank from which it flows back to the pressure pump. Usually, the oil is circulated in large quantities as the oil not only serves as lubricant but also act as a cooling medium to the bearings.

12.8.3 Crankpin Bearings

In small engines, the bearing pressure is low and the crankpins are sometimes lubricated by splashing oil. For this purpose, the bottom of the connecting rod is attached with a dipper which dips into the oil when the connecting rod comes down. This arrangement is illustrated in Fig.12.7(a).

Small horizontal engines and some two-stroke vertical engines use the centrifugal banjo oiler. Fig.12.7(b) shows this kind of arrangement. The oil hole leading to the surface of the crankpin is often drilled at an angle of about 30° before the dead centre, so that the upper shell receives oil before the ignition at a point of relatively low pressure. For a heavy duty engine, the oil is fed from the main bearing to the crankpin by a drilled hole. The details are illustrated in Fig.12.7(c).

12.8.4 Wristpin Bearing

In small horizontal engines the wristpin is lubricated by a sight feed oiler. The details of the arrangements are shown in Fig.12.8(a). A special scraper

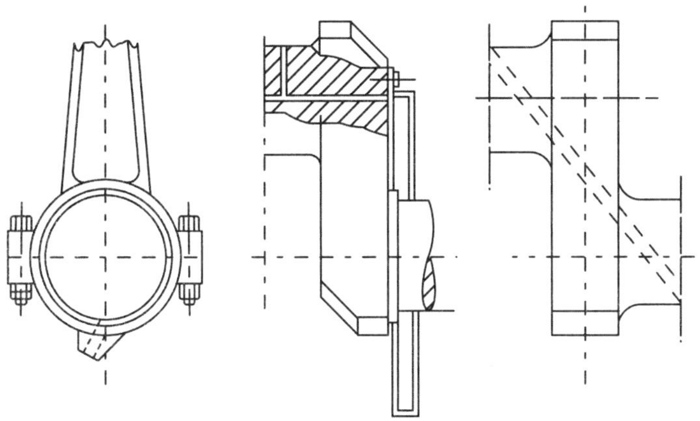

(a) (b) (c)

Fig. 12.7 Lubrication of crankpin bearings

scoop is provided to scrap the oil dripping from the cylinder walls and the arrangement is illustrated in Fig.12.8(b).

In other vertical engines where the lubricating oil delivered under pressure to the main and crankpin bearings, the wristpin is lubricated by excess oil from the crankpin bearing. For this purpose, a hole will be drilled through the connecting rod shown. This is illustrated in Fig.12.8(c).

12.9 LUBRICATION SYSTEM

The function of a lubrication system is to provide sufficient quantity of cool, filtered oil to give positive and adequate lubrication to all the moving parts of an engine. The various lubrication systems used for internal combustion engines may be classified as

(i) mist lubrication system

(ii) wet sump lubrication system

(iii) dry sump lubrication system

12.9.1 Mist Lubrication System

This system is used where crankcase lubrication is not suitable. In two-stroke engine, as the charge is compressed in the crankcase, it is not possible to have the lubricating oil in the sump. Hence, mist lubrication is adopted in practice. In such engines, the lubricating oil is mixed with the fuel, the usual ratio being 3% to 6%. The oil and the fuel mixture are inducted through the carburettor. The fuel is vaporized and the oil in the form of mist goes via the crankcase into the cylinder. The oil which strikes the crankcase walls lubricates the main and connecting rod bearings, and the rest of the oil lubricates the piston, piston rings and the cylinder.

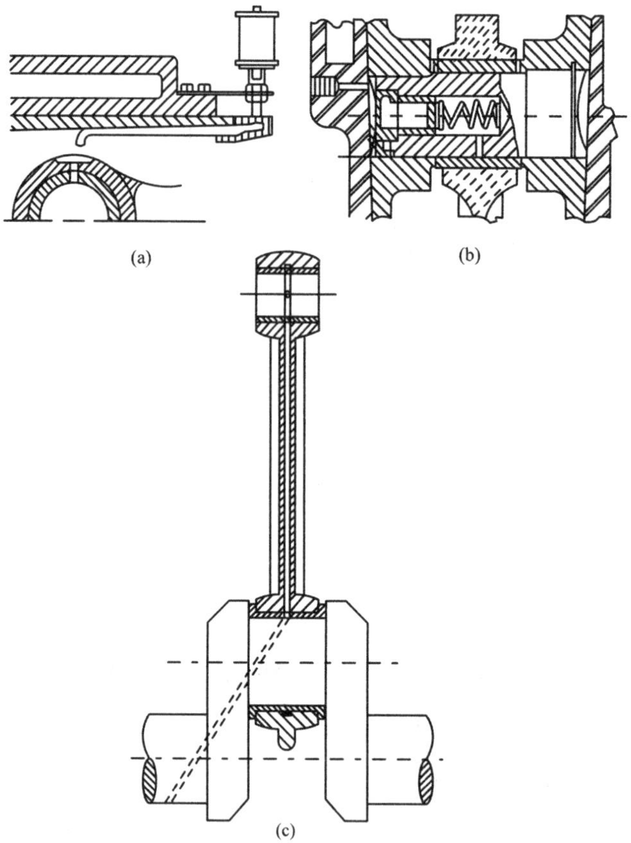

Fig. 12.8 Lubrication of wristpin bearings

The advantage of this system is its simplicity and low cost as it does not require an oil pump, filter, etc. However, there are certain disadvantages which are enumerated below.

(i) It causes heavy exhaust smoke due to burning of lubricating oil partially or fully and also forms deposits on piston crown and exhaust ports which affect engine efficiency.

(ii) Since the oil comes in close contact with acidic vapours produced during the combustion process gets contaminated and may result in the corrosion of bearing surface.

(iii) This system calls for a thorough mixing for effective lubrication. This requires either separate mixing prior to use or use of some additive to give the oil good mixing characteristics.

(iv) During closed throttle operation as in the case of the vehicle moving down the hill, the engine will suffer from insufficient lubrication as the supply of fuel is less. This is an important limitation of this system.

In some of the modern engines, the lubricating oil is directly injected into the carburettor and the quantity of oil is regulated. Thus the problem of oil deficiency is eliminated to a very great extent. In this system the main bearings also receive oil from a separate pump. For this purpose, they will be located outside the crankcase. With this system, formation of deposits and corrosion of bearings are also eliminated.

12.9.2 Wet Sump Lubrication System

In the wet sump system, the bottom of the crankcase contains an oil pan or sump from which the lubricating oil is pumped to various engine components by a pump. After lubricating these parts, the oil flows back to the sump by gravity. Again it is picked up by a pump and recirculated through the engine lubricating system. There are three varieties in the wet sump lubrication system. They are

(i) the splash system

(ii) the splash and pressure system

(iii) the pressure feed system

Splash System: This type of lubrication system is used in light duty engines. A schematic diagram of this system is shown in Fig.12.9.

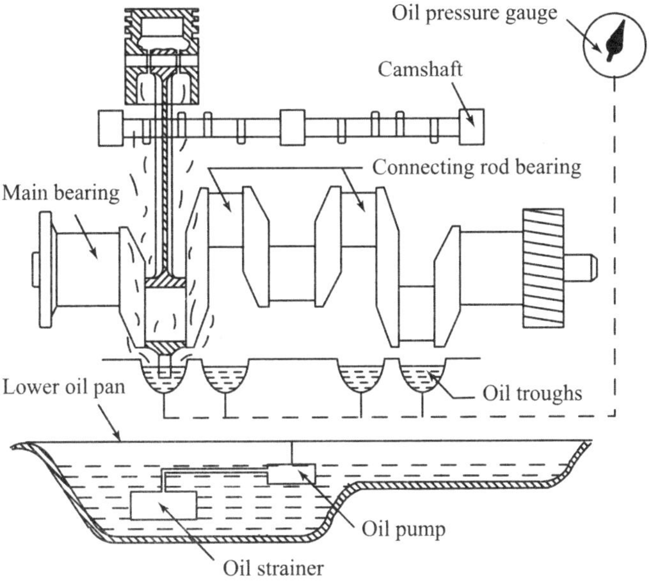

Fig. 12.9 Splash lubrication system

The lubricating oil is charged into in the bottom of the engine crankcase and maintained at a predetermine level. The oil is drawn by a pump and delivered through a distributing pipe extending the length of the crankcase into splash troughs located under the big end of all the connecting rods. These troughs were provided with overflows and the oil in the troughs is therefore kept at a constant level. A splasher or dipper is provided under each connecting rod cap which dips into the oil in the trough at every revolution of the crankshaft and the oil is splashed all over the interior of the crankcase, into the pistons and onto the exposed portions of the cylinder walls. A hole is drilled through the connecting rod cap through which oil will pass to the bearing surface. Oil pockets are also provided to catch the splashing oil over all the main bearings and also over the camshaft bearings. From the pockets the oil will reach the bearings surface through a drilled hole. The oil dripping from the cylinders is collected in the sump where it is cooled by the air flowing around. The cooled oil is then recirculated.

The Splash and Pressure Lubrication System: This system is shown in Fig.12.10, where the lubricating oil is supplied under pressure to main and camshaft bearings. Oil is also supplied under pressure to pipes which direct a stream of oil against the dippers on the big end of connecting rod bearing cup and thus the crankpin bearings are lubricated by the splash or spray of oil thrown up by the dipper.

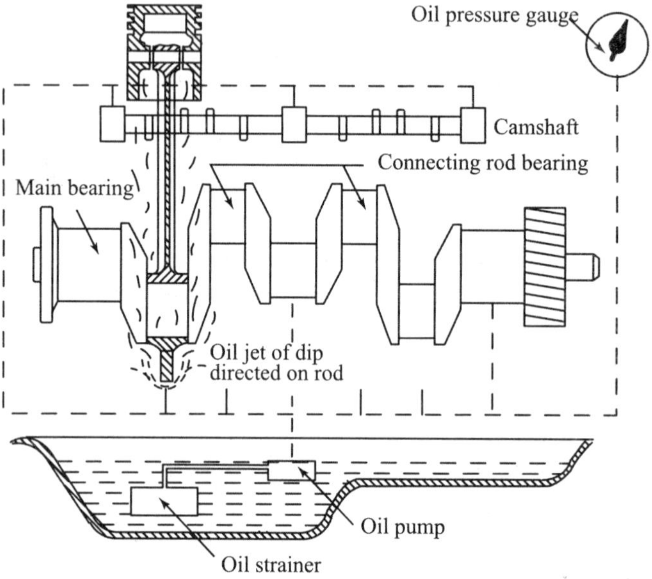

Fig. 12.10 Splash and pressure lubrication system

Pressure Feed System: The pressure feed system is illustrated in Fig.12.11 in which oil is drawn in from the sump and forced to all the main bearings of the crankshaft through distributing channels. A pressure relief valve will also be fitted near the delivery point of the pump which opens when the pressure in the system attains a predetermined value. An oil hole is drilled in the crankshaft from the centre of each crankpin to the centre of an adjacent main journal, through which oil can pass from the main bearings to the crankpin bearing. From the crankpin it reaches piston pin bearing through a hole drilled in the connecting rod. The cylinder walls, tappet rollers, piston and piston rings are lubricated by oil spray from around the piston pins and the main and connecting rod bearings. The basic components of the wet sump lubrication systems are (i) pump (ii) strainer (iii) pressure regulator (iv) filter (v) breather.

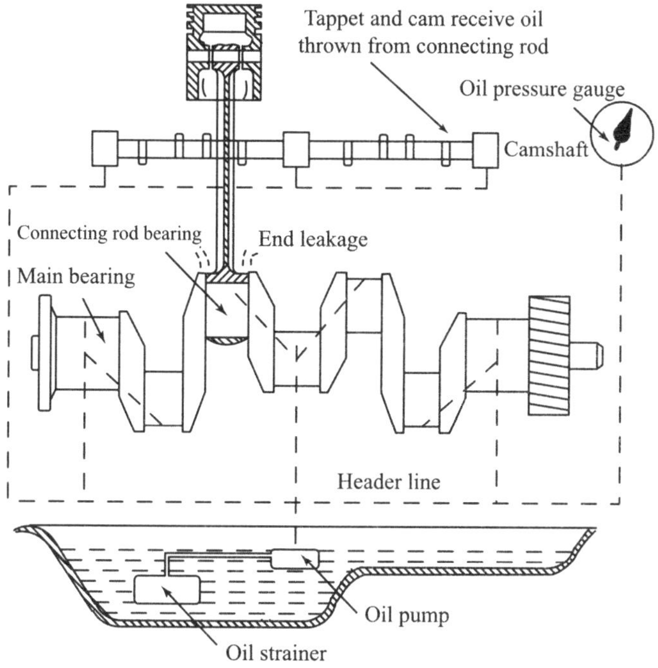

Fig. 12.11 Pressure feed lubrication system

A typical wet sump and its components are shown in Fig.12.12. Oil is drawn from the sump by a gear or rotor type of oil pump through an oil strainer. The strainer is a fine mesh screen which prevents foreign particles from entering the oil circulating systems. A pressure relief valve is provided which automatically keeps the delivery pressure constant and can be set to any value. When the oil pressure exceeds that for which the valve is set, the valve opens and allows some of the oil to return to the sump thereby relieving the oil pressure in the systems. Fig.12.13 shows a typical gear pump, pressure relief valve and by-pass. Most of the oil from the pump goes directly to the engine bearings and a portion of the oil passes through a cartridge filter which removes the solid particles from the oil. This reduces the amount of contamination from carbon dust and other impurities present in the oil. Since all the oil coming from the pump does not pass directly through the filter, this filtering system is called by-pass filtering system. All the oil will pass through the filter over a period of operation. The advantage of this system is that a clogged filter will not restrict the flow of oil to the engine.

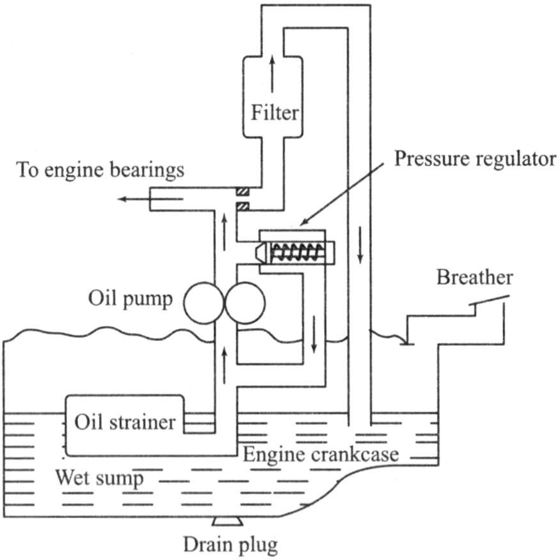

Fig. 12.12 Basic components of wet sump lubrication system

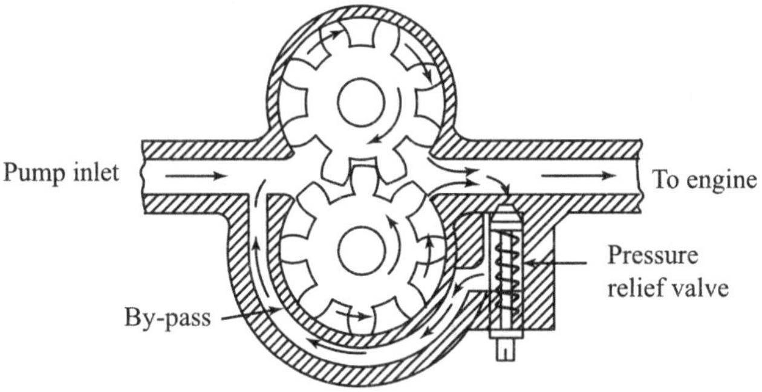

Fig. 12.13 Gear type lubricating pump

12.9.3 Dry Sump Lubrication System

A dry sump lubricating system is illustrated in Fig.12.14. In this, the supply of oil is carried in an external tank. An oil pump draws oil from the supply tank and circulates it under pressure to the various bearings of the engine. Oil dripping from the cylinders and bearings into the sump is removed by a scavenging pump which in turn the oil is passed through a filter, and is fed back to the supply tank. Thus, oil is prevented from accumulating in the base of the engine. The capacity of the scavenging pump is always greater than the oil pump. In this system a filter with a bypass valve is placed in between the scavenge pump and the supply tank. If the filter is clogged, the pressure relief valve opens permitting oil to by-pass the filter and reaches the supply tank. A separate oil cooler with either water or air as the cooling medium, is usually provided in the dry sump system to remove heat from the oil.

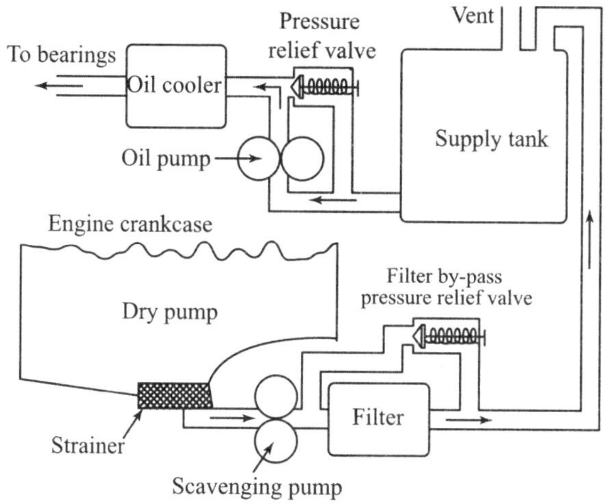

Fig. 12.14 Dry sump lubrication system

12.10 CRANKCASE VENTILATION

During the compression and the expansion strokes the gas inside the cylinder gets past the piston rings and enters the crankcase which is called the blowby. It contains water vapour and sulphuric acid if either the oil or the fuel contains appreciable amount of sulphur. They might cause corrosion of steel parts in the crankcase. This may also promote sludge formation in the lubricating oil. When the amount of water vapour condensed becomes considerable, in cold weather this may freeze and may cause damage to the lubricating oil pump. Hence, it is imperative to remove the blowby from the crankcase. This removal of the blowby can be achieved effectively by passing a constant stream of fresh air through the crankcase known as crankcase ventilation. By doing so, not only all the water vapour but also a considerable proportion of the fuel in the blowby may be removed from the crankcase. The problem of excessive crankcase dilution and the crankcase corrosion is at least materially lessened. This type of crankcase ventilation is illustrated in Fig.12.15.

The crankcase must have an air inlet and air outlet for the effective crankcase ventilation. The breather and oil filter (if any) forms a suitable inlet placed near the forward end of the case where the fan blows the cooling air and an outlet opening is then provided near the rear end of the engine block and a tube is taken from this outlet to a point below the crankcase where rapid flow of air flows past its outlet when the vehicle is in motion causing an ejector effect. Air enters through the breather on the right, passes through the crankcase and exits through a pipe down into the air stream at the bottom of the crankcase. The outlet from the crankcase should be located at a point where the air is comparatively quiescent and therefore does not hold much oil in suspension.

It is also possible to connect the crankcase outlet to the air cleaner, where the intake suction serves to ventilate the crankcase and the unburned fuel,

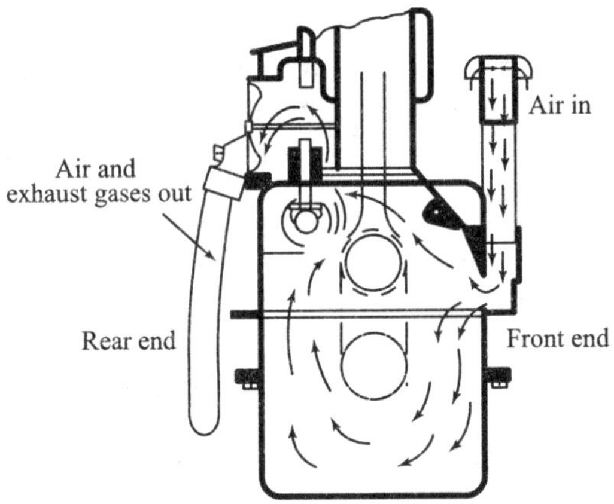

Fig. 12.15 Crankcase ventilation

gases as well as the water vapour is then drawn into the cylinders where the fuel has another chance to burn. This scheme, however has been given up evidently in the belief that corrosion might be promoted by circulating these vapours through the engine.

12.11 PROPERTIES OF LUBRICANTS

The duties of the lubricant in an engine are many and varied in scope. The lubricant is called upon to limit and control the following:

(i) friction between the components and metal to metal contact

(ii) overheating of the components

(iii) wear and corrosion of the components

To accomplish the above functions, the lubricant should have

(i) suitable viscosity

(ii) oiliness to ensure adherence to the bearings, and for less friction and wear when the lubrication is in the boundary region, and as a protective covering against corrosion

(iii) high strength to prevent the metal to metal contact and seizure under heavy load

(iv) should not react with the lubricating surfaces

(v) a low pour point to allow flow of the lubricant at low temperatures to the oil pump

(vi) no tendency to form deposits by reacting with air, water, fuel or the products of combustion

(vii) cleaning ability, nontoxic, non-inflammable, non-foaming characteristics

(viii) low cost

12.11.1 Viscosity

The viscosity of the oil at the temperature and pressure of the operation must be compatible with the load and speed to ensure hydrodynamic lubrication. In general, large clearances and high loads require high-viscosity oils whereas high speeds require low viscosity oils. Hence, the oil supplied must be in a position to meet the variable viscosity requirements.

Viscosity Index: The viscosity index is a measure of change in viscosity of an oil with temperature as compared to two reference oils having the same viscosity at 100 °C. It is an empirical number wherein typical Pennsylvania (paraffinic base) oil is assigned an index of 100 and Gulf Coast (naphthenic-base) oil is assigned an index of zero. In general, the high viscosity index number indicates relatively a smaller change in viscosity with temperature. A low index number for a given oil indicates relatively large change of viscosity with temperature.

Thus, the viscosity index of a lubricating oil is an important factor where extreme range of temperature is encountered. The oil must necessarily maintain sufficient viscosity at operating temperatures. Yet it should not be too viscous for starting of the engine especially at low temperature. Normally, a high viscosity index is preferred for engine lubrication, because of relatively smaller changes in viscosity of the oil with temperature.

12.11.2 Flash and Fire Points

The flash point of an oil is the minimum temperature at which sufficient flammable vapour is driven off to flash when brought into contact with a flame. The fire point is the minimum temperature at which the inflammable vapours will continue to form and steadily burn once ignited. Flash and fire points may vary with the nature of the original crude oil, the viscosity and the method of refining. For the same viscosities and degree of refinement, the paraffinic oils have higher flash and fire points than naphthenic oils.

12.11.3 Cloud and Pour Points

Petroleum oils when cooled may become plastic solids as a result of either of partial separation of wax or of congealing of the hydrocarbons. With some oils, the separation of wax becomes visible at temperatures slightly above the solidification point and this temperature (under prescribed condition) is known as the cloud point. With oils in which the separation is invisible, the cloud point cannot be determined. That temperature at which the oil will not flow when the test container is tilted under prescribed conditions is known as the pour point.

The pour point indicates the lowest temperature at which an oil stops flowing to the pump, bearings or cylinder walls. It is particularly important for immediate oil circulation in respect of starting of engines in very cold climates with gravity lubricating systems the fluidity is a factor of pour point and viscosity of the cold oil. Pour point depressants may be added to wax containing oils to lower the pour points instead of dewaxing the oil.

12.11.4 Oiliness or Film Strength

Oiliness or film strength of a lubricant is a measure of the protective film between shaft and bearing. Thus two oils of identical viscosity may show differences in their coefficients of friction in the boundary region because of the difference in their oiliness. Most probably, the lubricant reacts with the bearing on shaft to form a protective grease or soap, thus giving rise to the lower coefficient of friction (higher oiliness). Film strength refers to the ability of the lubricant to resist welding and scuffing. The lubricating oil used must be of enough film strength to take care of welding and scuffing.

12.11.5 Corrosiveness

The oil should be noncorrosive and should protect against corrosion. It is probable that the absorbed film that rises to the level of oiliness is also related to the protection of the surface against corrosion.

12.11.6 Detergency

An oil has the property of detergency if it acts to clean the engine deposits. A separate property is the dispersing ability which enables the oil to carry small particles uniformly distributed without agglomeration. In general, the term is the name for both detergent and dispersing properties.

12.11.7 Stability

The ability of oil to resist oxidation that would yield acids, lacquers and sludge is called stability. Oil stability demands low-temperature (under 90 °C) operation and the removal of all hot areas from contact with the oil.

12.11.8 Foaming

Foaming describes the condition where minute bubbles of air are held in the oil. This action accelerates oxidation and reduces the mass flow of oil to the bearings thus reducing the hydrodynamic pressure in the bearing and hence the load bearing capacity of the bearing.

12.12 SAE RATING OF LUBRICANTS

Selection of the lubricant for engine application is based on the temperature at which the engine is to be started and operated and the type of service to which the engine is to be subjected to. The SAE (Society of Automotive Engineers) has been the first organization that in June 1911 developed the SAE J300 standard that specifies Engine Oil Viscosity Classification. Therefore, grade of the engine oil is defined by SAE J300 standard. They have specified two grades for engine applications.

12.12.1 Single-grade

A single-grade engine oil cannot use a polymeric Viscosity Index Improver additive. SAE J300 has eleven viscosity grades, of which six are considered Winter-grades and given a W designation. The eleven viscosity grades are

0W, 5W, 10W, 15W, 20W, 25W, 20, 30, 40, 50, and 60. These numbers are often referred to as the 'weight' of a motor oil; and single-grade motor oils are often called "straight-weight" oils.

For single winter grade oils, the dynamic viscosity is measured at different cold temperatures in units of mPa or the equivalent older non-SI units, centipoise (cP), using two different test methods viz., the cold cranking simulator (ASTMD5293) and mini-rotary viscometer (ASTMD4684).

Based on the coldest temperature at which the oil can flow, it is graded as 0W, 5W, 10W, 15W, 20W, or 25W. The lower is the viscosity grade, the lower will be the temperature at which the oil can flow. For example, if an oil can flow at the specifications for 10W and 5W, but fails for 0W, then that oil must be labeled as an SAE 5W. That oil cannot be labeled as either 0W or 10W.

For single non-winter grade oils, the kinematic viscosity is measured at a temperature of 100 C in units of mm/s or the equivalent older non-SI units, centistokes (abbreviated cSt).

Based on the range of viscosity the oil falls in at that temperature, the oil is graded as SAE viscosity grade 20, 30, 40, 50, or 60. Higher the viscosity, the higher is the SAE grade.

For applications, where the temperature ranges in use are not very wide, single-grade motor oil is satisfactory; for example, lawn mower engines, industrial applications, and vintage or classic cars.

12.12.2 Multi-grade

The temperature range the oil is exposed to in most automobiles can be wide. For example it can range from cold temperatures in the winter before the vehicle is started up, to hot operating temperatures when the vehicle is fully warmed up in hot summer weather. A specific single-grade oil will have higher viscosity when cold and a lower viscosity at the engine's operating temperature. The difference in viscosities for most single-grade oil is too large between the extremes of temperature.

To bring the difference in viscosities closer together, special polymer additives called Viscosity Index Improvers or V I Is are added to the oil. These additives are used to make the oil a multi-grade though it is possible to have a multi-grade oil without the use of V I Is. The idea is to cause the multi-grade oil to have the viscosity of the base grade when cold and the viscosity of the second grade when hot. This enables one type of oil to be used all year. In fact, when multi-grades were initially developed, they were frequently described as all-season oil.

Present day engine oils are multi grade (viscosity) oils. The multi viscosity oil is one that has a low viscosity when cold (for easier cranking) and a higher viscosity when hot (to provide adequate lubrication). Multi grade oils are rated at two different temperatures. The SAE designation for multi-grade oils includes two viscosity grades. Multi grade oils are specified as SAE10W 30, 20W 40 etc. The first of the double numbers indicates the relative flow ability and the second number indicates the relative resistances to film break down. For example, a 10W 30 weight oil will flow easily (like a 10W oil) when starting a cold engine. It will then act as a thicker oil (like 30 weight) when the engine warms up to operating temperature. As such, it will provide adequate film strength (thickness) when the engine is at full operating temperature.

The service classification by API for diesel engine lubricating oils is subdivided into three classes ranging from the least to the most severe service, viz., DG, DM and DS. These correspond to the Diesel Good, Diesel Medium and Diesel Severe service respectively. There are five service ratings for petrol engine lubricating oils: SA,SB, SC, SD and SE. The oil differs in their properties and in the additives they contain.

Synthetic oils are now available for use in engines. The manufacturers claim that these have superior lubricating properties. There are several basic types of synthetic oils. The type most widely used at present is produced from organic acids and alcohols (from plants of various types). A second type is produced from coal and crude oil.

12.13 ADDITIVES FOR LUBRICANTS

The lubricating oil should possess all the above properties for the satisfactory engine performance. The modern lubricants for heavy duty engines are highly refined which otherwise may produce sludge or suffer a progressive increase in viscosity. For these reasons the lubricants are seasoned by the addition of certain oil-soluble organic compounds containing inorganic elements such as phosphorus, sulphur, amine derivatives. Metals are added to the mineral based lubricating oil to exhibit the desired properties. Thus oil soluble organic compounds added to the present day lubricants to impart one or more of the following characteristics.

(i) anti-oxidant and anticorrosive agents

(ii) detergent-dispersant

(iii) extreme pressure additives

(iv) pour point depressors

(v) viscosity index improvers

(vi) antifoam agent

(vii) oiliness and film-strength agents

12.13.1 Anti-oxidants and Anticorrosive Agents

Oxidation of the lubricating oil is slow at temperatures below 90 °C but increase at an exponential rate when high temperatures are encountered. Oxidation is undesirable, not only because sludge and varnish are formed but also because of the formation of acids which may be corrosive. Thus the additive has the dual purpose of preserving both the lubricant and the components of the engine. To accomplish these purposes, the additive must nullify the action of metals in catalyzing oxidation; copper is especially active as an oxidation catalyst of hydrocarbon. The additives may be alkaline to neutralize acids formed by oxidation, or, it may be non-alkaline and protect the metal by forming a surface film.

Some additives may unite with oxygen, either preferentially to the oil or else with some already oxidized portion of the oil or fuel contaminant. Other additives might act as metal deactivators and as corrosion shields by chemically combining with the metal. Thus a thin sulphide or phosphide coating on the metal deactivates those metals that act as catalysts while protecting other metals from corrosive attack. Zinc ditinophosphate serves as an anti-oxidant and anticorrosive additive.

12.13.2 Detergent-Dispersant

This type of additives improve the detergent action of the lubricating oil. These additives might be metallic salts or organic acids. The action due to the additive may arise either from direct chemical reaction or from polar attraction. Thus the additives may chemically combine with the compounds in the oil that would otherwise form sludge and varnish. On the other hand, if the additive and the deposits in the engine are polar compounds, the detergent action may arise from neutralization of the electric moment of the deposit molecules with that of the additive. In this manner the deposit could be neutralized and would not tend to cling to other molecules or to the surface. Therefore, agglomeration of deposits would be prevented.

12.13.3 Extreme Pressure Additives

At high loads and speeds with high surface temperatures, an extreme pressure additive is necessary. Such additives interact with the metal surface to form a complex inorganic film containing iron, oxygen, carbon and hydrogen. Welding is prevented by the presence of the film.

12.13.4 Pour Point Depressors

In order to obtain fluidity or flow of oil at low temperatures, pour point depressants is added to the lubricating oils to lower the pour point. An engine having a lubricant with higher pour point will not get adequate lubrication during starting at low ambient temperatures and excessive wear would result. These additives tend to prevent the formation of wax at the low temperatures encountered in starting.

12.13.5 Viscosity Index Improvers

High molecule polymers are added to the lubricating oils to increase their viscosity index. An increase in the viscosity index increases the resistance of an oil to change its viscosity with a change in temperature. A high viscosity index oil will have good starting characteristics plus satisfactory operation at high speed and heavy load conditions.

12.13.6 Oiliness and Film Strength Agents

Oiliness and high film-strength can be improved by adding organic sulphur, chlorine and phosphorus compounds.

12.13.7 Antifoam Agents

Foaming, to some extent is due to the violent agitation and aeration of the oil that occurs in an operating engine. The minute particles of air in a foaming oil increase oxidation and reduce the mass flow of oil to the bearings. In addition foaming may cause abnormal loss of oil through the crankcase breather. Antifoam agents are used to reduce the foaming tendencies of the lubricant. Although many chemical compounds are available for this purpose, the most effective are the silicone polymers.

Review Questions

12.1 Explain the six classes of mechanical friction and the various factors affecting them.

12.2 Explain the various mechanism of lubrication and their functions.

12.3 What are the various components to be lubricated in an engine and explain how it is accomplished?

12.4 Explain and compare the wet sump dry sump lubrication systems.

12.5 What is meant by crankcase ventilation? Explain the details.

12.6 What are the various desired properties of a lubricant and explain how additives help to achieve the desired properties.

Multiple Choice Questions (choose the most appropriate answer)

1. Mechanical efficiency is the ratio of

   (a) brake power to heat input
   (b) indicated power to heat input
   (c) brake power to indicated power
   (d) friction loss to heat input

2. Most commonly used lubrication system in automobiles is the

   (a) splash system
   (b) pressure system
   (c) petrol system
   (d) gravity system

3. Friction that occurs between the layers of oil film is called

   (a) viscous friction
   (b) greasy friction
   (c) dry friction
   (d) boundary friction

4. Crankcase ventilation is provided

   (a) to cool cylinder
   (b) to cool crankcase
   (c) to cool piston
   (d) to remove blowby

5. The most important property of the lubricant is

   (a) density
   (b) viscosity
   (c) thermal conductivity
   (d) none of the above

6. The maximum pressure in the lubrication system is controlled by

   (a) oil pump
   (b) oil filter
   (c) valve relief
   (d) supply voltage

7. The lubricants commonly used in the automobiles are

   (a) animal oils
   (b) vegetable oils
   (c) mineral oils
   (d) cooking oils

8. Detergents are oil additives used to

   (a) reduce viscosity
   (b) increase fire point
   (c) prevent sludge formation
   (d) prevent foaming

9. Oil pressure in the dry sump lubrication system is around

   (a) 5 bar – 10 bar
   (b) 11 bar – 15 bar
   (c) 3 bar – 8 bar
   (d) 1 bar

10. *fmep* decreases when using

    (a) single cylinder engine
    (b) smaller number of larger cylinders
    (c) larger number of smaller cylinders
    (d) none of the above

11. With increase in compression ratio, mechanical efficiency

    (a) increases
    (b) decreases
    (c) remains constant
    (d) compression ratio has nothing to do with η_{mech}

12. Blowby losses are

    (a) directly proportional to the inlet pressure
    (b) inversely proportional to the inlet pressure
    (c) proportional to the square root of inlet pressure
    (d) none of the above

13. Most lubrication system is mainly used in

    (a) four-stroke petrol engine
    (b) four-stroke diesel engine
    (c) two-stroke petrol engine
    (d) Wankle engine

14. Additives are added in lubricant to have

    (a) detergent-dispersant characteristics
    (b) pour point depression
    (c) antifoam characteristics
    (d) all of the above

15. The principal surfaces requiring lubrication in an IC engine are

    (a) cylinder head
    (b) crankcase
    (c) inlet and exhaust manifold
    (d) none of the above

Ans:	1. – (c)	2. – (b)	3. – (a)	4. – (d)	5. – (b)
	6. – (c)	7. – (c)	8. – (c)	9. – (c)	10. – (c)
	11. – (a)	12. – (c)	13. – (c)	14. – (d)	15. – (d)

13

HEAT REJECTION AND COOLING

13.1 INTRODUCTION

Internal combustion engines at best can transform about 25 to 35 per cent of the chemical energy in the fuel into mechanical energy. About 35 per cent of the heat generated is lost to the cooling medium, remainder being dissipated through exhaust and lubricating oil.

During the process of combustion, the cylinder gas temperature often reaches quite a high value. A considerable amount of heat is transferred to the walls of the combustion chamber. Therefore, it is necessary to provide proper cooling especially to the walls of the combustion chamber. Due to the prevailing high temperatures, chemical and physical changes in the lubricating oil may also occur. This causes wear and sticking of the piston rings, scoring of cylinder walls or seizure of the piston. Excessive cylinder-wall temperatures will therefore cause the rise in the operating temperature of piston head. This in turn will affect the strength of piston seriously.

In addition, overheated cylinder head may lead to overheated spark plug electrodes causing preignition. The exhaust valve may become hot enough to cause preignition or may fail structurally. Moreover, preignition can increase the cylinder head temperature to the extent of engine failure or complete loss of power.

As the last part of the charge to burn is in contact with the walls of the combustion space during the burning period, a high cylinder wall or cylinder head temperature will lead to auto-ignition in SI engines.

In view of the above, the inside surface temperature of the cylinder walls should be kept in a range which will ensure correct clearances between parts, promote vaporization of fuel, keep the oil at its best viscosity and prevent the condensation of harmful vapours. Therefore, the heat that is transferred into the walls of the combustion chamber is continuously removed by employing a cooling system. Almost 30 to 35 per cent of the total heat supplied by the fuel is removed by the cooling medium. Heat carried away by lubricating oil and heat lost by radiation amounts to 5 per cent of the total heat supplied. Unless the engine is adequately cooled engine seizure will result. In this chapter the details of engine heat transfer, heat rejection and cooling are considered.

13.2 VARIATION OF GAS TEMPERATURE

There is an appreciable variation in the temperature of the gases inside the engine cylinder during different processes of the cycle. Temperature inside the engine cylinder is almost the lowest at the end of the suction stroke. During combustion there is a rapid rise in temperature to a peak value which again drops during the expansion. This variation of gas temperature is illustrated in Fig.13.1 for various processes in the cycle.

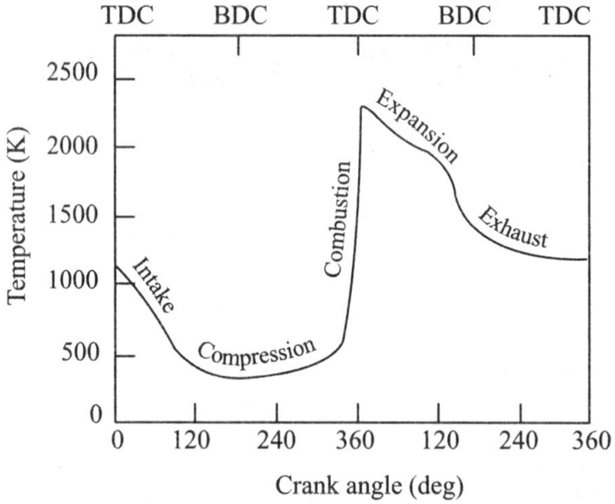

Fig. 13.1 Gas temperature variation during a cycle

13.3 PISTON TEMPERATURE DISTRIBUTION

The piston crown is exposed to very high combustion temperatures. Figure 13.2 gives the typical values of temperature at different parts of a cast iron piston. It may be noted that the maximum temperature occurs at the centre

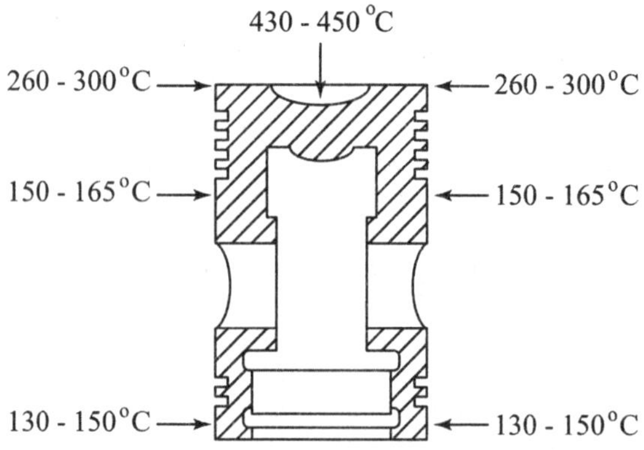

Fig. 13.2 Piston temperature distribution

of the crown and decreases with increasing distance from the centre. The temperature is the lowest at the bottom of the skirt. Poor design may result in the thermal overloading of the piston at the centre of the crown. The temperature difference between piston outer edge and the centre of the crown is responsible for the flow of heat to the ring belt through the path offered by metal section of the crown. It is, therefore, necessary to increase the thickness of the crown from the centre to the outer edge in order to make a path of greater cross-section available for the increasing heat quantity. The length of the path should not be too long or the thickness of the crown cross-section too small for the heat to flow. This will cause the temperature at the centre of crown to build up and thereby excessive temperature difference between the crown and the outer edge of the piston will result. This may even lead to cracking of piston during overload operation.

13.4 CYLINDER TEMPERATURE DISTRIBUTION

Whenever a moving gas comes into contact with a wall, there exists a relatively stagnant gas layer which acts as a thermal insulator. The resistance of this layer to heat flow is quite high. Heat transfer from the cylinder gases takes place through the gas layer and through the cylinder walls to the cooling medium. A large temperature drop is produced in the stagnant layer adjacent to the walls. The peak cylinder gas temperature may be 2800 K while the temperature of the cylinder inner wall surface may be only 450 K due to cooling, (Fig.13.3). Heat is transferred from the gases to the cylinder walls

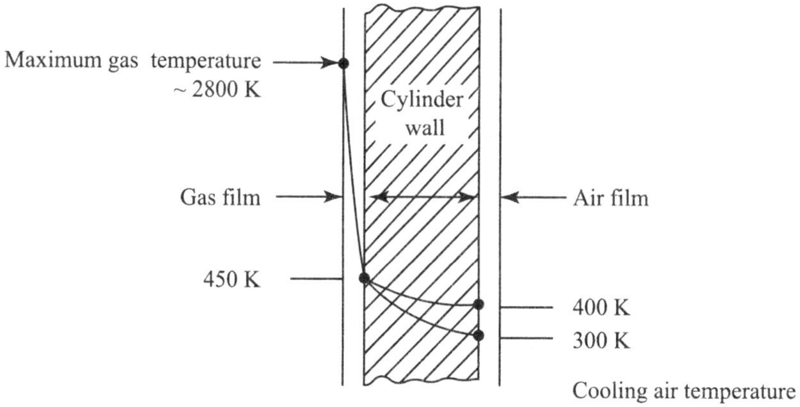

Fig. 13.3 Cylinder wall temperature distribution of a properly cooled cylinder

when the gas temperature is higher than the wall temperature. The rate and direction of flow of heat varies depending upon the temperature differential. If no cooling is provided, there could be no heat flow, so that the whole cylinder wall would soon reach an average temperature of the cylinder gases. By providing adequate cooling, the cylinder wall temperature can be maintained at optimum level.

13.5 HEAT TRANSFER

Heat transfer occurs when a temperature difference exists. As a result of combustion, high temperatures are produced, inside the engine cylinder. Consid-

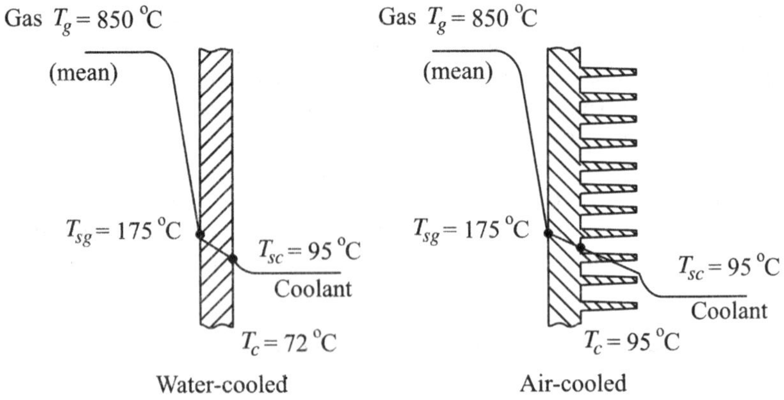

Fig. 13.4 Temperature profile across cylinder wall

erable heat flow occurs from the gases to the surrounding metal walls. In addition to this the shearing of the oil film (separating the bearing surfaces) transforms available energy into internal energy of the oil film. This increases the temperature of oil film and results in heat transfer from the oil to the bearing surfaces. However, the heat transfer on this account is quite small. Hence, the cylinder walls must be adequately cooled to maintain safe operating temperatures in order to maintain the quality of the lubricating oil.

Heat transfer from gases to the cylinder walls may occur predominantly by convection and radiation whereas the heat transfer through the cylinder wall occurs only by conduction. Heat is ultimately transferred to the cooling medium by all the three modes of heat transfer. The temperature profiles across the cylinder barrel wall are shown for both water-cooled and air-cooled engine in Fig.13.4.

In this case, T_g, is the mean gas temperature which may be as high as 850 °C. This may not be confused with the peak temperature of the cycle which may be two or three times this value. Largest temperature drop, however, occurs in the boundary-layer of the gas which lies adjacent to the cylinder wall. There is a corresponding boundary-layer in the cooling medium on the outer side of the cylinder. However, because of fins in the air-cooled engines the effect of external boundary-layer is reduced.

The conduction of heat through cylinder walls with corresponding temperature gradients is illustrated in Fig.13.5 The gas film, being of low conductivity, offers a relatively high resistance to the heat flow, whilst on the water jacket side there is usually a layer of corrosion products, scale etc., which are poor conductors of heat. The least resistance to the heat flow occurs through the metal cylinder wall, as shown by temperature gradient there.

In actual practice because of the cyclic operation of engines, there is a cyclic variation of the gas temperature within the cylinder the effect of which is to cause a wave of heat to travel into the metal which gradually dies out and after the warm-up period a steady flow condition prevails. It has been experimentally established that in internal combustion engines the cyclic temper-

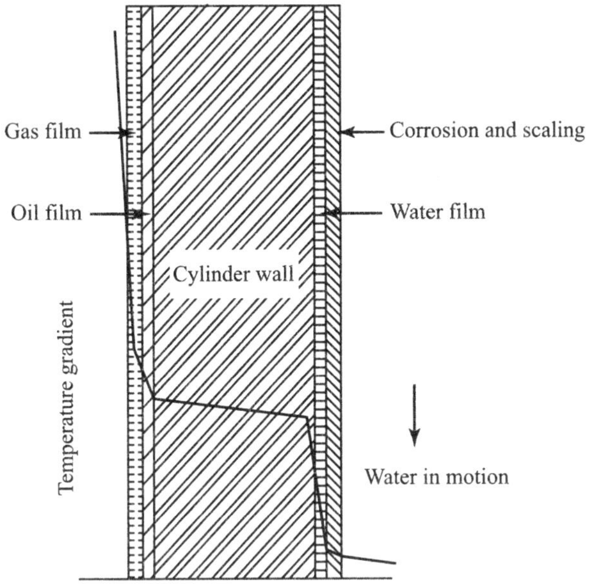

Fig. 13.5 Temperature gradient along cylinder wall

ature variations die out fast before the fluctuations reach the outside surface of the cylinder. Maximum temperature of the cylinder walls, in a properly designed engine, seldom exceeds 10 °C above the mean temperature.

13.6 THEORY OF ENGINE HEAT TRANSFER

In spite of its high temperature, the cylinder gas is a poor radiator and almost all the heat transfer to the cylinder walls from combustion space is by convection. In order to understand the engine heat transfer, a simple analysis can be followed for the flow of hot gases through a pipe.

For gases in pipes it can be shown by dimensional analysis and also through experiments that

$$\frac{hL}{k} = Z \times \left(\frac{\rho C L}{\mu}\right)^n \times \left(\frac{C_p \mu}{k}\right)^m \qquad (13.1)$$

where h = coefficient of heat transfer
L = any characteristic length (say stroke)
k = thermal conductivity of gases
Z = constant
ρ = mass density of gases
C = velocity of gases
C_p = specific heat of gas
μ = viscosity of gases
n, m = exponents

The term $(\rho CL/\mu)$ can be recognized as Reynolds number for cylinder gases. The term $(C_p\mu/k)$ is called the Prandtl number and is nearly constant for gases. Therefore, Prandtl number can be absorbed in the constant Z in Eq.13.1 so that

$$\frac{hL}{k} = Z \times \left(\frac{\rho CL}{\mu}\right)^n \tag{13.2}$$

Since Prandtl number is constant, $k \propto \mu C_p$ and substituting μC_p for k in Eq.13.2,

$$\frac{hL}{\mu C_p} = Z \times \left(\frac{\rho CL}{\mu}\right)^n \tag{13.3}$$

$$h = Z \times C_p \times (\rho C)^n \times \left(\frac{L}{\mu}\right)^{n-1} \tag{13.4}$$

The rate of heat transfer can be written as

$$\dot{q} = h \times A \times \Delta T$$

where ΔT is the temperature difference between the gas and the wall. Substituting the value of h from Eq.13.4, we get

$$\dot{q} = Z \times C_p \times (\rho C)^n \times \left(\frac{L}{\mu}\right)^{n-1} \times A \times \Delta T \tag{13.5}$$

In the above expression, A is the area of heat transfer which is proportional to L^2 and S is the mean piston speed which is proportional to gas velocity, C. When the average gas temperature is considered C_p and μ can be assumed to have constant values. Then,

$$\dot{q} = Z \times (\rho S)^n \times L^{n+1} \times \Delta T \tag{13.6}$$

Piston speed is proportional to the product of L and N where N is the rpm of the engine. Volumetric efficiency, η_v is proportional to the density of the charge, ρ. Then

$$\dot{q} = Z \times (\eta_v N)^n \times L^{2n+1} \times \Delta T$$

The average temperature of the cooling medium, the fuel-air ratio of the mixture and the compression ratio of the engine directly influence the value of ΔT. The density is mainly affected by the intake pressure, compression ratio and the volumetric efficiency. Those engines which have nearly equal value of ΔT, the heat transfer rate depends on the product of $\eta_v N$ and the size of the engine. For engines when ΔT is assumed to be invariant

$$\dot{q} = Z \times (\eta_v N)^n \times L^{2n+1} \tag{13.7}$$

The values of Z and n are determined from experiments on a particular type of engine under various operating conditions. The constants so obtained can be used for calculating heat transfer rate for other operating conditions of the same engine or for geometrically similar engines.

13.7 PARAMETERS AFFECTING ENGINE HEAT TRANSFER

From the above discussion, it may be noted that the engine heat transfer depends upon many parameters. Unless the effect of these parameters is known, the design of a proper cooling system will be difficult. In this section, the effect of various parameters on engine heat transfer is briefly discussed.

13.7.1 Fuel-Air Ratio

A change in fuel-air ratio will change the temperature of the cylinder gases and affect the flame speed. The maximum gas temperature will occur at an equivalence ratio of about 1.12 i.e., at a fuel-air ratio about 0.075. At this fuel-air ratio ΔT will be a maximum. However, from experimental observations the maximum heat rejection is found to occur for a mixture, slightly leaner than this value.

13.7.2 Compression Ratio

An increase in compression ratio causes only a slight increase in gas temperature near the top dead centre; but, because of greater expansion of the gases, there will be a considerable reduction in gas temperature near bottom dead centre where a large cylinder wall is exposed. The exhaust gas temperature will also be much lower because of greater expansion so that the heat rejected during blowdown will be less. In general, as compression ratio increases there tend to be a marginal reduction in heat rejection.

13.7.3 Spark Advance

A spark advance more than the optimum as well as less than the optimum will result in increased heat rejection to the cooling system. This is mainly due to the fact that the spark timing other than MBT value (Minimum spark advance for Best Torque) will reduce the power output and thereby more heat is rejected.

13.7.4 Preignition and Knocking

Effect of preignition is the same as advancing the ignition timing. Large spark advance might lead to erratic running and knocking. Though knocking causes large changes in local heat transfer conditions, the over-all effect on heat transfer due to knocking appears to be negligible. However, no quantitative information is available regarding the effect of preignition and knocking on engine heat transfer.

13.7.5 Engine Output

Engines which are designed for high mean effective pressures or high piston speeds, heat rejection will be less. Less heat will be lost for the same indicated power in large engines.

13.7.6 Cylinder Wall Temperature

The average cylinder gas temperature is much higher in comparison to the cylinder wall temperature. Hence, any marginal change in cylinder gas temperature will have very little effect on the temperature difference and thus on heat rejection.

13.8 POWER REQUIRED TO COOL THE ENGINE

Theoretically the thermal efficiency of the engine will improve if there is no cooling system, but actually the engine will cease to operate. It is mainly because of high temperature, the metals will lose their characteristics and piston will expand considerably resulting in engine seizure. In order to avoid seizure, cooling of the engine is a must. However, the power required to run the cooling system should come from the engine. In this section, the power required to run a cooling system for an air-cooled engine is briefly discussed.

In order to simplify the calculations and obtain an expression for the power required for cooling an engine, some assumptions have to be made. The important ones are:

(i) Engine is assumed to operate at constant fuel-air ratio.

(ii) Changes in fin or coolant temperature are assumed to be small enough so that ΔT, the temperature difference between cylinder gases and the cylinder wall may be assumed to be constant.

(iii) The density and temperature of cooling media are assumed to be unaffected by its flow through the engine or radiator fins.

With the above assumption, it can be shown that variation of cooling power required in terms of the indicated power of the engine can be shown to be

$$P_c = \frac{A_e(ip)^{2.25}}{(A_f \Delta T_f)^{3.75} \rho_a^2} \tag{13.8}$$

Equation 13.8 shows that, for a given power, a great reduction in required cooling power can be effected by increasing the fin area and the temperature difference as much as possible. In the above equation, A_e is the effective area, ip is the indicated power, A_f is the fin area and ΔT_f is the temperature difference between the air and the fin and ρ_a is the density of air. By reducing the air velocity, power required for the cooling, P_c, can be reduced. It can be shown that $P_c \propto C_a^3$, where C_a is the velocity of air. In order to reduce the air velocity, adjustable flaps are usually provided in the cooling air duct of air-cooled engines.

13.9 NEED FOR COOLING SYSTEM

From the discussion on heat rejection in the previous sections, it may be noted that during the process of converting thermal energy to mechanical energy, high temperatures are produced in the cylinders of the engine as a result of the combustion process. A large portion of the heat from the gases of combustion is transferred to the cylinder head and walls, piston and valves. Unless this excess heat is carried away and these parts are adequately cooled, the engine will be damaged. A cooling system must be provided not only to prevent damage to the vital parts of the engine, but the temperature of these components must be maintained within certain limits in order to obtain maximum performance from the engine. Adequate cooling is then a fundamental requirement associated with reciprocating internal combustion engines. Hence, a cooling system is needed to keep the engine from not getting so hot as to cause problems and yet to permit it to run hot enough to ensure maximum efficiency of the engine. The duty of cooling system, in other words, is to keep the engine from getting not too hot and at the same time not to keep it too cool either!

13.10 CHARACTERISTICS OF AN EFFICIENT COOLING SYSTEM

The following are the two main characteristics desired of an efficient cooling system:

(i) It should be capable of removing about 30% of heat generated in the combustion chamber while maintaining the optimum temperature of the engine under all operating conditions of the engine.

(ii) It should remove heat at a faster rate when engine is hot. However, during starting of the engine the cooling should be minimum, so that the working parts of the engine reach their operating temperatures in a short time.

13.11 TYPES OF COOLING SYSTEMS

In order to cool the engine a cooling medium is required. This can be either air or a liquid. Accordingly there are two types of systems in general use for cooling the IC engines. They are

(i) liquid or indirect cooling system

(ii) air or direct cooling system

13.12 LIQUID COOLED SYSTEMS

In this system mainly water is used and made to circulate through the jackets provided around the cylinder, cylinder-head, valve ports and seats where it extracts most of the heat.

The diagrammatic sketch of water circulating passage, viz., water jacket is shown in Fig.13.6. It consists of a long flat, thin-walled tube with an opening, facing the water pump outlet and a number of small openings along its length that direct the water against the exhaust valves. The tube fits in the water jacket and can be removed from the front end of the block.

The heat is transferred from the cylinder walls and other parts by convection and conduction. The liquid becomes heated in its passage through the

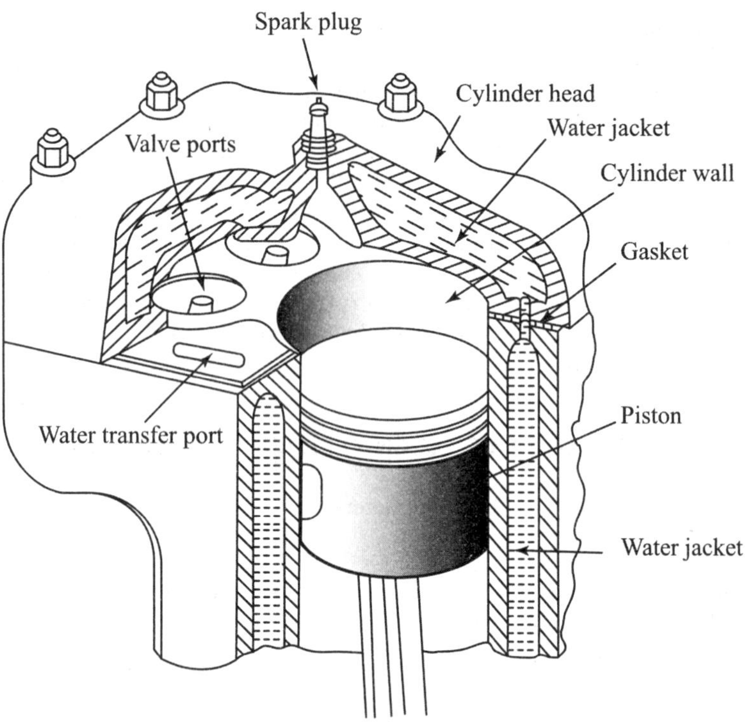

Fig. 13.6 Cooling water passages

jackets and is in turn cooled by means of an air-cooled radiator system. The heat from liquid in turn is transferred to air. Hence it is called the indirect cooling system.

Water-cooling can be carried out by any one of the following five methods:

(i) Direct or non-return system

(ii) Thermosyphon system

(iii) Forced circulation cooling system

(iv) Evaporative cooling system

(v) Pressure cooling system

13.12.1 Direct or Non-return System

This system is useful for large installations where plenty of water is available. The water from a storage tank is directly supplied through an inlet valve to the engine cooling water jacket. The hot water is not cooled for reuse but simply discharged.

13.12.2 Thermosyphon System

The basic principle of thermosyphon can be explained with respect to Fig.13.7. Heat is supplied to the fluid in the tank A. Because of the relatively lower density, the hot fluid travels up, its place being taken up by comparatively cold fluid from the tank B through the pipe p_2.

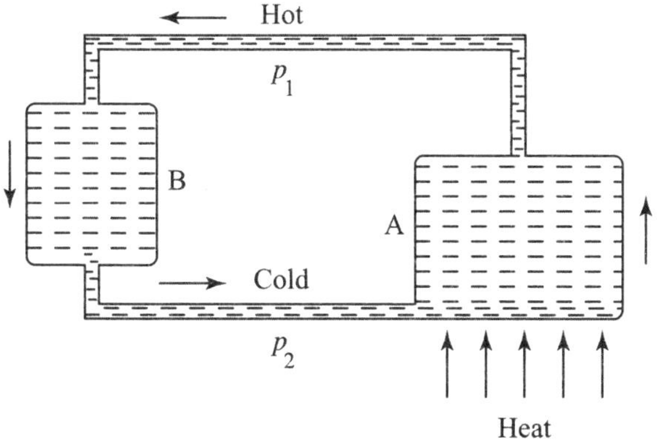

Fig. 13.7 Principle of thermosyphon system

The hot fluid flows through the pipe p_1 to the tank B where it gets cooled. Thus the fluid circulates through the system in the form of convection currents.

For engine application, tank A represents the cylinder jackets while tank B represents a radiator and water acts as the circulating fluid. In order to ensure that coolest water is always made available to cylinder jackets, the water jackets are located at a lower level than the radiator.

The main advantages of the system are its simplicity and automatic circulation of cooling water. The main limitation of the system is its inability to meet the requirement of large flow rate of water, particularly for high output engines.

13.12.3 Forced Circulation Cooling System

This system is used in a large number of automobiles like cars, buses and even heavy trucks. Here, flow of water from radiators to water jackets is by convection assisted by a pump.

The main principle of this system is explained with the help of a block diagram shown in Fig.13.8. The water or coolant is circulated through jackets around the parts of the engine to be cooled, and is kept in motion by a centrifugal pump which is driven by the engine. The water is passed through the radiator where it is cooled by air drawn through the radiator by a fan and by the air draft due to the forward motion of the vehicle. A thermostat is used to control the water temperature required for cooling. This system mainly consists of four components, viz., a radiator, fan, water pump and a thermostat. The details of these components are shown in Fig.13.9.

Radiator: The purpose of a radiator is to provide a large amount of cooling surface area so that the water passing downward through it in thin streams is

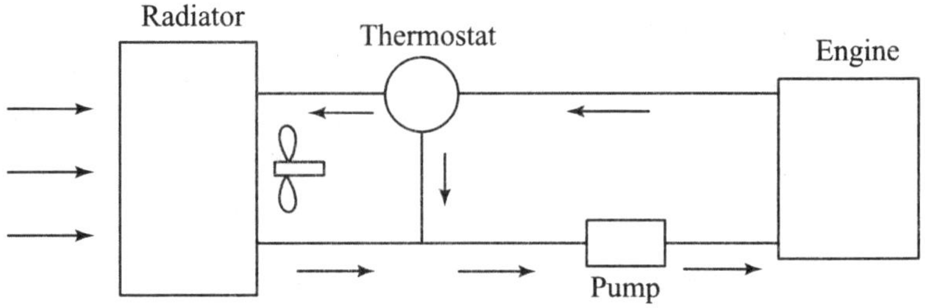

Fig. 13.8 Principle of Forced Circulation cooling system using the thermostat

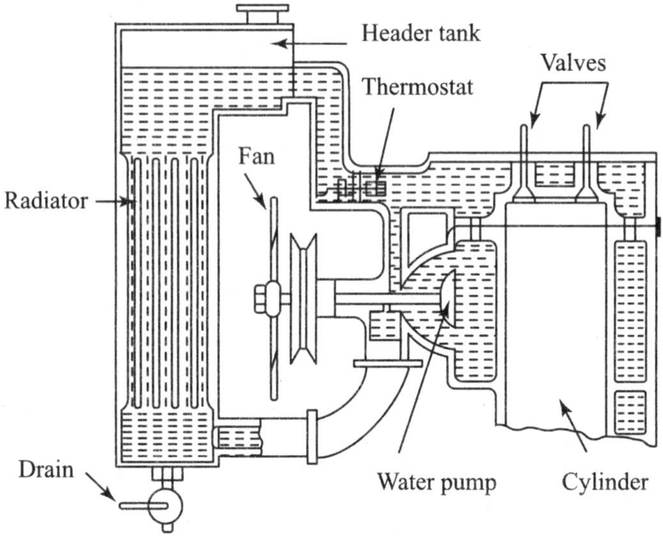

Fig. 13.9 Cooling of an automobile

cooled efficiently. To accomplish this, there are many possible arrangements. One such arrangement is shown in Fig.13.10.

The radiator consists essentially of an upper tank (header tank) and a lower tank. The upper tank in some design may contain a removable filter mesh to avoid dust particles going in into the radiator while filling water in the radiator. Between the two tanks is the core or radiating element. The upper tank is connected to the water outlets from the engine jacket by rubber hose, and the lower tank is connected by another rubber hose to the jacket inlet through the pump.

Radiator cores are classified as tubular or cellular. A tubular radiator, consists of a large number of elliptical or circular brass tubes pressed into a number of suitable punched brass fins. The tubes are finned to guard against corrosion and are staggered as shown in Fig.13.10. The main disadvantage is the great inconvenience to repair any of the damaged tubes. But initial cost of the system is comparatively less. The other type of radiator core arrangement, called *honey comb or cellular radiator core* is shown in Fig.13.11.

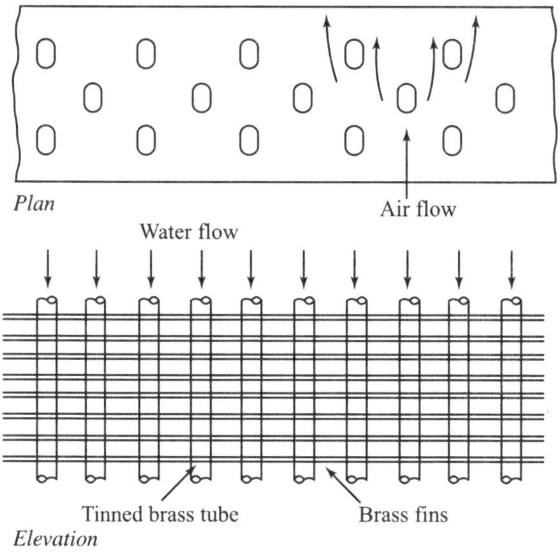

Fig. 13.10 Radiator construction

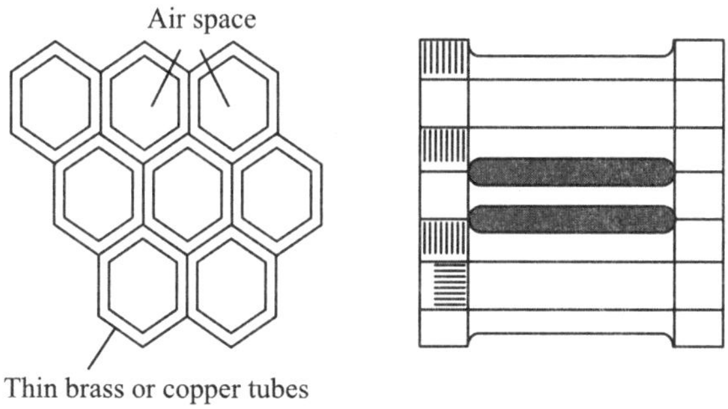

Fig. 13.11 Honey comb radiator core

The water used for cooling should be soft. If hard water is used, it forms sediments on water jackets and tubes, which acts as insulator and make the cooling inefficient. If soft water is not available, 30 g of sodium bichromate should be added for every 10 litres of water.

Fan: The fan mounted on the impeller spindle driven by a suitable belt pulley arrangement as shown in Fig.13.9 draws air through the spaces between the radiator tubes thus bringing down the temperature of the water appreciably.

Pump: The pump maintains the circulation of the water through the system. The bottom of radiator is connected to the suction side of the pump. The power is transmitted to the pump spindle from a pulley mounted on the end of the camshaft or crankshaft. A positive supply of water is achieved in all conditions by centrifugal pump placed in this system (Fig.13.9). This ensures good velocity of water circulation. Consequently less quantity of water and a smaller radiator would suit the purpose.

A pump is mounted conveniently on the engine and driven by the crankshaft with a fan belt. Adjustable packing glands are provided on the driving shaft to prevent water leakage. Lubrication of bearings is done by using high melting point grease. In certain cases special bushes are used which do not require lubrication. In case of multi-cylinder engines a header is usually employed to provide equal distribution of water to all the cylinders. The header is supplemented by tubes or ducts which give high rate of flow around critical sections of the engine such as the exhaust valve seats. This system is employed on most diesel and automotive spark-ignition engines. The rate of circulation is usually 3 to 4 litres per minute per kilowatt.

In some engines the pump is installed between the outlet of the radiator and the engine block and forces cool water from the radiator into the engine jacket. On automobiles, however, this arrangement would result in such a low location of the pump that the fan could not be well placed on the pump shaft. A disadvantage of this installation would seem to be that in case of loss of water, circulation stops as soon as the level drops to the bottom of the cylinder head jacket while with the pump in the supply line continues as long as there is any water left in the system.

Thermostat: Whenever the engine is started from cold, the coolant temperature has to be brought to the desired level in order to minimize the warmup time. This can be achieved by a thermostat fitted in the system which initially prevents the circulation of water below a certain temperature through the radiator so that the water gets heated up quickly. When the preset temperature is reached the thermostat allows the water to flow through the radiator. Usually a Bellow type thermostat is used, the details of which are shown in Fig.13.12. In modern engines, a wax-element type thermostat is normally employed.

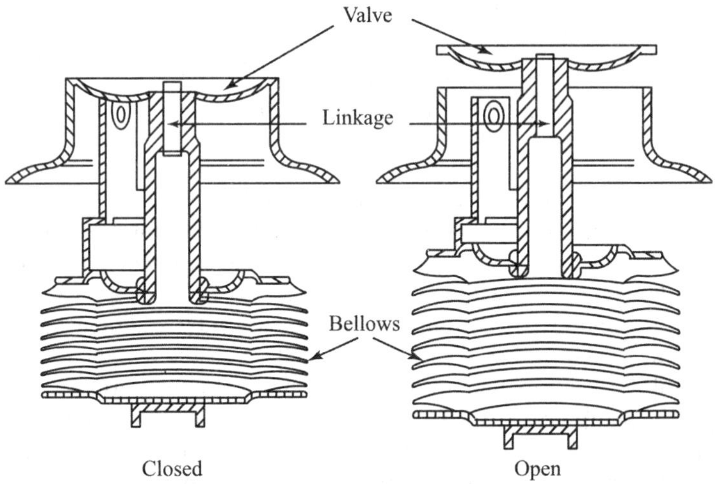

Fig. 13.12 Bellows type thermostat

The unit consists of a closed bellows with volatile liquid under reduced pressure. When the bellows is heated the liquid vaporizes and creates enough pressure to expand the bellows. The movement of bellows operates a linkage which opens the valve. When the unit is cooled, the gas condenses, the pressure is reduced and the bellows collapses to close the valve.

13.12.4 Evaporative Cooling System

This system is predominantly used in stationary engines. In this, the engine will be cooled because of the evaporation of the water in the cylinder jackets into steam. Here, the advantage is taken from the high latent heat of vapourization of water by allowing it to evaporate in the cylinder jackets. If the steam is formed at a pressure above atmospheric the temperature will be above the normal permissible temperature.

Figure 13.13 illustrates evaporative cooling with air-cooled condenser. In this case water is circulated by the pump A and when delivered to the overhead tank B part of it boils out. The tank has a partition C. The vapour rises above the partition C and because of the condensing action of the radiator tubes D, condensate flows into the lower tank E from which it is picked up and returned to the tank B by the small pump F. The vertical pipe G is in communication with the outside atmosphere to prevent the collapsing of the tanks B and E when the pressure inside them due to condensation falls below atmospheric.

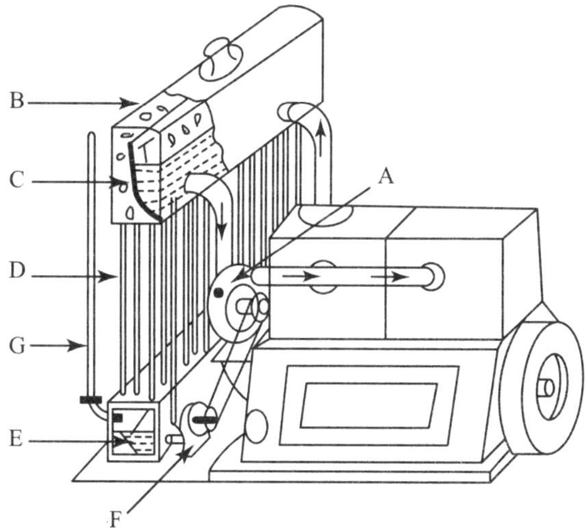

Fig. 13.13 Evaporative cooling with air-cooled condenser

Figure 13.14 illustrates evaporative cooling with the water-cooled condenser. In this case condensation of the vapour formed in the overhead tank B occurs in the heat exchanger C cooled by a secondary water circuit and the water returns to B by gravity. The pump A circulates the cooling water to the engine and the heated water from the engine is delivered to tank B thereby the circulation is maintained.

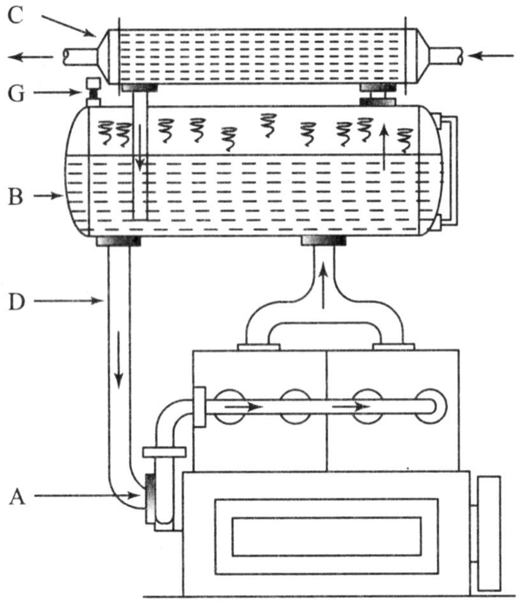

Fig. 13.14 Evaporative cooling with water-cooled condenser

13.12.5 Pressure Cooling System

As already mentioned, the rate of heat transfer depends upon the temperature difference between the two mediums, the area of exposed surface and conductivity of materials. In case of radiators, in order to reduce the size of radiator, it is proposed to seal the cooling system from the atmosphere and to allow a certain amount of pressure to build-up in the system, so that the advantage may be taken of the fact that the temperature of the boiling point of water increases as the pressure increases. Boiling point of water at various pressures is shown in Table 13.1.

Table 13.1 Boiling Point of Water at Various Pressures

Pressure (bar)	1.0	2.0	5.0	10.0
Temperature (°C)	100	121	153	180

In pressure cooling system moderate pressures, say upto 2 bar, are commonly used. As shown in Fig.13.15, a cap is fitted with two valves, a safety valve which is loaded by a compression spring and a vacuum valve. When the coolant is cold both valves are shut but as the engine warms up the coolant temperature rises until it reaches a certain preset value corresponding to the desired pressure when the safety valve opens; but if the coolant temperature falls during the engine operation the valve will close again until the temperature again rises to the equivalent pressure value. When the engine is switched off and the coolant cools down vacuum begins to form in the cooling system

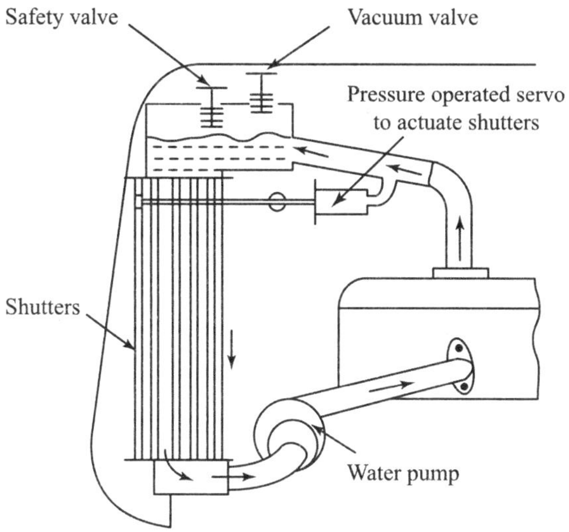

Fig. 13.15 Pressure cooling

but when the internal pressure falls below atmospheric the vacuum valve is opened by the higher outside pressure and the cooling system then attains atmospheric pressure.

A safety device is incorporated in the filler cap so that if an attempt is made to unscrew it while the system is under pressure, the first movement of the cap at once relieves the pressure and thus prevents the emission of scalding steam or the blowing off the cap due to higher internal pressure.

13.13 AIR–COOLED SYSTEM

In an air-cooled system a current of air is made to flow past the outside of the cylinder barrel, outer surface area of which has been considerably increased by providing cooling fins as shown in Fig.13.16. This method will increase the rate of cooling.

Application : This method is mainly applicable to engines in motor cycles, small cars, airplanes and combat tanks where motion of vehicle gives a good velocity to cool the engine. In bigger units a circulating fan is also used. In addition to these engines, air-cooling is also used in some small stationary engines. The value of heat transfer coefficient between metal and air is appreciably low. As a result of this the cylinder wall temperatures of the air-cooled cylinders are considerably higher than those of water-cooled type. In order to lower the cylinder wall temperature the area of the outside surface which directly dissipates heat to the atmosphere must be sufficiently high.

13.13.1 Cooling Fins

Cooling fins are either cast integral with the cylinder and cylinder head or can be fixed with the cylinder block separately. Various shapes of cooling fins are shown in Fig.13.17. The heat dissipating capacity of fins depends upon their

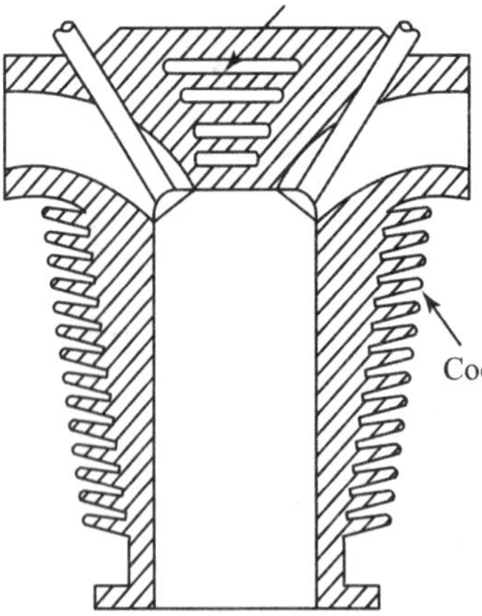

Fig. 13.16 Cooling fins on an engine cylinder increase the surface area of cooling

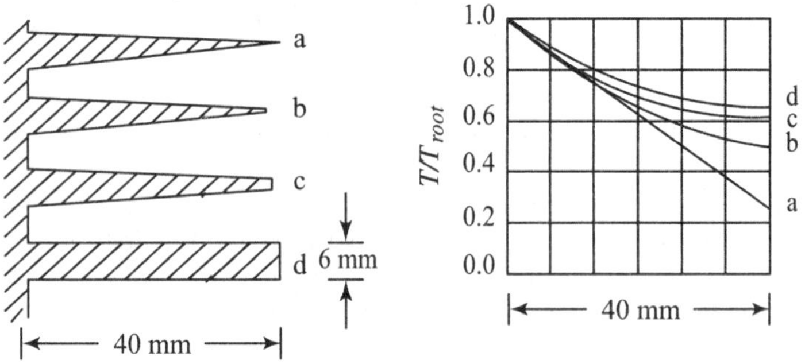

Fig. 13.17 Types of cooling systems

cross-section and length. At the same time as heat is gradually dissipated from the fin surface, the temperature of the fin decreases from its root to its tip. Hence, the fin surface nearer to the tip dissipates heat at a lower rate and is less efficient. On the other hand as the quantity of heat flowing towards the tip gradually decreases, the thickness of the fin can be decreased. The material of the fin is used most efficiently if the drop in temperature from the root to the tip is constant per unit length. A comparison of fins of different cross-sections is shown in Fig.13.17 with drop in temperature from root to tip. The rectangular section has least temperature drop whereas the maximum temperature drop is for the fin marked 'a'.

Fins are usually given a taper of 3 to 5 degrees in order to give sufficient draft to the pattern. The tip is made 0.5 to 1.25 mm thick and a clearance of 2.5 to 5 mm is allowed at the root. The fins are made 25 to 50 mm long. Too close spacing of the fins is undesirable as mutual interference of the boundary-layers of adjacent layers restricts the air flow and results in small quantity of heat dissipated.

13.13.2 Baffles

The rate of heat transfer from the cylinder walls can be substantially increased by using baffles which force the air through the space between the fins. Figure 13.18 shows various types of baffles commonly used on engines. The arrangement at 'a' has got the highest pressure drop. It is always desired to have negligible kinetic energy loss between the entrance and the exit. Usually the normal type of baffle, 'b', is used on petrol engines. The arrangement 'c' for minimizing the kinetic energy loss is shown with a well rounded entrance to reduce the entrance loss and an exit section that will transform the velocity head into pressure head and thus decrease the pressure drop. Arrangement 'd' is adopted for diesel engines.

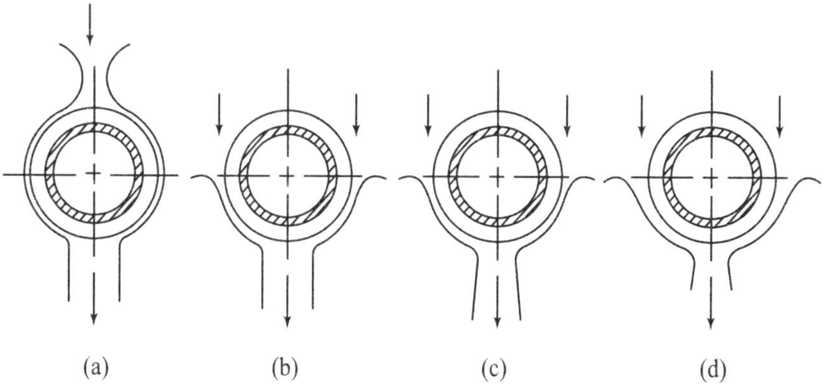

Fig. 13.18 Types of baffles in air-cooled engines

13.14 COMPARISON OF LIQUID AND AIR–COOLING SYSTEMS

In view of the wide spread use of these two alternative cooling systems for petrol as well as diesel engines it is of interest to summarize the respective advantages and limitations of these systems.

13.14.1 Advantages of Liquid-Cooling System

(i) Compact design of engines with appreciably smaller frontal area is possible.

(ii) The fuel consumption of high compression liquid-cooled engines are rather lower than for air-cooled ones.

(iii) Because of the even cooling of cylinder barrel and head due to jacketing makes it possible to reduce the cylinder head and valve seat temperatures.

(iv) In case of water-cooled engines, installation is not necessarily at the front of the mobile vehicles, aircraft etc. as the cooling system can be conveniently located wherever required. This is not possible in case of air-cooled engines.

(v) The size of engine does not involve serious problems as far as the design of cooling systems is concerned. In case of air-cooled engines particularly in high horsepower range difficulty is encountered in the circulation of requisite quantity of air for cooling purposes.

13.14.2 Limitations

(i) This is a dependent system in which water circulation in the jackets is to be ensured by additional means.

(ii) Power absorbed by the pump for water circulation is considerable and this affects the power output of the engine.

(iii) In the event of failure of the cooling system serious damage may be caused to the engine.

(iv) Cost of the system is considerably high.

(v) System requires considerable maintenance of its various parts.

13.14.3 Advantages of Air-Cooling System

(i) The design of the engine becomes simpler as no water jackets are required. The cylinder can have identical dimensions and be individually detachable and therefore cheaper to renew in case of accident etc.

(ii) Absence of cooling pipes, radiator, etc. makes the cooling system simpler thereby has minimum maintenance problems.

(iii) No danger of coolant leakage etc.

(iv) The engine is not subject to freezing troubles etc., usually encountered in case of water cooled engines.

(v) The weight of the air-cooled engine is less than that of water-cooled engine, i.e., power to weight ratio is improved.

(vi) In this case, the engine is rather a self-contained unit as it requires no external components like radiator, header, tank etc.

(vii) Installation of air-cooled engines is easier.

13.14.4 Limitations

(i) Can be applied only to small and medium sized engines

(ii) In places where ambient temperatures are lower

(iii) Cooling is not uniform

(iv) Higher working temperatures compared to water-cooling

(v) Produce more aerodynamic noise

(vi) Specific fuel consumption is slightly higher

(vii) Lower maximum allowable compression ratios

(viii) The fan, if used absorbs as much as 5% of the power developed by the engine

Review Questions

13.1 Explain with a figure the variation of gas temperature during a cycle.

13.2 Explain with sketches piston and cylinder temperature distribution.

13.3 Explain briefly the engine heat transfer. Develop the necessary equation for the rate of heat transfer.

13.4 Mention the various parameters which affect the engine heat transfer and explain their effect.

13.5 Explain the reasons for cooling an engine.

13.6 What are the various characteristics of an efficient cooling system?

13.7 Explain the two types of cooling systems and compare them.

13.8 Explain the following:

(i) thermosyphon cooling system

(ii) forced circulation cooling system

(iii) evaporative cooling system

(iv) pressure cooling system

13.9 What is an air-cooling system and in which engine it is normally used?

13.10 Why fins and baffles are required in an air-cooled engine? Explain.

13.11 What are advantages of liquid cooling system?

13.12 What are the limitations of liquid cooling system?

13.13 What are the advantages of air cooling system

13.14 What are the limitations of the air cooling system

13.15 Compare the air cooling and liquid cooling systems

Multiple Choice Questions (choose the most appropriate answer)

1. The heat given to cooling medium in IC engines is about
    (a) 50 – 60%
    (b) 30 – 40%
    (c) 10 – 20%
    (d) 60 – 70%
2. Radiator is provided to
    (a) cool the jacket water
    (b) pressurise the cooling water
    (c) provide additional water flow
    (d) none of the above
3. Thermostat is used in radiators to
    (a) control the velocity of water
    (b) control distribution of water to various cylinders
    (c) control the water temperature
    (d) control the pressure of water
4. As the compression ratio increases, there is a
    (a) large increase in heat rejection
    (b) large decrease in heat reduction
    (c) marginal increase in heat rejection
    (d) marginal reduction in heat rejection
5. Spark timing other than MBT results in
    (a) less heat rejection
    (b) more heat rejection
    (c) no effect on heat rejection
    (d) none of the above
6. Direct system of cooling air is one which
    (a) cooling water flows by gravity
    (b) hot water is continuously cooled and circulated
    (c) hot water is simply discharged
    (d) water is allowed to evaporate in the cylinder jacket

7. In evaporate cooling systems, heat absorbed per kg of coolant air is
   (a) $C_p \Delta t$
   (b) $C_v \Delta t$
   (c) latent heat of the coolant
   (d) $(C_p - C_v)\Delta t$

8. Pump used in the forced cooling system is normally
   (a) piston pump
   (b) gear pump
   (c) vane pump
   (d) centrifugal pump

9. Advantage of liquid cooling system is
   (a) dependent only on water supply
   (b) power absorbed by the pump is considerable
   (c) even cooling
   (d) very cheap

10. Limitations of air cooling systems are
    (a) applicable only to large engines
    (b) cooling is fast
    (c) higher working temperature compared to water cooling
    (d) all of the above

11. The main purpose of a thermostat in an engine cooling system is to
    (a) allow engine to warm-up quickly
    (b) prevent the coolant from boiling
    (c) pressurize the system
    (d) indicate to the driver the coolant temperature

12. The radiator cooling tubes are generally made of
    (a) rubber
    (b) plastic
    (c) brass
    (d) copper

13. Water circulation in a thermosyphon cooling system is due to

    (a) conduction currents
    (b) a gear driven water pump
    (c) change in the density of water
    (d) a belt driven water impeller

14. The main purpose of fan in a liquid cooling system is to

    (a) disperse engine fumes
    (b) pump cold air over the hot water
    (c) cool the external surface of the engine
    (d) drive air flow when the vehicle speed is low

15. Engine overheating may be due to

    (a) stuck radiator pressure cap
    (b) open thermostat
    (c) broken fan belt
    (d) excess coolant

Ans:					
	1. – (b)	2. – (a)	3. – (c)	4. – (d)	5. – (b)
	6. – (c)	7. – (c)	8. – (d)	9. – (c)	10. – (c)
	11. – (a)	12. – (d)	13. – (a)	14. – (b)	15. – (c)

14

ENGINE EMISSIONS AND THEIR CONTROL

14.1 INTRODUCTION

Internal combustion engines generate undesirable emissions during the combustion process. In this, both SI and CI engines are equally responsible for the same. The emissions exhausted into the surroundings pollute the atmosphere and causes the following problems

(i) global warming

(ii) acid rain

(iii) smog

(iv) odours

(v) respiratory and other health hazards

The major causes of these emissions are non-stoichiometric combustion, dissociation of nitrogen, and impurities in the fuel and air. The emissions of concern are: unburnt hydrocarbons (HC), oxides of carbon (CO_x), oxides of nitrogen (NO_x), oxides of sulphur (SO_x), and solid carbon particulates.

It is the dream of engineers and scientists to develop engines and fuels such that very few quantity of harmful emissions are generated, and these could be let into the surroundings without a major impact on the environment. However, with the present technology this is not possible, and after-treatment of the exhaust gases as well as in-cylinder reduction of emissions are very important. In case of after-treatment it consists mainly of the use of thermal or catalytic converters and particulate traps. For in-cylinder reduction, exhaust gas recirculation (EGR) and some fuel additives are being tried. In addition to exhaust emissions non-exhaust emissions also play a part. In this chapter we will look into the details of these emissions and their control.

14.2 AIR POLLUTION DUE TO IC ENGINES

Until the middle of the 20th century the number of IC engines in the world was so small that the pollution they caused was tolerable. During that period the environment, with the help of sunlight, stayed relatively clean. As world population grew, power plants, factories, and an ever-increasing number of automobiles began to pollute the air to the extent that it was no longer acceptable. During the late 1940s, air pollution as a problem was first recognized in the Los Angeles basin in California. Two causes of this were the large population density and the natural weather conditions of the area. Smoke and other pollutants from many factories and automobiles combined with fog that was common in this ocean area, and smog resulted. During the 1950s, the smog problem increased along with the increase in population density and automobile density. At this stage it was realized that the automobile was one of the major contributors to the problem. By the 1960s emission standards were beginning to be enforced in California.

During the next decade, emission standards were adopted in the rest of the United States and in Europe and Japan. By making engines more fuel efficient, and with the use of exhaust after-treatment, emissions per vehicle of HC, CO, and NO_x were reduced by about 95% during the 1970s and 1980s. Lead, one of the major air pollutants, was phased out as a fuel additive during the 1980s. More fuel-efficient engines were developed, and by the 1990s the average automobile consumed less than half the fuel used in 1970. However, during this time the number of automobiles greatly increased, resulting in no overall decrease in fuel usage.

Further reduction of emissions will be much more difficult and costly. As world population grows, emission standards have become more stringent out of necessity. The strictest laws are generally initiated in California, with the rest of the United States and world following. Although air pollution is a global problem, some regions of the world still have no emission standards or laws. However, many countries including India have started following emission norms. We will briefly go through the norms followed in India in the following section.

14.3 EMISSION NORMS

Emission norms are statutory requirements that set specific limits to the amount of pollutants that can be released into the environment. Norms focus on regulating pollutants released by automobiles and other powered vehicles. They can also regulate emissions from industry, power plants, and diesel generators. The pollutants in general that are regulated are the emissions of nitrogen oxides (NOx), sulfur oxides, particulate matter (PM) or soot, carbon monoxide (CO), or volatile hydrocarbons

In the United States, emissions standards are managed by the Environmental Protection Agency (EPA). The state of California has special dispensation to promulgate more stringent vehicle emissions standards. Other states may choose to follow either the national or California standards. The European Union has its own set of emissions standards that all new vehicles must meet. Currently, standards are set for all road vehicles, trains, barges and 'nonroad mobile machinery' (such as tractors). No standards apply to seagoing ships or airplanes.

The European Union is to introduce Euro 4 effective from January 1, 2008, Euro 5 effective from January 1, 2010 and Euro 6 effective from January 1, 2014. These dates have been postponed for two years to give oil refineries the opportunity to modernize their plants. The first Indian emission regulations were idle emission limits which became effective in 1989. These idle emission regulations were soon replaced by mass emission limits for both gasoline (1991) and diesel (1992) vehicles, which were gradually tightened during the 1990's. Since the year 2000, India started *adopting* European emission norms and fuel regulations for four-wheeled light-duty and for heavy-duty vehicles. Indian own emission regulations still apply to two- and three-wheeled vehicles.

14.3.1 Overview of the Emission Norms in India

1991 Idle CO Limits for Gasoline Vehicles and Free Acceleration Smoke for Diesel Vehicles, Mass Emission Norms for Gasoline Vehicles.

1992 Mass Emission Norms for Diesel Vehicles.

1996 Revision of Mass Emission Norms for Gasoline and Diesel Vehicles, mandatory fitment of Catalytic Converter for Cars in Metros on Unleaded Gasoline.

1998 Cold Start Norms Introduced.

2000 India 2000 (equivalent to Euro I) Norms, Modified IDC (Indian Driving Cycle), Bharat Stage II Norms for Delhi.

2001 Bharat Stage II (equivalent to Euro II) Norms for All Metros, Emission Norms for CNG and LPG Vehicles.

2003 Bharat Stage II (equivalent to Euro II) Norms for 11 major cities.

2005 From 1st April Bharat Stage III (equivalent to Euro III) Norms for 11 major cities.

2010 Bharat Stage III Emission Norms for 4-wheelers for entire country whereas Bharat Stage - IV (equivalent to Euro IV) for 11 major cities.

14.4 COMPARISON BETWEEN BHARAT STAGE AND EURO NORMS

The Bharat Stage norms have been styled to suit specific needs and demands of Indian conditions. The differences lie essentially in environmental and geographical needs, even though the emission standards are exactly the same. For instance, Euro-III is tested at sub-zero temperatures in European countries. In India, where the average annual temperature ranges between 24 and 28 degree Celsius, the test is done away with.

Another major distinction is in the maximum speed at which the vehicle is tested. A speed of 90 km/h is stipulated for BS-III, whereas it is 120 km/h for Euro-III, keeping emission limits the same in both cases. Further, the mass emission test measurements done in g/km on a chassis dynamometer requires a loading of 100 kg weight in addition to unloaded car weight in Europe. In India, BS-III norms require an extra loading of 150 kg weight to achieve the desired inertia weight mainly due to road conditions here. Details of the norms for petrol and diesel vehicles are given in Table 14.1.

Table 14.1 Indian emission norms for petrol and diesel vehicles

Petrol Vehicles

Two-Wheelers (g/km)			
Year	CO	HC	HC + NOx
1991	12 - 30	8-12	–
1996	4.50	-	3.60
2000	2.00	-	2.00
2005 (BS - II)	1.50	-	1.50

Three-Wheelers (g/km)			
Year	CO	HC	HC + NOx
1991	12 - 30	8–12	–
1996	6.75	-	5.40
2000	4.00	-	2.00
2005 (BS - II)	2.25	-	2.00

Cars (g/km)				
Year	CO	HC	NOx	HC + NOx
1991	14.30–27.10	2.00–2.90	–	–
1996	8.68–12.40	-	-	3.00 - 4.36
1998 *	4.34–6.20	-	-	1.50–2.18
2000	2.72–6.90	-	-	0.97–1.70
BS – II	2.20	–	–	0.50
BS – III	2.30	0.20	0.15	–

Diesel Vehicles (GVW Upto 3.5 Tons)

Engine Dynamometer (g/kW h)				
Year	CO	HC	NOx	PM
1992	14.00	3.50	18.00	-
1996	11.20	2.40	14.40	-
2000	4.50	1.10	8.00	0.36 / 0.61†
BS - II	4.00	1.10	7.00	0.15

Diesel Vehicles (GVW > 3.5 Tons) (Engine Dynamometer Test) (g/kW h)				
Year	CO	HC	NOx	PM
1992	17.30 - 32.60	2.70 - 3.70	-	-
1996	11.20	2.40	14.40	-
2000	4.50	1.10	8.00	0.36 / 0.61 †
BS - II	4.00	1.10	7.00	0.15
BS - III	2.10	0.66	5.0	0.10

* For Catalytic Converter Fitted Vehicles.

† For Engines with Power exceeding 85 kW / For Engines with power upto 85 kW. BS - III - Norms with effect from 1st April 2005 in major 11 Cities.

14.5 ENGINE EMISSIONS

Engine emissions can be classified into two categories:

(i) exhaust emissions and

(ii) non-exhaust emissions.

14.5.1 Exhaust Emissions

As already mentioned major exhaust emissions are

(i) unburnt hydrocarbons, (HC)

(ii) oxides of carbon, (CO and CO_2),

(iii) oxides of nitrogen, (NO and NO_2)

(iv) oxides of sulphur, (SO_2 and SO_3)

(v) particulates, soot and smoke.

The first four are common to both SI and CI engines and the last two are mainly from CI engines. The main non-exhaust emission is the unburnt hydrocarbons from fuel tank and crankcase blowby.

Figure 14.1 shows the variation of HC, CO and NO_x emissions as a function of equivalence ratio for an SI engine. It is clearly seen that all the three emissions are a strong function of equivalence ratio.

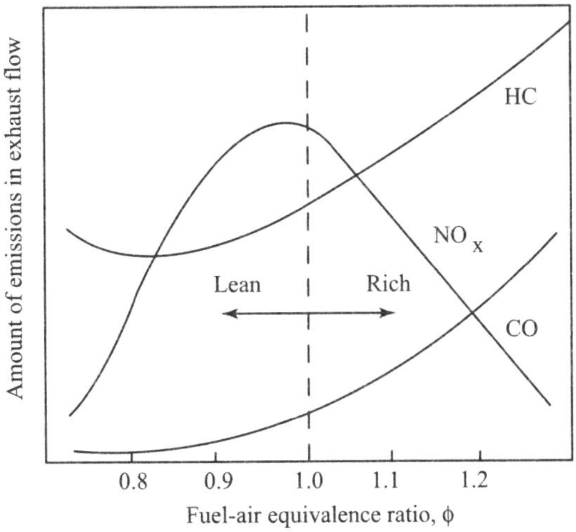

Fig. 14.1 Emissions as a function of equivalence ratio for a SI engine

As can be noticed from the Fig.14.1 that a rich mixture does not have enough oxygen to react with all the carbon and hydrogen, and both HC and CO emissions increase. For $\phi < 0.8$, HC emissions also increase due to poor combustion and misfire. The generation of nitrogen oxide emissions is a function of the combustion temperature, highest near stoichiometric conditions when temperatures are at the peak value. Maximum NO_x emissions occur at slightly lean conditions, where the combustion temperature is high and there is an excess of oxygen to react with the nitrogen.

Figure 14.2 shows a qualitative picture of HC, CO and NO_x emissions with respect to equivalence ratio, ϕ for a four-stroke DI Diesel engine. As can be seen HC will decrease slightly with increase in ϕ due to higher cylinder temperatures making it easier to burn up any over-mixed (very lean) or under-mixed (rich) fuel-air mixture. At high loads, however, HC may increase again if the amount of fuel in regions too rich to burn during primary combustion process. CO emissions will be very low at all equivalence ratio since excess air is always available. NO_x emission will steadily increase as ϕ increase due to increasing fraction of cylinder contents being burnt gases close to stoichiometric during combustion, and also due to higher peak temperatures and pressures. In the following sections the causes for these emissions and their controls will be dealt with in detail.

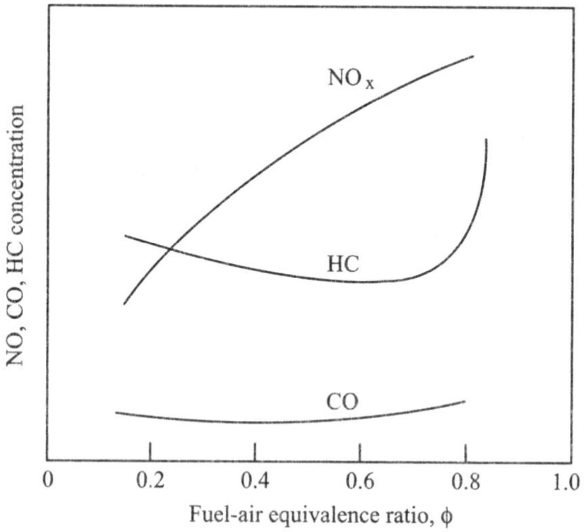

Fig. 14.2 Emissions as a function of equivalence ratio for a CI engine

14.6 HYDROCARBONS (HC)

Exhaust gases leaving the combustion chamber of an SI engine contain up to 6000 ppm of hydrocarbon components, the equivalent of 1-1.5% of the fuel. About 40% of this is unburned components of the fuel. The other 60% consists of partially reacted components that were not present in the original fuel. These consist of small non-equilibrium molecules, which are formed when large fuel molecules break up (thermal cracking) during the combustion reaction. It is often convenient to treat these molecules as if they contained one carbon atom, as CH_1.

Hydrocarbon emissions will be different for each gasoline blend, depending on the original fuel components. Combustion chamber geometry and engine operating parameters also influence the HC component spectrum.

When hydrocarbon emissions get into the atmosphere, they act as irritants and odorants; some are carcinogenic. All components except CH_4 react with atmospheric gases to form photochemical smog.

14.7 HYDROCARBON EMISSION

Figure 14.1 shows the variation of HC emission levels with respect to equivalence ratio for an SI engine. It is evident that it is a strong function of air-fuel ratio. With a fuel-rich mixture there is not enough oxygen to react with all the carbon, resulting in high levels of HC and CO in the exhaust products. This is particularly true during starting, when the air-fuel mixture is purposely made very rich. It is also true to a lesser extent during rapid acceleration under load. If air-fuel ratio is too lean poorer combustion occurs, again resulting in HC emissions. The extreme of poor combustion for a cycle is total misfire. This occurs more often as air-fuel ratio is made leaner. One misfire out of 1000 cycles gives exhaust emissions of 1 gm/kg of fuel used.

The causes for hydrocarbon emissions from SI engine are:

(i) Incomplete combustion

(ii) Crevice volumes and flow in crevices

(iii) Leakage past the exhaust valve

(iv) Valve overlap

(v) Deposits on walls

(vi) Oil on combustion chamber walls

We will discuss in details the various causes listed above.

14.7.1 Incomplete Combustion

Even when the fuel and air entering an engine are at the ideal stoichiometric condition, perfect combustion does not occur and some HC ends up in the exhaust. There are several reasons for this. Complete and homogeneous mixing of fuel and air is almost impossible. The incomplete combustion is due to:

(i) *Improper mixing*: Due to incomplete mixing of the air and fuel some fuel particles do not find oxygen to react with. This causes HC emissions.

(ii) *Flame quenching*: As the flame goes very close to the walls it gets quenched at the walls leaving a small volume of unreacted air-fuel mixture. The thickness of this unburned layer is of the order of 100 microns. However, it may be noted that some of this mixture near the wall that does not originally get burned as the flame front passes will burn later in the combustion process due to additional mixing, swirl and turbulence.

Another reason for flame quenching is the expansion of gases, which occurs during combustion and power stroke. As the piston moves down from TDC to BDC during power stroke, expansion of the gases lowers both pressure and temperature within the cylinder. This makes combustion slow and finally quenches the flame somewhere late in the expansion stroke. This leaves some fuel particles unreacted and causes HC emissions.

High exhaust gas contamination causes poor combustion and which in turn causes quenching during expansion. This is experienced at low load and idle conditions. High levels of EGR will also cause quenching of flame and will result in HC emission.

It has been found that HC emissions can be reduced by incorporating an additional spark plug at appropriate locations in the engine combustion chamber. By starting combustion at two points, the flame travel distance and total reaction time are both reduced, and less expansion quenching will result.

14.7.2 Crevice Volumes and Flow in Crevices

The volumes between the piston, piston rings, and cylinder wall are shown schematically in Fig.14.3. These crevices consist of a series of volumes (numbered 1 to 5) connected by flow restrictions such as the ring side clearance and ring gap. The geometry changes as each ring moves up and down in its ring groove, sealing either at the top or bottom ring surface. The gas flow, pressure distribution, and ring motion are therefore coupled.

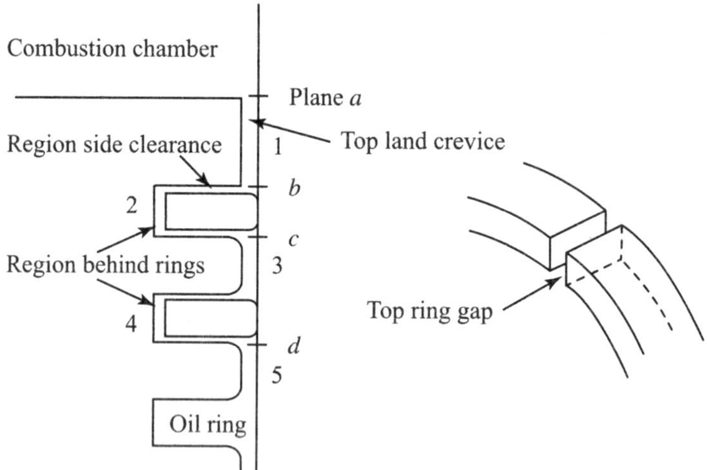

Fig. 14.3 Schematic of piston and ring assembly in automotive spark-ignition engine showing various crevice volume

During the compression stroke and early part of the combustion process, air and fuel are compressed into the crevice volume of the combustion chamber at high pressure. As much as 3.5% of the fuel in the chamber can be forced into this crevice volume. Later in the cycle during the expansion stroke, pressure in the cylinder is reduced below crevice volume pressure, and reverse blow-by occurs. Fuel and air, flow back into the combustion chamber, where most of the mixture is consumed in the flame. However, before the last elements of reverse blow-by occurs flame will be quenched and unreacted fuel particles come out in the exhaust. Location of the spark plug relative to the top compression ring gap will affect the amount of HC in engine exhaust. The farther the spark plug is from the ring gap, the greater is the HC in the exhaust. This is because more fuel will be forced into the gap before the flame front passes.

Crevice volume around the piston rings is greatest when the engine is cold, due to the differences in thermal expansion of the various materials. Up to 80% of all HC emissions can come from this source.

14.7.3 Leakage Past the Exhaust Valve

As pressure increases during compression and combustion, some amount of air-fuel mixture is forced into the crevice volume around the edges of the exhaust valve and between the valve and valve seat. A small amount even leaks past the valve into the exhaust manifold. When the exhaust valve opens, the air-fuel mixture which is still in this crevice volume gets carried into the exhaust manifold. This causes a momentary increase in HC concentration at the start of blowdown process.

14.7.4 Valve Overlap

Valve overlap is a must to obtain satisfactory performance from the engine. During valve overlap, both the exhaust and intake valves are open, simultaneously creating a path where the fresh air-fuel mixture can flow directly into the exhaust. A well-designed engine minimizes this flow, but a small amount of fresh fuel-air mixture escape is inevitable. The worst condition for this is at idle and low speed, when the overlap in terms of time (milliseconds) is the largest.

14.7.5 Deposits on Walls

Gas particles, including those of fuel vapor, are absorbed by the deposits on the walls of the combustion chamber. The amount of absorption is a function of gas pressure. The maximum absorption occurs during compression and combustion. Later in the cycle, when the exhaust valve opens and cylinder pressure gets reduced, absorption capacity of the deposit material becomes lower. Gas particles are desorbed back into the cylinder. These particles, including some HC, comes out from the cylinder during the exhaust stroke. This problem is greater in engines with higher compression ratios due to the higher pressure these engines generate. More gas absorption occurs as pressure goes up. Clean combustion chamber walls with minimum deposits will reduce HC emissions in the exhaust. Most gasoline blends include additives to reduce deposit buildup in engines. Older engines will typically have a greater amount of wall deposit buildup. This increases HC emissions correspondingly. This is due to age and to less swirl that was generally found in earlier engine design.

High swirl helps to keep wall deposits to a minimum. When unleaded gasoline is used HC emissions from wall deposits becomes more severe. When leaded gasoline is burned the lead compounds make the walls harder and less porous to gas absorption.

14.7.6 Oil on Combustion Chamber Walls

A very thin layer of oil gets deposited on the cylinder walls to provide lubrication between the walls and the moving piston. During the intake and compression strokes, the incoming air and fuel comes in contact with this oil film. In the same way as wall deposits, this oil film absorbs and desorbs gas particles, depending on gas pressure.

During compression and combustion, when cylinder pressure is high, gas particles, including fuel vapor, are absorbed into the oil film. When pressure is later reduced during expansion and blowdown, the absorption capability of the oil is reduced and fuel particles are desorbed back into the cylinder. Some of this fuel ends up in the exhaust.

As an engine ages, the clearance between piston rings and cylinder walls becomes greater, and a thicker film of oil is left on the walls. Some of this oil film is scraped off the walls during the compression stroke and gets burned during combustion. Oil is a high-molecular-weight hydrocarbon compound that does not burn as readily as gasoline. Some of it comes out as HC emissions. This happens at a very slow rate with a new engine but increases with engine age and wear.

Often as an engine ages, due to wear, clearance between the pistons and cylinder walls increases. This increases oil consumption contributes to an increase in HC emissions in three ways:

(i) there is added crevice volume,

(ii) there is added absorption-desorption of fuel in the thicker oil film on cylinder walls, and

(iii) there is more oil burned in the combustion process.

Figure 14.4 shows how HC emissions go up as oil consumption increases. Oil consumption increases as the piston rings and cylinder walls wear. In older engines, oil being burned in the combustion chamber is a major source of HC emissions. In addition to oil consumption going up as piston rings wear, blowby and reverse blowby also increase. The increase in HC emissions is therefore both from combustion of oil and from the added crevice volume flow.

14.8 HYDROCARBON EMISSION FROM TWO-STROKE ENGINES

Older two-stroke SI engines and many modern small two-stroke SI engines add HC emissions to the exhaust during the scavenging process. The intake air-fuel mixture is used to push exhaust residual out of the open exhaust port which is called scavenging. When this is done, some of the air and fuel mix with the exhaust gases and are expelled out of the cylinder before the exhaust

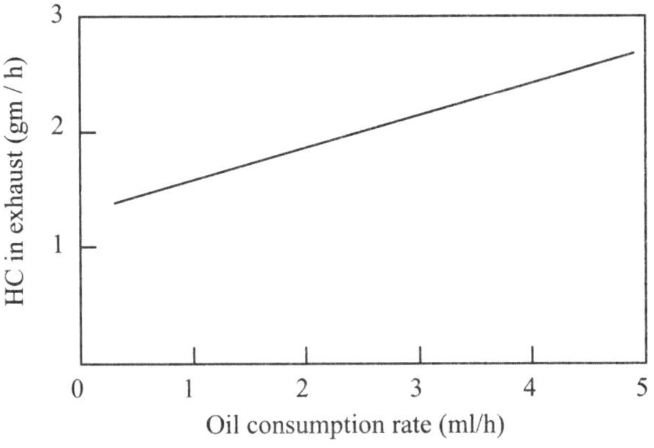

Fig. 14.4 HC exhaust emissions as a function of engine oil consumption

port closes. This can be a major source of HC in the exhaust and is one of the major reasons why there have been no modern two-stroke cycle automobile engines.

Some experimental automobile two-stroke cycle engines and just about all small engines use crankcase compression, and this is a second source of hydrocarbon emissions. The crankcase area and pistons of these engines are lubricated by adding oil to the fuel. The oil is vaporized with the fuel and lubricates the surfaces which come in contact with the air-fuel-oil mixture. Some of the oil vapor is carried into the combustion chamber and burned with the air-fuel mixture. Lubricating oil is mostly hydrocarbon components and acts like additional fuel. However, due to the high molecular weight of its components, oil does not fully burn as readily as fuel. This adds to HC emissions in the exhaust. Modern experimental two-stroke cycle automobile engines do not add fuel to the intake air, but scavenge the cylinders with pure air. This to a great extent avoid putting HC into the exhaust. After the exhaust port closes, fuel is added by injection directly into the cylinder. This creates a need for very fast and efficient vaporization and mixing of the air and fuel, but it eliminates a major source of HC emissions. Some automobile engines use superchargers instead of crankcase compression, and this eliminates HC pollution from that source.

14.9 HYDROCARBON EMISSION FROM CI ENGINES

Because CI engines operate with an overall fuel-lean equivalence ratio, CI engines have only about one-fifth the HC emissions of an SI engine. The components in diesel fuel have higher molecular weights on average than those in a gasoline blend, and this results in higher boiling and condensing temperatures. Therefore, soot formation is more in CI engines. Some HC particles condenses onto the surface of the solid carbon soot that is generated during combustion. Most of this is burned as mixing continues and the combustion process proceeds. Only a small percentage of the original carbon soot that is formed comes out of the cylinder. The HC components condensed on the surface of the carbon particles, in addition to the solid carbon particles themselves, contribute to the HC emissions of the engine.

In general, a CI engine has combustion efficiency of about 98%. This means that only about 2% of the HC fuel being emitted. Because of the non-homogeneity of fuel-air mixture some local spots in the combustion chamber will be too lean to combust properly. Other spots may be too rich, with not enough oxygen to burn all the fuel. Local spots range from very rich to very lean, and many flame fronts exist at the same time. With undermixing, some fuel particles in fuel-rich zones never react due to lack of oxygen. In fuel-lean zones, combustion is limited and some fuel does not get burned. With overmixing, some fuel particles will be mixed with already burned gas and will therefore not combust totally.

It is important that injectors be constructed such that when injection stops there is no dribble. However, a small amount of liquid fuel will be trapped on the tip of the nozzle. This very small volume of fuel is called sac volume, its size depending on the nozzle design. This sac volume of liquid fuel evaporates very slowly because it is surrounded by a fuel rich zone and, once the injector nozzle closes, there is no pressure pushing it into the cylinder. Some of this fuel does not evaporate until combustion has stopped, and this increases HC emissions.

CI engines also have HC emissions for some of the same reasons as SI engines do (i.e., wall deposit absorption, oil film absorption, crevice volume, etc).

14.10 CARBON MONOXIDE (CO) EMISSION

Carbon monoxide is a colorless and odorless but a poisonous gas. It is generated in an engine when it is operated with a fuel-rich equivalence ratio, as shown in Fig.14.1. When there is not enough oxygen to convert all carbon to CO_2, some fuel does not get burned and some carbon ends up as CO. Typically the exhaust of an SI engine will be about 0.2 to 5% carbon monoxide. Not only is CO considered an undesirable emission, but it also represents lost chemical energy. CO is a fuel that can be combusted to supply additional thermal energy:

$$CO + \frac{1}{2}\,O_2 \rightarrow CO_2 + \text{ heat} \tag{14.1}$$

Maximum CO is generated when an engine runs rich. Rich mixture is required during starting or when accelerating under load. Even when the intake air-fuel mixture is stoichiometric or lean, some CO will be generated in the engine. Poor mixing, local rich regions, and incomplete combustion will also be the source for CO emissions.

A well-designed SI engine operating under ideal conditions can have an exhaust mole fraction of CO as low as 0.001. CI engines that operate overall lean generally have very low CO emissions [Fig.14.2].

14.11 OXIDES OF NITROGEN (NO_x)

Exhaust gases of an engine can have up to 2000 ppm of oxides of nitrogen. Most of this will be nitrogen oxide (NO), with a small amount of nitrogen dioxide (NO_2). There will also be traces of other nitrogen-oxygen combinations. These are all grouped together NO_x, with x representing some suitable number. NO_x is very undesirable. Regulations to reduce NO_x emissions continue to become more and more stringent year by year. Released NO_x reacts in the atmosphere to form ozone and is one of the major causes of photochemical smog.

NO_x is created mostly from nitrogen in the air. Nitrogen can also be found in fuel blends. Further, fuel may contain trace amounts of NH_3, NC, and HCN, but this would contribute only to a minor degree. There are a number of possible reactions that form NO. All the restrictions are probably occurring during the combustion process and immediately after. These include but are not limited to:

$$O + N_2 \rightarrow NO + N \tag{14.2}$$

$$N + O_2 \rightarrow NO + O \tag{14.3}$$

$$N + OH \rightarrow NO + H \tag{14.4}$$

NO, in turn, can further react to form NO_2 by various means, including

$$NO + H_2O \rightarrow NO_2 + H_2 \tag{14.5}$$

$$NO + O_2 \rightarrow NO_2 + O \tag{14.6}$$

At low temperatures, atmospheric nitrogen exists as a stable diatomic molecule. Therefore, only very small trace amounts of oxides of nitrogen are found. However, at very high temperatures that occur in the combustion chamber of an engine, some diatomic nitrogen (N_2) breaks down to monatomic nitrogen (N) which is reactive:

$$N_2 \rightarrow 2N \tag{14.7}$$

It may be noted that the chemical equilibrium constant for Eq.14.7 is highly dependent on temperature. Significant amount of N is generated in the temperature range of 2500-3000 K that can exist in an engine. Other gases that are stable at low temperatures but become reactive and contribute to the formation of NO_x at high temperatures include oxygen and water vapor, which break down as follows:

$$O_2 \rightarrow 2O \tag{14.8}$$

$$H_2O \rightarrow OH + \frac{1}{2} H_2 \tag{14.9}$$

If one goes a little deep into combustion chemistry it can be understood that chemical Eqs.14.7 to 14.9 all react much further to the right as high combustion chamber temperatures are reached. The higher the combustion reaction temperature, the more diatomic nitrogen, N_2, will dissociate to monatomic nitrogen, N, and the more NO_x will be formed. At low temperatures very little NO_x is created.

Although maximum flame temperature will occur at a stoichiometric air-fuel ratio ($\phi = 1$), Fig.14.1 shows that maximum NO_x is formed at a slightly lean equivalence ratio of about $\phi = 0.95$. At this condition flame temperature is still very high, and in addition, there is an excess of oxygen that can combine with the nitrogen to form various oxides.

In addition to temperature, the formation of NO_x depends on pressure and air-fuel ratio. Combustion duration plays a significant role in NO_x formation within the cylinder. Figure 14.5 shows the NO_x versus time relationship and supports the fact that NO_x is reduced in modern engines with fast-burn combustion chambers. The amount of NO_x generated also depends on the location of spark plug within the combustion chamber. The highest concentration is formed around the spark plug, where the highest temperatures occur. Figure 14.6 shows how NO_x can be correlated with ignition timing. If spark is advanced, the cylinder temperature will be increased and more NO_x will be created. Because CI engines have higher compression ratios and higher temperatures and pressure, they with divided combustion chambers and indirect injection (IDI) tend to generate higher levels of NO_x.

14.11.1 Photochemical Smog

NO_x is one of the primary causes of photochemical smog, which has become a major problem in many large cities of the world. Smog is formed by the photochemical reaction of automobile exhaust and atmospheric air in the presence of sunlight. NO_2 decomposes into NO and monatomic oxygen:

$$NO_2 + \text{energy from sunlight} \rightarrow NO + O + \text{smog} \tag{14.10}$$

Monatomic oxygen is highly reactive and initiates a number of different reactions, one of which is the formation of ozone:

$$O + O_2 \rightarrow O_3 \tag{14.11}$$

Ground-level ozone is harmful to lungs and other biological tissue. It is harmful to plants and trees and causes very heavy crop losses each year. Damage is also caused through reaction with rubber, plastics, and other materials. Ozone also results from atmospheric reactions with other engine emissions such as HC, aldehydes, and other oxides of nitrogen.

14.12 PARTICULATES

The exhaust of CI engines contains solid carbon soot particles that are generated in the fuel-rich zones within the cylinder during combustion. These are seen as exhaust smoke and cause an undesirable odorous pollution. Maximum density of particulate emissions occurs when the engine is under load at WOT. At this condition maximum fuel is injected to supply maximum power,

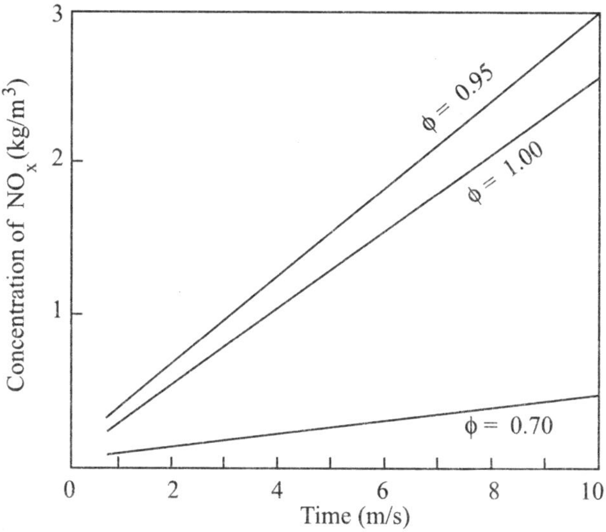

Fig. 14.5 Generation of NO_x as a function of combustion time in an engine

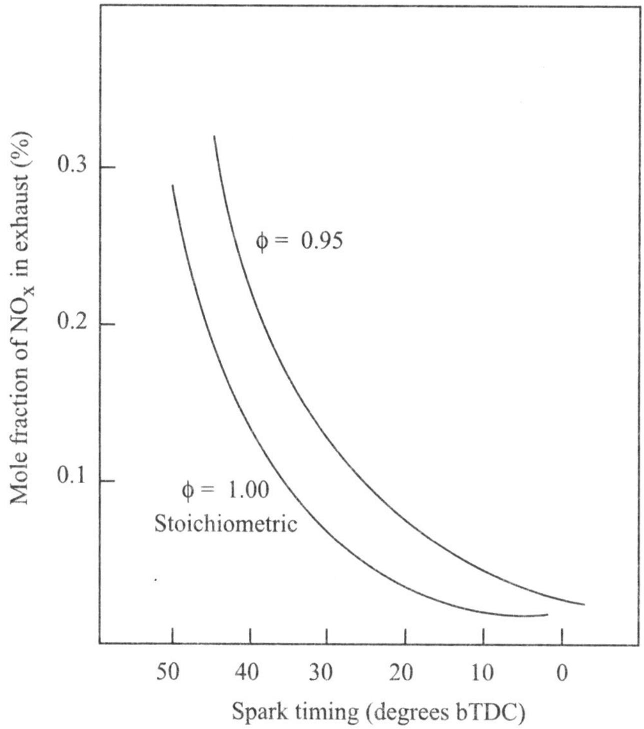

Fig. 14.6 Generation of NO_x in an SI engine as a function of spark timing

resulting in a rich mixture and poor fuel economy. This can be seen in the heavy exhaust smoke emitted when a truck or railroad locomotive accelerates up a hill or from a stop.

Soot particles are clusters of solid carbon spheres. These spheres have diameters from 9 nm to 90 nm (1 nm = 10^{-9} m). But most of them are within the range of 15-30 nm. The spheres are solid carbon with HC and traces of other components absorbed on the surface. A single soot particle may contain up to 5000 carbon spheres.

Carbon spheres are generated in the combustion chamber in the fuel-rich zones where there is not enough oxygen to convert all carbon to CO_2 :

$$C_x\ H_y + z\ O_2 \rightarrow a\ CO_2 + b\ H_2\ O + c CO + d C(s) \tag{14.12}$$

Then, as turbulence and mass motion continue to mix the components in the combustion chamber, most of these carbon particles $[C(s)]$ find sufficient oxygen to further react and are converted to CO_2:

$$C(s) + \ O_2 \rightarrow \ CO_2 \tag{14.13}$$

More than 90 to 95% of carbon particles originally generated within an engine are thus converted to CO_2 and never comes out as carbon particles. It should be remembered that if CI engines are made to operate with an overall stoichiometric air-fuel mixture, instead of overall lean as they do, particulate emissions in the exhaust would far exceed acceptable levels.

Up to about 25% of the carbon in soot comes from lubricating oil components which vaporize and then react during combustion. The rest comes from the fuel and amounts to 0.2-0.5% of the fuel. Because of the high compression ratios of CI engines, a large expansion occurs during the power stroke. This makes the gases within the cylinder cooled to a relatively low temperature. This causes the remaining high-boiling-point components found in the fuel and lubricating oil to condense on the surface of the carbon soot particles. This absorbed portion of the soot particles is called the soluble organic fraction (SOF), and the amount is highly dependent on cylinder temperature.

At light loads, cylinder temperatures are reduced and can drop to as low as 200 °C during final expansion and exhaust blow-down. Under these conditions, SOF can be as high as 50% of the total mass of soot. Under other operating conditions when temperatures are not so low, very little condensing occurs and SOF can be as low as 3% of total soot mass. SOF consists mostly of hydrocarbon components with some hydrogen, NO, NO_2, SO_2 and trace amounts of calcium, chromium, iron, phosphorus, silicon, sulphur and zinc. Diesel fuel contains calcium, chromium, iron, silicon, and sulphur, while lubricating oil additives contain calcium, phosphorus, and zinc.

Particulate generation can be reduced by engine design and control of operating conditions, but quite often this will create other adverse results. If the combustion time is extended by combustion chamber design and timing control, particulate amounts in the exhaust can be reduced. Soot particles originally generated will have a greater time to be mixed with oxygen and combusted to CO_2. However, a longer combustion time means a high cylinder temperature and more NO_x generation. Dilution with EGR lowers NO_x emissions but increases particulates and HC emissions. Higher injection pressure gives a finer droplet size. This will reduce HC and particulate emissions but increases cylinder temperature and NO_x emissions. Engine management systems are programmed to minimize CO, HC, NO_x, and particulate emissions by controlling ignition timing, injection pressure, injection timing, and/or valve timing. Obviously, some sort of compromise is necessary. In most cases exhaust particulate amounts cannot be reduced to acceptable levels solely by engine design and control.

14.13 OTHER EMISSIONS

Apart from major emissions like unburnt hydrocarbon, carbon monoxide and NO_x, there are other emissions that come out of the exhaust. A brief account of other emissions are given in the following sections.

14.13.1 Aldehydes

A major emission problem when alcohol fuel is used is the generation of aldehydes, an eye and respiratory irritant. These have the chemical formula of: where *R* denotes various chemical radicals. This is a product of incomplete

combustion and would be a major problem if as much alcohol fuel were used as presently as gasoline.

14.13.2 Sulphur

Many fuels used in CI engines contain small amounts of sulphur. When exhausted in the form of SO_2 and SO_3 (called SO_x) they contribute to the acid rain problem of the world. Unleaded gasoline generally contains 150-550 ppm sulphur by weight. Some diesel fuels contain up to 5500 ppm by weight, but in the developed countries this is restricted by law to a tenth of this value or less. At high temperatures, sulphur combines with hydrogen to form H_2S and with oxygen to form SO_2:

$$H_2 + S \rightarrow H_2S \tag{14.14}$$

$$O_2 + S \rightarrow SO_2 \tag{14.15}$$

Engine exhaust can contain up to 20 ppm of SO_2. SO_2 then combines with oxygen in the air to form SO_3

$$2\,SO_2 + O_2 \rightarrow 2\,SO_3 \tag{14.16}$$

These combine with water vapor in the atmosphere to form sulphuric acid (H_2SO_4) and sulphurous acid (H_2SO_3), which are ingredients in acid rain

$$SO_3 + H_2O \rightarrow H_2\,SO_4 \tag{14.17}$$

$$SO_2 + H_2O \rightarrow H_2\,SO_3 \tag{14.18}$$

Many countries have laws restricting the amount of sulphur allowed in fuel. These are continuously being made more stringent. During the 1990s, the developed countries reduced acceptable levels of sulphur in diesel fuel from 0.05% by weight to 0.01%.

The amount of sulphur in natural gas can range from little (sweet) to large (sour) amounts. This can be a major emissions problem when natural gas is used in a IC engine or any other combustion system.

14.13.3 Lead

Lead was a major gasoline additive from its introduction in 1920s to when it was phased out in the 1980s. The additive TEL (tetraethyl lead) was effectively used to increase gasoline octane number, which allowed higher compression ratios and more efficient engines. However, the resulting lead in the engine exhaust was a highly poisonous pollutant. During the first half of the 1900s, due to the lower number of automobiles and other engines, the atmosphere was able to absorb these emissions of lead without noticeable problems. As population and automobile density increased, the awareness of air pollution and its danger also increased. The danger of lead emissions was recognized, and a phase-out occurred during the 1970s and 1980s.

The use of lead could not be stopped immediately but had to be phased out over a number of years. First, low-lead gasoline was introduced, and then, years later no-lead gasoline. Lead was still the major additive to raise the octane number of gasoline, and alternate octane raisers had to be developed as lead was phased out. Millions of modern high-compression ratio engines could not use low-octane fuel.

Metals used in engines also had to be changed as lead in gasoline was phased out. When leaded fuel is burned, it hardens the surfaces in the combustion chamber and on the valves and valve seats. Engines designed to use leaded fuel had softer metal surfaces to start and relied on surface hardening effects that occurred in use. If these engines are used with unleaded fuel, surface hardening is not realized. Quick and serious wear problems were experienced. Catastrophic failures of valve seats or piston faces are common in a short period of time (i.e., 10,000–20,000 km in an automobile). Hence, harder metals and added surface treatments are being employed for engines designed to use unleaded fuel. It was necessary to phase out leaded gasoline over a period of time as older automobiles wore out and were taken out of operation.

Leaded gasoline contains about 0.15 gm/liter of lead in the fuel. 10 to 50% of this gets exhausted out with the other combustion products. The remaining lead gets deposited on the walls of the engine and exhaust system. The hardened combustion chamber surfaces which resulted from the burning of leaded gasoline were quite impervious to the absorption of gases such as fuel vapor. HC emissions were also, therefore, slightly reduced in these engines.

14.13.4 Phosphorus

Small amounts of phosphorus are emitted in engine exhaust. These come from impurities in the air and small amounts found in some fuel blends and lubricating oil.

14.14 EMISSION CONTROL METHODS

It is to be noted that combustion process in the four-stroke cycle occurs only for about 25 to 50 ms depending upon the operating conditions. After the combustion process ends, the exhaust gas constituents in the cylinder gas mixture that have been partially burned continue to react during the expansion stroke, during exhaust blowdown, and into the exhaust process. Over 90 to 95% of the HC remaining after combustion reacts during this time either in the cylinder, near the exhaust port, or in the upstream part of the exhaust manifold. CO and small component hydrocarbons react with oxygen to form CO_2 and H_2O and reduce undesirable emissions. The higher the exhaust temperature, the more these secondary reactions occur and the lower the engine emissions. Higher exhaust temperature can be caused by stoichiometric air-fuel combustion, high engine speed, retarded spark, and/or a low expansion ratio. Hence, in order to reduce emissions, some after-treatments are necessary with add on devices. The details are discussed in the following sections.

14.14.1 Thermal Converters

Secondary reactions occur much more readily and completely if the temperature is high. So some engines are equipped with thermal converters as a means of lowering emissions. Thermal converters are high-temperature chambers through which the exhaust gas flows. They promote oxidation of the CO and HC which remain in the exhaust.

$$\mathrm{CO} + \frac{1}{2}\,\mathrm{O_2} \quad \rightarrow \quad \mathrm{CO_2} \tag{14.19}$$

For this reaction to occur at a useful rate, the temperature must be held above 700 °C. Now consider the reaction

$$\mathrm{C}_x\,\mathrm{H}_y + z\,\mathrm{O_2} \quad \rightarrow \quad x\,\mathrm{CO_2} + y\,\mathrm{H_2\,O} \tag{14.20}$$

where $z = x + 0.25y$.

The above reaction needs a temperature above 600 °C for at least 50 milliseconds to substantially reduce HC. It is therefore necessary for a thermal converter to be effective, it should operate at a high temperature. Further, it should also be large enough to provide adequate residence time of the exhaust gases to promote the occurrence of these secondary reactions. Most thermal converters are essentially an enlarged exhaust manifold connected to the engine immediately outside the exhaust ports. This is necessary to minimize heat losses and keep the exhaust gases from cooling to nonreacting temperatures.

However, in automobiles this creates two very serious problems for the engine compartment. In modern, low-profile, aerodynamic automobiles, space in the engine compartment is very limited, and fitting in a large, usually insulated thermal converter chamber is almost impossible. Secondly, because the converter must operate above 700 °C to be efficient, even if it is insulated the heat losses create a serious temperature problem in the engine compartment.

Some thermal converter systems include an air intake which provides additional oxygen to react with the CO and HC. This increases the complexity, cost, and size of the system. Air addition is especially necessary during rich operating conditions such as startup. Because exhaust from engines is often at a lower temperature than is needed for efficient operation of a thermal converter, it is necessary to sustain the high temperatures by the reactions within the system. Adding outside air which is at a lower temperature, compounds this problem of maintaining the necessary operating temperature. Even though HC and CO emissions can be reduced by oxidation, NO_x emissions cannot be reduced using a thermal converter.

14.15 CATALYTIC CONVERTERS

The most effective aftertreatment for reducing engine emissions is the catalytic converter found on most automobiles and other modern engines of medium or large size. CO and HC can be oxidized to CO_2 and H_2O in exhaust systems and thermal converters if the temperature is held at 600–700 °C. If certain catalysts are present, the temperature needed to sustain these oxidation processes is reduced to 250–300 °C, making for a much more attractive system.

A catalyst is a substance that accelerates a chemical reaction by lowering the energy needed for it to proceed. The catalyst is not consumed in the reaction and so functions indefinitely unless degraded by heat, age, contaminants, or other factors.

Catalytic converters are chambers mounted in the flow system through which the exhaust gases pass through. These chambers contain catalytic material, which promotes the oxidation of the emissions contained in the exhaust flow. Generally, they are called three-way converters because they are used to reduce the concentration of CO, HC, and NO_x in the exhaust. It is usually a stainless steel container mounted somewhere along the exhaust pipe of the engine. Inside the container is a porous ceramic structure through which the exhaust gas flows. In most converters, the ceramic is a single honeycomb structure with many flow passages (Fig.14.7). Some converters use loose granular ceramic with the gas passing between the packed spheres. Volume of the ceramic structure of a converter is generally about half the displacement volume of the engine. This results in a volumetric flow rate of exhaust gas such that there are 5 to 30 changeovers of gas each second, through the converter. Catalytic converters for CI engines need larger flow passages because of the solid soot in the exhaust gases. The surface of the ceramic passages contains small embedded particles of catalytic material that promote the oxidation reactions in the exhaust gas as it passes. Aluminum oxide (alumina) is the base ceramic material used for most catalytic converters. Alumina can withstand the high temperatures, it remains chemically neutral, it has very low thermal expansion, and it does not thermally degrade with age. The catalyst materials most used are platinum, palladium, and rhodium.

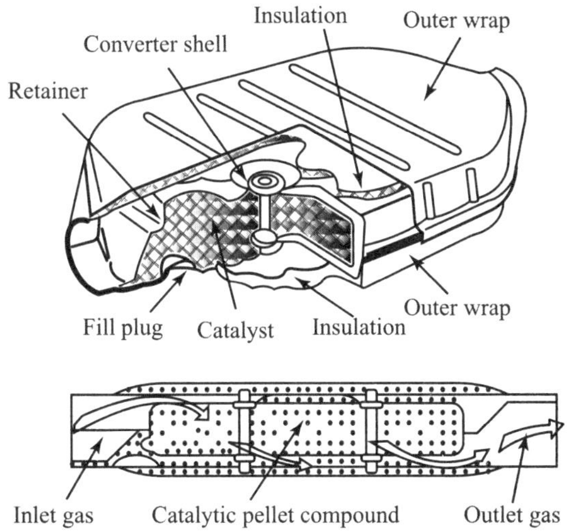

(a) Packed spheres

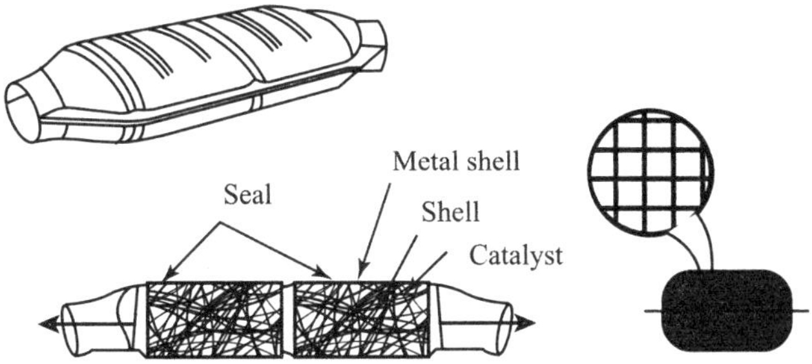

(b) Honey comb structure

Fig. 14.7 Catalytic converters for SI engines

Palladium and platinum promote the oxidation of CO and HC as in Eqs.14.19 and 14.20, with platinum especially active in the hydrocarbon reaction. Rhodium promotes the reaction of NO_x in one or more of the following reactions:

$$NO + CO \rightarrow \frac{1}{2} N_2 + CO_2 \qquad (14.21)$$

$$2\,NO + 5\,CO + 3\,H_2O \rightarrow 2\,NH_3 + 5\,CO_2 \qquad (14.22)$$

$$2\,NO + CO \rightarrow N_2O + CO_2 \qquad (14.23)$$

$$NO + H_2 \rightarrow \frac{1}{2} N_2 + H_2O \qquad (14.24)$$

$$2\,NO + 5\,H_2 \rightarrow 2\,NH_3 + 2\,H_2\,O \tag{14.25}$$

$$2\,NO + H_2 \rightarrow N_2\,O + H_2\,O \tag{14.26}$$

Also often used is cerium oxide, which promotes the so-called water gas shift

$$CO + H_2\,O \rightarrow CO_2 + H_2 \tag{14.27}$$

This reduces CO by using water vapor as an oxidant instead of O_2, which is very important when the engine is running rich.

Figure 14.8 shows that the efficiency of a catalytic converter is very much dependent on temperature. When a converter in good working order is operating at a fully warmed temperature of 400 °C or above, it will remove 98-99% of CO, 95% of NO_x, and more than 95% of HC from exhaust flow emissions.

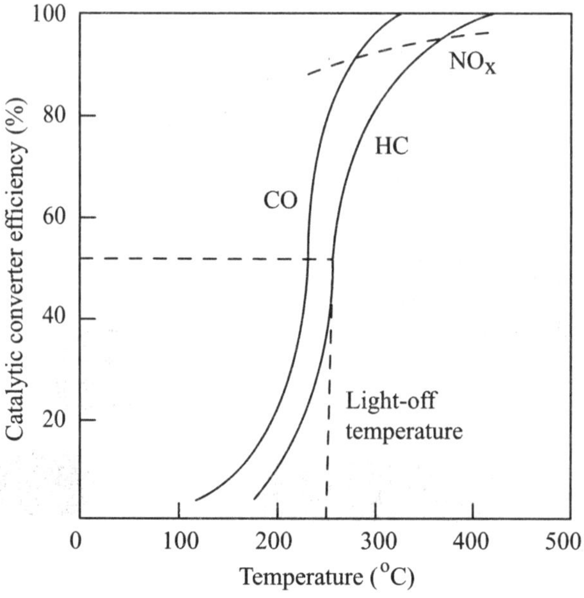

Fig. 14.8 Conversion efficiency of catalytic converters as a function of converter temperature

Figure 14.9 shows that it is also necessary to be operating at the proper equivalence ratio to get high converter efficiency. Effective control of HC and CO occurs with stoichiometric or lean mixtures while control of NO_x requires near stoichiometric conditions. Very poor NO_x control occurs with lean mixtures.

It is important that a catalytic converter be operated hot to be efficient, but not hotter. Engine malfunctions can cause poor efficiency and overheating of converters. A poorly tuned engine can have misfires and periods of too lean and/or too rich conditions. These cause the converter to be inefficient. A turbocharger lowers the exhaust temperature by removing energy, and this can make a catalytic converter less efficient.

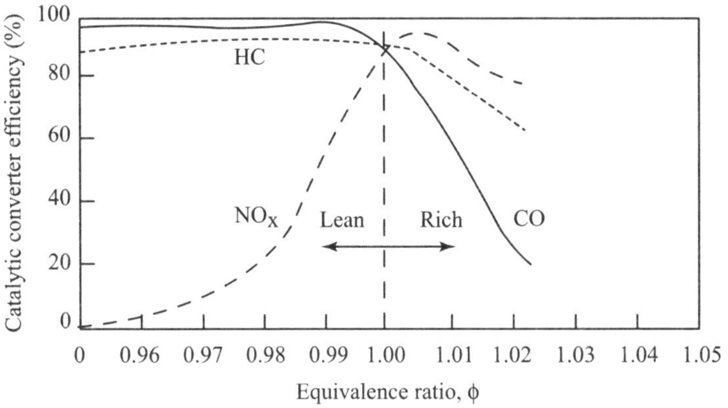

Fig. 14.9 Conversion efficiency of catalytic converters as a function of fuel equivalence ratio

It is desirable that catalytic converters have an effective life time equal to that of the automobile or at least 200,000 km. Converters lose their efficiency with age due to thermal degradation and poisoning of the active catalyst material. At high temperature the metal catalyst material can sinter and migrate together. This can cause larger active sites which are, overall, less efficient. Serious thermal degradation occurs in the temperature range of 500–900 °C. A number of different impurities contained in fuel, lubricating oil, and air find their way into the engine exhaust and poison the catalyst material. These include lead and sulphur from fuels, and zinc, phosphorus, antimony, calcium, and magnesium from oil additives.

Figure 14.10 shows how just a small amount of lead on a catalyst site can reduce HC emission reduction by a factor of two or three. Small amounts of lead impurities are found in some fuels, and 10 to 30% of this ends up in the catalytic converter. Up until the early 1990s leaded gasoline was quite common. Note that leaded gasoline cannot be used in engines equipped with catalytic converters. Use of leaded gasoline filled two times (full tank) would completely poison a converter and make it totally useless.

To reduce the chances of accidently using leaded gasoline with a catalytic converter, the fuel pump nozzle size and the diameter of the fuel tank inlet are made smaller for unleaded gasoline.

14.15.1 Sulphur

Sulphur offers unique problems for catalytic converters. Some catalysts promote the conversion of SO_2 to SO_3, which eventually gets converted to sulphuric acid. This degrades the catalytic converter and contributes to acid rain. New catalysts are being developed that promote the oxidation of HC and CO but do not change SO_2 to SO_3. Some of these create almost no SO_3 if the temperature of the converter is kept less than 400 °C.

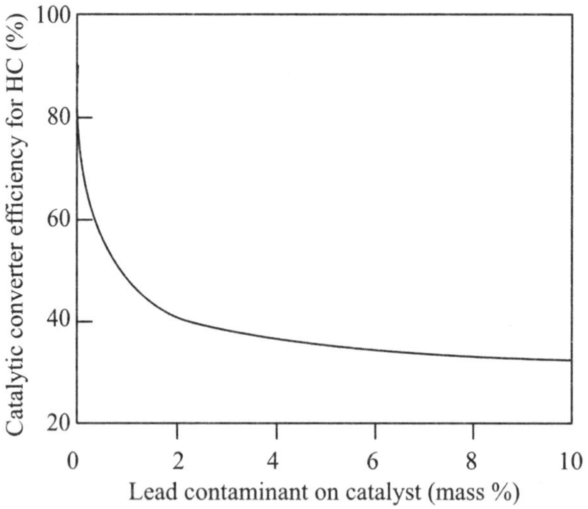

Fig. 14.10 Reduction of catalytic converter efficiency due to contamination by lead

14.15.2 Cold Start-Ups

As can be seen from Fig.14.8 catalytic converters are not very efficient when they are cold. When an engine is started after not being operated for several hours, it takes several minutes for the converter to reach an efficient operating temperature. The temperature at which a converter becomes 50% efficient is defined as the light-off temperature, and is in the range of 250–300 °C.

A large percentage of automobile travel is for short distances where the catalytic converter never reaches efficient operating temperature, and therefore emissions are high. Unfortunately, most short trips occur in cities where high emissions are more harmful. Further, all engines use a rich mixture when starting. Otherwise cold start-ups pose a major problem.

It is estimated that cold start-ups are the source of 70-90% of all HC emissions. A major reduction in emissions is therefore possible if catalytic converters could be preheated, at least to light-off temperature, before engine startup. Preheating to full steady-state operating temperature would be even better. Several methods of pre-heating have been tried with varying success. Because of the time involved and amount of energy needed, most of these methods preheat only a small portion of the total converter volume. This small section is large enough to treat the low exhaust flow rate which usually occurs at startup and immediately following. By the time higher engine speeds are used, most of the catalytic converter has been heated by the hot exhaust gas, and the higher flow rates are fully treated. Methods of catalytic converter preheating include the following.

(i) by locating the converter close to the engine

(ii) by having super-insulation

(iii) by employing electric preheating

(iv) by using flame heating

(v) incorporating thermal batteries

14.16 CI ENGINES

Catalytic converters are being tried with CI engines but are not efficient at reducing NO_x due to their overall lean operation. HC and CO can be adequately reduced, although there is greater difficulty because of the cooler exhaust gases of a CI engine (because of the larger expansion ratio). This is counter balanced by the fact that less HC and CO are generated in the lean burn of the CI engine. NO_x is reduced in a CI engine by the use of EGR, which keeps the maximum temperature down. EGR and lower combustion temperatures, however, contribute to an increase in solid soot.

Platinum and palladium are two main catalyst materials used for converters on CI engines. They promote the removal of 30–80% of the gaseous HC and 40–90% of the CO in the exhaust. The catalysts have little effect on solid carbon soot but do remove 30–60% of the total particulate mass by oxidizing a large percent of the HC absorbed on the carbon particles. Diesel fuel contains sulphur impurities, and this leads to poisoning of the catalyst materials. However, this problem is getting minimized as legal levels of sulphur in diesel fuels continue to be lowered.

14.16.1 Particulate Traps

Compression ignition engine systems are equipped with particulate traps in their exhaust flow to reduce the amount of particulates released to the atmosphere. Traps are filter-like systems often made of ceramic in the form of a monolith or mat, or else made of metal wire mesh. Traps typically remove 60–90% of particulates in the exhaust flow. As traps catch the soot particles, they slowly fill up with the particulates. This restricts exhaust gas flow and raises the back pressure of the engine. Higher back pressure causes the engine to run hotter, the exhaust temperature to rise, and fuel consumption to increase. To reduce this flow restriction, particulate traps are regenerated when they begin to saturate. Regeneration consists of combusting the particulates in the excess oxygen contained in the exhaust of the lean-operating CI engine.

Carbon soot ignites at about 550–650 °C, while CI engine exhaust is 150–350 °C at normal operating conditions. As the particulate trap fills with soot and restricts flow, the exhaust temperature rises but is still not high enough to ignite the soot and regenerate the trap. In some systems, automatic flame igniters are used which start combustion in the carbon when the pressure drop across the trap reaches a predetermined value. These igniters can be electric heaters or flame nozzles that use diesel fuel. If catalyst material is installed in the traps, the temperature needed to ignite the carbon soot is reduced to the 350–450 °C range. Some such traps can automatically regenerate by self-igniting when the exhaust temperature rises from increased back pressure. Other catalyst systems use flame igniters.

Another way of lowering the ignition temperature of the carbon soot and promoting self-regeneration in traps is to use catalyst additives in the diesel fuel. These additives generally consist of copper compounds or iron compounds, with about 6 to 8 grams of additive in 1000 liters of fuel is usually normal. To keep the temperatures high enough to self-regenerate in a catalytic system, traps can be mounted as close to the engine as possible, even before the turbocharger.

On some larger stationary engines and on some construction equipment and large trucks, the particulate trap is replaced when it becomes close to filled position. The removed trap is then regenerated externally, with the carbon being burned off in a furnace. The regenerated trap can then be used again.

Various methods are used to determine when soot buildup becomes excessive and regeneration is necessary. The most common method is to measure pressure drop in the exhaust flow as it passes through the trap. When a predetermined pressure drop Δp is reached, regeneration is initiated. Pressure drop is also a function of exhaust flow rate, and this must be programmed into the regeneration controls. Another method used to sense soot buildup is to transmit radio frequency waves through the trap and determine the percent that is absorbed. Carbon soot absorbs radio waves while the ceramic structure does not. The amount of soot buildup can therefore be determined by the percent decrease in radio signal. This method does not readily detect soluble organic fraction (SOF).

Modern particulate traps are not totally satisfactory, especially for automobiles. They are costly and complex when equipped for regeneration, and long-term durability does not exist. An ideal catalytic trap would be simple, economical, and reliable; it would be self-regenerating; and it would impose a minimum increase in fuel consumption.

14.16.2 Modern Diesel Engines

Carbon soot particulate generation has been greatly reduced in modern CI engines by advanced design technology in fuel injectors and combustion chamber geometry. With greatly increased mixing efficiency and speeds, large regions of fuel- rich mixtures can be avoided when combustion starts. These are the regions where carbon soot is generated, and by reducing their volume, far less soot is generated. Increased mixing speeds are obtained by a combination of indirect injection, better combustion chamber geometry, better injector design and higher pressures, heated spray targets, and air-assisted injectors. Indirect injection into a secondary chamber that promotes high turbulence and swirl greatly speeds the air-fuel mixing process. Better nozzle design and higher injection pressures create finer fuel droplets which evaporate and mix quicker. Injection against a hot surface speeds evaporation, as do air-assisted injectors. Some modern, top-of-the-line CI automobile engines have reduced particulate generation enough that they meet stringent standards without the need for particulate traps.

14.17 REDUCING EMISSIONS BY CHEMICAL METHODS

Development work has been done on large stationary engines using cyanuric acid to reduce NO_x emissions. Cyanuric acid is a low-cost solid material that sublimes in the exhaust flow. The gas dissociates, producing isocyanide that reacts with NO_x to form N_2, H_2O, and CO_2. Operating temperature is about 500 °C. Up to 95% NO_x reduction can be achieved with no loss of engine performance. At present, this system is not practical for automobile engines because of its size, weight, and complexity.

Research is being done using zeolite molecular sieves to reduce NO_x emissions. These are materials that absorb selected molecular compounds and catalyze chemical reactions. Using both SI and CI engines, the efficiency of NO_x reduction is being determined over a range of operating variables, including air-fuel ratio, temperature, flow velocity, and zeolite structure. At present, durability is a serious limitation with this method.

Various chemical absorbers, molecular sieves, and traps are being tested to reduce HC emissions. HC is collected during engine startup time, when the catalytic converter is cold, and then later released back into the exhaust flow when the converter is hot. The converter then efficiently burns the HC to H_2O and CO_2. A 35% reduction of cold-start HC has been achieved.

H_2S emissions occur under rich operating conditions. Chemical systems are being developed that trap and store H_2S when an engine operates rich and then convert this to SO_2 when operation is lean and excess oxygen exists. The reaction equation is

$$H_2\,S + O_2 \quad \rightarrow \quad SO_2 + H_2 \tag{14.28}$$

14.17.1 Ammonia Injection Systems

Some large marine engines and stationary engines reduce NO_x emissions with an injection system that sprays NH_3 into the exhaust flow. In the presence of a catalyst, the following reactions occur

$$4\,NH_3 + 4\,NO + O_2 \quad \rightarrow \quad 4\,N_2 + 6\,H_2O \tag{14.29}$$

$$6\,NO_2 + 8\,NH_3 \quad \rightarrow \quad 7\,N_2 + 12\,H_2\,O \tag{14.30}$$

Careful control must be adhered to, as NH_3 itself is an undesirable emission.

Ammonia injection systems are not practical in automobiles or on other smaller engines. This is because of the needed NH_3 storage and fairly complex injection and control system.

14.18 EXHAUST GAS RECIRCULATION (EGR)

The most effective way of reducing NO_x emissions is to hold combustion chamber temperatures down. Although practical, this is a very unfortunate method in that it also reduces the thermal efficiency of the engine. Those who have undergone thermodynamics course are aware that to obtain maximum engine thermal efficiency it should be operated at the highest temperature possible.

Probably the simplest and practical method of reducing maximum flame temperature is to dilute the air-fuel mixture with a non-reacting parasite gas. This gas absorbs energy during combustion without contributing any energy input. The net result is a lower flame temperature. Any nonreacting gas would work as a diluents, as shown in Fig.14.11. Those gases with larger specific heats would absorb the most energy per unit mass and would therefore require the least amount; thus less CO_2 would be required than argon for the same maximum temperature. However, neither CO_2 nor argon is readily available for use in an engine. Air is available as a diluents but is not totally nonreacting. Adding air changes the air-fuel ratio and combustion characteristics. The one nonreacting gas that is available to use in an engine is exhaust gas, and this is used in all modern automobile and other medium-size and large engines. Adding any non reacting neutral gas to the inlet air-fuel mixture reduces flame temperature and NO_x generation, Exhaust gas (EGR) is the one gas that is readily available for engine use.

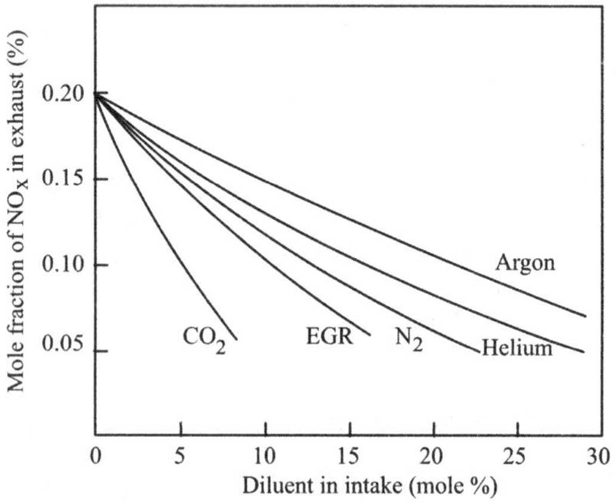

Fig. 14.11 NO_x reduction using non-combustible diluent gas to intake mixture

Exhaust gas recycle (EGR) is done by ducting some of the exhaust flow back into the intake system, usually immediately after the throttle. The amount of flow can be as high as 30% of the total intake. EGR combines with the exhaust residual left in the cylinder from the previous cycle to effectively reduce the maximum combustion temperature. The flow rate of EGR is controlled by the Engine Management System. EGR is defined as a mass percent of the total intake flow

$$\text{EGR} = \left(\frac{\dot{m}_{\text{EGR}}}{\dot{m}_{cyl}}\right) \times 100 \qquad (14.31)$$

where *cyl* is the total mass flow into the cylinders.

After EGR combines with the exhaust residual left from the previous cycle, the total fraction of exhaust in the cylinder during the compression stroke is

$$x_{ex} = \left(\frac{\text{EGR}}{100}\right) \times (1 - x_r) + x_r \qquad (14.32)$$

where x_r is the exhaust residual from previous cycle.

Not only does EGR reduce the maximum temperature in the combustion chamber, but it also lowers the overall combustion efficiency. Increase in

EGR results in some cycle partial burns and, in the extreme, total misfires. Thus, by using EGR to reduce NO_x emissions, a costly price of increased HC emissions and lower thermal efficiency must be paid.

The amount of EGR is controlled by the Engine Management System. By sensing inlet and exhaust conditions the flow is controlled, ranging from 0 upto 15–30%. Lowest NO_x emissions with relatively good fuel economy occur at about stoichiometric combustion, with as much EGR as possible without adversely affecting combustion. No EGR is used during WOT, when maximum power is desired. No EGR is used at idle and very little at low speeds. Under these conditions, there is already a maximum exhaust residual and greater combustion inefficiency. Engines with fast-burn combustion chambers can tolerate a greater amount of EGR. A problem unique to CI engines when using EGR is the solid carbon soot in the exhaust. The soot acts as an abrasive and breaks down the lubricant. Greater wear on the piston rings and valve train results.

14.19 NON-EXHAUST EMISSIONS

Apart from exhaust emissions there are three other sources in an automobile which emit emissions. They are

(i) *Fuel tank*: The fuel tank emits fuel vapours into the atmosphere.

(ii) *Carburetor*: The carburettor also gives out fuel vapours.

(iii) *Crankcase*: It emits blow-by gases and fuel vapours into the atmosphere.

The fourth source is the tail pipe exhaust emissions. The contribution of pollutants by sources, as shown in Fig.14.12 is (i) evaporative losses (both from fuel tank and carburetor), (ii) crankcase blowby (from crankcase), and tail pipe (from the exhaust pipe)

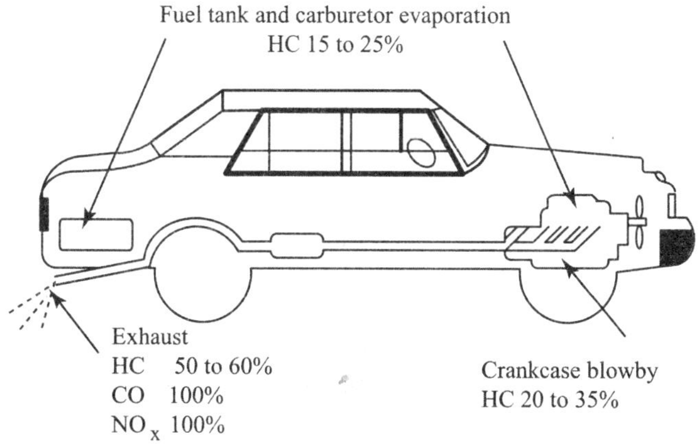

Fig. 14.12 Distribution of emissions by source (petrol engine powered vehicle)

Percentage emissions of various pollutants are as marked in Fig.14.12. The evaporative losses are the direct losses of raw gasoline from the engine fuel system; the blowby gases are the vapours and gases leaking into the crankcase from the combustion chamber and the pollutants from the exhaust pipe are due to incomplete combustion. The following sections discuss the details of the non-exhaust emissions and their control methods.

14.19.1 Evaporative Emissions

Evaporative emissions account for 15 to 25% of total hydrocarbon emission from a gasoline engine. The two main sources of evaporative emissions are the fuel tank and the carburettor.

Fuel tank losses: As the temperature inside the engine rises, the fuel tank heats up. The air inside the fuel tank expands, part of which goes out through the tank vent tube or leaves through the vent of the cap in the tank. This air is mixed with gasoline vapours.

As the temperature decreases, the tank cools. The air inside the tank contracts and there is more space inside the tank. Air enters the tank from the atmosphere and ventilates it. This process of ventilation is called *breathing.* Some of the gasoline is lost by the process of breathing. If the temperature is high, more gasoline is lost. The mechanism of tank loss is as follows:

When a partially filled fuel tank is open to atmosphere the partial pressure of the vapour phase hydrocarbons and vapour pressure of the liquid are equal and they are in equilibrium. If the temperature of the liquid is increased, say by engine operation, the vapour pressure of the liquid will increase and it will vapourize in an attempt to restore equilibrium. As additional liquid vapourize, the total pressure of the tank increases and since the tank is vented to atmosphere the vapour will flow out of the vent. This outflow of the vapour will increase if in addition to temperature rise of the liquefied gasoline the vapour temperature is also increased.

The evaporation from the tank is affected by a large number of variables of which the ambient and fuel tank temperature, the mode of vehicle operation, the amount of fuel in the tank and the volatility of the fuel are important. Other significant factors are the capacity, design and location of the fuel tank with respect to the exhaust system and the flow pattern of the heated air underneath the vehicle. Less the tank fill, greater is the evaporation loss. An approximate picture of the effect of tank fill and temperature are given in Table 14.2, This reflects the difference in the tank vapour space. Also when a vehicle is parked in a hot location the evaporation of the gasoline in the tank accelerates, so the loss due to evaporation are high.

Table 14.2 Effect of tank fill on evaporation loss

Tank fill	Ambient temperature (°C)	Loss during operation (%)
Quarter	10	5.8
Half	15	1.1
Three-fourth	18	0.1
Full	22	0.0

The operational mode substantially affect the evaporation loss. When the tank temperature raises the loss increases. The vapour which goes out from a partially filled tank during vehicle operation called soak, is a mixture of air and hydrocarbon. After a prolonged high speed operation the HC per cent in the soak is as high as 60 per cent as compared to about 30 per cent after an overnight soak. The fuel composition also affects the tank losses. About 75 per cent of the HC loss from tank are C_4 and C_5 hydrocarbons.

Carburettor losses: The operation of an engine depends on the level of gasoline in the float chamber inside the carburettor. The engine stops running when the gasoline has been completely utilized. Heat produced by the engine causes evaporation of some quantity of gasoline from the float chamber. The evaporation of gasoline constitutes the main reason for the loss of gasoline from the carburettor. Approximately, 10% of the total hydrocarbon emission of the engine into the atmosphere is through the fuel tank and the carburetor.

Carburettor losses result from (a) external venting of the float bowl relieving the internal pressure as the carburettor heats, and (b) 'hot soak' losses which occur after the engine has been stopped, as a result of evaporation of petrol stored in the bowl, loss being through vent pipe or through the air cleaner. Most of the loss from the carburettor occurs due to direct boiling of the fuel in the carburettor bowl during hot soak. Carburettor bowl temperature during hot soak rises by 15 to 45 ° C above the ambient. This can cause fuel boiling and the front end gasoline components, C5 and C6 hydrocarbons, vapourise. The amount of hydrocarbon emissions from the carburettor depend upon the design variables. In some designs the small passage from bowl leading to the throat after heating causes siphon action leading to HC loss. If the pressure in the fuel line becomes greater than the pressure holding the closed needle valve, after supply will occur. One of the possible reasons may be fuel evaporation in the carburettor bowl which presses down the bowl and increases the pressure in the fuel line. If the after-supply is more than the bowl volume the losses from the carburettor will change drastically. Thus bowl volume and maximum bowl temperature both significantly affect the evaporative losses from the carburettor. The losses of gasoline from the fuel tank and the carburettor should be prevented by special devices such as those used in evaporative emission control systems.

14.19.2 Evaporation Loss Control Device (ELCD)

This device aims at controlling all evaporative emissions by capturing the vapours and recirculating them at the appropriate time. The device, as shown in Fig.14.13, consists of an absorbent chamber, the pressure balance valve and the purge control valve. The adsorbent chamber, which consists of a charcoal bed or foamed polyurethane, holds the hydrocarbon vapour before they can escape to atmosphere.

The carburettor bowl and the fuel tank, main sources of HC emissions, are directly connected to the adsorbent chamber when engine is turned off, i.e. under hot soak. As already mentioned, hot soak is the condition when a warmed up car is stopped and its engine turned off. This results in some boiling in the carburettor bowl and significant amount of HC loss occurs. Thus

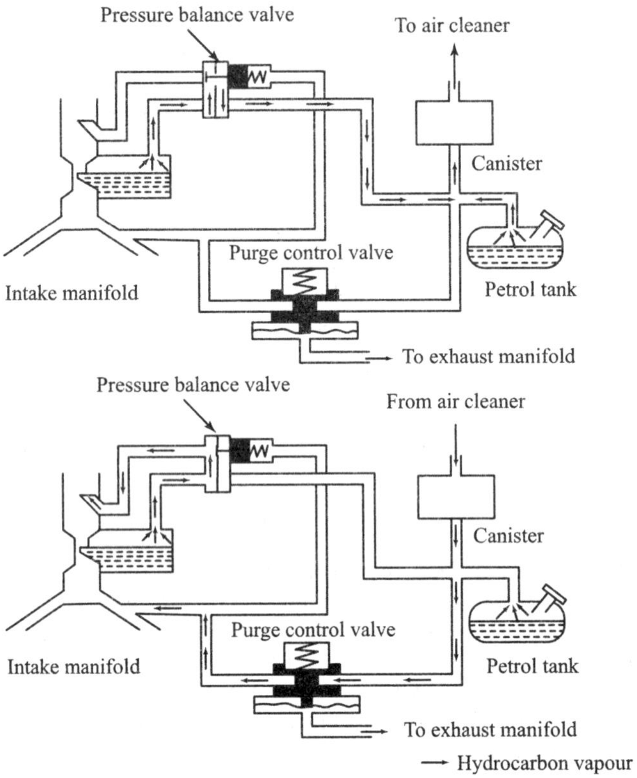

Fig. 14.13 Fuel system evaporation loss control device

the hot soak loss and also the running loss from the carburettor as well as the tank are arrested in the chamber and the absorbed there. Also diurnal cycle loss from the tank is taken care of. Diurnal cycle is the daily cyclic variation in the temperature which causes tank 'breathing' or forcing the gasoline out of tank. The adsorbent bed when saturated is relieved of the vapours by a stripping action allowing the air from the air cleaner to draw them to the intake manifold through the purge valve. The internal seat of the pressure valve at that time is so located that there is a direct pressure communication between the internal vent and the top of the carburettor bowl, maintaining designed carburettor metering forces. The operation of the purge control valve is taken care of by the exhaust back pressure. Under idling conditions the fuel supply is cut off so that the level of HC can be reduced. The ELCD completely controls all types of evaporative losses. However, the tolerance of the carburettor for supplying fuel-air ratio reduces to about 3 per cent only. This requires very accurate metering control.

14.20 MODERN EVAPORATIVE EMISSION CONTROL SYSTEM

A modern evaporative emission control system is illustrated in Fig.14.14. The fuel tank is fitted to the vapour-liquid separator which is in the form of a chamber on the fuel tank. Vapour from the fuel tank goes to the top of the separator where the liquid gasoline is separated and sent back to the fuel tank through the fuel return pipe. A vent valve or a vent hole is provided for the carburettor for the flow of fuel vapours. This vent hole is connected by a tube to the canister. Fuel vapours from the float chamber flow through the vent hole and the tube to the canister. The canister adsorbs the fuel vapours and stores them. *Adsorption* refers to the process of trapping of the gasoline vapours by the activated charcoal particles filled inside the canister. Vapour laden air from both the fuel tank and the carburettor passes through the canister. Hydrocarbons (HC) are left in the canister due to the process of adsorption, and air leaves from the canister into the atmosphere. When an engine is started, the inlet manifold sucks fresh air through the canister.

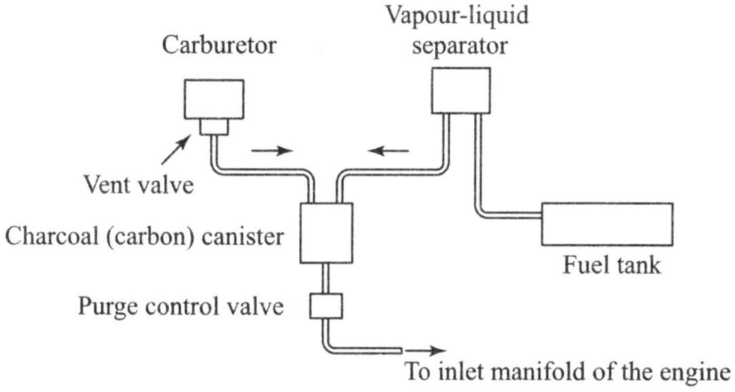

Fig. 14.14 Layout of vapour recovery system

The fresh air purges the gasoline vapours from the canister. 'Purging' is the process by which the gasoline vapours are removed from the charcoal particles inside the canister. The air carries the hydrocarbons (HC) through the purge control solenoid valve to the engine induction system. The purge control solenoid valve is controlled by the Electronic Control Module (ECM) of the Computer Command Control (CCC) system in modern automobiles.

14.20.1 Charcoal Canister

A charcoal canister used for trapping gasoline vapours is shown in Fig.14.15. This type of charcoal canister is used in the evaporative emission control system of a petrol engine. Fuel vapours from the float chamber of the carburetor enter into the canister though the left end passage.

Fuel vapours from the fuel tank enter through the mid passage into the canister. The flow of these vapours is shown by the arrows pointing downwards. When the engine is not running, the fuel vapours flow in this manner . The fuel vapours are absorbed by the charcoal particles present in the canister. When the engine runs, air reaches the charcoal, canister due to the suction provided by the engine. This air carries away the hydrocarbons (HC) in the fuel vapours to the engine manifold. This purging action is shown at the right end of the charcoal canister by the arrows pointing upwards. As charcoal is a form of carbon, the charcoal canister is also called the carbon canister.

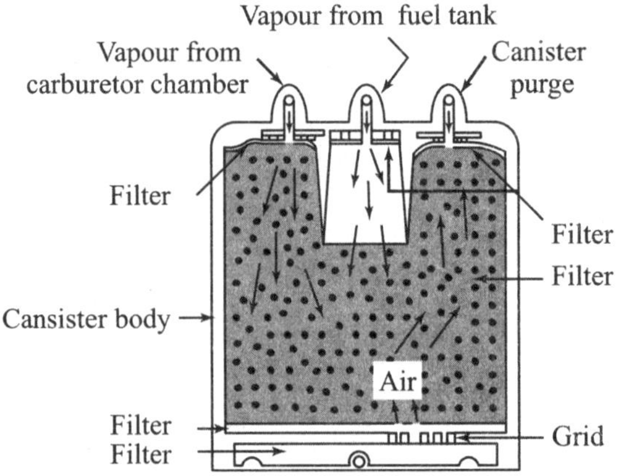

Fig. 14.15 Charcoal canister

14.21 CRANKCASE BLOWBY

The blowby is the phenomenon of leakage past the piston and piston rings from the cylinder to the crankcase. The blowby HC emission are about 20 per cent of the total HC emission from the engine. This is increased to about 35 per cent if the rings are worn.

The blowby rate is greatly affected by the top land clearance and the position of the top ring because some of quenched gas is recycled in the combustion chamber and the ability of this to burn will depend on nearness to spark plug and the flame speed etc. and it will burn only when favourable conditions are there, otherwise it will go in the form of HC.

14.21.1 Blowby Control

The basic principle of all types or crankcase blowby control is recirculation of the vapours back to the intake air cleaner. There are a large number of different systems in use. Figure 14.16 shows typical closed or positive crankcase ventilation systems. In the PCV system the draft tube as shown in Fig.14.17 is eliminated and the blowby gases are rerouted back into the intake manifold or inlet of the carburettor. The blowby gases are consequently reintroduced into the combustion chamber where they are burned along with fresh incoming air and fuel. Since the blowby handling devices place the crankcase under a slight vacuum, they quickly became known as positive crankcase ventilation (PCV) systems.

14.21.2 Intake Manifold Return PCV System (Open Type)

Figure 14.16 (a) shows the intake manifold return PCV or open type system. It has a tube leading from crankcase or else the rocker arm cover through a

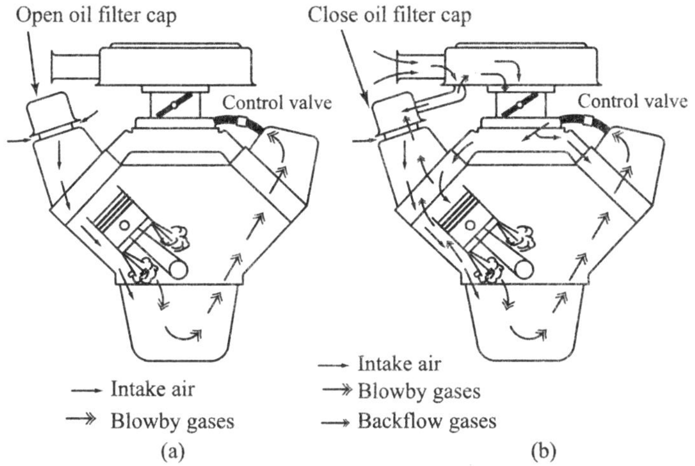

Fig. 14.16 Positive crankcase ventilation

flow control valve and into the intake manifold, usually, through an opening just below the carburettor. To provide proper ventilation of the interior of the engine, fresh air is usually drawn in through a rocker arm cover opposite that containing the PCV system. The closed PCV system Fig.14.16 (b) has a tube connected between the oil fill tube cap and the air cleaner, Both open and closed systems function in the same manner as long as the PCV valve remains unplugged. If the PCV valve plugs, using an open system, the blowby gases exhaust out of the oil fill tube cap and into the atmosphere. With PCV valve plugged it is no longer possible for fresh air crankcase ventilation to occur.

In closed PCV system if the PCV valve is plugged the blowby is rerouted through the tube to the air cleaner and subsequently into the air horn of the carburettor. As can be seen from Fig.14.16 (b) there is no possible escape of blowby into the atmosphere, even with 100 per cent PCV valve plugging. Again, with the PCV valve plugged, fresh air ventilation cannot take place. The closed system, however, requires the engine to digest all blowby developed regardless of the mechanical condition of the PCV system. The PCV valve, located between the crankcase and the intake manifold, controls the flow rate of blowby gas and fresh air mixture going into the intake manifold below the carburettor [Fig.14.16 (b)]. If there is no crankcase ventilation, the blowby will be passed on to the atmosphere as per the path shown in Fig.14.17.

Figure 14.18 shows the two positions of the PCV valve. The design of the valve is such that at high speed and power, i.e. at low manifold vacuum the valve opens and allows a free flow of blowby gases to the intake system. This is consistent with the high quantity of blowby gas which has to be transferred to carburettor at high speed. The valve restricts the flow at high manifold vacuum as the corresponding blowby gas is in small quantity. The air drawn for the ventilation of blowby gas has a very small tolerance. A small amount of air will not affect any circulation and too much air will lift the lubricating oil. Also the carburettor has to be modified and adjusted to account for the charge coming from the crankcase in order to meter exact fuel-air ratio into the

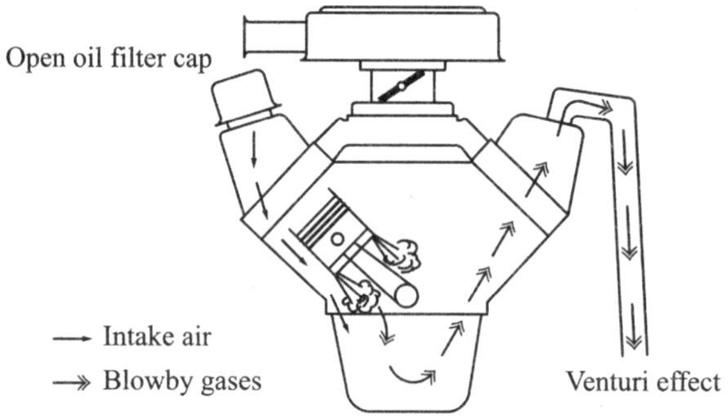

Fig. 14.17 Blowby path without positive crankcase ventilation

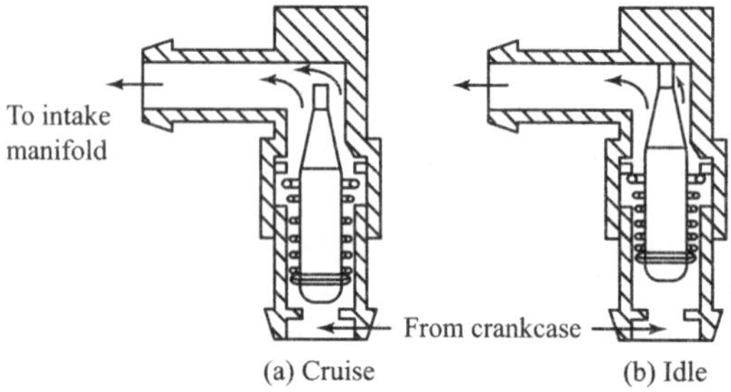

Fig. 14.18 Two positions of PCV valve

combustion chamber. The carburettor deposits and deposits on the blowby gas metering valve will significantly affect the performance of the carburettor. So high grade motor oil has to be used. In the closed ventilation system a provision is made for the blowby gases to escape to atmosphere in case of the metering valve failure.

Review Questions

14.1 What are the causes and problems of exhaust emissions?

14.2 Give a brief account of air pollution due to engines.

14.3 What are the emissions that come out of engine exhaust?

14.4 Describe the causes of hydrocarbon emissions from SI and CI engines.

14.5 How knock emissions are caused and what are their effects on environment?

14.6 Describe in detail about particulate emissions.

14.7 Give a brief account of other emissions from engines.

14.8 What is a thermal converter? How does it help to reduce emissions from engines?

14.9 What are catalytic converters? How do they help in reducing HC, CO and NO_x emissions?

14.10 How does catalytic converters help in reducing HC, CO and NO_x emissions?

14.11 Give a brief account of emissions from CI engines.

14.12 How can emissions be reduced using chemical methods?

14.13 What is EGR? and explain how it reduces the NO_x emission.

14.14 Explain with a sketch the non-exhaust emission from a vehicle.

14.15 Explain with sketches how non-exhaust emission are controlled.

14.16 Explain with a neat sketch fuel system evaporation loss control device.

14.17 Give a layout of a vapour recovery system and explain.

14.18 With a neat sketch explain a charcoal canister for controlling non-exhaust emission.

14.19 What is crankcase blowby? How it is controlled?

14.20 Explain intake manifold open type PCV system.

Multiple Choice Questions (choose the most appropriate answer)

1. Strictest emission norms are initiated in the world first in

   (a) London
   (b) New Delhi
   (c) Tokyo
   (d) California

2. One of the major exhaust emissions from CI engines compared to SI engine is

   (a) oxides of nitrogen
   (b) unburnt hydrocarbons
   (c) particulates
   (d) CO and CO_2

3. Decrease in air-fuel ratio in SI engines results in

   (a) increase of NO_x
   (b) decrease of CO and UBHC
   (c) increase of CO and UBHC
   (d) none of the above

4. NO_x emission is maximum in SI engines when the air-fuel ratio is
   (a) nearly stoichiometric
   (b) lean
   (c) rich
   (d) none of the above
5. NO_x emission in SI engines will be lowest during
   (a) cruising
   (b) idling
   (c) accelerating
   (d) decelerating
6. Photochemical smog is mainly due to
   (a) NO_x and HC
   (b) soot and particulate matter
   (c) CO and CO_2
   (d) excess O_2
7. Alcohol is the major source for the emission of
   (a) HC
   (b) aldehydes
   (c) oxides of nitrogen
   (d) soot
8. Fumigation technique is used to control
   (a) HC
   (b) NO_x
   (c) CO
   (d) smoke
9. Blue smoke in diesel engines indicate
   (a) NO_x
   (b) HC
   (c) CO
   (d) unburnt oil

10. What smoke in CI engines is noticed during

    (a) starting and idling
    (b) light loads
    (c) heavy loads
    (d) acceleration

11. Thermal converters cannot reduce emission of

    (a) CO
    (b) HC
    (c) NO_x
    (d) soot

12. Three way catalytic converters reduce emission of

    (a) CO, CO_2 and soot
    (b) CO, NO_x and HC
    (c) CO_2, NO_x and HC
    (d) CO, HC and soot

13. Platinum and Rhodium promote the oxidation of

    (a) CO, HC
    (b) CO, NO_x
    (c) CO
    (d) HC, NO_x

14. Rhodium promotes the reduction of

    (a) HC
    (b) CO
    (c) NO_x
    (d) CO and HC

15. Efficient operation of catalytic converters require maintenance of

    (a) temperature
    (b) equivalence ratio
    (c) (a) and (b)
    (d) pressure

16. EGR is the most effective way of reducing emission of

    (a) NO_x
    (b) CO
    (c) HC
    (d) CO and HC

17. Exhaust gas recirculation has the disadvantage of

    (a) decreasing thermal efficiency
    (b) increasing HC emission
    (c) (a) and (b)
    (d) increasing aldehydes

18. Evaporative emission in SI engines account for emission of

    (a) 50% CO
    (b) 50% HC
    (c) 100% HC
    (d) 25% HC

19. Chemiluminescence technique is used to measure

    (a) NO_x
    (b) CO
    (c) CO_2
    (d) smoke intensity

20. Lead compounds were added in gasoline to

    (a) reduce HC emissions
    (b) reduce knocking
    (c) reduce exhaust temperature
    (d) increase power output

Ans:					
	1. – (d)	2. – (c)	3. – (c)	4. – (a)	5. – (b)
	6. – (a)	7. – (b)	8. – (d)	9. – (d)	10. – (a)
	11. – (c)	12. – (b)	13. – (a)	14. – (c)	15. – (c)
	16. – (a)	17. – (c)	18. – (d)	19. – (a)	20. – (b)

15
MEASUREMENTS AND TESTING

15.1 INTRODUCTION

The basic task in the design and development of engines is to reduce the cost of production and improve the efficiency and power output. In order to achieve the above task, the development engineer has to compare the engine developed with other engines in terms of its output and efficiency. Towards this end he has to test the engine and make measurements of relevant parameters that reflect the performance of the engine. In general, he has to conduct a wide variety of engine tests. The nature and the type of the tests to be conducted depend upon a large number of factors. It is beyond the scope of this book to discuss all the factors. In this chapter certain basic as well as important measurements and tests are considered.

(i) Friction power

(ii) Indicated power

(iii) Brake power

(iv) Fuel consumption

(v) Air flow

(vi) Speed

(vii) Exhaust and coolant temperature

(viii) Emissions

(ix) Noise

(x) Combustion phenomenon

The details of measurement of these parameters are discussed in the following sections.

15.2 FRICTION POWER

The difference between the indicated and the brake power of an engine is known as friction power. The internal losses in an engine are essentially of two kinds, viz., pumping losses and friction losses. During the inlet and exhaust stroke the gaseous pressure on the piston is greater on its forward side (on the underside during the inlet and on the upper side during the exhaust stroke), hence during both strokes the piston must be moved against a gaseous pressure, and this causes the so called pumping loss. The friction loss is made up of the friction between the piston and cylinder walls, piston rings and cylinder walls, and between the crankshaft and camshaft and their bearings, as well as by the loss incurred by driving the essential accessories, such as the water pump, ignition unit etc.

It should be the aim of the designer to have minimum loss of power in friction. Friction power is used for the evaluation of indicated power and mechanical efficiency. Following methods are used to find the friction power to estimate the performance of the engine.

(i) Willan's line method

(ii) Morse test

(iii) Motoring test

(iv) From the measurement of indicated and brake power

(v) Retardation test

15.2.1 Willan's Line Method

This method is also known as fuel rate extrapolation method. A graph connecting fuel consumption (y-axis) and brake power (x-axis) at constant speed is drawn and it is extrapolated on the negative axis of brake power. The intercept of the negative axis is taken as the friction power of the engine at that speed. The method of extrapolation is shown in Fig.15.1 (dotted lines). As shown in the Fig.15.1, since, in most of the power range the relation between the fuel consumption and brake power is linear which permits extrapolation. Further, when the engine does not develop any power, i.e., $bp = 0$, it consumes a certain amount of fuel. The energy would have been spent in overcoming the friction. Hence, the extrapolated negative intercept of the x-axis will be the work representing the combined losses due to mechanical friction, pumping and blowby and as a whole it is termed the frictional loss of the engine. It should be noted that the measured frictional power by this method will hold good only for a particular speed and is applicable mainly to CI engines.

The main drawback of this method is the long distance to be extrapolated from data obtained between 5 and 40% load towards the zero line of fuel input. The directional margin of error is rather wide because the graph is not exactly linear. The changing slope along the curve indicates the effect of part load efficiency of the engine. The pronounced change in the slope of this line near full load reflects the limiting influence of the air-fuel ratio and of the quality of combustion. Similarly, there may be slight curvature at light loads. This is perhaps due to the difficulty in injecting accurately and consistently very small quantities of fuel per cycle. Therefore, it is essential that great care should be taken in extrapolating the line and as many readings as possible should be taken at light loads to establish the true nature of the curve. The accuracy obtained in this method is reasonably good and compares favourably with other methods if extrapolation is carefully done.

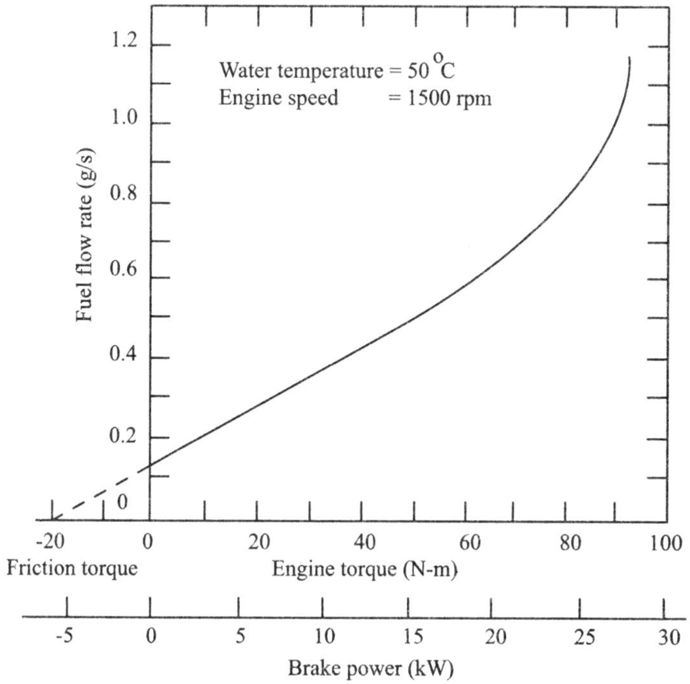

Fig. 15.1 Willan's line method

15.2.2 Morse Test

The Morse test consists of obtaining indicated power of the engine without any elaborate equipment. The test consists of making inoperative, in turn, each cylinder of the engine and noting the reduction in brake power developed. With a gasoline engine each cylinder is rendered inoperative by *shorting* the spark plug of the cylinder; with a diesel engine by cutting off the supply of fuel to each cylinder. It is assumed that pumping and friction losses are the same when the cylinder is inoperative as well as during firing. This test is applicable only to multi cylinder engines. Referring to the Fig.15.2, the unshaded area of the indicator diagram is a measure of the gross power, gp developed by the engine, the dotted area being the pumping power, pp.

$$\text{Net indicated power per cylinder} = gp - pp$$

In this test the engine is first run at the required speed by adjusting the throttle in SI engine or the pump rack in CI engine and the output is measured. The throttle rack is locked in this position. Then, one cylinder is cut out by short circuiting the spark plug in the SI engine or by disconnecting the injector in the CI engine. Under this condition all the other cylinders will *motor* the cut out cylinder and the speed and output drop. The engine speed is brought to its original value by reducing the load. This will ensure that the frictional power is the same while the brake power of the engine will be with one cylinder less.

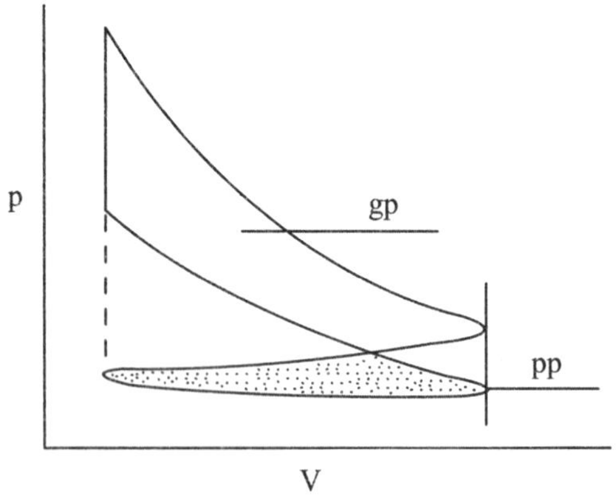

Fig. 15.2 p-V diagram of an Otto engine

If there are k cylinders, then

$$ip_1 + ip_2 + ip_3 + ip_4 + \ldots + ip_k = \sum_1^k bp_k + fp_k \qquad (15.1)$$

where ip, bp and fp are respectively indicated, brake and frictional power and the suffix k stands for the cylinder number.

If the first cylinder is cut-off, it will not produce any power but it will have friction, then

$$ip_2 + ip_3 + ip_4 + \ldots + ip_k = \sum_2^k bp_k + fp_k \qquad (15.2)$$

Subtracting Eqn.15.2 from Eqn.15.1

$$ip_1 = \sum_1^k bp_k - \sum_2^k bp_k$$

Similarly we can find the indicated power of the cylinders, viz., $ip_2, ip_3, ip_4, \ldots, ip_k$.

The total indicated power developed by the engine, ip_k, is given by

$$ip_k = \sum_1^k ip_k \qquad (15.3)$$

when all the k cylinders are working, it is possible to find the brake power, bp_k, of the engine.

The frictional power of the engine is given by

$$fp_k = ip_k - bp_k \qquad (15.4)$$

For a better understanding of this test refer to the worked out examples 17.24 and 17.25.

15.2.3 Motoring Test

In Motoring test the engine is steadily operated at the rated speed by its own power and allowed to remain under the given speed and load conditions for sufficient time so that the temperature of the engine components, lubricating oil and cooling water reaches a steady state. A swinging field type electric dynamometer is used to absorb the power during this period which is most suitable for this test. The ignition is then cut-off and by suitable electric switching devices the dynamometer is converted to run as a motor so as to crank the engine at the same speed at which it was previously operating. The power supply from the above dynamometer is measured which is a measure of the frictional power of the engine at that speed. The water supply is also cut-off during the motoring test so that the actual operating temperatures are maintained to the extent possible.

This method though determines the fp at conditions very near to the actual operating temperatures at the test speed and load, it does not give the true losses occurring under firing conditions due to following reasons:

(i) The temperatures in the motored engine are different from those in a firing engine.

(ii) The pressure on the bearings and piston rings is lower than in the firing engine.

(iii) The clearance between piston and cylinder wall is more (due to cooling) and this reduces the piston friction.

(iv) The air is drawn at a temperature much lower than when the engine is firing because it does not get heat from the cylinder (rather losses heat to the cylinder).

Motoring method, however, gives reasonably good results and is very suitable for finding the losses imparted by various engine components. This insight on the losses caused by various components and other parameters is obtained by progressive stripping off of the engine. First the full engine is motored, then the test is conducted under progressive dismantling conditions keeping water and oil circulation intact. Then the cylinder head can be removed to evaluate by difference, the compression loss. In this manner, piston rings, pistons, etc. can be removed and evaluated for their effect on overall friction.

15.2.4 From the Measurement of Indicated and Brake Power

This is an ideal method by which fp is obtained by computing the difference between indicated power obtained from an indicator diagram and brake power obtained by a dynamometer. This method is mostly used only in research laboratories as it is necessary to have elaborate equipment to obtain accurate indicator diagrams at high speeds.

15.2.5 Retardation Test

This test involves the method of retarding the engine by cutting the fuel supply. The engine is made to run at no load and rated speed taking into all usual precautions. When the engine is running under steady operating conditions the supply of fuel is cut-off and simultaneously the time of fall in speeds by say 20%, 40%, 60%, 80% of the rated speed is recorded. The tests are repeated once again with 50% load on the engine. The values are usually tabulated in an appropriate table. A graph connecting time for fall in speed (x-axis) and speed (y-axis) at no load as well as 50% load conditions is drawn as shown in Fig.15.3.

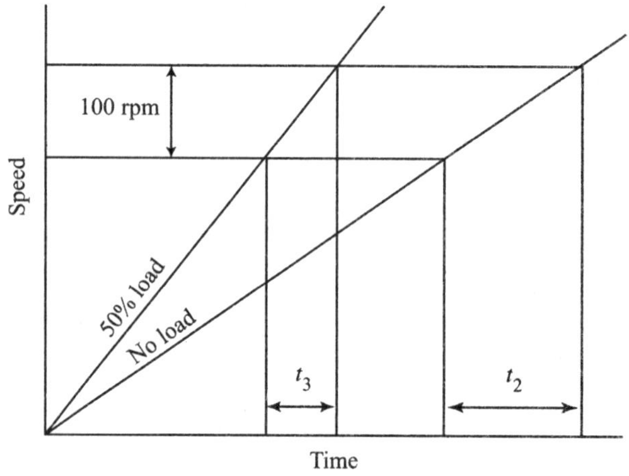

Fig. 15.3 Graph for retardation test

From the graph the time required to fall through the same range (say 100 rpm) in both, no load and load conditions are found. Let t_2 and t_3 be the time of fall at no load and load conditions respectively. The frictional torque and hence frictional power are calculated as shown below. Moment of inertia of the rotating parts is constant throughout the test.

$$\text{Torque} = \text{Moment of Inertia} \times \text{Angular Acceleration}$$

Let ω be the angular velocity and $\frac{d\omega}{dt}$ be the angular acceleration.

$$T = I\frac{d\omega}{dt} \qquad (15.5)$$

$$I = MK^2 \qquad (15.6)$$

therefore,

$$T = MK^2\frac{d\omega}{dt} \qquad (15.7)$$

$$d\omega = \frac{T}{MK^2}dt \qquad (15.8)$$

Now integrating between the limits ω_1 and ω_2 for time t_1 and t_2,

$$\int_{\omega_1}^{\omega_2} d\omega = \frac{T}{MK^2}\int_{t_1}^{t_2} dt \qquad (15.9)$$

therefore,

$$(\omega_2 - \omega_1) = \frac{T}{MK^2}(t_2 - t_1) \tag{15.10}$$

Let T_f be the friction torque and T_l the load torque. At no load the torque is only friction torque, T_f, and at load the torque is $T_l + T_f$. Hence at no load

$$\omega_0 - \omega_1 = \frac{T_f}{MK^2}(t_2 - 0) \tag{15.11}$$

The reference angular velocity, ω_0 is that at, say 1000 rpm, the time of fall for the same range at load

$$\omega_0 - \omega_1 = \frac{T_f + T_l}{MK^2}(t_3 - 0) \tag{15.12}$$

$$(T_f + T_l)t_3 = T_f \; t_2$$

$$\frac{t_2}{t_3} = \frac{T_l + T_f}{T_f} = 1 + \frac{T_l}{T_f} \tag{15.13}$$

$$\frac{T_l}{T_f} = \frac{t_2}{t_3} - 1 = \frac{t_2 - t_3}{t_3} \tag{15.14}$$

$$T_f = T_l\left(\frac{t_3}{t_2 - t_3}\right) \tag{15.15}$$

T_l is the load torque which can be measured from the loading, t_2 and t_3 are observed values. From the above T_f can be calculated and thereby the frictional power. For a better understanding of this test refer the worked out example 16.26.

15.2.6 Comparison of Various Methods

The Willan's line method and Morse tests are comparatively easy to conduct. However, both these tests give only an overall idea of the losses whereas motoring test gives a very good insight into the various causes of losses and is a much more powerful tool. As far as accuracy is concerned, the $ip - bp$ method is the most accurate if carefully done. Motoring method usually gives a higher value for fp as compared to that given by the Willan's line method. Retardation method, though simple, requires accurate determination of the load torque and the time for the fall in speed for the same range.

15.3 INDICATED POWER

Indicated power of an engine tells about the health of the engine and also gives an indication regarding the conversion of chemical energy in the fuel into heat energy. Indicated power is an important variable because it is the potential output of the cycle. Therefore, to justify the measurement of indicated power, it must be more accurate than motoring and other indirect methods of measuring frictional power. For obtaining indicated power the cycle pressure must be determined as a function of cylinder volume. It may be noted that it is of no use to determine pressure accurately unless volume or crank angle can be accurately measured.

In order to estimate the indicated power of an engine the following methods are usually followed.

(i) using the indicator diagram

(ii) by adding two measured quantities viz. brake power and friction power

15.3.1 Method using the Indicator Diagram

The device which measures the variation of the pressure in the cylinder over a part or full cycle is called an *indicator* and the plot of such information obtained is called an *indicator diagram*. Indicator diagram is the only intermediate record available in the account of total liberated energy before it is measured at the output shaft. Thus an indicator diagram gives a very good indication of the process of combustion and in the associated factors such as rate of pressure rise, ignition lag, etc. by its analysis. Also the losses occurring in the suction and exhaust strokes can be studied. It is very rare that an indicator diagram is taken to find indicated power only. It is almost invariably used to study engine combustion, knocking, tuning of inlet and exhaust manifolds, etc.

Pressure-volume, p-V and pressure-crank angle, p-θ, are the two types of indicator diagrams that can be obtained from an engine. Both these indicator diagrams are mutually convertible. An actual indicator diagram is shown in Fig.15.4(a) for a working cycle whereas Fig.15.4(b) is for a missed cycle. During a missed cycle of operation there is no power developed and therefore the entire area is shaded. The direction of the arrows shows the path to be

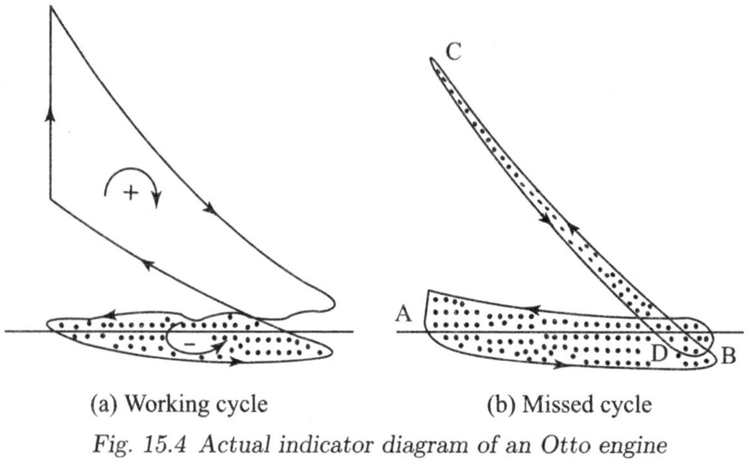

(a) Working cycle (b) Missed cycle

Fig. 15.4 Actual indicator diagram of an Otto engine

followed in the diagram. The sign of an area depends upon the direction in which it is traced and since the shaded area is traced in the reverse direction compared to the unshaded area, which has the opposite sign. The shaded area represents the work done in charging and discharging the cylinder. The elasticity of the column of exhaust gas results in a wavy line on the exhaust stroke. The unshaded area represents the gross power, *gp*, developed and the shaded one represents the pumping power, *pp*. Therefore, the indicated power, $ip = (gp - pp)$. In practice *pp* is generally ignored since it is very small. Thus the area of the indicator diagram if accurately measured will represent the indicated power of the engine.

15.3.2 Engine Indicators

Basically an engine indicating device consists of

(i) a pressure sensing device

(ii) a device for sensing the piston displacement or the angular position of the crankpin over the complete cycle and

(iii) a display device which can depict both pressure and piston displacement on paper or screen.

Some indicators also need additional equipment such as preamplifier to amplify the pressure signal before it can be displayed.

The main types of engine indicators are

(i) Piston indicator

(ii) Balanced diaphragm type indicator

(iii) Electronic indicator

In addition to this, optical indicators are also used. Thus, a large number of indicators are in use. Of the above types, only electronic indicators are in common use at present.

15.3.3 Electronic Indicators

In order to investigate the individual cycles or a part of the cycle, electronic indicators have been developed which consist of four main parts.

(i) a pressure pick-up

(ii) a preamplifying device

(iii) a time-base recording device

(iv) a display unit

The pressure pick-up shown in Fig.15.5 is usually called a pressure transducer. It generates an electric signal in proportion to the pressure to which it is subjected. The transducer is usually fitted in the cylinder head just like a spark plug without projecting into the combustion space. The pressure is picked-up with respect to displacement of a diaphragm. This diaphragm is made very stiff in order to reduce the displacement and hence the inertia effects are reduced to minimum. The displacement of the diaphragm is transmitted to the transducer element which may be any one of the following.

(i) piezo electric crystal

(ii) electromagnetic type

(iii) capacitance type

(iv) strain gauge-type element

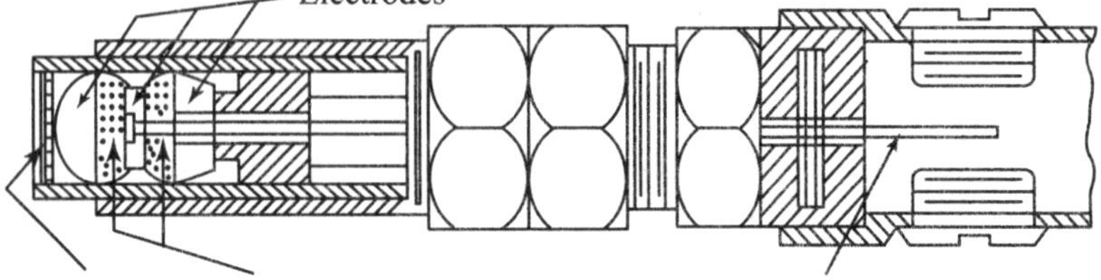

Fig. 15.5 Pressure transducer

The detailed description of these transducer elements and their characteristics is beyond the scope of this book and is not discussed. The transducer element produces an electrical signal which is usually too small to be displayed on any device. Therefore, a preamplifying device is used to augment the signal so that it can be displayed on the oscilloscope or recorded in a recorder.

The pick-up used for measuring the cylinder pressure must have a linear output and a good frequency response. Its temperature behaviour should also be satisfactory, i.e., the effect of heat should not affect its performance. Also it must have low acceleration sensitivity. Of all the pressure transducers currently available the piezo electric quartz transducers are most satisfactory for all normal uses in internal combustion engine measurements as far as the sensitivity is concerned. The quartz transducer, which has a natural frequency greater than 50 kHz, has a sensitivity of about one-tenth of the other types of pressure transducers in which inductive, capacitive or strain-gauge principles are applied. The temperature effect is about 0.005 per cent per degree centigrade change in temperature of the crystal.

The use of electrical pressure pickups avoids almost all the difficulties of a mechanical indicator and gives inertia free operation. However, the greatest problem when using these transducers is the difficulty in calibrating them. A notable exception is strain gauge type transducer which can be satisfactorily calibrated.

Usually the device used to display the p-θ diagram is the storage type cathode ray oscilloscope, CRO. The CRO provides almost inertia free recording and displaying of the pressure signal. The principle of CRO is that a cathode ray can be deflected by the variation of an electric current. It can be of electromagnetic or electrostatic type. Usually the pressure signal from the pressure transducer and the time signal from the time-base pick-up are applied to the two beams of dual beam oscilloscope. This produces a p-θ or p-t diagram on the screen of the oscilloscope which can be observed or photographed. A typical time base unit consists of a permanent magnet with coil and a V-shaped pole piece and a rotating disc having slots in which a magnetic material is fixed. When the disc rotates and a slot passes the permanent magnet it generates a voltage according to its depth and produces a peak on the oscilloscope screen. Usually slots are 1° apart with deeper slots at 10° intervals and still deeper at 90° interval so that a complete degree timing diagram is produced. The disc is so adjusted on the engine shaft that when the deepest slot is against the magnet poles it shows the top dead centre. This type of time base device does not work below about 150 rpm because of weak impulse signal. Hence an oscilloscope triggering circuit is used. A typical p-θ diagram obtained from the electronic indicator is shown in Fig.15.6(a) for 0 to 360° and Fig.15.6(b) for 360 to 720°.

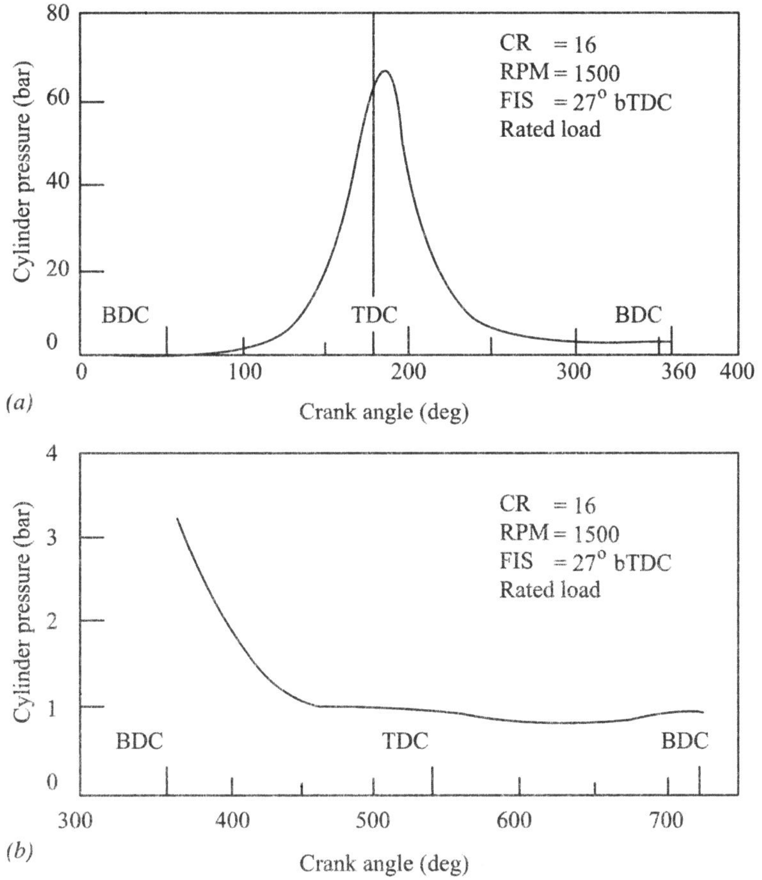

Fig. 15.6 A typical p-θ diagram

15.4 BRAKE POWER

Measurement of brake power is one of the most important measurements in the test schedule of an engine. It involves the determination of the torque and the angular speed of the engine output shaft. The torque measuring device is called a dynamometer. Figure 15.7 shows the basic principle of a dynamometer. A rotor driven by the engine under test, is mechanically, hydraulically or electromagnetically coupled to a stator. For every revolution

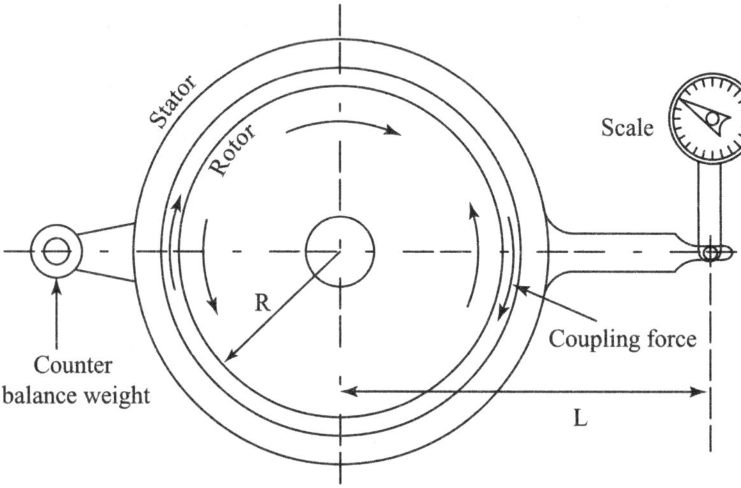

Fig. 15.7 Principle of a dynamometer

of the shaft, the rotor periphery moves through a distance $2\pi R$ against the coupling force, F. Hence the work done per revolution is

$$W = 2\pi RF \tag{15.16}$$

The external moment or torque is equal to $S \times L$, where S is the scale reading and L is the arm length. This moment balances the turning moment $R \times F$, i.e.,

$$S \times L = R \times F \tag{15.17}$$

Therefore

$$\text{Work done/revolution} = 2\pi SL$$

$$\text{Work done/minute} = 2\pi SLN$$

Hence brake power is given by

$$bp = 2\pi NT \text{ Watts} \tag{15.18}$$

where T is the torque and N is rpm.

Dynamometers can be broadly classified into two main types:

(i) *Absorption Dynamometers*: These dynamometers measure and absorb the power output of the engine to which they are coupled. The power absorbed is usually dissipated as heat by some means. Examples of such dynamometers are prony brake, rope brake, hydraulic, eddy current dynamometers, etc.

(ii) *Transmission Dynamometer*: In transmission dynamometers the power is transmitted to the load coupled to the engine after it is indicated on some type of scale. These are also called torquemeters.

The terms brake and dynamometer mean the same. A dynamometer is also a brake except the measuring devices are included to indicate the amount of force required in attempting to stop the engine.

15.4.1 Prony Brake

One of the simplest methods of measuring power output of an engine is to attempt to stop the engine by means of a mechanical brake on the flywheel and measure the weight which an arm attached to the brake will support, as it tries to rotate with the flywheel. This system is known as the *prony brake* and from its use, the expression brake power has come. The prony brake consists of a frame with two brake shoes gripping the flywheel (see Fig.15.8).

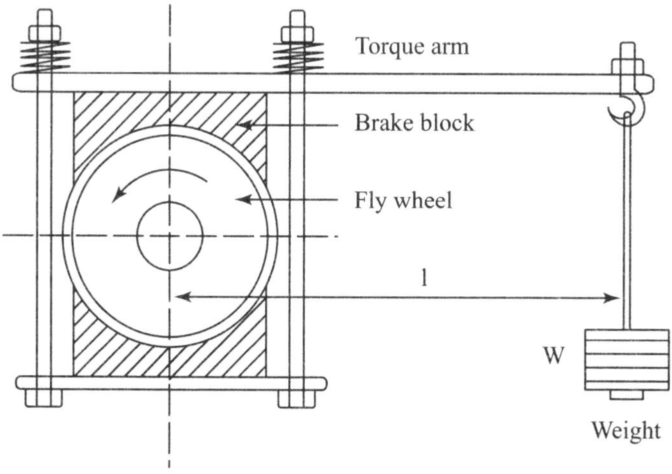

Fig. 15.8 Prony brake

The pressure of the brake shoes on the fly wheel can be varied by the spring loaded using nuts on the top of the frame. The wooden block when pressed into contact with the rotating drum opposes the engine torque and the power is dissipated in overcoming frictional resistance. The power absorbed is converted into heat and hence this type of dynamometer must be cooled. The brake power is given by

$$bp = 2\pi NT \tag{15.19}$$

$$T = Wl \tag{15.20}$$

W being the weight applied at a distance l.

15.4.2 Rope Brake

The rope brake as shown in Fig.15.9 is another simple device for measuring *bp* of an engine. It consists of a number of turns of rope wound around the rotating drum attached to the output shaft. One side of the rope is connected to a spring balance and the other to a loading device. The power absorbed is due to friction between the rope and the drum. The drum therefore requires cooling.

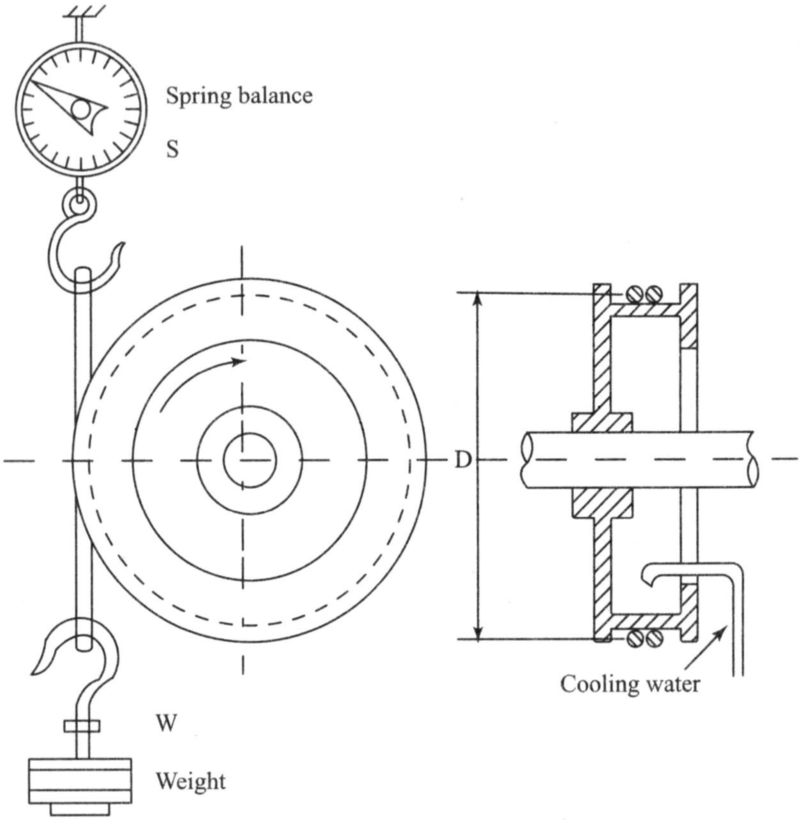

Fig. 15.9 Rope brake

Rope brake is quite cheaper and can be easily fabricated but not very accurate because of changes in the friction coefficient of the rope with temperature.

The *bp* is given by

$$bp = \pi DN(W - S) \tag{15.21}$$

where D is the brake drum diameter, W is the weight and S is the spring scale reading.

15.4.3 Hydraulic Dynamometer

The hydraulic dynamometer (Fig.15.10) works on the principle of dissipating the power in fluid friction rather than in dry friction. In principle its construction is similar to that of a fluid flywheel. It consists of an inner rotating member or impeller coupled to the output shaft of the engine. This impeller

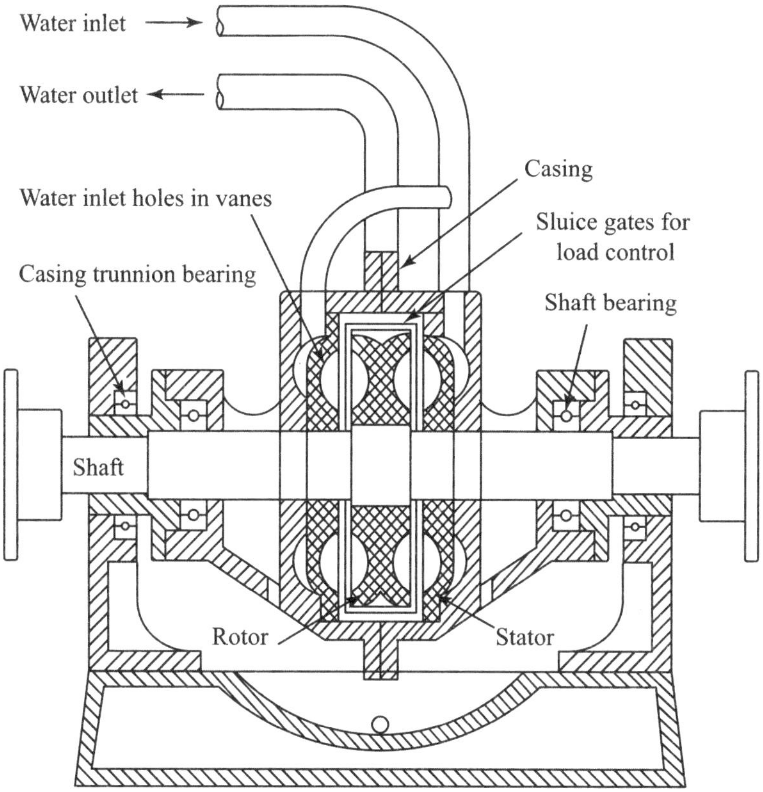

Fig. 15.10 Hydraulic dynamometer

rotates in a casing filled with some hydraulic fluid. The outer casing, due to the centrifugal force developed, tends to revolve with the impeller, but is resisted by a torque arm supporting the balance weight. The frictional forces between the impeller and the fluid are measured by the spring-balance fitted on the casing. The heat developed due to dissipation of power is carried away by a continuous supply of the working fluid, usually water. The output can be controlled by regulating the sluice gates which can be moved in and out to partially or wholly obstruct the flow of water between impeller and the casing.

15.4.4 Eddy Current Dynamometer

The details of eddy current dynamometer are shown in Fig.15.11. It consists of a stator on which are fitted a number of electromagnets and a rotor disc made of copper or steel and coupled to the output shaft of the engine. When the rotor rotates eddy currents are produced in the stator due to magnetic flux set up by the passage of field current in the electromagnets. These eddy currents oppose the rotor motion, thus loading the engine. These eddy currents are dissipated in producing heat so that this type of dynamometer also requires some cooling arrangement. The torque is measured exactly as in other types of absorption dynamometers i.e., with the help of a moment arm. The load is controlled by regulating the current in the electromagnets.

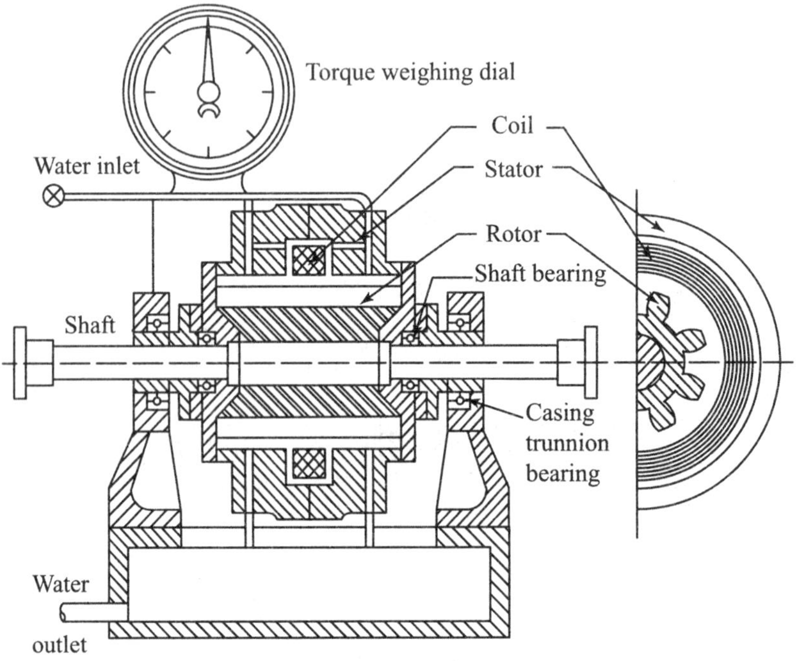

Fig. 15.11 Eddy current dynamometer

The main advantages of eddy current dynamometers are:

(i) Capable of measuring high power per unit weight of the dynamometer.

(ii) They offer the highest ratio of constant brake power to speed range (up to 5:1).

(iii) Level of field excitation is below 1 per cent of total power being handled by dynamometer, thus easy to control and operate.

(iv) Development of eddy current is smooth hence the torque is also smooth and continuous under almost all conditions.

(v) Relatively higher torque under low speed conditions.

(vi) Has no intricate rotating parts except shaft bearing.

(vii) No natural limit to size, either small or large.

15.4.5 Swinging Field DC Dynamometer

Basically a swinging field DC dynamometer is a DC shunt motor so supported in *trunnion* bearings to measure the reaction torque that the outer case and field coils tend to rotate due to the magnetic drag. Hence the name *swinging field*. The torque is measured with an arm and weighing equipment in the usual manner.

These dynamometers are provided with suitable electric connections to run as motor also. Then the dynamometer is reversible, i.e., works as a motoring as well as power absorbing device. When used as an absorption dynamometer it works as a DC generator and converts mechanical energy into electric energy which is dissipated in an external resistor or fed back to the mains. When used as a motoring device an external source of DC voltage is needed to drive the motor. The load is controlled by changing the field current.

15.4.6 Fan Dynamometer

A fan dynamometer is shown in Fig.15.12. This dynamometer is also an absorption type of dynamometer in that when driven by the engine it absorbs the engine power. Such dynamometers are useful mainly for rough testing and running in. The accuracy of the fan dynamometer is very poor. It is also quite difficult to adjust the load. The power absorbed is determined by using previous calibration of the fan brake.

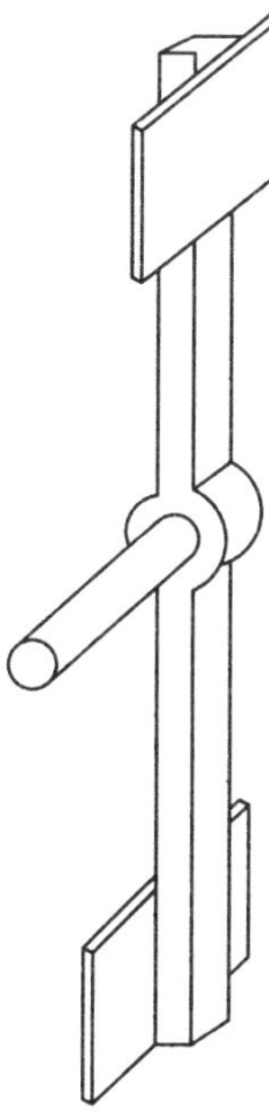

Fig. 15.12 Fan dynamometer

15.4.7 Transmission Dynamometer

Transmission dynamometers, also called torquemeters, mostly consist of a set of strain gauges fixed on the rotating shaft and the torque is measured by the angular deformation of the shaft which is indicated as strain of the strain gauge. Usually a four-arm bridge is used to reduce the effect of temperature to minimum and the gauges are arranged in pairs such that the effect of axial or transverse load on the strain gauges is avoided.

Figure 15.13 shows a transmission dynamometer which employs beams and strain-gauges for a sensing torque.

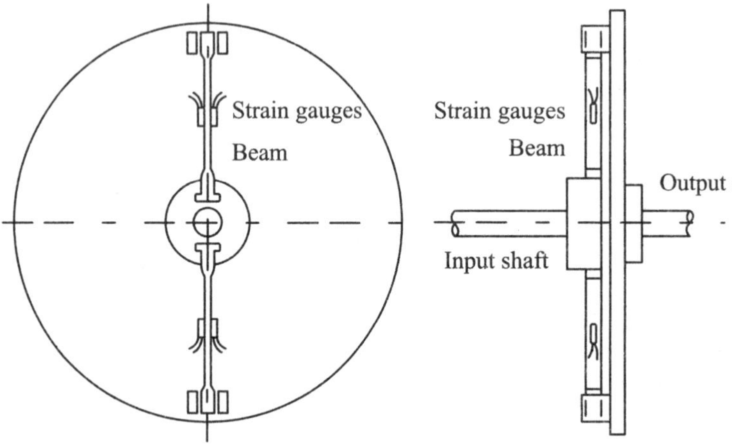

Fig. 15.13 Transmission dynamometer

Transmission dynamometers are very accurate and are used where continuous transmission of load is necessary. These are used mainly in automatic units.

15.4.8 Chassis Dynamometer

In order to test the complete vehicle a *chassis dynamometer* is used. Use of chassis dynamometer allows the test engineer to simulate road load conditions in a laboratory and it can be termed as *all weather road* for the test vehicle. The *road load* on the vehicle can be put on the engine on a chassis dynamometer and quick results can be obtained. However, this dynamometer is quite expensive to install.

15.5 FUEL CONSUMPTION

There is two ways of expressing fuel consumption viz. by volume or by weight during a specified time. For automobiles it is expressed in terms of kilometers per litre.

Accurate measurement of fuel consumption is very important in engine testing work. Though this seems to be a simple matter, it is by no means so as apparent from the occurrence of the following phenomena:

(i) Due to engine heat, vapour bubbles are formed in the fuel line. When the bubble grows the fuel volume increases and back flow of fuel take place. Some fuel flowmeters measure this backflow as if it was forward flow. Some meters do not count backward flow but when the bubble collapses a forward flow takes place which is counted.

(ii) If bubbles are formed before or inside the flowmeter the measured flow can be much higher than actual.

(iii) If there is any swirl in the fuel flow especially in the case of turbine type flowmeter it may register a higher flow rate.

(iv) The density of the fuel is dependent on temperature which can vary over a wide range (-10 °C to 70 °C) giving rise to an error in measurement.

(v) Some flowmeters which use a light beam, the measurement may be affected by the colour of the fuel.

(vi) The needle valve in the float bowl of the carburettor opens and closes periodically allowing fuel to surge into the float bowl. This may cause water hammer type effect making the turbine type flowmeter to continue to rotate even when fuel flow has stopped, thereby producing errors in flow measurements.

As already mentioned two basic type of fuel measurement methods are

(i) Volumetric type

(ii) Gravimetric type

15.5.1 Volumetric Type Flowmeter

The simplest method of measuring volumetric fuel consumption is using glass bulbs of known volume and having a mark on each side of the bulb. Time taken by the engine to consume this volume is measured by a stop watch. Volume divided by time will give the volumetric flow rate.

Burette Method: It consists of two spherical glass bulbs having 100 cc and 200 cc capacity respectively (Fig.15.14). They are connected by three way cocks so that one may feed the engine while the other is being filled. The glass bulbs are of different capacities so as to make the duration of the tests approximately constant irrespective of the engine load whilst the spherical form combines strength with a small variation of fuel head which is most important particularly in case of carburettor engines.

In order to avoid the error in sighting the fuel level against the mark on the burette photocells are used. Figure 15.14 shows such an arrangement in which the measurement is made automatic.

Automatic Burette Flowmeter: Figure 15.15 shows an automatic volumetric type fuel flow measuring system which is commercially available. It consists of a measuring volume (A) which has a photocell (B) and a light source (C) fitted in tubular housings. These housings are put opposite to each other at an angle such that a point of light is formed on the axis of the

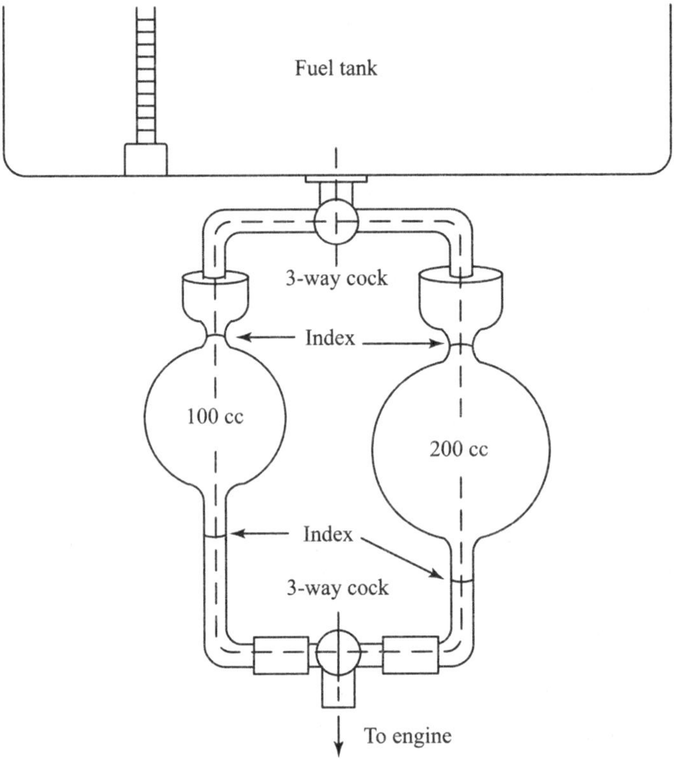

Fig. 15.14 Burette method of measuring fuel consumption

measuring volume as shown in Fig.15.15 and one each is put on lower and upper portions of the measuring cylinder. An equalization chamber (D) is connected to the measuring tube via the air tube (E) and magnetic valve (F) and equalization pipe (G) to provide an air cushion at supply line pressure and to store fuel during measurement.

On pressing the start button the lamps in the two photoelectric systems light up and the magnetic valve stops the flow through the instrument. The fuel level in the measuring volume starts falling at a rate depending upon the engine consumption. At the same time an equal amount of the flows through the equalization tube to the equalization chamber. When the fuel level reaches the upper measuring level (H), the focused beam of light from the lamp is reflected on to the opposite photocell and converted into an electrical signal to start a timer counter. When the fuel level has fallen further to reach the lower measuring level the new signal generated stops the timer counter. The lamps are automatically switched off and the valve opened and the regular flow is restored. The time period for the consumption of the chosen volume of fuel is thus recorded.

Orifice Flowmeters: Sometimes flowmeters are also used for this purpose. Flowmeters depend on the pressure drop across an orifice. Two orifices, X and Y are shown in Fig.15.16. These orifices are pre-calibrated in terms of

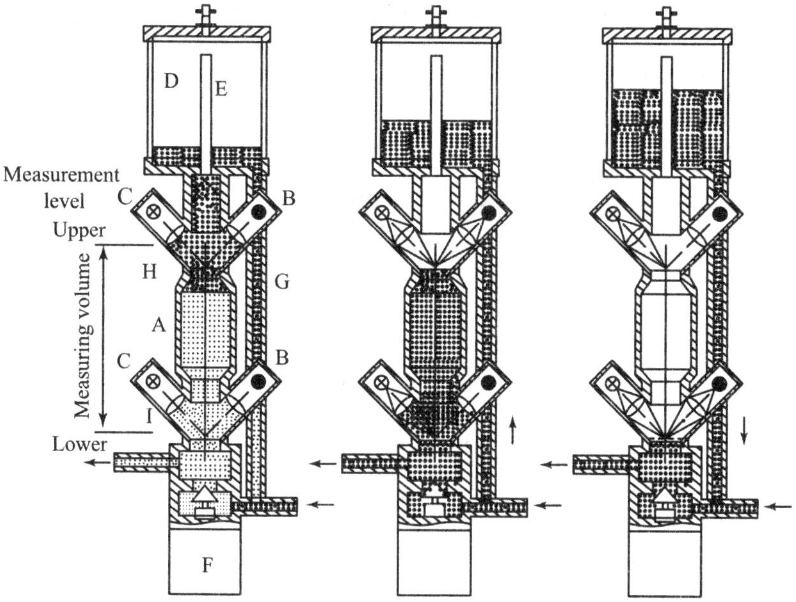

Fig. 15.15 Automatic volumetric fuel flowmeter

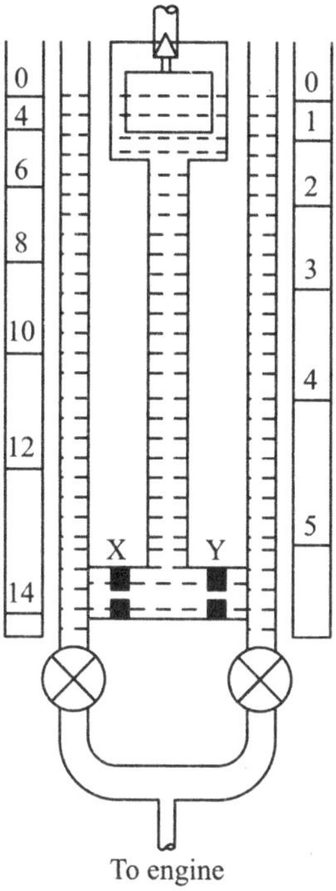

Fig. 15.16 Orifice flowmeter

the fuel being used and direct observations in terms of volume of fuel supplied per hour may be recorded. One or two orifices may be used at a time. Orifices can also be changed for different rates of flow. In that case calibration scales have also got to be changed.

15.5.2 Gravimetric Fuel Flow Measurement

The efficiency of an engine is generally related to the kilograms of fuel which are consumed and not to the number of litres. The method of measuring volume flow and then correcting it for specific gravity variations is quite inconvenient and inherently limited in accuracy. Instead if the weight of the fuel consumed is directly measured a great improvement in accuracy and cost can be obtained.

The method involves weighing the fuel supplied to the engine by an arrangement as shown in Fig.15.17. In this method the valve A is opened whenever the engine is to be run without measuring the rate of fuel supply and valve B is closed so that fuel from tank directly flows to the engine. The fuel from the tank is supplied to the flask by opening valves A and B whenever measurement of the fuel is to be done. On the balance the amount of fuel is weighed. Keeping the valve B open the valve A is closed so that the fuel from flask is syphoned off to the engine. This method avoids separate determination of the specific gravity of the fuel. The time taken to syphon off the weighed fuel completely is noted by means of a stop watch. Thus the fuel consumption in gravimetric units is obtained.

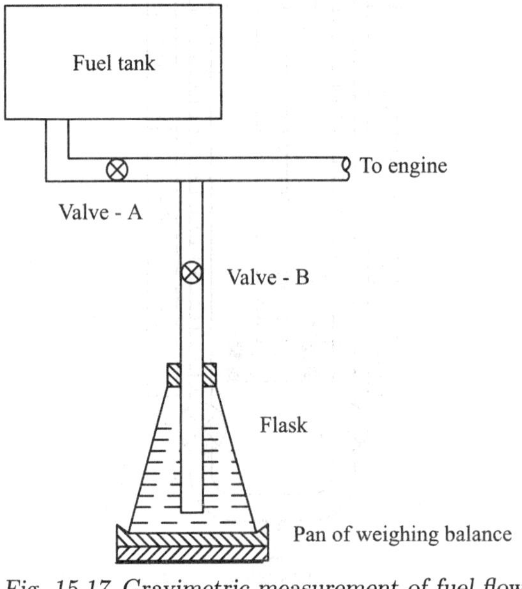

Fig. 15.17 Gravimetric measurement of fuel flow

15.5.3 Fuel Consumption Measurement in Vehicles

The third way of expressing fuel consumption is by measuring the fuel consumption in kilometers per litre. The instrument as shown in Fig.15.18 is usually used which accurately checks the amount of fuel used by any vehicle under test. A glass burette of 1 litre capacity is connected by tubes and control valves so that the precise number of km/litre is observed on an actual road test. The instrument shows the effect of speed, traffic, loading, driver's habits and engine conditions on fuel consumption. The tester is hung on the top edge of the right front door glass or similarly suitable location and connection is made by special plastic tubes and the adapters provided. The surplus capacity of the fuel pump fills the glass burette when the needle valve is opened, and when a test run is made the control tap directs the fuel to the intake side of the fuel pump. Thus the carburettor is supplied at normal working pressure. Speedometer readings in kilometers and tenths for each 0.5 litres used, make calculations of actual consumption simple and accurate.

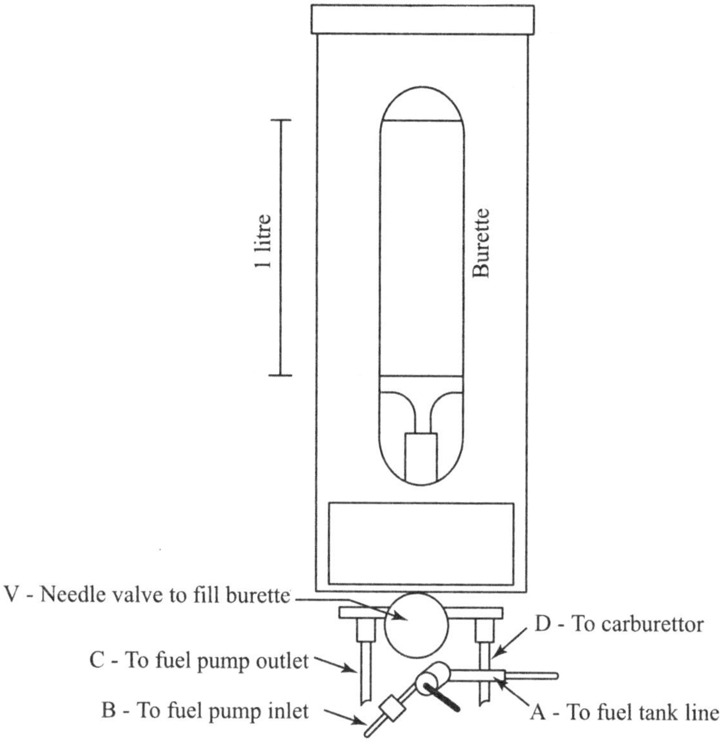

Fig. 15.18 Fuel consumption measurements in vehicles

15.6 AIR CONSUMPTION

The diet of an engine consists of air and fuel. For finding out the performance of the engine accurate measurement of both the quantities is essential.

In IC engines the satisfactory measurement of air consumption is quite difficult because *the flow is pulsating due to the cyclic nature of the engine* and because the air is a compressible fluid. Therefore, the simple method of using an orifice in the induction pipe is not satisfactory since the reading will be pulsating and unreliable.

All kinetic flow inferring systems such as nozzles, orifices and venturies have a square law relationship between flow rate and differential pressure which gives rise to severe errors on unsteady flow. Pulsation produced errors are roughly inversely proportional to the pressure across the orifice for a given set of flow conditions.

15.6.1 Air Box Method

The orifice method can be used if pressure pulsations could be damped out by some means. The usual method of damping out pulsations is to fit an air box of suitable volume (500 to 600 times the swept volume in single cylinder engines and less in the case of multi-cylinder engines) to the engine with an orifice placed in the side of the box remote from the engine (Fig.15.19).

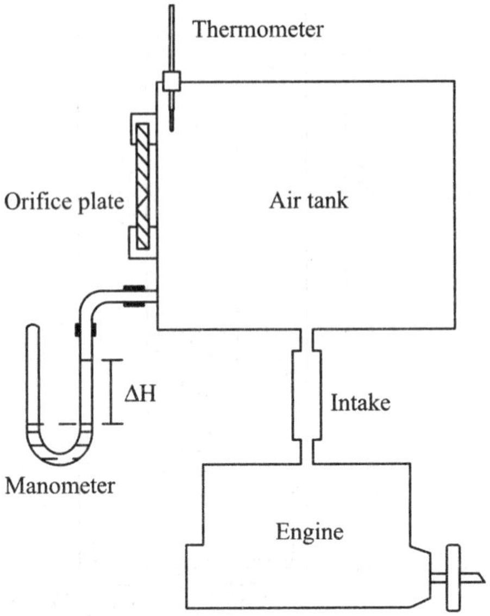

Fig. 15.19 Measurement of air by air box method

15.6.2 Viscous-Flow Air Meter

The use (Fig.15.20) of viscous flow airmeter gives accurate reading for pulsating flows. This meter uses an element where viscous resistance is the principal source of pressure loss and kinetic effects are small. This gives a linear relationship between pressure difference and flow instead of a square-law. From this it follows that a true mean-flow indication is obtained under pulsating flow conditions.

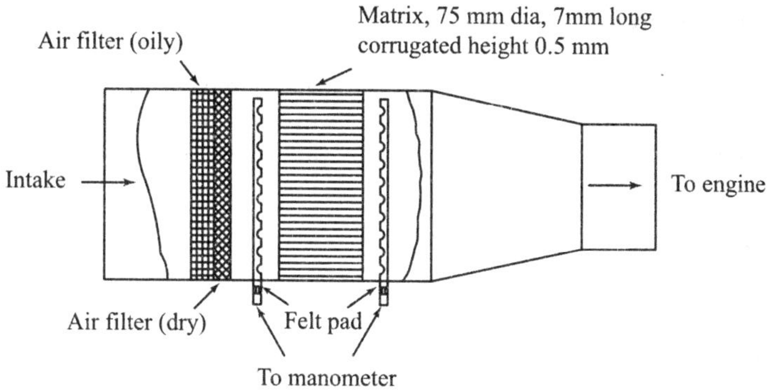

Fig. 15.20 Alcock viscous-flow air meter

The viscous element is in the form of a honeycomb passage (a very large number of passages, Reynolds number being less than 200). The passages are triangular of the size approximately $0.5 \times 0.5 \times 75$ mm.

The chief source of error in viscous meters arises from surface contamination of the small triangular passages. However, by ensuring good filtration at the entry to the meter, and not passing air through the meter unless readings are required, this trouble can be minimized. An advantage of viscous-flow meter is that larger range of flow can be measured without pressure head being too small. Nowadays positive displacement type of flowmeters is also used for the measurement of air consumption.

15.7 SPEED

Speed measurement is an art. Speed of the engine is widely used in the computation of power, design and development. Measurement of speed is accomplished by instruments like mechanical counters and timers, mechanical tachometers, stroboscope, electric counters, tachometers, electric generators, electronic pulse counters etc. The best method of measuring speed is to count the number of revolution in a given time. This gives an accurate measurement of speed. Many engines are fitted with such revolution counters. A mechanical or electrical tachometer can also be used for measuring speed. Both these types are affected by temperature variation and are not very accurate. For accurate and continuous measurements of speed a magnetic pick-up placed near a toothed wheel coupled to the engine shaft can be used. The magnetic pick-up will produce a pulse for every revolution and a pulse counter will accurately measure the speed.

15.8 EXHAUST AND COOLANT TEMPERATURE

Simplest way of measuring the exhaust temperature is by means of a thermocouple. Nowadays electronic temperature sensitive transducers are available which can be used for temperature measurements. Ultra violet radiation analyzers also have come into use for measuring temperatures. Coolant temperatures are normally measured using suitable thermometers.

15.9 EMISSION

From the point of view of pollution control, measurement of emissions from engines is very important. Emissions may be divided into two groups, viz., invisible emissions and visible emissions. The exhaust of an engine may contain one or more of the following:

(i) carbon dioxide

(ii) water vapour

(iii) oxides of nitrogen

(iv) unburnt hydrocarbons

(v) carbon monoxide

(vi) aldehydes

(vii) smoke and

(viii) particulate

Out of the eight the first six may be grouped as invisible emissions and the last two as visible emissions. Out of the various invisible emissions carbon dioxide and water vapour are considered harmless compared to others. Hence, their measurements are not discussed. We will briefly describe the measurement of other invisible emissions.

15.9.1 Oxides of Nitrogen

Oxides of nitrogen which also occur only in the engine exhaust are a combination of nitric oxide (NO) and nitrogen dioxide (NO_2). Nitrogen and oxygen react at relatively high temperatures. Therefore, high temperatures and availability of oxygen are the two main reasons for the formation of NO_x. When the proper amount of oxygen is available, the higher the peak combustion temperature the more is the NO formed.

The NO_x concentration in exhaust is affected by engine design and the mode of vehicle operation. Air-fuel ratio and the spark advance are the two important factors which significantly affect NO_x emissions. The maximum NO_x is formed at ratios between 14:1 and 16:1. At lean and rich air-fuel mixtures the NO_x concentration is comparatively low. Increasing the ignition advance will result in lower peak combustion temperatures and higher exhaust temperatures. This will result in high NO_x concentration in the exhaust.

Internationally accepted method for measuring oxides of nitrogen is by chemiluminescence analyzer. The details are shown in Fig.15.21. The principle of measurement is based on chemiluminescence reaction between ozone and NO resulting in the formation of excited NO_2. This excited NO_2 emits light whose intensity is proportional to NO concentration. The light intensity is measured by a photo multiplier tube. The analyzer measures only nitric oxide, NO, and not NO_2. To analyze all the oxides of nitrogen a converter

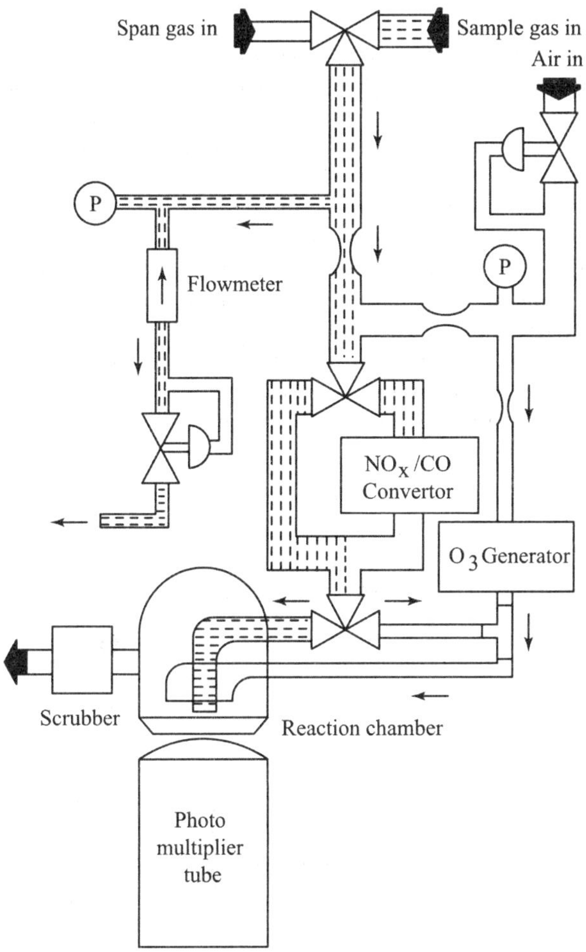

Fig. 15.21 Chemiluminescence method of measuring oxides of nitrogen

is usually fitted ahead of the reaction chamber to convert all the oxides of nitrogen into nitric oxide. Thereby, the light intensity can be taken to be proportional to the oxides of nitrogen concentration in the sample.

15.9.2 Carbon Monoxide

Carbon monoxide occurs only in engine exhaust. It is a product of incomplete combustion due to insufficient amount of air in the air-fuel mixture or insufficient time in the cycle for completion of combustion. Theoretically, the gasoline engine exhaust, can be made free of CO by operating it at air-fuel mixture ratios greater than 16:1. However, that some CO is always present in the exhaust even at lean mixtures.

The percentage of CO decreases with speed. In passenger cars CO percentage has been found to be as high as 5 per cent with rich mixtures and

1% with near stoichiometric mixtures. The complete elimination of CO is not possible and 0.5 per cent CO should be considered a reasonable goal. Carbon monoxide emissions are high when the engine is idling and reach a minimum value during deceleration. They are the lowest during acceleration and at steady speeds. Closing of the throttle which reduces the oxygen supply to engine is the main cause of CO production, so deceleration from high speed will produce highest CO in exhaust gases.

Non Dispersive Infra-Red analyzer (NDIR) as shown in Fig.15.22 is the widely accepted instrument for measuring CO. This instrument is presently used for the testing and legal certification of some automotive exhaust emissions. In the NDIR analyzer the exhaust gas species being measured are used to detect themselves. The method of detection is based on the principle of selective absorption of the infrared energy of a particular wave length peculiar to a certain gas which will be absorbed by that gas.

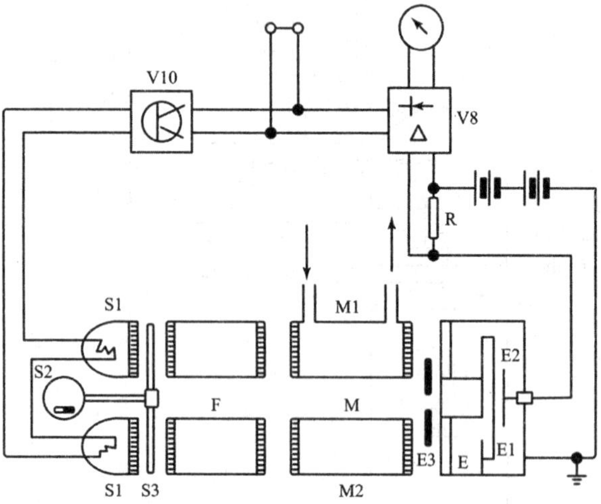

E	Receiver	M1	Sample cell
E1	Diaphragm	M2	Reference cell
E2	Fixed counter electrode	R	High impedance resistor
E3	Receiver trimmer	S1	I R sources
F	Filter cell	S2	Motor
G	DC supply	S3	Shutter wheel
M	Measuring cell	V8	Amplifier
		V10	Mains stabilization

Fig. 15.22 NDIR method of measuring carbon monoxide

15.9.3 Unburned Hydrocarbons

Unburnt hydrocarbons emissions are the direct result of incomplete combustion. The pattern of hydrocarbon emissions is closely related to many design and operating variables. Two of the important design variables are induction system design and combustion chamber design, while main operating variables are air-fuel ratio, speed, load and mode of operation. Maintenance is also an important factor. Induction system design and engine maintenance affect the operating air-fuel ratio of the engine and hence the emission of hydrocarbons and carbon monoxide. Induction system determines fuel distribution of cylinders, fuel economy, available power etc. And the quantity of engine maintenance determines whether the engine will operate at the designed air-fuel ratio and for how long. This will include piston ring wear, lubrication, cooling, deposits and other factors which are likely to affect the air-fuel ratio supplied or its combustion in the combustion chamber.

The design of the combustion chamber is important. A portion of the fuel-air mixture in the combustion chamber comes into direct contact with the chamber walls and are quenched and do not burn. Some of this quenched fuel-air mixture is forced out of the chamber during the exhaust stroke and, because of the high local concentration of hydrocarbon in this mixture, contributes to the high hydrocarbon exhaust from the engine. A small displacement engine will have a higher surface-to-volume ratio than an engine with a large displacement. Factors like combustion chamber shape, bore diameter, stroke and compression ratio affect the surface-to-volume ratio and hence the hydrocarbon emission. Lower compression ratio, higher stroke to bore ratio, larger displacement per cylinder and fewer cylinders, all lower the surface-to-volume ratio and hence the hydrocarbons. The effect of air-fuel ratio on the HC emission is exactly like that on carbon monoxide. At near stoichiometric fuel-air mixtures both hydrocarbon and carbon monoxide (HC/CO) emissions are higher and lean fuel mixtures have substantially low HC/CO emission.

Flame Ionization Detector (FID) is used for measuring hydrocarbons. This instrument as shown in Fig.15.23 is a well established and accepted method for measuring HC. Ionization is a characteristic of HC compound. This principle is employed in the FID detector. Formation of electrically charged particles of ionized carbon atoms from the hydrocarbons in a hydrogen-oxygen flame is achieved in the FID analyzer. Current flow in micro amperes (amplified for measurements) is a measure of the concentration of hydrocarbons.

15.9.4 Aldehydes

The emission of odourous oxygenated hydrocarbons from the engines is generally carcinogenic. The use of alcohol based fuels can lead to higher levels of oxygenated hydrocarbon emissions. These aldehydes are responsible for the pungent smell of the engine exhaust and a trained human personnel specifies the odour ratings for the emission sample by comparison. The methods of measurement for aldehydes are based on wet chemical methods (analytical methods) like iodine titration technique (ITT), chromotropic acid (CA) method, 3-methyl 2-benzo-thiazolene hydrazone (MBTH) method and 2,4 Dinitrophenyl hydrazine (DNPH) method. While the first two methods are meant to measure total aldehydes, the DNPH method is for individual aldehydes and the CA method is only for the formaldehyde.

All the above described wet chemical methods excepting the improved DNPH method, even though time consuming and cumbersome, are economical. Various other methods available are Fourier Transform-Infrared Spectroscopy (FT-IR), Derivative Spectrophotometry and Portable Polarigraph.

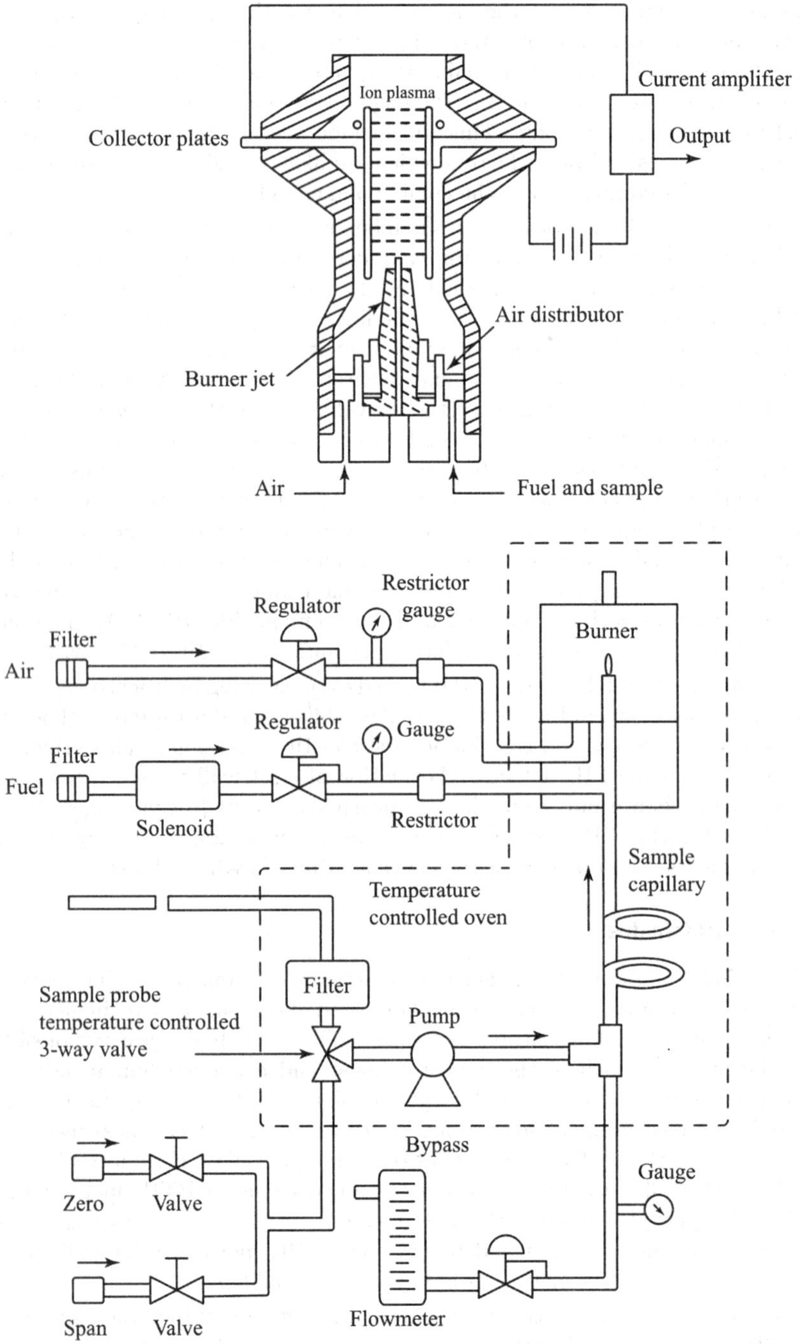

Fig. 15.23 Flame ionization method for measuring unburnt hydrocarbons

15.10 VISIBLE EMISSIONS

Compared to harmful and invisible emissions, visible emissions are more irritating and cause nuisance. Especially in diesel engines, smoke is one of visible emissions. The details are discussed in the following sections.

15.10.1 Smoke

The smoke of the engine exhaust is a visible indicator of the combustion process in the engine. Smoke is due to incomplete combustion. Smoke in diesel engine can be divided into three categories viz., blue, white and black. Visible method of analysis is used for quantifying the above three types of smokes. Smoke measurements can be broadly classified into two groups viz. comparison method and obscuration method.

Comparison Method: Most ordinances regulating smoke emissions are based on estimation of the density of the smoke as it emerges from the exhaust. Of the several available methods, the one of the commonly used method is the Ringelmann Chart. The chart shows four shades of gray, as well as a pure white and an all-black section. To overcome the difficulty of reproducing various shades of gray, the intermediate shades are built from black lines of various widths (Fig.15.24). The four intermediate charts are printed by the United States Bureau of Mines on a single 70 cm $\times$ 25 cm sheet. They may be reproduced as follows:

0 All white

1 Black lines 1 mm thick, 10 mm apart, leaving white spaces 9 mm square.

2 Lines 2.3 mm thick, spaces 7.7 mm square.

3 Lines 3.7 mm thick, spaces 6.3 mm square.

4 Lines 5.5 mm thick, spaces 4.5 mm square.

5 All black.

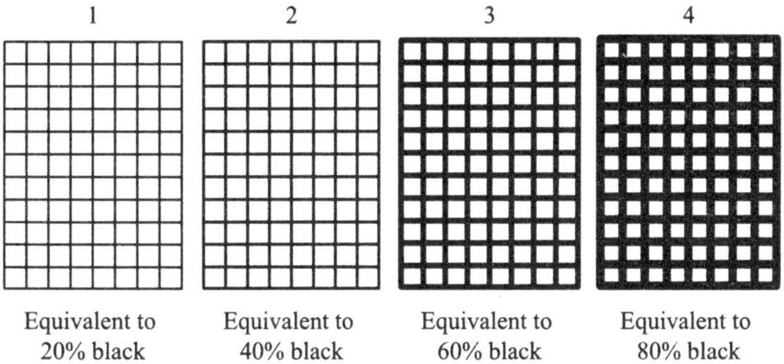

Fig. 15.24 Ringelmann chart

In use, the chart is set up at eye level in line with the stack at such distances (10 m or more) that the sections appear to be different degrees of uniform gray shades. The appearance of the smoke at the top of the stack is matched against one of the shades on the card and reported as a specific *Ringelmann number* ranging from 0 (no smoke) to No.5 (dense black smoke). With practice, an observer can estimate smoke density to half a number, particularly in the Nos.2 to 4 ranges. Readings below No.2 Ringelmann are subject to considerable error.

Obscuration Method: It is basically divided into light extinction type, continuous filtering type and spot filtering type.

Light Extinction Type: In this method of testing, the intensity of a light beam is reduced by smoke which is a measure of smoke intensity. Schematically this method is shown in Fig.15.25.

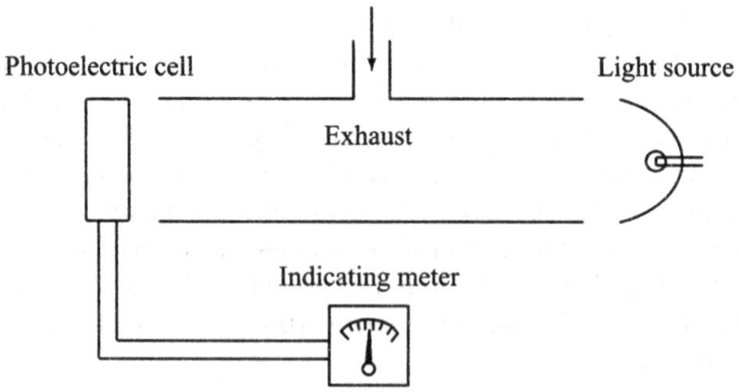

Fig. 15.25 Obscuration method for measuring smoke

A continuously taken exhaust sample is passed through a tube of about 45 cm length which has light source at one end and photocell at the other end. The amount of light passed through this column is used as an indication of smoke level or smoke density. *The smoke level or smoke density is defined as the ratio of electric output from photocell when sample is passed through the column to the electric output when clean air is passed through it.*

The Hartridge smokemeter is a very commonly used instrument based on this principle. Schematically it is represented in Fig.15.26.

Light from a source is passed through a standard length tube containing the exhaust gas sample from the engine and at its other end the transmitted light is measured by a suitable device. The fraction of the light transmitted through the smoke, (T) and the length of the light path (L_ℓ) are related by the Beer-Lambert law.

$$T = e^{-K_{ac}L_\ell} \qquad (15.22)$$

where $K_{ac} = nA\theta$.

K_{ac} is called the optical absorption coefficient of the obscuring matter per unit length, n the number of soot particles per unit volume, A the average projected area of each particles and θ the specific absorbance per particle.

Continuous Filtering Type: In this method provision is made for continuous reading and observing transient conditions. Measurement of smoke intensity is achieved by continuously passing exhaust gas through a moving strip of filter paper and collecting particles. The instrument is schematically

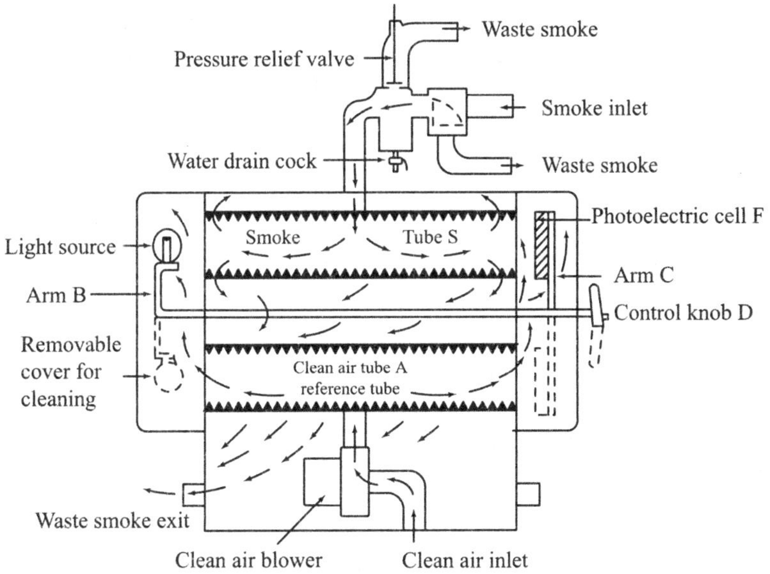

Fig. 15.26 Hartridge smokemeter

represented in Fig.15.27. Van Brand smokemeter is the popular instrument based on this principle. Van Brand smokemeter is also filter darkening type. The exhaust sample is passed at a constant rate through a strip of filter paper moving at a preset speed. A stain is imparted to the paper. The intensity of the stain is measured by the amount of light which passes through the filter and is indication of the smoke density of exhaust. In Van Brand smokemeter the amount of light passing through the filter is used to indicate smoke level.

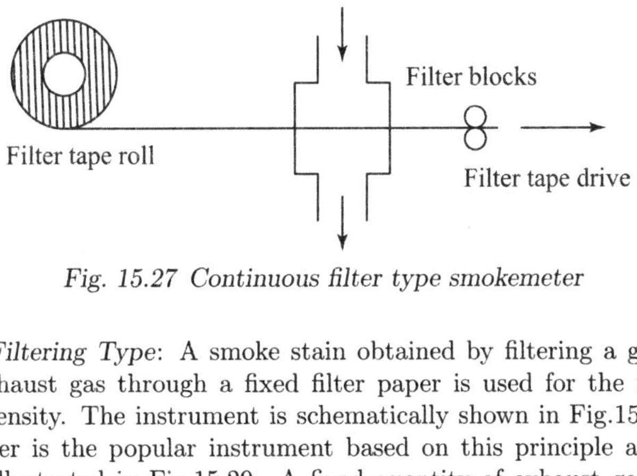

Fig. 15.27 Continuous filter type smokemeter

Spot Filtering Type: A smoke stain obtained by filtering a given quantity of exhaust gas through a fixed filter paper is used for the measure of smoke intensity. The instrument is schematically shown in Fig.15.28. Bosch smokemeter is the popular instrument based on this principle and the details are illustrated in Fig.15.29. A fixed quantity of exhaust gas is passed through a fixed filter paper and the density of the smoke stains on the paper is evaluated optically. In a recent modification of this type of smokemeter, a pneumatically operated sampling pump and a photo-electric unit are used for the measurement of the intensity of smoke stain on filter paper.

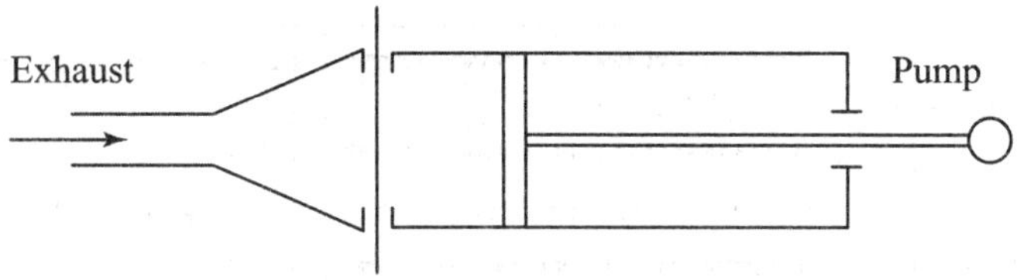

Fig. 15.28 Spot filtering type smokemeter

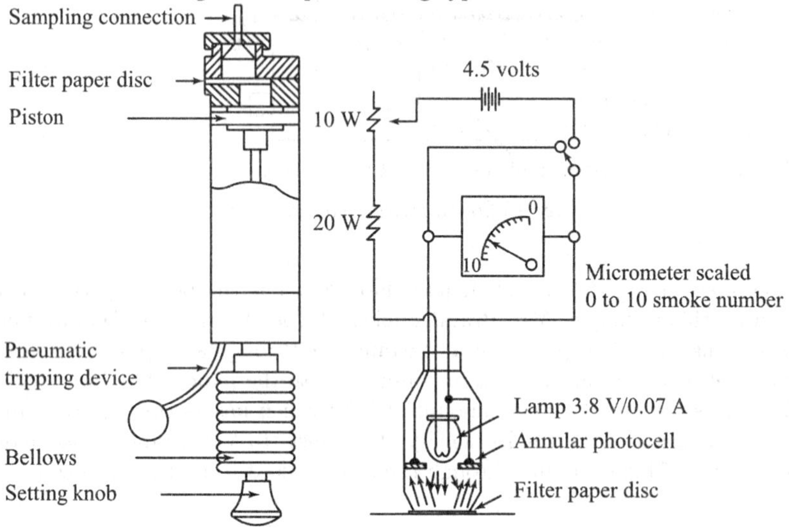

Fig. 15.29 Bosch smokemeter

15.11 NOISE

Noise is a mixture of various sounds which is a source of irritation for the listener. Sound is created by a vibrating object. The vibrations are transmitted to the surrounding air in the form of pressure waves. If the frequency and intensity of the pressure waves are within specified range they produce sensation of sound (15 to 15000 Hz and 0 to 120 dB intensity). Sound level meter consists of a microphone, calibrated attenuator, an electronic amplifier and an indicator meter which reads in decibels (dB) as shown in Fig.15.30. Octave band frequency analyzer is suitable for obtaining the frequency distribution in light bands in frequency region between 20 and 10,000 Hz. The measurement of the noise emitted by motor vehicles is based on a moving vehicle, since it is the total noise emitted by motor vehicle including gear box and transmission.

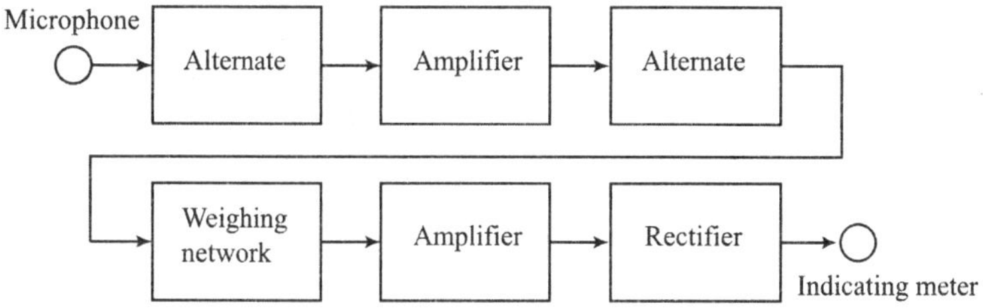

Fig. 15.30 Sound level meter

15.12 COMBUSTION PHENOMENON

Combustion in internal combustion engine is very complex and still it is not fully understood. In order to have an insight into the combustion it is necessary to measure flame temperature, flame propagation, details of combustion and knock.

15.12.1 Flame Temperature Measurement

Flame temperature measurement is a difficult task especially inside the cylinder. Infrared and spectrographic methods are some of the methods currently employed. Figure 15.31 shows a schematic of the infrared method. Principle of the method is based on the fact that if infrared waves from a black body source pass through a cylinder containing gas at a temperature T, then the black body temperature T_b equals the cylinder temperature when the rate of absorption of the infrared waves by the gas in the cylinder equals the rate of emission from the gas. Water vapour is taken as the sensing element (that is the detector and optical system is set to record the emissions at one of the wavelengths for water vapour – 2.6 μm). The black body source for an optical filter is kept ahead of the detector to absorb the unwanted wave lengths. The cylinder consists of two quartz windows so that there is a direct optical path from the infrared source to the detector. During the suction stroke there is minimum infrared absorption by the cylinder gases so that infrared waves transmitted from the black body source will pass through the cylinder with almost no change in intensity.

As shown in Fig.15.31 a horizontal line AB will be recorded. The intensity, I will correspond to the black body temperature, T_b measured by the thermocouple. It should be noted that this will not be the same as the gas temperature. Suppose if T_b is set above the suction temperature, then at the beginning of the compression stroke as the temperature raises there will be some absorption of the infrared by the cylinder gas and the emission level will be less than from the black body. The detector will record a decrease in intensity. Further increase in temperature of the cylinder gas will produce a further decrease in recorded intensity until a minimum is reached. As the stroke continues the intensity will now increase until at C the rate of absorption of the infrared waves from the black body source equals the rate of emission from the cylinder gases. At this point the cylinder temperature equals the black body temperature T_b. The crank angle at which this occurs can be measured in

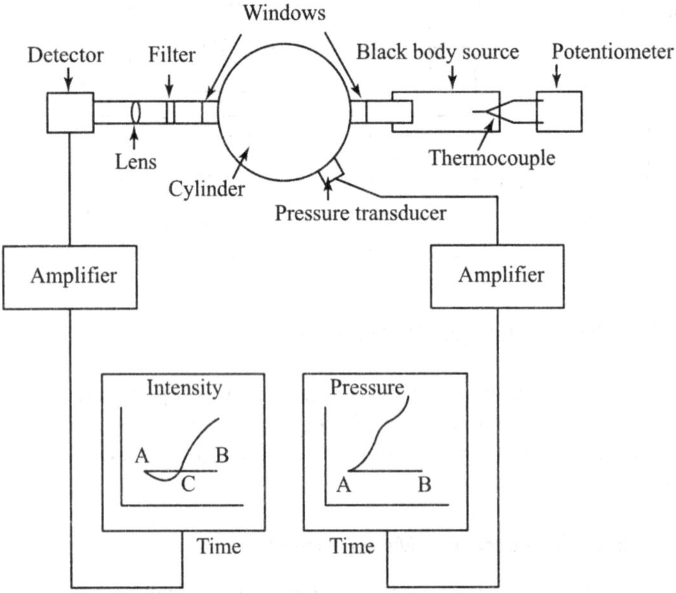

Fig. 15.31 Infrared spectrographic method

the normal manner. As series of black body temperatures T_b is taken and the procedure is repeated, a temperature-crank angle diagram can be obtained. Cleanliness of the quartz windows, window radiation, absorption and homogeneity of the cylinder temperature, cycle-to-cycle variations are factors upon which the accuracy of the method depends.

Another technique is the spectrographic method which is not only used for measuring the local gas temperature but also for studying the chemical reactions in the cylinder. Basis of this method depends on the measurement of the light intensities associated with reacting species at defined wavelengths at which the intensities are at a maximum. One method which has been successfully used to study the formation of oxides of nitrogen during combustion is described. Figures 15.32(a) and 15.32(b) show the details.

A number of quartz windows, W are fitted in the cylinder head. The light source is of 2×2 mm size fitted in the combustion chamber. The core of light emitted from the cylinder is split into four separate beams in mirror M_2, each of which is brought to a separate focus by mirrors M_3 and M_4. Three beams (2, 3 and 4) are focused onto a photo-multiplier with an interference filter to pass wave lengths 0.38 μm and 0.61 μm with a band pass of 100°A and a wave length of 0.75 μm at a band pass of 300°A. The fourth channel is monitored with a monochromator and photomultiplier. The light intensities I at the wave length 0.38 μm, 0.68 μm and 0.61 μm are recorded on a oscillograph relative to the crank angle as shown in Fig.15.32(c). The 0.38 μm wavelength corresponds to the reaction

$$CO + O \rightarrow CO_2 + h\nu \tag{15.23}$$

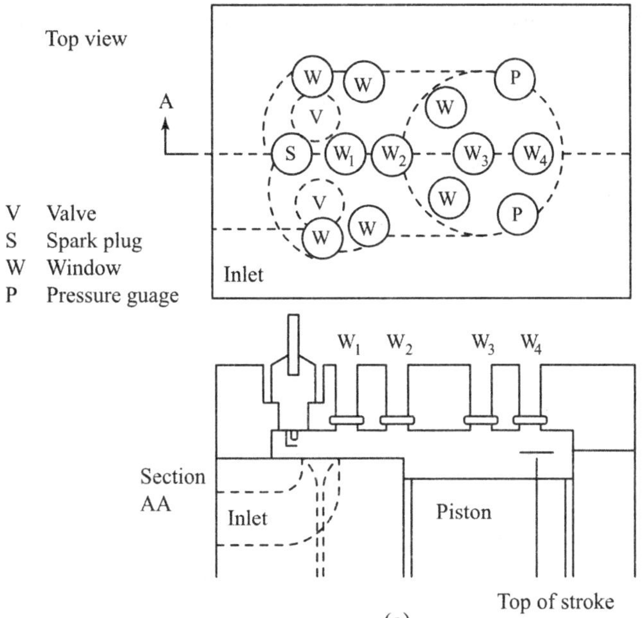

(a)

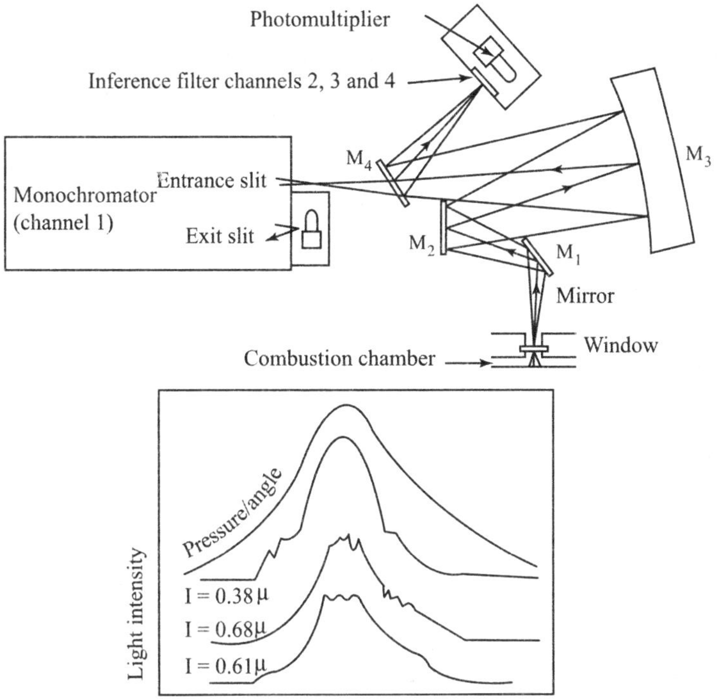

(b)

Fig. 15.32 Spectrographic method to study the formation of oxygen where the emitted light is mainly associated with the discreet energy pocket $h\nu$. The 0.61 μm and 0.68 μm wave lengths are associated with the reaction

$$NO + O \rightarrow NO_2 + h\nu \qquad (15.24)$$

For the above two reactions the intensities of emitted light I associated with the energy packets $h\nu$ are related to the concentrations by

$$I_{CO} = K_1 \text{ [CO] [O]} \qquad (15.25)$$

$$I_{NO} = K_2 \text{ [NO] [O]} \qquad (15.26)$$

K_1 andK_2 parameters are functions of the instantaneous temperature T and the wave length λ. It is assumed that the carbon-hydrogen-oxygen reactions are in equilibrium. Thus for each temperature T there is a known value for [CO][O] from the equilibrium constant. Also for each temperature and wave length there is a known value for K_1. It follows therefore that at a given wave length

$$K_1 \text{ [CO] [O]} = f(T) \qquad (15.27)$$

when this function equals the numerical value of the emitted light I_{CO} we know the temperature and the oxygen concentration. In this way by measuring the intensity I_{CO} at the wave length 0.38 μm we can determine the local temperature T.

For the nitric oxide reaction, if I_{NO} is known at the appropriate wave length, then, since we know the temperature T and the oxygen concentration [O] and K_2 is a known function of the wave length and temperature, the nitric oxide concentration can be calculated from

$$\text{[NO]} = \frac{I_{NO}}{K_2\text{[O]}} \qquad (15.28)$$

15.12.2 Flame Propagation

Slow combustion and the propagation of a combustion wave are the two phenomena that occur whenever ignition of combustible mixture takes place. During slow combustion, the fuel molecules that are already burning raise the temperature of adjacent molecules by conduction and radiation causing them to ignite. At the same time the temperature rise of the gas molecules increases their velocity. This raises the pressure in that point and results in an expansion that assists in propagating the ignition.

Turbulence created in the charge before ignition increase materially the velocity of flame propagation which in this case occurs not only through conduction and radiation but also through convection. It is not easy to segregate all these processes. Whenever a compression wave occurs its velocity may reach several metres per second and passing through the explosive mixture accompanied by almost instantaneous generation of very high pressures it may cause serious trouble in the engine. That is why the measurement of flame propagation is necessary in the evaluation of the performance of IC engine.

Flame location with time is directly measured by the use of ionization gauges. The gauges are made up of a wire in an annulus. The wire is insulated from the body of the gauge. Whenever flame reaches the annulus it becomes conducting since an electrical circuit is completed between the wire and the gauge body. A DC voltage is normally applied to the wire and an electronic timing circuit connected to the gauge body as well as some reference time location. When the flame arrives at the gauge the timing circuit is triggered and the time from the reference time is measured. By locating a number of gauges in the combustion chamber a quantitative picture of the flame propagation may be made. Allowance must be made for expansion of the hot gas zone which is superimposed on the flame speed during the analysis of the results. Air-fuel ratio affects the minimum voltage.

15.12.3 Combustion Process

High speed colour photography has been successfully used for qualitative combustion analysis notably by Ricardo (Fig.15.33).

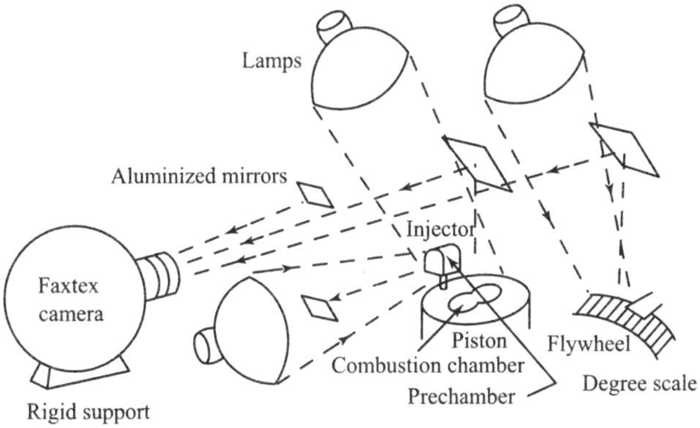

Layout of optical system and camera

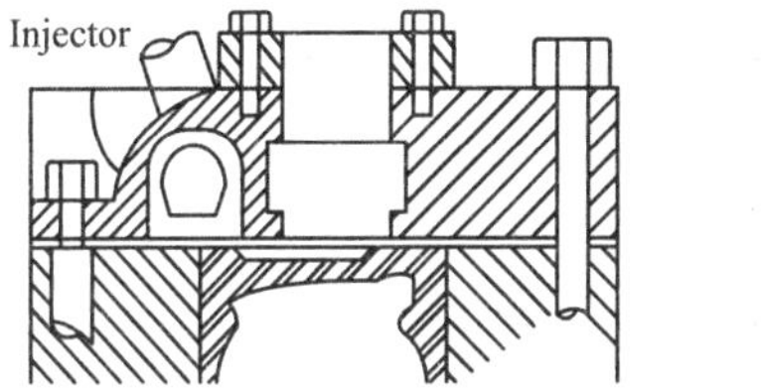

Location of transparent windows in comet V combustion chamber

Fig. 15.33 High speed photographic technique for combustion analysis

The cylinder has either a quartz or perspex window. A high speed rotating prism camera, operating up to 16,000 frames per second is mounted on a rigid support and mirrors are arranged to record the combustion and crankshaft simultaneously. The fuel is normally doped with copper oleate to render low luminosity flames visible. A better understanding of the combustion process can be obtained from combustion films. Nowadays software is developed to analyze these chemical films and thereby analysis of the process is accurately possible using computers.

Review Questions

15.1 List various methods available for finding friction power of an engine.

15.2 State the limitations experienced in the evaluation of friction power using Willan's line method.

15.3 Why Morse test is not suitable for single cylinder engine? Describe the method of finding friction power using Morse test.

15.4 Explain the method of motoring test for obtaining friction power of an engine.

15.5 Explain the principle involved in the measurement of brake power.

15.6 Why the method of obtaining friction power by computing the difference between indicated power and brake power is mostly used in research laboratories?

15.7 Explain the use of prony brake and rope brake in measuring the power output of an engine.

15.8 Explain the basic principle and working of hydraulic dynamo-meter.

15.9 With a neat sketch, explain an Eddy current dynamometer.

15.10 What is transmission dynamometer? Explain.

15.11 Enumerate the advantage of gravimetric fuel flow measurement over volumetric fuel flow measurement.

15.12 Explain an automatic fuel flow meter.

15.13 Classify the meters used for measuring air flow and explain.

15.14 "Air flow to engines cannot be measured with the same precision as can fuel flow", explain the significance of the above statement.

15.15 What is the need for measurement of speed of an I.C. engine?

15.16 List the types of exhaust temperature measurement.

15.17 List the emissions that are considered significant for measurement and performance study.

15.18 Explain the internationally accepted methods of measuring the following invisible emission. (i) Oxides of nitrogen; (ii) Carbon monoxide; (iii) Unburned hydrocarbons; (iv) Aldehydes.

15.19 What is smoke and classify the measurement of smoke?

15.20 Explain the method of measurement of smoke by comparison method.

15.21 In obscuration method of measuring smoke, list the types and give the name of popular instruments with the principle of working.

15.22 Define noise and explain the method of measurement of noise using sound level meter.

15.23 What parameters are necessary for measurement in order to have an insight into combustion?

15.24 Explain the method of determining the local temperature (flame temperature) by spectrographic method.

15.25 Explain how the flame propagation during the combustion process can be measured using high speed photographic techniques.

Multiple Choice Questions (choose the most appropriate answer)

1. The range of mechanical efficiency for automobile engines is

   (a) 0 – 30%
   (b) 30 – 50%
   (c) 70 – 80%
   (d) 90 – 100%

2. The measurement of frictional power by Willans line is applicable to

   (a) SI engines at a particular speed
   (b) CI engines at a particular speed
   (c) any engine at a particular speed only
   (d) none of the above

3. Morse test is applicable only to

   (a) single cylinder SI engines
   (b) single cylinder CI engines
   (c) multicylinder CI engines
   (d) single and multicylinder SI and CI engines

4. The most accurate method of determining fp is by

   (a) Willan's line
   (b) Morse test
   (c) measurement of brake and indicated power
   (d) motoring test

5. In the air box method of measuring air flow, the air box is provided to

    (a) have constant temperature
    (b) have constant flow
    (c) damp out the pulsations
    (d) provide constant velocity of flow

6. The air box/swept volume ratio should be in the range for single-cylinder engines

    (a) 10 – 100%
    (b) 200 – 300%
    (c) 500 – 600%
    (d) > 1000%

7. The best method of measuring speed is by

    (a) mechanical tachometer
    (b) electrical tachometer
    (c) magnetic pickup
    (d) none of the above

8. Flame ionization detector is used for measuring

    (a) CO
    (b) HC
    (c) NO_x
    (d) CO_2

9. Chemiluminescence analyzer is used for measuring

    (a) NO_x
    (b) CO
    (c) HC
    (d) CO_2

10. Non-dispersive infra-red analyzer is widely accepted instrument for measuring

    (a) NO_x
    (b) HC
    (c) CO
    (d) CO_2

Ans:					
	1. – (c)	2. – (b)	3. – (c)	4. – (c)	5. – (c)
	6. – (c)	7. – (c)	8. – (b)	9. – (a)	10. – (c)

16
PERFORMANCE PARAMETERS AND CHARACTERISTICS

16.1 INTRODUCTION

Internal combustion engine generally operates within a useful range of speed. Some engines are made to run at fixed speed by means of a speed governor which is its rated speed. At each speed within the useful range the power output varies and it has a maximum usable value. The ratio of power developed to the maximum usable power at the same speed is called the load. The specific fuel consumption varies with load and speed. The performance of the engine depends on inter-relationship between power developed, speed and the specific fuel consumption at each operating condition within the useful range of speed and load.

The following factors are to be considered in evaluating the performance of an engine:

(i) Maximum power or torque available at each speed within the useful range of speed.

(ii) The range of power output at constant speed for stable operation of the engine. The different speeds should be selected at equal intervals within the useful speed range.

(iii) Brake specific fuel consumption at each operating condition within the useful range of operation.

(iv) Reliability and durability of the engine for the given range of operation.

Engine performance characteristics can be determined by the following two methods.

(i) By using experimental results obtained from engine tests.

(ii) By analytical calculation based on theoretical data.

Engine performance is really a relative term. It is represented by typical characteristic curves which are functions of engine operating parameters. The term performance usually means how well an engine is doing its job in relation to the input energy or how effectively it provides useful energy in relation to some other comparable engines.

Some of the important parameters are speed, inlet pressure and temperature, output, air-fuel ratio etc. The useful range of all these parameters is limited by various factors, like mechanical stresses, knocking, over-heating etc. Due to this, there is a practical limit of maximum power and efficiency obtainable from an engine. The performance of an engine is judged from the point of view of the two main factors, viz., engine power and engine efficiency. Besides the overall efficiency, various other efficiencies are encountered when dealing with the theory, design and operation of engines. These factors are discussed in more detail in the following two sections.

16.2 ENGINE POWER

In general, as indicated in section 1.7, the energy flow through the engine is expressed in three distinct terms. They are indicated power, *ip*, friction power *fp* and brake power, *bp*. Indicated power can be computed from the measurement of forces in the cylinder and brake power may be computed from the measurement of forces at the crankshaft of the engine. The friction power can be estimated by motoring the engine or other methods discussed in Chapter 15. It can also be calculated as the difference between the *ip* and *bp* if these two are known, then,

$$ip = bp + fp \tag{16.1}$$

$$fp = ip - bp \tag{16.2}$$

In the following sections, the usually employed formulae for the computation of power are discussed.

16.2.1 Indicated Mean Effective Pressure (p_{im})

It has been stated in section 16.2 that *ip* can be computed from the measurement of forces developed in the cylinder, viz., the pressure of the expanding gases. As already described, in chapters dealing with cycles, the pressure in the cylinder varies throughout the cycle and the variation can be expressed with respect to volume or crank angle to obtain p-V or p-θ diagrams respectively. However, such a continuous variation does not readily lend itself to simple mathematical analysis in the computation of *ip*. If an average pressure for one cycle can be used, then the computations becomes far less difficult.

As the piston moves back and forth between TDC and BDC (Fig.16.1), the process lines on the p-V diagram indicate the successive states of the working fluid through the cycle. The indicated net work of the cycle is represented by the area 1234 enclosed by the process lines for that cycle. If the area of rectangle ABCD equals area 1234, the vertical distance between the horizontal lines AB and CD represents the *indicated mean effective pressure*, *imep*. It is a mean value expressed in N/m^2, which, when multiplied by the displacement volume, V_s, gives the same indicated net work as is actually produced with the varying pressures.

$$p_{im} \times (V_1 - V_2) = \text{Net work of cycle} \tag{16.3}$$

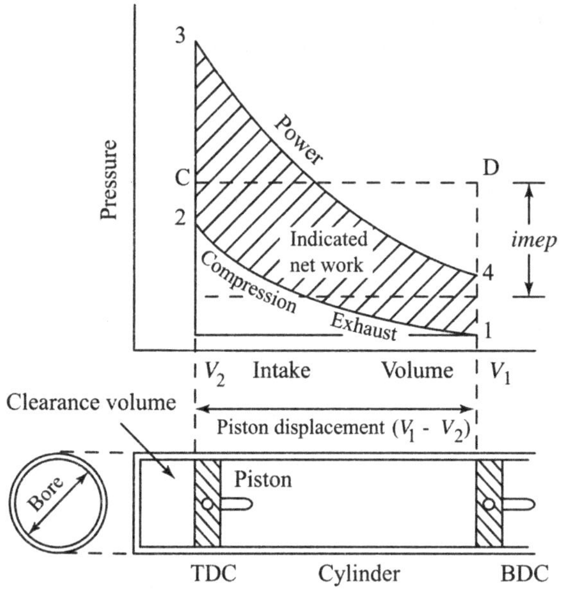

Fig. 16.1 p-V diagram for an ideal four-stroke cycle engine

$$p_{im} = \frac{\text{Net work of cycle}}{V_1 - V_2} \tag{16.4}$$

$$= \frac{\text{Area of the indicator diagram}}{\text{Length of the indicator diagram}} \tag{16.5}$$

On an actual engine, the p-V diagram (called the *indicator diagram*) is obtained by a mechanical or electrical instrument attached to the cylinder taking into consideration the spring constant. The area enclosed by the actual cycle on the indicator card may be measured by a planimeter. The value of the area measured, when divided by the piston displacement, results in the mean ordinate, or indicated mean effective pressure, p_{im}.

16.2.2 Indicated Power (ip)

Power is defined as the rate of doing work. In the analysis of cycles the net work is expressed in kJ/kg of air. This may be converted to power by multiplying by the mass flow rate of air through the engine in kg per unit time. Since, the net work obtained from the p-V diagram is the net work produced in the cylinder as measured by an indicator diagram, the power based there on is termed indicated power, ip.

$$ip = \dot{m}_a \times \text{net work} \tag{16.6}$$

where $\dot{m}_a$ is in kg/s, network is in kJ/kg of air and ip is in kW.

In working with actual engines, it is often desirable to compute ip from a given p_{im} and given engine operating conditions. The necessary formula may be developed from the equation of net work based on the mean effective pressure and piston displacement. From Eq.16.3,

$$\text{Indicated net work/cycle} = p_{im}\ V_s \tag{16.7}$$

By definition,

$$\text{Indicated power} = \text{Indicated net work} \times \text{cycles/s}$$

$$ip = \frac{p_{im} V_s n K}{1000 \times 60} = \frac{p_{im} L A n K}{60000} \text{ kW} \tag{16.8}$$

where ip = indicated power (kW)

p_{im} = indicated mean effective pressure (N/m^2)

L = length of the stroke (m)

A = area of the piston (m^2)

N = speed in revolutions per minute

n = number of power strokes per minute

$N/2$ for a four-stroke engine

N for a two-stroke engine

K = number of cylinders

16.2.3 Brake Power (*bp*)

Indicated power is based on indicated net work and is thus a measure of the forces developed within the cylinder. More practical interest is the rotational force available at the delivery point, at the engine crankshaft (termed the drive-shaft), and the power corresponding to it. This power is interchangeably referred to as brake power, shaft power or delivered power. In general, only the term *brake power, bp*, has been used in this book to indicate the power actually delivered by the engine.

The *bp* is usually measured by attaching a power absorption device to the drive-shaft of the engine. Such a device sets up measurable forces counter-acting the forces delivered by the engine, and the determined value of these measured forces is indicative of the forces being delivered.

By using the geometry of a simple prony brake as the basis, a formula can now be developed for computing the *bp* delivered by an engine. Work has been defined as the product of a force and the distance through which the point of application of force moves. Then the drive-shaft of the engine turns through one revolution, any point on the periphery of the rigidly attached wheel moves through a distance equal to $2\pi r$ (Fig.16.2). During this movement, a friction force, f is acting against the wheel. The force, f is thus acting through the distance $2\pi r$, and producing work. Thus,

$$\text{Work during one revolution} = \text{Distance} \times \text{Force}$$

$$= (2\pi r) \times f \tag{16.9}$$

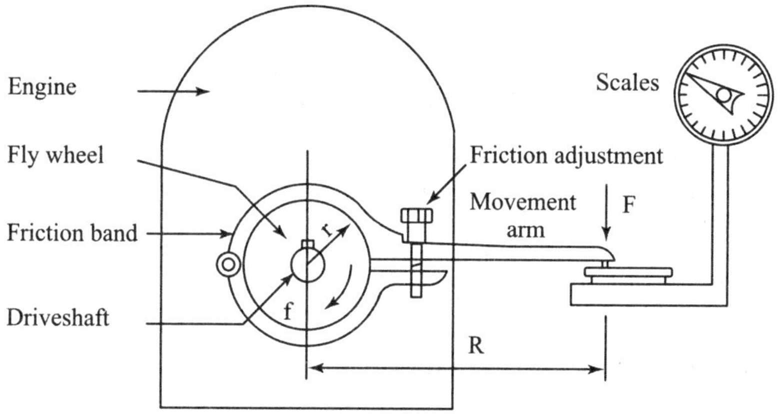

Fig. 16.2 Adaptation of prony brake for power measurement

The torque, rf, produced by the drive-shaft is opposed by a turning moment equal to the product of the length of the moment arm R and the force F measured by the scale

$$T = rf = RF \tag{16.10}$$

$$\text{Work during one revolution} = 2\pi RF$$

$$\text{Power} = \frac{\text{Work}}{\text{Time}} = 2\pi RF\frac{N}{60} \tag{16.11}$$

where N = revolutions per minute of the drive-shaft. Therefore,

$$bp = \frac{2\pi RFN}{60 \times 1000} \text{ kW} \tag{16.12}$$

It should be noted that N is the rpm of the engine. The friction force is acting during every revolution of the crankshaft, regardless of whether or not that revolution contains a power stroke.

The product of the moment arm R and the measured force, F is termed the torque of the engine and is usually expressed in Nm. *Torque*, T is the uniform or fluctuating turning moment, or twist, exerted by a tangential force acting at a distance from the axis of rotation. For an engine operating at a given speed and delivering a given power, the torque must be a fixed amount, or the product of F and R must be constant ($T = FR$). In such a case, if R is decreased, F will increase proportionately and vice versa.

The brake power, *bp*, can also be written as

$$bp = \frac{2\pi NT}{60000} \text{ kW} \tag{16.13}$$

In practice, the length of the moment arm R of the measuring equipment is so designed that the value of the constants 2π and the constant R and 60000 combine to give a convenient number (i.e., in thousands and ten-thousands) in order to simplify computations.

$$bp = \frac{FN}{60000/2\pi R} = \frac{FN}{C_1} \tag{16.14}$$

In order to have $C_1 = 10000$, R should be 0.955 m.

The reader may recollect that the *torque is the capacity of an engine to do work while power is the rate at which an engine does work.* A simple example is that a tractor pulling a given load. The torque developed will determine whether or not the tractor is *capable* of pulling the load, and the power delivered will determine how *fast* the load can be pulled.

16.2.4 Brake Mean Effective Pressure (p_{bm})

Indicated mean effective pressure may be considered to consist of *fmep* and *bmep*, two hypothetical pressures. Friction mean effective pressure is that portion of *imep* which is required to overcome friction losses, and brake mean effective pressure is the portion which produces the useful power delivered by the engine.

$$imep = bmep + fmep$$

Since *bmep* is that portion of *imep* which goes into the development of useful power, it has the same relationship to *bp* as *imep* has to *ip*, or

$$\frac{bmep}{imep} = \frac{bp}{ip} \tag{16.15}$$

Equation 16.8 was developed as a means of computing *ip* when *imep* is determined from an engine indicator diagram

$$ip = \frac{p_{im}LAnK}{60000}$$

For a given engine, L, A, n and K are constants. Since *bp* and *bmep* have the same relationship to one another as do *ip* and *imep*, *bp* can be expressed as

$$bp = \frac{p_{bm}LAnK}{60000} \tag{16.16}$$

where p_{bm} is brake mean effective pressure (N/m^2).

And due to the same relationship, the mechanical efficiency, η_m of the engine can be expressed as the ratio of *bmep* to *imep*.

$$\eta_m = \frac{bp}{ip} = \frac{bmep}{imep} \tag{16.17}$$

It should be noted that for a given engine operating under given conditions, the torque developed is proportional to the *bmep*. This relationship, may be obtained by equating Eq.16.13 and Eq.16.16.

Brake mean effective pressure is very useful in comparing engines or in establishing engine operating limits.

16.3 ENGINE EFFICIENCIES

Apart from expressing engine performance in terms of power, it is also essential to express in terms of efficiencies. Various engine efficiencies are:

(i) Air-standard efficiency

(ii) Brake thermal efficiency

(iii) Indicated thermal efficiency

(iv) Mechanical efficiency

(v) Relative efficiency

(vi) Volumetric efficiency

(vii) Scavenging efficiency

(viii) Charge efficiency

(ix) Combustion efficiency

Most of these efficiencies have already been discussed in various chapters. Generally these efficiencies are expressed in percentage or decimal fractions. We will briefly review them again here.

16.3.1 Air-Standard Efficiency

The air-standard efficiency is also known as thermodynamic efficiency. It is mainly a function of compression ratio and other parameters. It gives the upper limit of the efficiency obtainable from an engine.

16.3.2 Indicated and Brake Thermal Efficiencies

The indicated and brake thermal efficiencies are based on the *ip* and *bp* of the engine respectively. These efficiencies give an idea of the output generated by the engine with respect to heat supplied in the form of fuel. In modern engines an indicated thermal efficiency of almost 28 per cent is obtainable with gas and gasoline spark-ignition engines having a moderate compression ratio and as high as 36 per cent or even more with high compression ratio oil engines.

16.3.3 Mechanical Efficiency

Mechanical efficiency takes into account the mechanical losses in an engine. Mechanical losses of an engine may be further subdivided into the following groups:

(i) Friction losses as in case of pistons, bearings, gears, valve mechanisms. With the development in bearing design and materials, improvements in gears etc., these losses are usually limited from 7 to 9 per cent of the indicated output.

(ii) Power is absorbed by engine auxiliaries such as fuel pump, lubricating oil pump, water circulating pump, radiator, magneto and distributor, electric generator for battery charging, radiator fan etc. These losses may account for 3 to 8 per cent of the indicated output.

(iii) Ventilating action of the flywheel. This loss is usually below 4 per cent of the indicated output.

(iv) Work of charging the cylinder with fresh charge and discharging the exhaust gases during the exhaust stroke. In case of two-stroke engines the power absorbed by the scavenging pump etc. These losses may account for 2 to 6 per cent of the indicated output. In general, mechanical efficiency of engines varies from 65 to 85%.

16.3.4 Relative Efficiency

The relative efficiency or efficiency ratio as it is sometimes called is the ratio of the actual efficiency obtained from an engine to the theoretical efficiency of the engine cycle. Hence,

$$\text{Relative efficiency} = \frac{\text{Actual brake thermal efficiency}}{\text{Air-standard efficiency}}$$

Relative efficiency for most of the engines varies from 75 to 95% with theoretical air and decreases rapidly with insufficient air to about 75% with 90% air.

16.3.5 Volumetric Efficiency

Volumetric efficiency is a measure of the success with which the air supply, and thus the charge, is inducted into the engine. It is a very important parameter, since it indicates the breathing capacity of the engine. It has been discussed in detail in section 4.5.2. Volumetric efficiency is defined as *the ratio of the actual mass of air drawn into the engine during a given period of time to the theoretical mass which should have been drawn in during that same period of time, based upon the total piston displacement of the engine, and the temperature and pressure of the surrounding atmosphere.*

$$\eta_v = \frac{\dot{m}_{act}}{\dot{m}_{th}} \tag{16.18}$$

$$\dot{m}_{th} = \rho_a n V_s$$

where n is the number of intake strokes per minute. For a four-stroke engine $n = N/2$ and for a two-stroke engine $n = N$, where N is the speed of the engine in rev/min. The actual mass is a measured quantity. The theoretical mass is computed from the geometry of the cylinder, the number of cylinders, and the speed of the engine, in conjunction with the density of the surrounding atmosphere.

16.3.6 Scavenging Efficiency

In case of two-stroke engines (discussed in detail in the next chapter) scavenging efficiency is defined as the ratio of the amount of air or gas-air mixture, which remains in the cylinder, at the actual beginning of the compression to the product of the total volume and air density of the inlet. Scavenging efficiency for most of the two-stroke engines varies from 40 to 95 per cent depending upon the type of scavenging provided.

16.3.7 Charge Efficiency

The charge efficiency shows how well the piston displacement of a four-stroke engine is utilized. Various factors affecting charge efficiency are:

(i) the compression ratio.

(ii) the amount of heat picked up during passage of the charge through intake manifold.

(iii) the valve timing of the engine.

(iv) the resistance offered to air-fuel charge during its passage through induction manifold.

16.3.8 Combustion Efficiency

Combustion efficiency is the ratio of heat liberated to the theoretical heat in the fuel. The amount of heat liberated is less than the theoretical value because of incomplete combustion either due to dissociation or due to lack of available oxygen. Combustion efficiency in a well adjusted engine varies from 92% to 97%.

16.4 ENGINE PERFORMANCE CHARACTERISTICS

Engine performance characteristics are a convenient graphical presentation of an engine performance. They are constructed from the data obtained during actual test runs of the engine and are particularly useful in comparing the performance of one engine with that of another. In this section some of the important performance characteristics of the SI engines are discussed.

It is to be noted that there is a certain speed, within the speed range of a particular engine, at which the charge inducted per cylinder per cycle will be the maximum. At this point, the maximum force can therefore be exerted on the piston. For all practical purposes, the torque, or engine capacity to do work will also be maximum at this point. Thus, *there is a particular engine speed at which the charge per cylinder per cycle is a maximum, and at approximately this same speed, the torque of the engine will be a maximum.*

As the speed of the engine is increased above this speed the quantity of the indicated charge will decrease. However, the power output of the engine increases with speed due to more number of cycles are executed per unit time. It should be noted that the air consumption will continue to increase with increased engine speed until some point is reached where the charge per cylinder per stroke decreases very rapidly than the number of strokes per unit time is increasing. Engines are so designed that the maximum air consumption point is not reached within the operating speed of the engine. Increase in air consumption means that increased quantities of fuel can be added per unit time increasing the power output. In fact the *ip* produced in the cylinder is almost directly proportional to the engine air consumption.

The relationship between air charge per cylinder per cycle and torque, as well as air consumption and *ip* is illustrated in Fig.16.3. Note that the maximum torque occurs at a lower speed than the maximum *ip*.

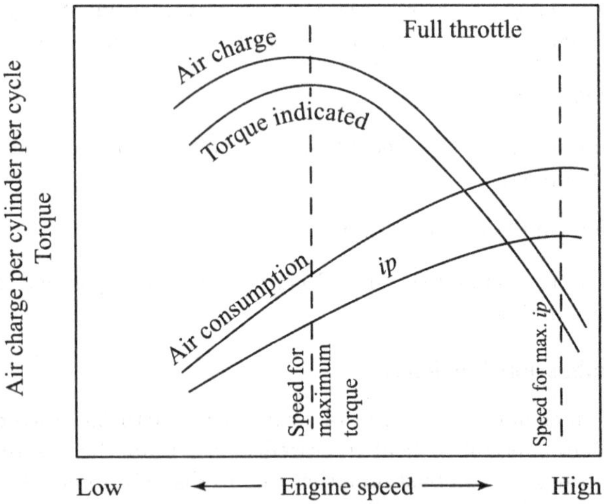

Fig. 16.3 Typical performance plot with respect to speed

Figure 16.4 shows some of the other important performance characteristics for a typical SI engine. In this figure, torque, *ip*, *bp* and *fp* are plotted against engine speed throughout the operating range of the engine, at full throttle and variable load. The difference between the *ip* produced in the cylinder, and the *bp* realized at the drive-shaft, is the *fp*. At low engine speeds, the *fp* is relatively low, and *bp* is close to *ip*. As engine speed increases, the *fp* increases at a greater rate. At engine speeds above the usual operating range, *fp* increases very rapidly. Also, at these higher speeds, *ip* will reach a maximum and then fall off. At some point, *ip* and *fp* will be equal, and *bp* will then drop to zero. Note that the torque reaches a maximum at approximately 60% of the rated rpm of the engine, while the *ip* has not reached maximum even at the rated speed.

Figure 16.5 shows fuel consumption and *bsfc* plotted against the engine speed, for the same engine operating under the same conditions. The quantity of fuel consumed increases with engine speed. The *bsfc*, on the other hand, drops as the speed is increased in the low speed range, nearly levels off at medium speeds, and increases in the high speed range, At low speeds, the heat loss to the combustion chamber walls is proportionately greater and combustion efficiency is poorer, resulting in higher fuel consumption for the

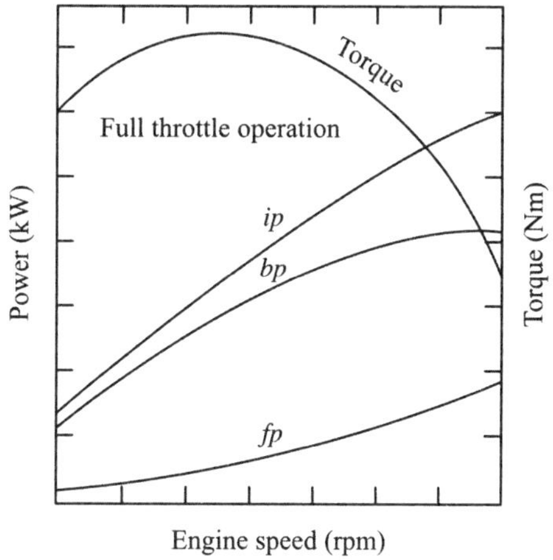

Fig. 16.4 Typical SI engine performance curves

power produced. At the high speeds, the fp is increasing at a rapid rate, resulting in a slower increase in bp than in fuel consumption, with a consequent increase in $bsfc$.

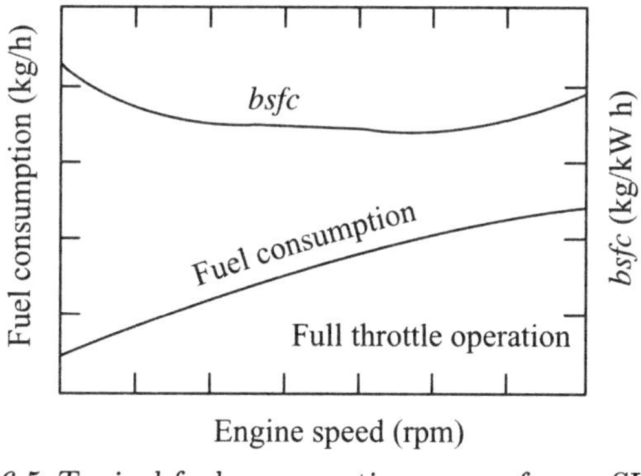

Fig. 16.5 Typical fuel consumption curves for an SI engine

The $bsfc$ curve of Fig.16.5 is for full throttle, variable speed operation. At any one speed, it represents the $bsfc$ which will result when the engine is carrying its maximum load at that speed. By reducing throttle opening and load, that same speed may be obtained, but at loads less than the maximum. A family of curves for various speeds can be obtained, each showing the effect on $bsfc$ of varying the load at constant speed. Under these conditions of constant speed and variable load, and at a constant air-fuel ratio, the $bsfc$ will rise consistently and rapidly as the load (and throttle opening) is decreased. Figure 16.6 illustrates the general shape of the curve for any given rpm. The reason for the rapid increase in $bsfc$ with the reduction in throttle opening is that the fp remains essentially constant, while the ip is being reduced. The bp drops more rapidly than fuel consumption, and thereby the $bsfc$ rises.

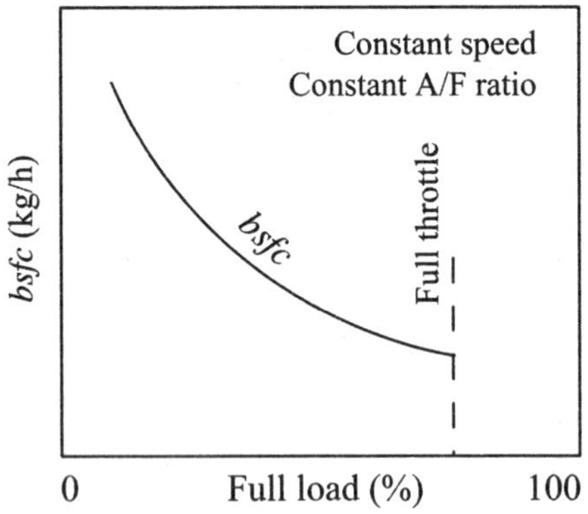

Fig. 16.6 bsfc curve at constant speed and variable load

Performance curves can be constructed for other operating factors such as *imep*, *bmep*, air consumption etc. However, the curves presented are typical, and are among the more important. Probably the most important of these are the curves of torque, *bp* and *bsfc* plotted against engine speed at full throttle operation. These curves are the ones most generally published by engine manufacturers with the descriptive literature on their engine models. Such a plot would look similar to Fig.16.7.

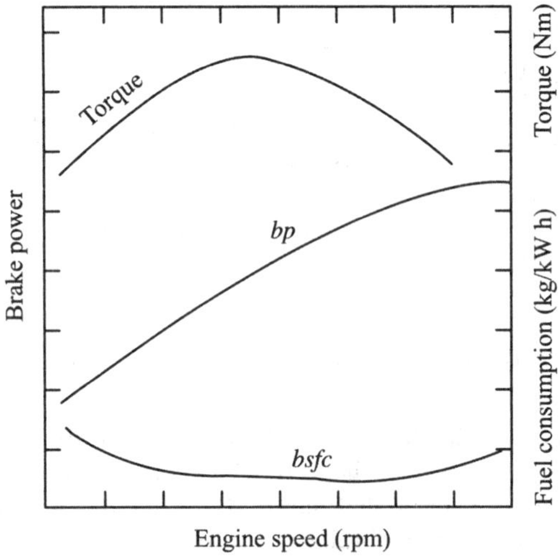

Fig. 16.7 Variation of bsfc, torque and bp with respect to speed for an SI engine

For selecting a particular capacity engine, one can refer to the curves published by the various engine manufacturers which will meet his needs. Then comprehensive performance curves may be studied to determine the appropriate engine.

Figure 16.8 shows full-load indicated and brake power and mean effective pressure for naturally aspirated DI and IDI compression-ignition engines. Except at high engine speeds, brake torque and *mep* vary only modestly with engine speed since the intake system of the diesel can have larger flow areas than the intake of SI engines with their intake-system fuel transport requirements. The part-load torque and bmep characteristics (at fixed amount of fuel injected/cycle) have a similar shape to the full-load characteristics in Fig.16.8.

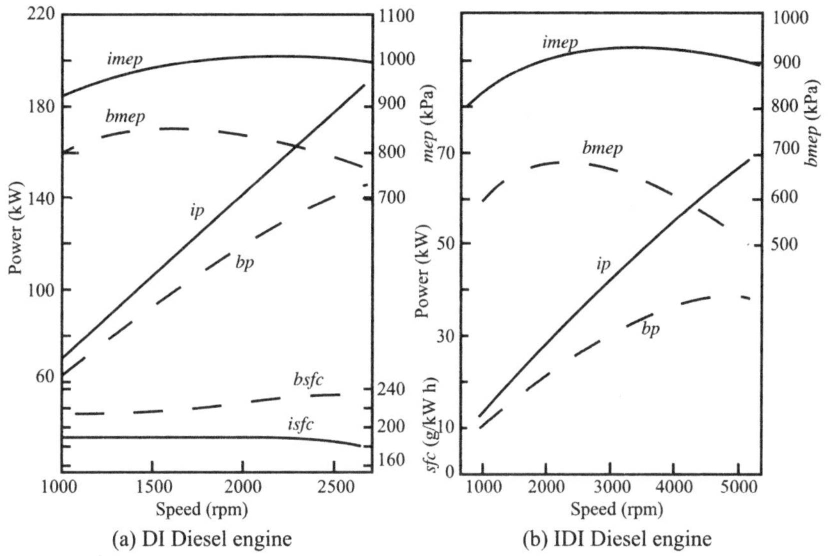

Fig. 16.8 Performance graph of DI and IDI CI engine

16.5 VARIABLES AFFECTING PERFORMANCE CHARACTERISTICS

In the preceding section, engine performance curves were discussed. The shape of these curves, or the engine performance is determined by the regulation of many design and operating variables. Some of the important variables will be briefly discussed and summarized in this section.

16.5.1 Combustion Rate and Spark Timing

The spark should be timed and the combustion rate controlled such that the maximum pressure occurs as close to the beginning of the power stroke as possible, consistent with a smooth running engine. As a general rule, the spark timing and combustion rate are regulated in such a way that approximately one half of the total pressure rise due to combustion has occurred as the piston reaches *TDC* on the compression stroke.

16.5.2 Air-Fuel Ratio

This ratio must be set to fulfill engine requirements. Consistent with these requirements, however, it is usually set as close as possible to the best economy proportions during normal cruising speeds, and as close as possible to the best power proportions when maximum performance is required.

16.5.3 Compression Ratio

An increase in compression ratio increases the thermal efficiency, and is, therefore, generally advantageous. The compression ratio in most SI engines is limited by knock, and the use of economically feasible antiknock quality fuels. Increasing compression ratio also increases the friction of the engine, particularly between piston rings and the cylinder walls, and there is a point at which further increase in compression ratio would not be profitable, though this point appears to be rather high.

16.5.4 Engine Speed

At low speeds, a greater length of time is available for heat transfer to the cylinder walls and therefore a greater proportion of heat loss occurs. Up to a certain point, higher speeds produce greater air consumption and therefore greater *ip*. Higher speeds, however, are accompanied by rapidly increasing *fp* and by greater inertia in the moving parts. Consequently, the engine speed range must be a compromise, although most present day designs appear to favour the higher speeds.

16.5.5 Mass of Inducted Charge

The greater the mass of the charge inducted, the higher the power produced. For a given engine, the geometry is fixed, and it is desirable to induct a charge to a maximum possible density giving the highest volumetric efficiency.

16.5.6 Heat Losses

It should be noted that the large proportion of the available energy is lost in a non-usable form, i.e., heat losses. Any method which can be employed to prevent the excessive heat loss and cause this energy to leave the engine is a usable form will tend to increase engine performance. Higher coolant temperatures, for instance, provide a smaller temperature gradient around combustion chamber walls and a reduction in heat loss, but are limited by the possibility of damage to engine parts.

16.6 METHODS OF IMPROVING ENGINE PERFORMANCE

The engine designer is always interested in methods through which engine performance may be improved. By referring to Fig.1.13, it can be seen that there are two general areas in which methods can be utilized to improve performance:

(i) the energy put into the engine at the start may be increased, and/or

(ii) the efficiency with which the fuel energy is converted to mechanical energy may be increased (Areas A and B of Fig.1.13).

Energy supply may be increased by increasing the mass of charge entering the combustion chamber. Supercharging is one method of accomplishing this. Larger piston displacement is another solution, but is limited by engine weight and cooling problems. Improvement in volumetric efficiency would also increase the mass of charge. Higher engine speeds may be utilized, but these result in increased friction losses, and above a certain point, in lowered volumetric efficiency. Improvements in fuels resulting in greater usable energy content without detonation would also help.

The use of higher compression ratios would increase the efficiency of conversion of the energy in the fuel into useful mechanical energy. This requires the development of economically feasible higher antiknock quality fuels. Even with such fuels, as pointed out earlier, there appears to be a limit to the advantage in increasing the compression ratio. Another solution would be to reduce the losses between the air cycle and the actual cycle, and thereby increase the proportion of energy which can be mechanically utilized.

Also, it is possible to take advantage of the kinetic energy in the exhaust gas to increase the engine output through use of exhaust driven turbines. In this case, the exhaust gas from engine cylinders drives a turbine which is connected to the engine crankshaft, thus increasing engine output. Engines having this type of power booster are known as *turbocompound engines.*

Many of the parameters entering into the performance of four-stroke CI engine are similar to those already analyzed for SI engines. Hence, the performance characteristics of CI engines are not discussed separately.

16.7 HEAT BALANCE

Energy supplied to an engine is the heat value of the fuel consumed. As has been repeatedly pointed out, only a part of this energy is transformed into useful work. The rest of it is either wasted or utilized in special application like turbocompounding. The two main parts of the heat not available for work are the heat carried away by the exhaust gases and the cooling medium. Figure 16.9 illustrates the same for spark-ignition engines. A typical heat balance for compression-ignition engines is illustrated in Fig.16.10.

To give sufficient data for the preparation of a heat balance sheet, a test should include a method of determining the friction power and the measurement of speed, load, fuel consumption, air consumption, exhaust temperature, rate of flow of cooling water and its temperature rise while flowing through the water jackets. Besides, the small losses, such as radiation and incomplete combustion, the above enumerated data makes it possible to account for the heat supplied by the fuel and indicate its distribution.

It may be argued that same amount of frictional power, is accounted in the rise of cooling water temperature and lubricating oil temperature etc. However, it is taken into account here to show that the frictional losses also

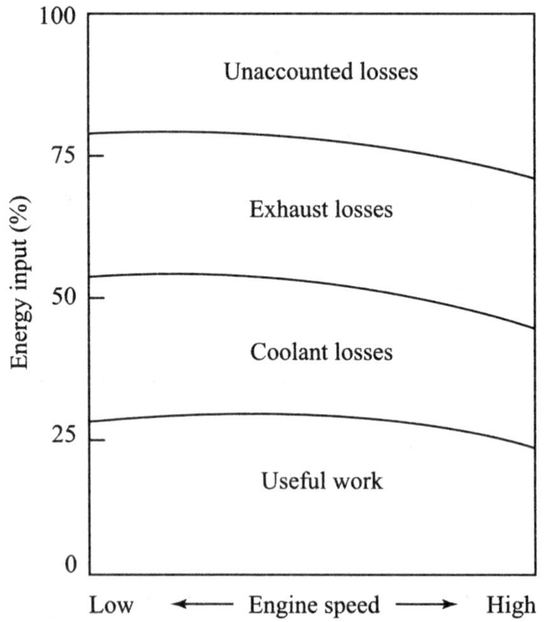

Fig. 16.9 Heat balance diagram for a typical SI engine

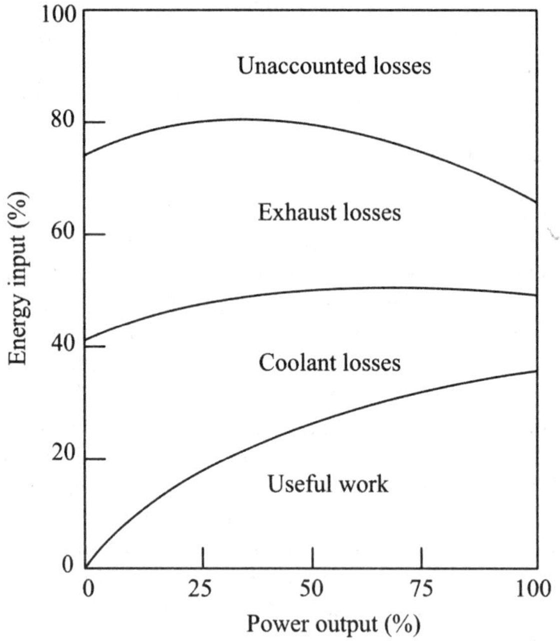

Fig. 16.10 Heat balance diagram for a typical CI engine

include blowdown and pumping losses and therefore it is not appropriate to put it in the heat balance. Since, there are always certain losses which cannot be accounted for, by including fp in the heat balance, the unaccounted losses will reduce.

The heat balance may be external or internal. Typical external heat balance is shown in Fig.16.11.

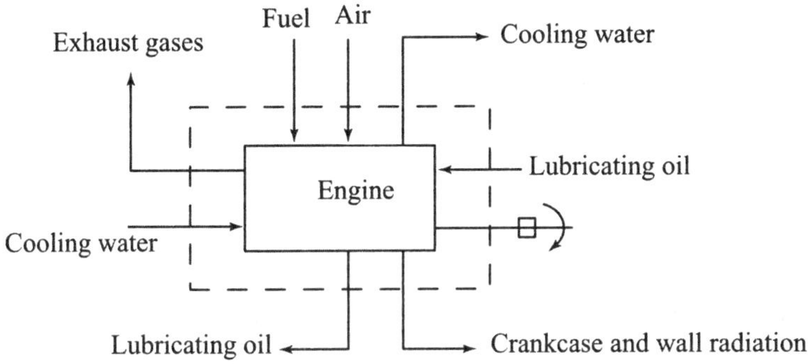

Fig. 16.11 External heat balance

Usually the amount of heat carried by lubricating oil is comparatively small and are normally not included. A further method of representing heat balance is by means of the Sankey diagram. This is a stream type diagram in which the width of the stream represents the heat quantity being considered, usually as a percentage of the heat supplied, as shown in Fig.16.12.

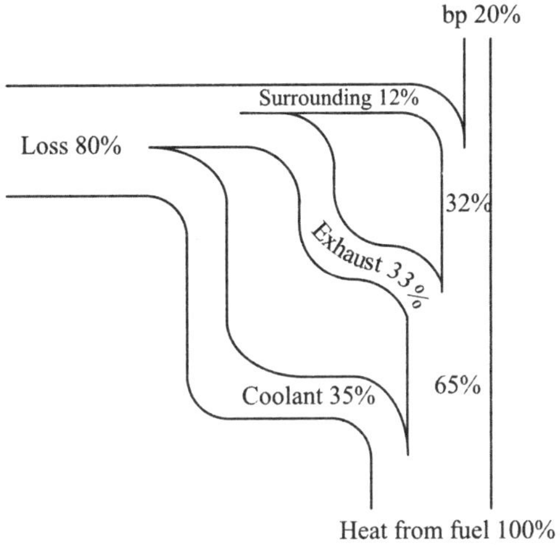

Fig. 16.12 Sankey diagram

It may be observed that the diagram starts at the bottom with a stream width which represents the heat input from the fuel which is 100% of the heat input and is marked as such. Moving up the diagram, first the coolant loss stream is let off to the left.

The width of this stream represents the percentage loss to the coolant. Still higher the exhaust loss stream is let off to the left and finally the loss to the surroundings appears. The loss streams finally meet a single loss stream as shown of the original vertical stream, only the brake power output stream is left at the top of the diagram. The figures on the diagram are percentages of the heat supplied in the fuel. A more detailed diagram for a spark-ignition engine is shown in Fig.16.13. In this case, actually the heat distribution is much more involved. During the suction or scavenging period the entering fresh charge receives heat from the residual gases and from the cylinder walls. Part of the indicated work on the piston is transformed through friction into heat, which goes mostly into the cooling medium but partly into the exhaust gases and lubricating oil and also is dissipated through the crankcase to the surrounding air.

16.8 PERFORMANCE MAPS

For critical analysis the performance of an IC engine under all conditions of load and speed is shown by a performance map. Figure 16.14 shows the performance map of an automotive SI engine and Fig.16.15 the performance map of a four-stroke prechamber CI engine. Figure 16.14 also includes a typical curve of *bmep* vs piston speed for level road operation in high gear. Note that these maps can be used for comparing different sized engines, as performance parameters have been generalized by converting rpm into piston speed and power per unit piston area. Generally speaking, all the engines show a region of lowest specific fuel consumption (highest efficiency) at a relatively low piston speed with a relatively high *bmep*.

16.8.1 SI Engines

Constant Speed Line : Reduced $bsfc$ is obtained by moving upward along constant speed line. Mixture enrichment at high load more than offsets increase in mechanical efficiency. Moving to lower *bmeps*, the $bsfc$ increases because of the reduced mechanical efficiency.

Constant *bmep* Line : Moving from the region of highest efficiency along a line of constant *bmep*, the $bsfc$ increases due to increased friction at higher piston speeds. Moving to the left towards lower piston speed, although friction *mep* decreases, indicated efficiency falls off owing to poor fuel distribution and increased heat losses.

16.8.2 CI Engines

In the CI engine the $bsfc$ increases at high loads owing to the increased fuel waste (smoke) associated with high fuel-air ratios. At lower load $bsfc$ increases due to decrease in mechanical efficiency (same as in the SI engine).

As the speed is reduced from the point of best economy along a line of constant *bmep*, the product of mechanical and indicated thermal efficiency

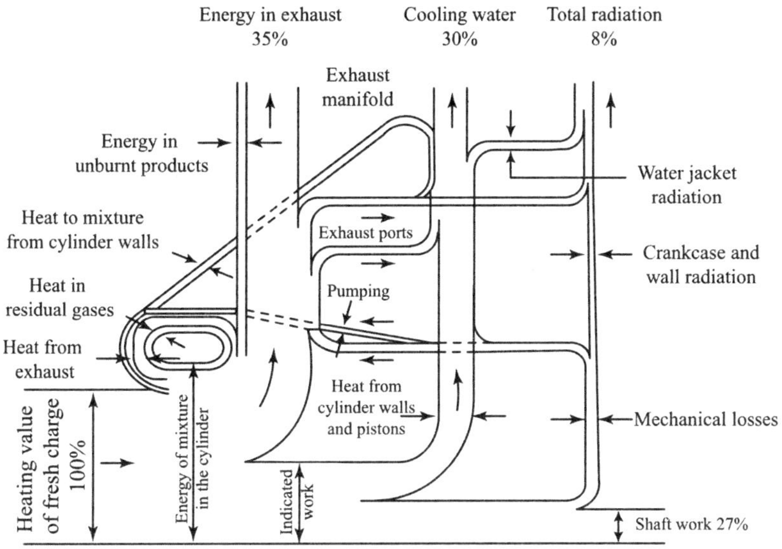

Fig. 16.13 Sankey diagram for an SI engine

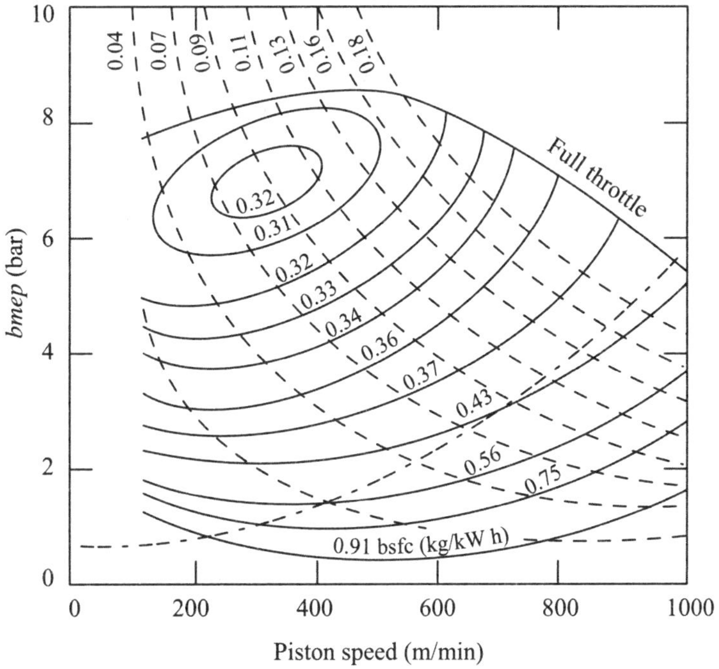

Fig. 16.14 Generalized performance map of automotive SI engine

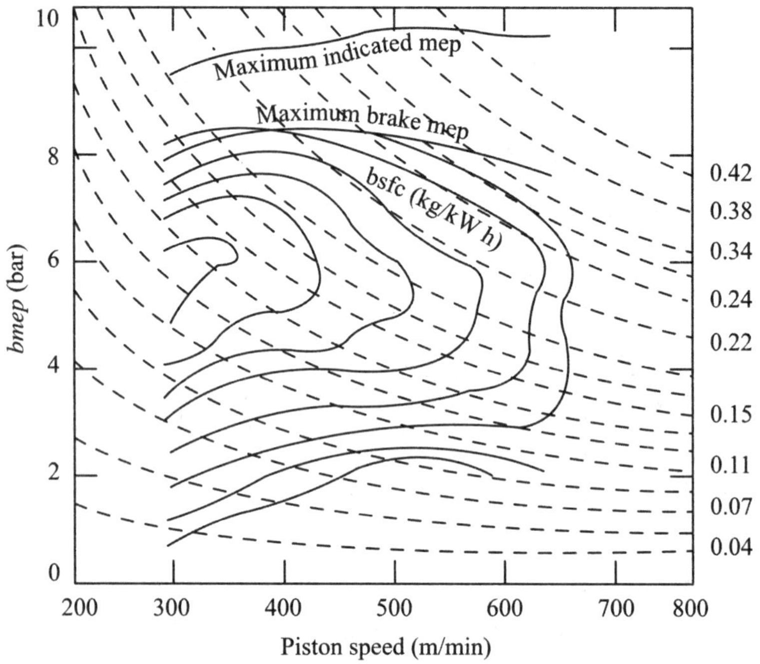

Fig. 16.15 Performance map of a four-stroke prechamber diesel engine

appears to remain a constant down to the lowest operating speed. The reduction in *fmep* with speed is apparently balanced by a reduction is indicated thermal efficiency due to poor spray characteristics at very low speeds. An interesting feature of the performance curves is that they show the power at maximum economy is about half of the maximum power.

16.9 ANALYTICAL METHOD OF PERFORMANCE ESTIMATION

Performance data of engine obtained from theoretical analysis are very useful for the design of a new engine. Due to complex nature of the processes taking place in an engine (such as combustion with variable specific heat and dissociation, mixing of different gases, heat transfer, etc.) the theoretical calculations are rather very difficult and some simplifying assumptions are to be made. Therefore, results obtained from theoretical calculations must be compared with experimental results obtained from engine of similar design for validation. The theoretical results are accepted only when they are reasonably close to the experimental results.

The brake output of an engine depends on brake mean effective pressure, *bmep*, and the piston speed, $\bar{s}_p$. Brake mean effective pressure depends on indicated mean effective pressure, *imep*, and the frictional mean effective pressure, *fmep*. When the speed of the engine changes from N_1 to N_2, the piston speed changes from $\bar{s}_{p1}$ to $\bar{s}_{p2}$ and the brake output changes from bp_1

to bp_2. Now the ratio of bp_2 to bp_1 can be written as

$$\frac{bp_2}{bp_1} = \frac{imep_2 - fmep_2}{imep_1 - fmep_1} \times \frac{\bar{s}_{p2}}{\bar{s}_{p1}} \tag{16.19}$$

where bp_1 and bp_2 are the power output in kW at speeds N_1 and N_2 respectively.

The ratio of indicated mean effective pressure at N_2 and N_1 is given by

$$\epsilon = \frac{imep_2}{imep_1} = \frac{\rho_{in_2}}{\rho_{in_1}} \frac{\eta_{v_2}}{\eta_{v_1}} \frac{(\dot{m}_f \eta_{ith})_2}{(\dot{m}_f \eta_{ith})_1} \tag{16.20}$$

Dividing numerator and denominator on the right hand side of Eq.16.19 by $imep_1$, we get

$$\frac{bp_2}{bp_1} = \frac{\frac{imep_2}{imep_1} - \frac{fmep_2}{fmep_1}}{1 - \frac{fmep_1}{imep_1}} \times \frac{\bar{s}_{p2}}{\bar{s}_{p1}}$$

$$= \frac{\epsilon - \frac{fmep_2}{imep_1}}{1 - \frac{fmep_1}{imep_1}} \times \frac{\bar{s}_{p2}}{\bar{s}_{p1}} \tag{16.21}$$

From the above relation the power output at condition 2 (bp_2 at mean effective pressure, $imep_2$ and speed, N_2) can be obtained if the bp_1 at $imep_1$ and N_1 are known. In order to determine the complete performance at condition 2, the brake specific fuel consumption at condition 2 should be determined. The brake specific fuel consumption, $bsfc$, which indicates the economy of the engine operation, is related to the indicated specific fuel consumption, $isfc$ by the following relation:

$$bsfc = \frac{isfc}{\frac{bmep}{imep}} = \frac{isfc}{1 - \frac{fmep}{imep}} \tag{16.22}$$

Therefore, the ratio of specific fuel consumption at condition 2 to that at condition 1 is given by the following relation,

$$\frac{bsfc_2}{bsfc_1} = \frac{isfc_2}{isfc_1} \left(\frac{1 - \frac{fmep_1}{imep_1}}{1 - \frac{fmep_2}{imep_2}} \right)$$

$$= \frac{isfc_2}{isfc_1} \left(1 - \frac{\frac{fmep_1}{imep_1}}{\frac{fmep_2}{\epsilon \times imep_1}} \right) \tag{16.23}$$

When engine speed is constant, power developed is proportional to $bmep_2$ and therefore, bp_2 can be obtained from the relation

$$\frac{bp_2}{bp_1} = \frac{bmep_2}{bmep_1} = \frac{imep_2 - fmep_2}{imep_1 - fmep_1} \tag{16.24}$$

For four-stroke cycle unsupercharged engine, the change in $fmep$ with change in power output at constant speed is negligibly small.

Therefore, we can assume

$$fmep_1 = fmep_2 = fmep$$

Therefore, the ratio of brake outputs is given by

$$\frac{bp_2}{bp_1} = \frac{\frac{imep_2}{imep_1} - \frac{fmep}{imep_1}}{1 - \frac{fmep}{imep_1}} = \frac{\epsilon - \frac{fmep}{imep_1}}{1 - \frac{fmep}{imep_1}} \tag{16.25}$$

$$\frac{bsfc_2}{bsfc_1} = \frac{isfc_2}{isfc_1}\left(\frac{1 - \frac{fmep}{imep_1}}{1 - \frac{fmep}{imep_2}}\right)$$

$$= \frac{isfc_2}{isfc_1}\left(\frac{1 - \frac{fmep}{imep_1}}{1 - \frac{fmep}{\epsilon \times imep_1}}\right) \tag{16.26}$$

Value of air capacity is given by the product of inlet density and volumetric efficiency ($\rho_{in} \times \eta_v$) for a spark-ignition engine and it increases with increase in average piston speed and reaches a maximum value at a particular piston speed. The indicated thermal efficiency is nearly constant with increasing speed if the fuel-air ratio and the spark timing are adjusted to best power condition at each speed. Therefore, the ratio of indicated mean effective pressures, *imep*, is approximately equal to the ratio of air capacities at different speeds. The mean effective pressure, due to mechanical losses, *fmep* changes with change in average piston speed. The variation of *fmep* with variation of piston speed for different designs of engine are obtained from motoring tests. The values of $fmep_1$ and $fmep_2$ are taken from the test data of similar engine at piston speeds $\bar{s}_{p1}$ and $\bar{s}_{p2}$. The air capacities and *fmep* at two condition being known, the power output and brake specific fuel consumption at condition 2 can be calculated (by Eqs.16.21 and 16.23. When the power output of the engine is decreased at a constant speed, the value of $\rho_{in}\eta_v$ decreases appreciably (resistance at inlet increases due to throttling). The indicated thermal efficiency, η_{ith}, also decreases and the change in indicated thermal efficiency being known, the ratio of indicated mean effective pressures, ϵ can be calculated. The power output and brake specific fuel consumption at condition 2 can be calculated using Eqs.16.25 and 16.26.

When the speed of a compression-ignition engine increases the value of air capacity $\rho_{in}\eta_v$ first increases and then decreases after reaching its maximum value. The indicated thermal efficiency η_{ith} increases with increase in speed as long as the fuel feed system operates satisfactorily and the air capacity remains sufficiently high. Therefore, the ratio of indicated mean effective pressures, ϵ increases with speed upto a particular value. The *fmep* also increases with speed of the engine (average piston speed). The variation of *fmep* with piston speed is obtained from motoring tests. Knowing the value of ϵ and $fmep_2$ the power output and brake specific fuel consumption at condition 2 can be calculated.

When the power developed at a constant speed is reduced by decreasing the amount of fuel injected the volumetric efficiency and indicated thermal efficiency increases with decrease in power developed. Therefore, though the fuel-air ratio decreases, the net effect is an increase in the indicated mean effective pressure. Therefore, the value of ϵ increases with decrease in load at constant speed. The $fmep$ at constant speed and varying power output (varying load) practically remains constant and knowing the value of ϵ output and brake specific fuel consumption at condition 2 can be determined.

Other factors (except the speed and load of the engine) commonly affecting engine performance are the atmospheric conditions (pressure, temperature and humidity), the fuel-air ratio and the compression ratio. The effects of variation of these factors on the volumetric efficiency, indicated thermal efficiency and mechanical efficiency within the range of speed and output of the engine have been discussed in previous chapters.

If the fuel-air ratio is maintained nearly constant during change of inlet conditions (other factors remain constant), the indicated thermal efficiency may be assumed constant. Therefore, the indicated mean effective pressure will depend on $\rho_a \times \eta_v$. Under this condition, the volumetric efficiency is inversely proportional to $\sqrt{T_0}$ ($p_{in} = p_{ex}$ at all conditions). Therefore, $\rho_a \times \eta_v$ is proportional to $p_0/T_0 \times \sqrt{T_0}$ or $p_0/\sqrt{T_0}$. Therefore,

$$\frac{imep_2}{imep_1} = \frac{p_{02}}{p_{01}}\left(\frac{T_{01}}{T_{02}}\right)^{\frac{1}{2}} = \epsilon \qquad (16.27)$$

Using this value of ϵ the performance of the engine at condition 2 can be obtained if their performance at rated condition is known.

The effect of altitude on engine performance is important when the engine operates at different heights in mountainous region or for the aircraft engines. With change in altitude both the inlet pressure and temperature (also the exhaust pressure) change. Therefore, their performance using constant fuel-air ratio can be obtained as in the previous case.

Fuel-air ratio has a marked effect on the indicated thermal efficiency of an engine. Its effect on volumetric efficiency, is however, small (may be neglected). Therefore,

$$\frac{imep_2}{imep_1} = \frac{(\dot{m}_f\ \eta_{ith})_2}{(\dot{m}_f\ \eta_{ith})_1} = \epsilon \qquad (16.28)$$

when all other conditions remain the same but the fuel-air ratio of the charge is changed. The performance at condition 2 can be obtained if the performance at conditions 1 is known.

Compression ratio has significant effect on indicated thermal efficiency. Therefore, when the compression ratio is changed all other conditions of operation remaining the same, the ratio of indicated mean effective pressures is given by,

$$\frac{imep_2}{imep_1} = \frac{(\eta_{ith})_2}{(\eta_{ith})_1} = \epsilon \qquad (16.29)$$

Worked out Examples

16.1 A four-stroke gas engine has a bore of 20 cm and stroke of 30 cm and runs at 300 rpm firing every cycle. If air-fuel ratio is 4:1 by volume and volumetric efficiency on NTP basis is 80%, determine the volume of gas used per minute. If the calorific value of the gas is 8 MJ/m^3 at NTP and the brake thermal efficiency is 25% determine the brake power of the engine.

Solution

$$V_s = \frac{\pi}{4}D^2L = \frac{\pi}{4} \times 20^2 \times 30 = 9424.8 \text{ cc}$$

Total charge taken in per cycle

$$\dot{V}_C = 0.8 \times 9424.8 = 7.54 \times 10^{-3} \text{ m}^3$$

Volume of gas used per minute

$$\dot{V}_g = \frac{7.54 \times 10^{-3}}{4+1} \times \frac{300}{2}$$

$$= 0.2262 \text{ m}^3 \text{ at NTP/min}$$

$$\text{Heat input} = 8000 \times 0.2262 = 1809.6 \text{ kJ/min}$$

$$bp = \eta_{bth} \times \text{ Heat input} = \frac{0.25 \times 1809.6}{60}$$

$$= \mathbf{7.54 \text{ kW}}$$ Ans ⟸

16.2 The following observations have been made from the test of a four-cylinder, two-stroke gasoline engine. Diameter = 10 cm; stroke = 15 cm; speed = 1600 rpm; Area of the positive loop of the indicator diagram = 5.75 sq cm; Area of the negative loop of the indicator diagram = 0.25 sq cm; Length of the indicator diagram = 55 mm; Spring constant = 3.5 bar/cm; Find the indicated power of the engine.

Solution

Net area of diagram = 5.75 – 0.25 = 5.5 cm^2

Average height of the diagram $= \dfrac{5.5}{5.5} = 1$ cm

$$p_{im} = \text{Average height of the diagram} \times \text{ Spring constant}$$

$$= 1 \times 3.5 = 3.5 \text{ bar}$$

$$ip = \frac{p_{im}LAnK}{60000} = \frac{3.5 \times 10^5 \times 0.15 \times \frac{\pi}{4} \times 0.1^2 \times 1600 \times 4}{60000}$$

$$= \mathbf{43.98 \text{ kW}}$$ Ans ⟸

16.3 A single-cylinder engine running at 1800 rpm develops a torque of 8 Nm. The indicated power of the engine is 1.8 kW. Find the loss due to friction power as the percentage of brake power.

Solution

$$bp = \frac{2\pi NT}{60000} = \frac{2 \times \pi \times 1800 \times 8}{60000} = 1.508 \text{ kW}$$

$$\textit{Friction power} = 1.8 - 1.508 = 0.292$$

$$\textit{Percentage loss} = \frac{0.292}{1.508} \times 100 = \mathbf{19.36\%}$$ Ans ⟸

16.4 A gasoline engine working on Otto cycle consumes 8 litres of gasoline per hour and develops 25 kW. The specific gravity of gasoline is 0.75 and its calorific value is 44000 kJ/kg. Determine the indicated thermal efficiency of the engine.

Solution

$$\eta_{ith} = \frac{\text{Heat equivalent of } ip}{\text{Heat input}}$$

$$= \frac{25 \times 60 \times 60}{(8 \times 10^{-3} \times 750) \times 44000} \times 100 = \mathbf{34.1\%}$$ Ans ⟸

16.5 A four cylinder engine running at 1200 rpm delivers 20 kW. The average torque when one cylinder was cut is 110 Nm. Find the indicated thermal efficiency if the calorific value of the fuel is 43 MJ/kg and the engine uses 360 grams of gasoline per kW h.

Solution

$$\text{Avg. bp for 3 cylinders} = \frac{2\pi NT}{60000} = \frac{2\pi \times 1200 \times 110}{60000} = 13.82 \text{ kW}$$

$$\text{Avg. } ip \text{ with 1 cylinder} = 20 - 13.82 = 6.18 \text{ kW}$$

$$\text{Total } ip = 4 \times 6.18 = 24.72 \text{ kW}$$

$$isfc = bsfc \times \frac{bp}{ip} = 360 \times \frac{20}{24.72}$$

$$= 291.26 \text{ g/kW h}$$

$$\text{Fuel consumption} = \frac{isfc \times ip}{3600 \times 1000} = \frac{291.26 \times 24.72}{3600 \times 1000}$$

$$= 2 \times 10^{-3} \text{ kg/s}$$

$$\eta_{ith} = \frac{ip}{\dot{m}_f \times CV} = \frac{24.72}{2 \times 10^{-3} \times 43000} \times 100$$

$$= \mathbf{28.74\%} \qquad \overset{\text{Ans}}{\Longleftarrow}$$

16.6 The bore and stroke of a water-cooled, vertical, single-cylinder, four-stroke diesel engine are 80 mm and 110 mm respectively and the torque is 23.5 Nm. Calculate the brake mean effective pressure of the engine.

Solution

$$P = \frac{2\pi NT}{60000} = \frac{p_{bm} LAn}{60000}$$

$$p_{bm} = \frac{2\pi NT}{LAn} = \frac{2\pi NT}{L \times \frac{\pi}{4} \times D^2 \frac{N}{2}} = \frac{16T}{D^2 L}$$

$$= \frac{16 \times 23.5}{0.08^2 \times 0.11} = 5.34 \times 10^5 \text{ Pa} = \mathbf{5.34 \text{ bar}} \qquad \overset{\text{Ans}}{\Longleftarrow}$$

16.7 Find the mean effective pressure and torque developed by the engine in the previous problem if its rating are 4 kW at 1500 rpm.

Solution

$$p_{bm} = \frac{P \times 60000}{\frac{\pi}{4} D^2 L \frac{N}{2}} \times 10^{-5} \text{ bar}$$

$$= \frac{4 \times 60000}{\frac{\pi}{4} \times 0.08^2 \times 0.11 \times \frac{1500}{2}} \times 10^{-5} = \mathbf{5.78 \text{ bar}} \qquad \overset{\text{Ans}}{\Longleftarrow}$$

$$T = \frac{P \times 60000}{2\pi N} = \frac{4 \times 60000}{2 \times \pi \times 1500} = \mathbf{25.46 \text{ Nm}} \qquad \overset{\text{Ans}}{\Longleftarrow}$$

16.8 Find the brake specific fuel consumption in kg/kW h of a diesel engine whose fuel consumption is 5 grams per second when the power output is 80 kW. If the mechanical efficiency is 75%, calculate the indicated specific fuel consumption.

Solution

$$bsfc = \frac{\dot{m}_f}{bp} = \frac{5}{80} = 0.0625 \text{ g/kW s}$$

$$= \frac{0.0625}{1000} \times 3600 = \mathbf{0.225 \text{ kg/kW h}} \qquad \overset{\text{Ans}}{\Longleftarrow}$$

$$isfc = bsfc \times \eta_m 0.225 \times 0.75 = \mathbf{0.169 \text{ kg/kW h}} \qquad \overset{\text{Ans}}{\Longleftarrow}$$

16.9 For engine in the previous problem find the brake specific energy consumption, *bsec*, given the fuel consumption 5.55 g/s and the lower heating value of the fuel as 43 MJ/kg. Find also the indicated specific energy consumption.

Solution

$$bsec = \frac{\text{kW } heat\ input}{\text{kW } work\ output} = \frac{CV \times \dot{m}_f}{P} = CV \times bsfc$$

$$bsfc = \frac{5.55}{80} = 0.069 \text{ g/kW s} = 0.069 \times 10^{-3} \text{ kg/kW s}$$

$$CV = 43 \text{ MJ/kg} = 43 \times 10^3 \text{ kJ/kg}$$

$$bsec = bsfc \times CV = 43 \times 10^3 \times 0.069 \times 10^{-3} = \mathbf{2.97} \quad \overset{\text{Ans}}{\Longleftarrow}$$

$$isec = bsec \times \eta_m = 2.97 \times 0.75 = \mathbf{2.23} \quad \overset{\text{Ans}}{\Longleftarrow}$$

16.10 Find the air-fuel ratio of a four-stroke, single-cylinder, air-cooled engine with fuel consumption time for 10 cc is 20.4 s and air consumption time for 0.1 m^3 is 16.3 s. The load is 17 kg at the speed of 3000 rpm. Find also brake specific fuel consumption in g/kW h and brake thermal efficiency. Assume the density of air as 1.175 kg/m^3 and specific gravity of fuel to be 0.7. The lower heating value of fuel is 43 MJ/kg and the dynamometer constant is 5000.

Solution

$$Air\ consumption = \frac{0.1}{16.3} \times 1.175 = 7.21 \times 10^{-3} \text{ kg/s}$$

$$Fuel\ consumption = \frac{10}{20.4} \times 0.7 \times \frac{1}{1000} = 0.343 \times 10^{-3} \text{ kg/s}$$

$$Air\text{-}fuel\ ratio = \frac{7.21 \times 10^{-3}}{0.343 \times 10^{-3}} = \mathbf{21} \quad \overset{\text{Ans}}{\Longleftarrow}$$

$$Power\ output,\ P = \frac{WN}{5000} = \frac{7 \times 3000}{5000} = 4.2 \text{ kW}$$

$$bsfc = \frac{Fuel\ consumption\ \ (g/h)}{Power\ output}$$

$$= \frac{0.343 \times 10^{-3} \times 3600 \times 1000}{4.2}$$

$$= \mathbf{294\ g/kW\ h} \quad \overset{\text{Ans}}{\Longleftarrow}$$

$$\eta_{bth} = \frac{4.2}{0.343 \times 10^{-3} \times 43000} \times 100 = \mathbf{28.48\%} \quad \overset{\text{Ans}}{\Longleftarrow}$$

16.11 A six-cylinder, gasoline engine operates on the four-stroke cycle. The bore of each cylinder is 80 mm and the stroke 100 mm. The clearance volume per cylinder is 70 cc. At a speed of 4000 rpm the fuel consumption is 20 kg/h and the torque developed is 150 Nm. Calculate (i) the brake power (ii) the brake mean effective pressure (iii) brake thermal efficiency if the calorific value of the fuel is 43000 kJ/kg and (iv) the relative efficiency on a brake power basis assuming the engine works on the constant volume cycle. $\gamma = 1.4$ for air.

Solution

$$bp = \frac{2\pi NT}{60000} = \frac{2 \times \pi \times 4000 \times 150}{60000} = \mathbf{62.8\ kW} \quad \stackrel{\text{Ans}}{\Longleftarrow}$$

$$p_{bm} = \frac{bp \times 60000}{LAnK} = \frac{62.8 \times 60000}{0.1 \times \frac{\pi}{4} \times 0.08^2 \times \frac{4000}{2} \times 6}$$

$$= 6.25 \times 10^5 \text{ Pa} = \mathbf{6.25\ bar} \quad \stackrel{\text{Ans}}{\Longleftarrow}$$

$$\eta_{bth} = \frac{bp}{\dot{m}_f \times CV} = \frac{62.8 \times 3600}{20 \times 43000} \times 100 = \mathbf{26.3\%} \quad \stackrel{\text{Ans}}{\Longleftarrow}$$

$$r = \frac{V_s + V_{cl}}{V_{cl}}$$

$$V_s = \frac{\pi}{4} D^2 L = \frac{\pi}{4} \times 8^2 \times 10 = 502.65 \text{ cc}$$

$$r = \frac{502.65 + 70}{70} = 8.18$$

$$\eta_{Otto} = 1 - \frac{1}{8.18^{0.4}} = 0.568$$

$$\eta_{rel} = \frac{0.263}{0.568} \times 100 = \mathbf{46.3\%} \quad \stackrel{\text{Ans}}{\Longleftarrow}$$

16.12 An eight-cylinder, four-stroke engine of 9 cm bore and 8 cm stroke with a compression ratio of 7 is tested at 4500 rpm on a dynamometer which has 54 cm arm. During a 10 minutes test the dynamometer scale beam reading was 42 kg and the engine consumed 4.4 kg of gasoline having a calorific value of 44000 kJ/kg. Air 27 °C and 1 bar was supplied to the carburettor at the rate of 6 kg/min. Find (i) the brake power delivered (ii) the brake mean effective pressure (iii) the brake specific fuel consumption (iv) the brake specific air consumption (v) the brake thermal efficiency (vi) the volumetric efficiency and (vii) the air-fuel ratio.

Solution

$$bp = \frac{2\pi NT}{60000}$$

$$= \frac{2 \times \pi \times 4500 \times 42 \times 0.54 \times 9.81}{60000} = \mathbf{104.8\ kW} \quad \stackrel{\text{Ans}}{\Longleftarrow}$$

$$bmep = \frac{bp \times 60000}{LAnK} = \frac{104.8 \times 60000}{0.08 \times \frac{\pi}{4} \times 0.09^2 \times \frac{4500}{2} \times 8}$$

$$= 6.87 \times 10^5 \text{ Pa} = \mathbf{6.87\ bar} \quad \stackrel{\text{Ans}}{\Longleftarrow}$$

$$bsfc = \frac{\frac{4.4}{10} \times 60}{104.8} = \mathbf{0.252\ kg/kW\ h} \quad \stackrel{\text{Ans}}{\Longleftarrow}$$

$$bsac = \frac{6 \times 60}{104.8} = \mathbf{3.435\ kg/kW\ h} \quad \stackrel{\text{Ans}}{\Longleftarrow}$$

$$\eta_{bth} = \frac{bp}{\dot{m}_f \times CV} = \frac{104.9 \times 60}{\frac{4.4}{10} \times 44000} \times 100 = \mathbf{32.5\%} \quad \stackrel{\text{Ans}}{\Longleftarrow}$$

Volume flow rate of air at intake condition

$$\dot{V}_a = \frac{\dot{m}_a RT}{p} = \frac{6 \times 287 \times 300}{1 \times 10^5} = 5.17 \text{ m}^3\text{/min}$$

$$V_s = \frac{\pi}{4} D^2 LnK = \frac{\pi}{4} \times 0.09^2 \times 0.08 \times \frac{4500}{2} \times 8 = 9.16 \text{ m}^3\text{/min}$$

$$\eta_v = \frac{5.17}{9.16} \times 100 = \mathbf{56.44\%} \quad \stackrel{\text{Ans}}{\Longleftarrow}$$

$$A/F = \frac{6.0}{0.44} = \mathbf{13.64} \quad \stackrel{\text{Ans}}{\Longleftarrow}$$

16.13 The following details were noted in a test on a four-cylinder, four-stroke engine, diameter = 100 mm; stroke = 120 mm; speed of the engine = 1600 rpm; fuel consumption = 0.2 kg/min; calorific value of fuel is 44000 kJ/kg; difference in tension on either side of the brake pulley = 40 kg; brake circumference is 300 cm. If the mechanical efficiency is 80%, calculate (i) brake thermal efficiency (ii) indicated thermal efficiency (iii) indicated mean effective pressure and (iv) brake specific fuel consumption

Solution

$$bp = \frac{2\pi NT}{60000} = \frac{2\pi NWR}{60000} = \frac{WN2\pi R}{60000}$$

$$= \frac{40 \times 9.81 \times 1600 \times 3}{60000} = 31.39 \text{ kW}$$

$$\eta_{bth} = \frac{bp}{\dot{m}_f \times CV} \times 100 = \frac{31.39 \times 60}{0.2 \times 44000} \times 100 = \mathbf{21.40\%} \quad \stackrel{\text{Ans}}{\Longleftarrow}$$

$$\eta_{ith} = \frac{\eta_{bth}}{\eta_m} \times 100 = \frac{0.214}{0.80} \times 100 = \mathbf{26.75\%} \quad \stackrel{\text{Ans}}{\Longleftarrow}$$

$$imep = \frac{\frac{bp}{\eta_m} \times 60000}{LAnK} = \frac{\frac{31.39}{0.8} \times 60000}{0.12 \times \frac{\pi}{4} 0.1^2 \times \frac{1600}{2} \times 4}$$

$$= 7.8 \times 10^5 \text{ Pa} = \mathbf{7.8\ bar}$$ Ans

$$bsfc = \frac{\dot{m}_f}{bp} = \frac{0.2 \times 60}{31.39} = \mathbf{0.382\ kg/kW\ h}$$ Ans

16.14 The air flow to a four cylinder, four-stroke oil engine is measured by means of a 5 cm diameter orifice having a coefficient of discharge of 0.6. During a test on the engine the following data were recorded : bore = 10 cm; stroke = 12 cm; speed = 1200 rpm; brake torque = 120 Nm; fuel consumption = 5 kg/h; calorific value of fuel = 42 MJ/kg; pressure drop across orifice is 4.6 cm of water; ambient temperature and pressure are 17 °C and 1 bar respectively. Calculate (i) the thermal efficiency on brake power basis; (ii) the brake mean effective pressure and (iii) the volumetric efficiency based on free air condition.

Solution

$$bp = \frac{2\pi NT}{60000} = \frac{2 \times \pi \times 1200 \times 120}{60000} = 15.08 \text{ kW}$$

$$\eta_{bth} = \frac{15.08 \times 60}{\frac{5}{60} \times 42000} \times 100 = \mathbf{25.85\%}$$ Ans

$$p_{im} = \frac{bp \times 60000}{LAnK}$$

$$= \frac{15.08 \times 60000}{0.12 \times \frac{\pi}{4} \times 0.1^2 \times \frac{1200}{2} \times 4} = 4 \times 10^5 \text{ Pa} = \mathbf{4\ bar}$$ Ans

$$\dot{V}_a = C_d A \sqrt{2g\Delta h_w \frac{\rho_w}{\rho_a}}$$

$$\rho_a = \frac{p}{RT} = \frac{10^5}{287 \times 290} = 1.20 \text{ kg/m}^3$$

$$\dot{V}_a = 0.6 \times \frac{\pi}{4} \times 0.05^2 \times \sqrt{2 \times 9.81 \times 0.046 \times \frac{1000}{1.2}} \times 60$$

$$= 1.938 \text{ m}^3/\text{min}$$

$$V_s = \frac{\pi}{4} d^2 LnK$$

$$= \frac{\pi}{4} \times 0.1^2 \times 0.12 \times \frac{1200}{2} \times 4 = 2.262 \text{ m}^3/\text{min}$$

$$\eta_v = \frac{1.938}{2.262} \times 100 = \mathbf{85.7\%}$$ Ans

16.15 The following observations were recorded during a trial of a four-stroke, single-cylinder oil engine. Duration of trial is 30 min; oil consumption is 4 litres; calorific value of the oil is 43 MJ/kg; specific gravity of the fuel = 0.8; average area of the indicator diagram = 8.5 cm^2; Length of the indicator diagram = 8.5 cm; spring constant = 5.5 bar/cm; brake load = 150 kg; spring balance reading = 20 kg; effective brake wheel diameter = 1.5 m; speed = 200 rpm; cylinder diameter = 30 cm; stroke = 45 cm; jacket cooling water = 10 kg/min; temperature rise is 36 °C. Calculate (i) indicated power (ii) brake power (iii) mechanical efficiency (iv) brake specific fuel consumption in kg/kW h and (v) indicated thermal efficiency.

Solution

$$p_{im} = \frac{\text{Area of the diagram}}{\text{Length of the diagram}} \times \text{Spring const.}$$

$$= \frac{8.5}{8.5} \times 5.5 = 5.5 \text{ bar}$$

$$ip = \frac{p_{im}LAn}{60000}$$

$$= \frac{5.5 \times 10^5 \times 0.45 \times \frac{\pi}{4} \times 0.3^2 \times \frac{200}{2}}{60000}$$

$$= \mathbf{29.16\ kW} \qquad \text{Ans}$$

$$bp = \frac{2\pi NWR}{60000} = \frac{\pi NWd}{60000}$$

$$= \frac{\pi \times 200 \times (150 - 20) \times 9.81 \times 1.5}{60000}$$

$$= \mathbf{20.03\ kW} \qquad \text{Ans}$$

$$\eta_m = \frac{20.03}{29.16} \times 100 = \mathbf{68.7\%} \qquad \text{Ans}$$

$$\dot{m}_f = \frac{4}{30} \times 60 \times 10^{-3} \times 800 = 6.4 \text{ kg/h}$$

$$bsfc = \frac{6.4}{20.03} = \mathbf{0.3195\ kg/kW\ h} \qquad \text{Ans}$$

$$\eta_{ith} = \frac{ip}{\dot{m}_f \times CV} = \frac{29.16 \times 3600}{6.4 \times 43000} \times 100 = \mathbf{38.14\%} \qquad \text{Ans}$$

16.16 A four-stroke cycle gas engine has a bore of 20 cm and a stroke of 40 cm. The compression ratio is 6. In a test on the engine the indicated mean effective pressure is 5 bar, the air to gas ratio is 6:1 and the calorific value of the gas is 12 MJ/m^3 at NTP. At the beginning of the compression stroke the temperature is 77 °C and pressure 0.98 bar. Neglecting residual gases, determine the indicated power, the thermal efficiency and the relative efficiency of the engine at 250 rpm.

Solution

$$V_s = \frac{\pi}{4}D^2L = \frac{\pi}{4} \times 20^2 \times 40 = 12566.4 \text{ cc}$$

Volume of gas in the cylinder

$$= \frac{1}{1 + A/F} \times V_1$$

$$V_1 = V_s + \frac{V_s}{r-1} = V_s \times \frac{6}{5} = \frac{1}{6+1} \times 12566.4 \times \frac{6}{5}$$

$$= 2154.24 \text{ cc/cycle}$$

Since the residual gases are to be neglected, one can assume a volumetric efficiency of 100%

Normal pressure = 1 bar

$$\left(\frac{pV}{T}\right)_{NTP} = \left(\frac{p_2V_2}{T_2}\right)_{working}$$

Volume of gas at NTP conditions

$$= 2154.24 \times \frac{0.98}{1} \times \frac{273}{350} = 1646.7 \text{ cc}$$

$$\textit{Heat added} = 1646.7 \times 10^{-6} \times 12 \times 10^3 = 19.76 \text{ kJ/cycle}$$

$$ip = \frac{p_{im}V_sn}{60000} = \frac{5 \times 10^5 \times 12566.4 \times 10^{-6} \times \frac{250}{2}}{60000}$$

$$= \mathbf{13.09 \text{ kW}}$$ Ans

$$\eta_{ith} = \frac{ip}{\textit{Heat added (in kW)}} \times 100 = \frac{13.09}{19.76 \times \frac{250}{2\times60}} \times 100$$

$$= \mathbf{31.8\%}$$ Ans

$$\eta_{air-std} = 1 - \frac{1}{6^{0.4}} = 0.512$$

$$\eta_{rel} = \frac{0.318}{0.512} \times 100 = \mathbf{62.11\%}$$ Ans

16.17 A four-stroke, four-cylinder gasoline engine has a bore of 60 mm and a stroke of 100 mm. On test it develops a torque of 66.5 Nm when running at 3000 rpm. If the clearance volume in each cylinder is 60 cc the relative efficiency with respect to brake thermal efficiency is 0.5 and the calorific value of the fuel is 42 MJ/kg, determine the fuel consumption in kg/h and the brake mean effective pressure.

Solution

$$V_s = \frac{\pi}{4} \times 0.06^2 \times 0.1 = 2.83 \times 10^{-4} \ \text{m}^3/\text{cylinder}$$

$$= 283 \ \text{cc/cylinder}$$

$$r = \frac{283 + 60}{60} = 5.71$$

$$\eta_{air-std} = 1 - \frac{1}{5.71^{0.4}} = 0.50$$

$$\eta_{bth} = \textit{Relative } \eta \times \textit{Air-standard } \eta = 0.5 \times 0.5 = 0.25$$

$$bp = \frac{2 \times \pi \times 3000 \times 66.5}{60000} = 20.89 \ \text{kW}$$

$$\textit{Heat supplied} = \frac{20.89}{0.25} = 83.56 \ \text{kJ/s}$$

$$\text{Fuel consumption} = \frac{83.56 \times 3600}{42000} = \mathbf{7.16\ kg/h} \quad \overset{\text{Ans}}{\Longleftarrow}$$

$$p_{bm} = \frac{P \times 60000}{V_s n K} = \frac{20.89 \times 60000}{2.83 \times 10^{-4} \times \frac{3000}{2} \times 4}$$

$$= 7.38 \times 10^5 \ \text{N/m}^2 = \mathbf{7.38\ bar} \quad \overset{\text{Ans}}{\Longleftarrow}$$

16.18 The power output of a six cylinder four-stroke engine is absorbed by a water brake for which the law is $WN/20000$ where the brake load, W is in Newton and the speed, N is in rpm. The air consumption is measured by an air box with sharp edged orifice system. The following readings are obtained.

Orifice diameter	=	30 mm
Bore	=	100 mm
Stroke	=	120 mm
Brake load	=	560 N
C/H ratio by mass	=	83/17
Coefficient of discharge	=	0.6
Ambient pressure	=	1 bar
Pressure drop across orifice	=	14.5 cm of Hg
Time taken for 100 cc of fuel consumption	=	20 s
Ambient temperature	=	27 °C
Fuel density	=	831 kg/m^3

Calculate (i) the brake power (ii) the torque (iii) the brake specific fuel consumption (iv) the percentage of excess air and (v) the volumetric efficiency

Solution

$$\rho_a = \frac{p}{RT} = \frac{1 \times 10^5}{287 \times 300} = 1.16 \text{ kg/m}^3$$

$$\dot{V}_a = C_d A \sqrt{2g\Delta H_g \frac{\rho_{Hg}}{\rho_a}}$$

$$= 0.6 \times \frac{\pi}{4} \times 0.03^2 \times \sqrt{2 \times 9.81 \times 0.145 \times \frac{13600}{1.16}}$$

$$= 0.077 \text{ m}^3\text{/s}$$

$$V_s = \frac{\pi}{4} \times 0.1^2 \times 0.12 \times \frac{2400}{2} \times \frac{6}{60}$$

$$= 0.113 \text{ m}^3\text{/s}$$

$$\eta_v = \frac{0.077}{0.113} \times 100 = \mathbf{68.1\%}$$ Ans

$$bp = \frac{WN}{20000} = \frac{560 \times 2400}{20000} = \mathbf{67.2\ kW}$$ Ans

$$bmep = \frac{bp \times 60000}{LAnK}$$

$$= \frac{67.2 \times 60000 \times 10^{-5}}{0.12 \times \frac{\pi}{4} \times 0.1^2 \times \frac{2400}{2} \times 6} = 5.94 \text{ bar}$$

$$T = \frac{bp \times 60000}{2\pi N}$$

$$= \frac{67.2 \times 60000}{2 \times \pi \times 2400} = \mathbf{267.3\ Nm}$$ Ans

$$\dot{m}_f = \frac{100}{20} \times 10^{-6} \times 831 \times 3600 = 14.96 \text{ kg/h}$$

$$bsfc = \frac{14.96}{67.2} = \mathbf{0.223\ kg/kW\ h}$$ Ans

$$O_2 \text{ required/kg of fuel} = 0.83 \times \frac{32}{12} + 0.17 \times \frac{8}{1}$$

$$= 3.57 \text{ kg/kg of fuel}$$

Since, air contains 23.3% of O_2 by weight,

$$\text{Air required/kg of fuel} = \frac{3.57}{0.233} = 15.32 \text{ kg}$$

$$\text{Actual mass flow rate of air} = 0.077 \times 1.16 = 0.089 \text{ kg/s}$$

$$\text{Actual mass A/F ratio} = \frac{0.089 \times 3600}{14.96} = 21.42$$

$$\text{\%of excess air} = \frac{21.42 - 15.32}{15.32} \times 100 = \mathbf{39.8\%}$$ Ans

16.19 A six-cylinder, four-stroke cycle gasoline engine with a bore of 120 mm and a stroke of 200 mm under test was supplied with gasoline of composition C = 82% and H_2 = 18% by mass. The dry exhaust composition by volume was CO_2 = 11.2%, O_2 = 3.6% and N_2 = 85.2%. Determine the mass of air supplied per kg of gasoline at 17 °C and 1 bar which were the conditions for the mixture entering the cylinder during the test. Also determine the volumetric efficiency of the engine based on intake conditions when the mass of gasoline used per hour was 30 kg and the engine speed was 1400 rpm. The gasoline is completely evaporated before entering the cylinder and the effect of its volume on the volumetric efficiency should be included. Take the density of gasoline vapour as 3.4 times that of air at the same temperature and pressure. One kg of air at 0 °C and 1 bar occupies 0.783 m^3. Air contains 23% oxygen by mass.

Solution

$$\text{Stoichiometric air-fuel ratio} = \frac{0.82 \times \frac{32}{12} + 0.18 \times \frac{8}{1}}{0.23} = 15.77$$

Let y mol of air be supplied per kg of fuel then

$$\frac{0.82}{12}\text{C} + \frac{0.18}{2}\text{H}_2 + 0.21y\text{O}_2 + 0.79y\text{N}_2 = a\text{CO}_2 + b\text{O}_2 + c\text{H}_2\text{O} + d\text{N}_2$$

$$\text{From carbon balance, } \frac{0.82}{12} = a = 0.068$$

$$\text{From hydrogen balance, } \frac{0.18}{2} = c = 0.09$$

$$\text{From oxygen balance, } 0.21y = a + b + \frac{c}{2}$$

$$= 0.068 + b + 0.045$$

$$= 0.113 + b$$

$$\text{From nitrogen balance, } 0.79y = d$$

$$\text{From exhaust gas analysis.} \quad \frac{0.068}{d} = \frac{11.2}{85.2}$$

$$d = \frac{85.2}{11.2} \times 0.068 = 0.517$$

$$0.79y = 0.517$$

$$y = 0.655 \text{ mol of air/kg of fuel}$$

$$\text{Molecular wt of air} = 0.23 \times 32 + 0.77 \times 28$$

$$= 28.92 \text{ kg/mol}$$

$$\text{Actual air-fuel ratio} = 0.655 \times 28.92$$

$$= \mathbf{18.94} \quad \overset{\text{Ans}}{\Longleftarrow}$$

$$\%\ \text{excess air} = \frac{18.94 - 15.77}{15.77} \times 100$$

$$= 20.1\%$$

$$\text{Volume of air} = V_a \times m$$

$$V_a = 0.783 \times \frac{290}{273} = 0.832 \text{ m}^3\text{/kg}$$

$$= 0.832 \times 18.94 = 15.76 \text{ m}^3$$

$$\text{Volume of fuel} = V_f \times m$$

$$= \frac{0.832}{3.4} \times 1 = 0.245 \text{ m}^3$$

$$\text{Total volume} = 15.76 + 0.245$$

$$= 16.005 \text{ m}^3\text{/kg of fuel}$$

$$\text{Mixture evaporated} = \frac{16.005 \times 30}{60} = 8.002 \text{ m}^3\text{/min}$$

$$V_s/\text{min} = 6 \times \frac{\pi}{4} \times 0.12^2 \times 0.20 \times \frac{1400}{2}$$

$$= 9.5 \text{ m}^3\text{/min}$$

$$\eta_v = \frac{8.002}{9.5} \times 100 = \mathbf{84.2\%} \quad \overset{\text{Ans}}{\Longleftarrow}$$

16.20 An indicator diagram taken from a single-cylinder, four-stroke CI engine has a length of 100 mm and an area of 2000 mm^2. The indicator pointer deflects a distance of 10 mm for pressure increment of 2 bar in the cylinder. If the bore and stroke of the engine cylinder are both 100 mm and the engine speed is 1000 rpm. Calculate the mean effective pressure and the indicated power. If the mechanical efficiency is 75% what is the brake power developed.

Solution

Mean height of the indicator diagram

$$= \frac{2000}{100} = 20 \text{ mm}$$

$$mep = \frac{20}{10} \times 2 = \mathbf{4\ bar} \quad \overset{\text{Ans}}{\Longleftarrow}$$

$$ip = \frac{p_{im} LAn}{60000}$$

$$= \frac{4 \times 10^5 \times 0.1 \times \frac{\pi}{4} \times 0.1^2 \times \frac{1000}{2}}{60000}$$

$$= \mathbf{2.62\ kW} \quad \overset{\text{Ans}}{\Longleftarrow}$$

$$bp = ip \times \eta_m = 2.62 \times 0.75 = \mathbf{1.96\ kW} \quad \overset{\text{Ans}}{\Longleftarrow}$$

16.21 A single-cylinder, four-stroke gas engine has a bore of 180 mm and a stroke of 330 mm and is governed on the hit and miss principle. When running at 400 rpm at full load indicator card are taken which give a working loop mean effective pressure of 6 bar and a pumping loop mean effective pressure of 0.4 bar. Diagrams from the dead cycle give a mean effective pressure of 0.6 bar. When running on no load a mechanical counter recorded 50 firings strokes per minute. Calculate at the full load with regular firing, brake power and the mechanical efficiency of the engine.

Solution

Assume fp to be constant at a given speed and is independent of load.

$$\text{Net } imep = 6.0 - 0.4 = 5.6 \text{ bar}$$

$$\text{Working cycle/minute} = 50$$

$$\text{Dead cycles/minute} = \frac{400}{2} - 50 = 150$$

In hit and miss governing the working cycle has the same indicated diagram at any load. Since at no load, bp is zero

$$fp = ip - \text{pumping power of dead cycles}$$

$$V_s = \frac{\pi}{4} \times 0.18^2 \times 0.33 = 8.4 \times 10^{-3} \text{ m}^3$$

$$fp = \frac{p_{im} \times V_s \times n}{60000} - \frac{p_{fm} \times V_s \times n}{60000}$$

$$= \frac{5.6 \times 10^5 \times 8.4 \times 10^{-3} \times 50}{60000} - \frac{0.6 \times 10^5 \times 8.4 \times 10^{-3} \times 150}{60000}$$

$$= 3.92 - 1.26 = 2.66$$

At full load, with regular firing ($n = 400/2$) per minute

$$ip = \frac{p_{im}LAn}{60000}$$

$$= \frac{5.6 \times 10^5 \times 8.4 \times 10^{-3} \times \frac{400}{2}}{60000}$$

$$= 15.68 \text{ kW}$$

$$bp = 15.68 - 2.66 = \mathbf{13.02\ kW} \quad \stackrel{\text{Ans}}{\Longleftarrow}$$

$$\eta_{mech} = \frac{13.02}{15.68} \times 100 = \mathbf{83.03\%} \quad \stackrel{\text{Ans}}{\Longleftarrow}$$

16.22 A six-cylinder, four-stroke, direct-injection oil engine is to deliver 120 kW at 1600 rpm. The fuel to be used has a calorific value of 43 MJ/kg and its percentage composition by mass is carbon 86.0%, hydrogen 13.0%, non combustibles 1.0%. The absolute volumetric efficiency is assumed to 80%, the indicated thermal efficiency 40% and the mechanical efficiency 80%. The air consumption to be 110% in excess of that required for theoretically correct combustion.

(i) Estimate the volumetric composition of dry exhaust gas

(ii) Determine the bore and stroke of the engine, taking a stroke to bore ratio as 1.5.

Assume the volume of 1 kg of air at the given conditions as 0.77 m^3. Oxygen in air is 23% by mass and 21% by volume.

Solution

$$\text{Stoichiometric air-fuel ratio} = \frac{0.86 \times \frac{32}{12} + 0.13 \times \frac{8}{1}}{0.23}$$

$$= 14.49$$

$$A/F = \left(1 + \frac{110}{100}\right) \times 14.49 = 30.43$$

$$\text{Mol wt of air} = 0.23 \times 32 + 0.769 \times 28$$

$$= 28.9 \text{ kg/K mol} \quad \stackrel{\text{Ans}}{\Longleftarrow}$$

Let y mol of air be supplied per kg of fuel and the equation of combustion per kg of fuel is

$$\frac{0.86}{12}C + \frac{0.14}{2}H_2 + 0.21yO_2 + 0.79yN_2 = aCO_2 + bH_2O + cO_2 + dN_2$$

$$\text{From carbon balance, } \frac{0.86}{12} = a = 0.0717$$

$$\text{From hydrogen balance, } \frac{0.13}{2} = b = 0.065$$

$$\text{From oxygen balance, } 0.21y = a + \frac{b}{2} + c = 0.0717 + 0.0325 + c$$

$$= 0.1042 + c$$

Number of kilo moles of air for per kg of fuel

$$\frac{30.43}{28.9} = 1.05 = y$$

$$0.21 \times 1.05 = 0.1042 + c$$

$$c = 0.116$$

$$\text{From nitrogen balance, } 0.79y = d$$

$$d = 0.79 \times 1.05 = 0.8295$$

Volumetric composition of dry exhaust gas **Ans** ⟸

Constituent	mols	% Vol
CO_2	0.0717	7.05
O_2	0.1160	11.40
N_2	0.8295	81.55
Total	**1.0172**	**100.00**

$$ip = \frac{bp}{\eta_m} = \frac{120}{0.8} = 150 \text{ kW}$$

$$\text{Heat input} = \frac{\text{Heat equivalent of } ip}{\eta_{ith}}$$

$$= \frac{150 \times 60}{0.40} = 22500 \text{ kJ/min}$$

$$\dot{m}_f = \frac{22500}{43000} = 0.523 \text{ kg/min}$$

$$\dot{m}_a = \dot{m}_f \times \text{Actual A/F} = 0.523 \times 30.43 = 15.92 \text{ kg/min}$$

$$\dot{V}_a = \dot{m}_a V_a = 15.92 \times 0.770 = 12.26 \text{ m}^3\text{/min}$$

$$V_s = \frac{12.26}{0.8} = 15.32 \text{ m}^3\text{/min}$$

$$V_s = \frac{\pi}{4} D^2 LnK$$

$$15.32 = \frac{\pi}{4} D^2 \times 1.5D \times \frac{1600}{2} \times 6$$

$$D^3 = \frac{15.32 \times 4 \times 2}{\pi \times 1.5 \times 1600 \times 6} = 2.71 \times 10^{-3}$$

$$D = 0.14 \text{ m} = \mathbf{14 \text{ cm}}$$ Ans

$$L = 1.5 \times 0.14 = 0.21 \text{ m} = \mathbf{21 \text{ cm}}$$ Ans

16.23 A six cylinder, four-stroke gasoline engine having a bore of 90 mm and stroke of 100 mm has a compression ratio 7. The relative efficiency is 55% when the indicated specific fuel consumption is 300 gm/kW h. Estimate (i) the calorific value of the fuel and (ii) corresponding fuel consumption, given that imep is 8.5 bar and speed is 2500 rpm.

Solution

$$\eta_{air-std} = 1 - \frac{1}{r^{\gamma-1}} = 1 - \frac{1}{7^{0.4}} = 0.541$$

$$\eta_{rel} = \frac{\text{Thermal efficiency}}{\text{Air-standard efficiency}}$$

$$\eta_{ith} = 0.55 \times 0.541 = 0.297$$

$$\eta_{ith} = \frac{1}{isfc \times CV}$$

$$CV = \frac{1}{\eta_{ith} \times isfc} = \frac{3600}{0.3 \times 0.297}$$

$$= \mathbf{40404 \text{ kJ/kg}}$$ Ans

$$ip = \frac{p_{im} LAnK}{60000}$$

$$= \frac{8.5 \times 10^5 \times 0.1 \times \frac{\pi}{4} \times 0.09^2 \times \frac{2500}{2} \times 6}{60000}$$

$$= 67.6 \text{ kW}$$

$$\text{Fuel consumption} = isfc \times ip = 0.3 \times 67.6 = \mathbf{20.28 \text{ kg/h}}$$ Ans

16.24 A gasoline engine working on four stroke develops a brake power of 20.9 kW. A Morse Test was conducted on this engine and the brake power (kW) obtained when each cylinder was made inoperative by short circuiting the spark plug are 14.9, 14.3, 14.8 and 14.5 respectively. The test was conducted at constant speed. Find the indicated power, mechanical efficiency and *bmep* when all the cylinders are firing. The bore of the engine is 75 mm and the stroke is 90 mm. The engine is running at 3000 rpm.

Solution

$$ip_1 = bp_{1234} - bp_{234}$$

$$= 20.9 - 14.9 = 6.0 \text{ kW}$$

$$ip_2 = bp_{1234} - bp_{134}$$

$$= 20.9 - 14.3 = 6.6 \text{ kW}$$

$$ip_3 = bp_{1234} - bp_{124}$$

$$= 20.9 - 14.8 = 6.1 \text{ kW}$$

$$ip_4 = bp_{1234} - bp_{123}$$

$$= 20.9 - 14.5 = 6.4 \text{ kW}$$

$$ip_1 + ip_2 + ip_3 + ip_4 = ip_{1234} = 6.0 + 6.6 + 6.1 + 6.4$$

$$= \mathbf{25.1\ kW} \quad \overset{\text{Ans}}{\Longleftarrow}$$

$$\eta_m = \frac{20.9}{25.1} \times 100$$

$$= \mathbf{83.3\%} \quad \overset{\text{Ans}}{\Longleftarrow}$$

$$p_{bm} = \frac{bp \times 60000}{LAnK}$$

$$= \frac{20.9 \times 60000}{0.09 \times \frac{\pi}{4} \times 0.075^2 \times \frac{3000}{2} \times 4}$$

$$= 5.25 \times 10^5 \text{ Pa}$$

$$= \mathbf{5.25\ bar} \quad \overset{\text{Ans}}{\Longleftarrow}$$

16.25 A Morse test on a 12 cylinder, two-stroke compression-ignition engine of bore 40 cm and stroke 50 cm running at 200 rpm gave the following readings:

Condition	Brake load (Newton)	Condition	Brake load (Newton)
All firing	2040	7th cylinder	1835
1st cylinder	1830	8th cylinder	1860
2nd cylinder	1850	9th cylinder	1820
3rd cylinder	1850	10th cylinder	1840
4th cylinder	1830	11th cylinder	1850
5th cylinder	1840	12th cylinder	1830
6th cylinder	1855	All firing	2060

The output is found from the dynamometer using the relation

$$bp = \frac{WN}{180}$$

where W, the brake load is in Newton and the speed, N is in rpm. Calculate *ip*, mechanical efficiency and *bmep* of the engine.

Solution

$$\text{Power output when all cylinders fire} = \frac{2040 + 2060}{2} \times \frac{200}{180}$$

$$= 2277.8 \text{ kW}$$

Power output, *bp* when kth cylinder is cut-off $= \frac{N}{180} \sum_{k=1}^{12} W_k$

Ans ⟸

Cylinder number cut-off	ip of kth cylinder $ip_k = 2277.8 - \frac{N}{180} \sum W_i$ (kW)
1	244.5
2	222.2
3	222.2
4	244.5
5	233.4
6	216.7
7	238.9
8	211.1
9	255.6
10	233.4
11	222.2
12	244.5

$$\text{Total indicated power} = ip_1 + ip_2 + \ldots + ip_{12}$$

$$= \mathbf{2789.2}$$

Ans ⟸

$$\eta_{mech} = \frac{2277.8}{2789.2} = \mathbf{81.66\%}$$

Ans ⟸

$$bmep = \frac{bp \times 60000}{LAnK}$$

$$= \frac{2277.8 \times 60000}{0.5 \times \frac{\pi}{4} \times 0.4^2 \times 200 \times 12}$$

$$= 9.06 \times 10^5 \text{ Pa} = \mathbf{9.06\ bar}$$ Ans

16.26 The observations recorded after the conduct of a retardation test on a single-cylinder diesel engine are as follows:

Rated power : 8 kW Rated speed : 475 rpm

S.No.	Drop in speed (rpm)	Time for fall of speed at no load, t_2 (s)	Time for fall of speed at 50% load, t_3 (s)
1.	475 → 400	7.0	2.2
2.	475 → 350	10.6	3.7
3.	475 → 325	12.5	4.8
4.	475 → 300	15.0	5.4
5.	475 → 275	16.6	6.5
6.	475 → 250	18.9	7.2

Calculate frictional power and mechanical efficiency.

Solution

First draw a graph of drop in speed versus time taken for the drop.

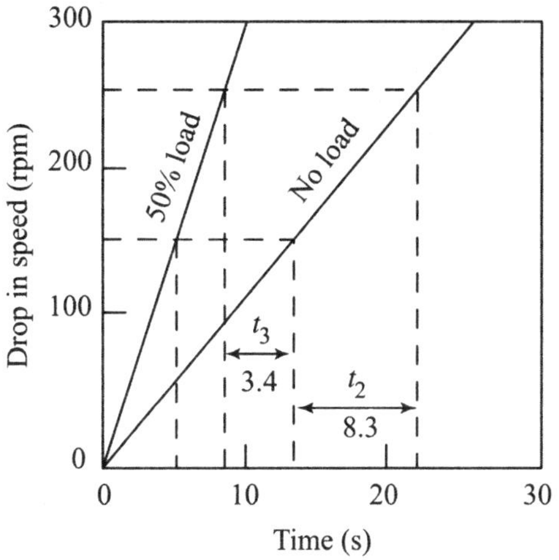

$$P = \frac{2\pi NT}{60000} \text{ kW}$$

$$\text{Full load torque, } T = \frac{P \times 60000}{2\pi N}$$

$$= \frac{8 \times 60000}{2 \times \pi \times 475} = 160.8 \text{ Nm}$$

$$\text{Torque at half load, } T_{\frac{1}{2}} = 80.4 \text{ Nm}$$

From the graph, time for the fall of 100 rpm at no load, $t_2 = 8.3$ s and time for the fall of same 100 rpm at half load, $t_3 = 3.4$ s.

$$T_f = \frac{t_3}{t_2 - t_3} T_{\frac{1}{2}}$$

$$= \left(\frac{3.4}{8.3 - 3.4}\right) \times 80.4 = 55.8 \text{ Nm}$$

$$fp = \frac{2\pi N T_f}{60000}$$

$$= \frac{2 \times \pi \times 475 \times 55.8}{60000} = \mathbf{2.77\ kW} \quad \stackrel{\text{Ans}}{\Longleftarrow}$$

$$\eta_m = \frac{bp}{bp + fp} = \frac{8}{8 + 2.77} \times 100$$

$$= \mathbf{74.28\%} \quad \stackrel{\text{Ans}}{\Longleftarrow}$$

16.27 A single-cylinder gas engine, with bore x stroke of 25 x 50 cm and running at 240 rpm fires 100 times per min. The quantity of coal gas used is 0.3 m^3 per minute at 100 cm of water (gauge) (barometer pressure 1 bar) at 17 °C while the amount of air used is 3 kg/min. Assuming that an extra volume of air is taken in during a missed cycle equal to that of a coal gas normally taken in, if both are measured at NTP, find (i) the charge of air per working cycle as measured at NTP and (ii) the volumetric efficiency. Assume 760 mm of Hg as 1 bar.

Solution

$$\text{Gas pressure} = 1 + \frac{100}{13.6} \times \frac{1}{76}$$

$$= 1.097 \text{ bar}$$

$$\text{Volume of coal gas at NTP} = 0.3 \times \frac{1.097}{1} \times \frac{273}{290}$$

$$= 0.31 \text{ m}^3/\text{min}$$

$$\text{Volume of coal gas used/explosion} = \frac{0.31}{100}$$

$$= 0.0031 \text{ m}^3 \text{ at NTP}$$

$$\text{Extra air missed/cycle} = 0.0031 \text{ m}^3 \text{ at NTP}$$

$$\text{Volume of air taken at NTP} = \frac{mRT}{p}$$

$$= \frac{3 \times 287 \times 273}{1 \times 10^5}$$

$$= 2.35 \text{ m}^3/\text{min}$$

The engine is running at 240 rpm and therefore there must be 120 firing cycles per minute. However, there are only 100 cycles per minute. Hence, there are 20 missed cycles. The 2.35 m^3 of air per minute at NTP must be made up of 120 normal air charges, V, together with 20 missed cycles each equivalent to 0.0031 m^3 at NTP

$$20 \times 0.0031 + 120V = 2.35$$

$$V = 0.019 \text{ m}^3$$

$$\text{Total volume of charge at NTP} = 0.019 + 0.0031$$

$$= \mathbf{0.022 \text{ m}^3} \qquad \text{Ans}$$

$$V_s = \frac{\pi}{4} \times 0.25^2 \times 0.5 = 0.0245 \text{ m}^3$$

$$\eta_v = \frac{0.022}{0.0245} \times 100$$

$$= \mathbf{89.8\%} \qquad \text{Ans}$$

16.28 A trial was conducted on a single-cylinder oil engine having a cylinder diameter of 30 cm and stroke 45 cm. The engine is working on the four-stroke cycle and the following observations were made:

Duration of trial	=	54 minutes
Total fuel used	=	7 litres
Calorific value	=	42 MJ/kg
Total number of revolution	=	12624
Gross *imep*	=	7.25 bar
Pumping *imep*	=	0.35 bar
Net load on the brake	=	150 kg
Diameter of the brake wheel drum	=	1.78 m
Diameter of the rope	=	4 cm
Cooling water circulated	=	550 litres
Cooling water temperature rise	=	48 °C
Specific heat of water	=	4.18 kJ/kg K
Specific gravity of oil	=	0.8

Calculate the mechanical efficiency and also the unaccounted losses.

Solution

$$ip = \frac{(7.25 - 0.35) \times 10^5 \times 0.45 \times \frac{\pi}{4} \times 0.3^2 \times \frac{12624}{45 \times 2}}{60000}$$

$$= 51.3 \text{ kW}$$

$$\text{Heat supplied} = \frac{7 \times 10^{-3} \times 800}{45} \times 42000 = 5226.67 \text{ kJ/min}$$

$$bp = \frac{9.8 \times 150 \times \pi \times (1.78 + 0.4) \times 12624}{60000 \times 54}$$

$$= 39.23 \text{ kW}$$

$$\eta_m = \frac{bp}{ip} \times 100 = \frac{39.23}{51.3} \times 100 = \mathbf{76.47\%}$$ Ans

$$\text{Heat equivalent of } bp = 39.23 \times 60 = 2353.8 \text{ kJ/min}$$

$$\text{Heat lost in cooling water} = \frac{550 \times 48 \times 4.18}{45} = 2452.3 \text{ kJ/min}$$

$$\text{Unaccounted losses} = 5226.67 - (2353.8 + 2452.3)$$

$$= \mathbf{420.57 \text{ kJ/min}}$$ Ans

16.29 A four-stroke gas engine has a cylinder diameter of 25 cm and stroke 45 cm. The effective diameter of the brake is 1.6 m. The observations made in a test of the engine were as follows:

Duration of test	=	40 min
Total number of revolutions	=	8080
Total number of explosions	=	3230
Net load on the brake	=	90 kg
Mean effective pressure	=	5.8 bar
Volume of gas used	=	7.5 m^3
Pressure of gas indicated in meter	=	136 mm water of gauge
Atmospheric temperature	=	17 °C
Calorific value of gas	=	19 MJ/m^3 at NTP
Rise in temperature of jacket cooling water	=	45 °C
Cooling water supplied	=	180 kg

Draw up a heat balance sheet and estimate the indicated thermal efficiency and brake thermal efficiency. Assume atmospheric pressure as 760 mm of Hg.

Solution

$$ip = \frac{p_{im} L A n}{60000}$$

$$= \frac{5.8 \times 10^5 \times 0.45 \times \frac{\pi}{4} \times 0.25^2 \times \frac{3230}{40}}{60000} = 17.25$$

$$bp = \frac{9.81 \times 90 \times \pi \times 1.6 \times \frac{8080}{40}}{60000} = 14.94 \text{ kW}$$

Pressure of the gas supplied

$$= 760 + \frac{136}{13.6} = 770 \text{ mm of Hg}$$

Volume of gas used at NTP

$$= 7.5 \times \frac{273}{290} \times \frac{770}{760} = 7.15 \text{ m}^3$$

$$\text{Heat supplied} = \frac{7.15 \times 19000}{40} = 3396.25 \text{ kJ/min}$$

Heat equivalent of *bp*

$$= 14.94 \times 60 = \mathbf{896.4 \text{ kJ/min}}$$ Ans

Heat loss in cooling medium

$$= \frac{180 \times 45}{40} \times 4.18 = \mathbf{846.5 \text{ kJ/min}}$$ Ans

Heat lost to exhaust, radiation, etc. (by difference)

$$= 3396.25 - 896.4 - 846.5 = \mathbf{1653.35 \text{ kJ/min}}$$ Ans

$$\eta_{ith} = \frac{ip \times 60}{\text{Heat supplied/min}} \times 100$$

$$= \frac{17.25 \times 60}{3396.25} \times 100 = \mathbf{30.47\%}$$ Ans

$$\eta_{bth} = \frac{bp \times 60}{\text{Heat supplied}} = \frac{14.94 \times 60}{3396.25} \times 100$$

$$= \mathbf{26.39\%}$$ Ans

Heat input (per minute)	(kJ)	Heat expenditure (per minute)	(kJ)
Heat supplied by fuel	3396.25	1. Heat equivalent to *bp*	896.40
		2. Heat lost to cooling medium	846.50
		3. Heat lost in exhaust	1653.35
		Total	**3396.25**

16.30 The following observations were made during a trial of a single-cylinder, four-stroke cycle gas engine having cylinder diameter of 18 cm and stroke 24 cm.

Duration of trial	=	30 min
Total number of revolution	=	9000
Total number of explosion	=	4450
Mean effective pressure	=	5 bar
Net load on the brake wheel	=	40 kg
Effective diameter of brake wheel	=	1 m
Total gas used at NTP	=	2.4 m^3
Calorific value of gas at NTP	=	19 MJ/m^3
Total air used	=	36 m^3
Pressure of air	=	720 mm Hg
Temperature of air	=	17 °C
Density of air at NTP	=	1.29 kg/m^3
Temperature of exhaust gas	=	350 °C
Room temperature	=	17 °C
Specific heat of exhaust gas	=	1 kJ/kg K
Cooling water circulated	=	80 kg
Rise in temperature of cooling water	=	30 °C

Draw up a heat balance sheet and estimate the mechanical and indicated thermal efficiencies of the engine. Take $R = 287$ J/kg K.

Solution

$$ip = \frac{p_{im}LAn}{60000} = \frac{5 \times 10^5 \times 0.24 \times \frac{\pi}{4} \times 0.18^2 \times 4450}{60000 \times 30}$$

$$= 7.55 \text{ kW}$$

$$bp = \frac{\pi N d W}{60000}$$

$$= \frac{\pi \times 9000 \times 1 \times 40 \times 9.81}{60000 \times 30} = 6.16 \text{ kW}$$

$$\text{Heat supplied at NTP} = \frac{2.4}{30} \times 19000 = 1520 \text{ kJ/min}$$

$$\text{Heat equiv. of bp} = 6.16 \times 60 = \mathbf{369.6\ kJ/min} \quad \overset{\text{Ans}}{\Longleftarrow}$$

$$\text{Heat lost to cooling medium} = \frac{80}{30} \times 30 \times 4.18 = \mathbf{334.4\ kJ/min} \quad \overset{\text{Ans}}{\Longleftarrow}$$

$$\text{Total air used} = 36 \text{ m}^3 \text{ at 720 mm of Hg}$$

$$\text{Volume of air used at NTP} = 36 \times \frac{273}{290} \times \frac{720}{760} = 32.1 \text{ m}^3$$

$$\text{Mass of air used} = \frac{32.1 \times 1.29}{30} = 1.38 \text{ kg/min}$$

$$\text{Mass of gas at NTP, } m_g = \frac{pV}{RT} = \frac{1 \times 10^5 \times 2.4}{287 \times 273} = 3.06 \text{ kg}$$

$$\text{Mass of gas/min} = \frac{3.06}{30} = 0.102 \text{ kg}$$

$$\text{Total mass of exhaust gas} = 1.38 + 0.102 = 1.482 \text{ kg}$$

$$\text{Heat lost to exhaust gas} = 1.482 \times (350 - 17) \times 1$$

$$= \mathbf{493.5 \text{ kJ/min}}$$ Ans

$$\text{Heat lost by radiation} = 1520 - (369.6 + 334.4 + 493.5)$$

$$= \mathbf{322.5 \text{ kJ/min}}$$ Ans

$$\eta_m = \frac{bp}{ip} \times 100 = \frac{6.16}{7.55} \times 100 = \mathbf{81.6\%}$$ Ans

$$\eta_{ith} = \frac{ip \times 60}{\text{Heat supplied}} = \frac{7.55 \times 60}{1520} \times 100$$

$$= \mathbf{29.8\%}$$ Ans

Heat input (per minute)	(kJ)	Heat expenditure (per minute)	(kJ)
Heat supplied by fuel	1520	1. Heat equivalent to *bp*	369.6
		2. Heat lost to cooling medium	334.4
		3. Heat lost in exhaust	493.5
		4. Unaccounted losses	322.5
		Total	**1520.0**

16.31 The following results were obtained in a test on a gas engine:

Gas used	=	0.16 m^3/min at NTP
Calorific value of gas at NTP	=	14 MJ/m^3
Density of gas at NTP	=	0.65 kg/m^3
Air used	=	1.50 kg/min
Specific heat of exhaust gas	=	1.0 kJ/kg K
Temperature of exhaust gas	=	400 °C
Room temperature	=	20 °C
Cooling water per minute	=	6 kg
Specific heat of water	=	4.18 kJ/kg K
Rise in temp. of cooling water	=	30 °C
ip	=	12.5 kW
bp	=	10.5 kW

Draw a heat balance sheet for the test on per hour basis in kJ.

Solution

Heat supplied at NTP $=$ $0.16 \times 14000 \times 60 = 134400$ kJ/h

Heat equivalent of *bp* $=$ $10.5 \times 60 \times 60 =$ **37800 kJ/h** Ans

Heat lost in cooling medium

$=$ $6 \times 30 \times 4.18 \times 60$

$=$ **45144 kJ/h** Ans

Mass of gas used $=$ $0.16 \times 0.65 = 0.104$ kg/min

Mass of air used $=$ 1.50 kg/min

Mass of exhaust gas $=$ $0.104 + 1.50 = 1.604$ kg/min

Heat carried away in exhaust gases

$=$ $1.604 \times 1 \times (400 - 20) \times 60$

$=$ **36571.2 kJ/h** Ans

Unaccounted losses $=$ $134400 - (37800 + 45144 + 36571.2)$

$=$ **14884.8 kJ/h** Ans

Heat input (per minute)	(kJ)	Heat expenditure (per minute)	(kJ)
Heat supplied by fuel	134400	1. Heat equivalent to *bp*	37800.0
		2. Heat lost to cooling medium	45144.0
		3. Heat lost in exhaust	36571.2
		4. Unaccounted losses	14884.8
		Total	**134400.0**

16.32 A test on a two-stroke engine gave the following results at full load:

Speed	=	350 rpm
Net brake load	=	65 kg
mep	=	3 bar
Fuel consumption	=	4 kg/h
Jacket cooling water flow rate	=	500 kg/h
Jacket water temperature at inlet	=	20 °C
Jacket water temperature at outlet	=	40 °C
Test room temperature	=	20 °C

Temperature of exhaust gases	=	400 °C
Air used per kg of fuel	=	32 kg
Cylinder diameter	=	22 cm
Stroke	=	28 cm
Effective brake diameter	=	1 m
Calorific value of fuel	=	43 MJ/kg
Proportion of hydrogen in fuel	=	15%
Mean specific heat of dry exhaust gas	=	1 kJ/kg K
Mean specific heat of steam	=	2.1 kJ/kg K
Sensible heat of water at room temp.	=	62 kJ/kg
Latent heat of steam	=	2250 kJ/kg

Find *ip*, *bp* and draw up a heat balance sheet for the test in kJ/min and in percentage.

Solution

$$ip = \frac{p_{im}LAn}{60000}$$

$$= \frac{3 \times 10^5 \times 0.28 \times \frac{\pi}{4} \times 0.22^2 \times 350}{60000}$$

$$= \mathbf{18.63\ kW} \qquad \text{Ans}$$

$$bp = \frac{W\pi Nd}{60000} = \frac{65 \times 9.81 \times \pi \times 350 \times 1}{60000}$$

$$= \mathbf{11.68\ kW} \qquad \text{Ans}$$

$$\text{Heat supplied/min} = \frac{4 \times 43000}{60}$$

$$= \mathbf{2866.7\ kJ = 100\%}\ \text{(let)} \qquad \text{Ans}$$

$$\text{Heat equivalent of } bp = 11.68 \times 60$$

$$= \mathbf{700.8\ kJ/min = 24.4\%} \qquad \text{Ans}$$

$$\text{Heat lost to cooling water} = \mathbf{696.7\ kJ/min = 24.3\%} \qquad \text{Ans}$$

1 kg of H_2 produces 9 kg of H_2O. Therefore,

H_2O produced per kg of fuel burnt

$$= 9 \times \%H_2 \times \text{ mass of fuel/min}$$

$$= 9 \times 0.15 \times \frac{4}{60} = 0.09 \text{ kg/min}$$

$$\text{Mass of wet exhaust gases/min} = \text{Mass of air/min} + \text{Mass of fuel/min}$$

$$= \frac{(32+1)\times 4}{60} = 2.2 \text{ kg/min}$$

Mass of dry exhaust gases/min = Mass of wet exhaust gases/min − Mass of H_2O produced/min

$$= 2.2 - 0.09 = 2.11 \text{ kg}$$

Heat lost to dry exhaust gases/minute

$$= 2.11 \times 1 \times (400 - 20)$$

$$= \mathbf{801.8\ kJ/min = 28\%}$$ Ans

Assuming that steam in exhaust exists as super heated steam at atmospheric pressure and at exhaust gas temperature, total heat of 1 kg of steam at atmospheric pressure (1 bar) and 400° reckoned above room temperature,

Heat in steam $= H_{sup} - h$

where h is the sensible heat of water at room temperature.

$$C_{pw}(100 - T_R) + C_{ps}(T_{sup} - 100) + L - h$$

$$= [-h + 100C_{pw} + L + C_{ps}(T_{sup} - 100)] - h$$

$$= 100C_{pw} + L + C_{ps}(T_{sup} - 100) - 2h$$

$$= [100 \times 4.18 + 2250 + 2.1 \times (400 - 100)] - 2 \times 4.18 \times 293 = 848.52 \text{ kJ/kg}$$

Heat carried away by steam in exhaust gases per minute

$$= 0.09 \times 848.52$$

$$= \mathbf{76.4\ kJ/min = 2.7\%}$$ Ans

Unaccounted losses $= 2866.7 - (700.8 + 696.7 + 801.8 + 76.4)$

$$= \mathbf{591\ kJ = 20.6\%}$$ Ans

Heat input (per min)	(kJ)	%	Heat expenditure (per minute)	(kJ)	%
Heat supplied by fuel	2866.7	100	1. Equivalent of *bp*	700.8	24.4
			2. Lost to cooling water	696.7	24.3
			3. Lost to dry exhaust gas	801.8	28.0
			4. Carried away by steam	76.4	2.7
			5. Unaccounted losses	591.0	20.6
			Total	**2866.7**	**100.0**

16.33 During the trial of a single-cylinder, four-stroke oil engine, the following results were obtained.

Cylinder diameter	=	20 cm
Stroke	=	40 cm
Mean effective pressure	=	6 bar
Torque	=	407 Nm
Speed	=	250 rpm
Oil consumption	=	4 kg/h
Calorific value of fuel	=	43 MJ/kg
Cooling water flow rate	=	4.5 kg/min
Air used per kg of fuel	=	30 kg
Rise in cooling water temperature	=	45 °C
Temperature of exhaust gases	=	420 °C
Room temperature	=	20 °C
Mean specific heat of exhaust gas	=	1 kJ/kg K
Specific heat of water	=	4.18 kJ/kg K

Find the *ip*, *bp* and draw up a heat balance sheet for the test in kJ/h.

Solution

$$ip = \frac{p_{im}LAn}{60000} = \frac{6 \times 10^5 \times 0.4 \times \frac{\pi}{4} \times 0.2^2 \times \frac{250}{2}}{60000}$$

$$= \mathbf{15.7\ kW} \qquad \stackrel{\text{Ans}}{\Longleftarrow}$$

$$bp = \frac{2\pi NT}{60000} = \frac{2 \times \pi \times 250 \times 407}{60000}$$

$$= \mathbf{10.6\ kW} \qquad \stackrel{\text{Ans}}{\Longleftarrow}$$

$$\text{Heat supplied} = 4 \times 43000 = 172000 \text{ kJ/h}$$

$$\text{Heat equivalent of } bp = 10.6 \times 60 \times 60 = \mathbf{38160\ kJ/h} \qquad \stackrel{\text{Ans}}{\Longleftarrow}$$

Heat carried away by cooling water

$$= \quad 4.5 \times 60 \times 45 \times 4.18 = \mathbf{50787\ kJ/h} \qquad \underleftarrow{\text{Ans}}$$

Heat carried away by exhaust

$$= \quad 4 \times (30 + 1) \times 1 \times (420 - 20)$$

$$= \quad \mathbf{49600\ kJ/h} \qquad \underleftarrow{\text{Ans}}$$

Unaccounted loss by difference

$$= \quad \mathbf{33453\ kJ/h} \qquad \underleftarrow{\text{Ans}}$$

Heat input (per hour)	(kJ)	Heat expenditure (per hour)	(kJ)
Heat supplied by fuel	172000	1. Heat equivalent to *bp*	38160
		2. Heat lost to cooling medium	50787
		3. Heat lost in exhaust	49600
		4. Unaccounted losses	33453
		Total	**172000**

16.34 In a test of an oil engine under full load condition the following results were obtained.

ip	=	33 kW
brake power	=	27 kW
Fuel used	=	8 kg/h
Rate of flow of water through gas calorimeter	=	12 kg/min
Cooling water flow rate	=	7 kg/min
Calorific value of fuel	=	43 MJ/kg
Inlet temperature of cooling water	=	15 °C
Outlet temperature of cooling water	=	75 °C
Inlet temperature of water to exhaust gas calorimeter	=	15 °C
Outlet temperature of water to exhaust gas calorimeter	=	55 °C
Final temperature of the exhaust gases	=	80 °C
Room temperature	=	17 °C
Air-fuel ratio on mass basis	=	20
Mean specific heat of exhaust gas	=	1 kJ/kg K
Specific heat of water	=	4.18 J/kg K

Draw up a heat balance sheet and estimate the thermal and mechanical efficiencies.

Solution

$$\text{Heat supplied} \quad = \quad \frac{8 \times 43000}{60} = 5733.3\ \text{kJ/min}$$

$$\text{Heat equivalent of } bp = 27 \times 60 = \mathbf{1620\ kJ/min} \quad \overset{\textbf{Ans}}{\Longleftarrow}$$

$$\text{Heat carried away by cooling water} = 7 \times 4.18 \times (75 - 15)$$

$$= \mathbf{1755.6\ kJ/min} \quad \overset{\textbf{Ans}}{\Longleftarrow}$$

Heat lost by exhaust gases in exhaust calorimeter in kJ/min

$$= 12 \times 4.18 \times (55 - 15) = 2006.4$$

$$\text{Mass of exhaust gases (fuel + air)} = \frac{8}{60} + 20 \times \frac{8}{60}$$

$$= 2.8 \text{ kg/min}$$

$$\text{Heat lost in exhaust gases} = \dot{m}_{ex} C_{p_{ex}} (t_{ex} - t_R)$$

$$= 2.8 \times 1 \times (80 - 17)$$

$$= 176.4 \text{ kJ/min}$$

Total heat carried away by the exhaust gases

$$= 2006.4 + 176.4$$

$$= \mathbf{2182.8\ kJ/min} \quad \overset{\textbf{Ans}}{\Longleftarrow}$$

$$\text{Total heat accounted} = 1620 + 1755.6 + 2182.8$$

$$= 5558.4\ \mathbf{kJ/min} \quad \overset{\textbf{Ans}}{\Longleftarrow}$$

$$\text{Unaccounted loss} = 5733.3 - 5558.4$$

$$= \mathbf{174.9\ kJ/min} \quad \overset{\textbf{Ans}}{\Longleftarrow}$$

$$\eta_{ith} = \frac{ip \times 60}{\text{Heat supplied/min}} \times 100$$

$$= \frac{33 \times 60}{5733.3} \times 100$$

$$= \mathbf{34.5\%} \quad \overset{\textbf{Ans}}{\Longleftarrow}$$

$$\eta_{bth} = \frac{27 \times 60}{5733.3} \times 100 = \mathbf{28.3\%} \quad \overset{\textbf{Ans}}{\Longleftarrow}$$

$$\eta_m = \frac{bp}{ip} \times 100 = \frac{27}{33} \times 100$$

$$= \mathbf{81.8\%} \quad \overset{\textbf{Ans}}{\Longleftarrow}$$

Heat input (per minute)	(kJ)	Heat expenditure (per minute)	(kJ)
Heat supplied by fuel	5733.3	1. Heat equivalent of *bp*	1620
		2. Heat lost to cooling medium	1755.6
		3. Heat lost in exhaust	2182.8
		4. Unaccounted losses	174.9
		Total	**5558.4**

16.35 A gasoline engine has a stroke volume of 0.0015 m^3 and a compression ratio of 6. At the end of the compression stroke, the pressure is 8 bar and temperature 350°C. Ignition is set so that the pressure rises along a straight line during combustion and attains its highest value of 25 bar after the piston has travelled 1/30 of the stroke. The charge consists of a gasoline-air mixture in proportion by mass 1 to 16. Take R = 287 J/kg K, calorific value of the fuel = 42 MJ/kg and C_p = 1 kJ/kg K. Calculate the heat lost per kg of charge during combustion.

Solution

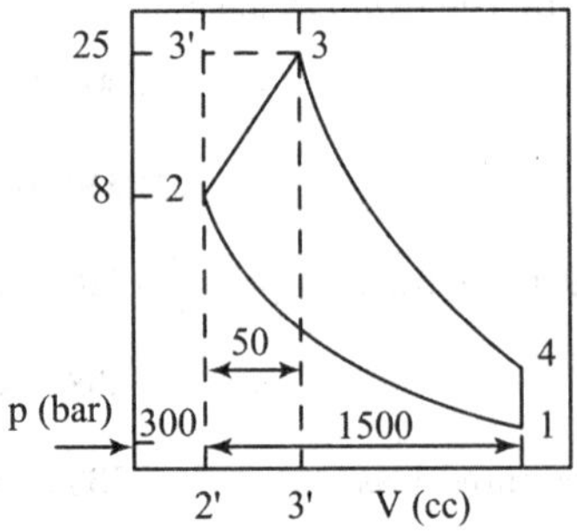

$$V_1 - V_2 = 0.0015 \times 10^6 = 1500 \text{ cc}$$

$$V_2 = \frac{1500}{6-1} = 300 \text{ cc}$$

$$V_3 = \frac{1500}{30} + 300 = 350 \text{ cc}$$

$$T_2 = 350 + 273 = 623K$$

$$T_3 = T_2\frac{p_3V_3}{p_2V_2} = 623 \times \frac{25}{8} \times \frac{350}{300} = 2271 \text{ K}$$

In order to estimate the heat added to the mixture during the process 2→3, it is required to calculate the work done and the increase in internal energy between 2 and 3.

$$W_{2-3} = \left(\frac{25+8}{2}\right) \times 10^5 \times (350 - 300) \times 10^{-6}$$

$$\text{Area of trapezoid } 2'23'3 = 82.5 \text{ J}$$

$$\text{Mixture mass, } m = \frac{pV}{RT}$$

$$= \frac{8 \times 10^5 \times 300 \times 10^{-6}}{287 \times 623} = 1.342 \times 10^{-3} \text{ kg}$$

$$\Delta E = E_3 - E_2$$

$$= 1.342 \times 10^{-3} \times (1 - 0.287) \times (2271 - 623)$$

$$= 1.5772 \text{ kJ}$$

$$Q = 0.0825 + 1.5772 = 1.6597 \text{ kJ}$$

This is the quantity of heat actually given to the mixture in one cycle. But the heat liberated in one cycle must have been

$$\frac{1}{17} \times 1.342 \times 10^{-3} \times 42000 = 3.3155 \text{ kJ}$$

$$\text{Heat lost during explosion} = 3.3155 - 1.6597 = 1.6558 \text{ kJ}$$

$$\text{Heat lost in kJ/kg} = \frac{1.6558}{1.342 \times 10^{-3}}$$

$$= \mathbf{1234.1 \text{ kJ/kg of charge}}$$ Ans ⟸

16.36 The air flow to a four-cylinder four-stroke gasoline engine was measured by means of a 8 cm diameter sharp edged orifice with $C_d = 0.65$. During a test the following data were recorded:

Bore	=	10 cm
Stroke	=	15 cm
Engine speed	=	2500 rpm
Brake power	=	36 kW
Fuel consumption	=	10 kg/h
Calorific value of fuel	=	42 MJ/kg
Pressure drop across the orifice	=	4 cm of water

Atmospheric temperature and pressure are 17 °C and 1 bar respectively. Calculate

(i) brake thermal efficiency

(ii) brake mean effective pressure

(iii) volumetric efficiency based on free air condition

Solution

$$\eta_{bth} = \frac{36 \times 60}{\frac{10}{60} \times 42000} \times 100 = \mathbf{30.86\%}$$ Ans

$$p_{bm} = \frac{bp \times 60000}{LAnK} = \frac{36 \times 60000}{0.15 \times \frac{\pi}{4} \times 0.1^2 \times \frac{2500}{2} \times 4}$$

$$= 3.67 \times 10^5 \text{ Pa} = \mathbf{3.67 \text{ bar}}$$ Ans

$$V_s = \frac{\pi}{4} d^2 LK = \frac{\pi}{4} \times 10^2 \times 15 \times 4 = 4712.4 \text{ cc}$$

Velocity of air through the orifice,

$$C_a = \sqrt{2g\Delta h_a}$$

$$\Delta h_w \rho_w = \Delta h_a \rho_a$$

$$\rho_a = \frac{p}{RT} = \frac{1 \times 10^5}{287 \times 290} = 1.20 \text{ kg/m}^3$$

$$C_a = \sqrt{2g \times \frac{\Delta h_w}{1000} \times \frac{1000}{\rho_a}}$$

where Δh_w is the pressure drop in mm of water column

$$C_a = \sqrt{2 \times 9.81 \times \frac{40}{1.2}} = 25.57 \text{ m/s}$$

$$\dot{m}_a = C_d A \rho_a C_a$$

$$= 0.65 \times \frac{\pi}{4} \times 0.08^2 \times 1.20 \times 25.57 \times 3600$$

$$= 360.9 \text{ kg/h}$$

$$\text{Volume of air} = \frac{mRT}{p} = \frac{360.9 \times 287 \times 290}{1 \times 10^5} = 300.4 \text{ m}^3/\text{h}$$

$$V_s = 4712.4 \times 10^{-6} \times \frac{2500}{2} \times 60 = 353.43 \text{ m}^3/\text{h}$$

$$\eta_v = \frac{300.4}{353.43} \times 100 = \mathbf{85\%}$$ Ans

16.37 A test on a single-cylinder, four-stroke oil engine having a bore of 15 cm and stroke 30 cm gave the following results: speed 300 rpm; brake torque 200 Nm; indicated mean effective pressure 7 bar; fuel consumption 2.4 kg/h; cooling water flow 5 kg/min; cooling water temperature rise 35 °C; air-fuel ratio 22; exhaust gas temperature 410 °C; barometer pressure

1 bar; room temperature 20 °C. The fuel has a calorific value of 42 MJ/kg and contains 15% by weight of hydrogen. Take latent heat of vapourization as 2250 kJ/kg. Determine,

(i) the indicated thermal efficiency

(ii) the volumetric efficiency based on atmospheric conditions

Draw up a heat balance in terms of kJ/min. Take C_p for dry exhaust gas = 1 kJ/kg K and super heated steam C_p = 2.1 kJ/kg K; R=0.287 kJ/kg K.

Solution

$$ip = \frac{p_{im}LAn}{60000}$$

$$= \frac{7 \times 10^5 \times 0.3 \times \frac{\pi}{4} \times 0.15^2 \times \frac{300}{2}}{60000}$$

$$= 9.28 \text{ kW}$$

$$\eta_{ith} = \frac{9.28 \times 3600}{2.4 \times 42000} \times 100 = \mathbf{33.1\%} \quad \stackrel{\text{Ans}}{\Longleftarrow}$$

$$\dot{m}_a = \frac{2.4 \times 22}{60} = 0.88 \text{ kg/min}$$

$$\rho_a = \frac{p}{RT} = \frac{1 \times 10^5}{287 \times 293} = 1.19 \text{ kg/m}^3$$

$$\text{Volume of air consumed} = \frac{0.88}{1.19} = 0.739 \text{ m}^3\text{/min}$$

$$V_s/\text{min} = \frac{\pi}{4} \times 0.15^2 \times 0.30 \times \frac{300}{2}$$

$$= 0.795 \text{ m}^3\text{/min}$$

$$\eta_v = \frac{0.739}{0.795} \times 100 = \mathbf{93\%} \quad \stackrel{\text{Ans}}{\Longleftarrow}$$

$$bp = \frac{2\pi NT}{60000} = \frac{2\pi \times 300 \times 200}{60000} = 6.28 \text{ kW}$$

$$\text{Heat input} = \frac{2.4 \times 42000}{60} = \mathbf{1680 \text{ kJ/min}} \quad \stackrel{\text{Ans}}{\Longleftarrow}$$

$$\text{Heat equivalent of } bp = 6.28 \times 60 = \mathbf{376.8 \text{ kJ/min}} \quad \stackrel{\text{Ans}}{\Longleftarrow}$$

$$\text{Heat in cooling water} = 5 \times 4.18 \times 35 = \mathbf{731.5 \text{ kJ/min}} \quad \stackrel{\text{Ans}}{\Longleftarrow}$$

One kg of H_2 in the fuel will be converted to 9 kg of H_2O during combustion. Assuming the steam in the exhaust is in the superheated state, heat carried away by steam can be calculated as

$$C_{pw}(100 - T_a) + h_{fg} + C_{pa}(T_{sup} - 100)$$

where h_{fg} is the latent heat of vapourization = 2250 kJ/kg.

$$\text{Enthalpy of steam} = 4.18 \times (100 - 20) + 2250 + 2.1 \times (410 - 100)$$

$$= 3235.4 \text{ kJ/kg}$$

Heat carried away by steam

$$= \dot{m}_s(h - C_{pw}t_R)$$

$$= 9 \times 0.15 \times \frac{2.4}{60} \times (3225.4 - 4.18 \times 20)$$

$$= \mathbf{170.2 \text{ kJ/min}} \quad \text{Ans}$$

Heat carried away by exhaust gas

$$= \left(0.88 + \frac{2.4}{60} - 9 \times 0.15 \times \frac{2.4}{60}\right) \times 1 \times (410 - 20)$$

$$= \mathbf{337.7} \quad \text{Ans}$$

Unaccounted loss (by difference)

$$= 1680 - (376.8 + 731.5 + 170.2 + 337.7)$$

$$= \mathbf{63.8 \text{ kJ/min}} \quad \text{Ans}$$

Heat input (per minute)	(kJ)	Heat expenditure (per minute)	(kJ)
Heat supplied by fuel	1680	1. Heat equivalent to *bp*	376.8
		2. Heat lost to cooling medium	731.5
		3. Heat carried away by steam	170.2
		4. Heat lost in exhaust	337.7
		5. Unaccounted losses	63.8
		Total	**1680.0**

16.38 A four-stroke cycle gasoline engine has six single-acting cylinders of 8 cm bore and 10 cm stroke. The engine is coupled to a brake having a torque radius of 40 cm. At 3200 rpm, with all cylinders operating the net brake load is 350 N. When each cylinder in turn is rendered inoperative, the average net brake load produced at the same speed by the remaining 5 cylinders is 250 N. Estimate the indicated mean effective pressure of the engine. With all cylinders operating the fuel consumption is 0.33 kg/min; calorific value of fuel is 43 MJ/kg; the cooling water flow rate and temperature rise is 70 kg/min and 10 °C respectively. On test, the engine is enclosed in a thermally and acoustically insulated box through which the output drive, water, fuel, air and exhaust connections pass. ventilating air blown up through the box at the rate of 15 kg/min enters at 17 °C and leaves at 62 °C. Draw up a heat balance of the engine stating the items as a percentage of the heat input.

Solution

$$bp = \frac{2\pi NT}{60000}$$

$$= \frac{2 \times \pi \times 3200 \times 350 \times 0.4}{60000}$$

$$= 46.91 \text{ kW}$$

bp of engine when each cylinder is cut-off in turn

$$= \frac{2 \times \pi \times 3200 \times 250 \times 0.4}{60000}$$

$$= 33.51 \text{ kW}$$

$$ip = 6 \times (46.91 - 33.51) = 80.4 \text{ kW}$$

$$imep = \frac{ip \times 60000}{LAnK}$$

$$= \frac{80.4 \times 60000}{0.1 \times \frac{\pi}{4} \times 0.08^2 \times \frac{3200}{2} \times 6}$$

$$= 10 \times 10^5 \text{ Pa} = 10 \text{ bar}$$

$$\text{Heat input} = 0.33 \times 43000$$

$$= 14190 \text{ kJ/min} = \mathbf{100\%} \text{ (let)}$$ Ans

$$\text{Heat equivalent of } bp = 46.91 \times 60$$

$$= \mathbf{2814.6} \text{ kJ/min} = \mathbf{19.8\%}$$ Ans

$$\text{Heat in cooling water} = 70 \times 4.18 \times 10$$

$$= \mathbf{2926} \text{ kJ/min} = \mathbf{20.6\%}$$ Ans

Heat carried away by ventilating air

$$= 15 \times 1.005 \times (62 - 17)$$

$$= \mathbf{678.4 \text{ kJ/min}} = \mathbf{4.8\%}$$ Ans

Unaccounted loss (by difference)

$$= 14190 - (2814.6 + 2926 + 678.4)$$

$$= \mathbf{7771\ kJ/min = 54.8\%} \quad \text{Ans}$$

Heat input (per min)	(kJ)	%	Heat expenditure (per minute)	(kJ)	%
Heat supplied by fuel	2866.7	100	1. Equivalent of *bp*	2814.6	19.8
			2. Lost to cooling water	2926.0	20.6
			3. Lost to dry exhaust gas	678.4	4.8
			4. Unaccounted losses	7771.0	54.8
			Total	**14190.0**	**100.0**

16.39 A full load test on a two-stroke engine yielded the following results: speed 440 rpm; brake load 50 kg; *imep* 3 bar; fuel consumption 5.4 kg/h; rise in jacket water temperature 36 °C; jacket water flow 440 kg/h; air-fuel ratio by mass 30; temperature of exhaust gas 350 °C; temperature of the test room 17 °C; barometric pressure 76 cm of Hg; cylinder diameter 22 cm; stroke 25 cm; brake diameter 1.2 m; calorific value of fuel is 43 MJ/kg; proportion of hydrogen by mass in the fuel 15%; R = 0.287 kJ/kg of mean specific heat of dry exhaust gases = 1 kJ/kg K; specific heat of dry steam 2 kJ/kg K. Assume enthalpy of super heated steam to be 3180 kJ/kg. Determine,

(i) the indicated thermal efficiency

(ii) the specific fuel consumption in g/kW h

(iii) volumetric efficiency based on atmospheric conditions

Draw up a heat balance for the test on the percentage basis indicating the content of each item in the balance.

Solution

$$bp = \frac{2\pi NT}{60000} = \frac{2\pi \times 440 \times 50 \times 9.81 \times 0.6}{60000}$$

$$= 13.56 \text{ kW}$$

$$ip = \frac{p_{im} LAn}{60000}$$

$$= \frac{3 \times 10^5 \times 0.25 \times \frac{\pi}{4} \times 0.22^2 \times 440}{60000}$$

$$= 20.91 \text{ kW}$$

$$\eta_{ith} = \frac{20.91 \times 60}{\frac{5.4}{60} \times 43000} \times 100 = \mathbf{32.4\%} \quad \text{Ans}$$

$$bsfc = \frac{5.4 \times 1000}{13.56} = \mathbf{398.2\ g/kW\ h} \quad \stackrel{\text{Ans}}{\Longleftarrow}$$

$$V_s = \frac{\pi}{4}D^2Ln = \frac{\pi}{4} \times 0.22^2 \times 0.25 \times 440$$

$$= 4.18\ \text{m}^3/\text{min}$$

$$\dot{m}_a = A/F \times \dot{m}_f = 30 \times \frac{5.4}{60} = 2.7\ \text{kg/min}$$

$$\rho = \frac{p}{RT} = \frac{1 \times 10^5}{287 \times 290} = 1.20\ \text{m}^3/\text{kg}$$

$$\text{Air consumption in m}^3 = \frac{2.7}{1.2} = 2.25\ \text{m}^3/\text{min}$$

$$\eta_v = \frac{2.25}{4.18} \times 100 = \mathbf{53.8\%} \quad \stackrel{\text{Ans}}{\Longleftarrow}$$

$$\text{Heat input} = \frac{5.4}{60} \times 43000$$

$$= \mathbf{3870\ kJ/min} = \mathbf{100\%}\ \text{(let)} \quad \stackrel{\text{Ans}}{\Longleftarrow}$$

$$\text{Heat equivalent of } bp = 13.56 \times 60 = 813.6\ \text{kJ/min} = \mathbf{21\%} \quad \stackrel{\text{Ans}}{\Longleftarrow}$$

Heat lost to cooling water

$$= \frac{440}{60} \times 4.18 \times 36 = 1103.5\ \text{kJ/min}$$

$$= \mathbf{28.5\%} \quad \stackrel{\text{Ans}}{\Longleftarrow}$$

Heat carried away by dry exhaust gas

$$= \frac{5.4}{60} \times (30 + 1 - 9 \times 0.15) \times 1 \times (350 - 17)$$

$$= 888.6\ \text{kJ/min} = \mathbf{23\%} \quad \stackrel{\text{Ans}}{\Longleftarrow}$$

Heat carried away by the steam in the exhaust gas

$$= 9 \times 0.15 \times \frac{5.4}{60} \times (3180 - 4.18 \times 17)$$

$$= 377.7\ \text{kJ/min} = \mathbf{9.8\%} \quad \stackrel{\text{Ans}}{\Longleftarrow}$$

Unaccounted loss (by difference)

$$= 3870 - (813.6 + 1103.5 + 888.6 + 377.7)$$

$$= 686.6\ \text{kJ/min} = \mathbf{17.7\%} \quad \stackrel{\text{Ans}}{\Longleftarrow}$$

Heat input (per minute)	%	Heat expenditure (per minute)	%
Heat supplied by fuel	100	1. Heat equivalent to *hp*	21.0
		2. Heat lost to cooling water	28.5
		3. Heat carried away by dry exhaust	23.0
		4. Heat lost in steam	9.8
		5. Unaccounted losses	17.7
		Total	**100**

16.40 A gas engine working on the constant-volume cycle gave the following results during a one-hour test run. Cylinder diameter 24 cm; stroke 48 cm; torque 770 Nm; average speed 220 rpm; average explosion per minute 77; *mep* 7.5 bar; volume of gas used 12 m^3 at 17 °C and 770 mm of mercury pressure; lower calorific value of gas 21 MJ/m^3 at NTP; inlet and outlet temperature of cooling water are 25 °C and 60 °C respectively; cooling water used 600 kg. Determine (i) the mechanical efficiency (ii) the indicated specific gas consumption in m^3/kW h and (iii) the indicated thermal efficiency.

Draw up a heat balance for the engine on minute basis, explaining why friction power has been included in or omitted from your heat balance. NTP conditions are 760 mm of Hg and 0 °C.

Solution

$$bp = \frac{2 \times \pi \times 220 \times 770}{60000} = 17.74 \text{ kW}$$

$$ip = \frac{7.5 \times 10^5 \times 0.48 \times \frac{\pi}{4} \times 0.24^2 \times 77}{60000}$$

$$= 20.9 \text{ kW}$$

$$\eta_m = \frac{17.74}{20.9} \times 100 = \mathbf{84.9\%} \quad \text{Ans}$$

Gas consumption at NTP, $\dot{V}_f$

$$= 12 \times \frac{770}{760} \times \frac{273}{290} = \mathbf{11.44\ m^3/h} \quad \text{Ans}$$

$$\eta_{ith} = \frac{ip}{\dot{V}_f \times CV}$$

$$= \frac{20.9 \times 60 \times 60}{11.44 \times 21000} \times 100 = \mathbf{31.3\%} \quad \text{Ans}$$

$$\text{Heat input} = \frac{11.44 \times 21000}{60} = 4004 \text{ kJ/min}$$

$$\text{Heat equivalent of} bp = 17.74 \times 60 = \mathbf{1064.4\ kJ/min} \quad \text{Ans}$$

$$\text{Heat in cooling water} = \frac{600}{60} \times 4.18 \times (60 - 25)$$

$$= \mathbf{1463\ kJ/min} \qquad \stackrel{\text{Ans}}{\Longleftarrow}$$

Heat in exhaust, radiation etc. (by difference)

$$= 4004 - (1064.4 + 1463)$$

$$= \mathbf{1476.6\ kJ/min} \qquad \stackrel{\text{Ans}}{\Longleftarrow}$$

Heat input (per minute)	(kJ)	Heat expenditure (per minute)	(kJ)
Heat supplied by fuel	4004	1. Heat equivalent to *bp*	1064.4
		2. Heat lost to cooling medium	1463.0
		3. Heat lost in exhaust	1476.6
		Total	**4004.0**

The friction heat is not included since it is assumed that friction heat is rejected to cooling water, exhaust, radiation etc.

Review Questions

16.1 Mention the basic aspects covered by the engine performance.

16.2 List the parameters by which performance of an engine is evaluated.

16.3 Define mean effective pressure and distinguish between brake mean effective pressure and indicated mean effective pressure.

16.4 Develop an expression for the calculation of indicated mean effective pressure.

16.5 Derive the expression for calculating indicated power of an engine.

16.6 How is the torque of an engine is evaluated from them nomenclature of the engine?

16.7 Distinguish between the power and specific output.

16.8 Briefly discuss the various efficiency terms associated with an engine.

16.9 Define air-fuel ratio and briefly state its effect on power output, fuel consumption and combustion pressure.

16.10 What is the importance of specific fuel consumption?

16.11 Schematically explain the use of the study of the heat balance of an engine.

16.12 Explain the effect of the following factors on the performance of an SI engine: (i) compression ratio (ii) air-fuel ratio (iii) spark timing (iv) engine speed (v) mass of inducted charge and (vi) heat losses.

16.13 Briefly explain the reason of poor part load thermal efficiency of the SI engine compared with CI engine.

16.14 What limits the brake power and brake mean effective pressure of a CI engine?

16.15 What are the methods available for improving the performance of an engine?

16.16 Draw a typical performance map for a four-stroke fast burn SI engine showing contours of constant bsfc.

16.17 Draw a typical performance map showing the effect of fuel injection parameters, air swirl and bowl in piston design and fraction of exhaust gas recirculation.

16.18 By means of a Sankey diagram explain the energy flow through an engine.

16.19 Draw a detailed Sankey diagram for SI engine and explain.

16.20 Explain the details of the analytical method of performance estimation.

Exercise

16.1 Find the bore of the single-cylinder diesel engine working on the four-stroke cycle and delivers 40 kW at 200 rpm from the following data:

Compression ratio	:	14:1
Fuel cut-off	:	5% of stroke
Index of compression curve	:	1.4
Index for expansion curve	:	1.3
Pressure at beginning of compression	:	1 atm
Ratio of stroke to bore	:	1.5 to 1

Ans: 34.5 cm

16.2 Determine the diameter of a gas engine cylinder to develop 18 kW when making 100 explosions per minute, gives clearance volume 1/3 swept volume, law of compression and explosion $pV^{1.3}$, absolute maximum pressure is 3 times the absolute pressure at the end of the stroke. Take length of stroke to be twice the bore. *Ans:* 24.7 cm

16.3 A four-stroke gas engine having a cylinder of 250 mm diameter and stroke 450 mm has a volumetric efficiency of 80%, ratio of air to gas is 8 to 1, calorific value of gas is 20 MJ/m^3 at NTP. Find the heat supplied to the engine per working cycle. If the compression ratio is 5, what is the heating value of the mixture per working stroke per m^3 of total cylinder volume? *Ans:* (i) 40 kJ (ii) 1428.6 kJ/m^3

16.4 The swept volume of a gas engine is 9 litre and the clearance volume is 2.25 litre. The engine consumes 3500 litre of gas per hour, when running at 160 rpm firing every cycle and developing 4 kW. It has a mechanical efficiency of 75%. What is the relative efficiency of the engine compared with air-standard cycle if the calorific value of gas is 20 MJ/m^3. Assuming a volumetric efficiency of 0.87, find the ratio of air to gas used by 1 m^3 of the mixture in the cylinder. *Ans:* (i) 57.68% (ii) 9.73

16.5 In order to study the effect of mixture strength on the thermal efficiency of the engine, tests were made on a four-stroke gas engine and the following heat balance results were obtained.

Test	Engine A Lean mixture	Engine B Rich mixture
Indicated work	37	33
Heat in exhaust gas	42	39
Heat lost	21	28
	100	1000

In the test A the supply of gas was 0.23 m^3 per minute and in test B was 0.30 m^3 per minute. The calorific value of the gas used was 20 MJ/m^3. Calculate the indicated power and the heat loss to the cylinder walls and piston per minute in the two cases. Calculate the indicated thermal efficiencies of the two engines and comment on the result. *Ans:* (i) 1702 kJ/min; 1980 kJ/min (ii) 966 kJ; 1680 kJ (iii) 37%; 33%

Reasons for higher thermal efficiency on lean mixtures

(i) With a weak mixture the temperature rise for a given heat input is greater than with rich mixture since there is a little or no dissociation and the specific heat is less at the lower temperature.

(ii) The smaller maximum temperature reduces the heat flow to the cylinder walls.
The more nearly the maximum temperature approaches the temperature at the end of compression will the Otto efficiency approaches the Carnot.

16.6 An engine of 175 mm bore and 375 mm stroke is governed by hit and miss type governor to 220 rpm. With a fixed setting of the gas supply and ignition advance, indicator diagrams gave the following values of mean effective pressure. Firing, positive loop 5.7 bar, negative loop 0.25 bar; missing negative loop 0.42 bar. When developing 6 kW the explosions were 100 per minute and the gas used was 0.1 m^3 per minute. Calculate the friction power and assuming uniform gas supply per explosion, find the gas consumption per minute at no load. *Ans:* (i) 2.13 kW (ii) 0.032 m^3

16.7 Calculate the maximum brake power which can be developed in the cylinder of a four-stroke gas engine which runs at 200 rpm. The diameter of the piston is 300 mm and stroke 400 mm. Clearance volume is 25% of the swept volume. The gas supplied consists of CO = 19.7%; H_2 = 28.8%; CO_2 = 14.4%; N_2 = 37.1%. Assume that the total mixture at NTP admitted per suction stroke is 0.875 of total volume behind the piston at the end of the stroke and that the thermal efficiency is 35%. Calorific value of H_2 = 121.4 MJ/kg; Calorific value of carbon burning from CO to CO_2 = 23.4 MJ/kg; Density of air = 1.2 kg/m^3.

Ans: 47 kW

16.8 The following observations were made in a test of a gas engine in which a waste heat boiler served as an exhaust gas calorimeter. Gross calorific value of gas 20.0 MJ/m^3 at NTP; gas consumption 9.35 m^3/h at NTP; density of gas = 0.706 kg/m^3; mass of water vapour of combustion produced per m^3 of gas (at NTP) = 0.72 kg; air consumption = 77.4 kg/h; temperature of air and gas = 17 °C; rate of flow of water through boiler = 168 kg/h; inlet and outlet temperature of water is 20 °C and 80 °C. Temperature of exhaust gases leaving the boiler 127 °C. Calculate the heat per hour leaving the engine and express as a percentage of heat supplied. Assume the dew point of the exhaust gases as 50 °C; the total heat of dry saturated steam at 50 °C = 2580 kJ/kg; the mean specific heat of steam as 2 kJ/kg K and the specific heat of flue gas as 1 kJ/kg K. Take atmospheric temperature = 17 °C as datum.

Ans: (i) 187000 kJ/h (ii) 36.39%

16.9 In olden days in order to compare the various forms and sizes of the engine a factor known as Tookey factor is defined. It is given by

$$TF = \frac{\text{mep of the cycle in bar}}{\text{Heat equivalent of 1 m}^3\text{ of cylinder mixture in MJ}}$$

Calculate the value of the Tookey factor for an engine developing 10 kW using the following data. Piston diameter = 200 mm; stroke = 300 mm; explosion per minute = 100; calorific value of gas = 19 MJ/m^3 gas per hour 6 m^3; clearance volume = 25% of swept volume; volumetric efficiency = 87.5%. (Note: Modern engines will have a TF > 4).

Ans: 3.45

16.10 In a test of a gas engine, the gas used had the following composition by volume : CH_4 = 65%; H_2 = 2%; N_2 = 2%; CO_2 = 31%. The dry exhaust gas analysis gave O_2 = 5.3%; N_2 = 83%; CO = 0.3% and CO_2 = 11.4%. Find (i) the air-fuel ratio by volume, to give complete combustion (ii) the percentage of excess air actually used in the test. Air contains 79% by volume of nitrogen.

Ans: (i) 6.238 (ii) 36.7%

16.11 Assume that an oil engine cylinder is not cooled. One kg of air and 0.00518 of fuel are introduced into the cylinder at 17 °C and 1 bar and compressed to 4 bar. Taking the specific heat of the product to 0.717 kJ/kg K, find the maximum temperature and pressure at the end of explosion. The calorific value of the fuel is 46 MJ/kg. Take γ = 1.4.

Ans: (i) 761.55 K (ii) 7.07 bar

16.12 Assuming a volumetric efficiency of 75%, estimate the probable indicated power of a four-cylinder petrol engine, given the following data, diameter of cylinder = 180 mm; stroke = 210 mm; speed = 1000 rpm; air-fuel ratio = 16:1. Engine works on a four-stroke cycle, net calorific value of the fuel = 44 MJ/kg; thermal efficiency is 30%. Assume $\rho_a = 1.3$.
Ans: 140.8 kW

16.13 A nine-cylinder petrol engine of bore 150 mm and stroke 200 mm has a compression ratio of 6:1 and develops 360 kW at 2000 rpm when running on a mixture of 20% rich. The fuel used has a calorific value of 43 MJ/kg and contains 85.3% carbon and 14.7% hydrogen. Assuming volumetric efficiency of 70% at 17 °C and mechanical efficiency of 90%, find the indicated thermal efficiency of the engine. Air contains 23.3% by mass of oxygen.
Ans: 30.84%

16.14 In a test the percentage analysis of petrol is found to be C = 83.2%; H = 14.3% O_2 = 2.5%. Calculate the mixture strength theoretically required for complete combustion of this fuel. Tests were conducted on a petrol engine at full throttle and constant speed, the quantity of fuel supplied to the engine being varied by means of an adjustable needle valve fitted to the jet of the carburettor. The results obtained were as follows:

Speed (rpm)	Torque (Nm)	Fuel (kg/min)	Air (kg/min)	Air-fuel ratio
1570	122.9	0.097	1.570	16.20
1570	128.5	0.100	1.560	15.60
1573	131.5	0.103	1.570	15.20
1569	138.0	0.110	1.560	14.20
1572	139.3	0.113	1.560	13.80
1563	141.5	0.118	1.560	13.20
1560	142.7	0.123	1.560	12.70
1572	141.2	0.129	1.560	12.10

Calorific value of fuel is 42 MJ/kg. Find the mixture strength for maximum brake power and maximum thermal efficiency.
Ans: (i) 12.1 (ii) 15.6

16.15 A four-cylinder automobile engine of 90 mm bore and 115 mm stroke was tested at constant speed over the complete practical range of mixture strength. The speed, the brake loads and the fuel consumption are as follows:

Test Number	Brake load (kg)	Speed (rpm)	Fuel consumption (kg/h)
1	17.35	1510	10.99
2	17.39	1500	10.80
3	17.44	1510	10.53
4	17.48	1512	10.35
5	17.48	1510	9.99
6	17.48	1510	9.72
7	17.21	1509	9.17
8	16.35	1493	8.54
9	15.08	1513	8.08

The brake arm length was 1 m. Plot *sfc* vs *bmep* curve and find the mixture strength for maximum power and maximum economy.

Ans: (i) 0.335 kg/kW h (ii) 0.36 kg/kW h

16.16 The following results were obtained from a set of trials at full throttle on a single cylinder four-stroke kerosene engine working of constant volume cycle has a bore of 110 mm and stroke of 200 mm. The speed was kept constant at 1500 rpm and the compression ratio varied.

Compression ratio	3.8	4.2	4.6	5.0	5.4	5.8
Fuel consumption/kg/min	0.113	0.112	0.112	0.112	0.111	0.111
Brake torque (Nm)	112.03	119.77	126.69	131.99	135.92	139.32
Frictional torque (Nm)	16.97	17.38	17.92	18.33	18.87	19.28

Calorific value of kerosene = 42 MJ/kg. Plot the curves of indicated mean effective pressure and thermal efficiency with respect to a compression ratio and obtain the values at compression ratio of 5.5. Also find the relative efficiency at the above compression ratio. *Ans:* 58.3%

16.17 In a test of a four-cylinder, four-stroke petrol engine of 75 mm bore and 100 mm stroke, the following results were obtained at full throttle at a constant speed and with a fixed setting of the fuel supply of 0.082 kg/min.

$$
\begin{aligned}
bp \text{ with all cylinders working} &= 15.24 \text{ kW}\\
bp \text{ with cylinder number 1 cut-off} &= 10.45 \text{ kW}\\
bp \text{ with cylinder number 2 cut-off} &= 10.38 \text{ kW}\\
bp \text{ with cylinder number 3 cut-off} &= 10.23 \text{ kW}\\
bp \text{ with cylinder number 4 cut-off} &= 10.45 \text{ kW}
\end{aligned}
$$

Estimate the indicated power of the engine under these conditions. If the calorific value of the fuel is 44 MJ/kg, find the indicated thermal efficiency of the engine. Compare this with the air-standard efficiency, the clearance volume of one cylinder being 115 cc.

Ans: (i) $ip_1 = 4.79; ip_2 = 4.86; ip_3 = 5.01; ip_4 = 4.79;$
$ip_{1234} = 19.45$; (ii) 32.35% (iii) 69.1%

16.18 A six-cylinder petrol engine of 100 mm bore and 125 mm stroke was run at full throttle at a constant speed of 1500 rpm over the practical range of air-fuel ratio, and the following results were deduced from the series:

bmep (bar)	*sfc* (kg/kW h)	Air-fuel ratio (mass basis)
6.19	0.555	11.0
6.53	0.494	11.5
6.67	0.438	12.9
6.63	0.383	14.7
6.60	0.352	16.1
6.26	0.339	17.6
5.71	0.352	19.2
5.07	0.407	20.8

The engine has a compression ratio of 5. The fuel used has a calorific value of 44300 kJ/kg and the stoichiometric air-fuel ratio is 14.5. Plot on a base of air-fuel ratio, curves of brake mean effective pressure and the specific fuel consumption. Point out these characteristics of petrol engine in general and this engine in particular, revealed by these curves. Calculate the highest brake thermal efficiency given by these tests.
Ans: 24%

16.19 A four-cylinder, four-stroke automobile engine of 60 mm bore and 115 mm stroke was tested at a constant speed over the complete range of mixture strength. The arm of the brake was 1 m. The following data were recorded.

Speed (rpm)	Brake load (kg)	Fuel consumption (kg/h)
1510	8.67	5.50
1500	8.70	5.40
1510	8.72	5.27
1510	8.74	5.18
1510	8.74	5.00
1510	8.74	4.86
1509	8.60	4.59
1493	8.17	4.27
1513	7.10	4.04

Plot a diagram showing the relation between fuel consumption in kg/kW h and *bmep*. Discuss the information which this diagram provides with respect to the performance of the engine. Calculate the power output at the most economical point and also the corresponding brake thermal efficiency if the calorific value of the fuel is 44 MJ/kg h.
Ans: (i)12.54 kW (ii) 24.1%

16.20 The fuel supplied to a Diesel engine has a gross calorific value of 44800 kJ/kg and contains 85.4% C and 12.3% H_2. The average temperature of the exhaust gases is 260 °C and their volumetric analysis gives CO_2 : 5.77%, CO : 0.12%, O_2 : 13.09%, N_2 (by difference) : 81.02%. Find (i) the heat carried away by the exhaust expressed as a percentage of the heat supplied and (ii) the mass of air per kg of fuel in excess of that theoretically required for complete combustion. Take mean specific heat of the dry exhaust gases as 1 kJ/kg K and atmospheric temperature as 17 °C. Air contains 23% oxygen on mass basis.
Ans: (i) 26.61% (ii) 21.42 kg

16.21 The following set of observations refer to a trial on a single-cylinder, four-stroke solid injection diesel engine of 200 mm bore and 400 mm stroke; gross mep = 6.20 bar, pumping mep = 0.44 bar, speed 262 rpm, brake torque = 468 Nm; fuel used 3.85 kg of oil per hour of gross calorific value 46600 kJ/kg, cooling water 6 kg/min raised 47 °C. Draw up a heat balance sheet for the trial expressing various quantitative in kJ/min and calculate the mechanical efficiency of the engine. If the fuel contains 13.5% H_2 (by mass) and the air supply to the engine 1.71 kg/min at 17 °C. Estimate the heat carried away per minute by the exhaust gases when their temperature is 280 °C. Assume a mean specific heat of 1 kJ/kg and specific heat of fuel to be 4 kJ/kg K. Take sensible heat of air and fuel also in the heat balance. *Ans:* (i) 81.2% (ii) 678.26 kJ/min

16.22 A four-cylinder, four-stroke diesel engine develops 28 kW at 2000 rpm. Its *bsfc* is 0.26 kg/kW h. Calculate the power output of the engine and its *bsfc* when the fuel rate is reduced by 40% at the same speed. Mechanical efficiency is 0.80. Assume that the indicated thermal efficiency changes linearly with equivalence ratio and there is 1% increase in indicated thermal efficiency for 6% increase in the equivalence ratio. Equivalence ratio (ϕ) at higher fuel flow rate is 0.6666.
Ans: (i) 16.1 kW (ii) 0.271 kg/kW h

16.23 An eight-cylinder SI engine with 90 mm bore and 110 mm stroke produces 100 kW at a mean piston speed of 660 m/min at full throttle and the *bsfc* is 0.39 kg/kW h. What will be the power produced by the engine and the *bsfc* when the engine runs with a mean piston speed of 440 m/min with the throttle set at the same position. The fuel-air ratio and spark timing are adjusted for best power at each speed. From experimental curves of similar engine it is found that for the given percentage reduction in piston speed the air capacity of the engine is reduced by 20%. Friction mep at piston speeds of 660 and 440 m/min are 1.9 and 1.2 bar respectively. *Ans:* (i) 56.3 kW (ii) 0.369 kg/kW h

16.24 An eight-cylinder automobile petrol engine of 100 mm bore and 90 mm stroke has a compression ratio of 7. The engine develops 136 kW at 4000 rpm. The engine operates at 20% rich in fuel and the atmospheric conditions are 27 °C and 760 mm of Hg barometer. The *bsfc* is 0.34 kg/kW h. Estimate the power output and *bsfc* when

(i) barometer is 740 mm of Hg and temperature is 47 °C.

(ii) barometer is 775 mm of Hg and temperature is 7 °C. *fmep* at 4000 rpm is 2.10 bar.

Ans: (i) 125.9 kW; 0.346 kg/kW h
(ii) 145.8 kW; 0.335 kg/kW h

16.25 A four-cylinder, four-stroke cycle diesel engine produces 60 kW at 2200 rpm (under maximum fuel delivery position) with a *bsfc* of 0.28 kg/kW h at sea level (barometer 760 mm of Hg and 27 °C). Cylinder bore of the engine is 110 mm and stroke is 140 mm. The friction mean effective pressure obtained from motoring test at 2200 rpm is 2 bar. Estimate the *bsfc* of the engine at 2200 rpm, when it is taken to a hill top at 3000 m altitude. Effect of humidity may be neglected. The fuel-air ratio is maintained at a constant value. At 3000 m altitude barometer is 540 mm of Hg and temperature is 270 K. *Ans:* 0.314 kg/kW h

Multiple Choice Questions (choose the most appropriate answer)

1. Thermal efficiency varies

   (a) inversely as *sfc*
   (b) directly as *sfc*
   (c) as square as *sfc*
   (d) as root as *sfc*

2. Mechanical efficiency is ratio of

   (a) *fp* to *bp*
   (b) *fp* to *ip*
   (c) *bp* to *ip*
   (d) *ip* to *fp*

3. If N is the rpm, number of power strokes/min in a four-stroke engine is

   (a) 2N
   (b) N/2
   (c) N
   (d) 4N

4. If N is the rpm, number of power strokes/min in a two-stroke engine is

   (a) N
   (b) 2N
   (c) N/2
   (d) 4N

5. An indicator from an engine has a length of 100 mm and an area of 2000 mm^2. If the indicator pointer deflects 10 mm for a pressure increment of 2 bar, the *mep* is

   (a) 2 bar
   (b) 4 bar
   (c) 8 bar
   (d) 1 bar

6. The spark timing and combustion rate should be such that

   (a) peak pressure occurs at TDC
   (b) one half of the total pressure occurs at TDC
   (c) ignition delay is reduced
   (d) none of the above

7. Volumetric efficiency is a measure of

   (a) speed of the engine
   (b) power of the engine
   (c) breathing capacity of the engine
   (d) pressure rise in the cylinder

8. Indicated power is directly proportional to

   (a) torque
   (b) air consumption
   (c) cylinder peak pressure
   (d) none of the above

9. Turbocharger engines are those in which charge density is increased by

   (a) separate air compressors
   (b) compressors driven by exhaust gas turbine
   (c) cooling inlet air
   (d) none of the above

10. Brake thermal efficiency of SI engine is in the range

    (a) 35% to 60%
    (b) 25% to 35%
    (c) 60% to 80%
    (d) none of the above

11. Sankey diagram represents

    (a) η_{bth} vs bp
    (b) air consumption vs speed
    (c) heat balance of the engine
    (d) torque vs speed

12. Performance *mep* shows

    (a) indicated power vs speed
    (b) *bmep* vs piston speed under various conditions
    (c) η_{bth} vs speed under various conditions
    (d) η_{ith} vs speed under various conditions

13. The *bp* of a four-cylinder engine is 30 with all cylinder firing and 20 with one cylinder cut. The mechanical efficiency is

    (a) 60%
    (b) 80%
    (c) 75%
    (d) none of the above

14. The bore and stroke of a single cylinder four-stroke engine are 100 mm and 160 mm respectively. If the brake torque is 50 NM the bmep is

    (a) 15 bar
    (b) 10 bar
    (c) 5 bar
    (d) 7.6 bar

15. The volumetric efficiency of a well designed engine is in the range

    (a) 30 to 40%
    (b) 40 to 60%
    (c) 60 to 70%
    (d) 75 to 90%

16. The normal efficiency of petrol engine as compared to diesel engine is

    (a) lower
    (b) higher
    (c) equal
    (d) none of the above

17. For SI engine with engine speed torque

    (a) increases
    (b) decreases
    (c) increases and then decreases
    (d) remains constant

18. For SI engine, air consumption with engine speed

    (a) increases and then decreases
    (b) increases
    (c) decreases
    (d) remains constant

19. Charge efficiency depend on

    (a) mechanical efficiency
    (b) compression ratio
    (c) air-fuel ratio
    (d) combustion efficiency

20. Indicated mean effective pressure is given by

    (a) $imep = fmep - bmep$
    (b) $imep = fmep/bmep$
    (c) $imep = fmep \times bmep$
    (d) $imep = fmep + bmep$

21. At constant speed and constant air-fuel ratio for an SI engine

    (a) $bsfc$ is maximum at full load
    (b) $bsfc$ is minimum at full load
    (c) $bsfc$ is minimum at no load
    (d) $bsfc$ does not depend on load

Ans:					
	1. – (a)	2. – (c)	3. – (b)	4. – (a)	5. – (b)
	6. – (b)	7. – (c)	8. – (b)	9. – (b)	10. – (b)
	11. – (c)	12. – (b)	13. – (c)	14. – (c)	15. – (d)
	16. – (a)	17. – (c)	18. – (a)	19. – (b)	20. – (d)
	21. – (b)				

17 ENGINE ELECTRONICS

17.1 INTRODUCTION

Engine development has become a challenge mainly because the user expects improved performance levels with reduced fuel consumption. Further, environmental considerations necessitate adopting the use of methods which lower emissions. Achieving the twin goal of low emissions with good performance and drivability is a difficult task. It is in this context that electronic engine management has gained importance. The principal aims of an engine developer is to achieve:

(i) High reliability and durability with lowest possible initial cost

(ii) High power output and torque

(iii) Low levels of gaseous and particulate emissions

(iv) Low fuel consumption

(v) Low noise levels and vibrations

Over the years, lots of developments in electronics have taken place. Therefore, in gasoline engines control of the following parameters is easily monitored by using sensors and actuators linked to an electronic control module. The important parameters that can be controlled are:

(i) Air-fuel ratio

(ii) Mixture distribution between cylinders

(iii) Ignition timing

(iv) Injection timing of the fuel

(v) Idle speed

As known a diesel engine uses a heterogeneous fuel air mixture. The load is controlled by varying the amount of fuel injected. The fuel that is injected has to be atomized and mixed with air without leaving rich pockets so that combustion can take place properly. Too much mixing may lead to very lean mixtures. Again the fuel will not burn completely and this will result in hydrocarbon emission. Insufficient mixing will lead to high smoke, HC, CO emissions and fuel consumption. Proper timing of the ignition can lead to low combustion temperatures and smooth engine operation. This will also reduce NO_x emissions.

Modern emission standards and performance requirements cannot be met by conventional fuel injection systems operated mechanically. Injection timing, pressure, duration etc. can be easily controlled electronically to minimize fuel consumption and emissions. Here again a set of sensors determines the engine operating conditions and this data is fed to the electronic control module to take suitable steps in order to control the engine operation via actuators. Electronic controls can also be used for engine speed governing. These systems can give very close control over the engine speed under transients and wide load fluctuations.

In both SI and CI engines the electronic control module works on software specially developed which uses sensor inputs and previously stored data about the engine. Using this information it controls various parameters. The control is achieved through actuators. The data about the engine is stored as a table that is analyzed to take appropriate decisions. In most cases the electronic control module has to work in conjunctions with mechanical systems. In this chapter we will introduce different instrumentation and sensors that can be used in practice.

17.2 TYPICAL ENGINE MANAGEMENT SYSTEMS

In order to get an idea of the different types of sensors that are used in an engine let us take the example of a typical gasoline fuel injection system as shown in Fig.17.1. We can see that different sensors are used to detect crank shaft position, coolant temperature, engine speed, air flow rate, exhaust oxygen level, camshaft position, EGR valve position, exhaust manifold pressure, knock, manifold air pressure and manifold temperature.

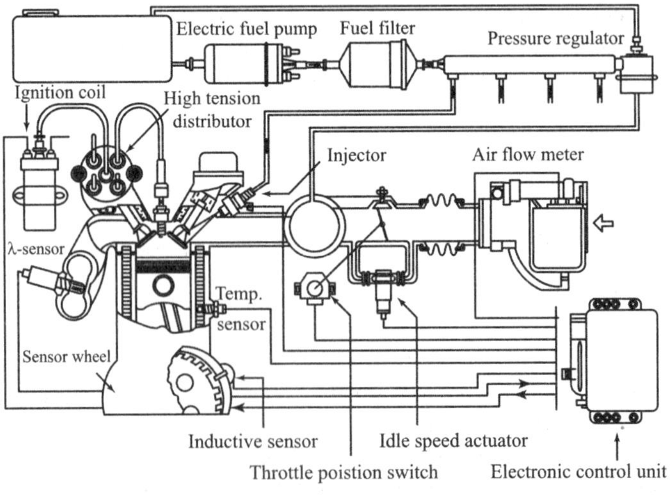

Fig. 17.1 Bosch motronic system

Figure 17.2 shows a typical common rail diesel fuel injection system. In this case we have sensors for engine speed, air mass flow, crank speed, cam shaft position, turbo air boost pressure, fuel rail pressure, air temperature,

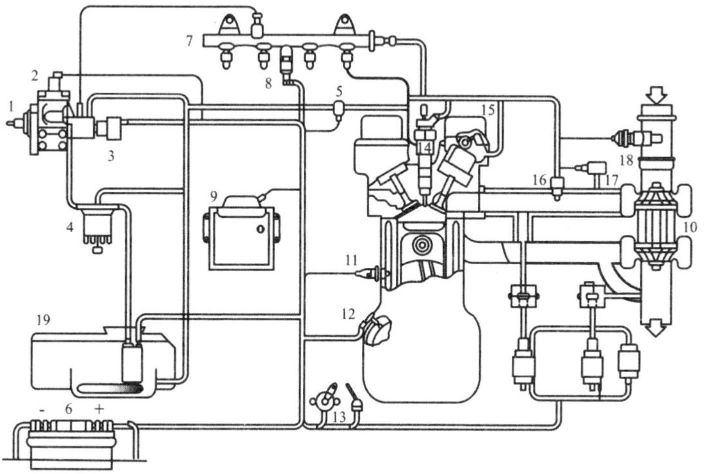

1	High pressure pump	7	High pressure accumulator	13	Accelerator pedal sensor
2	Element shutoff valve	8	Rail pressure sensor	14	Injector
3	Pressure control valve	9	ECU	15	Camshaft speed sensor
4	Fuel filter	10	Turbocharger	16	Intake air temperature sensor
5	Fuel temperature sensor	11	Coolant temperature sensor	17	Boost pressure sensor
6	Battery	12	Crankshaft speed	18	Air mass meter

19 Fuel tank with prefilter and presupply pump

Fig. 17.2 Bosch common rail diesel injection system

coolant temperature, accelerator pedal position etc. Thus it is clear that the functioning of all electronically controlled fuel control systems depends on the inputs from different types of sensors. The ECU (Electronic Control Unit) receives these signals from sensors and after manipulation and calculations sends outputs to vary the injection timing, fuel quantity, ignition timing etc. It also controls systems like the fuel injection pump, idle speed control unit, particulate trap regenerator (in a diesel engine), coolant supply etc. Thus any engine management system consists of the following main units: sensor, signal conditioner, analogue to digital converter, electronic control unit, output signal, driver and actuator. There will be more than one input and also more than one output which will be involved in controlling the engine at any given instant. We will look at different kinds of sensors that are normally used along with their measuring principle. For clarity, the discussion is divided depending on the parameter that is measured and applicable sensors are discussed under each category.

17.3 POSITION DISPLACEMENT AND SPEED SENSING

Position displacement and speed sensing are very important in the engine management system. For such sensing inductive, hall effect, potentiometric, electro optical, differential transformer and strain gauge sensors are extensively used for these applications particularly in automobiles and engine laboratories. The details and working principle of various sensors are discussed in the following sections.

17.3.1 Inductive Transducers

A typical inductive transducer is shown in Fig.17.3. As can be seen, there is a permanent magnet. When the toothed piece moves it changes the permeance of the magnetic circuit and this changes the magnetic flux. Thus a voltage gets developed when the flux field varies as the toothed piece moves. The voltage output alternates about the mean on the plus and minus sides. It can be further sent to an electronic circuit to shape it into a square pulse. The toothed piece can be the teeth on the crank shaft of the engine as shown in Fig.17.1, so that the frequency of the pulses can give the speed of the shaft.

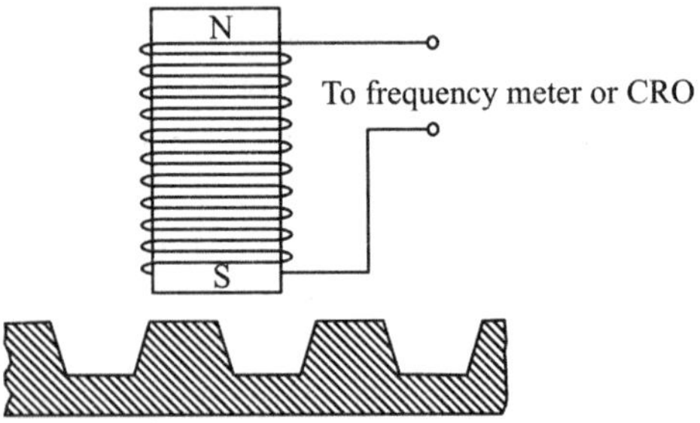

Fig. 17.3 Variable reluctance pickup

These transducers are often used for this application. Their output becomes stronger as the variation in the flux rate becomes faster. Thus they are used only for dynamic applications. They can also be used to determine the position of the cam shaft if at some point on the shaft a tooth is removed as shown in Fig.17.1. In that case the signals will be as seen in Fig.17.4. The signal being essentially a sine wave where a tooth is missing that will be indicted as a missed pulse (Fig.17.4). The ECU can use this information effectively. The speed is determined from the frequency of the pulses and the number of pulses before or after the missed pulse can give the crank position. The crank position will be used by the ECU to initiate the injection and/or the ignition process(es). The zero of the sine wave occurs when the pickup is near the apex of every tooth.

Inductive pickups can also be used to detect the actual timing of the injection in a diesel engine. Inductive transducers can also be used in the rotor of distributors to initiate spark on the correct cylinder. Inductive pickups are simple and reliable and give a strong voltage if the movement is rapid or the sensor is close to the moving part.

17.3.2 Hall Effect Pickup

In a hall effect pick up a suitable semiconductor material is supplied with a constant current. When this sensor is subjected to a magnetic field which is perpendicular to the direction of the current, an emf gets developed at right

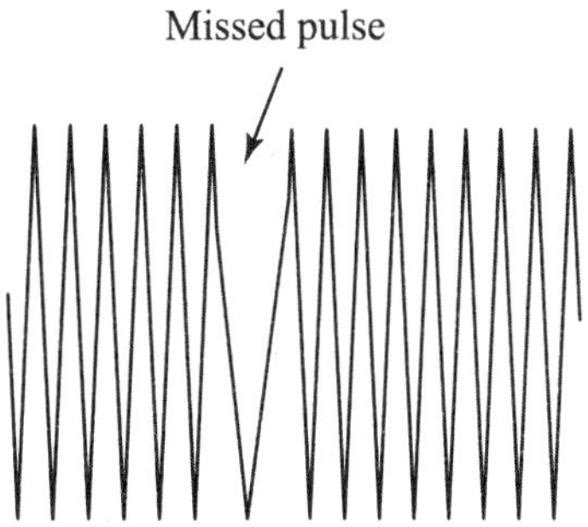

Fig. 17.4 Output signal

angles to the supply current as seen in Fig.17.5. A permanent magnet can be attached to the moving object. This sensor can be used to detect motion and here unlike the inductive transducer the velocity of the moving object is immaterial. The sensor output varies with the strength of the magnetic field. The output is normally modified to give a square pulse which can be fed to the ECU. This sensor can be used to detect shaft position and speed. It can also be used to trigger the ignition system.

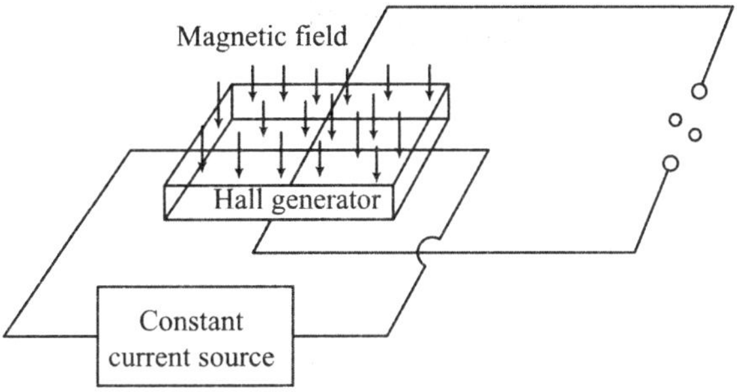

Fig. 17.5 Hall effect sensor

17.3.3 Potentiometers

Normally the position of the throttle is determined using a potentiometer. The potentiometer is a passive device and does not give any voltage output unless it is exited. The potentiometer is basically a variable resistance. Across the resistance a constant voltage is applied. A moving leg slides on the resistance and the voltage across the moving leg and one end of the resistance is the output. The contact motion can be rotational or translational. It can also be helical in the case of multi turn devices. The resistance elements can be wire wound, made of a conductive plastic or made with a conductive ceramic. The resolution depends on the type of resistance element. To get a sufficiently high resistance, wound wires are used. But in this case the resistance varies in small steps. The turns are usually 500 to 1000 per inch.

Non-wire wound potentiometers are used for applications like throttle position sensing etc. They have infinite resolution. A typical device is seen in

Fig.17.6. Here a resistance is in the form of a strip that is deposited on a base insulator.

The main advantage here is that the deposition can be varied in such a way to achieve any type of resistance variation with the position of the slider contact or wiper. This means that any non-linearity in the associated hard ware can be compensated for by suitably designing the potentiometer. The output varies about a mean due to roughness and small variations in the resistance in the strip as it is composed of a mixture of conductive and non-conductive powders. So there is a high resolution but also an associated roughness which really limits the resolution. The life of potentiometers is limited. Typical values of cycles are two million for wire wound, ten million for hybrid and fifty million for conductive plastic. A potentiometric device is typically used for position measurement. It is not suitable for speed measurement.

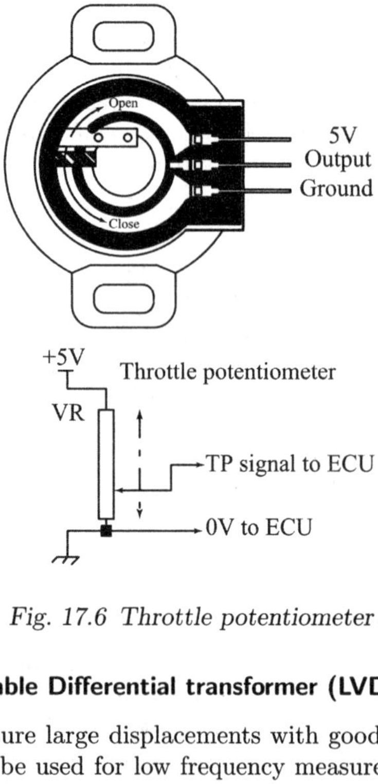

Fig. 17.6 Throttle potentiometer

17.3.4 Linear Variable Differential transformer (LVDT)

The LVDT can measure large displacements with good linearity and resolution. They can only be used for low frequency measurements and are somewhat bulky. These transducers are ideal for measurement in the laboratory for parameters like valve lift, injector needle lift, fuel injection pump rack travel measurement etc. They are not commonly used on a moving automobile. LVDTs have been used to detect the movement of the diaphragms of manifold pressure sensors. The schematic of a LVDT is seen in Fig.17.7. The device needs an alternating current input. This is usually of a very high frequency, which is several times higher than the frequency at which the displacement will vary. This is frequency of the input signal is called the carrier frequency which can typically be about 5 kHz.

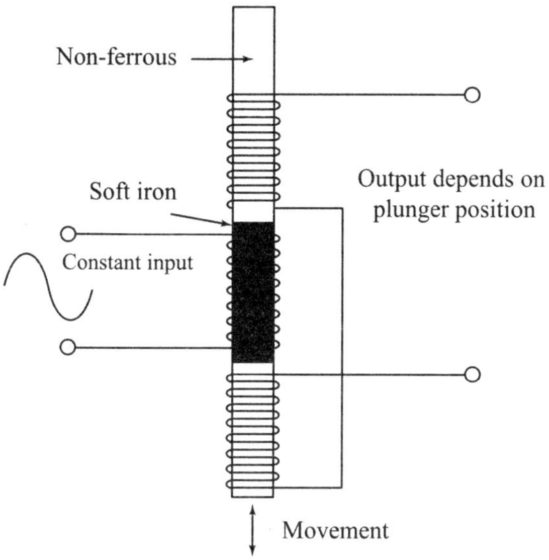

Fig. 17.7 LVDT

The primary is used for excitation and the two secondaries are connected in opposition. In the core at mean or null position there will not be any output voltage. The output is the difference between the voltages produced in both the secondary windings. The core is made of a ferromagnetic material. When it is moved the voltage in one of the windings becomes different from the other. The output is an alternating voltage and is in phase or out of phase with the input depending on the direction of motion of the core and is proportional to the displacement from null. A phase sensitive detector is needed to determine the magnitude and direction of motion of the object which is actually attached to the core. The output signal is actually superimposed on the carrier signal and hence has to be separated. This process is called demodulation.

17.3.5 Electro Optical Sensors

Electro-optical sensors can be used for position and speed measurement. These devices can operate on high frequencies and thus can detect fast moving objects. Normally shaft encoders have two optical pickups, one gives a signal at definite crank angle intervals and the other gives one pulse per revolution so that the absolute angle can be detected. Incremental encoders accumulate pulses to determine the crank angle (Fig.17.8). However, they cannot be used in situations where the direction changes. In such cases two crankangle based pulses with a phase shift of 1/4th of the degree resolution can be used. The phase difference between the signals can then be used to get the direction. In the case of all these types of incremental encoders loss of power or noise signals can lead to total loss of position detection at least for a small duration. Absolute encoders solve these problems and have several tracks and outputs which are a binary representation of the actual position.

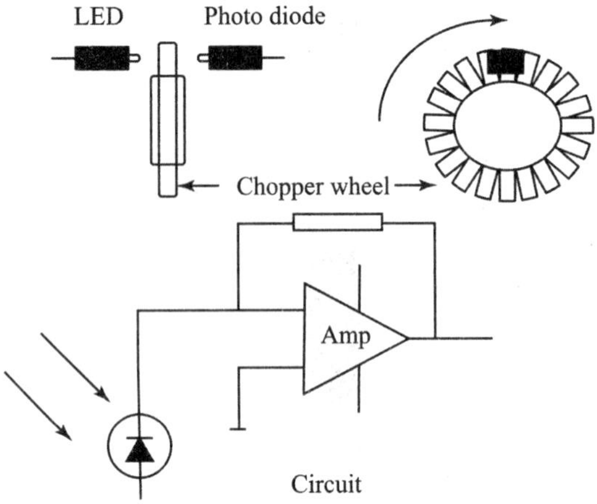

Fig. 17.8 Photo detector

17.4 MEASUREMENT OF PRESSURE

The measurement of manifold pressure, ambient pressure, cylinder pressure, lubricating oil pressure etc will involve the use of transducers like variable capacitance, strain gauge, LVDT, Piezoelectric and piezoresistive. In most cases, only an average variation in the pressure is needed. In others instantaneous variations within a crank angle may be needed. For engine control average pressure variations are sufficient. But in the laboratory when manifolds or the combustion and injection systems are being optimized one will need pressure sensors with high frequency response. All pressure sensors will have a diaphragm and the method of detecting the movement of this diaphragm varies. Sometimes the detecting element itself resists the movement of the diaphragm in others the diaphragm itself does this job by acting like a spring.

17.4.1 Strain Gauge Sensors

The strain gauge consists of a conductor which changes its dimensions along with the member whose strain is to be measured. The change in dimension as well as the stress in the wire leads to a change in the resistance of the wire. Thus the change in the resistance of the strain gauge element can be used to determine the strain on the element which is itself the strain on the member. Conventional strain gauges are indicated in Fig.17.9. Several types of strain gauges are available. The most important ones are the:

(i) wire bonded on the member

(ii) wire or metal foil sandwiched between two insulators and bonded on the member

(iii) Thin metal film vacuum deposited on the member

(iv) Semiconductor bonded on the member

(v) Semiconductor diffused on a base material

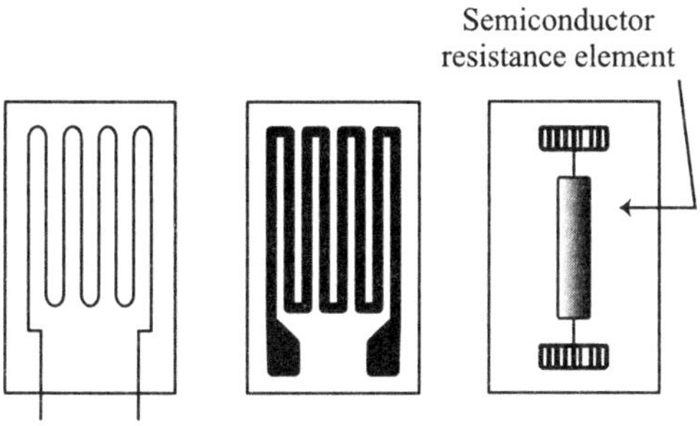

Fig. 17.9 Conventional strain gauges

Metallic strain gauges have a gauge factor of about 2 normally. Gauge factor is the change in resistance per unit initial resistance divided by the strain. Semiconductor gauges can have a very high gauge factor. A bridge circuit such as the one indicated in Fig.17.10 is used to measure the change in resistance and hence the strain.

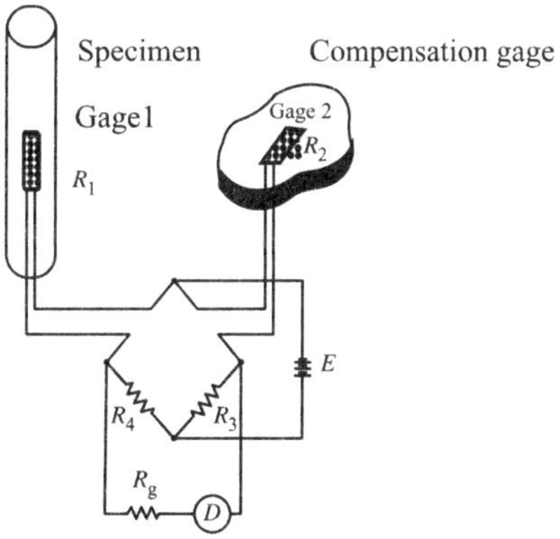

Fig. 17.10 Temperature compensation

All strain gauges are sensitive to temperature. In order to overcome this problem temperature compensation is done as seen in Fig.17.10. In this case two are four strain gauges that are connected to the opposite arms of the Wheatstone's bridge. The resistance change due to temperature thus gets compensated. The system also becomes more sensitive if the strain gauges on the opposite arms can have opposite strains.

Strain gauges can be pasted on the upper and lower sides of the diaphragm of pressure sensors to detect the deformation and hence the pressure. This system will also have temperature compensation. Diffused semiconductor strain gauges with a very high sensitivity can be used to measure low pressures. A typical Manifold pressure gauge is seen in Fig.17.11. Here the strain gauges are diffused on the diaphragm that is square in shape.

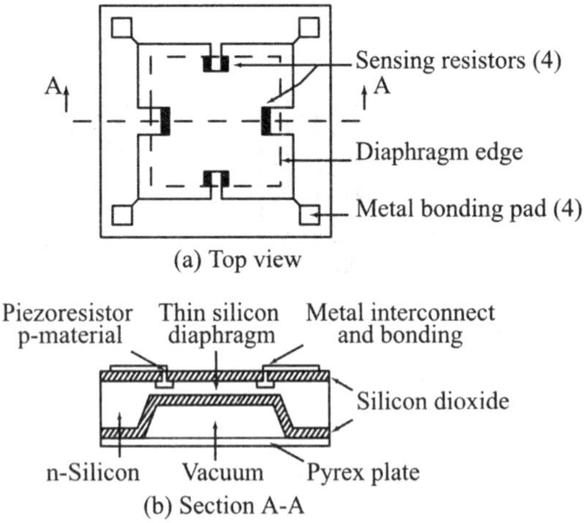

Fig. 17.11 Manifold pressure sensor

17.4.2 Capacitance Transducers

Capacitance transducers as seen in Fig.17.12 can be used to detect the movement of the diaphragm of pressure transducers. These sensors can have high frequency response. Here the capacitor formed at the diaphragm is used in one arm of an AC bridge. The bridge is itself exited by a high frequency supply.

17.4.3 Peizoelectric Sensors

Engine research always involves the measurement of cylinder pressure. For this purpose fast acting (high natural frequency) piezoelectric pickups are used. Piezoelectric pickups use quartz or other crystals, which are stressed when a pressure is applied. This causes two opposite sides of the crystal to get oppositely charged. The charge is proportional to the applied stress/pressure. A charge amplifier is used to convert this charge to an equivalent voltage and amplify it. Normally charge amplifiers give a 0 to 10 volt output. They can have natural frequencies of the order of 100 kHz. The choice of the time constant is very important as it can affect the frequency response. The entire pressure measuring system has to have a very high insulation resistance so that the charge does not leak and cause drifts. Further the internal leakage of the charge in the transducer and amplifier, which is inevitable, makes the system unsuitable for static measurements. This system is ideally suited for dynamic measurements in engine cylinders. The measurement of cylinder pressure is complicated because:

(i) The peak temperature in the cylinder is high

(ii) The peak maximum pressure is also quite high

(iii) The pressure varies from a very low (suction pressure) to a very high values(combustion pressure)

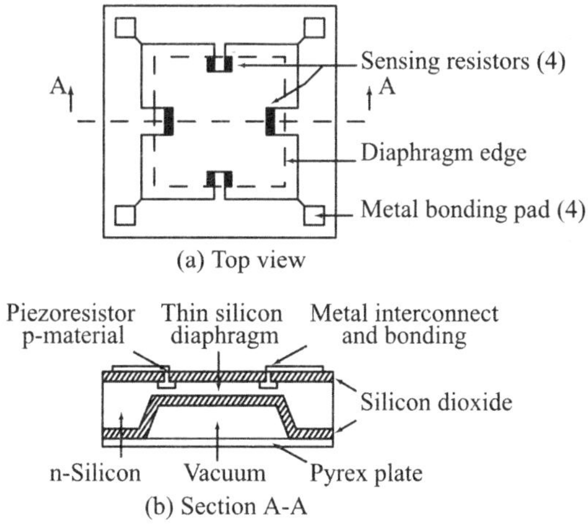

Fig. 17.12 Capacitance transducers

(iv) The pressure signal may have small amplitude but high frequency variations

(v) The cylinder temperature fluctuates rapidly

These mean we need a system with:

(i) high natural frequency,

(ii) high temperature and high pressure capability,

(iii) high thermal shock resistance,

(iv) high sensitivity, and

(v) extremely good linearity and accuracy.

One disadvantage of the piezoelectric pressure measuring pickup is that it can only give pressure differences and not the absolute value. Thus we must know the pressure at some point in the cycle already to get the pressure at every other point. This process is called pegging. Typical pressure pickups are seen in Figs.17.13 and 17.14.

17.5 TEMPERATURE MEASUREMENT

Temperature of the manifold air, coolant, lubricant etc. can be measured by thermistors, Resistance Temperature Detectors (RTD) and Thermocouples.

17.5.1 Thermistors

These transducers are commonly used. Most of them have a negative temperature coefficient. They give a large change in resistance for a given variation in the temperature. This is ideal. Thermistors are constructed out of semiconductor materials like cobalt or nickel oxides. Electrons break away from

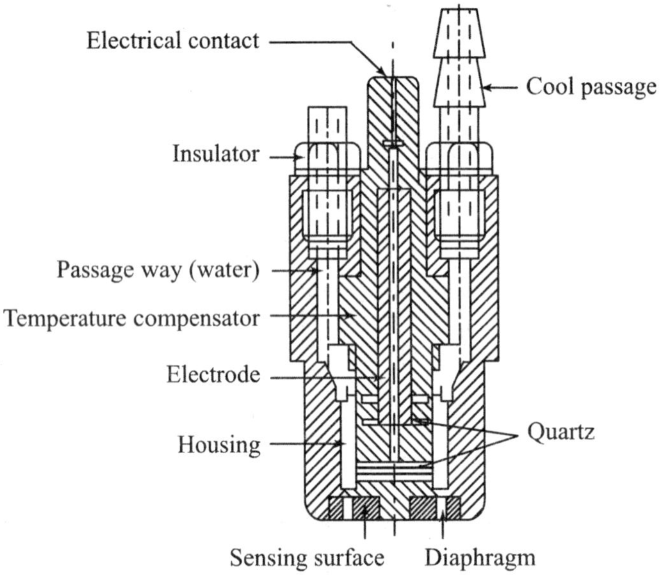

Fig. 17.13 Piezoelectric transducers

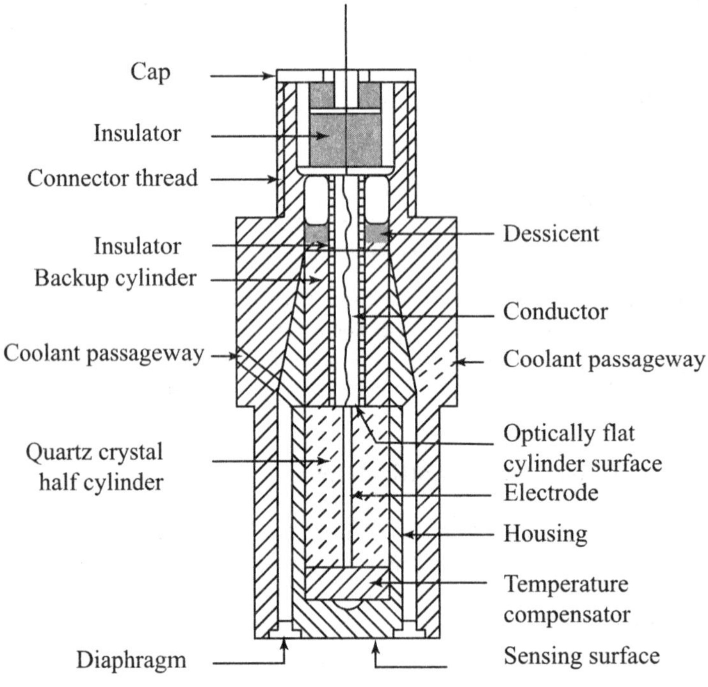

Fig. 17.14 Piezoelectric transducers

covalent bonds at high temperatures and thus the resistance falls. A thermistor is suitable for temperature measurements below 300 °C. It gives a highly nonlinear output and linearizing circuits are essential. A typical thermistor and the sensing circuit are shown in the Fig.17.15.

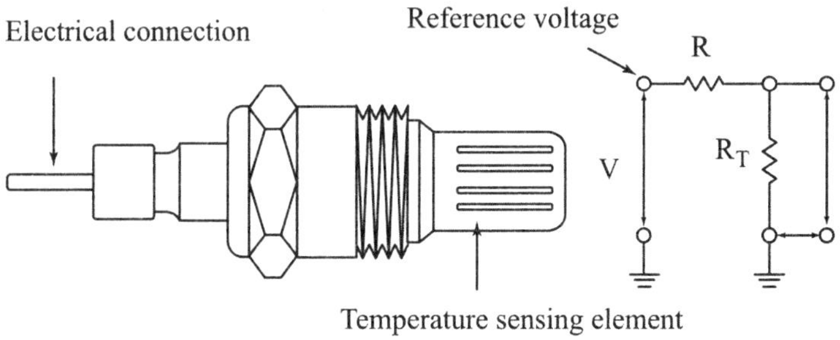

Fig. 17.15 Thermistor and sensing circuit

17.5.2 Thermocouples

When two dissimilar metals are joined and the junctions are maintained at different temperatures an emf is developed. The emf depends on the difference in temperature and the materials. This is called the Seebeck effect. One of the junctions has to be at a known temperature for us to measure the other temperature. One of the junctions can be at room temperature and we can separately measure it. Thermocouples can be used generally for high temperature measurement such as exhaust gas temperature in turbochargers. Platinum rhodium alloys can be used. The junctions can be welded, soldered or formed by mechanical contact. Typical thermocouples and cold junction compensating circuits using a thermistor are shown in Figs.17.16 and 17.17 respectively.

17.5.3 Resistance Temperature Detector (RTD)

A resistance temperature detector is a thermo-resistive element like the thermistor. However it has a positive coefficient of resistance. It is made up of good conductors of electricity like copper, platinum, nickel etc. It provides a highly linear variation and has high temperature range. They can be used upto temperatures of 1000 °C. The wire is wound over an insulating material. Figures 17.18 and 17.19 indicate a RTD and measuring circuit. A typical measuring circuit is shown in Fig.17.19. This one has automatic compensation for the variation in lead resistance with temperature.

17.6 INTAKE AIR FLOW MEASUREMENT

Intake air flow measurement is very essential to determine the amount of fuel to be injected to obtain a given air fuel ratio. Generally hot wire or flap type sensors are used.

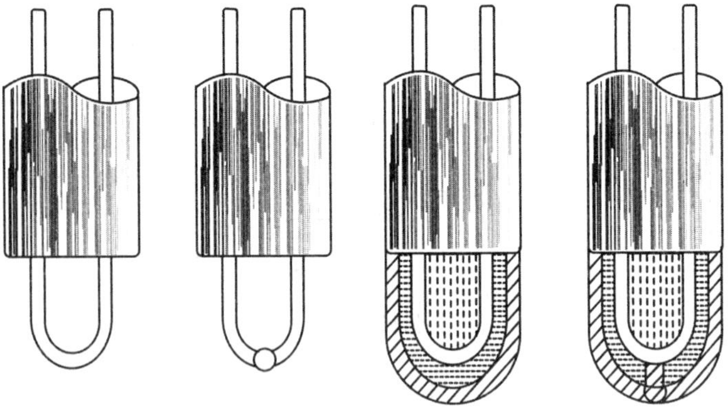

Fig. 17.16 Thermocouples

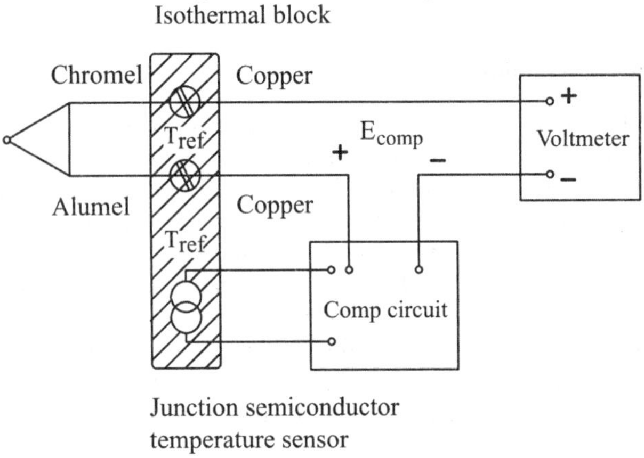

Fig. 17.17 Compensating circuit

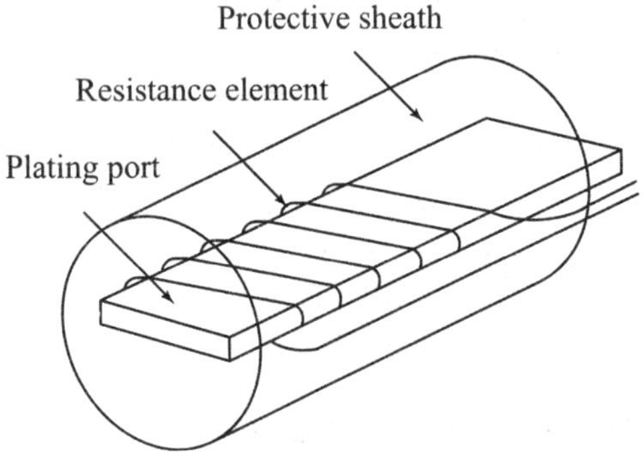

Fig. 17.18 A resistance temperature detector

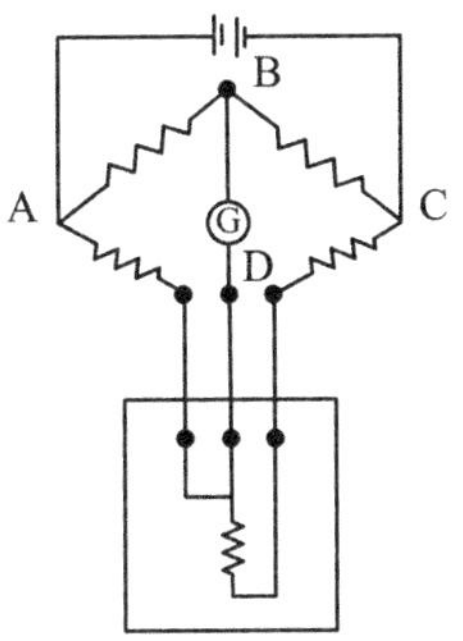

Fig. 17.19 Measuring circuit

17.6.1 Hot Wire Sensor

A hot wire sensor directly measures the mass flow rate of air. Measuring the air flow directly rather than calculating it from the throttle position and engine speed offers the advantage of automatically accounting for changes due to wear, deposits, incorrect valve setting etc. The hot-wire mass sensor is positioned between the air filter and the throttle valve. It is in the form of a thin platinum wire of about 70 μm diameter with a low thermal inertia, placed inside a measuring venturi. The hot wire sensor is indicated in Figs.17.20 and 17.21. This operates on the constant temperature principle. The hot-wire forms on arm of a bridge. Initially, the bridge is balanced. This occurs at a particular temperature of the hot wire i.e., at a particular resistance of the wire. As the air flows over the hot wire probe, it gets cooled and its temperature and hence resistance reduces. The bridge then gets unbalanced. The control circuit senses this and corrects the situation by increasing the heating current. The heating current thus is an indication of the airflow and is a measure of the air mass drawn into the engine. The current for heating causes the voltage across the precision resistor to vary and this is the sensed parameter. The temperature-compensating resistor is used to take care of temperature changes. The time constant is a few milliseconds. In order to remove any dirt from the hot wire, which can affect the output, it is heated to a high temperature for a short time before the engine is switched off. The main advantages of the hot wire sensor are:

(i) precise measurement,

(ii) fast response,

(iii) adaptability to engine operating conditions,

(iv) no errors due to variation in altitude,

(v) no errors due to pulsations,

(vi) no errors due to temperature variations, and

(vii) simple design with no moving parts.

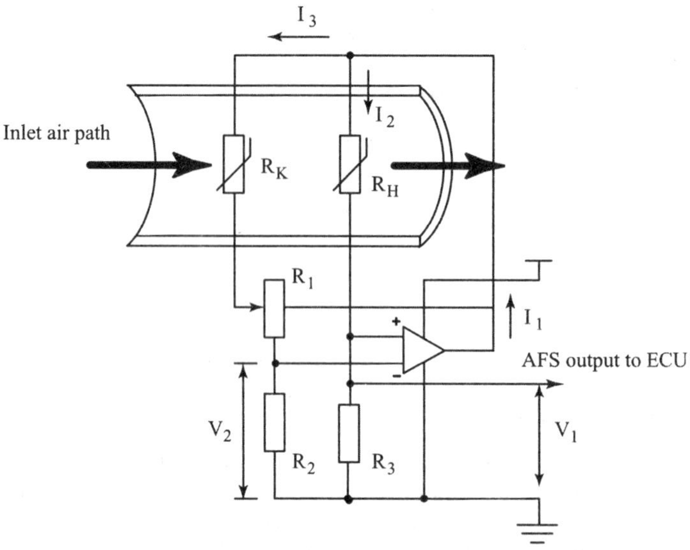

Fig. 17.20 Hot wire mass flow meter

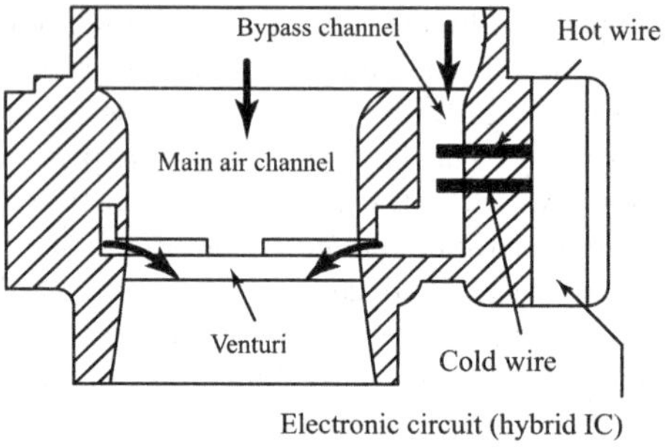

Fig. 17.21 Hot wire mass flow meter

Generally a portion of the air alone is made to flow around the hot wire so that the wire does not get damaged due to back firing and also less dirt gets accumulated.

17.6.2 Flap Type Sensor

This type of sensor has a flap which moves against a spring. The movement is proportional to the air mass flow rate. The flap movement is determined using a potentiometer. The problems with this arrangement are that the flap fluctuates when the air mass flow varies with the strokes of the engine. A compensating flap is used so that it also varies as the flow fluctuates and this is used to compensate for the fluctuations in the flap movement. A typical sensor is seen in Fig.17.22.

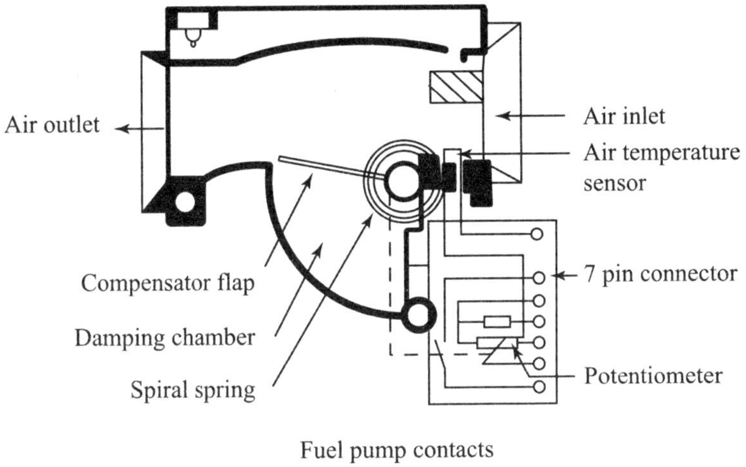

Fig. 17.22 Flap type mass sensor

17.6.3 Vortex Sensor

Here a bluff body as seen in Fig.17.23 is located in the intake manifold. As the air passes vortices are shed by the bluff body. The frequency at which they are shed linearly depends on the flow velocity. These vortices produce pressure disturbances which can be sensed by a microphone or piezo pressure detector located on the downstream side of the bluff body. There are no moving parts and wear. At idling this system produces signals of about 50 Hz and at maximum speed it may be about 1000 kHz. The output is shaped and sent out as a square pulse of varying frequency.

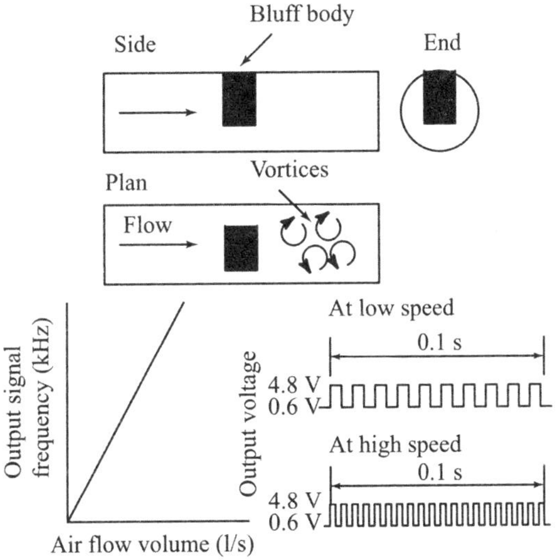

Fig. 17.23 Vortex flow meter principle

17.7 EXHAUST OXYGEN SENSOR

Catalytic converters can operate efficiently only in a narrow band of air fuel ratios. In order to maintain the excess air ratio, λ, within a narrow range, a closed loop control of the air fuel ratio is needed. A schematic of the lambda (λ) sensor is indicated in Fig.17.24. The outer section of the ceramic body is in contact with the exhaust whilst the inner section is in contact with ambient air. The ceramic is made of zirconium dioxide. The surfaces are coated with porous platinum which acts as electrodes. A porous protective ceramic coating is also applied on the outer surface.

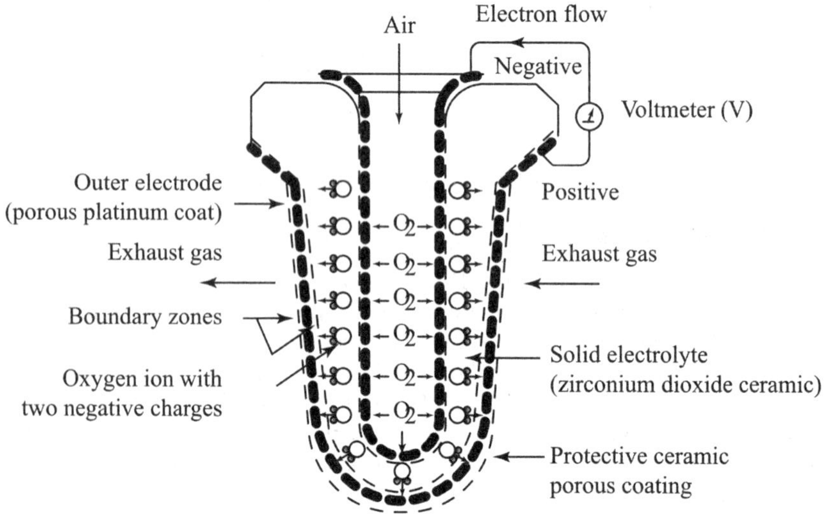

Fig. 17.24 Oxygen level sensor

The lambda sensor measures the oxygen concentration in the exhaust gases. When the oxygen concentration on both sides of the cell is different there is a voltage output. The voltage characteristics of this sensor are indicated in Fig.17.25. The voltages given are for a sensor operating at about 600 °C. The temperature of the sensor affects the conductivity of the ions. Thus the curve depends strongly on the sensor temperature. The response also depends on the sensor temperature. At the ideal operating temperature of about 600 °C, the response time is less than 50 ms. Hence, the Lambda sensor and the closed loop control are active only after the sensor reaches a temperature of about 350 °C. The sensor must not be placed very close to the exhaust valve because temperatures in excess of about 850 °C can damage it. The sensor is heated electrically at low load conditions and by the exhaust at high loads. A heated sensor can be located far away from the exhaust valve and also becomes operational fast.

17.7.1 Knock Sensor

On line knock control can allow the engine to be operated at high thermal efficiencies without damage due to knock. Knock control systems use a sensor,

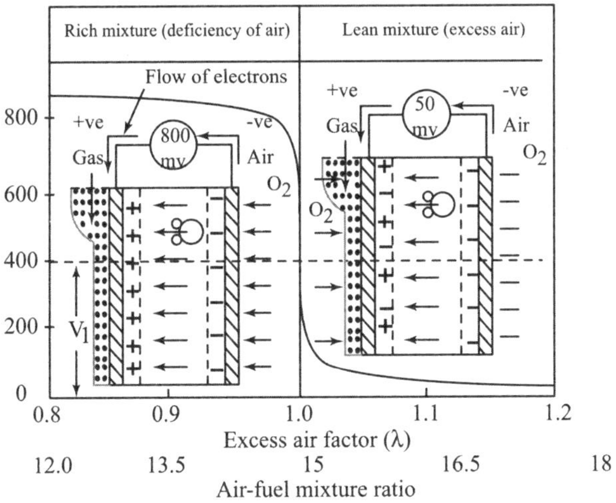

Fig. 17.25 Voltage characteristics

which is basically a piezoelectric vibration pickup. A typical knock sensor is seen in Fig.17.26. This is mounted on the cylinder block at a suitable location. This sensor has a high natural frequency. It has a mass held on a piezoelectric crystal. Any vibration makes the mass to alternatively compress and relieve the piezoelectric crystal thus producing a voltage variation as seen in the figure. This system will respond to engine vibrations also. However knock frequency is particular to a given engine and depends on the size of the cylinder. Thus the signal is filtered to get the knock output. The intensity of this signal determined the knock level.

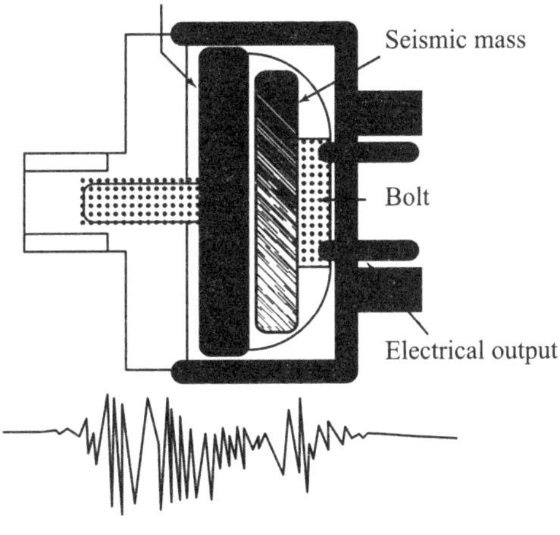

Fig. 17.26 Knock sensor

The various sensors discussed above are attached to the engine at appropriate places and the outputs are monitored by the ECU. The information about the engine is already stored in the ECU. From the input from all the sensors helps the ECU to alter the ignition and injection timings as well as the fuel flow rates. It makes the engine to run at optimum condition thereby the engine gives the best performance possible at all operating conditions. Thus engine electronics will play a major role in the engine management in the future.

Review Questions

17.1 What are the principle aims of an engine developer?

17.2 What are the important parameters that could be controlled in an engine?

17.3 Why modern engines are electronically controlled?

17.4 Briefly explain a typical electronic engine management system.

17.5 What are various sensors that can be used for displacement and position sensing in an engine? Briefly explain them.

17.6 Explain the various sensors that can be used for pressure measurements.

17.7 Explain the sensors used for temperature measurements.

17.8 Explain with figures the various methods and sensors that are used for inlet air flow measurements.

17.9 Give a brief account of exhaust oxygen sensor.

17.10 Explain briefly the working of a knock sensor.

Multiple Choice Questions (choose the most appropriate answer)

1. Hall effect pickup use
   (a) inductive transducers
   (b) potentiometers
   (c) thermistors
   (d) semiconductors

2. LVDT is used to measure
   (a) crank angle
   (b) engine speed
   (c) large displacements
   (d) gas temperature

3. The disadvantage of the piezoelectric pressure pickup is that
   (a) it can only give pressure difference
   (b) it can measure only low pressure
   (c) it is not suitable for dynamic measurement
   (d) has too much sensitivity
4. Thermistors are desirable because of their
   (a) linear output
   (b) large temperature coefficient
   (c) suitability for high temperature
   (d) none of the above
5. Seebeck effect is used in
   (a) thermistors
   (b) thermocouples
   (c) RTD
   (d) hot-wire sensor
6. Hot-wire sensors are used for measurement of
   (a) temperature
   (b) pressure
   (c) mass flow rate
   (d) smoke intensity
7. Knock sensors use
   (a) thermistors
   (b) thermocouples
   (c) piezoelectric pickup
   (d) flap type sensors
8. Catalytic converters use lambda (λ) sensors to keep
   (a) exhaust temperature constant
   (b) exhaust pressure constant
   (c) excess air ratio within a range
   (d) flow rate of air constant

9. Strain gauges are mainly used to measure
   (a) pressure
   (b) temperature
   (c) velocity
   (d) viscosity

10. Electro-optical sensors are used for
    (a) lubricating oil flow measurement
    (b) cooling water flow measurement
    (c) position and speed measurement
    (d) piston temperature measurement

Ans: 1. – (d) 2. – (c) 3. – (a) 4. – (b) 5. – (b)
6. – (c) 7. – (c) 8. – (c) 9. – (a) 10. – (c)

18 SUPERCHARGING

18.1 INTRODUCTION

It will be the principal aim of the engine designer, to achieve the twin goals of improved power output and minimum exhaust emissions. The power output of a naturally aspirated engine depends mainly on the following five factors:

(i) Amount of air inducted into the cylinder.

(ii) Extent of utilization of the inducted air.

(iii) The speed of the engine.

(iv) Quantity of fuel admitted and its combustion characteristics.

(v) Thermal efficiency of the engine.

The last two factors are inter-dependent and major modifications might be required to achieve complete combustion and therefore may not be a preferred method. The brake power of the engine is given by

$$bp = \frac{p_{bm} \times V_s \times n \times K}{60000} \tag{18.1}$$

There are two factors in the expression apart from number of cylinders and cubic capacity of the engine can increase the power output. They are (i) n, and p_{bm}. Hence, for a given cubic capacity of the engine, $(V_s \times K)$ by increasing the speed (number of power strokes) power output can be increased. However, friction will also increase and therefore, there will be a limit to the speed.

The most preferred method of increasing the power output is by means of increasing the mean effective pressure. This can be achieved by supplying air or air-fuel mixture at a pressure which is higher than the atmospheric pressure. This will increase the density, thereby the mass of air or air-fuel mixture inducted for the same swept volume. This in turn will increase the power output of the engine.

This method of supplying air or fuel-air mixture higher than the pressure at which the engine naturally aspirates, by means of a boosting device is called the supercharging. The device which boosts the pressure is called supercharger.

18.2 SUPERCHARGING

Supercharging of internal combustion engines is in practice for a long time as a method for improving engine power output. Entering the millennium, a new trend is appearing. The trend points to small displacement engines in order to meet emission legislation on fuel consumption and emission control. The consumers, however, still demand equally the same or better performance they are used to.

A good way to meet these needs is to have supercharging which may be called forced induction. As already stated, the purpose of supercharging an engine is to raise the density of the air charge, before it enters the cylinders. Thus, the increased mass of air will be inducted which will then be compressed in each cylinder. This makes more oxygen available for combustion than the conventional method of drawing the fresh air charge into the cylinder (naturally aspirated). Consequently, more air and fuel per cycle will be forced into the cylinder, and this can be effectively burnt during the combustion process to raise the engine power output to a higher value than would otherwise be possible.

The points to be noted in supercharging an engine summarized as:

(i) Supercharging increases the power output of the engine. It does not increase the fuel consumption, per brake kW hour.

(ii) Certain percentage of power is consumed in compressing the air. This power has to be taken from the engine itself. This will lead to some power loss. However, it is seen that the net power output will be more than the power output of an engine of the same capacity, without supercharging.

(iii) The engine should be designed to withstand the higher forces due to supercharging.

(iv) The increased pressure and temperature as a result of supercharging, may lead to detonation, Therefore the fuel used must have better anti-knock characteristics.

In practice, racing car engines use supercharging. The most important areas where supercharging is of vital importance are :

(i) Marine and automotive engines where weight and space are important.

(ii) Engines working at high altitudes. The power loss due to altitude can be compensated by supercharging.

18.3 TYPES OF SUPERCHARGERS

Supercharger is a pressure-boosting device which supplies air (or mixture) at a higher pressure. A centrifugal or axial flow or displacement type compressor is normally used. If the supercharger is driven by the engine crankshaft, then it is called mechanically driven supercharger. Some superchargers are driven by a gas turbine, which derives its power from the engine exhaust gases. Such a supercharger is called turbocharger. There are three types of superchargers

(i) Centrifugal type

(ii) Root's type

(iii) Vane type

18.3.1 Centrifugal Type Supercharger

The centrifugal type supercharger is commonly used in automotive engines (Fig.18.1). A V-belt from the engine pulley runs the supercharger. First, the air-fuel mixture enters the impeller at the centre. It then passes through the impeller and the diffuser vanes. Finally, air or mixture enters the volute casing and then goes to the engine from the casing. The mixture will come out at higher pressure and this condition is called supercharged condition.

Because of higher pressure more air-fuel mixture is forced into the cylinder. About 30% more air-fuel mixture can be forced into the combustion chamber. The impeller runs at very high speeds, about 80,000 revolutions per minute. Therefore the impeller should be able to withstand the high stresses produced at this speed. Impellers are usually made of duralumin, or alloy steels, to withstand the high stresses.

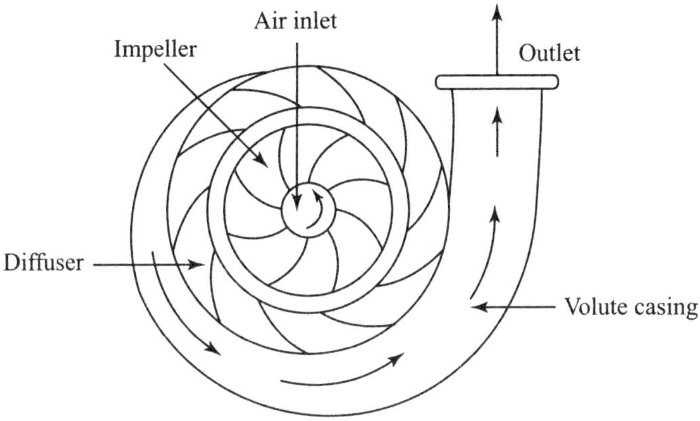

Fig. 18.1 Centrifugal type of supercharger

18.3.2 Root's Supercharger

The details of Root's supercharger is shown in Fig.18.2. The Root's supercharger has two rotors of epicycloids shape, with each rotor keyed to its shaft. One rotor is connected with the other one by means of gears. The gears are of equal size and therefore both the rotors rotate at the same speed. The Root's supercharger operates like a gear pump. The mixture at the outlet of this supercharger will be at much higher pressure than the inlet.

18.3.3 Vane Type Supercharger

Details of a typical vane type supercharger is shown in Fig.18.3. A number of vanes are mounted on the drum which is inside the body of the supercharger. The vanes can slide in or out, against the force of the spring. Because of this arrangement, the vanes are always in contact with the inner surface of the body. The space between the inner surface of the body and the drum decreases from the inlet to the outer side. In this way, the quantity of the mixture which enters at the inlet, decreases in volume, because of which the pressure of the mixture will increase as it reaches the exit.

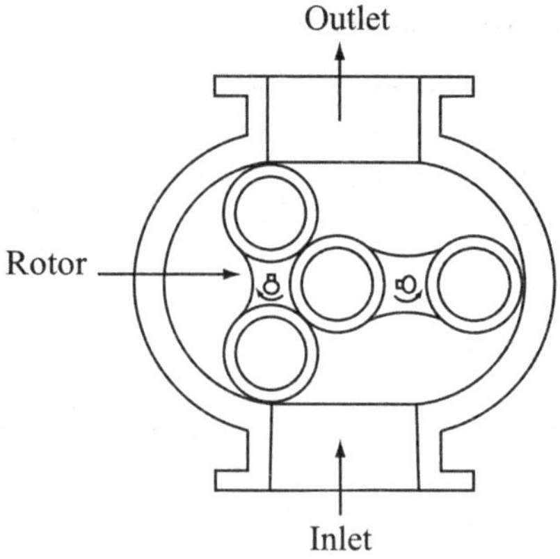

Fig. 18.2 Root's supercharger

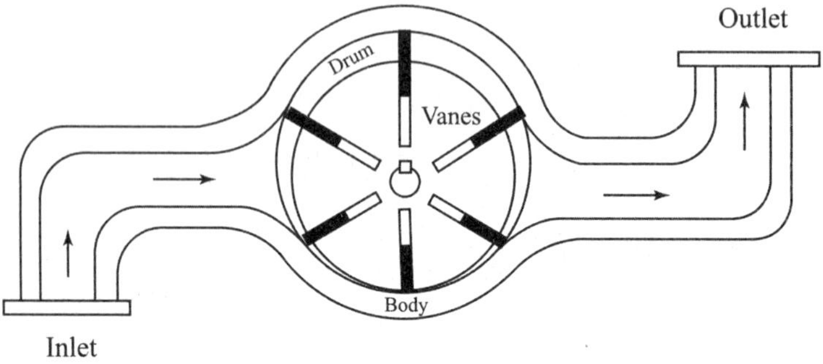

Fig. 18.3 Vane type supercharger

18.3.4 Comparison between the Three Superchargers

The required characteristics of a centrifugal type supercharger is poor and suitable for only low speeds. The root's supercharger is simple in construction, requires only minimum maintenance and has longer life. The vane type supercharger has a special problem of wear of tips of the vanes with time. Therefore, one has to take into account the application and then decide the type of supercharger for that application.

18.4 METHODS OF SUPERCHARGING

Necessary amount of compressed air (or mixture) can be supplied to the engine in the following ways.

(i) Independently driven compressor or blower, usually driven by an electric motor.

(ii) Ram effect.

(iii) Underpiston supercharging.

(iv) Kadenacy system (applied to two stroke engines).

(v) Engine driven compressor or blower.

The details of the above five methods of supercharging are briefly discussed in the following sections.

The two other important superchargers viz., gear driven supercharger and exhaust driven superchargers will be discussed in detail in subsequent sections.

18.4.1 Electric Motor Driven Supercharging

In this type the compressor is driven independently usually by an electric motor. The speed of the supercharger can be varied independent of engine speed and therefore control is comparatively easier.

18.4.2 Ram Effect of Supercharging

The ram effect of supercharging system consists primarily of tuned inlet pipes. These pipes induce resonant harmonic air oscillations. The kinetic energy of these oscillations provides a ramming effect. For the efficient operation of this system, the engine speed must be kept constant.

18.4.3 Under Piston Supercharging

Under piston method of supercharging has so far been confined to large marine four stroke engines of the crosshead type. It utilizes the bottom side of the piston for compressing the air. The bottom ends of the cylinder are closed off and provided with suitable valves. This system gives an adequate supply of compressed air, as there are two delivery strokes to each suction stroke of the cycle.

18.4.4 Kadenacy System of Supercharging

The kadenacy system utilizes the energy in the exhaust system to cause a depression of pressure in the cylinder. This depression makes the scavenge air to flow into the cylinder. A blower may also be used with this system, but it is not an essential.

The kadenacy system is based on the following principle: When the exhaust ports or valves are opened rapidly during the end of expansion stroke, there is, within the first interval of a few thousandths of a second, an urge or impulse in the gases to escape very rapidly from the cylinder. The escaping gases leave behind a pressure depression.

At the above moment, the fresh charge of air (or mixture) is allowed to enter the cylinder behind the exhaust gases by suitable timing of the admission valve or ports. For the best result a proper timing and skillful design of the exhaust system is a must.

The exhaust blowdown must be rapid to get a good-sized puff. In this respect, the exhaust ports are better than valves, and the ports with square upper edges are better than those with rounded upper edges. The impulse must arrive at the exhaust duct of the concerned cylinder at the right time some 15 to 20°, before exhaust valve closure. This will depend upon the timing of the blow down and the travel time of the wave from the source of its origin. In this method, the exhaust pressure is low (even sub-atmospheric during the greater part of the scavenging period). Hence, scavenging takes place against lower resistance and the intake pressure need not be high. This type of supercharging is also called exhaust pulse supercharging.

18.5 EFFECTS OF SUPERCHARGING

Before supercharging an engine one should understand its effects. The following are the effects of supercharging engines. Some of the points refer to CI engines:

(i) Higher power output

(ii) Greater induction of charge mass

(iii) Better atomization of fuel

(iv) Better mixing of fuel and air

(v) Better scavenging of products

(vi) Better torque characteristic over the whole speed range

(vii) Quicker acceleration of vehicle

(viii) More complete and smoother combustion

(ix) Inferior or poor ignition quality fuel usage

(x) Smoother operation and reduction in diesel knock tendency

(xi) Increased detonation tendency in SI engines

(xii) Improved cold starting

(xiii) Reduced exhaust smoke

(xiv) Reduced specific fuel consumption, in turbocharging

(xv) Increased mechanical efficiency

(xvi) Increased thermal stresses

(xvii) Increased heat losses due to increased turbulence

(xviii) Increased gas loading

(xix) Increased valve overlap period of 60 to 160° of crank angle

(xx) Increased cooling requirements of pistons and valves

18.6 LIMITATIONS TO SUPERCHARGING

Due to supercharging, thermal load on the various parts of the engine increases. In some engines, the piston crown is provided with a hollow space. Oil or water is circulated through this space and thereby the piston crown is cooled. In some engines, the piston crown and the seat and the edges of the exhaust valves are usually made of better materials that can withstand higher temperatures. Increased gas loading caused by supercharging necessitates the use of larger bearing areas and heavier engine components

In an existing engine if supercharging has to be adopted, one should first study the factors that limit the extent of supercharging that can be tried. Further certain modifications have to be made to the engine to safeguard the same and to get the full benefit of supercharging. These are discussed below:

The permissible extent of supercharging depends upon the ability of the engine to withstand the increased gas loading and thermal stresses. Durability, reliability and fuel economy are the main considerations that limit the degree of supercharging of an engine Because of the increased heat generation and heat transfer, there is a greater tendency to bum the piston crown and the seat and edges of the exhaust valves. To overcome this problem, the valve overlap is usually greater in supercharged engines. The valve overlap may vary from about 80 to 160 degree of crank travel. Increased valve overlap permits greater time during which cooler air will flow past the valves and the piston crown. This cools the exhaust valve seat, the exhaust valves and the piston crown.

18.7 THERMODYNAMIC ANALYSIS OF SUPERCHARGED ENGINE CYCLE

The ideal dual-combustion cycle of a mechanically driven supercharged engine is shown in Fig.18.4. The corresponding cycle for a naturally aspirated engine is shown in Fig.18.5. The pressure p_1 represents the supercharging pressure and $p_6 = p_7$, is the exhaust pressure. Area $9 - 10 - 1 - 11 - 9$ represents the work supplied from the engine to the super charger as it is mechanically driven. The various processes for the supercharged and naturally aspirated engine are given in Table 18.1.

Table 18.1 Various processes for the supercharged and naturally aspirated engine

Process	S.C. engine	N.A. engine
Induction	$8 \rightarrow 1$	$7{-}6'$
Compression	$1 \rightarrow 2$	$1' - 2'$
Heat addition	$2 \rightarrow 3 - 4$	$2' - 3' - 4'$
Expansion	$4 - 5$	$4' - 5'$
Heat rejection	$5 - 1$	$5' - 1'$

As could be seen from the Figs.18.4 and Fig.18.5 the supercharged engine inducts air at a higher pressure ($p_8 = p_1$) compared to naturally aspirated engine ($p_7 = p'_6$ = atmospheric). Hence the density and thereby the mass of air (m) going into supercharged engine will be higher than the mass of air going into the naturally aspirated engine (m'). That is to say $m > m'$.

From the Fig.18.4, it can be noted that the net work output of the supercharged engine cycle is a function of two positive work and one negative. It is given by

$$\begin{aligned} W_{sc} &= \text{Engine work output (+ve)} + \text{Gas exchange work (+ve)} - \\ &\quad \text{Supercharger work (-ve)} \qquad (18.2) \\ &= (\text{Area } 1-2-3-4-5-1) + (\text{Area } 8-1-6-7-8) - \\ &\quad (\text{Area } 9-10-11-12-9) \qquad (18.3) \end{aligned}$$

It is to be noted that positive gas exchange area 8-1-6-7-8 may be greater than the negative area 9-10-11-12-9. It should be noted that there is a loss of work which is not recoverable. Further, it is to be kept in mind that with increase in supercharging pressure the negative work, will also increase and therefore there will be a limit for supercharging. The ideal efficiency of the supercharged engine will decrease with increase in supercharging pressure. However, it is to be understood that the net increase in power output is due to *increase in mass of charge at condition 1* (Fig.18.4) for supercharged engine compared to the mass of charge for naturally aspirated engine at conditions 1′ (Fig.18.5). The density of charge at 1 is greater than the density of charge at 1′ for the same stroke volume V_s. Further, in naturally aspirated actual engines, there is a negative work due to gas exhaust process.

It is to be emphasized again that the gain in output of supercharged engine is mainly due to increase in the mass of air inducted for the same swept volume. The additional mass of air inducted may also be due to compression of the residual gas volume to higher pressure. The rate of increase of maximum cylinder pressure is less than the rate of increase of brake mean effective pressure for supercharged engine. Thus mechanical efficiency of supercharged engine is better than that of a naturally aspirated engine.

18.8 POWER INPUT FOR MECHANICAL DRIVEN SUPERCHARGER

Assuming adiabatic compression of air, the work done on the supercharger per kg of air is given by

$$w = -\int v dp = h_2 - h_1 \qquad (18.4)$$

$$= C_p(T_2 - T_1) = C_p T_1 \left[\left(\frac{p_2}{p_1} \right)^{\frac{\gamma-1}{\gamma}} - 1 \right] \qquad (18.5)$$

where T_1 = initial temperature, p_1 = initial pressure p_2 = delivery pressure. And, with the isentropic efficiency of η_c

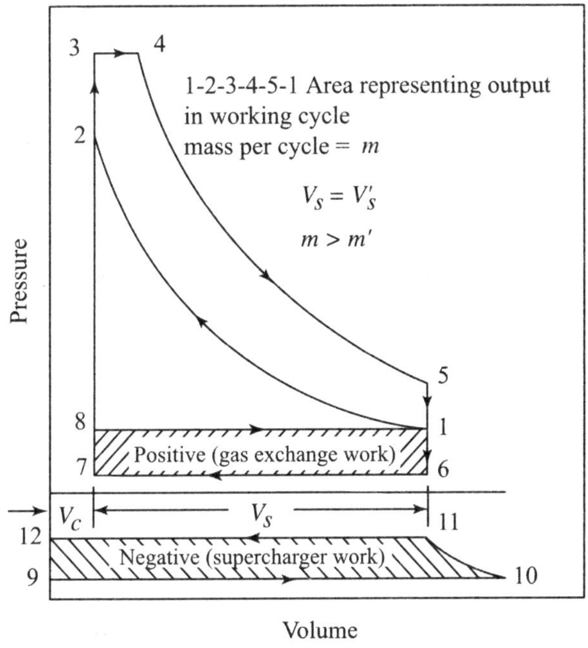

Fig. 18.4 Ideal dual-fuel cycle of a supercharged engine

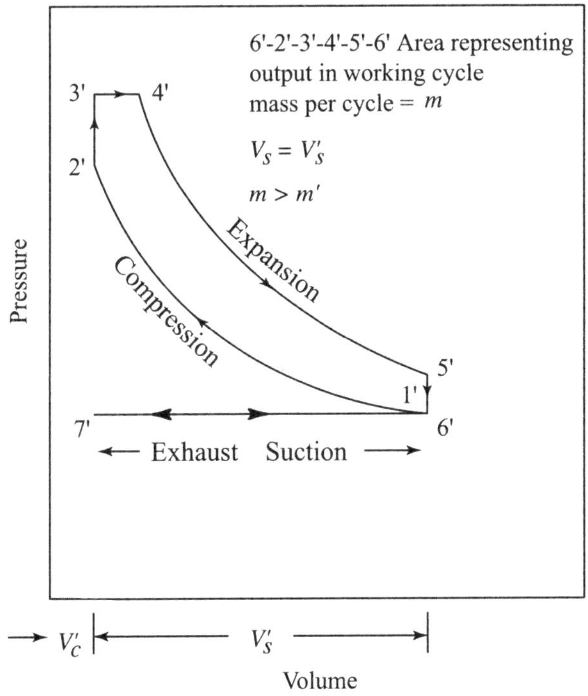

Fig. 18.5 Ideal dual-fuel cycle of a naturally aspirated engine

$$w = \frac{C_p T_1}{\eta_c}\left[\left(\frac{p_2}{p_1}\right)^{\frac{\gamma-1}{\gamma}} - 1\right] \quad (18.6)$$

where $w$is the power input to the compressor per unit mass flow rate, η_c is the isentropic efficiency of the compressor and T_1 is the inlet temperature to the compressor. Thus power required to drive the compressor is given by

$$= \frac{\dot{m}_a C_p T_1\left[\left(\frac{p_2}{p_1}\right)^{\frac{\gamma-1}{\gamma}} - 1\right]}{60 \times \eta_c} \text{ kW} \quad (18.7)$$

where $\dot{m}_a$ is mass of air supplied by supercharger in kg/min and C_p is specific heat of air in kJ/kg K. This power may be supplied by

(i) a separate drive viz. by a motor or any other prime mover driving the super charger

(ii) connecting the supercharger to engine output shaft

(iii) exhaust gas driven gas turbine which is called turbocharging .

18.9 GEAR DRIVEN AND EXHAUST DRIVEN SUPERCHARGING ARRANGEMENTS

Two main types of supercharging arrangements are shown in Fig.18.6 and 18.7. Figure 18.6(a) shows the compressor coupled to the engine with step up gearing to increase the rotational speed of compressor. In this case a certain percentage of engine output is utilized to drive the compressor. The net output increase due to supercharging is obtained by subtracting this power from the engine gross output. The ideal indicator diagrams shown in Fig.18.4 are based on this method. Aftercooler is also shown, by which the cool air to the engine can be sent if so desired. This will further increase the density of the intake air.

Figure 18.6(b) shows an engine with free exhaust driven compressor. The engines, so equipped are said to be turbo-supercharged. In this case the exhaust energy of the engine is used to drive the turbine which is coupled to a compressor. There is no mechanical coupling of compressor or turbine with the engine. The exhaust pipe of engine is however connected to inlet of turbine. In this case engine output is not utilized to drive the compressor.

In Fig.18.7(a), compressor, engine, and turbine are all geared together. The Wright Turbo-compound air plane engine is an example. In this case, if the turbine output is insufficient to run the compressor particularly at part loads, the engine power takes care of the remaining load of compressor. Also, the additional power from the turbine can be fed to the engine.

Figure 18.7(b) shows the gas generator type of arrangement. In this case engine drives only the compressor. Air from the compressor flows through the engine and the exhaust gases drive a power turbine. Most free-piston engines work on this principle.

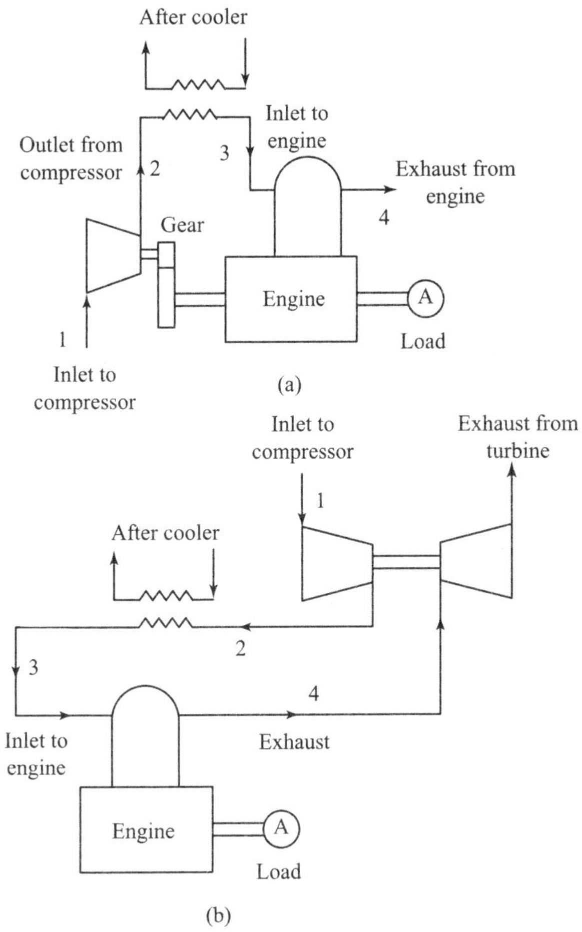

Fig. 18.6 Supercharging arrangements

18.10 TURBOCHARGING

In turbocharging, the supercharger is being driven by a gas turbine which uses the energy in the exhaust gases. There is no mechanical linkage between the engine and the supercharger. The major parts of a turbocharger are turbine wheel, turbine housing, turboshaft, compressor wheel, compressor housing and bearing housing. Figures 18.8 and 18.9 show the principle of exhaust turbocharging of a single cylinder engine and a Vee type engine with charge cooling unit respectively.

During engine operation, hot exhaust gases blowout through the exhaust valve opening into the exhaust manifold. The exhaust manifold and the connecting tubing route these gases into the turbine housing. As the gases pass through the turbine housing, they strike on the fins or blades on the turbine wheel. When the engine load is high enough, there is enough gas flow and

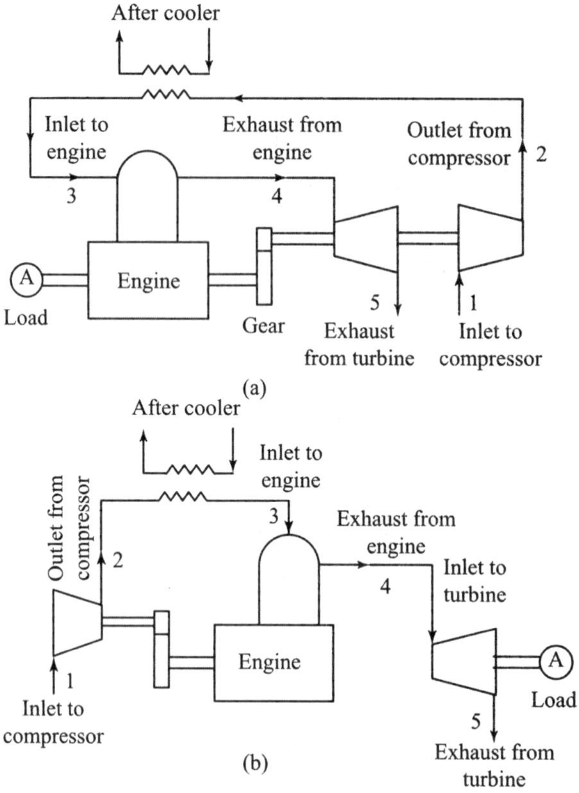

Fig. 18.7 Methods of supercharging

this makes the turbine wheel to spin rapidly. The turbine wheel is connected to the compressor wheel by the turboshaft. As such, the compressor wheel rotates with the turbine which sucks air into the compressor housing. Centrifugal force throws the air outward. This causes the air to flow out of the turbocharger and into the engine cylinder under pressure. In the case of turbocharging, there is a phenomena called turbolag. It refers to the short delay period before the boost or manifold pressure increases. This is due to the time the turbocharger assembly takes the exhaust gases to accelerate the turbine and compressor wheel to speed up.

In the turbocharger assembly, there is a control unit called waste gate. This unit limits the maximum boost pressure to prevent detonation in SI engines and the maximum pressure and engine damage. It is a diaphragm operated valve that can bypass part of the gases around the turbine wheel when manifold pressure is quite high.

The computer controlled turbocharging system uses engine sensors, a microprocessor and a waste gate solenoid. The solenoid when energized or deenergized by the computer, can open or close the waste gate. By this way, the boost pressure can be controlled closely. The exhaust smoke comparison for a

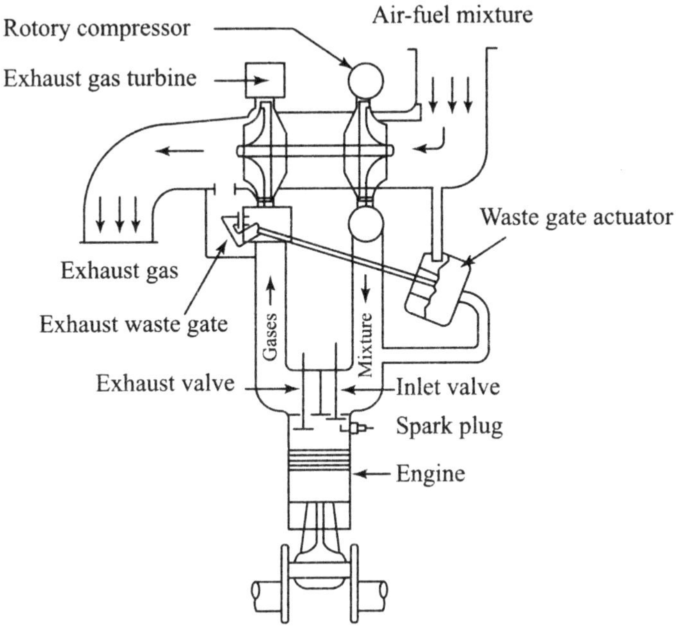

Fig. 18.8 Principles of exhaust turbocharging of a single-cylinder engine

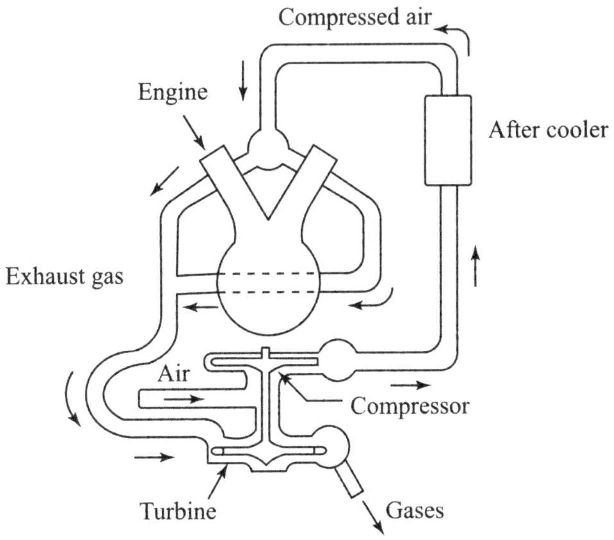

Fig. 18.9 Exhaust turbocharging of a "V" type engine

diesel engine for a naturally aspirated and turbocharged version, for different loads can be seen in Fig.18.10 There is an appreciable reduction in smoke in the case of turbocharged engine in the overload operation.

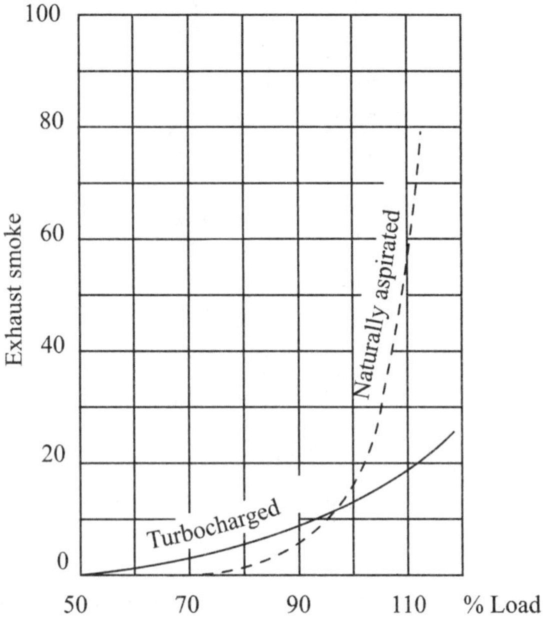

Fig. 18.10 Exhaust smoke comparison for naturally aspirated and turbocharged diesel engines

18.10.1 Charge Cooling

When air charge is compressed, it becomes hot. When air charge leaves the compressor, it is at a much higher temperature than ambient air temperature. During supercharging, the temperature of air increases from 60 to 95 °C. When air gets heated, it expands and the density reduces. Because of this, the mass of air entering the cylinder becomes lesser. This reduces oxygen availability in the cylinder for combustion. Further, supply of hot air to the engine may increase engine operating temperature. As such, charge is cooled by way of intercooling and/or after cooling to overcome these problems. However, this adds to the complexity of the system.

Worked out Examples

18.1 A three-litre four-stroke diesel engine develops 12 kW per m^3 of free air inducted per minute. The volumetric efficiency is 82% at 3600 rpm referred to atmospheric condition of 1 bar and 27 °C. A rotary compressor which is mechanically coupled to the engine is used to supercharge the engine. The pressure ratio and the isentropic efficiency of the compressor are 1.6 and 75% respectively. Calculate the percentage increase in brake power due to supercharging.

Assume mechanical efficiency of the engine to be 85% and air intake to the cylinder to be at the pressure equal to delivery pressure from compressor and temperature equal to 5.6 °C less than the delivery temperature of the compressor. Also assume that cylinder contains volume of charge equal to swept volume.

Solution

Naturally aspirated engine

$$\text{Swept volume, } V_s = \frac{3}{1000} \times \frac{3600}{2} = 5.4 \text{ m}^3/\text{min}$$

Actual volume/min of air inducted

$$\dot{V}_a = \dot{V}_s \times \eta_v = 5.4 \times 0.82 = 4.428 \text{ m}^3/\text{min}$$

Indicated power developed by the engine

$$\dot{V}_a \times P = 4.428 \times 12 = 53.136 \text{ kW}$$

$$\text{Brake power developed} = 0.75 \times 53.136 = 39.852$$

Pressure ratio of the compressor

$$\frac{p_2}{p1} = r = 1.6$$

Delivery pressure of the compressor,p_a

$$= 1 \times 1.6 = 1.6 \text{ bar}$$

$$\frac{T_2'}{T_1} = (r)^{\frac{\gamma-1}{\gamma}} = (1.6)^{\frac{0.4}{1.4}} = 1.144$$

$$T_2' = 300 \times 1.144 = 343.2 \text{ K}$$

$$\eta_c = \frac{T_2' - T_1}{T_2 - T_1} = T$$

$$T_2 = T_1 + \frac{1}{\eta_c}(T_2' - T_1)$$

$$= 300 + \frac{1}{0.7} \times (343.2 - 300) = 361.7 \text{ K}$$

Actual temperature at the exit of the compressor

$$= 361.6 - 273 = 88.7 \text{ K}$$

Actual intake temperature of the engine

$$= 88.7 - 5.7 = 83^\circ \text{ C} = 356 \text{ K}$$

When supercharged, the engine takes in air at a pressure p_2 of 1.6 bar , a pressure p_2 and temperature T_2 of 356 K. The swept volume is still 5.4

m^3/min and η_v will be $> 100\%$. At atmospheric conditions the corresponding volume, (V_1) will be

$$\frac{p_1 V_1}{T_1} = \frac{p_2 V_2}{T_2}$$

$$V_1 = \frac{p_2}{p_1} \times \frac{T_1}{T_2} \times V_2 = \frac{1.6}{1} \times \frac{300}{356} \times 5.4$$

$$= 7.281 \text{ m}^3/\text{min} \quad (\text{Note } \eta_v > 100$$

Increased intake volume rate of air due to supercharging is given by

$$= 7.281 - 4.428 = 2.853 \text{ m}^3/\text{min}$$

The corresponding increase in indicated power of the engine due to supercharging

$$= 2.853 \times 12 = 34.236 \text{ kW}$$

Additional indicated power developed due to positive gas exchange work because of increase in intake pressure

$$= \frac{\Delta p \times \dot{V}_s}{1000 \times 60}$$

$$= \frac{(1.6 - 1) \times 10^5 \times 5.4}{1000 \times 60}$$

$$= 5.4 \text{ kW}$$

$$\text{Total increase in } ip = 34.236 + 5.4 = 39.636 \text{ kW}$$

$$\text{Total increase in } bp = \eta_{mech} \times ip = 0.75 \times 39.636 = 29.727$$

$$\dot{m}_a = \frac{1.6 \times 10^5 \times 5.4}{0.287 \times 356} = 8.46 \text{ kg/min}$$

(Note that the delivery temperature from compressor is 361.6 K but mass is calculated at 356 K since volume occupied by this mass is known only at 356 K being the swept volume of cylinder)

Power required to run the compressor

$$= \dot{m}_a C_p \Delta T_{ac}$$

$$= \frac{8.46}{60} \times 1.005 \times (361.6 - 300) = 8.73 \text{ kW}$$

$$\text{Net increase in } bp = 29.73 - 8.73 = 21 \text{ kW}$$

$$\% \text{ increase in } bp = \frac{21}{39.852} = \mathbf{52.7\%}$$

Ans ⟸

18.2 A four-stroke diesel engine working at sea level (pressure : 1 bar and temperature 17°C) develops a brake power of 280 kW with a volumetric efficiency of 80% at sea level conditions. The engine works at an air-fuel ratio of 18:1, with a specific fuel consumption of 0.240 kg/kW h. The engine runs at 1800 rpm. Determine the engine capacity and the *bmep*.

This engine is taken to an altitude of 3 km where the ambient temperature and pressure are −23°C and 0.715 bar. A mechanically coupled supercharger is fitted to the engine which consumes 12% of the total power developed by the engine. The temperature of air leaving the supercharger is 37 °C. Determine the degree of supercharging required to maintain the same brake power of sea level. Also calculate the isentropic efficiency of the compressor. Assume that air-fuel ratio, thermal efficiency and volumetric efficiency remain the same for naturally aspirated and supercharged engine.

Solution

Consider the naturally aspirated engine at sea level condition

Fuel consumption rate,

$$\dot{m}_f = \frac{0.24 \times 280}{60} = 1.12 \text{ kg/min}$$

$$\dot{m}_a = 1.12 \times 18 = 20.16 \text{ kg/min}$$

$$\text{Volumetric efficiency } \eta_v = \frac{\text{Actual air consumption/cycle}}{\text{Displacement volume/cycle}}$$

$$0.8 = \frac{20.16 \times \frac{2}{1800}}{\frac{1 \times 10^5 \times V_s}{287 \times 290}}$$

$$V_s = \frac{20.16 \times 2}{1800} \times \frac{287 \times 290}{1 \times 10^5 \times 0.8} = \mathbf{0.0233\ m^3} \quad \xleftarrow{\text{Ans}}$$

$$p_{bm} = \frac{60000 \times bp}{V_s n K} = \frac{60000 \times 280}{0.0233 \times \frac{1800}{2} \times 1 \times 10^5} = \mathbf{8.01\ bar} \quad \xleftarrow{\text{Ans}}$$

Consider the supercharged engine:

The supercharger takes 12% of the total power produced by the engine. Since the net power at altitude should be equal to power developed by naturally aspirated engine at sea level viz. 280 kW, the supercharged engine should produce the power

$$= \frac{280}{0.88} = 318.18 \text{ kW}$$

$$\text{Mass flow rate required} = \frac{318.18 \times 20.16}{280} = \mathbf{22.91\ kg/min}$$

Since η_v is to remain the same,

$$0.8 = \frac{22.91 \times \frac{2}{1800}}{\frac{p_s \times 10^5 \times 0.0233}{287 \times (273+37)}}$$

where p_s is the pressure from the supercharger.

$$p_s = \frac{22.91 \times 2}{1800} \times \frac{287 \times 310}{0.0233 \times 10^5 \times 0.8} = 1.215 \text{ bar}$$

Pressure increase required

$$= 1.215 - 0.715 = 0.5 \text{ bar}$$

Degree of supercharging

$$= \frac{0.5}{0.715} \times 100 = \mathbf{69.9\%}$$ $\overset{\text{Ans}}{\Longleftarrow}$

$$\frac{T_2}{T_1} = \left(\frac{p_2}{p_1}\right)^{\frac{\gamma-1}{\gamma}}$$

$$T_2 = 250 \times \left(\frac{1.215}{0.715}\right)^{\frac{0.4}{1.4}} = 290.9 \text{ K}$$

$$\eta_{isen} = \frac{290.9 - 250}{310 - 250} = 0.682 = 68.2\%$$

18.3 A four-stroke engine working on dual-combustion cycle is supercharged by a turbocharger. Air from the atmosphere at 1 bar and 27 °C is compressed isentropically to 1.6 bar. Both compressor and turbine have isentropic efficiency of 75%. The air is cooled to 37 °C before entering the engine cylinder. The compression ratio of the engine is 18 and the peak pressure not to exceed 125 bar. The total heat input is 1200 kJ/kg. The heat rejection is at constant volume. The exhaust gases, assumed to obey gas laws, is throttled to 1.6 bar before entering the turbine where is expands isentropically to atmospheric pressure. Neglecting all the pressure and frictional losses, calculate the extra work available from turbocharger.

Solution

The flow process is assumed to be steady. The compression and expansion pressure ratio is 1.6. If T_1' is the isentropic compression temperature then,

$$\frac{T_1'}{T_8} = \left(\frac{p_1}{p_8}\right)^{\frac{\gamma-1}{\gamma}}$$

$$T_1' = 300 \times 1.6^{0.286} = 343.16 \text{ K}$$

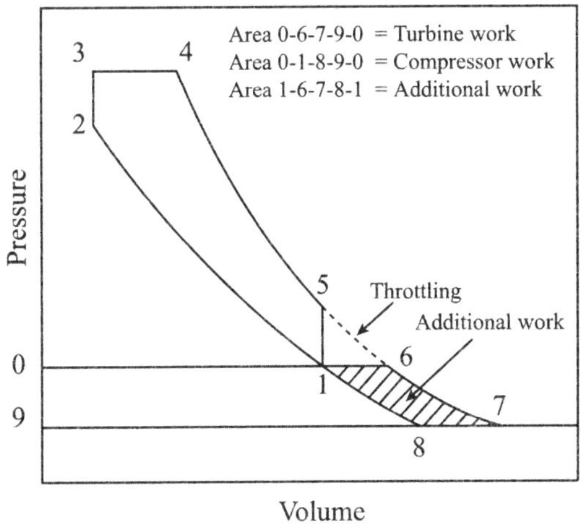

1-2-3-4-5-1	Ideal dual combustion cycle
8-1-6-7	Turbocharged cycle
8-1	Isentropic compression
6-7	Isentropic expansion

$$T_1 = T_8 + \frac{T_1' - T_8}{\eta_c} = 300 + \frac{343.16 - 300}{0.75}$$

$$= 357.55$$

Now work of compression in the turbocharger for unit mass flow rate

$$W_c = C_p \Delta T_{actual} = 1.005 \times (357.55 - 300)$$

$$= 57.84 \text{ kJ/kg}$$

The air is cooled in the after-cooler from 357.55 K to (273+37) = 310 K. Consider the engine cycle.

The temperature after compression

$$T_2 = T_1 r^{\gamma-1} = 310 \times 18^{0.4} = 985.1 \text{ K}$$

$$p_2 = p_1 r^{\gamma} = 1.6 \times 18^{1.4} = 91.52 \text{ bar}$$

$$T_3 = \frac{p_3}{p_2} \times T_2 = \frac{125}{91.52} \times 985.1 = 1345.5 \text{ K}$$

Heat supplied during constant volume

$$q_v = C_v(T_3 - T_2) = 0.717 \times (1345.5 - 985.1)$$

$$= 258.41 \text{ kJ/kg}$$

The heat added during constant pressure process

$$q_p = 1200 - 258.41 = 941.59$$

$$C_p(T_4 - T_3) = 941.59$$

$$T_4 = \frac{941.59}{1.005} + 1345.5 = 2282.4 \text{ K}$$

$$\text{Cut-off ratio } \frac{V_4}{V_3} = \frac{T_4}{T_3} = \frac{2282.4}{1345.5} = 1.7$$

$$\text{Expansion ratio} = \frac{r}{r_c} = \frac{18}{1.7} = 10.6$$

$$T_5 = \frac{T_4}{\left(\frac{V_5}{V_4}\right)^{\gamma-1}} = \frac{2282.4}{10.6^{0.4}} = 887.71 \text{ K}$$

It is assumed that the gas throttles from pressure p_5 to $p_6 = 1.6$ bar as perfect gas. Thus $T_6 = 908.64$. The isentropic temperature T_7' after expansion in the turbine

$$T_7' = \frac{T_6}{\left(\frac{p_6}{p_7}\right)^{\frac{\gamma-1}{\gamma}}} = \frac{887.71}{1.6^{0.286}} = 776.06$$

$$T_7 = T_6 - (T_6 - T_7') \times \eta_T$$

$$= 887.71 - (887.71 - 776.06) \times 0.75 = 803.97$$

$$W_T = C_p(T_6 - T_7) = 1.005 \times (887.71 - 803.97)$$

$$= 84.16$$

$$\text{Extra work available} = W_T - W_C = 84.16 - 57.84$$

$$= \mathbf{26.32\ kJ/kg}$$

Ans ⟸

18.4 Two identical vehicles are fitted with engine having the following specifications:

Engine 1: (Naturally aspirated)

Swept volume, V_s	:	3.6 litres
Brake mean effective pressure	:	9 bar
Speed	:	5000 rpm
Compression ratio	:	8
Efficiency ratio $\left(\frac{\eta_{ith}}{\eta_{air-std}}\right)$	:	0.5
Mechanical efficiency, η_m	:	90%
Mass	:	250 kg

Engine 2: (Super charged)

Swept volume, V_s	:	3.6 litres
Brake mean effective pressure	:	12 bar

Speed	:	5000 rpm
Compression ratio (lowered to avoid knocking)	:	6
Efficiency ratio $\left(\frac{\eta_{ith}}{\eta_{air-std}}\right)$	:	0.5
Mechanical efficiency, η_m	:	90%
Mass	:	260 kg

Identify the engine first. If both engines are supplied with just enough fuel for the test run, determine the duration of the test run so that specific mass (engine mass + fuel) is the same for both the arrangements. Take the calorific value of the fuel as 43 MJ/kg.

Solution

Since compression ratio is less than 10, they must be petrol engines. Consider first the naturally aspirated engine.

$$bp_1 = \frac{p_{bm}V_s nK}{60000} = \frac{9\times 10^5}{60000}\times\frac{3.6}{1000}\times\frac{5000}{2}$$

$$= \mathbf{135\ kW} \qquad \text{Ans}$$

$$ip_1 = \frac{bp_1}{\eta_m} = \frac{135}{0.9} = 150\text{ kW}$$

$$\eta_{air-std} = 1-\frac{1}{r^{\gamma-1}} = 1-\frac{1}{8^{0.4}} = 0.5647 = 56.47\%$$

$$\eta_{ith1} = \eta_{air}\times\eta_{ratio} = 0.5647\times 0.5 = 0.2824$$

Mass flow rate of fuel $\dot{m}_{f_{na}}$

$$\dot{m}_{f_{na}} = \frac{ip}{\eta_{ith}}\times\frac{3600}{CV} = \frac{150}{0.2824}\times\frac{3600}{43000} = 44.47\text{ kg/h}$$

If the test duration is t hours then specific mass is given by

$$\left.\frac{\text{mass}}{ip_1}\right|_{na} = \frac{250+44.47t}{150} = 1.67+0.2965\,t \qquad (1)$$

Now consider the supercharged engine

$$bp_2 = \frac{p_{bm}LAnK}{60000} = \frac{12\times 10^5}{60000}\times\frac{3.6}{1000}\times\frac{5000}{2}$$

$$= \mathbf{180\ kW} \qquad \text{Ans}$$

$$ip_2 = \frac{bp_2}{\eta_m} = \frac{180}{0.9} = 200\text{ kW}$$

$$\eta_{air-std} = 1-\frac{1}{r^{\gamma-1}} = 1-\frac{1}{6^{0.4}} = 0.5116 = \mathbf{51.16\%} \qquad \text{Ans}$$

$$\eta_{ith2} = \eta_{air} \times \eta_{ratio} = 0.5116 \times 0.5 = 0.2558$$

$$\dot{m}_{f_{sc}} = \frac{ip}{\eta_{ith}} \times \frac{3600}{CV} = \frac{200}{0.2558} \times \frac{3600}{43000} = 65.46 \text{ kg/h}$$

If the test duration is t hours then specific mass is given by

$$\left.\frac{\text{mass}}{ip_2}\right|_{sc} = \frac{260 + 65.46t}{180} = 1.44 + 0.3637\,t \qquad (2)$$

For the given condition,

$$1.67 + 0.2965t = 1.44 + 0.3637t$$

$$t = \mathbf{3.42\ h}$$

Ans

18.5 A mechanically coupled supercharger is run by a four-stroke four-cylinder square diesel engine with a bore of 100 mm as per the arrangements shown in figure below.

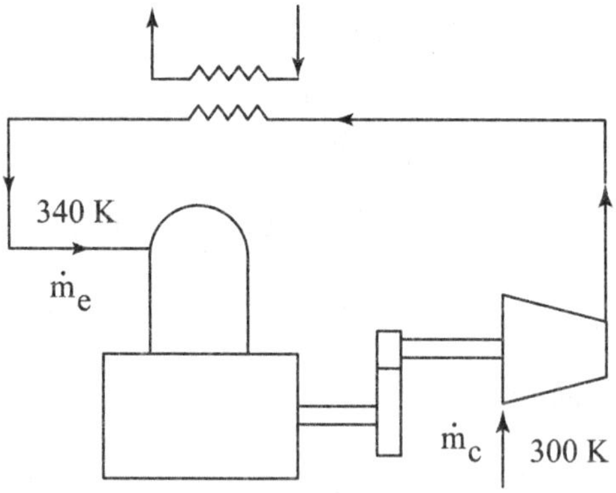

Air enters the compressor at 27 °C and the compressor pressure ratio is 1.6. From the compressor the air is passed on to a cooler where 1200 kJ/min of heat is rejected. The air leaves the cooler at 67 °C. Some air from the compressor is bled after the cooler to supercharge the engine. The volumetric efficiency is 85% based on intake manifold pressure and temperature. The other details about the engine are: *bp* is 50 kW, speed is 3000 rpm and mechanical efficiency η_m is 85%.

Determine

(i) *imep* of the engine

(ii) air consumption rate of the engine

(iii) the air handling capacity of the compressor in kg/min.

Take isentropic efficiency the compressor to be 85%.

Solution

$$ip = \frac{bp}{\eta_m} = \frac{50}{0.85} = 58.82 \text{ kW}$$

$$ip \text{ per cylinder} = \frac{58.82}{4} = 14.7 \text{ kW}$$

$$imep = \frac{ip}{LAn}$$

$$= \frac{14.7 \times 60000}{0.1 \times \frac{\pi}{4} \times 0.1^2 \times \frac{3000}{2}} \times 10^{-5}$$

$$= \mathbf{7.49\ bar}$$ Ans

$$\text{Swept volume} = \frac{\pi}{4} D^2 L = \frac{\pi}{4} \times 0.1^2 \times 0.1$$

$$= 7.85 \times 10^{-4} \text{ m}^3$$

Total volume of air swept per minute

$$= \frac{N}{2} K \dot{V}_s$$

$$= \frac{3000}{2} \times 4 \times 7.85 \times 10^{-4}$$

$$= 4.71 \text{ m}^3/\text{min}$$

Actual volume of air inducted,

$$\dot{V}_a = \eta_v \times \dot{V}_s = 0.85 \times 4.71$$

$$= 4 \text{ m}^3/\text{min}$$

Actual mass flow rate of air

$$= \rho \dot{V}_a = \frac{1.6 \times 10^5 \times 4.0}{287 \times 340}$$

$$= 6.56 \text{ kg/min}$$

Actual compressor work required comes from the engine output

$$\text{Compressor work, } W_c = \dot{m}_a C_p \frac{\Delta T}{\eta_c}$$

$$50 = \dot{m}_c \times 1.005 \times \frac{(T_2 - 300)}{0.85}$$

$$\dot{m}_c = \frac{50 \times 0.85}{1.005 \times (T_2 - 300)} \text{ kg/s} \qquad (1)$$

Heat balance in the cooler gives

$$\dot{m}_c(T_2 - 340) = \frac{\text{Heat rejected in the cooler/min}}{60 \times C_p}$$

$$\dot{m}_c = \frac{1200}{60 \times 1.005 \times (T_2 - 340)} \qquad (2)$$

$$\frac{50 \times 0.85}{1.005 \times (T_2 - 300)} = \frac{1200}{60 \times 1.005 \times (T_2 - 340)}$$

$$\frac{42.5}{T_2 - 300} = \frac{20}{T_2 - 340}$$

$$T_2 = 375.6 \text{ K}$$

$$\dot{m}_c = \frac{42.5}{375.6 - 300} = 0.5622 \text{ kg/s}$$

$$= 0.5622 \times 60$$

$$= \mathbf{33.732 \text{ kg/min}}$$ Ans

Review Questions

18.1 What are the factors that affect the power output of an engine? Explain how supercharging helps to improve the power output.

18.2 What is meant by supercharging? What is its effect on engine performance?

18.3 Briefly explain the working of the following:

(i) Centrifugal supercharger
(ii) Roots supercharger
(iii) Vane type supercharger

Compare all the above superchargers.

18.4 Briefly explain the various methods of supercharging an engine.

18.5 Mention the effect of supercharging on engine performance.

18.6 What are the limitations of supercharging in an IC engine?

18.7 Make the thermodynamic analysis of a supercharged engine cycle.

18.8 With a neat sketch explain gear driven and exhaust driven supercharging methods.

18.9 What do you understand by the term turbocharging?

18.10 Explain with a neat sketch the principle of exhaust turbocharging of a single-cylinder engine.

Exercise

18.1 A 2.5-litre four-stroke diesel engine develops 10 kW per m^3 of free air inducted per minute. The volumetric efficiency is 82% at 3600 rpm referred to atmospheric condition of 1 bar and 27 °C.

A rotary compressor which is mechanically coupled to the engine is used to supercharge the engine. The pressure ratio and the isentropic efficiency of the compressor are 1.6 and 75% respectively. Calculate the percentage increase in brake power due to supercharging.

Assume mechanical efficiency of the engine to be 82% and air intake to the cylinder to be at the pressure equal to delivery pressure from compressor and temperature equal to 7 °C less than the delivery temperature of the compressor. Also assume that cylinder contains volume of charge equal to swept volume. *Ans:* 77.26%

18.2 A four-stroke diesel engine working at sea level (pressure : 1 bar and temperature 17°C) develops a brake power of 300 kW with a volumetric efficiency of 85% at sea level conditions. The engine works at an air-fuel ratio of 17:1, with a specific fuel consumption of 0.25 kg/kW-h. The engine runs at 2000 rpm. Determine the engine capacity and the *bmep*.

This engine is taken to an altitude of 3 km where the ambient temperature and pressure are −23°C and 0.715 bar. A mechanically coupled supercharger is fitted to the engine which consumes 12% of the total power developed by the engine. The temperature of air leaving the supercharger is 35 °C. Determine the degree of supercharging required to maintain the same brake power of sea level. Also calculate the isentropic efficiency of the compressor. Assume that air-fuel ratio, thermal efficiency and volumetric efficiency remain the same for naturally aspirated and supercharged engine. *Ans:* (i) 0.0208 m^3 (ii) 8.65 bar (iii) 68.83% (iv) 69.6%

18.3 A four-stroke engine working on dual-combustion cycle is supercharged by a turbocharger. Air from the atmosphere at 1 bar and 30 °C is compressed isentropically to 1.5 bar. Both compressor and turbine have isentropic efficiency of 80%. The air is cooled to 37 °C before entering the engine cylinder. The compression ratio of the engine is 17 and the peak pressure not to exceed 125 bar. The total heat input is 1200 kJ/kg. The heat rejection is at constant volume. The exhaust gases, assumed to obey gas laws, is throttled to 1.5 bar before entering the turbine where is expands isentropically to atmospheric pressure. Neglecting all the pressure and frictional losses, calculate the extra work available from turbocharger. *Ans:* 49.52 kJ/kg

18.4 Two identical vehicles are fitted with engine having the following specifications:

Engine 1: (Naturally aspirated)

Swept volume, V_s	=	4 litres
Brake mean effective pressure	=	10 bar
Speed	=	5000 rpm
Compression ratio	=	8
Efficiency ratio $\left(\frac{\eta_{ith}}{\eta_{air-std}}\right)$	=	0.55
Mechanical efficiency, η_m	=	92%
Mass	=	258 kg

Engine 2: (Super charged)

Swept volume, V_s	=	4 litres
Brake mean effective pressure	=	15 bar
Speed	=	5000 rpm
Compression ratio (lowered to avoid knocking)	=	6
Efficiency ratio $\left(\frac{\eta_{ith}}{\eta_{air-std}}\right)$	=	0.55
Mechanical efficiency, η_m	=	92%
Mass	=	270 kg

Identify the engine first. If both engines are supplied with just enough fuel for the test run, determine the duration of the test run so that specific mass (engine mass + fuel) is the same for both the arrangements. Take the calorific value of the fuel as 43 MJ/kg.

Ans: (i) Because of lower compression ratio the engine is a petrol engine. (ii) 1.79 h

18.5 A mechanically coupled supercharger is run by a four-stroke four-cylinder square diesel engine with a bore of 120 mm as per the arrangements shown in figure below.

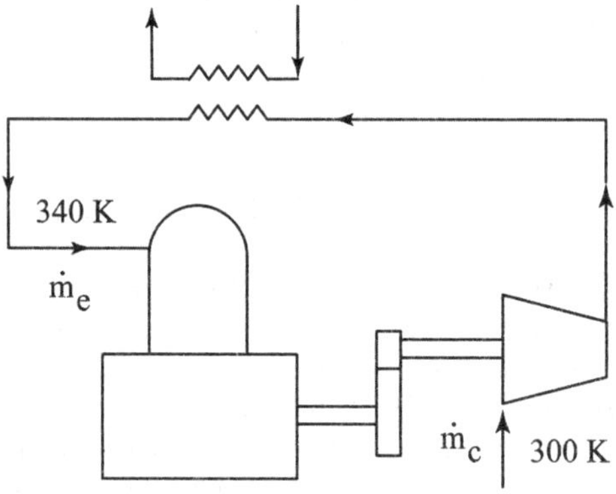

Air enters the compressor at 25 °C and the compressor pressure ratio is 1.7. From the compressor the air is passed on to a cooler where 1250 kJ/min of heat is rejected. The air leaves the cooler at 67 °C. Some air from the compressor is bled after the cooler to supercharge the engine. The volumetric efficiency is 85% based on intake manifold pressure and temperature. The other details about the engine are: *bp* is 55 kW, speed is 3500 rpm and mechanical efficiency η_m is 85%.

Determine

(i) *imep* of the engine
(ii) actual air consumption rate of the engine
(iii) the air handling capacity of the compressor in kg/min.

Take isentropic efficiency the compressor to be 85%.

Ans: (i) 4.09 bar (ii) 14.068 kg/min (iii) 35.95 kg/min

Multiple Choice Questions (choose the most appropriate answer)

1. Supercharging increases the power output of the engine by
   (a) increasing the charge temperature
   (b) increasing the charge pressure
   (c) increasing the speed of the engine
   (d) quantity of fuel admitted
2. The centrifugal type supercharger is preferable only for
   (a) low speeds
   (b) high speeds
   (c) high pressures
   (d) none of the above
3. The advantage of Root's supercharger is
   (a) high pressure
   (b) minimum maintenance
   (c) consumes less power
   (d) occupies less space
4. Supercharging air compressor is driven by
   (a) exhaust gas turbine
   (b) engine itself
   (c) separate electrical motor
   (d) none of the above
5. If turbochargers compressor is driven by
   (a) exhaust gas turbine
   (b) engine itself

(c) separate electrical motor

(d) none of the above

6. Cooling after compression is necessary to

(a) increase the density of air

(b) reduce engine operating temperatures

(c) both (a) and (b)

(d) increase exhaust temperature

7. Volumetric efficiency of supercharged engine is

(a) between 100 – 110%

(b) between 90 – 100%

(c) between 80 – 90%

(d) between 70 – 80%

8. Supercharging is normally done in

(a) racing cars

(b) marine engines

(c) automotive diesel engines

(d) none of the above

9. Compared to engine driven supercharger the exhaust driven supercharger is

(a) easy to handle

(b) supplies more air

(c) utilizes the exhaust energy of the engine

(d) matching with engine is easy

10. Types of supercharger are

(a) reciprocating type

(b) gear type

(c) centrifugal type

(d) none of the above

Ans: 1. – (b) 2. – (a) 3. – (b) 4. – (b) 5. – (a)
6. – (c) 7. – (a) 8. – (d) 9. – (c) 10. – (c)

19 TWO–STROKE ENGINES

19.1 INTRODUCTION

A two-stroke engine is one which completes its cycle of operation in one revolution of the crankshaft or in two strokes of the piston. In this engine the functions of the intake and exhaust processes of the four-stroke engine are taken care of by the incoming fresh charge which is compressed either in the crankcase or by means of a separate blower while the engine piston is near the bottom dead center. The engine piston needs only to compress the fresh charge and expand the products of combustion. Since a two-stroke engine will have twice as many cycles per minute as a four-stroke engine operating at the same speed and with the same number of cylinders, theoretically it will develop twice the power when operating at the same mean effective pressure. As with the four-stroke engine, the power output of this engine also depends upon the number of kilograms of air per minute available for combustion.

In many two-stroke engines the mechanical construction is greatly simplified by using the piston as a slide valve in conjunction with intake and exhaust ports cut in the side of the cylinder. If the engine is running on Otto cycle, the charge consists of correct mixture of fuel and air whereas for the diesel or dual combustion cycles the charge will consist of pure air. The application of two-stroke principle to small high speed CI engines involves many difficulties, although these are by no means insurmountable. In case of SI engines, the two-stroke cycle principle has been applied to a large number of engines ranging from tiny single cylinder model engines developing a fraction of a kW to the largest of the aircraft units developing 2500 kW or more.

19.2 TYPES OF TWO-STROKE ENGINES

Depending upon the scavenging method used there are basically two types of two-stroke engines:

(i) crankcase scavenged engine

(ii) separately scavenged engine

The details of the above two types of two-stroke engines are discussed briefly in the following sections.

19.2.1 Crankcase Scavenged Engine

One of the simplest types of two-stroke engines is shown in Fig.19.1. In this engine, the charge (fuel-air mixture in SI engine and air in CI engine) is compressed in the crankcase by the underside of the piston during the expansion stroke. There are three ports in this engine.

(i) intake port at the crankcase

(ii) transfer port

(iii) exhaust port

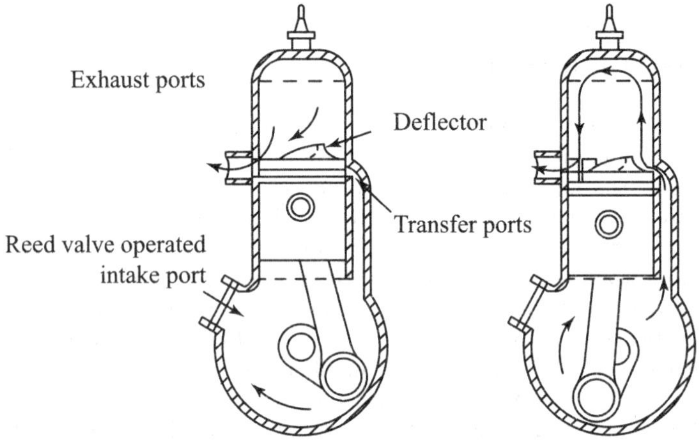

Fig. 19.1 Crankcase-scavenged two-stroke engine

The compressed charge passes through the transfer port into the engine cylinder flushing the products of combustion. This process is called scavenging and this type of engines is called the crankcase-scavenged engines.

As the piston moves down, it first uncovers the exhaust ports, and the cylinder pressure drops to atmospheric level as the combustion products escape through these ports. Further, downward motion of the piston uncovers the transfer ports, permitting the slightly compressed mixture or air (depending upon the type of the engine) in the crankcase to enter the engine cylinder. The top of the piston and the ports are usually shaped in such a way that the fresh air is directed towards the top of the cylinder before flowing towards the exhaust ports. This is for the purpose of scavenging the upper part of the cylinder of the combustion products and also to minimize the flow of the fresh fuel-air mixture directly through the exhaust ports. The projection on the piston is called the deflector. As the piston returns from bottom center, the transfer ports and then the exhaust ports are closed and compression of the charge begins. Motion of the piston during compression lowers the pressure in the crankcase so that the fresh mixture or air is drawn into the crankcase through the inlet reed valve. Ignition and expansion take place in the usual way, and the cycle is repeated. Due to the flow restriction in the inlet reed valve and the transfer ports the engine gets charged with less than one cylinder displacement volume.

19.2.2 Separately Scavenged Engine

Another type of engine which uses an external device like a blower to scavenge the products of combustion is called the externally or separately scavenged engine. The details of this type of engine are shown in Fig.19.2. In these engines air-fuel mixture is supplied at a slightly higher pressure at the inlet manifold. As the piston moves down on the expansion stroke, it uncovers the exhaust ports at approximately 60° before bottom center. About 10° later, when the cylinder pressure has been considerably reduced the inlet ports are uncovered and the scavenging process takes place. The inlet ports are shaped in such a way that most of the air flows to the top of the cylinder on the inlet side and move down on the exhaust side forming a loop (Fig.19.2) before reaching the exhaust ports. This ensures scavenging of the upper cylinder volume. Piston deflectors are not used as they are heavy and tend to become overheated at high output. The scavenging process is more efficient in these types of engines than in the usual crankcase scavenged engine with deflector piston.

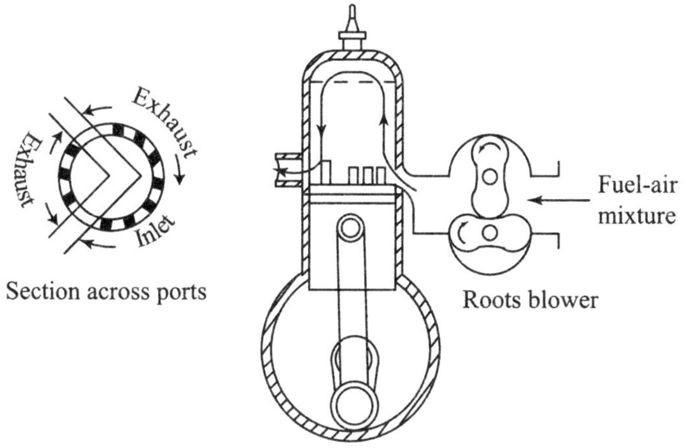

Fig. 19.2 Loop-scavenged two-stroke engine

Opposed Piston or End-to-End Scavenged Engine :

Another type of two-stroke engine is the opposed piston type or sometime called *end-to-end* scavenged engine. The details of this type of engine are shown in Fig.19.3. In this type the exhaust ports are opened first. The inlet ports are shaped in such a way that the air or mixture enters tangentially, thereby imparting a swirling motion (Fig.19.3). The swirl helps to prevent mixing of fresh charge and combustion products during the scavenging process. Early on the compression stroke, the exhaust ports close first. Because of the flow through the inlet port the cylinder pressure start rising and when the pressure is close to inlet manifold pressure the inlet ports close. In this opposed piston engine it may be noted that two pistons are a little out of phase (Fig.19.3). In the loop-scavenged engine the port timing is symmetrical, so that the exhaust port must close after the inlet port closes. The timing prevents this type of engine from filling its cylinder at full inlet pressure. In the end-to-end scavenged engines, counterflow within the cylinder is eliminated, and there is less opportunity for mixing of fresh and spent gases. The scavenging should therefore be more efficient.

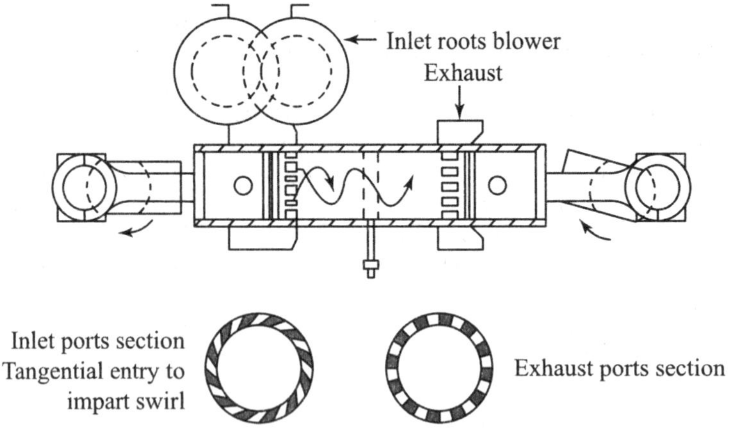

Fig. 19.3 Port arrangement of a two-stroke end-to-end scavenged compression-ignition engine

19.3 TERMINOLOGIES AND DEFINITIONS

In the absence of a terminology that is commonly accepted or at least commonly understood, it is necessary to explain and define the terms used in connection with two-stroke engines. In this section a list of terminologies used are explained. The terminologies can be easily understood from the diagram showing the charging process of the engine. The flow of gases through a two-stroke cycle engine is diagrammatically represented in Fig.19.4. The

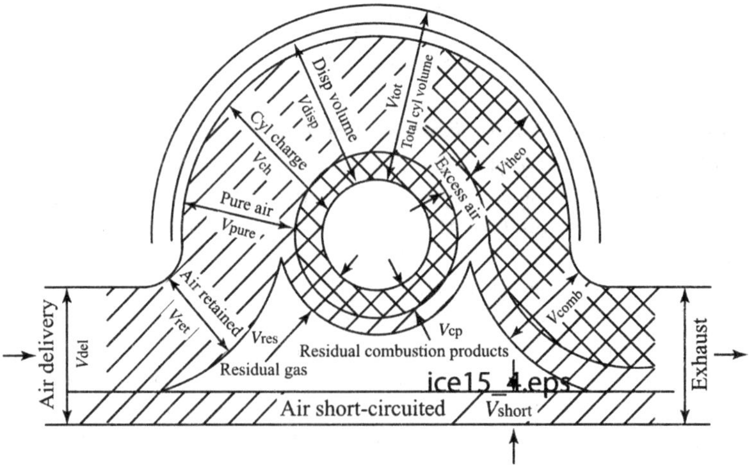

Fig. 19.4 Scavenging diagram for two-stroke cycle SI engine

hatched areas represent fresh air or mixture and the cross hatched areas represent combustion gases. The width of the channels represents the quantity of the gases expressed by volume at NTP condition.

19.3.1 Delivery Ratio (R_{del})

In two-stroke cycle engines, air or mixture is supplied to the cylinders either by a separate pump or blower, or by the piston of the working cylinder acting as a pump. Depending on the relative capacity of the blower, the air delivered, V_{del}, may be either more or less than the swept volume.. The delivery ratio is usually defined as

$$R_{del} = \frac{V_{del}}{V_{ref}} \tag{19.1}$$

The reference volume, V_{ref}, has been variously chosen to be displacement volume, effective displacement volume, total cylinder volume, or total effective cylinder volume. Since, it is only the quantity of charge in the remaining total cylinder volume at exhaust port closure that enters into the combustion, it is recommended that the total effective cylinder volume should be preferred.

The delivery ratio, nowadays, is defined on mass basis. According to it, the delivery ratio is mass of fresh air delivered to the cylinder divided by a reference mass, i.e.

$$R_{del} = \frac{M_{del}}{M_{ref}} \tag{19.2}$$

Thus the delivery ratio is a measure of the air supplied to the cylinder relative to the cylinder content. If $R_{del} = 1$, it means that the volume of the scavenging air supplied to the cylinder is equal to the cylinder volume (or displacement volume whichever is taken as reference). Delivery ratio usually varies between 1.2 and 1.5 except for crankcase scavenged engines where it is less than unity.

19.3.2 Trapping Efficiency

The air or mixture delivery, V_{del}, is split into two parts (Fig.19.4): the short circuiting air, V_{short} which leaves through the exhaust port or valve without remaining in the cylinder, and the retained air or mixture, V_{ret}, which is trapped in the cylinder and takes part in the subsequent combustion. Therefore, an additional term, trapping efficiency, is used to indicate the ability of the cylinder to retain the fresh charge. It is defined as the ratio of the amount of charge retained in the cylinder to the total charge delivered to the engine i.e.

$$\eta_{trap} = \frac{V_{ret}}{V_{del}} \tag{19.3}$$

Trapping efficiency indicates that fraction of the fresh air or mixture supplied to the cylinder which is retained in the cylinder the rest being wasted through the exhaust. Short circuiting is naturally equal to $(1 - \eta_{trap})$. The trapping efficiency, therefore, is a measure of the success of trapping the supplied air or mixture with minimum waste. It is mainly controlled by the geometry of the ports and the overlap time.

19.3.3 Relative Cylinder Charge

The air or mixture retained, V_{ret}, together with the residual gas, V_{res}, remaining in the cylinder after flushing out the products of combustion constitutes the cylinder charge, V_{ch}. Relative cylinder charge is a measure of the success of filling the cylinder irrespective of the composition of charge and defined as

$$C_{ret} = \frac{V_{ch}}{V_{ref}} = \frac{V_{ret} + V_{res}}{V_{ref}} \qquad (19.4)$$

The relative cylinder charge may be either more or less than unity depending upon the scavenging pressure and the port heights.

It must be noted that all volumes referred to are at NTP condition. However, some authors, recommend the use of inlet temperature and exhaust pressure as the reference. *In view of the use of different reference volumes as well as different reference conditions, it should always be kept in mind that the published values may not be directly comparable.*

The cylinder charge may also be considered as composed of pure air and residual combustion products. By denoting

$$p_{ar} = \frac{V_{pure}}{V_{ret}}$$

as pure air ratio and

$$\frac{V_{cp}}{V_{ret}}$$

as residual combustion products ratio.

$$C_{rel} = p_{ar} + \frac{V_{cp}}{V_{ret}}$$

During combustion, part of the air (or, rather of the oxygen in the air) contained in the cylinder charge burns, while the remainder, the excess air, is not involved in the attendant chemical reactions. Part of this excess air escapes through the exhaust with the combustion products, and another part, $V_{res} - V_{cp}$, remains in the cylinder and participates in the subsequent cycle, where V_{cp} represents combustion products in the residual gas. Therefore, the cylinder charge consists of three parts: the retained portion of the air delivered, part of the combustion products from the preceding cycle, and part of the excess air from the preceding cycle. As the cylinder charge, V_{ch} is contaminated by combustion products, V_{cp},

$$\eta_p = \frac{V_{pure}}{V_{ch}} = \frac{V_{ch} - V_{cp}}{V_{ch}} = 1 - \frac{V_{cp}}{V_{ch}}$$

represents the purity of the charge and $\frac{V_{cp}}{V_{ch}}$ constitutes the pollution. It should be realized that V_{pure} is more than that part of the air delivered which is retained in the cylinder; it includes some pure air contained in the residual gas remaining in the cylinder from the previous cycle.

19.3.4 Scavenging Efficiency

The purity of charge is a measure of the success of scavenging the cylinder from the combustion products of the preceding cycle. It is largely controlled by the shape of the combustion chamber and the scavenging arrangement (cross, loop or uniflow). Experimental determination of the purity is relatively simple, consisting only of analysis of a gas sample taken during the compression stroke. The difficulty lies in representative sample.

In German technical literature the term *scavenging efficiency (spuelwirkungs-grad)* has been widely used. It is defined as

$$\eta_{sc} = \frac{V_{ret}}{V_{ch}} = \frac{V_{ret}}{V_{ret} + V_{res}}$$

It can be shown that the delivery ratio, scavenging and trapping efficiencies are related by the following equation

$$R_{del} = \frac{C_{rel}\ \eta_{sc}}{\eta_{trap}} \qquad (19.5)$$

Scavenging efficiency is a term somewhat similar to purity and expresses the measure of the success in clearing the cylinder of residual gases from the preceding cycle.

Scavenging efficiency indicates to what extent the residual gases in the cylinder are replaced with fresh air. If it is equal to unity, it means that all the gases existing in the cylinder at the beginning of scavenging have been swept out.

The scavenging efficiency in diesel engines can be measured by drawing off a small sample of the products of combustion just before the exhaust valve opens or during the earlier part of blowdown. This sample is analyzed and the results obtained are compared with standard curves of exhaust products versus fuel-air ratio. This determines the fuel-air ratio that must have existed in the cylinder before combustion. Knowing the quantity of fuel injected per cycle, the quantity of fresh air retained in the cylinder per cycle can be calculated. Air in the residual gas is not considered as it represents a constant quantity which does not take part in combustion.

19.3.5 Charging Efficiency

The amount of fresh charge in the cylinder is a measure of the power output of the engine. The useful fresh charge divided by the displacement volume is the charging efficiency defined as

$$\eta_{ch} = \frac{V_{ret}}{V_{ref}}$$

Charging efficiency is a measure of the success of filling the cylinder with fresh air. Naturally

$$\eta_{ch} = R_{del}\ \eta_{trap}$$

as can be seen from Eqn.19.1 and 19.3. The charging efficiency is an important index as it most directly affects the power output of the engine.

19.3.6 Pressure Loss Coefficient (P_l)

The pressure loss coefficient is the ratio between the main upstream and down-stream pressures during the scavenging period and represents the loss of pressure to which the scavenge air is subjected to when it crosses the cylinder.

19.3.7 Index for Compressing the Scavenge Air (n)

This index is proportional to the power required for compressing the scavenge air and is calculated on the basis of the delivery ratio and pressure loss coefficient measurements. It allows, along with scavenging efficiency evaluation, a comparison of different types of scavenging systems.

19.3.8 Excess Air Factor (λ)

The value ($R_{del} - 1$) is called the excess air factor, λ. For example, if the delivery ratio is 1.7, the excess air factor is 0.7.

19.4 TWO-STROKE AIR CAPACITY

Except when large valve overlaps are used, a four-stroke engine retains almost all the charge entering the cylinder during the intake process, i.e. nothing is lost through the exhaust valve. An air meter at the engine inlet will therefore measure $\dot{m}_a$, the amount of air available for combustion, and the engine output will be proportional to $\dot{m}_a$.

The exhaust ports of a two-stroke engine would remain open during most of the scavenging process. This makes it impossible to avoid some loss of fresh air or mixture at that time through the open exhaust port. With the increasing quantity of charge coming into the cylinder, increased amount of charge would be lost through the exhaust port. The power output of a two-stroke engine is therefore proportional not to the amount of charge entering the engine but to the amount of charge retained in the cylinder. The amount of charge that can be retained in the cylinder is called the air capacity of the two-stroke engine.

19.5 THEORETICAL SCAVENGING PROCESSES

The amount of charge retained in the cylinder depends upon the scavenging ability of the engine. Three theoretical scavenging processes are illustrated in Fig.19.5. These are perfect scavenging, perfect mixing and complete short circuiting. The details are explained in the following sections.

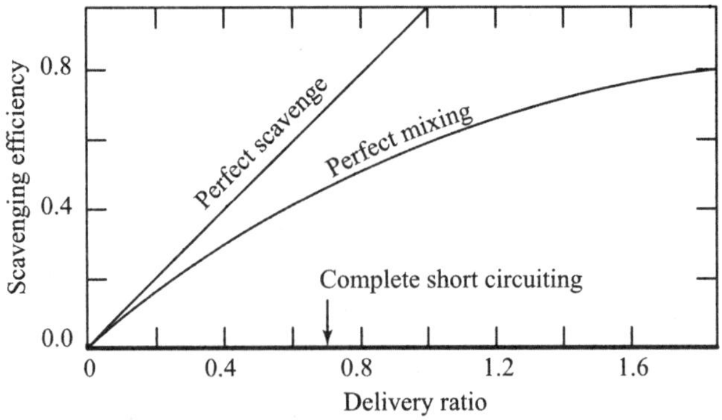

Fig. 19.5 Theoretical scavenging processes

19.5.1 Perfect Scavenging

Ideally the fresh fuel-air mixture should remain separated from the residual products of combustion with respect to both mass and heat transfer during the scavenging process. Fresh charge is pumped into the cylinder by the blower through the inlet ports at the lower end of the cylinder. This in turn, pushes the products of combustion in the cylinder out through the exhaust port/valve at the other end. It is assumed that there is no mixing of fresh charge and the products and as long as any products remain in the cylinder the flow through the exhaust ports is considered to be products of combustion only. However, when sufficient fresh air has entered to fill the entire cylinder volume the flow abruptly changes from one of products to one of air. This ideal process would represent perfect scavenging without any short circuiting loss.

19.5.2 Perfect Mixing

The second theoretical scavenging process is perfect mixing, in which the incoming fresh charge mixes completely and instantaneously with the cylinder contents, and a portion of this mixture passes out through the exhaust ports at a rate equal to that of the charge entering the cylinder. This homogeneous mixture consists initially of products of combustion only and then gradually changes to pure air. This mixture flowing through the exhaust ports is identical with that momentarily existing in the cylinder and changes with it. For the case of perfect mixing the scavenging efficiency can be represented by the following equation

$$\eta_{sc} = 1 - e^{-R_{del}} \tag{19.6}$$

where η_{sc} and R_{del} are scavenging efficiency and delivery ratio respectively. This is plotted in Fig.19.5. The result of this theoretical process closely approximates the results of many actual scavenging processes, and is thus often used as a basis of comparison.

19.5.3 Short Circuiting

The third type of scavenging process is that of short circuiting in which the fresh charge coming from the scavenge manifold directly goes out of the exhaust ports without removing any residual gas. This is a dead loss and its occurrence must be avoided.

19.6 ACTUAL SCAVENGING PROCESS

The actual scavenging process is neither one of perfect scavenging nor of perfect mixing. It probably consists partially of perfect scavenging, mixing and short circuiting. Figure 19.6 shows the variation of delivery ratio and trapping efficiency with crank angle for three different scavenging modes, i.e. perfect scavenging, perfect mixing and intermediate scavenging.

The scavenging parameters for the intermediate scavenging are shown in Fig.19.7. This represents the actual scavenging process. It can be seen from this figure that a certain amount of combustion products is initially pushed

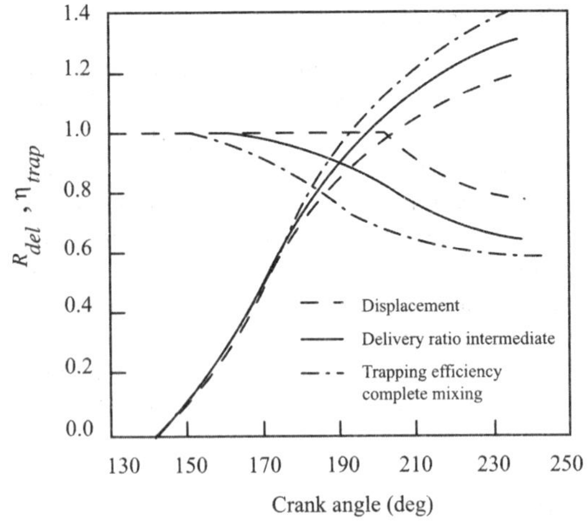

Fig. 19.6 Delivery ratio and trapping efficiency variation for a crankcase scavenged engine (different scavenging modes)

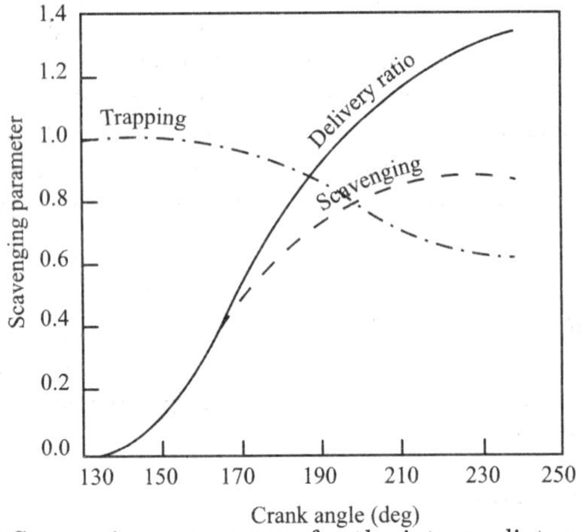

Fig. 19.7 Scavenging parameters for the intermediate scavenging

out of the cylinder without being diluted by fresh air. Gradually, mixing and short circuiting causes the outflowing products to be diluted by more and more fresh air until ultimately the situation is the same as for perfect mixing, i.e. the first phase of the scavenging process is a perfect scavenging process which then gradually changes into a complete mixing process.

19.7 CLASSIFICATION BASED ON SCAVENGING PROCESS

The simplest method of introducing the charge into the cylinder is to employ crankcase compression as shown in Fig.19.1. This type of engine is classified as the crankcase scavenged engine. In another type, a separate blower or a pump (Fig.19.2) is used to introduce the charge through the inlet port, which are classified as the separately scavenged engines.

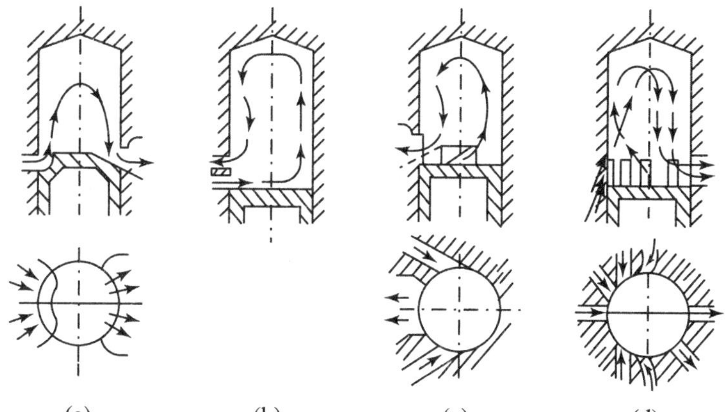

(a) Cross scavenging (c) Loop scavenging, Schnuerle type

(b) Loop scavenging M.A.N. type (d) Loop scavenging, Curtis type

Fig. 19.8 Methods of scavenging

Another classification of two-stroke cycle engines is based on the air flow. The most common arrangement is cross scavenging, illustrated in Fig.19.8(a). The incoming airs is directed upward, and then down to force out the exhaust gases through the oppositely located exhaust ports. With loop or reverse scavenging, the fresh air first sweeps across the piston top, moves up and then down and finally out through the exhaust. In the M.A.N. type of loop scavenge, Fig.19.8(b), the exhaust and inlet ports are on the same side, the exhaust above the inlet. In the Schnuerle type, Fig.19.8(c), the ports are side by side. The Curtis type of scavenging, Fig.19.8(d), is similar to the Schnuerle type, except that upwardly directed inlet ports are placed also opposite the exhaust ports.

The most perfect method of scavenging is the uniflow method, where the fresh air charge is admitted at one end of the cylinder and the exhaust escapes at the other end. The air flow is from end to end, and little short-circuiting between the intake and exhaust openings is possible. The three available arrangements for uniflow scavenging are shown in Fig.19.9. A poppet valve is used in *a* to admit the inlet air or for the exhaust, as the case may be. In *b* the inlet and exhaust ports are both controlled by separate pistons that move in opposite directions. In *c* the inlet and exhaust ports are controlled by the combined motion of piston and sleeve. In an alternative arrangement one set of ports is controlled by the piston and the other set by a sleeve or slide valve. All uniflow systems permit unsymmetrical scavenging and supercharging. Reverse flow scavenging is shown in Fig.19.10.

In this type the inclined ports are used and the scavenging air is forced on to the opposite wall of the cylinder where it is reversed to the outlet ports. One obvious disadvantage of this type is the limitation on the port area. For long stroke engines operating at low piston speeds, this arrangement has proved satisfactory.

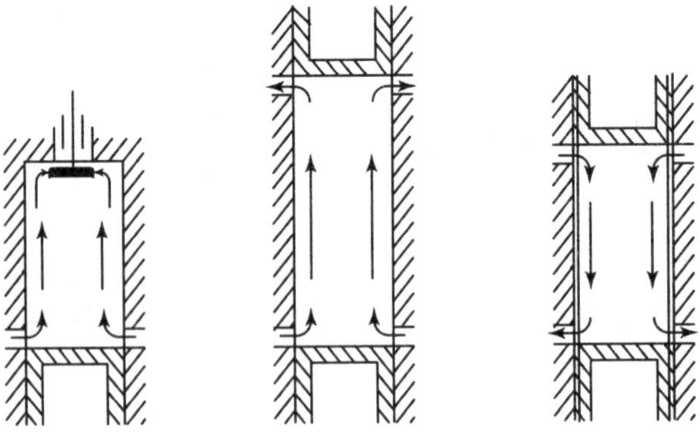

(a) Poppet valve (b) Opposed piston (c) Sleeve valve

Fig. 19.9 Uniflow scavenging

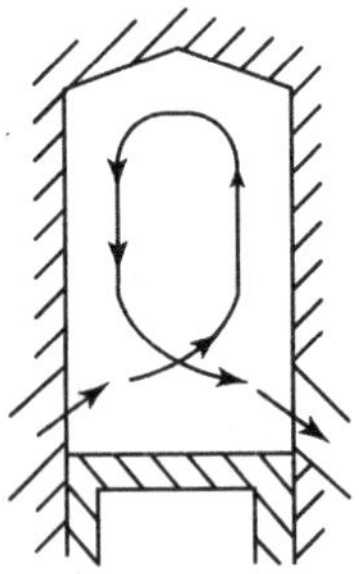

Fig. 19.10 Reverse flow scavenging

19.8 COMPARISON OF SCAVENGING METHODS

An interesting comparison of the merits of two cycle engine air scavenging methods is illustrated in Fig.19.11. In fact, specific output of the engine is largely determined by the efficiency of the scavenging system and is directly related to the brake mean effective pressure. As shown in Fig.19.11 scavenging efficiency varies with the delivery ratio and the type of scavenging. In this respect cross scavenging is least efficient and gives the lowest brake mean effective pressure. The main reason for this is that the scavenging air flows through the cylinder but does not expel the exhaust residual gases effectively. Loop scavenging method is better than the cross scavenging method. Even with a delivery ratio of 1.0 in all cases the scavenging efficiencies are about 53, 67 and 80 per cent for cross scavenging, loop scavenging and uniflow scavenging systems with corresponding values of *bmep* as 3.5, 4.5 and 5.8 bar.

19.9 SCAVENGING PUMPS

The performance of a two-stroke engine will depend largely on the characteristics of the type of compressor used as a scavenging pump. Figure 19.12 illustrates various types of scavenging pumps used. Displacement type of pumps

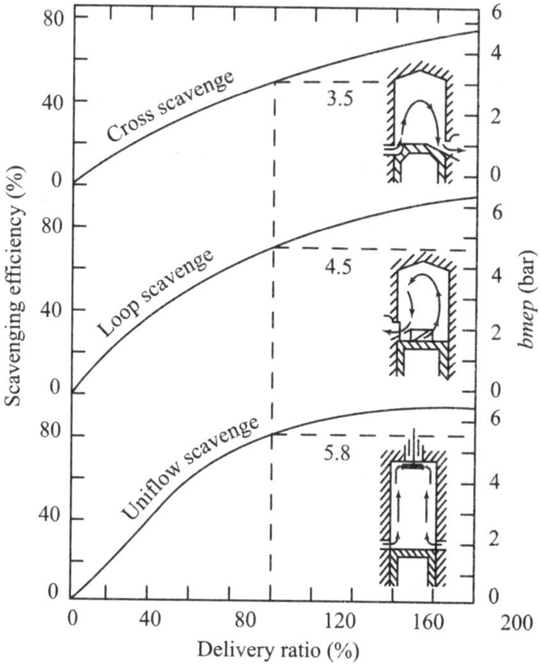

Fig. 19.11 Scavenging efficiency

include crankcase scavenging, piston and roots type blowers. An important characteristic of the displacement pumps is that their volumetric efficiency, and therefore, the mass of air delivered per unit time are not seriously reduced even by considerable increase in the outlet pressure. Thus it tends to maintain constant scavenging ratio even though ports may become partially clogged with deposits etc.

In case of centrifugal pumps, however, the mass flow is heavily influenced by the engine and exhaust system resistance. The pressure ratio in this case varies almost linearly with the rpm squared. Thus, the centrifugal type scavenging pump is a very satisfactory type provided the resistance of the flow system is not suddenly altered.

19.10 ADVANTAGES AND DISADVANTAGES OF TWO-STROKE ENGINES

Two-stroke engines have certain advantages as well as disadvantages compared to four-stroke engines. In the following sections the main advantages and disadvantages are discussed briefly.

19.10.1 Advantages of Two-stroke Engines

(i) As there is a working stroke for each revolution, the power developed will be nearly twice that of a four-stroke engine of the same dimensions and operating at the same speed.

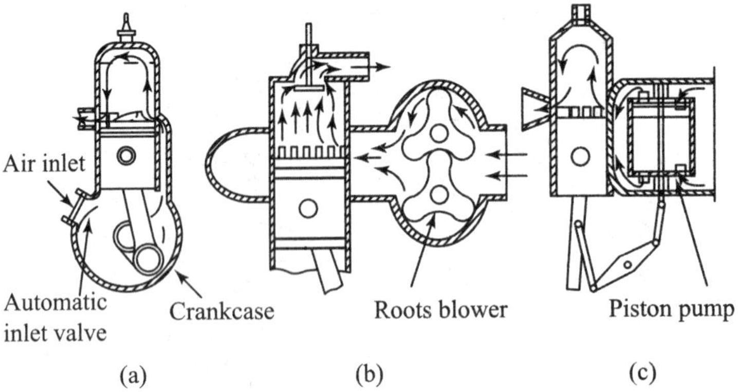

Fig. 19.12 Scavenging pumps

(ii) The work required to overcome the friction of the exhaust and suction strokes is saved.

(iii) As there is a working stroke in every revolution, a more uniform turning moment is obtained on the crankshaft and therefore, a lighter flywheel is required.

(iv) Two-stroke engines are lighter than four-stroke engines for the same power output and speed.

(v) For the same output, two-stroke engines occupies lesser space.

(vi) The construction of a two-stroke cycle engine is simple because it has ports instead of valves. This reduces the maintenance problems considerably.

(vii) In case of two-stroke engines because of scavenging, burnt gases do not remain in the clearance space as in case of four-stroke engines.

19.10.2 Disadvantages of Two-Stroke Engines

(i) High speed two-stroke engines are less efficient owing to the reduced volumetric efficiency.

(ii) With engines working on Otto cycle, a part of the fresh mixture is lost as it escapes through the exhaust port during scavenging. This increases the fuel consumption and reduces the thermal efficiency.

(iii) Part of the piston stroke is lost with the provision of the ports thus the effective compression is less in case of two-stroke engines.

(iv) Two-stroke engines are liable to cause a heavier consumption of lubricating oil.

(v) With heavy loads, two-stroke engines gets heated due to excessive heat produced. Also at light loads, the running of engine is not very smooth because of the increased dilution of charge.

19.11 COMPARISON OF TWO–STROKE SI AND CI ENGINES

The two-stroke SI engine suffers from two big disadvantages—fuel loss and idling difficulty. The two-stroke CI engine does not suffer from these disadvantages and hence CI engine is more suitable for two-stroke operation.

If the fuel is supplied to the cylinders after the exhaust ports are closed, there will be no loss of fuel and the indicated thermal efficiency of the two-stroke engine will be as good as that of a four-stroke engine. However, in an SI engine using carburettor, the scavenging is done with fuel-air mixture and only the fuel mixed with the retained air is used for combustion. To avoid the fuel loss, fuel-injection just before the exhaust port closure may be used instead of a carburettor.

The two-stroke SI engine picks up only gradually and may even stop at low speeds when mean effective pressure is reduced to about 1.2 bar. This is because a large amount of residual gas (more than in four-stroke engine) mixing with small amount of charge. At low speeds there may be backfiring due to slow burning rate. Fuel-injection improves idling and also eliminates backfiring as there is no fuel present in the inlet system.

In CI engines there is no loss of fuel as the charge is only air and there is no difficulty at idling because the fresh charge (air) is not reduced.

Worked out Examples

19.1 Show that the *imep* of a two-stroke engine in terms of scavenging efficiency and indicated thermal efficiency can be given by

$$imep = \rho_{sc}\left(\frac{r}{r-1}\right)\eta_{sc}\eta_{ith}\frac{F}{A} \times CV \times 6 \times 10^4$$

Solution

$$\eta_{sc} = \frac{\text{Actual mass of air}}{\text{Ideal mass of air}}$$

$$\dot{m}_{ideal} = V_s\left(\frac{r}{r-1}\right)\rho_{sc} \times N$$

$$\dot{m}_a = \eta_{sc}\rho_{sc}NV_s\left(\frac{r}{r-1}\right)$$

$$\eta_{ith} = \frac{ip}{\dot{m}_f CV}$$

$$= \frac{ip}{\dot{m}_a\left(\frac{F}{A}\right)CV}$$

$$ip = p_{im}V_s\frac{N}{60 \times 10^3}$$

$$p_{im}V_s\frac{N}{60000} = \eta_{ith}\dot{m}_a\frac{F}{A}CV$$

$$p_{im}V_s\frac{N}{60000}\rho_{sc}\frac{r}{r-1} = \eta_{ith}\dot{m}_a\frac{F}{A}CV\rho_{sc}\frac{r}{r-1}$$

$$p_{im}\dot{m}_{ideal} = \eta_{ith}\dot{m}_a\frac{F}{A}CV\rho_{sc}\frac{r}{r-1}\times 60000$$

$$p_{im}\frac{\dot{m}_a}{\eta_{sc}} = \eta_{ith}\dot{m}_a\frac{F}{A}CV\rho_{sc}\frac{r}{r-1}\times 60000$$

$$p_{im} = \rho_{sc}\left(\frac{r}{r-1}\right)\eta_{sc}\eta_{ith}\times\frac{F}{A}CV\times 60000$$

19.2 A two-stroke Diesel engine having a stroke to bore ratio of 1.2. The compression ratio is 16 and runs at 1500 rpm. During a trial run the following observations were made:

Exhaust pressure	:	1.05 bar
Inlet air temperature	:	37 °C
Fuel flow rate	:	3 kg/h
Air assumed is	:	130 kg/h
Diameter of the cylinder	:	100 mm

The fuel-air ratio was 0.045. Calculate the scavenging efficiency and the scavenging delivery ratio of the engine.

Solution

$$\text{Fuel-air ratio} = 0.045$$

$$\text{Mass of air, } \dot{m}_a = \frac{3.0}{0.045} = 66.67 \text{ kg/h}$$

$$\text{Swept volume, } V_s = \frac{\pi}{4}\times\left(\frac{100}{1000}\right)^2\times\left(\frac{120}{1000}\right)$$

$$= 9.425\times 10^{-4}\text{ m}^3$$

$$V_{tot} = 0.0009425\times\frac{16}{15} = 0.001005\text{ m}^3/\text{cycle}$$

Mass of air supplied/cycle

$$\dot{m}_{as} = \frac{66.67}{60\times 1500}$$

$$= 0.00074\text{ m}^3/\text{cycle}$$

$$\dot{m}_{ref} = 0.001005\times\left(\frac{1.05\times 10^5}{287\times 300}\right) = 0.00122$$

$$\eta_{sc} = \frac{\dot{m}_{as}}{\dot{m}_{ref}} = \frac{0.00074}{0.00122} = \mathbf{0.606} \qquad \underleftarrow{\text{Ans}}$$

$$\text{Scavenging ratio} = \frac{\text{Fresh air supplied}}{V_{ref}}$$

$$= \frac{\frac{130}{60} \times \frac{1}{1500}}{0.00122} = \mathbf{1.18} \qquad \underleftarrow{\text{Ans}}$$

19.3 A twin cylinder two-stroke cross-scavenged diesel engine of 25 cm bore and 30 cm stroke runs at 400 rpm. The compression ratio is 16. The following observations are made:

Fuel flow	:	15 kg/h
Inlet air temperature	:	35 °C
Exhaust pressure	:	1.05 bar
Exhaust gas composition	:	
CO_2	:	7.5%
O_2	:	9.0
CO	:	negligible

Calculate the scavenging efficiency and indicated mean effective pressure of the engine. Take indicated thermal efficiency of the engine as 0.40. The light diesel oil ($C_{12}H_{26}$) has a heating value of 42.2 MJ/kg.

Solution

The exhaust gas composition is given. If the exhaust contains CO, CO_2, CO and N_2 then we can write a dimensionally homogeneous equation as

$$\frac{\text{kg of fuel}}{\text{kg of air}} = \frac{\frac{\text{k mole of C}}{\text{k mole of gas}} \times \frac{\text{kg of C}}{\text{k mole of C}} \times \frac{\text{kg of N}_2}{\text{kg of air}}}{\frac{\text{k mole of N}_2}{\text{k mole of gas}} \times \frac{\text{kg of N}_2}{\text{k mole of N}_2}} \times \frac{\text{kg of C}}{\text{kg of fuel}}$$

$$= \frac{(\text{CO}_2 + CO) \times 12 \times 0.768}{\text{N}_2 \times 28 \times \left(\frac{1}{1+h}\right)}$$

$$= 0.33 \times (1+h) \times \frac{\text{CO}_2 + \text{CO}}{\text{N}_2}$$

where h is the carbon to hydrogen ratio.

$$h = \frac{26 \times 1}{12 \times 12} = 0.18$$

$$\text{Fuel-air ratio} = 0.33 \times (1 + 0.18) \times \left(\frac{7.5}{83.5}\right) = 0.035$$

$$\text{Mass flow of air} = \frac{15}{0.035} = 428.6 \text{ kg/h} = 7.14 \text{ kg/min}$$

$$V_{tot} = V_{disp} \times \frac{r}{r-1}$$

$$= \frac{\pi}{4}d^2L \times \frac{r}{r-1} = \frac{\pi}{4} \times 0.25^2 \times 0.30 \times \frac{16}{15} \times 2$$

$$= 0.032 \text{ m}^3/\text{cycle}$$

$$\rho_{sc} = \frac{1.05 \times 10^5}{287 \times 308} = 1.19$$

Theoretical mass flow

$$= 0.032 \times 400 \times 1.19 = 15.23 \text{ kg/s}$$

$$\eta_{sc} = \frac{7.14}{15.23} = \mathbf{0.47}$$ **Ans**

$$imep = \eta_{sc}\ \rho_{sc}\ \frac{r}{r-1}\ \eta_{ith}\ \frac{F}{A}\ CV$$

$$= 0.47 \times 1.19 \times \frac{16}{15} \times 0.4 \times 0.035 \times 42200$$

$$= 352.46 \text{ kN/m}^2 = \mathbf{3.53 \text{ bar}}$$ **Ans**

19.4 A two-stroke SI engine having a cylinder volume of 1100 cc and compression ratio of 8 runs at 2800 rpm. The exhaust pressure is 1.07 bar and the inlet temperature to the engine is 37 °C. The scavenging efficiency is 0.5. Calculate the trapping efficiency and scavenging ratio for a charge flow of 4 kg per minute. If the brake thermal efficiency of the engine is 0.25, fuel-air ratio is 0.068, calculate the brake power developed and the $bsfc$. Also calculate, the short circuiting loss per hour. Take calorific value of fuel as 45 MJ/kg.

Solution

$$\rho_{sc} = \frac{1.07 \times 10^5}{287 \times 310} = 1.20 \text{ kg/m}^3$$

$$\eta_{sc} = \frac{\dot{m}_a}{V_{tot} \times \rho_{sc}}$$

$$\dot{m}_a = 0.5 \times 0.0011 \times 1.20 = 0.00066 \text{ kg/cycle}$$

$$R_{sc} = \frac{4}{2800 \times 0.0011 \times 1.20} = 1.08$$

$$\eta_{tr} = \frac{\eta_{sc}}{R_{sc}} = \frac{0.5}{1.08} = 0.46 \text{ (quite low)}$$

$$bp = \frac{\dot{m}_a \times \frac{F}{A} \times CV \times \eta_{bth}}{60}$$

$$= \frac{0.00066 \times 2800 \times 0.068 \times 45000 \times 0.25}{60}$$

$$= \mathbf{23.562\ kW} \quad \stackrel{\text{Ans}}{\Longleftarrow}$$

$$bsfc = \frac{4 \times 60 \times 0.068}{23.562} = \mathbf{0.693\ kg/kW\ h} \quad \stackrel{\text{Ans}}{\Longleftarrow}$$

Short circuiting

$$= 4 \times (1 - 0.46) \times 60 \times 0.068$$

$$= \mathbf{8.813\ kg/h} \quad \stackrel{\text{Ans}}{\Longleftarrow}$$

19.5 A six-cylinder engine having 20 cm bore and 25 + 25 cm stroke opposed piston two-stroke cycle diesel engine develops 110 kW per cylinder at the rated speed of 720 rpm. Compression ratio is 20. The engine has a scavenge pressure of 1.14 bar. Exhaust pressure of 1.04 bar and air inlet temperature at blower inlet is 27 °C. Scavenging efficiency for scavenge ratio of 1.2 and a scavenge pressure of 1.15 bar is 0.85. *bsfc* of the engine is 0.21 kg/kW h. Calculate the *bmep* and indicated thermal efficiency of the engine if the total mechanical loss is 1.5 times the power to drive the blower. Also calculate the fuel-air ratio of the engine if the lower calorific value of the fuel is 43 MJ/kg. Take atmospheric pressure as 1 bar.

Solution

$$V_{tot} = kV_{disp}\frac{r}{r-1} = k\frac{\pi}{4}d^2(2l)\frac{r}{r-1}$$

$$= 6 \times \frac{\pi}{4} \times 0.2^2 \times 0.5 \times \frac{20}{19}$$

$$= \mathbf{0.0992\ m^3/cycle} \quad \stackrel{\text{Ans}}{\Longleftarrow}$$

$$\rho_{sc} = \frac{1.04 \times 10^5}{287 \times 300} = 1.21\ \text{kg/m}^3$$

$$\eta_{sc} = 0.85$$

$$= \frac{\text{Actual mass flow rate}}{\text{Theoretical mass flow rate}}$$

Actual mass flow rate

$$= 0.85 \times 0.0992 \times 1.21 = 0.102\ \text{kg/cycle}$$

$$R_{sc} = 1.2$$

$$= \frac{\text{Mass flow rate of air supplied by the blower}}{\text{Theoretical mass flow rate}}$$

Mass flow rate of air supplied by the blower

$$= 1.2 \times 0.0992 \times 1.21 = 0.144 \text{ kg/cycle}$$

$$\eta_{blower} = \frac{\Delta T_{isen}}{\Delta T_{actual}}$$

$$\frac{T_2'}{T_1} = r^{\frac{\gamma-1}{\gamma}}$$

$$T_2' = 300 \times \left(\frac{1.15}{1}\right)^{0.286} = 312.2 \text{ K}$$

$$\Delta T_{actual} = \frac{312.2 - 300}{0.75} = 16.3 \text{ K}$$

$$T_2 = 300 + 16.3 = 316.3 \text{ K}$$

$$W_c = \dot{m} C_p \Delta T = 0.102 \times 1.005 \times 16.3$$

$$= 1.6709 \text{ kJ/cycle}$$

$$= 1.6709 \times \frac{720}{60} = 20 \text{ kW}$$

$$V_{disp} = k\frac{\pi}{4}d^2 2l = 6 \times \frac{\pi}{4} \times 0.2^2 \times 0.5$$

$$= 0.0942 \text{ m}^3\text{/cycle}$$

$$bmep = \frac{bp}{V_s N} = \frac{120 \times 6}{0.0942 \times 720 \times 10^5} \times 60 \times 1000$$

$$= \mathbf{6.37 \text{ bar}}$$ Ans ⟸

Total mechanical loss

$$= 1.5 \times 20 = 30 \text{ kW}$$

$$ip = bp + fp = 6 \times 120 + 30 = 750 \text{ kW}$$

Fuel consumed per hour

$$= bsfc \times bp = 0.21 \times 720 = 151.2 \text{ h}$$

$$\eta_{ith} = \frac{ip}{\dot{m}_f CV} \times 100 = \frac{750 \times 3600}{151.2 \times 44000}$$

$$= 0.406 = \mathbf{40.6\%}$$ Ans ⟸

$$\textit{Fuel-air ratio} = \frac{151.2}{60 \times 720 \times 0.0992} = \mathbf{0.0353}$$ Ans ⟸

Review Questions

19.1 What is a two-stroke engine and how does it differ from a four stroke engine?

19.2 Explain with neat sketches the two different types of two-stroke engines.

19.3 What is an opposed piston engine? Explain.

19.4 Define the following :

- *(i) delivery ratio*
- *(ii) trapping efficiency*
- *(iii) relative cylinder charge*
- *(iv) scavenging efficiency*
- *(v) charging efficiency*
- *(vi) pressure loss coefficients*
- *(vii) excess air factor*
- *(viii) index of compression*

19.5 Explain with a graph the three possible theoretical scavenging processes.

19.6 How does the actual scavenging process differ from the theoretical one? Explain by means of suitable graphs.

19.7 Briefly explain the classification of two-stroke engines based on scavenging process.

19.8 Compare the various scavenging methods.

19.9 Explain the various scavenging pumps used in a two-stroke engine.

19.10 What are the advantages and disadvantages of a two-stroke engine? Compare two-stroke SI and CI engines.

Exercise

19.1 A two-stroke SI engine with a cubic capacity of 1.5 litres and compression ratio of 7 consumes 0.5 kg of fresh charge per minute when running at 2500 rpm. The exhaust pressure is 1.02 bar and inlet temperature is 37 °C. If η_{sc} = 0.6. Calculate the scavenging ratio and trapping efficiency.

If the indicated thermal efficiency of the engine is 0.29, fuel-air ratio is 0.07 and calorific value of the fuel is 43 MJ/kg. Calculate the indicated power developed by the engine. *Ans:* (i)1.395 (ii) 0.43 (iii) 43.75 kW

19.2 A two-stroke petrol engine having a bore of 10 cm and stroke of 14 cm runs at 2000 rpm. Compression ratio is 7. The engine develops an indicated power of 27.2 kW. The fuel-air ratio is 0.075. Exhaust pressure is 1.03 bar and intake temperature is 40 °C. The indicated thermal efficiency is 0.304 and calorific value of the fuel is 44 MJ/kg. If the charge flow measured at inlet to scavenge pump is 3 kg/minute. Calculate the scavenge ratio and trapping efficiency. *Ans:* (i) 1.02 (ii) 0.542

19.3 A two-stroke cycle twin cylinder diesel engine has a bore of 10 cm and stroke of 12.5 cm has a compression ratio of 17 and runs at 2000 rpm. It consumes 7 kg of air at rated speed. The exhaust pressure is 1.05 bar and the inlet temperature is 50°. If the scavenging efficiency of the engine is 0.8. Calculate scavenging ratio and the trapping efficiency. If the indicated thermal efficiency is 0.36 and fuel-air ratio is 0.04, calculate the power developed by the engine. Calorific value of fuel is 44 MJ/kg.
Ans: (i) 1.55 (ii) 0.516 (iii) 38.18 kW

19.4 A loop scavenged two-stroke cycle diesel engine for locomotive has six cylinders with 75 cm bore and 100 cm stroke and runs at 150 rpm. Compression ratio is 15. During a test at rated speed and power, the following assumptions were made.

Fuel consumption	:	780 kg/h
Inlet air temperature at receiver	:	45 °C
Exhaust pressure	:	1.03 bar

The composition of exhaust gas collected during the blowdown process is CO = 9.4% by volume and O_2 = 7.4% by volume.

Calculate the scavenging efficiency and the *bmep* of the engine if the brake thermal efficiency of the engine is 0.3. The fuel used is $C_{14}H_{30}$ having a lower calorific value of 42000 kJ/kg.

Ans: (i) 0.62 (ii) 4.12 bar

19.5 A single-cylinder two-stroke SI engine with 8 cm bore and 12 cm stroke has a compression ratio of 8. The engine runs at 3000 rpm and the following observations have been made.

Indicated power	:	17 kW
Fuel-air ratio	:	0.08
Initial temperature	:	72 °C
Exhaust pressure	:	1.02 bar
Calorific value	:	44000 kJ/kg
Indicated thermal efficiency	:	29%

Determine (i) V_{dis} (ii) *imep* (iii) η_{sc}.

Ans: (i)6 $\times 10^{-4}$ m^3 (ii) 5.67 bar (iii) 0.472

19.6 A single cylinder two-stroke diesel engine of 125 mm bore and 152 mm stroke has a compression ratio of 15. The engine runs at 1800 rpm. The following measurements were made:

$\dot{m}_a$	:	245 kg/h
T_i	:	300 K
p_e	:	1.0275 bar

Calculate (i) the scavenge ratio (ii) the scavenging efficiency (iii) trapping efficiency. *Ans:* (i) 1.02 (ii) 0.639 (iii) 0.627

Multiple Choice Questions (choose the most appropriate answer)

1. A two-stroke engine can be identified by
   (a) cooling system
   (b) lubrication system
   (c) absence of valves
   (d) piston size

2. Advantage of two-stroke engine is
   (a) more uniform torque
   (b) lighter flywheel
   (c) no valves
   (d) all of the above

3. Charge pressure at the inlet port of a two-stroke engine is
   (a) 20 bar
   (b) vacuum
   (c) atmospheric
   (d) higher than atmospheric

4. The most perfect method of scavenging is
   (a) cross scavenging
   (b) uniflow scavenging
   (c) loop scavenging
   (d) reverse flow scavenging

5. Two-stroke SI engines suffer from
   (a) fuel loss
   (b) idling difficulty
   (c) both (a) and (b) together
   (d) none of the above

6. At the same speed two-stroke engine of the same size as a four-stroke engine will develop

   (a) same power
   (b) half the power
   (c) twice the power
   (d) four times the power

7. Two wheelers without deflector type piston use

   (a) loop scavenging
   (b) uniflow scavenging
   (c) reverse flow scavenging
   (d) cross scavenging

8. Crankcase scavenged engines have delivery ratio of

   (a) greater than 1
   (b) less than 1
   (c) equal to 1
   (d) none of the above

9. Short-circuiting in the case of two-stroke engines is equal to

   (a) $1 - \eta_{trap}$
   (b) $\eta_{trap}/2$
   (c) $\eta_{trap} - 0.5$
   (d) none of the above

10. If the delivery ratio is 1.8, the excess air factor in the case of a two-stroke engine is

    (a) 0.8
    (b) 0.9
    (c) 1.0
    (d) none of the above

Ans:	1. – (c)	2. – (d)	3. – (d)	4. – (b)	5. – (a)
	6. – (c)	7. – (d)	8. – (c)	9. – (a)	10. – (a)

20 NONCONVENTIONAL ENGINES

20.1 INTRODUCTION

So far we have seen the details of the conventional engines, viz., Spark Ignition (SI) and Compression ignition (CI) engines. Conventionally, SI engine uses carburetion and CI engine employs mechanical injection. During the last few decades a lot of research has been carried out to improve the performance of these engines. Because of the sustained efforts a number of nonconventional engines have been developed. In this chapter we will look into some of the nonconventional engines in a comprehensive manner. The typical nonconventional engines arranged in alphabetical order are:

(i) Common Rail Direct Injection (CRDI) engine

(ii) Dual fuel and multi-fuel engine

(iii) Free piston engine

(iv) Gasoline Direct Injection (GDI) engine

(v) Homogeneous Charge Compression Ignition (HCCI) engine

(vi) Lean burn engine

(vii) Stirling engine

(viii) Stratified charge engine

(ix) Variable Compression Ratio (VCR) engine

(x) Wankel engine

20.2 COMMON RAIL DIRECT INJECTION ENGINE

Conventional SI and CI engines use gasoline and diesel respectively as fuel. The problem with diesel fuel is that diesel particles are larger and heavier than gasoline. Therefore, it is comparatively more difficult to atomize. Imperfect atomization leads to more unburnt particles, causing more pollution, lower fuel efficiency and less power. In order to overcome these problems high pressure fuel injection systems for both gasoline and diesel engines have been developed. *Engines that use this technology is called CRDI engines.* However, CRDI is more suitable for diesel engines because common-rail technology is intended to improve the atomization process by means of very high (upto

1800 bar) injection pressures. Conventional DI diesel engines generates fuel pressure (around 300 bar) for each injection repeatedly. But in CRDI engines the pressure is built up independently of the injection sequence and is available constantly in the fuel line. CRDI system uses appropriate sensors to provide real-time combustion data for each cylinder.

The common rail which is placed upstream of the cylinders acts as an accumulator. It distributes the fuel to the injectors at a constant pressure of up to 1800 bar. High speed solenoid valves are used which are regulated by an electronic engine management system. They separately control the injection timing and the amount of fuel to be injected for each cylinder as a function of the cylinder's actual need. In other words, pressure generation and fuel injection are independent of each other. This is an important advantage of common-rail injection over conventional injection.

Common rail direct injection increases the controllability of the individual injection processes and improves fuel atomization. This helps in saving fuel and also in reducing emissions. It is reported that fuel economy of around 30% is possible over a conventional diesel engine. A substantial noise reduction is also achieved due to a more synchronized timing operation. The principle of CRDI can also be employed in gasoline engines as Gasoline Direct Injection, which removes to a great extent the draw backs of the conventional carburetors and the multi-point fuel injection system. GDI engines are discussed in detail in section 20.6.

20.2.1 The Working Principle

As already mentioned CRDI is meant for direct injection of the fuel into the cylinders of a diesel engine via a single, common line, called the common rail which is connected to all the fuel injectors. A typical CRDI system is shown in Fig.20.1. As can be seen, fuel from the fuel tank passes through a fuel filter to a low pressure pump where the pressure is raised to a reasonably high value. The fuel temperature is monitored by a temperature sensor. Then the fuel goes to high pressure pump. A pressure regulator valve controls the pressure. In the modern CRDI system, the outlet pressure can be as high as 1800 bar. The highly pressurized fuel goes to an accumulator, which is called common rail. The pressure in the common rail is monitored by the rail pressure sensor.

In the common rail system, a high pressure pump stores a reservoir of fuel at very high pressure and supplies this high pressure fuel to the multiple injectors. This simplifies the purpose of the high pressure pump because the system has to maintain only the designed pressure either mechanically or electronically. The fuel injectors are typically ECU-controlled. When the fuel injectors are electrically activated, a hydraulic valve (consisting of a nozzle and plunger) is mechanically or hydraulically opened and fuel is sprayed into the cylinders at the desired pressure.

20.2.2 The Injector

A typical fuel injector used in CRDI is shown in Fig.20.2(a). The injector is nothing but an electronically controlled valve. It is supplied with pressurized

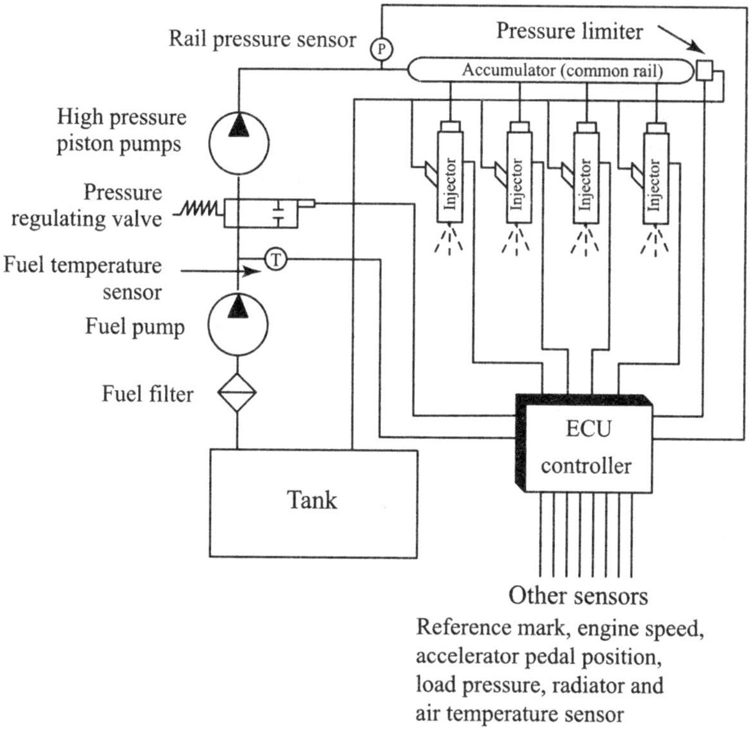

Fig. 20.1 Schematic of common rail injection system

fuel by the fuel pump, and is capable of opening and closing many times per second. When the injector is energized, an electromagnet moves a plunger that opens the valve, allowing the pressurized fuel to squirt out through a tiny nozzle. Each injector is complete and self-contained with nozzle, hydraulic intensifier, and electronic digital valve. At the end of each injector, a rapid-acting solenoid valve adjusts both the injection timing and the amount of fuel injected. A microcomputer controls each valve's opening and closing sequence. The nozzle is designed to atomize the fuel – to make as fine a mist as possible so that it can evaporate very fast and burn easily. The amount of fuel supplied to the engine is determined by the amount of time the fuel injector stays open. This is called the pulse width, and it is controlled by the ECU. This division of labour necessitates a special chamber to maintain the high injection pressure of up to 1,800 bar. Since the pressure energy of the fuel is stored remotely and the injectors are electrically actuated, the injection pressure at the start and end of injection is very close to the pressure in the accumulator (rail), thus producing a square injection rate. If the accumulator, pump and plumbing are sized properly, the injection pressure and rate will be the same for each of the multiple injection events.

The high-pressure injectors are available with different nozzles for different spray configurations. Swirler nozzle to produce a cone-shaped spray and a slit nozzle for a fan-shaped spray. The details can be seen in Fig.20.2(b).

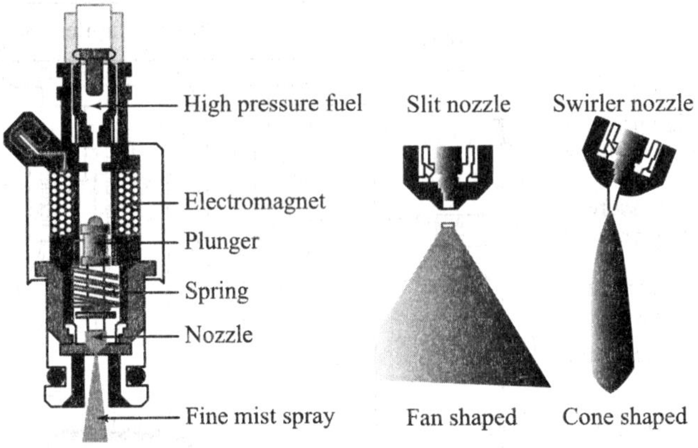

(a) CRDI injector (b) Spray pattern

Fig. 20.2 A typical CRDI injector

20.2.3 Sensors

Apart from the temperature and pressure sensors, the other input sensors include throttle position sensor, crank position sensor, pressure sensor, lambda sensor etc. The use of sensors and microprocessor to control the engine makes most efficient use of the fuel. This improves the power, fuel-economy and performance of the engine by managing it in a much better way. The electronic control unit (ECU) adjusts injection pressure precisely and as needed, based on data obtained from various sensors on the cam and crankshafts. There is also an electronic display unit (EDU) which displays all important data.

20.2.4 Electronic Control Unit (ECU)

Solenoid or piezoelectric valves make it possible for fine electronic control over the fuel injection time, quantity and the pressure. As already stated, the common rail technology provides better fuel atomisation. In order to lower the engine noise, the engine's electronic control unit can inject a small amount of diesel just before the main injection event ("pilot" injection). This will reduce explosiveness and vibration. Further, ECU can optimise injection timing and quantity considering the variations in fuel quality, cold starting and so on. Because of the precise timing control by ECU, common-rail injection system can introduce a post-combustion process also. During this process, a small amount of fuel is injected during the expansion stroke thus creating small scale combustion after the normal combustion ends. This eliminates the unburned particles and increases the exhaust gas temperature. It also reduces the pre-heat time of the catalytic converter. In short, post-combustion can reduce emissions.

The drive torque and pulsation inside the high-pressure lines are minimal, since the pump supplies only as much fuel as the engine actually requires. Some advanced common rail fuel systems perform as many as five injections per stroke which is precisely controlled by ECU. Thus CRDI is an intelligent way of controlling a diesel engine employing modern electronics.

In a conventional non-CRDI system, the interval between injections and the fuel quantity is determined by mechanical components, but in a CRDI system this time interval and timing etc. are all controlled by a central computer or microprocessor based electronic control unit. In the current first generation design, the pipe withstands pressures as high as 1,600 bar. Precise timing reduces the characteristic "Diesel Knock" common to all diesel engines, direct injection or not.

To run a CRDI system effectively, the microprocessor must be programmed to ably handle input from multiple sensors. Based on the input from these sensors, the microprocessor can calculate the precise amount of the diesel and the timing when the diesel should be injected inside the cylinder. Using these calculations, the CRDI control system delivers the right amount of diesel at the right time to allow best possible output with least emissions and least possible wastage of fuel.

20.2.5 Microcomputer

In modern CRDI system, direct-injection motors are regulated by a powerful microcomputer linked via CAN (Controller Area Network) data bus to other control devices on board. These devices are programmed to exchange data. The engine's electrical controls are the central element of the common rail system. It regulates injection pressure and, controls the solenoid valves fitted in each cylinder. It is indispensable for variable control of the motor. This electronic engine management network is a critical element of the common rail system because only the speed and spontaneity of electronics can ensure immediate pressure injection adjustment and cylinder-specific control of the injector solenoid valves.

The microcomputer regulates the amount of time the valves stay open and thus the amount of fuel injected, depending on operating conditions and how much output is needed. When it shuts the solenoid valves, fuel injection stops immediately. With the state-of-the-art common-rail direct fuel injection, an ideal compromise can be achieved between economy, torque, ride comfort and long life.

20.2.6 Status of CRDI Engines

This technology generates an ideal swirl in the combustion chamber. Coupled with the common-rail injectors' superior fuel-spray pattern and optimized piston head design, allows the air-fuel mixture to form a perfect vertical vortex. This results in uniform combustion and greatly reduces NO_X (nitrogen oxide) emissions by some 50% over the current generation of diesel engines.

The new common-rail engine (in addition to other improvements) cuts fuel consumption by 30%, doubles torque at low engine speeds and increases power by 25%. It also brings a significant reduction in the noise and vibrations of conventional diesel engines. In emission, greenhouse gases (CO_2) is reduced by 30%. At a constant level of NO_X, carbon monoxide (CO) emissions are reduced by 40%, unburnt hydrocarbons (HC) by 50%, and particulate emissions by 60%.

20.2.7 Principle of CRDI in Gasoline Engines

Gasoline engines were using carburetors for supply of air-fuel mixture before the introduction of MPFI system. But even now carburetors are in use for its simplicity and low cost. CRDI principle can be applied to gasoline engines also. Now a days the new technology, viz. Gasoline Direct Injection (GDI) is in use for gasoline engines. This is discussed in more detail in section20.6.

20.2.8 Advantages of CRDI Systems

By the introduction of CRDI a lot of advantages can be achieved, some of them are:

(i) Improved power, increased fuel efficiency and reduced noise.

(ii) Less emissions and reduced particulates in the exhaust.

(iii) Precise injection timing, very high injection pressure and better stability.

(iv) Better pulverization of fuel.

(v) Increased combustion quality due to pilot and post injection.

(vi) Doubling the torque at lower speeds.

The main disadvantage is that this technology increases the initial cost and the maintenance of the engine.

20.3 DUAL FUEL AND MULTI-FUEL ENGINE

Conventional internal combustion engines operate on a mono fuel either liquid or gaseous. However, many large sized stationary engines operate on dual fuels. Of the two fuels, normally, one is gaseous and the other is liquid. The two fuels can be taken in varying proportion to run the engine. *Such an engine is usually called dual fuel engine.* It may be noted that the very first diesel engine patented by Dr. Diesel was a dual fuel engine. The engine ran on gaseous fuel ignited by oil injection into the cylinder. World War I was the turning point when attention started to focus on dual-fuel engines. It was due to the shortage of liquid fuels at that time. Further gaseous fuels were far more cheaper than liquid fuels. This has led to increased attention on the dual-fuel technology.

Large reserves of natural gas is available and this can be utilized locally to produce power. The gaseous fuels require a high compression ratio to burn efficiently because they have high self-ignition temperatures. Natural gas is composed of mainly (about 95 percent) methane and other light paraffins. It has a higher self- ignition temperature of 740 °C compared to 470 °C for gasoline. For this reason, mainly diesel engines are more suitable as dual-fuel engines. Moreover, a diesel engine has the ability to run, over a wide range of fuels ranging from light fuels like JP-4 and kerosene to heavier fuels and crude oils.

In short, dual-fuel operation combines in a simple manner the possibility of operating a diesel engine on liquid fuels such as diesel oil or gas oil and on gaseous fuels such as natural gas, sewage gas and cook oven gas, etc. The engine can be switched over from dual-fuel operation to diesel operation almost instantaneously in case of emergency.

20.3.1 The Working Principle

The dual-fuel engine works on diesel cycle. The gaseous fuel which is called the primary fuel is inducted by the engine. If the engine is supercharged then it is supplied by the supercharger at a pressure slightly above the atmospheric pressure. In a four-stroke cycle engine the gas is supplied in the inlet manifold where it mixes with the incoming air to form a homogeneous mixture. In two-stroke cycle engines the gas may be injected at low pressures (1.5 to 3.5 bar) directly into the combustion chamber after the exhaust ports are closed. This mixture of air and gaseous fuel is compressed in the cylinder just like air in a normal diesel operation. At some point in the compression stroke, near top dead centre, a small charge of liquid fuel (about 5 to 7 per cent) called pilot fuel (or the secondary fuel), is injected through a conventional diesel fuel system. This pilot injection acts as a source of ignition. The gas-air mixture in the vicinity of the injected spray ignites at number of places establishing a number of flame-fronts. Thus combustion starts smoothly and rapidly.

It may be noted that in a dual-fuel engine the combustion starts in a fashion similar to the CI engine. However, the flame front propagates in a manner similar to the SI engine. The power output of the engine is normally controlled by changing the amount of primary gaseous fuel. The pilot oil quantity is usually kept constant for a given engine and is about 5 to 7 percent of the total heat of the engine at full load. The dual-fuel engine is capable of running on either gas or diesel oil or a combination of these two over a wide range of mixture ratios. Figure 20.3 shows a typical p-θ variation for a dual-fuel engine showing the weak limit and rich limit of operation. It can be seen that transition from one fuel to another is quite smooth.

20.3.2 Combustion in Dual-Fuel Engines

The ignition of the gaseous fuel in a dual-fuel engine is achieved by introducing a small amount of liquid fuel in the form of fine spray near TDC. The combustion following this injection is strongly dependent on the amount of gaseous fuel supplied. The process of combustion can be divided into three main stages:

(i) Without the gaseous fuel the pilot fuel burns similar to, in a diesel engine. However, it is not sufficient to maintain the speed of the engine at the desired level. It requires at least 10 to 14 percent of full load fuel to run the engine at no load. As already stated the pilot fuel injected is only about 5 to 7 percent of full load value. As the gaseous fuel is introduced, the weak gas-air mixture comes in contact with the injected spray of the pilot fuel. Only that part of the mixture which is within the combustible limit of the spray gets oxidized. The rest of the gas remains unaffected and goes in exhaust. This results in very low efficiency at part load operation of the engine.

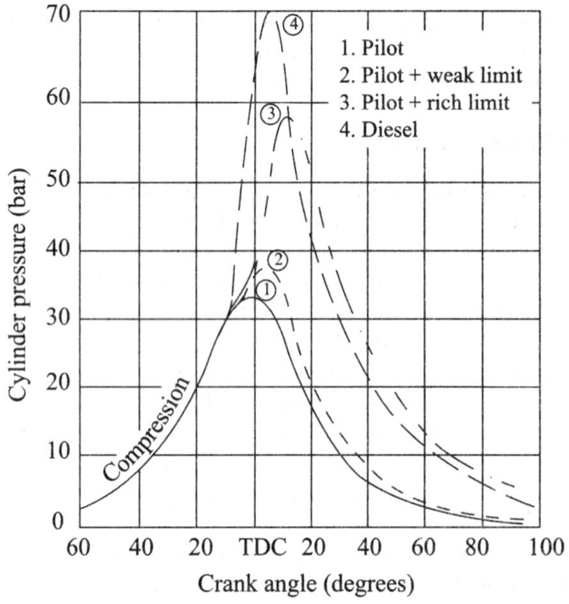

Fig. 20.3 Typical $p - \theta$ diagram for a dual fuel engine

(ii) As the amount of the gaseous fuel is increased, the gas air mixture in the vicinity of the injected fuel spray also gets oxidized and starts burning at a number of places. Flame-fronts start traveling from these ignition points and combustion takes place rapidly and almost completely. The combustion then is exactly similar to combustion in an SI engine. The p-θ diagram will be as shown in 20.4(a).

(iii) Further admission of the gaseous fuel results in very fast reaction rates. This is followed by ignition with very high rates of pressure rise and combustion becomes uncontrollable. This is the onset of knock. The high rates of pressure rise result in combustion noise and a marked change in the shape of pressure-crank angle diagram as seen in Fig.20.4(b).

The very high peak pressure and the oscillations on the expansion curve are exactly similar to the knocking condition usually seen in SI engine. The transition from 'normal' to knocking condition is quite sharp. A small increase in the gaseous fuel beyond a limit can result in very severe knock which can damage the engine. The ignition quality and the amount of pilot fuel seem to have little influence on the quality of the charge at knocking conditions.

20.3.3 Nature of Knock in a Dual-Fuel Engine

The phenomenon of knock in a dual-fuel engine is of the nature of auto-ignition of gaseous mixture in the neighbourhood of injected spray. When the pilot fuel is injected a series of pre-combustion reactions of chain type occur and heat energy is released. If this heat energy is more than that dissipated by the fuel droplets, the temperature in the vicinity of spray increases. This results

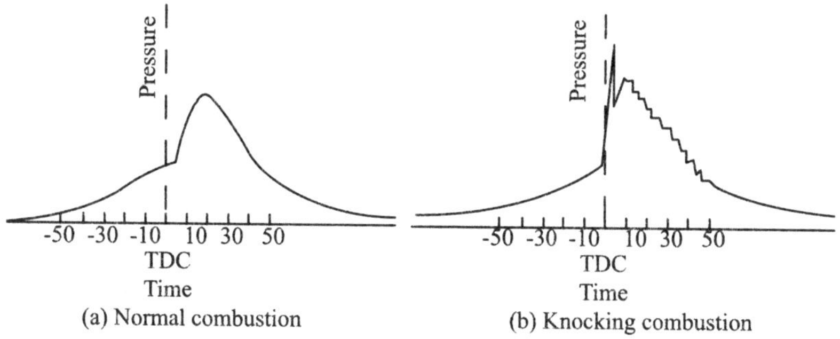

Fig. 20.4 Typical pressure time diagram for a dual fuel engine

in the increased number of active radicals and the reactions are automatically speeded up. There is a sudden rise in the temperature of the gas in the neighbourhood of the spray and it gets ignited and a flame front starts from the ignition point. This flame front consumes gas in its immediate surrounding and more thermal energy is released which speeds up reactions everywhere. Thus it is to be noted that the processes determining the onset of knocking are essentially similar to the auto-ignition of fuel in an SI engine.

20.3.4 Weak and Rich Combustion Limits

Refer the four curves in Fig.20.3. With only pilot injection (curve 1) of fuel the rise in pressure after ignition is noticeable but cannot sustain the load since only 5 to 7 per cent of the full load requirements is injected. Actually the engine requires 10–14% of the full load fuel. Now, when a small quantity of gaseous fuel is introduced the pressure trend will remain the same (curve 1). It may be due to the small quantity of gaseous fuel might have dispersed into regions where the mixture strength is too lean to autoignite. If a little more gaseous fuel is introduced, combustion become self sustaining. There is a noticeable change in pressure rise (curve 2). This is the weak combustion limit for the particular gaseous fuel.

Similarly, when the gaseous mixture strength is increased, there is considerable pressure rise as can be seen from curve 3. At the same time, there is an increase in ignition delay. If there is further increase in gaseous mixture strength, there will be no rise in the combustion pressure (curve 3). Under these conditions more heat is lost than released by the precombustion reaction due to long delay periods. This limit is called rich combustion limit. These limits are mainly dependent on the ignition delay as these are strongly affected by the energy losses during the pre-combustion reactions. Hence, the type of fuel and operating conditions affect these limits. The trend can be clearly observed in Fig.20.3. Curve 4 shows the p-θ variation for pure diesel operation.

20.3.5 Factors Affecting Combustion in a Dual-Fuel Engine

A large number of factors affect the combustion in a dual-fuel engine. Among them the important ones are:

(i) amount of the pilot fuel injection,

(ii) injection timing

(iii) Cetane number of pilot fuel

(iv) throttling

(v) nature of the gaseous fuel,

(vi) the mixture strength and its initial pressure and temperature.

20.3.6 Advantages of Dual Fuel Engines

In addition to the inherent advantage of using efficiently the available cheaper gaseous fuel from various sources the dual fuel engine has substantial advantages over a single fuel engine. They are:

(i) The gas burns neatly and therefore the exhaust is clean which indirectly helps in reducing air pollution.

(ii) The clean combustion results in reduced wear of the engine parts and reduced consumption of the lubricating oil. Further it reduces the contamination of the lubricating oil.

(iii) The utility of the power plant is highly increased by its ability of instantaneous change over from gas to diesel and vice-versa.

(iv) Only a small amount of liquid fuel is needed to run the engine and thereby there is a saving of precious fossil liquid fuel.

(v) The dual-fuel engine is highly suitable for total energy installation. For example the exhaust heat of the engine can be used for digesting the sludge in a sewage disposal plant and the sewage gas produced can be used to run the engine itself.

(vi) A typical use of the dual-fuel engine has been to produce synthetic gas, which is a mixture of CO and H_2 by burning methane in it and also producing power at the same time.

(vii) For LPG tankers, these engines are ideally suited as they can utilize the gas which mainly evaporates during transportation, by suitably arresting it.

20.4 MULTIFUEL ENGINES

A multi-fuel engine is one which can be satisfactorily operated with comparable performance and efficiency on a wide variety of fuels ranging from diesel oil, crude oil, JP-4 to lighter fuels like gasoline, and even the normal lubricating oil. The main reasons for developing multi-fuel engines have been mainly for the military requirements. The need of an engine which can satisfactorily run on any automotive fuel in case of emergency, a situation very often occurring during the war.

Multifuel engine have a good idling and part-load efficiency, and low exhaust smoke and noise under these operating conditions to avoid any possible detection by the enemy. Further, shortage of middle range distillates has started a trend for diesel engines seeking alternate fuels for their operation. The interest in the multifuel engine has further increased by the realization of the possibilities, of getting fuel economy of CI engines using gasoline.

20.4.1 Characteristics of a Multi-Fuel Engine

Almost all diesel engines are capable of burning a wide variety of fuels. The use of low ignition quality fuels requires a higher compression ratio for satisfactory burning. It may be noted that raising the compression ratio of an SI engine is difficult because of knocking. Therefore, CI engines are most suitable for multi-fuel operations. A multi-fuel engine must fulfill the following requirements:

(i) must have good combustion efficiency.

(ii) combustion chamber temperature must be comparatively higher.

(iii) easy starting under sub-zero temperature conditions.

(iv) must have low exhaust smoke and noise levels.

The above requirements give an indication of the design features essential for multi-fuel operation. These are:

(i) *Higher compression ratio*: Gasoline have a cetane number of less than 20 which is an indication of their low ignition quality for use in a diesel engine. Therefore, the compression ratios of multi-fuel engines are usually around 23:1 to increase the temperature at the end of compression stroke for proper burning. Higher compression ratio will also ensure better mixing of fuel and air at higher temperatures. This will reduce the misfiring tendency of the engine when running on low ignition quality fuels.

(ii) *Stroke to bore ratio*: It is very important to maintain the combustion chamber hot under all conditions of speed and load. A large stroke to bore ratio gives a compact combustion chamber. Stroke to bore ratio as high as 1.35:1 has been used.

(iii) *Combustion chamber*: An open combustion chamber is better suited for multi-fuel operation than a pre-combustion chamber. It is because in the latter additional heat losses due to throat occur during compression. A spherical combustion chamber is ideally suitable for such engines due to lowest surface to volume ratio. However, its air utilization is not optimum.

(iv) *Injection pump*: The conventional jerk-type fuel pump can satisfactorily meet the requirements of multi-fuel operation.

The difficulties of multi-fuel operation are:

(i) Tendency of vapour lock in the fuel pump while using lighter fuels.

(ii) Tendency of increased wear in fuel pump due to lower lubricity of the fuel.

(iii) Requirement of injecting different volumes of fuels due to differences in their heating values and compressibility effect.

20.5 FREE PISTON ENGINE

Extensive use of fossil fuels as an energy source for both sea and land based transport leads to significant production of CO_2 and other pollutants. Further there is always a quest for increased power from a given cylinder size. Lot of research, particularly within the automotive industry, is in progress to develop more environmental friendly fuel chains. However, the complete fuel chain ('well-to-wheel') efficiencies are not yet superior to those of conventional technology. Important steps in this direction are:

(i) improvements in the fuel properties and

(ii) component design changes for higher efficiencies, lower cost and weight.

However, a different approach in the direction of using different cycles of operation or modifications of existing cycle has also been pursued with great interest. In this respect to start with naturally aspirated I.C. engine was first supercharged to get increased power. Further, improvements in the supercharger design resulted in turbocharged engine development. Turbocharger utilizes exhaust heat to drive the compressor with the help of an exhaust gas driven turbine. This idea of using exhaust energy has culminated to its logical end in a free piston engine

After being abandoned in the mid-20th century, free-piston engines are being investigated nowadays by a number of research groups worldwide. It is considered as an alternative to conventional engine-generator sets or for generating hydraulic power in off-highway vehicles. Reasons for the interest in developing the free-piston engine include:

(i) optimized combustion through variable compression ratio,

(ii) higher part load efficiency,

(iii) possible multi-fuel operation,

(iv) reduced frictional losses

(v) simple design

(vi) few moving parts.

20.5.1 Free-Piston Engine Basics

Due to the breadth of the term free-piston, many engine configurations will fall under this category. *The free-piston term is most commonly used to distinguish a linear engine from a rotating crankshaft engine.* The piston is 'free' because its motion is not controlled by the position of a rotating crankshaft, as in the conventional engines. It is determined by the interaction between the gas forces and load acting upon it. This gives the free-piston engine some distinct characteristics, including variable stroke length and the need for active control of piston motion. Other important features of the free-piston engine are potential reductions in frictional losses and possibilities to optimize engine operation using the variable compression ratio.

20.5.2 Categories of Free Piston Engine

Free-piston engines are usually divided into three categories based on the piston/cylinder configuration. A fourth category is free-piston gas generators in which the load is extracted purely from an exhaust turbine. There is no separate load device mechanically coupled to the engine. Various categories of free-piston engines are described in the following sections.

20.5.3 Single Piston

A single piston free-piston engine is shown in Fig.20.5. This engine essentially consists of a combustion cylinder, a load device, and a rebound device to store the energy required to compress the next cylinder charge.

The hydraulic cylinder in the engine serves as both load and rebound device. In some other designs these may be two individual devices, for example an electric generator and a gas filled bounce chamber. A simple design with high controllability is the main strength of the single piston design compared to the other free-piston engine configurations. The rebound device may give the opportunity to accurately control the amount of energy put into the compression process and thereby regulating the compression ratio and stroke length.

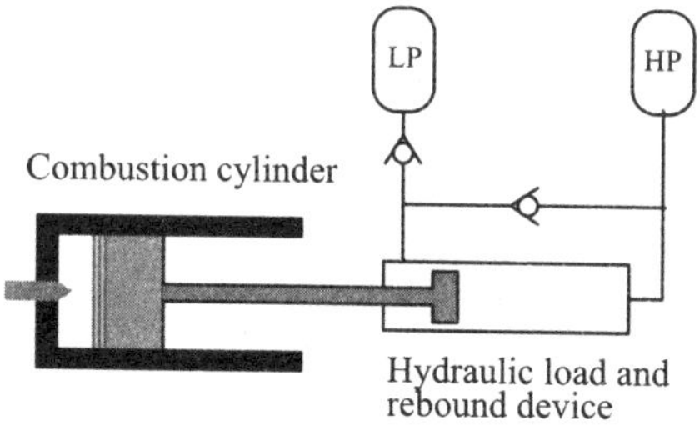

Fig. 20.5 Single piston free-piston engine

20.5.4 Dual Piston

A typical dual piston (or dual combustion chamber) configuration is shown in Fig.20.6. It has been the topic for much of the recent research in free-piston engine technology. A number of dual piston designs have been proposed and a few prototypes have emerged, both with hydraulic and electric power output. This configuration eliminates the need for a rebound device. It is because at any time working piston provides the work to drive the compression process in the other cylinder. This allows a simple and more compact device with higher power to weight ratio.

Some problems with the dual piston design have, however, been reported. The control of piston motion, in particular stroke length and compression ratio, has proved difficult. This is due to the fact that the combustion process in one cylinder drives the compression in the other. A small variations in the combustion will have large influence on the next compression. This is a control challenge because the combustion process is to be controlled accurately in order to optimize emissions and/or efficiency. Experimental work with this type of dual piston engines has reported high sensitivity to load variations and high cycle-to-cycle variations.

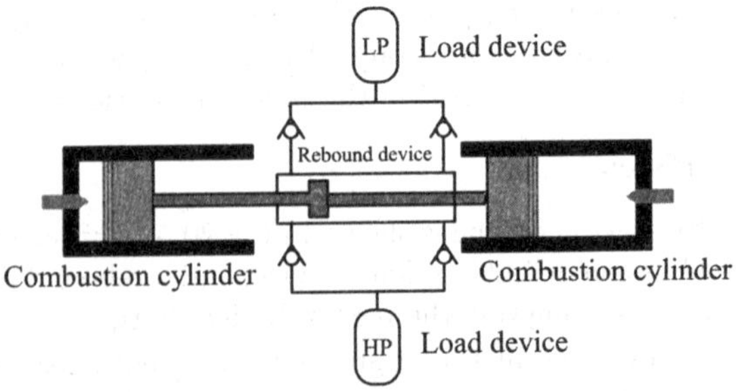

Fig. 20.6 Dual piston free-piston engine

20.5.5 Opposed Piston

An opposed piston type free-piston engine essentially consists of two single piston units with a common combustion chamber. Each piston requires a re-bound device, and a load device. The load device may be coupled to one or both of the pistons. Figure 20.7 shows an opposed piston type free-piston engine, with a mechanical piston synchronization mechanism.

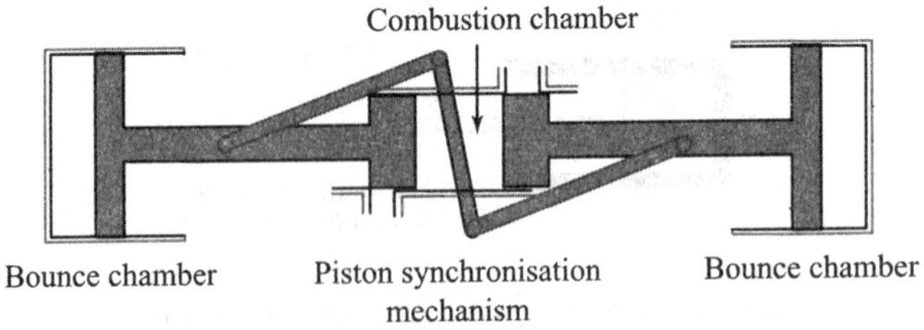

Fig. 20.7 Opposed piston free-piston engine

The opposed piston principle was used almost exclusively in the early free-piston engine designs (1930-1960), and mechanical linkages connected the two pistons to ensure symmetric piston motion, as illustrated in Fig.20.7. These engines served successfully as air compressors and later as gas generators in large-scale plants. A number of units are often used to feed a single power turbine.

The main advantage of this opposed piston configuration is the perfectly balanced and vibration-free design. This feature is not available with any of the other free-piston configurations. Therefore, in other designs alternative means of controlling vibrations is required. A further advantage of the opposed piston design is reduced heat transfer losses due to the opposed piston cylinder eliminating the cylinder head. This also allows uniflow scavenging to be used, giving high scavenging efficiency. The main disadvantage of this design is the absolute need for a piston synchronization mechanism. This, together with the need for a dual set of the main components, makes the engine complicated and bulky.

20.5.6 Free Piston Gas Generators

These are free-piston engines feeding hot gas to a power turbine. The only 'load' for the engine is that to supercharge the intake air. The output work is taken entirely from the power turbine. Free-piston gas generators were used in some large-scale marine and stationary power plants in the mid-20th century. Attempts were also made to use this principle in automotive applications. Figure 20.8 illustrates an opposed piston free-piston gas generator plant.

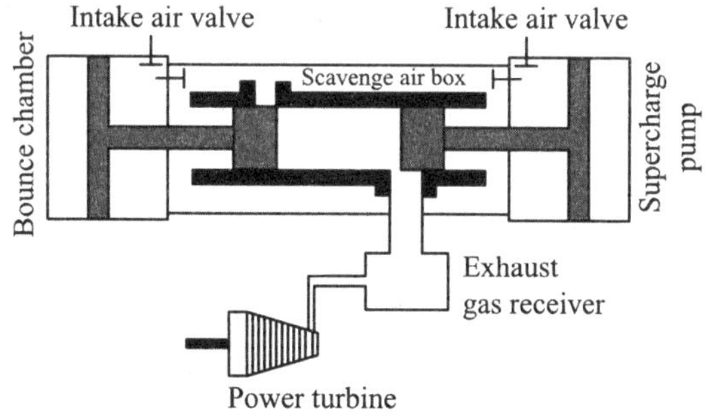

Fig. 20.8 Gas generator free-piston engine

Compared to a conventional gas turbine, the free-piston gas generator has the advantage of high compression and pressure ratios. In this arrangement the work needed to compress the intake air is extracted from the gas which is supplied to the power turbine. Consequently, the gas fed to the turbine holds a lower temperature which reduces the materials requirements. Further, it allows the turbine to be placed away from the combustor without extensive heat transfer losses. The operational characteristics of a free-piston gas generator do not differ much from those of other free-piston engines of the same configuration. The opposed piston free-piston gas generator was the topic of much research in the mid-20th century. However, as conventional gas turbine technology matured, the free-piston gas generator concept was abandoned.

20.5.7 Loading Requirements

Free-piston engines require a linear load. Further, for the overall system to be efficient the load must provide efficient energy conversion. Internal combustion engines and gas turbines are the main devices for many years for electric power generation. A challenge for free-piston engine developers is to find linear equivalents of these machines with comparable performance. The mechanical requirements for free-piston engine load devices are high since the load is coupled directly to the mover. Moreover, the load will be subjected to high acceleration forces. Secondary effects from the high accelerations such as cavitations in hydraulic cylinders must also be considered. Furthermore, the load device may be subjected to heat transfer from the engine cylinders. Known free-piston engine loads include electric generators, hydraulic pumps and air compressors.

20.5.8 Design Features

The simple design of the free-piston engine compared to conventional technology is one of the driving forces behind many of the recent free-piston engine developments. The elimination of the crank mechanism reduces the number of parts. The major design features of the free-piston engines are:

(i) *Low frictional losses*: Fewer moving parts in the free-piston engine give reduced frictional losses. Absence of a crankshaft eliminates losses due to crankshaft bearing friction and pure linear motion leads to very low side loads on the piston. This also reduces the cylinder lubrication requirements

(ii) *Reduced manufacturing costs*: The reduced number of parts in the free-piston engine results in lower manufacturing costs

(iii) *Compactness*: This is again due to reduced number of parts. The size and weight of the free-piston engine can be reduced, giving a more compact unit.

(iv) *Low maintenance costs and increased life*: The reduced frictional losses due to reduced number of parts reduce the maintenance costs of the free-piston engine which increases life.

20.5.9 The Combustion Process

It is believed that the combustion in free-piston engines benefits from the high piston speed around TDC. This leads to higher air velocity and turbulence level in the cylinder. It helps air-fuel mixing and increase the reaction rate and flame speed. The high piston acceleration just after TDC leads to a rapid expansion. The time dependent chemical reactions, such as NO_X formation, are potentially reduced.

A particular feature of the free-piston engine is the ability of the combustion process to influence the speed of the expansion. It is due to the direct coupling of the combustion cylinder to the low-inertia moving part. A rapid combustion process and pressure rise may lead to a faster expansion and vice versa. In a conventional engine, the inertia of the crank system and flywheel ensures that the speed of the engine stays constant in the time frame of the combustion process.

20.5.10 Combustion Optimization

The variable compression ratio in the free piston engine may allow for optimization of the combustion process not achievable in conventional engines. Nowadays, a sufficiently accurate piston motion control system can be realized. The compression ratio can be regulated even during operation to achieve best possible performance in terms of efficiency or emissions. Free-piston engines with compression ratio as high as 50:1 has been reported in the mid-20th century.

20.5.11 Advantages and Disadvantages of Free Piston Engine

Advantages:

(i) *Simplicity*: Vibration is very much reduced due to inherently balanced configuration of opposed piston The absence of crankshaft and connecting rods results in great mechanical simplicity.

(ii) *Flexibility and reliability*: Compared to conventional engines, the free-piston engine has certain flexibility of installation and the plant life for a free-piston engine is much higher compared to conventional engines.

(iii) *Multifuel capability*: The free piston engine has a characteristic of adjusting to the ignition requirements by changing its compression ratio. The compression ratio varies from about 30 to 50. This property allows it to utilize a wider variety of fuels than the conventional high speed diesel engine.

(iv) *Power to weight ratio*: The power to weight ratio of a free piston engine is quite favorable

(v) *Lower turbine operating temperatures*: In gas generator free piston engines, the gas turbine in the free-piston engine does not have to supply compression work to the compressor, unlike the conventional gas turbine power-plant. Turbine inlet temperatures of about 750 to 800 K are common in the free-piston engine as compared to that of about 1200 to 1400 K in the conventional gas turbine plants.

(vi) *Vibrations, noise and maintenance*: Due to better balancing the vibrations and structure-borne noise are lower compared to diesel engine. All these, along with lower operating temperatures, result in low maintenance requirements.

(vii) *Starting and control*: Due to variable compression ratio, it is easy to start a free-piston engine. The air required for starting the free piston engine is much less compared to diesel engine of corresponding size.

(viii) *Waste heat recovery*: Free piston engine is highly suitable for waste heat recovery. The nearly constant temperature and constant mass flow rate with load allows efficient waste heat recovery giving a reasonably constant output under all loads.

(ix) *Application for marine or land traction*: In marine application, it gives a high degree of maneuverability and the reverse speed compared to diesel engines or steam turbines. In road or rail traction the torque converter requirements are reduced, thereby, less elaborate transmission system is required.

(x) *Manufacturing cost*: The manufacturing cost is much less compared to conventional engines due to reduced number of parts.

Disadvantages:

Though the free piston engine has many advantages it also suffers from the following disadvantages.

(i) *Poor fuel economy*: The specific fuel consumption of a free piston engine is much higher than the diesel engine.

(ii) *Stability*: Free-piston engines require a certain quantity of fuel per stroke which varies according to load to maintain a stable operation. Any fluctuation in the fuel or air supply will make the operation unstable.

(iii) *Part load efficiency*: At part loads the pistons reciprocate within a narrow limit as the compression ratio is decided by the combustion pressure inside the cylinder. This results in poor part load efficiency especially at very low load and at this condition a part of the gas has to be blown-off.

(iv) *High combustion rates*: Due to higher supercharge the rate of combustion per cylinder volume is 4 to 6 times higher compared to conventional diesel engines. This causes difficulty in wall lubrication, higher ring wear and cooling problems.

(v) *Reduction gearing*: The gearing arrangement necessary to couple high speed turbine with the load, for example a marine propeller tends to increase the initial cost and weight of the plant.

20.5.12 Applications of Free Piston Engine

As on today the free-piston engine has not established itself very much and has limited use. However, with intensive research and development, it may find large number of industrial and other applications in the future such as

(i) submarine air compressor units,

(ii) power generation in medium power range,

(iii) ship propulsion, road and rail traction and even in aircrafts,

(iv) high speed centrifugal air compressors,

(v) pumping oil as no fire wall is necessary, and

(vi) mixed gas-steam cycle.

20.6 GASOLINE DIRECT INJECTION ENGINE

Until 1995, carburetor was the device that supplied fuel to the four-wheeler engine. Even today on many other machines, such as two-wheelers, lawnmowers and chainsaws, it still is. With improvements in the automobile design and development, the carburetor got more and more complicated trying to handle all of the operating requirements. To handle some of these tasks, carburetors had five different circuits:

(i) *Main circuit*: Provides just enough fuel for fuel-efficient cruising

(ii) *Idle circuit*: Provides just enough fuel to keep the engine idling

(iii) *Accelerator pump* Provides an extra burst of fuel when the accelerator pedal is depressed, reducing hesitation before the engine speeds up

(iv) *Power enrichment*: Provides extra fuel when the vehicle is going up a hill or towing a trailer

(v) *Choke*: Provides extra rich mixture when the engine is cold so that it will start effortlessly

In order to meet stricter emissions requirements, catalytic converters were introduced. For the catalytic converter to be effective very careful control of the air-fuel ratio is a must. Oxygen sensors, monitor the amount of oxygen in the exhaust. The engine control unit (ECU) uses this information to adjust the air-to-fuel ratio in real-time. This is called closed loop control. It was not feasible to achieve this control with carburetors. There was a brief period of electrically controlled carburetors before fuel injection systems took over. However, these electrical carburetors were even more complicated than the mechanical ones.

The development of fuel feed system for SI engines can be seen from Fig.20.9. The carburettors were in vogue until 1995. Then carburetors slowly got replaced with throttle body fuel injection systems between 1980 and 1995. They are also called as single point or central fuel injection systems. They were electrically controlled fuel-injector valves into the throttle body. These were almost a bolt-in replacement for the carburetor. The automakers did not have to make any drastic changes to their engine designs. Gradually, as new engines were designed, throttle body fuel injection was replaced by multi-port fuel injection (1995–2005). These are also known as port, multipoint or sequential fuel injection. These systems have a fuel injector for each cylinder. They are usually located in such a way that they spray right at the intake valve. These systems provide more accurate fuel metering and quicker response. Between 1995 and 2005, gasoline direct injection slowly got into four-wheelers. After 2005, all major car manufacturers appear to be switching over to this new gasoline engine technology. *In internal combustion engines,*

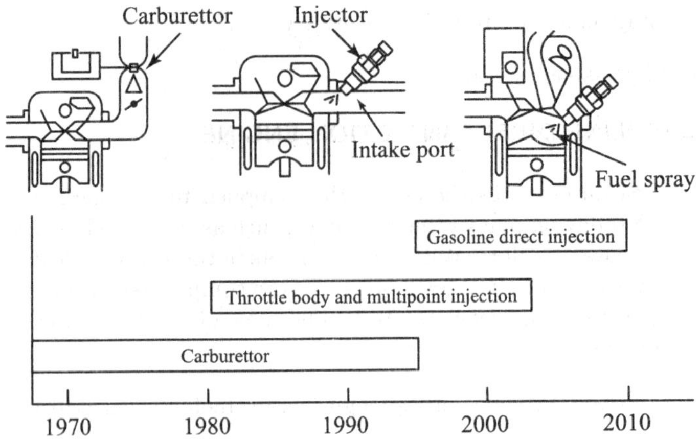

Fig. 20.9 History for carburettor

gasoline direct injection (GDI) is a variant of fuel injection employed in modern two-stroke and four-stroke gasoline engines. This is similar to CRDI in diesel engine. The gasoline is pressurized, and injected via a common rail fuel line directly into the combustion chamber of each cylinder. This is different from conventional multi-point fuel injection (MPFI) in which injection takes place in the intake manifold, or cylinder port. In some applications, gasoline direct injection enables a stratified fuel charge (ultra lean burn) combustion for improved fuel efficiency, and reduced emission levels at low load.

20.6.1 Modes of Operation

The major advantages of a GDI are increased fuel efficiency and higher power output. Emission levels can also be more accurately controlled with the GDI system. The cited gains are achieved by the precise control over the amount of fuel and injection timings that are varied according to the load conditions. In addition, there are no throttling losses in most GDI engines. In such engines the efficiency is greatly improved. Further, pumping losses are considerably reduced because of the absence of the throttle plate. Engine speed is controlled by the engine control unit or engine management system (EMS). It regulates fuel injection function and ignition timing. Adding this function to the EMS requires considerable enhancement of its processing and memory of ECU. Direct injection plus the engine speed management must have very precise algorithms for good performance and driveability.

The engine management system continually chooses among three combustion modes: ultra lean burn, stoichiometric, and full power output. Each mode is characterized by the air-fuel ratio. The gravimetric stoichiometric air-fuel ratio for gasoline is 14.7:1. But, ultra lean mode can involve ratios as high as 60:1 for even higher in some engines, for very limited periods. These mixtures are much leaner than in a conventional engine and reduce fuel consumption quite considerably. Let us see the details of the three modes of operation briefly.

(i) *Ultra lean burn mode* is used for light-load running conditions, at constant or reducing road speeds, where no acceleration is required. The fuel is not injected during the intake stroke but rather at the latter stages of the compression stroke. By this a small amount of air-fuel mixture is optimally placed near the spark plug. This stratified charge is surrounded mostly by air. This keeps the fuel and the flame away from the cylinder walls by which lowest emissions and heat losses are achieved. The combustion takes place in a toroidal (donut-shaped) cavity on the piston head. The cavity is displaced towards the fuel injector side. This technique enables the use of ultra-lean mixtures that would be impossible with carburetors or conventional fuel injection.

(ii) *Stoichiometric* mode is used for moderate load conditions. Fuel is injected during the intake stroke. This creates a homogenous fuel-air mixture in the cylinder. From the stoichiometric mixture, an optimum combustion results. There is a good possibility of clean exhaust emission, further cleaned by the catalytic converter.

(iii) *Full power* mode is used for rapid acceleration and heavy loads (climbing a hill). The air-fuel mixture is homogenous and the ratio is slightly richer than stoichiometric. This can help in preventing knock. In this mode fuel is injected during the intake stroke.

Direct injection may also be accompanied by other engine technologies such as variable valve timing (VVT) and tuned/multi path or variable length intake manifolding (VLIM, or VIM). Water injection or more commonly employed exhaust gas recirculation (EGR) may help in reducing the high nitrogen oxides (NO_X) emissions that can result from burning ultra lean mixtures.

Because of electronic control, it is also possible to inject more than once during a single cycle. After the first fuel charge has been ignited, it is possible to add fuel as the piston descends. The benefits are more power and economy. However, certain octane fuels have been seen to cause exhaust valve erosion. For this reason, most manufacturers have ceased to use the Fuel Stratified Injection (FSI) operation during normal running. Tuning up an early generation FSI engine to generate higher power is difficult. This is because, only one injection is possible during the induction phase.

Conventional injection engines can inject throughout the four-stroke sequence, as the injector squirts onto the back of a closed valve. A direct injection engine, where the injector injects directly into the cylinder, is limited to the suction stroke of the piston. As the engine speed increases, the time available to inject fuel decreases. Newer FSI systems that have sufficient fuel pressure to inject even late in compression phase do not suffer from this deficiency. However, they still do not inject during the exhaust cycle (they could but it would just waste fuel). Hence, all other factors being equal, an FSI engine needs higher-capacity injectors to achieve the same power as a conventional engine.

20.7 HOMOGENEOUS CHARGE COMPRESSION IGNITION ENGINE

Homogeneous charge compression ignition (HCCI) is a form of internal combustion in which well-mixed fuel and air are compressed to the auto-ignition temperature of the fuel. The exothermic reaction releases chemical energy into a sensible form that can be transformed in an engine into work and heat.

HCCI has characteristics of the two most popular forms of combustion used in engines:

(i) homogeneous charge spark ignition and

(ii) stratified charge compression ignition.

However, rather than using a spark to ignite the mixture, the density and temperature of the mixture are raised by compression. When the entire mixture reaches its self ignition temperature it reacts spontaneously.

The main characteristic of HCCI is that the ignition occurs at several places. This makes the fuel-air mixture burn nearly simultaneously. There is no direct initiator of combustion. This poses a real challenge to control the combustion. However, advances in microprocessors and physical understanding of the ignition process come to our help.

HCCI concept, if properly implemented, can achieve gasoline engine-like emissions along with diesel engine-like efficiency. In fact, HCCI engines have been shown to achieve extremely low levels of nitrogen oxide (NO_X) emissions without after-treatment in a catalytic converter. The unburned hydrocarbon and carbon monoxide emissions are still high (due to lower peak temperatures), as in gasoline engines. Therefore, exhaust gases must be treated to meet automotive emission regulations.

Recent research has shown that the use of two fuels with different reactivities (such as gasoline and diesel) can help to solve some of the difficulties of controlling HCCI ignition and burn rates. Reactivity Controlled Compression Ignition (RCCI) has been demonstrated to provide highly efficient, low emission operation over wide load and speed ranges. HCCI engines have a long history. However, it may be noted that HCCI has not yet been as widely implemented as spark ignition or diesel injection.

HCCI engine is essentially works on an Otto cycle. In fact, HCCI was popular before electronic spark ignition was used. One example is the hot-bulb engine which used a hot vaporization chamber to help mix fuel with air. The extra heat combined with compression induced conditions for combustion to occur.

A mixture of fuel and air will ignite when the concentration and temperature of reactants are sufficiently high. The concentration and/or temperature can be increased either by increasing compression ratio, or pre-heating of induction gases, or forced induction, or retained or re-inducted exhaust gases.

Once ignited, combustion proceeds very rapidly. When auto-ignition occurs too early or with too much chemical energy, combustion is too fast. This can cause very high in-cylinder pressures and may destroy the engine. For this reason, HCCI is typically operated at lean overall fuel mixtures. Therefore, the challenging job in HCCI is the appropriate control of combustion.

20.7.1 Control

Controlling HCCI is a major problem, which causes major hurdle to more widespread commercialization. In a typical gasoline engine, a spark is used to ignite the pre-mixed fuel and air. In diesel engines, combustion begins when the fuel is injected into compressed air. In both cases, the timing of combustion is explicitly controlled. In an HCCI engine, however, the homogeneous mixture of fuel and air is compressed and combustion begins whenever the appropriate conditions are reached. This means that there is no well-defined combustion initiator that can be directly controlled.

Engines can be designed so that the ignition conditions occur at a desirable timing. To achieve this in an HCCI engine, the control system must come into effect to bring the conditions that induce combustion. As already mentioned, the control must be effected either by

(i) variable compression ratio, or

(ii) variable induction temperature, or

(iii) variable exhaust gas percentage, or

(iv) variable valve actuation, or

(v) variable fuel ignition quality.

Various control approaches mentioned above are briefly discussed in the following sections.

20.7.2 Variable Compression Ratio

There are several methods for changing both the geometric and effective compression ratio. For example,

(i) The geometric compression ratio can be changed with a movable plunger at the top of the cylinder head.

(ii) The effective compression ratio can be changed from the geometric ratio by closing the intake valve either very late or very early with some form of variable valve actuation mechanism.

Both the approaches mentioned above require some additional power to achieve fast responses. Further, implementation is expensive. However, control of an HCCI engine using variable compression ratio strategies is found to be effective. The effect of compression ratio on HCCI combustion has been studied extensively.

20.7.3 Variable Induction Temperature

In HCCI engines, the auto-ignition event is highly sensitive to temperature. Various methods have been tried, using temperature to control combustion timing. The simplest method uses resistance heaters to vary the inlet temperature, but this approach is slow. It cannot change the temperature on a cycle-to-cycle basis. Another technique is known as fast thermal management (FTM) method. It is achieved by rapidly varying the cycle to cycle intake charge temperature by rapidly mixing hot and cold air streams. It is also equally expensive to implement and has limited range of application.

20.7.4 Variable Exhaust Gas Percentage

Incylinder exhaust gas is very hot if retained or relatively cool if re-inducted from the previous cycle through the intake as in conventional EGR systems. Both hot EGR and cool EGR have been tried. The exhaust has dual effects on HCCI combustion. Cool EGR dilutes the fresh charge, delaying ignition and reducing the chemical energy and engine work. Hot EGR conversely will increase the temperature of the gases in the cylinder and will advance ignition. Control of combustion timing in HCCI engines using EGR has also been studied extensively.

20.7.5 Variable Valve Actuation

Variable valve actuation (VVA) has proven to extend the HCCI operating region by giving finer control over the temperature-pressure-time history within the combustion chamber. VVA can achieve this by two distinct methods:

(i) *Controlling the effective compression ratio*: A variable valve actuation system on intake can control the point at which the intake valve closes. If this is retarded past bottom dead center, then the compression ratio will change, altering the in-cylinder pressure-time history prior to combustion.

(ii) *Controlling the amount of hot exhaust gas retained in the combustion chamber*: A VVA system can be used to control the amount of hot internal exhaust gas recirculation (EGR) within the combustion chamber. This can be achieved either by including valve re-opening and changes in valve overlap. By balancing the percentage of cool EGR with the hot internal EGR generated by a VVA system, it may be possible to control the in-cylinder temperature.

While electro-hydraulic and camless VVA systems can be used to give a great deal of control over the valve event, manufacturing of components for such systems is currently complicated and expensive. Mechanical variable lift and duration systems, however, are far cheaper and less complicated. If the desired VVA characteristic is known, then it is relatively simple to configure such systems to achieve the necessary control over the valve lift curve

20.7.6 Variable Fuel Ignition Quality

Another means to extend the operating range is to control the onset of ignition and the heat release rate by manipulating fuel ignition quality itself. This is usually carried out by adopting multiple fuels and blending. Examples could be blending of commercial gasoline and diesel or natural gas or ethanol. This can be achieved by the following ways:

(i) *Blending fuels upstream of the engine*: Two fuels are mixed in the liquid phase, one with lower resistance to ignition (such as diesel fuel) and a second with a greater resistance (gasoline). The timing of ignition is controlled by varying the ratio of these fuels. Fuel is then delivered using either as port or direct injection.

(ii) *Having two fuel circuits*: Dual fuel concept can be adopted. Fuel A can be injected in the intake duct (port injection) and Fuel B using a direct injection (in-cylinder). The proportion of these fuels can be used to control ignition, heat release rate and exhaust emissions.

20.7.7 Power

In both spark ignition and compression ignition engines, power can be increased by introducing more fuel into the combustion chamber. These engines can withstand the increased power, because the heat release rate in these engines is slow. However, in HCCI engines the entire mixture burns nearly simultaneously. Increasing the fuel-air ratio will result in even higher peak pressures and heat release rates. In addition, many of the viable control strategies for HCCI require thermal preheating of the charge. This will reduce the density and hence, the mass of the fuel-air charge in the combustion chamber, reducing power. These factors make it a challenging task to improve the power output in HCCI engines.

One way to increase power is to use fuels with different autoignition properties. This will lower the heat release rate and peak pressures and will make it possible to increase the equivalence ratio. Another way is to thermally stratify the charge. This will make different points in the compressed charge to have different temperatures and will burn at different times lowering the heat release rate. By this approach it is possible to increase power. A third way is to run the engine in HCCI mode only at part load conditions and run it as a diesel or spark ignition engine at full or near full load conditions. Since more research is required to successfully implement thermal stratification in the compressed charge, the last approach is being pursued more vigorously.

20.7.8 Emissions

Because HCCI operates on lean mixtures, the peak temperatures are lower in comparison to spark ignition and compression ignition engines. The lower peak temperatures reduces the formation of NO_X . This leads to lower NO_X emissions than those found in conventional engines. However, the low peak temperatures also lead to incomplete burning of fuel, especially near the walls of the combustion chamber. This leads to high carbon monoxide and hydrocarbon emissions. An oxidizing catalyst is required in removing the regulated species because the exhaust is still oxygen rich.

20.7.9 Difference in Engine Knock

In conventional spark-ignition engine knock or pinging occurs when some of the unburnt gases ahead of the flame spontaneously auto ignite. This causes a shock wave to traverse from the end gas region and an expansion wave to traverse into the end gas region. The two waves reflect off the boundaries of the combustion chamber and interact to produce high amplitude standing waves. In HCCI engines, ignition occurs due to piston compression. In this engine, the entire reactant mixture ignites (nearly) simultaneously. Since there are very little or no pressure differences between the different regions of the gas, there is no shock wave propagation and hence, no knocking. However, at high loads (i.e. high fuel-air ratios), knocking is a remote possibility even in HCCI.

20.7.10 Advantages and Disadvantages of HCCI Engine

Advantages:

(i) Thirty per cent fuel savings, while meeting current emissions norms.

(ii) They are fuel-lean and operate at a Diesel-like compression ratios.

(iii) It can achieve higher efficiencies than conventional SI engines.

(iv) Homogeneous mixing leads to cleaner combustion and lower emissions.

(v) Peak temperatures are lower than the typical SI engines,

(vi) NO_X and soot emissions are almost negligible.

(vii) It can operate on gasoline and diesel; and almost all alternative fuels.

(viii) HCCI efficiency is comparatively more due to low throttling losses.

Disadvantages

(i) High in-cylinder peak pressures may cause damage to the engine.

(ii) Fast heat release and pressure rise rates contribute to engine wear.

(iii) The auto-ignition is difficult to control, unlike the SI and CI engine

(iv) HCCI engines have a small power range.

(v) There are constraints at low loads due to lean flammability limits.

(vi) Problem at high loads due to in-cylinder pressure restrictions.

(vii) CO emissions are higher compared conventional engines.

(viii) Pre-catalyst hydrocarbon emissions are higher.

20.8 LEAN BURN ENGINE

Conventional engines using gasoline and diesel operating at full throttle employ an air-fuel mixture close to stoichiometric. For most of the hydrocarbon fuels the stoichiometric air-fuel ratio can be taken as 15:1. Beyond this ratio, the engine begins to misfire resulting in an unsteady combustion cycle. In the past, the air-fuel ratio was kept close to this figure, to prevent any combustion problems. Since the end of World War II, however, governments all over the world have started pushing the automotive industry to reduce automobile exhaust emissions. This, along with the realisation of diminishing oil reserves, have forced automotive designers to look at higher air-fuel ratio engines, in order to increase fuel efficiency. *These higher than average air-fuel ratio engines are called lean burn engines* and are being developed since the 1960s. The way that these engines work smoothly, despite burning air-fuel mixtures of about 18:1 has led to many new design features in lean burn technology. For smooth combustion, the amount of fuel and air entering the combustion chamber must be closely monitored. Even small variations when the mixture is so lean, can greatly affect the performance of the engine. The introduction of fuel injection combats this problem. Spraying of fuel directly before the inlet valve closure provides more or less an uniform mixture distribution. Modern lean burn engines use a lean mixture even greater than 20:1. Because of this, considerably less fuel compared to the stoichiometric ratio will be used.

In a lean burn engine the fuel must be injected into the combustion chamber where there is intensive swirling air motion. This concentrates the fuel around the spark plug which keeps the ignition duration constant for every cycle, preventing misfiring. In order to concentrate the fuel around the spark plug, the combustion chamber should be designed in such a way that the air motion swirls up towards the spark plug. At the same time, the spark plug should be placed in the centre of the combustion chamber. This makes the spark plug closer to the fuel. It prevents the fuel particles farthest from the spark plug self-igniting. This means that the compression ratio can be increased and higher fuel efficiency can be achieved. The above improvements enable the air-fuel ratio to be increased thereby decreasing the specific fuel consumption of the engine by 5–25%.

Lean burn engines also have the advantage of decreasing emissions. The amount of carbon monoxide emitted is less, as there is plenty of oxygen available to produce carbon dioxide. Unburned hydrocarbon emission is reduced by up to 80% in lean burn engines. This is because unburned hydrocarbons are released when combustion is not complete. Fuel injection prevents fuel droplets settling in the intake passage, by spraying them directly just behind the inlet valves. This helps to produce a homogeneous air-fuel mixture.

To put it in a nutshell, lean burn engines (both gasoline and diesel) enjoy higher fuel economy and cleaner emissions than conventionally tuned engines. They use less fuel and emit fewer unburned hydrocarbons and greenhouse gases while producing equivalent power of a like-sized "normal" combustion engine. They achieve lean burn status by employing higher compression ratios which develop higher cylinder pressure, significant air intake swirl and precise lean metered direct fuel injection.

The negative side of lean burn technology is increased exhaust NO_X emissions (due to higher heat and cylinder pressure) and a somewhat narrower speed-power-band (due to slower burn rates of lean mixtures). Vehicles that use these types of engines require more complex catalytic converters and are often limited to light duty uses (passenger vehicles).

20.8.1 Basics of Lean Burn Technology

A lean burn mode is a way to reduce throttling losses. An engine in a typical vehicle is designed for providing the power required for acceleration. At the same time must operate well below that point in normal steady-speed operation. Ordinarily, in SI engine, the power is reduced by partially closing a throttle. However, the extra work done in pumping air through the throttle reduces efficiency. If the air-fuel ratio is increased, then lower power can be achieved even at full throttle. At the same time the efficiency during normal driving can be higher. The engines designed for lean burning can employ higher compression ratios and thus provide better performance, efficient fuel use and low exhaust hydrocarbon emissions than those found in conventional gasoline engines. Ultra lean mixtures with very high air-fuel ratios can be achieved by direct injection engines only. Lean burn engines do not work well with modern three-way catalytic converter because they require a pollutant balance at the exhaust port so that they can carry out both oxidation and reduction reactions. Most modern engines run at or near the stoichiometric point. Alternatively, ultra-lean ratios can reduce NO_X emissions. Therefore, the main drawback of lean burning is that a complex catalytic converter system is required to reduce NO_X emissions.

20.8.2 Lean Burn Combustion

Gaseous fuels are well suited for lean burn operation. Any air-fuel reaction requires an energy source to initiate combustion. In lean burn engines, the combustion process is enhanced by pre-mixing the air and fuel upstream of the turbocharger before introduction into the cylinder. This creates a more homogenous mixture in the combustion chamber and reduces the occurrence of "knocking" or detonation. To prevent either knocking or misfiring, the combustion process must be controlled within a narrow operating window. Charge air temperatures and volume, together with air to fuel ratio, are constantly monitored. Engine controller regulates the fuel flow and air-gas mixture and ignition timing. Modern lean burn engines are designed to operate at a lean air-gas ratio of $\lambda = 1.7$. (Traditional stoichiometric natural gas engines have an air-gas ratio of $\lambda = 1.0$). A richer mixture (< 0.7) can potentially produce knocking and higher NO_X emissions; leaner mixture greater than $\lambda = 1.7$ may not combust reliably and cause misfiring, which raises HC emissions. Fully instrumented electronic engines with sensors and microprocessors in the new lean burn engines are critical for maintaining combustion within these boundaries.

The design of the lean burn engine incorporates a simple open combustion chamber housed in the piston crown. The shape of the piston crown introduces turbulence to the incoming air-fuel mixture that promotes more complete combustion by thoroughly exposing it to the advancing flame front. The cylinder head is flat and the spark plug is centrally located. The air and gaseous fuel are correctly mixed under the control of the engine management system.

20.8.3 Combustion Monitoring

In-cylinder sensors provide important data on the timing and quality of the combustion process, which is specifically important when engines are operated with lean mixtures or heavy EGR. Presently available techniques used to evaluate these data are direct pressure measurement with a pressure sensor and indirect monitoring through spark-plug ionization current. The spark-plug voltage ion method detects the ion density within the combustion chamber by measuring the decay time of voltage after a spark. Using this technique, the limits of lean burn or EGR can easily be detected. Another much cheaper method is to derive a combustion quality value from piston acceleration. To obtain this the crankshaft speed fluctuations are measured using the crank speed sensor.

20.8.4 Lean Burn Emissions

Potential application for lean burn technology is for gas engine and electric generation. One of the benefits of this technology is significantly reduced emissions in the exhaust. New lean burn gas engine generators have NO_X emissions as low as 0.85 g/bp-h, and produce low amounts of HC, CO and particulate matter. This allows the generator sets to meet the most stringent air quality regulations without after-treatment devices in the exhaust stream. For lower emissions, lean burn gas engine generator sets are frequently coupled with integrated after-treatment options such as Selective Catalytic Reduction (SCR) and Oxidation Catalysts, resulting in NO_X levels at or below 0.15 g/bp-h. With these after-treatment options, the gas engine generators have been shown to meet the most stringent prime power emissions regulations anywhere in the world

20.8.5 Fuel Flexibility

Another advantage of the lean burn technology with full-fledged electronic engine controls is the ability to operate on gas with a wide range of quality. A measurement called the Methane Number (MN) is used to determine fuel gas suitability as an engine fuel. Most natural gas has an MN from 70 to 97, and pipeline quality gas typically has MN of about 75. Resource recovery gas from landfills or sewage treatment facilities is typically of lower quality, but is often suitable for use in lean burn engines. Modern lean burn gas engine generators operate on gas with an MN of 50 or greater, providing excellent fuel flexibility. However, gas with a MN below 70 may require derating of the generator output.

Lean burn gas engine generator sets are setting a new standard for fuel efficiency, high power output for their size, and for low emissions. In regions with abundance of natural gas, these generator sets are providing highly reliable electric power for utility peaking, distributed generation, prime power and for combined heat and power systems.

20.8.6 Toyota Lean Burn Engine

A lean burn engine control system developed by Toyota is shown in Fig.20.10. It uses in-cylinder sensors to monitor combustion pressure (5), and a sequential individual injection system (1) to control fuelling on a cylinder-by-cylinder basis. The A/F ratio for the engine is monitored through a wide-range oxygen sensor installed in the exhaust down-pipe before the three-way catalytic converter (7).

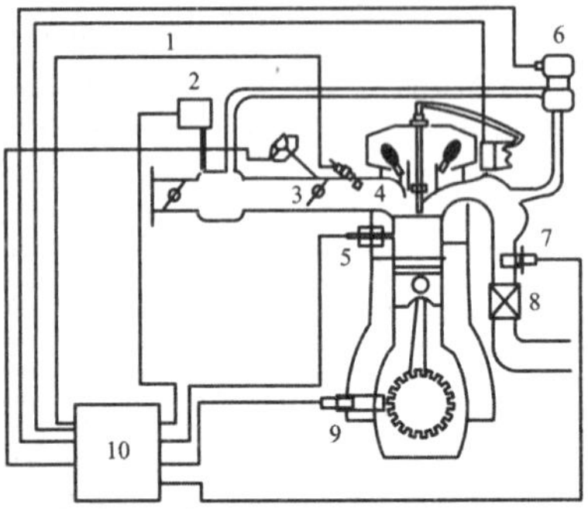

Fig. 20.10 Lean burn engine control system used on a Toyota engine

A novel feature incorporated is the use of a swirl control valve (3) mounted in the intake system. The intake tract for each cylinder is divided into two passages. One passage is smooth, which allows maximum gas flow for good cylinder charging. The other passage is fitted with a corkscrew-shaped flange (not shown) with helical port (4), which introduces swirl into the incoming air. The engine electronic control unit (10) can switch air flow in one of the two tracts by actuating the SCV. The engine operates in a lean burn mode when it is running under light to medium load conditions. The ECU directs the SCV to open-up the curved inlet passage to have well mixed incoming vapour due to a high level of turbulence through swirl. During combustion, the ECU monitors the pressure sensor signals for any signs of slow or incomplete burning and then appropriately modifies the A/F ratio using electronically controlled valve (2) or ignition timing on a cylinder-by-cylinder basis. Because of the continuous monitoring of the exhaust gas oxygen concentration, these facilities permit the engine to produce high efficiency at A/F ratios upto 25:1. Further, the engine speed is monitored by the speed sensor (9). There is also an EGR valve (6) to reduce NO_X emissions. A three-way catalytic converter (8) is fitted in the exhaust pipe to reduce harmful emissions. When the engine runs under high load conditions, specifically during overtaking or hill climbing, the ECU switches to stoichiometric operation for maximum power. To achieve this the ECU directs the SCV to open the smooth intake passage and uses the oxygen sensor signal to maintain an A/F ratio of 14.7:1.

20.8.7 Honda Lean Burn Systems

The newer Honda stratified charged lean burn engines operate on air-fuel ratios as high as 22:1 using precise control of fuel injection with strong air-fuel swirl created in the combustion chamber. It employs new linear air-fuel sensor and lean burn NO_X catalyst to further reduce the NO_X.

The amount of fuel drawn into the engine is much lower than a typical gasoline engine, which operates at 14.7:1. This lean burn ability by the necessity of the limits of physics, and the chemistry of combustion as it applies to a current gasoline engine must be limited to light load and lower RPM conditions. A "top" speed cut-off point is required since leaner gasoline fuel mixtures burn slower. For power to be produced combustion must be "complete" by the time the exhaust valve opens. This stratified-charge approach to lean burn combustion means that the air-fuel ratio is not equal throughout the cylinder. Instead, precise control over fuel injection and intake flow dynamics allows a denser concentration of fuel closer to the spark plug tip (richer), which is required for successful ignition and flame spread for complete combustion. The remainder of the cylinder's intake charge is progressively leaner with an overall average air-fuel ratio falling into the lean burn category of up to 22:1.

The older Honda engines that used lean burn (not all did) accomplished this by having a parallel fuel and intake system that fed a pre-chamber with the "ideal" ratio for initial combustion. This is called Compound Vortex Controlled Combustion (CVCC), which allowed lower emissions without the need for a catalytic converter. It had a normal inlet and exhaust valves plus a small auxiliary inlet valve which provided a relatively rich mixture near the spark plug. The remaining leaner air-fuel mixture is drawn into the cylinder through the main inlet valve. The volume near the spark plug is contained by a small perforated metal plate. Upon ignition, flame fronts emerge from perforations and ignite the remainder of the air-fuel charge. This combination of rich mixture near the spark plug and the lean mixture in the cylinder allows stable running. Complete combustion could be achieved with reduction in CO and HC emissions. It may be noted that these were carbureted engines and the relative *imprecise* nature of such system limited their applications.

20.8.8 Mitsubishi Ultra Lean Burn Combustion Engines

The ultra lean burn control system developed by Mitsubishi is shown in Fig.20.11. It uses a catalytic converter to reduce NO_X emissions. As air pollution has become more important to automotive companies and governments, the lean burn combustion technology is being developed and improved. Mitsubishi have created a lean burn engine that will operate a 40:1 air-fuel ratio mixture.

It may be noted that the "ultra lean burn mode" is not used for starting or accelerating the vehicle. For these tasks the engine uses a "superior output mode" which uses a leaner mixture. The reason is that the lean burn technique is not used during start up, is because more HC and CO emissions are created at this stage. This means that there is no advantage in using the lean burn to lower the performance engine at the start up stage. The "ultra lean burn" engine does, however contain new technologies. Instead of making the air-fuel mixture spiral around the combustion chamber, [Fig.20.12(a)], the Mitsubishi injector forces the mixture to tumble clockwise [Fig.20.12(b)] into

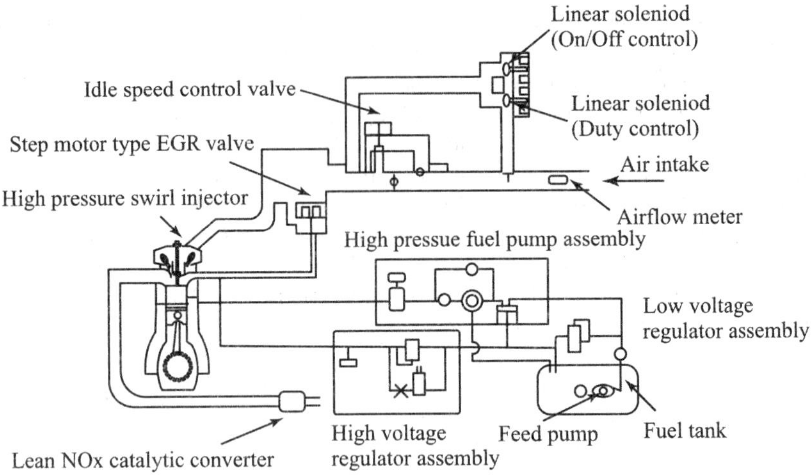

Fig. 20.11 Mitsubishi ultra lean burn engine

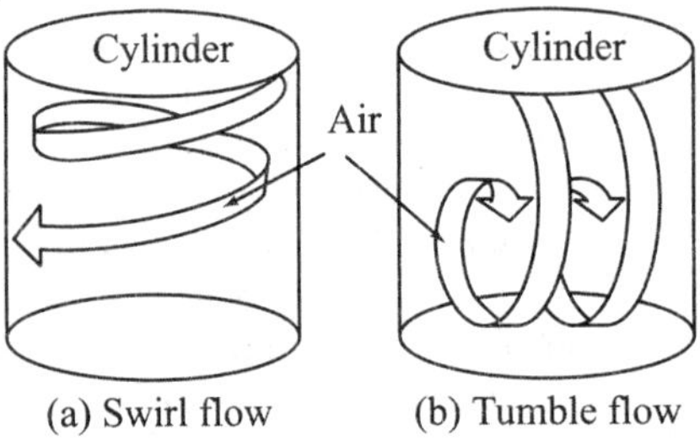

Fig. 20.12 Diagrams of swirl and tumble flows

the chamber, using upright and straight intake ports. This system breaks up as the piston compresses, forming eddies that push the fuel even closer to the spark plug. A new injector system has also been introduced which provides a more reliable source of ignition for lean burn engines. The stratified charge system atomises the fuel across the spark plug. The particles of fuel produced are much smaller than conventional processes, less than nine microns as opposed to 27 microns in a high pressure direct injection system.

20.9 STIRLING ENGINE

A Stirling engine is a heat engine operating on cyclic compression and expansion of air or any other gas. It was once called hot air engine. This engine was invented much before the invention of gasoline and diesel engines. In Stirling engine the working fluid is kept at different temperature levels. Because of this, there is a net conversion of heat energy to mechanical work.

The Stirling engine is vastly different from the internal-combustion engine used in automobiles. Invented by Robert Stirling in 1816, the Stirling engine has the potential to be much more efficient than a gasoline or diesel engine.

But, as of now, Stirling engines are used only in some very specialized applications, like in submarines or auxiliary power generators for yachts, where quiet operation is important. Although there hasn't been a successful mass-market application for the Stirling engine, many people are still working on it.

Like the steam engine, the Stirling engine is traditionally classified as an external combustion engine. All heat transfers to and from the working fluid take place through the engine wall. This contrasts with an internal combustion engine where heat addition is by combustion of a fuel within the engine. It is also different from steam engine (or more generally a Rankine cycle engine) where the working fluid is both in its liquid and gaseous phases.

In Stirling engine a fixed quantity of gaseous fluid such as air is used as the working medium. In a typical heat engine, the general cycle consists of compressing the cool gas, heating the gas, expanding the hot gas, and finally cooling the gas before repeating the cycle. The efficiency of the process is restricted by the efficiency of the Carnot cycle, which depends on the temperature difference between the hot and cold reservoir. Stirling engine uses the Stirling cycle, which is different from the cycles used in internal combustion engines. For example:

- The gasses used inside a Stirling engine never leave the engine. There are no exhaust valves that vent high-pressure gasses, as in a gasoline or diesel engine. There is no combustion taking place inside the engine. Because of this, Stirling engines are very quiet.

- The Stirling cycle uses an external heat source, which could be anything from gasoline to solar energy to the heat produced by decaying plants.

The Stirling engine is noted for its high efficiency (compared to steam engines), quiet operation, and the ease with which it can use almost any heat source. This compatibility with alternative and renewable energy sources has become increasingly significant as the price of conventional fuels rises. Further, there is great concern regarding oil crisis and climate change. This engine is evincing a lot of interest as the core component of combined heat and power (CHP) units, in which it is more efficient and safer than a comparable steam engine.

20.9.1 Principle of Operation

The engine is designed in such a way that the working gas is generally compressed in the colder portion of the engine and expanded in the hotter portion, resulting in a net conversion of heat into work. An internal Regenerative heat exchanger increases the Stirling engine's thermal efficiency compared to simpler hot air engines which are lacking this feature.

The key principle of a Stirling engine is that there is always a fixed amount of a gas sealed inside the engine. The Stirling cycle involves a series of events that change the pressure of the gas inside the engine, causing it to do work. There are several properties of gasses that are critical to the operation of Stirling engines. Important principles to keep in mind are:

(a) If the temperature of a fixed amount of gas in a fixed volume of space is raised then the pressure of that gas will increase.

(b) If a fixed amount of gas is compressed (decrease the volume of its space), then the temperature of that gas will increase.

Figure 20.13 shows a simplified sketch of the Stirling engine. Let us go through each part of the Stirling cycle. Our simplified engine uses two cylinders. One cylinder is heated by an external heat source (such as flame), and the other is cooled by an external cooling source (such as ice). The gas chambers of the two cylinders are connected as shown in Fig.20.13. The pistons are connected to each other mechanically by a linkage (not shown in figure) that determines how they will move in relation to one another.

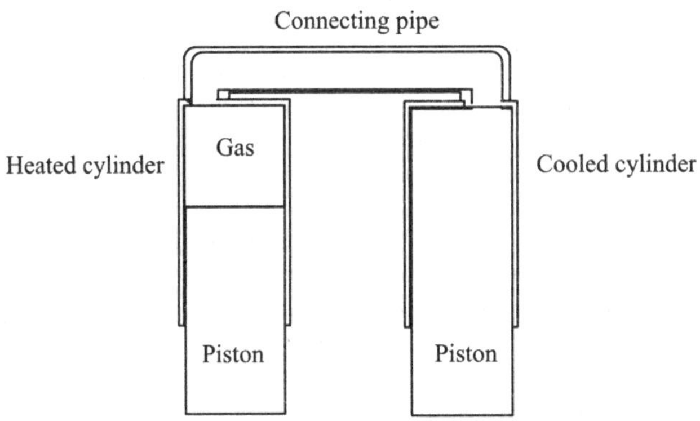

Fig. 20.13 Working Principle of a Stirling Engine

There are four processes in the Stirling cycle. The two pistons in the Fig.20.13 accomplish all of the following processes of the cycle:

(i) Heat is added to the fixed mass of gas inside the heated cylinder (left), causing pressure to build as per principle (a). This forces the piston to move down. During this stage of the cycle the work is done.

(ii) The left piston will be made to move up while the right piston moves down by means of a suitable link mechanism (not shown in the figure). This pushes the hot gas into the cooled cylinder, which quickly cools the gas to the temperature of the cooling source, lowering its pressure. This makes it easier to compress the gas in the next stage of the cycle.

(iii) The piston in the cooled cylinder (right) starts to compress the gas. Heat generated by this compression is removed by the cooling source.

(iv) The right piston moves up while the left piston moves down. This forces the gas into the heated cylinder, where it quickly heats up, building pressure, at which point the cycle repeats.

It may be noted that the Stirling engine develops power only during the first process (stage 1) of the cycle. There are two ways to increase the power output of a Stirling cycle:

(i) *Increase power output in stage one*: In stage one of the cycle, the pressure of the heated gas which pushes the piston down performs work. Increasing the pressure during this stage of the cycle will increase the power output of the engine. One way of increasing the pressure is by increasing the temperature of the gas. When we take a look at a two-piston Stirling engine, we will see how a device called a regenerator can improve the power output of the engine by temporarily storing heat.

(ii) *Decrease power usage in stage three*: In stage three of the cycle, the pistons perform work on the gas, using some of the power produced in stage one. Lowering the pressure during this stage of the cycle can decrease the power required during this stage of the cycle. In effect this will increase the power output of the engine. One way to decrease the pressure is to cool the gas to a lower temperature.

To summarize, the Stirling engine uses the temperature difference between its hot end and cold end to establish a cycle of a fixed mass of gas, heated and expanded, and cooled and compressed, thus converting thermal energy into mechanical energy. Greater the temperature difference between the hot and cold sources, greater will be the thermal efficiency. The maximum theoretical efficiency is equivalent to the Carnot cycle, however the efficiency of a real engine is less than this value due to friction and other losses.

20.9.2 Types of Stirling Engines

There are two major types of Stirling engines. They are distinguished by the way they move the air between the hot and cold sides of the cylinder:

(i) *The two piston alpha type*: In this design, pistons are in two independent cylinders, and gas is driven between the hot and cold spaces.

(ii) *The displacement type*: This design is known as *beta and gamma* types. This type uses an insulated mechanical displacer to push the working gas between the hot and cold sides of the cylinder. The displacer is large enough to insulate the hot and cold sides of the cylinder thermally and to displace a large quantity of gas. There must be enough gap between the displacer and the cylinder wall to allow gas to flow around the displacer easily.

20.9.3 Alpha Stirling Engine

An alpha Stirling contains two power pistons in separate cylinders, one hot and one cold. The hot cylinder is situated inside the high temperature heat exchanger and the cold cylinder is situated inside the low temperature heat exchanger. This type of engine has a high power-to-volume ratio. However, it has technical problems due to high temperature of the hot piston and the durability of its seals. In practice, this piston usually carries a large insulating head to move the seals away from the hot zone at the expense of some additional dead space.

20.9.4 Working Principle of Alpha Stirling Engine

Figures 20.14 shows the working of an alpha Stirling engine. But they do not show internal heat exchangers in the compression and expansion spaces, which are needed to produce power. A regenerator would be placed in the pipe connecting the two cylinders. The crankshaft has also been omitted. There are four steps involved

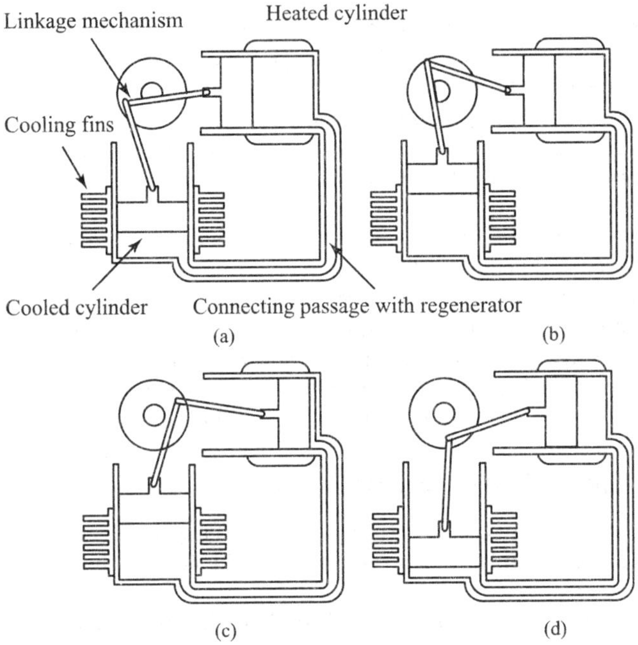

Fig. 20.14 Stirling engine

(i) Refer Fig.20.14(a). Most of the working gas is in contact with the hot cylinder walls. During the first part of the cycle, the gas is heated and pressure builds up. This forces the piston to move to the left *doing work*. The gas in the hot cylinder is at its maximum volume. The cooled piston stays approximately stationary because it is at the point of revolution where it changes direction.

(ii) In the second stage [refer Fig.20.14(b)] both the pistons move. The heated piston moves to the right and the cooled piston moves up. This makes most of the hot gas to move into the cooled piston cylinder through the connecting passage with regenerator.

The regenerator is a device that can temporarily store heat. It may be a heated mesh of wire through which the hot gas pass through. The large surface area of the wire must quickly absorb most of the heat. This leaves less heat to be removed by the cooling fins. Because of cooling the pressure drops.

(iii) In this stage all the gas is in the cooled cylinder and cooling continues [refer Fig.20.14(c)]. The cooled piston, powered by flywheel momentum starts to compress the gas. The heat generated by the compression is removed by the cooling fins. The gas in the cooled cylinder reaches the maximum volume.

(iv) In the last phase of the cycle, both pistons move – the cooled piston moves down while the heated piston moves to the left. This forces the gas across the regenerator (where it picks up the heat that was stored there during the previous cycle) and into the heated cylinder. At this point, the cycle begins again.

20.9.5 Beta Stirling Engine

A beta Stirling has a single power piston arranged within the same cylinder on the same shaft as a displacer piston. The displacer piston is a loose fit and does not extract any power from the expanding gas but only serves to shuttle the working gas from the hot heat exchanger to the cold heat exchanger. When the working gas is pushed to the hot end of the cylinder it expands and pushes the power piston. When it is pushed to the cold end of the cylinder it contracts and the momentum of the machine, usually enhanced by a flywheel, pushes the power piston the other way to compress the gas. Unlike the alpha type, the beta type avoids the technical problems of hot moving seals.

20.9.6 Working Principle of Beta Stirling Engine

The following Fig.20.15(a–d) gives the details of beta Stirling engine, but do not show the internal heat exchangers or a regenerator, which will be placed in the gas path around the displacer. The working principle is as follows:

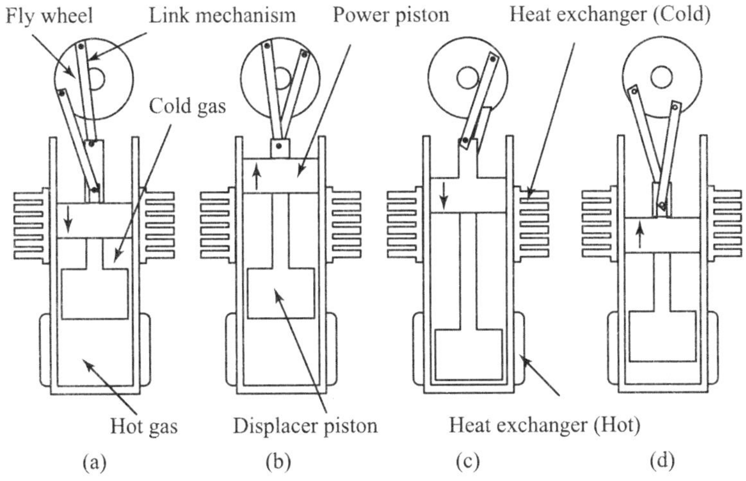

Fig. 20.15 Working Principle of a Beta Type Stirling Engine

(i) To start with, power piston compresses the cooled gas in the cold heat exchanger space passing it through the displacer piston towards the hot heat exchanger [Fig.20.15(a)].

(ii) Because of the heat addition from the hot exchanger, pressure of the gas increases and pushes the power piston to the farthest limit of the power stroke [Fig.20.15(b)].

(iii) The displacer piston now moves down, shunting the gas to the cold end of the cylinder [Fig.20.15(c)] where it gets cooled quickly.

(iv) The cooled gas is now compressed by the power piston due to the fly-wheel momentum. This takes less energy, since when gas is cooled its pressure drops [Fig.20.15(d)] and the cycle repeats.

A gamma Stirling is simply a beta Stirling in which the power piston is mounted in a separate cylinder alongside the displacer piston cylinder, but is still connected to the same flywheel. The gas in the two cylinders can flow freely between them and remains a single body. This configuration produces a lower compression ratio but is mechanically simpler and often used in multi-cylinder Stirling engines.

20.9.7 The Stirling Cycle

The ideal p-V diagram of a Stirling cycle consists of four thermodynamic processes acting on the working fluid (Fig.20.16).

(i) *Isothermal expansion*: The expansion-space and associated heat exchanger are maintained at a constant high temperature, and the gas undergoes near-isothermal expansion (1–2) absorbing heat from the hot source.

(ii) *Constant-volume heat-removal*: The gas is passed through the regenerator, where it cools transferring heat to the regenerator for use in the next cycle (2–3).

(iii) *Isothermal compression*: The compression space and associated heat exchanger are maintained at a constant low temperature so the gas undergoes near-isothermal compression rejecting heat to the cold sink (3–4).

(iv) *Constant-volume heat-addition*: The gas passes back through the regenerator where it recovers much of the heat transferred in (2–3), heating up on its way to the expansion space (4–1).

Theoretical thermal efficiency of the cycle equals that of the hypothetical Carnot cycle - i.e. the highest efficiency attainable by any heat engine. However, the efficiency of actual engines is much less due to:

(i) limits of convective heat transfer, and viscous flow (friction).

(ii) practical mechanical considerations, such as kinematic linkage

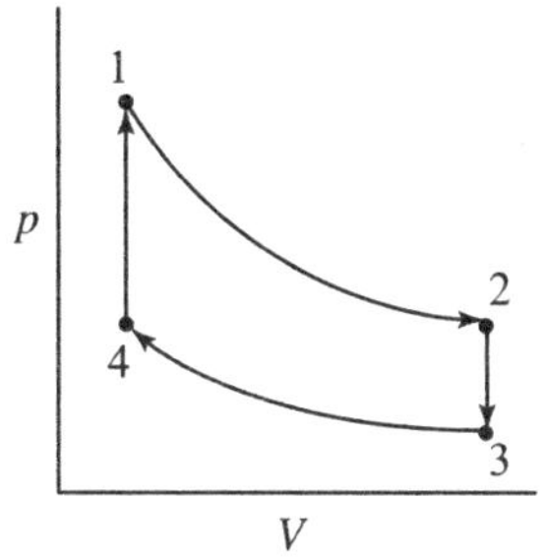

Fig. 20.16 p-V diagram of the ideal the Stirling cycle

(iii) limitations imposed by available non-ideal materials such as non-ideal properties of the working gas, thermal conductivity, tensile strength, creep, rupture strength, etc.

(iv) ideal isothermal expansion and compression is difficult to achieve

20.9.8 Displacer Type Stirling Engine

In this design there is one piston and one displacer. A temperature difference is required between the top and bottom of the large cylinder in order to run the engine. In the case of the low-temperature difference (LTD) stirling engine, even the temperature difference between your hand and the surrounding air is enough to run the engine. The power piston in the displacer type stirling engine, is tightly sealed and is controlled to move up and down as the gas inside expands. The displacer on the other hand is very loosely fitted so that air can move freely between the hot and cold sections of the engine as the piston moves up and down. The displacer moves up and down to control the heating and cooling of the gas in the engine.

20.9.9 Pressurization

In most high power Stirling engines, both the minimum pressure and mean pressure of the working fluid are above atmospheric. The initial engine pressurization can be realized by any one of the following methods.

(i) a pump,

(ii) filling the engine from a compressed gas tank,

(iii) just by sealing the engine when the mean temperature is lower than the mean operating temperature.

All of the above methods increase the mass of working fluid in the thermodynamic cycle. The heat exchangers must be sized appropriately to supply the necessary heat transfer rates. If the heat exchangers are well designed they can supply the heat flux needed for convective heat transfer. The engine will in a first approximation produce power in proportion to the mean pressure. In practice, the maximum pressure is limited to the safe pressure of the pressure vessel. A difficulty of pressurization is that while it improves the power, the heat input to the pressurized gas also increases proportionately to the increased power. The higher heat transfer rate is difficult with pressurization. The increased pressure demands increased thicknesses of the walls of the engine. This, in turn, will increase the resistance to heat transfer.

20.9.10 Lubricants and Friction

A modern Stirling engine and generator can produce 55 kW electrical output, for combined heat and power (CHP) applications. At high temperatures and pressures, the oxygen in air-pressurized crankcases, or in the working gas of hot air engines, can combine with the engine's lubricating oil and explode. Lubricants can also clog heat exchangers, especially the regenerator. For these reasons, designers prefer non-lubricated, low-coefficient of friction materials (such as rulon or graphite), with low normal forces on the moving parts, especially for sliding seals. Some designs avoid sliding surfaces altogether by using diaphragms for sealed pistons. These are some of the factors that allow Stirling engines to have lower maintenance requirements and longer life than internal-combustion engines.

20.9.11 Comparison with Internal Combustion Engines

In contrast to internal combustion engines, Stirling engines have the potential to use renewable heat sources more easily, to be quieter, and to be more reliable with lower maintenance. They are preferred for applications that value these unique advantages, particularly if the cost per unit energy generated is more important than the capital cost per unit power. On this basis, Stirling engines are cost competitive up to about 100 kW.

Compared to an internal combustion engine of the same power rating, Stirling engines currently have a higher capital cost and are usually larger and heavier. However, they are more efficient than most internal combustion engines. Their lower maintenance requirements make the overall energy cost comparable. The thermal efficiency is also comparable (for small engines), ranging from 15% to 30%. For applications such as micro-CHP, a Stirling engine is often preferable to an internal combustion engine. However, Stirling engines are generally not price-competitive as an automobile engine, due to high cost per unit power, low power density and high material costs.

20.9.12 Advantages and Disadvantages of Stirling Engine

Advantages:

(i) Stirling engines can run directly on any available heat source, not just one produced by combustion, so they can run on heat from biological, geothermal, nuclear sources, solar or waste heat from industrial processes.

(ii) A continuous combustion process can be used to supply heat, so those emissions associated with the intermittent combustion processes of a reciprocating internal combustion engine can be reduced.

(iii) Most types of Stirling engines have the bearing and seals on the cool side of the engine. They require only less lubricant and last longer than other reciprocating engine types.

(iv) The engine mechanisms are in some ways simpler than other reciprocating engine types. No valves are needed, and the burner system can be relatively simple. Crude Stirling engines can be made using common household materials.

(v) A Stirling engine uses a single-phase working fluid which maintains an internal pressure close to the design pressure. Thus for a properly designed system the risk of explosion is low. In comparison, a steam engine uses a two-phase gas/liquid working fluid, so a faulty release valve can cause an explosion.

(vi) In some cases, low operating pressure allows the use of lightweight cylinders.

(vii) They can be built to run quietly and without an air supply, for air-independent propulsion use in submarines.

(viii) They start easily (albeit slowly, after warmup) and run more efficiently in cold weather, whereas the internal combustion which starts quickly in warm weather, but not in cold weather.

(ix) A Stirling engine used for pumping water can be configured so that the water cools the compression space. This is most effective when pumping cold water.

(x) They are extremely flexible.

(xi) They can be used as CHP in the winter and as a cooler in summer.

(xii) Waste heat is easily harvested (compared to waste heat from an internal combustion engine) making Stirling engines useful for dual-output heat and power systems.

Disadvantages: Size and cost issues

(i) Stirling engine designs require heat exchangers for heat input and for heat output. They must be able to withstand the pressure of the working fluid. Note that the pressure is proportional to the engine power output. In addition, the expansion-side heat exchanger is often at very high temperature, so the materials must resist the corrosive effects of the heat source, and have low creep (deformation). Typically these material requirements substantially increase the cost of the engine. The materials and assembly costs for a high temperature heat exchanger typically accounts for 40% of the total engine cost.

(ii) All thermodynamic cycles require large temperature differentials for efficient operation. In an external combustion engine, the heater temperature always equals or exceeds the expansion temperature. This means that the metallurgical requirements for the heater material are very demanding, which is similar to a gas turbine. But is in contrast to gasoline or diesel engine, where the expansion temperature can far exceed the metallurgical limit of the engine materials. This is because the input heat source is not conducted through the engine, so engine materials operate closer to the average temperature of the working gas.

(iii) Dissipation of waste heat is especially complicated because the coolant temperature is kept as low as possible to maximize thermal efficiency. This increases the size of the radiators, which can make packaging difficult. Along with materials cost, this has been one of the factors limiting the adoption of Stirling engines as automotive prime movers. For other applications such as ship propulsion and stationary micro-generation systems using combined heat and power (CHP) high power density is not required.

Power and torque issues

(i) Stirling engines, especially those that run on small temperature differentials, are quite large for the amount of power that they produce (i.e., they have low specific power). This is primarily due to the heat transfer coefficient of gaseous convection which limits the heat flux that can be attained in a typical cold heat exchanger to about 500 $W/(m^2K)$, and in a hot heat exchanger to about 500-5000 $W/(m^2K)$.

Compared with internal combustion engines, this makes it more challenging for the engine designer to transfer heat into and out of the working gas. Because of the thermal efficiency, the required heat transfer increases with decrease in temperature difference. The heat exchanger surface (and cost) per kW output increases with $1/\Delta T^2$. Therefore, the specific cost of very low temperature difference engines is very high.

(ii) A Stirling engine cannot start instantly. It literally needs to "warm up". This is true for all external combustion engines, but the warm up time may be longer for Stirling engines than for others such as steam engines. Stirling engines are best option for constant speed engines.

(iii) Power output of a Stirling tends to be constant and to adjust it can sometimes require careful design and additional mechanisms. Typically, changes in output are achieved by varying the displacement of the engine (often through use of a swashplate crankshaft arrangement), or by changing the quantity of working fluid, or by altering the piston/displacer phase angle, or in some cases simply by altering the engine load.

Gas choice issues

(i) The used gas should have a low heat capacity, so that a given amount of transferred heat leads to a large increase in pressure. Considering this issue, helium would be the best gas because of its very low heat capacity.

Air is a viable working fluid, but the oxygen in a highly pressurized air engine can cause fatal accidents caused by lubricating oil explosions.

(ii) Hydrogen's low viscosity and high thermal conductivity make it the most powerful working gas, primarily because the engine can run faster than with other gases. However, due to hydrogen absorption, and given the high diffusion rate associated with this low molecular weight gas, particularly at high temperatures, H_2 will leak through the solid metal of the heater. Diffusion through carbon steel is too high to be practical, but may be acceptably low for metals such as aluminum, or even stainless steel. Certain ceramics also greatly reduce diffusion.

Hermetic pressure vessel seals are necessary to maintain pressure inside the engine without replacement of lost gas. For high temperature differential (HTD) engines, auxiliary systems may need to be added to maintain high pressure working fluid. These systems can be a gas storage bottle or a gas generator. Hydrogen can also cause the embrittlement of metals. Hydrogen is a flammable gas, which is a safety concern if released from the engine.

(iii) Most technically advanced Stirling engines, like those developed for United States government labs, use helium as the working gas. It is because it functions close to the efficiency and power density of hydrogen with fewer of the material containment issues. Helium is inert, which removes all risk of flammability, both real and perceived. Helium is relatively expensive, and must be supplied as bottled gas.

(iv) Some engines use air or nitrogen as the working fluid. These gases have much lower power density (which increases engine costs). However, they are more convenient to use and they minimize the problems of gas containment and supply (which decreases costs). The use of compressed air in contact with flammable materials or substances such as lubricating oil, introduces an explosion hazard, because compressed air contains a high partial pressure of oxygen. However, oxygen can be removed from air through an oxidation reaction or bottled nitrogen can be used, which is nearly inert and very safe.

20.9.13 Applications

Applications of the Stirling engine range from heating and cooling to underwater power systems. A Stirling engine can function in reverse as a heat pump for heating or cooling. Other uses include: combined heat and power, solar power generation, Stirling cryocoolers, heat pump, marine engines, and low temperature difference engines

20.9.14 Future of Stirling Engines

There are a couple of key characteristics that make Stirling engines impractical for use in many applications, including in most cars and trucks. Because the heat source is external, it takes a little while for the engine to respond to changes in the amount of heat being applied to the cylinder – it takes time for the heat to be conducted through the cylinder walls and into the gas inside the engine. This means that:

(i) The engine requires some time to warm up before it can produce useful power.

(ii) The engine cannot change its power output quickly.

These shortcomings all but guarantee that it won't replace the internal-combustion engine in cars. However, a Stirling engine powered hybrid car might be feasible

20.10 STRATIFIED CHARGE ENGINE

Conventionally there are two types of internal combustion engines, viz., gasoline and diesel which are well established. However, each one of them has its own limitations. Gasoline engines have very good full load power characteristics, but have rather poor part load efficiency. Diesel engines have good part load characteristics but have low smoke-limited power and higher weight-to-power ratio. The use of higher compression ratios poses additional problems of maintenance and higher losses in diesel operation. For an automotive engine both part load efficiency and full load power are very important because during the operating life of the engines most of the time they work under part load conditions. The maximum power is controlled by the speed, acceleration and other characteristics of the vehicle.

Therefore, there is a need to develop an engine which combines the advantages of both gasoline and diesel engines. At the same time it should avoid, as far as possible, their disadvantages. *Stratified charge engine is an attempt in this direction.* It is an engine which is midway between the homogeneous charge spark-ignition engine, and the heterogeneous charge compression ignition engine.

Charge stratification means providing different fuel-air mixture strengths at various places in the combustion chamber – a relatively rich mixture at and in the vicinity of the spark plug and a leaner mixture in the rest of the combustion chamber. That is, the whole fuel-air mixture is distributed in layers or strata of different mixture strengths across the combustion chamber while the overall mixture is rather lean.

Thus, the stratified charge engine is usually defined as a spark ignition internal combustion engine in which the mixture in the zone of spark plug is very much richer than that in the rest of the combustion chamber, i.e. one which burns leaner overall fuel-air mixtures.

20.10.1 Advantages of Burning Leaner Overall Fuel-Air Mixtures

(i) *Higher thermodynamic efficiency*: The spark ignition engine output is controlled by means of a throttle. This varies the quantity of the mixture inducted during the suction stroke while keeping the mixture strength nearly constant. The diesel engine which is unthrottled, the output is controlled by varying the amount of fuel injected into a constant amount of air every cycle. Thus the gasoline engine operates within a very narrow range of fuel air ratios whereas the diesel engine operates over a much wider range of lean mixture strength.

The thermodynamic efficiency of the Otto cycle is given by

$$\eta = 1 - \frac{1}{r^{\gamma-1}} \tag{20.1}$$

The value of γ for air is 1.4 and for chemically correct carburetted fuel air mixture is around 1.3. A leaner mixture will have higher values of γ which will be between 1.3 and 1.4. It is evident that the eqn.20.1 would result in slightly higher thermodynamic efficiency for lean mixture, refer curve 1 in Fig.20.17. It is to be noted that the range of mixture strength is quite narrow for spark-ignition engine (between 0.8 and 1.2). However, for diesel engine the range (between 0.1 and 0.8) is quite wide (curve 2). This is one of the reasons for better part load efficiency of the diesel engine. The unthrottled diesel engine has an excess air of about 20 to 40 per cent at full load which increases progressively at part load as reduced amounts of fuel are injected. This is in contrast to the almost constant mixture strength operation of the gasoline engine.

Figure 20.17 shows the variation of theoretical efficiencies of Otto (1), diesel ((2) and stratified charge engine (3) for different mixture strengths under ideal conditions. It can be seen that the part load efficiency of the stratified charged engine is much better than the gasoline engine of comparable compression ratio, and almost approaches the efficiency of the diesel engine. However, it is to be noted that the diesel engine has a much higher compression ratio and hence, has an advantage due to this factor.

Thus, with the use of leaner mixtures and a slightly higher compression ratio in a SI engine, a performance level approaching that of the CI engine can be achieved. This helps to overcome many disadvantages of diesel operation. For example a mandatory high compression ratio for better starting and good combustion over a wide range of mixture strength, and poor air utilization are the main concern of the diesel engines. Use of high compression ratio brings with it a host of problems. It involves greater maintenance, higher mechanical losses and higher weight to power ratio. The poor air utilization results in poor fuel economy and smoky operation at higher loads.

As already mentioned, another important point to note in Fig.20.17 is the limited range of mixture strength (0.8 to 1.2) which can be used in a gasoline engine. For complete combustion, propagation of flame throughout the mixture is a must. In other words only those mixtures through which flame propagation is possible can be used. In a single-cylinder engine, a mixture strength below a relative fuel-air ratio of 0.8 will result in misfiring. For a multi-cylinder engine this becomes 0.85 due to imperfect distribution among the cylinders. The maximum output mixture strength is about 1.05 to 1.1 (1.2 for multi-cylinder

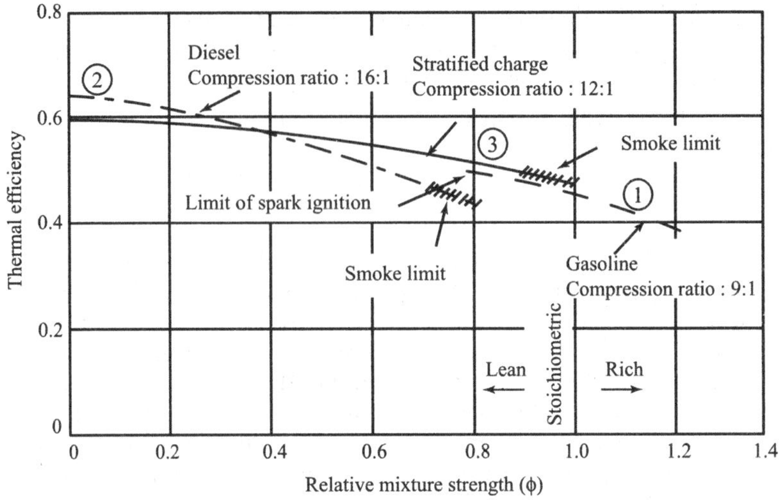

Fig. 20.17 Theoretical efficiencies of Otto, Diesel and stratified charge engine cycles for various mixture strength

engine). Minimum specific fuel consumption is obtained at a relative fuel-air ratio of 0.85 to 0.9 below which flame propagation becomes slow and cycle to cycle fluctuations occur. This limits the use of leaner mixtures and hence limits the gain in thermodynamic efficiency in SI engine. In the stratified charge engine a relative fuel-air ratio as low as 0.2 (corresponding to idling conditions) can be used.

Another disadvantage of the nearly constant mixture strength operation of the gasoline engine is that it results in almost constant peak cycle temperature over the full load range. This means that the losses due to heat transfer, dissociation at high temperature, and variable specific heats would be much higher at part loads. This shortcoming of the gasoline engine can be avoided by using charge stratification.

(ii) *Reduced air pollution*: The use of overall lean mixture in stratified charge engine results in reduced amount of oxides of nitrogen (NO_x) and carbon monoxide. The hydrocarbons are also low. In SI engine, higher hydrocarbons in exhaust are due to flame quenching at the combustion chamber walls. If charge stratification is used, this quenching effect is drastically reduced. It is because, almost pure air will be present near the cold combustion chamber walls at part loads. There are three distinct advantages of using charge stratification:

(a) no throttling losses,

(b) less prone for knock due to reduced residence time under high pressure and temperature conditions, and

(c) multi-fuel capability.

20.10.2 Methods of Charge Stratification

The stratified charge engines can be classified into two main categories, according to the method of formation of the heterogeneous mixture in the combustion chamber.

(i) Those using fuel injection and positive ignition (including swirl stratified charge engines).

(ii) Those using carburetion alone.

20.10.3 Stratification by Fuel Injection and Positive Ignition

The first attempt to obtain charge stratification was made by Ricardo around 1922. The details of which are shown in Fig.20.18. A relatively rich mixture was formed at the vicinity of the spark plug by an auxiliary spray while another spray of fuel in the combustion chamber formed a leaner mixture. This arrangement could give combustion over a relatively wide range of mixture strengths with overall very lean operation giving efficiencies as high as 35 percent. However, the range was limited at higher speed. At loads higher than about 50 per cent of the full load the engine did not work satisfactorily, presumably due to too rich a mixture near the spark plug.

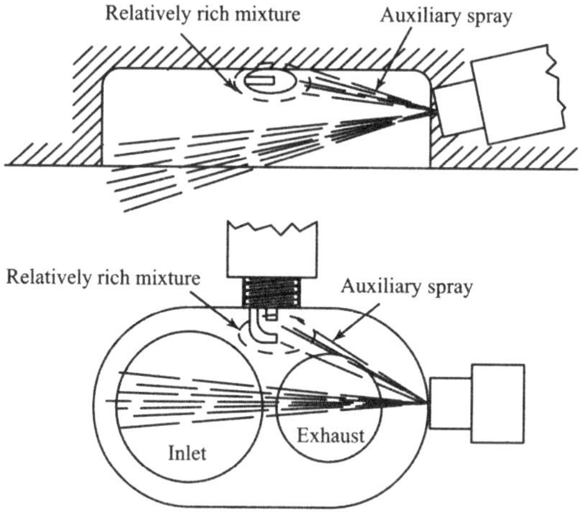

Fig. 20.18 Ricardo's first charge stratification approach

Prechamber stratified charge engine: Later Ricardo used a small prechamber (Fig.20.19) fitted with injector and the spark plug.

In this arrangement a rich mixture is formed near the spark plug by fuel supply from the injector. A carburettor supplies lean mixture to the main combustion chamber. The auxiliary charge burns in prechamber and comes out through its throat into the main chamber and burns the lean mixture present there. Thus a leaner overall mixture can be burned.

This approach involves many problems of engine operations such as

(i) getting good performance at the full load operation.

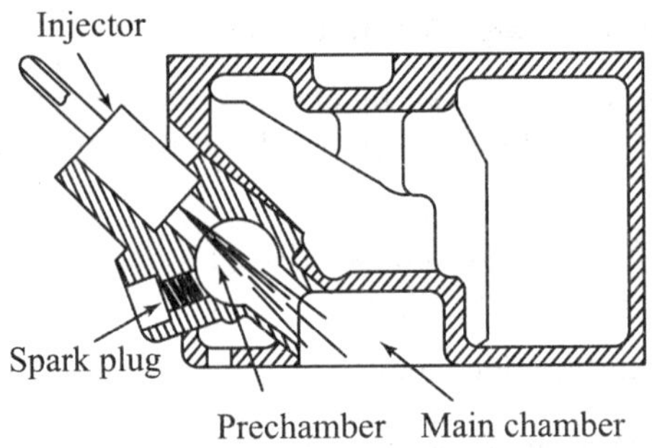

Fig. 20.19 Ricardo's prechamber stratification

(ii) improper burning of rich mixture at full load due to improper fuel distribution and incomplete scavenging of the prechamber.

(iii) loss of thermal efficiency due to throttling.

20.10.4 Volkswagen PCI stratified charge engine

Figure 20.20 shows the Volkswagen PCI stratified charge engine. It consists of a spherical un-scavenged pre-chamber comprises approximately 25-30 per cent of the compression volume. It is linked to the main combustion chamber by a relatively large prechamber opening through a flow passage. The main combustion chamber is disc-shaped. It has no squish surfaces but a slight swirl is induced by the intake port. The injection nozzle and spark plug are arranged in sequence in the flow direction during compression. It is for the purpose of spark plug to receive a mixture of incoming air with fuel already dispersed in air. This is expected to avoid over-richment at the spark plug. The total fuel volume is divided and is injected partly into the prechamber and partly in the intake manifold respectively. A relatively rich mixture is made available at spark plug under all operating conditions. Load regulation is achieved primarily by adjusting the mixture strength introduced into the main combustion chamber.

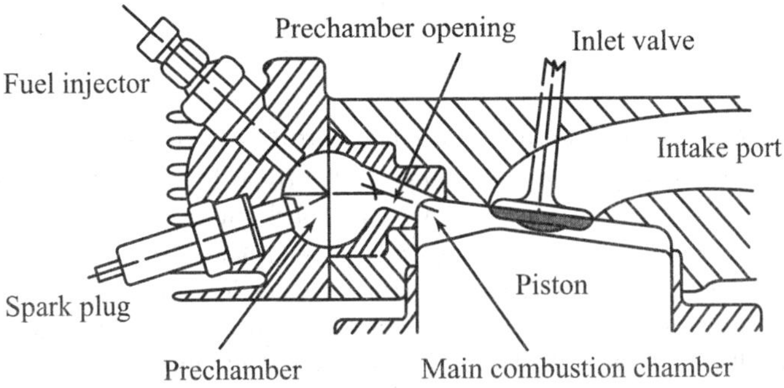

Fig. 20.20 Volkswagen PCI stratified charge engine

The main advantage of this system is that unlike other stratification processes, the fuel injection timing need not to be varied. This is a good simplification. The octane requirement is comparatively low, especially at higher speeds. It can be easily operated on very lean mixtures (relative air-fuel ratios greater than 2) which is also advantageous from exhaust emission point of view.

20.10.5 Broderson Method of Stratification

Part load and full load performance of gasoline engines are not the same. There are two possibilities to tackle the problems of part load and full load performance. One way is to use fuel injection alone. Control the mixture strengths in auxiliary and main combustion chambers by means of injection timings. Another way is to use carburetion alone to obtain stratification with or without prechamber.

Figure 20.21 shows the Broderson method of charge stratification. It consists of an engine with a divided combustion chamber. The small or auxiliary chamber contains the injector, the intake valve and the spark plug. Entire fuel is injected into the auxiliary chamber.

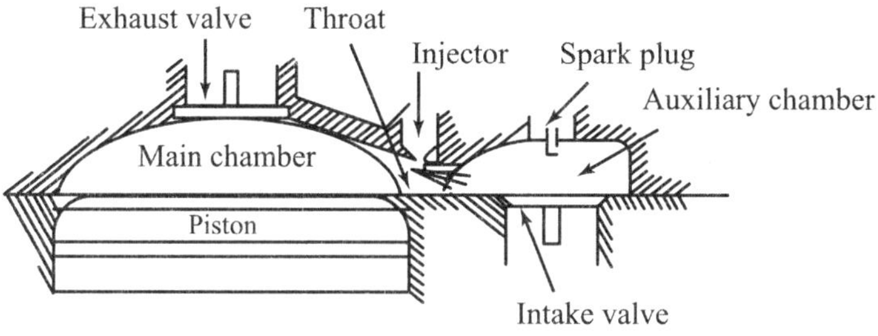

Fig. 20.21 Broderson method of stratification

At light loads the fuel can be injected after bdc, i.e. after the start of compression stroke. This is a situation in which the air is moving from main chamber into the auxiliary chamber. Almost all the fuel injected into the auxiliary chamber will remain there and will form an ignitable mixture near the spark plug. The main chamber will contain only air or very lean mixture. Due to the blast of flame from the auxiliary chamber due to torch effect, the lean mixture in the main chamber is burnt. For rapid and complete burning of this lean mixture the main chamber must be designed to ensure proper turbulence. This will enable mixing of the hot burning mixture coming out of the chamber with the mixture in the main chamber.

At full load the fuel is injected before bdc, i.e. during the suction stroke. It is intimately mixed with whole of the air resulting in a mixture of uniform strength throughout the combustion space. The flame produced by the spark plug will spread into both the chambers just like in the normal spark ignition operation.

The Broderson method possess the advantage of altogether avoiding the pumping losses due to throttling. In addition, a higher part load efficiency due to lean mixture and knockless operation at full load are achieved. This method also gives lower exhaust temperatures compared to conventional gasoline engines. The fact that at part loads very lean mixture remains in the main chamber emissions will also be less.

This type of divided chamber stratified charge engine can burn almost any fuel such as propane, kerosene, diesel or gasoline fuels. It has little sensitivity to octane number, i.e. it has multifuel capability inherent in it.

The disadvantages of this method are:

(i) It requires greater attention for matching the injection and ignition timing. Therefore, great care must be exercised in the design of auxiliary chamber and main chamber.

(ii) A sharp, hollow sound is produced at idling due to rapid expulsion of gases from the auxiliary chamber. Further, this noise increases with increase in load.

20.10.6 Charge Stratification by Swirl

It is known that by properly tuning the injection system a wide range of air-fuel ratio can be burnt in an open combustion chamber itself. Thereby the disadvantages associated with a divided chamber engine can be overcome. For this the fuel injection and air swirl are to be properly matched to give charge stratification in an open combustion chamber. Consequently, quite a few designs of stratified charge engines utilizing air swirl in an open combustion chamber have been developed over the years. These are :

(i) Ford combustion process (FCP)

(ii) Ford PROCO

(iii) Texaco combustion process (TCP)

(iv) Witzky swirl stratification process

20.10.7 Ford Combustion Process (FCP)

Ford combustion process also attempts to obtain part load stratification by proper coordination of air swirl and fuel injection ensuring positive ignition. At the same time it also maintains the full load potential of the homogenous fuel-air mixture. However, spray characteristics play an important role.

Figure 20.22 shows the layout of the Ford combustion process. The injector is located radially at a specified angle (56°) as shown in the Fig.20.22(a). This location is found to provide good mixing at all loads and speeds. A long electrode is used in the spark plug. It is positioned in such a way that the spark gap is about 10 mm ahead of the injector along its centre line. A recessed and shrouded intake valve Fig.20.22(b) is used to impart the appropriate air motion with high turbulence. The use of the stationary shroud reduces the anti-swirl in air flow. A directional intake port is used to properly guide the intake flow. Therefore, intake port design is very critical for this system.

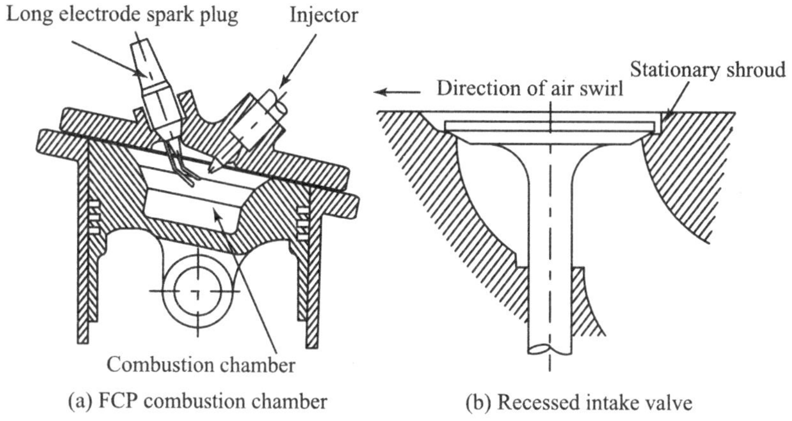

Fig. 20.22 Ford combustion process

The working principle is as follows. The injection of the fuel spray moves a substantial amount of air forward and creates a low pressure region in front of the injector as shown in Fig.20.23(a). Air behind the injector tip moves into this low pressure region. This helps to drag some of the smaller droplets. They get vapourised and form an ignitable air-fuel mixture some 5 to 10 mm ahead of the injector tip. Due to higher inertia to drag forces the heavy droplets do not get closer to the spark plug. This ignitable mixture, which is at or near the bore centre, rotates without drifting away from the spark plug. At the same time it gets mixed properly by the swirling air.

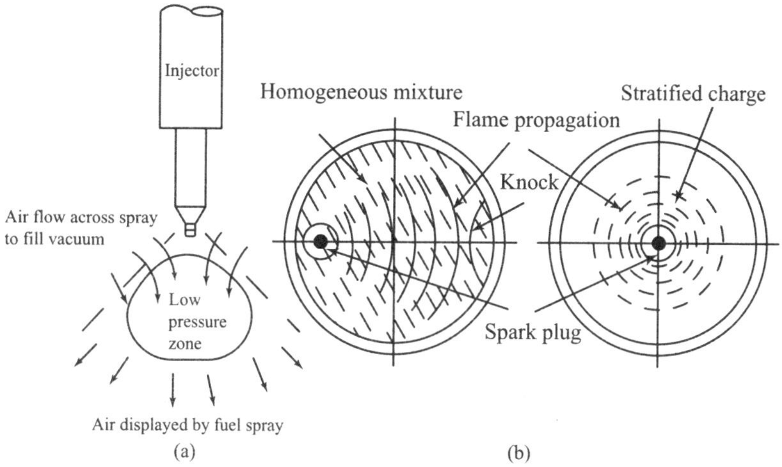

Fig. 20.23 Air flow pattern in FCP combustion chamber

Possible stratification in the combustion chamber at different loads and speeds is shown in Fig.20.23(b). As can be seen, there is a significant difference in the mixture distribution pattern at part load and full load. Therefore, injection and ignition timings should be changed as per the load and speed for proper and complete combustion. The injection timing is advanced with increase in load for better air utilization. The spark timing is adjusted to achieve maximum cycle efficiency. This requires a spark advance mechanism as in normal gasoline engine. Though flame velocity increases with engine speed it is not good enough to give appropriate heat release.

20.10.8 Ford PROCO

The Ford PROCO engine is the second generation of Ford combustion process (FCP). This was developed to give fuel economy and maximum power close to a carburetted engine. PROCO process aims at minimising the exhaust emissions with maximum fuel economy. Unlike FCP, it uses air throttling for this purpose.

Intake port design (Fig.20.24) is the most important in Ford PROCO engine. It is shaped to impart a swirl around the cylinder bore axis. The swirl speed in the engine is about 4 to 5 times the crankshaft speed. The swirling charge is compressed into a cup-shaped combustion chamber situated concentrically in the piston with about 70% squish area. The compression ratio is 11:1. Fuel is injected during the compression stroke. The injector is located close to the centre of the cylinder bore. Injection provides a soft, low-penetrating, wide-angle conical spray. This results in a rich mixture at the centre, surrounded by a lean mixture and excess air. The spark plug with its gap located either near the bore centerline or just above the spray, ignites the charge near tdc. Combustion is fast in rich mixture and then spreads into the leaner regions.

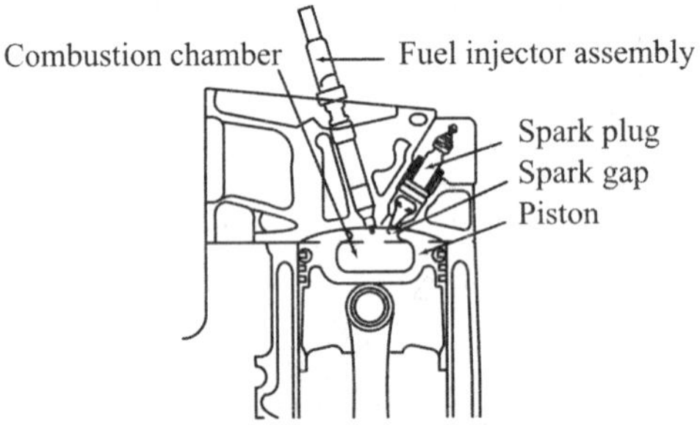

Fig. 20.24 Ford PROCO engine

20.10.9 Texaco Combustion Process (TCP)

Figure 20.25 shows the Texaco combustion process. In this process a high degree of swirl is imparted to the incoming air by the suitable designs of inlet manifold. The fuel is injected across the swirling air in the downstream directions. This enables the entire air to be impregnated by fuel. The ignition source, which may be a glow plug or a spark plug, is positioned directly downstream and close to the injector. The spark plug is situated within the swirling air but is outside the spray envelope.

The fuel is injected towards the end of the compression stroke. The normal practice is to inject about 30° before tdc or just after the initiation of the spark. The first part of the injected fuel which mixes with air during its passage to the spark plug forms a flame front.

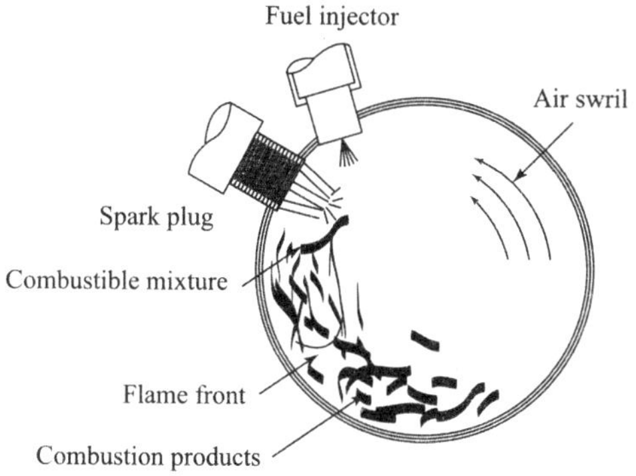

Fig. 20.25 Texaco combustion process engine

The rest of the injected fuel is now continuously fed into this already established flame front after mixing with the swirling air. There must be a good coordination between air swirl and injection. Further, a positive ignition is to be guaranteed for proper operation of TCP.

There are two important characteristics of this process.

(i) The residence time of the fuel-air mixture in the combustion zone is quite small. This results in almost knock-free operation. Further, it is insensitive to the octane numbers of the fuel. In other words it gives the engine the multifuel capability.

(ii) Very lean mixtures can be burned easily by terminating the fuel injection before the complete utilization of the swirling air.

At part loads a small patch near the spark plug has an ignitable mixture while the rest of the chamber has very lean mixture. As the load increases the area of this patch also increases. At full load it is just like the homogeneously charged gasoline engine.

The TCP gives good performance over the whole range of load and speed. A wide range of fuels ranging from premium gasoline to high cetane diesel fuel can be used. In addition to giving better part load efficiency the starting and warm-up characteristics of TCP are quite good. This is due to employment of the cup combustion chamber. The inherent knock resistance of TCP allows the use of higher compression ratio or turbocharging. The lean overall mixtures can be used. The exhaust smoke is also very low.

The major difference between TCP and Ford PROCO system is the timing of the fuel injection. In Texaco engine, combustion occurs near the end of the compression stroke when fuel is injected into the compressed air and immediately ignited by the spark plug. In Ford engine, the fuel is injected into the cylinder over a longer period of time.

20.10.10 Witzky Swirl Stratification Process

The Witzky swirl stratification process is shown in Fig.20.26. This is basically an unthrottled spark ignition process with fuel injection. There is no carburetion. By the appropriate design of the intake port, high velocity swirl is imparted to the intake air during the suction stroke. The fuel is injected during the compression stroke against the swirl direction at some suitable angle. The swirling air, forces the fuel droplets to follow a spiral path by virtue of drag forces and directs them towards the centre of the combustion chamber. A spark plug is located at the carburettor for initiating the combustion. This produces a good degree of stratification – a rich ignitable mixture near the spark plug over the full load range and leaner mixture away from the spark plug. Close to the wall almost pure air is present. The thickness of this pure air layers decreases as the load is increased.

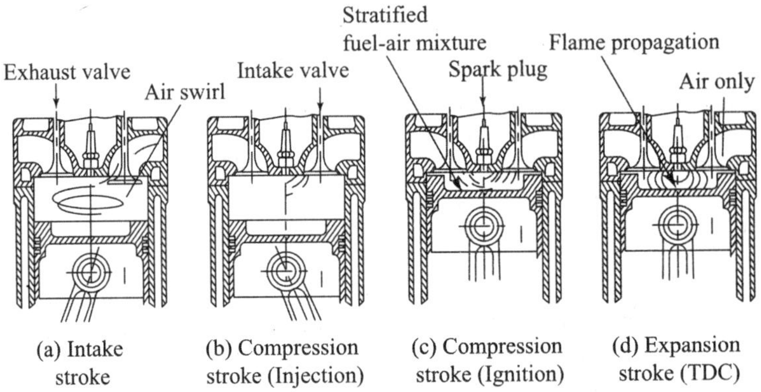

Fig. 20.26 Witzky swirl stratification process

20.10.11 Honda CVCC Engine

Even though stratification are attempted by injection, there are attempts to achieve stratification by carburetion alone. In this compound vortex controlled combustion, Honda CVCC is a bold attempt.

The Honda Compound Vortex Controlled Combustion (CVCC) engine obtains charge stratification using a three barrel carburetor. The engine has two chambers. Prechamber is filled with a rich mixture. The prechamber is connected to the main chamber which is filled with lean mixture. Chambers are filled using carburettors. Figure 20.27 shows the Honda CVCC engine. The basic structure of the engine is same as that of a conventional four-stroke gasoline engine. However, it has an auxiliary combustion chamber around the spark plug. There is also a small additional intake valve which is fitted to each cylinder. Two separate intake valves are used on each cylinder. One valve is located in the prechamber and the other in the main chamber. The smallest venturi of the three barrel carburettor supplies a rich mixture to each prechamber. The other two venturies supply a very lean mixture to the main chamber. A conventional ignition system and spark plugs (one

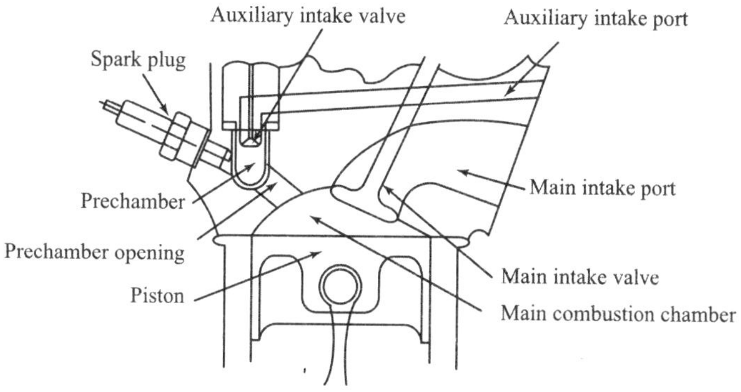

Fig. 20.27 Honda CVCC engine combustion chamber

plug per prechamber) are used to initiate combustion. Figure 20.28 shows the schematic of the combustion system. The combustion sequence is as follows:

(i) A large amount of lean mixture and a small amount of rich mixture is supplied through the main and auxiliary intake valves respectively. On the whole the overall mixture is lean.

(ii) At the end of the compression stroke there is a rich mixture around the spark plug, a moderate mixture in the vicinity of the outlet of the auxiliary chamber and a lean mixture in rest of the mean combustion chamber.

(iii) The rich mixture in the auxiliary chamber is ignited by the spark plug.

(iv) The moderate mixture at, the outlet of auxiliary chamber is ignited which ignites the lean mixture in the main combustion chamber.

(v) Lean mixture continues to burn slowly.

(vi) The temperature of the burned gas remains relatively high for a long duration.

The overall air-fuel ratio of the CVCC engine is much leaner than stoichiometric ratio. It has good emission characteristics. The resulting lower peak combustion temperatures lean mixture, and sufficiently high temperature during exhaust result in reduced NO_X, CO and HC respectively.

20.10.12 Advantages and Disadvantages of Stratified Charge Engines

Advantages:

(i) It can use a wide range of fuels.

(ii) It has low exhaust emission levels.

Disadvantages:

(i) For a given engine size, charge stratification results in reduced power.

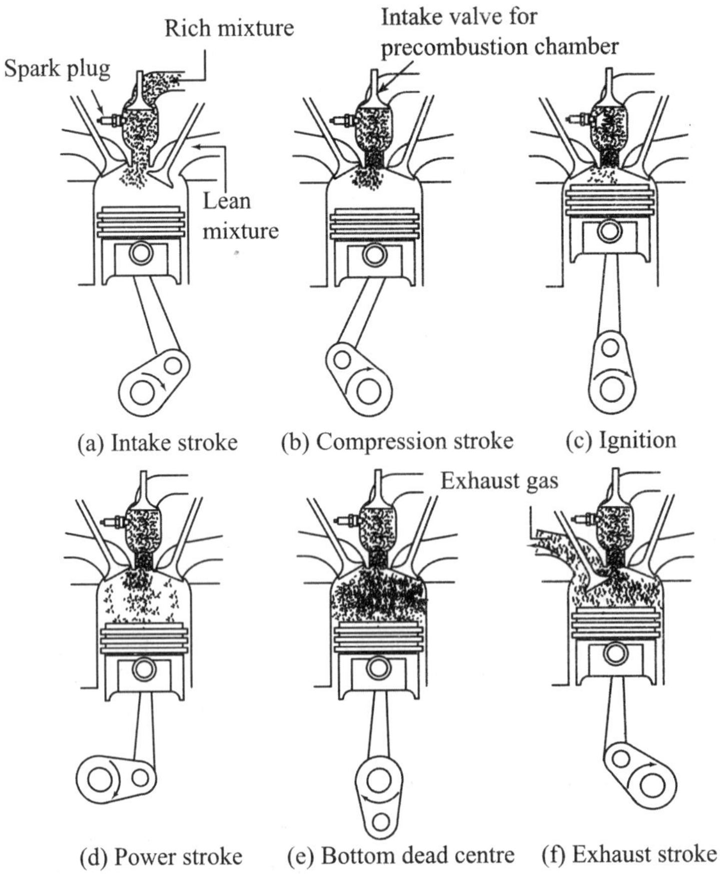

Fig. 20.28 Combustion sequence of Honda CVCC engine

(ii) Compared to conventional engines, its weight is higher for the comparable power and its manufacturing cost is also higher. Its reliability and durability are yet to be well established.

20.11 VARIABLE COMPRESSION RATIO ENGINE

There is a need for developing high specific power output engine from the point of view of specific fuel consumption and emission. Further, the engine must have high reliability and longer life. The maximum power output depends on the utilization of full air capacity of the engine i.e. when maximum amount of fuel can be burnt effectively.

All the methods of increasing power output of an engine have their own problems. For example, increasing engine speed imposes dynamic loads and increased wear. This reduces reliability and life. Further, increasing the speed increases the pumping losses which may become unacceptable especially under part load operation.

Use of turbochargers results in very high cycle peak pressures and subjects the engine to higher thermal loads. Further, the turbocharger cannot maintain good isentropic efficiencies over a wide range of pressure ratios and airflows. Difficulties do arise in matching the turbocharger and the engine at higher specific outputs. At lower speeds torque becomes quite low for certain applications such as for automotive use. Adding a positive displacement supercharger to overcome this difficulty creates more problems than the solution.

One method of solving the high peak pressure problem, when the specific output is increased, is to reduce the compression ratio at full load. At the same time keeping the compression ratio sufficiently high for good starting and part load operation is a must. Thus, it becomes clear that a fixed compression ratio engine cannot meet these requirements of high specific output. *Hence, there is a need for the development of a variable compression ratio (VCR) engine.*

In the VCR engine a high compression ratio is employed for good stability at low load operation. A lower compression ratio is used at full load to allow the turbocharger to boost the intake pressures without increasing the peak cycle pressure. At starting, the turbocharger output is almost zero, so a high compression ratio is needed. As the load increases the engine exhaust temperature increases. More energy becomes available for the turbocharger to boost the pressure. At full load the turbocharger boost capacity is quite high. Therefore, to utilize it efficiently without increasing the peak cycle pressure, lowering of the compression ratio is necessary. It should be noted that larger clearance volume at lower compression ratio would result in increased air intake for the same peak compression pressure and would give higher output.

VCR principle can be employed in both SI and CI engines. However, the concept of variable compression ratio is more appropriate for turbocharged diesel engines because of the following reasons:

(i) It is beneficial only at part load and the part load efficiency of the diesel engine is higher than that of the gasoline engine.

(ii) Diesel engine has better multifuel capability.

20.11.1 Cortina Variable Compression Engine

American inventor Paul Cortina is the latest entry into variable compression engine development. The Cortina engine is the only variable compression concept that slides the entire reciprocating assembly toward and away from the cylinder head. The advantage of this approach is that there is no complication to the workings of the reciprocating assembly itself, nor is there any complication outside the engine. The way this is accomplished is by sliding the reciprocating assembly on a splined shaft that is positioned perpendicular to a typical engine's output shaft. In other words the output shaft is inline or parallel with the sweep of the pistons such that the cylinders can be arranged radially around it. This can be accomplished by two ways.

Model 1 : It uses a conventional crankshaft mounted in an internal subhousing with bevel gears to shift the rotational force 90 degrees. See Fig.20.29(a).

This method uses a more tried and true crankshaft approach, but has more parts and lacks features compared with the barrel cam concept.

Model 2 : It uses a barrel cam. The novelty is in the use of a barrel cam in place of a tradition crankshaft. The barrel cam uses fewer parts and adds the option of a true Atkinson cycle. It also has a more favorable leverage curve that a traditional crankshaft. Since the connecting rods stay strait with a barrel cam cycling the pistons it also is possible to box in the lower cylinder for use as an internal supercharger. For these reasons this method would be preferred if the durability proves adequate (Fig.20.29(b)). For a barrel or cylindrical cam to survive the high stress environment of cranking an internal combustion engine a cam with an external rib with complicated variable thickness would be necessary. This style of cam is just now becoming common in industrial machinery.

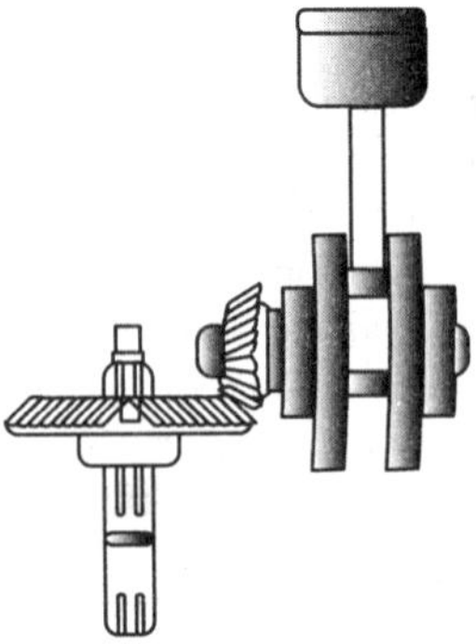
(a) Model 1

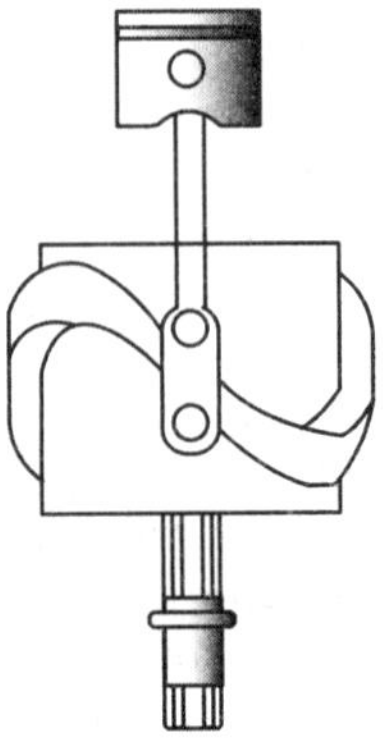
(b) Model 2

Fig. 20.29 Cortina VCR engine

20.11.2 Cycle Analysis

Figure 20.30 shows *p*-*V* diagram of ideal diesel (constant pressure) cycle for CCR and VCR engines with a constant pressure combustion. The full lines correspond to the CCR engine and the dotted to the VCR engine. Figure 20.30 refers to the engine running at constant fuel-air ratio and at full load. Note that at full load compression ratio for VCR engine is lower. The combustion pressure can be kept constant by increasing the boost pressure, fuel rate, and output when the compression ratio is lowered. The following observations can be made from the *p*-*V* diagram shown in 20.30.

(i) Both the pressure (Fig.20.30) and the temperature (Fig.20.31) of VCR engine lie above those for constant compression ratio engine during expansion, indicating that the expansion is slower at low compression ratios.

(ii) The gas temperature for the VCR engine is lower than that for constant compression ratio engine during entire compression stroke and up to

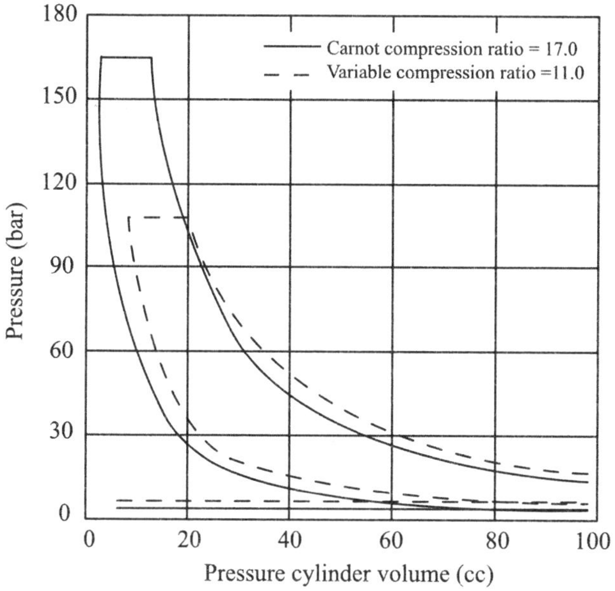

Fig. 20.30 p – V diagram for CCR and VCR engines

about 50° after tdc. After this the temperature drops slowly due to slower expansion and thus, it is clear that the exhaust valves of VCR engines run hotter.

(iii) Boost pressure and mean cycle temperature increases with load but the maximum cycle temperature for VCR engine is lower at higher loads.

(iv) Both bsfc and isfc significantly increase with increase in load for VCR engines.

20.11.3 The CFR Engine

In the CFR engine, developed by Coordinating Fuel Research Committee, the cylinder head assembly is raised or lowered by means of a fine screw-threaded adjustment mechanism. This allows in changing the dimensions between the axis of the crankshaft and the cylinder head and permits variation of clearance volume by only changing the height. This engine is ideal for laboratory studies but is not suitable either for multi-cylinder version or for mass production.

20.11.4 Performance of Variable Compression Ratio Engines

Power output and compactness: VCR engines can develop much more power for the same engine dimensions of CCR engine, i e. it is quite compact and has a high power to weight ratio without any penalty on specific fuel consumption.

Thermal and structural loads: The overall duration of heat release is shortened, i.e. as the load is increased the rate of heat release is also increased. This results in smoother combustion at both lower and higher compression ratios.

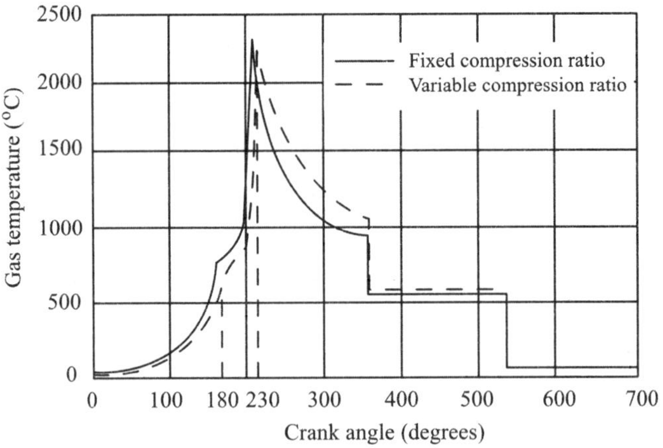

Fig. 20.31 Theoretical gas temperature versus crank angle for CCR and VCR engines

Lower compression ratio effects: With lower compression ratio, the temperature of the combustion chamber decreases and the charging efficiency increases. There is a slight increase in the exhaust temperature. As the ignition lag increases, the maximum pressure decreases. The overall result of using VCR principle is lower thermal and structural loads and to obtain a very high specific output.

Specific fuel consumption: It is known that the thermal efficiency of the engine decreases drastically with a decrease in the compression ratio. However, this effect is countered by the following factors :

(i) The higher mechanical efficiency is achieved due to higher bmep and relatively lower fmep. The friction mep depends upon the peak cylinder pressure and increases in direct proportion to peak pressure. Since in the VCR operation, the peak cylinder pressure remains constant the frictional losses remain almost constant.

(ii) Lower-rate of expansion during combustion allows sufficient time for complete combustion.

(iii) A greater benefit can be obtained from after-cooling since the boost pressure is high.

Due to these factors it is expected that bsfc of the VCR engine should be comparable to CCR engine.

Engine noise: The maximum pressure in the cylinder and the rate of pressure rise both significantly affect the noise emanating from the engine. The first factor determines the low frequency noise and the second the high frequency noise. Thus the VCR engine by virtue of having a constant peak pressure reduces the low frequency noise. However, as the compression ratio is reduced, there is a pressure rise which causes high frequency noise.

Cold starting and idling: Due to use of a higher compression ratio at low loads the VCR engine has a good cold starting and idling performance even at low ambient temperatures.

Multifuel capability: Due to higher compression ratio at starting and part load operation the VCR engine has good multifuel capability. The opposed piston type engine is especially suited to multifuel operation.

20.11.5 Variable Compression Ratio Applications

In earlier days VCR engines were designed only in laboratories for the purposes of studying combustion processes. These designs usually have a second adjustable piston set in the head opposing the working piston. Variable compression engines are highly desirable but technically not feasible for production vehicles. It is mainly due to the mechanical complexity and difficulty of controlling all of the parameters. However, the advances in low cost microcontrollers and the experience gained over the years in their application to engine management now makes the control possible.

20.12 WANKEL ENGINE

Conventionally IC engines are reciprocating type. However, in the twentieth century, a rotary engine was invented. *The engine invented by German engineer Felix Wankel, is a type of internal combustion engine using a rotary design to convert pressure into a rotating motion instead of using reciprocating pistons.* Its four-stroke cycle takes place in a space between the inside of an oval-like epitrochoid-shaped housing and a rotor that is similar in shape to a Reuleaux triangle but with sides that are somewhat flatter. This design delivers power smoothly even at very high speed. The engine is quite compact in size. It is the only internal combustion engine invented in the twentieth century to go into production. Since its introduction the engine has been commonly considered rotary engine. However, this name is also applied to several completely different designs. Figure 20.32 shows the anatomy of a Wankel engine kept in Deutsches Museum in Munich, Germany.

Fig. 20.32 A Wankel engine in Deutsches Museum in Munich, Germany

Because of its compact design, Wankel rotary engines have been installed in a variety of vehicles and devices such as automobiles (including racing cars), along with aircraft, personal water craft, chain saws, and auxiliary power units. The most extensive automotive use of the Wankel engine has been by the Japanese company Mazda. Figure 20.33 illustrates the Mazda's first Wankel engine, at the Mazda Museum in Hiroshima, Japan

Fig. 20.33 Mazda's first Wankel engine, at the Mazda Museum in Hiroshima, Japan

20.12.1 Basic Design

A typical design of the Wankel engine is shown in the Fig.20.34. There are three apexes as seen in the figure. The (8) marked in the figure is one of the three apexes of the rotor. The (4) marked is the eccentric shaft and (7) is the lobe of the eccentric shaft. The shaft turns three times for each rotation of the rotor around the housing. It rotates once for each orbital revolution around the eccentric shaft.

In the Wankel engine, the four strokes (Fig.20.35) of a typical Otto cycle occur in the space between a three-sided symmetric rotor and the inside of a housing. The expansion phase of the Wankel cycle is much longer than that of the Otto cycle. In the basic single-rotor Wankel engine, the oval-like epitrochoid-shaped housing (2) surrounds a rotor. The configuration of rotor is triangular with bow-shaped flanks. It has three-pointed curve of constant width (Fig.20.34) having the bulge in the middle of each side. The shape of the rotor between the fixed corners is so designed to achieve minimum volume of the geometric combustion chamber and to maximize the compression ratio.

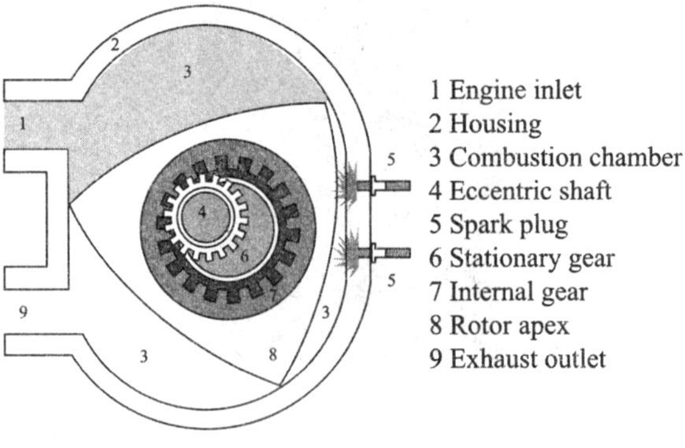

Fig. 20.34 A typical design of the Wankel engine

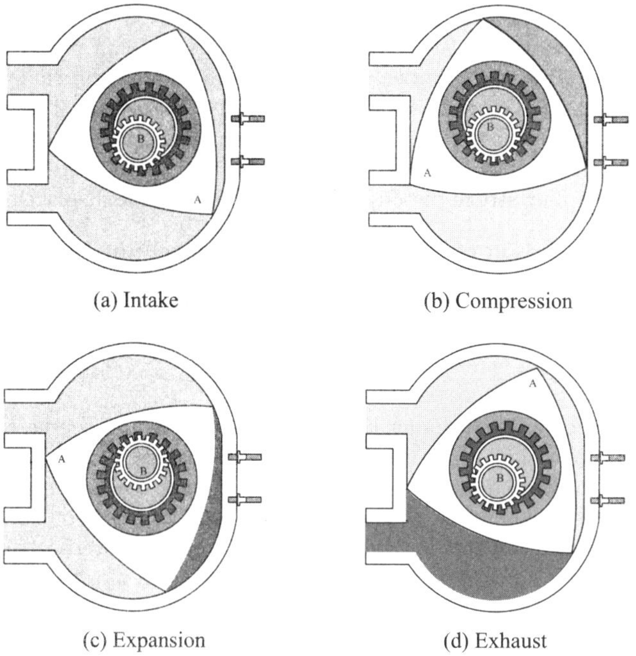

Fig. 20.35 Working of Wankel engine

The central drive shaft, called the eccentric shaft or e-shaft, passes through the center of the rotor. It is supported by fixed bearings. The rotors ride on eccentrics (analogous to cranks) integral to the eccentric shaft (analogous to a crankshaft). The rotors rotate around the eccentrics and at the same time make orbital revolutions around the eccentric shaft. Seals at the corners of the rotor seal against the periphery of the housing, dividing it into three moving combustion chambers. The rotation of each rotor on its own axis is caused and controlled by a pair of synchronizing gears. A fixed gear mounted on one side of the rotor housing engages a ring gear attached to the rotor and ensures the rotor moves exactly 1/3 turn for each turn of the eccentric shaft. The power output of the engine is not transmitted through the synchronizing gears. The force of gas pressure on the rotor (to a first approximation) goes directly to the center of the eccentric, part of the output shaft.

The Wankel engine is actually a variable-volume progressing-cavity system. Thus there are 3 cavities per housing, all repeating the same cycle. Note as well that points A and B on the rotor and e-shaft turn at different speed, point B moves 3 times faster than point A, so that one full orbit of the rotor equates to 3 turns of the e-shaft.

As the rotor rotates and orbitally revolves, each side of the rotor is brought closer to and then away from the wall of the housing, compressing and expanding the combustion chamber like the strokes of a piston in a reciprocating engine. The power vector of the combustion stage goes through the center of the offset lobe.

A four-stroke piston engine makes one combustion stroke per cylinder for every two rotations of the crankshaft (that is, one-half power stroke per crankshaft rotation per cylinder). However, each combustion chamber in the Wankel generates one combustion stroke per each driveshaft rotation. That is to say, one power stroke per rotor orbital revolution and three power strokes per rotor rotation. Thus, power output of a Wankel engine is generally higher than that of a four-stroke piston engine of similar engine displacement.

20.12.2 Comparison of Reciprocating and Wankel Rotary Engine

In the following sections, we will compare the Wankel engine with reciprocating engine with respect to materials, sealing, fuel consumption and emissions.

20.12.3 Materials

In a piston engine, the cylinder is cooled by the incoming charge after being heated by combustion. However, Wankel rotor housings are constantly heated on one side and cooled on the other. This causes high local temperatures and unequal thermal expansion. While this places high demands on the materials used, the simplicity of the Wankel makes it easier to use alternative materials like exotic alloys and ceramics. With water cooling in a radial or axial flow direction, with the hot water from the hot bowl heating the cold bowl, the thermal expansion remains tolerable.

20.12.4 Sealing

Early engine designs experienced sealing problems. The losses take place both between the rotor and the housing and also between the various pieces making up the housing. Also, in earlier model Wankel engines carbon particles could become trapped between the seal and the casing. This started jamming the engine, requiring a partial rebuild.

It was common for very early Mazda engines to require rebuilding (now solved) in less than 100,000 km operation. Further, sealing problems arose from the uneven thermal distribution within the housings causing distortion and loss of sealing and compression. This thermal distortion also causes uneven wear between the apex seal and the rotor housing. Problem is encountered when the engine is stressed before reaching operating temperature. However, Mazda seems to have solved these problems.

20.12.5 Fuel consumption and emissions

It may be noted that the shape of the Wankel combustion chamber is resistant to preignition. Therefore, it can run on lower-octane rating gasoline than a comparable piston engine. This also leads to relatively incomplete combustion of the air-fuel charge, with a larger amount of unburned hydrocarbons released into the exhaust. However, NO_X emissions are relatively low. Inexpensive 'thermal reactor' can be used where the unburned hydrocarbons (HC) can be oxidized. It is worth noting that piston-engine requires expensive catalytic converters to deal with both unburned hydrocarbons and NO_X emissions. Higher unburnt hydrocarbon emission raises fuel consumption. This is a weak point for the Wankel engine

20.12.6 Advantages and Disadvantages of Wankel Engines

Advantages:

(i) Wankel engines are considerably lighter, simpler, and contain far fewer moving part

(ii) There are no valves or complex valve trains

(iii) There are no connecting rods and there is no crankshaft.

(iv) The elimination of reciprocating mass and the elimination of the most highly stressed and failure prone parts of piston engines gives the Wankel engine high reliability, a smoother flow of power, and a high power-to-weight ratio.

(v) It has higher volumetric efficiency and a lower pumping loss

(vi) It is very quick to react to throttle changes and is able to quickly deliver a surge of power when the demand arises, especially at higher rpm.

(vii) A further advantage of the Wankel engine for use in remotely piloted aircrafts is the fact that a Wankel engine generally has a smaller frontal area than a piston engine of equivalent power, allowing a more aerodynamic nose to be designed around it.

(viii) The simplicity of design and smaller size of the Wankel engine also allows for savings in construction costs, compared to piston engines of comparable power output.

(ix) Due to a 50% longer stroke duration compared to a four-cycle engine, there is more time to complete the combustion. This leads to greater suitability for direct injection.

(x) A Wankel rotary engine has stronger flow of air-fuel mixture and a longer operating cycle than a reciprocating engine

Disadvantages:

(i) In two dimensions the sealing system of a Wankel looks to be simpler than that of a corresponding multi-cylinder piston engine. However, in three dimensions the opposite is true. The rotor must also seal against the chamber ends which is comparatively difficult.

(ii) The less effective sealing of the Wankel is one factor reducing its efficiency, limiting its use mainly to applications such as racing engines and sports vehicles where neither efficiency nor long engine life are major considerations.

(iii) The time available for fuel to be port-injected into a Wankel engine is significantly shorter, compared to four-stroke piston engines, due to the way the three chambers rotate.

(iv) The fuel-air mixture cannot be pre-stored as there is no intake valve.

(v) Also the Wankel engine, compared to a piston engine, has 50% longer stroke duration. The four stroke Otto cycles last 1080° for a Wankel engine, whereas it is 720° for a four-stroke reciprocating piston engine.

(vi) The trailing side of the rotary engine's combustion chamber develops a squeeze stream which pushes back the flamefront. That is why there can be more carbon monoxide and unburnt hydrocarbons in a Wankel's exhaust stream

(vii) All Wankel rotaries burn a small quantity of lubricating oil by design. periodically small amounts of oil is to be added, marginally increasing running costs

Review Questions

20.1 Name the nonconventional engines known to you.

20.2 Explain the working principle of CRDI engine.

20.3 Discuss the requirements for ECU and microcomputer in CRDI operation.

20.4 What are the advantages and disadvantages of CRDI engine?

20.5 Why should we go for a dual fuel operation?

20.6 Describe the working principle of a dual fuel engine.

20.7 Explain the process of combustion in dual fuel engines.

20.8 What are the factors those affect the combustion in dual fuel engine?

20.9 What is a multi fuel engine and what are its characteristics?

20.10 What is a free piston engine and what are its characteristics?

20.11 Explain with sketches the working principle of various free piston engine configurations.

20.12 With a neat sketch explain the working principle of free piston gas generator.

20.13 Mention the various advantages and disadvantages of a free piston engine.

20.14 Explain the evolution GDI engine over the period with a sketch.

20.15 Explain the principle of operation of a GDI engine.

20.16 Explain the concept of HCCI. Describe the various control mechanisms for HCCI.

20.17 What are the advantages and disadvantages of HCCI engine?

20.18 Why should one go for lean burn operation? Explain the basics of lean burn technology.

20.19 With a neat sketch explain Toyota lean burn engine.

20.20 Give a brief account of Honda lean burn system.

20.21 With a neat sketch describe the Mitsubishi ultra lean burn combustion engine.

20.22 Explain the principle of operation of Stirling engine.

20.23 With neat sketches explain the working principle of alpha and beta Stirling engines.

20.24 Compare the Stirling engine with internal combustion engine.

20.25 What are the advantages and disadvantages of Stirling engine.

20.26 What are the applications of Stirling engine and what is its future?

20.27 What do you understand by charge stratification?

20.28 Explain the various methods of charge stratification.

20.29 Explain the various engines that use stratification by injection and positive ignition.

20.30 With a sketch explain any one engine that uses the concept of charge stratification by swirl.

20.31 What are the advantages and the disadvantages of the stratified charge engine.

20.32 What is the advantage of variable compression ratio concept?

20.33 Explain the principle of Cortina variable compression ratio engine.

20.34 Explain the performance of VCR engine over CCR engine.

20.35 What are the applications of VCRE?

20.36 What are the basic defects in a reciprocating engine? Why rotary engine is necessary?

20.37 With a diagram explain the configuration of a Wankel engine.

20.38 With neat sketches explain the working principle of a Wankel engine.

20.39 Compare the rotary Wankel engine with reciprocating I C engine.

20.40 What are the advantages and disadvantages of Wankel engine?

Multiple Choice Questions (choose the most appropriate answer)

1. Modern CRDI engines uses injection pressure of the order of
   (a) 400 bar
   (b) 800 bar
   (c) 1200 bar
   (d) 1600 bar
2. A dual fuel engine use two fuels in which
   (a) one is gaseous and the other liquid
   (b) both are liquid fuels
   (c) both are gaseous fuels
   (d) one is liquid and the other can be anything
3. A free piston engine will have
   (a) a combustion chamber
   (b) a load device
   (c) a rebound device
   (d) all of the above
4. GDI concept came in the year
   (a) 1985
   (b) 1990
   (c) 1995
   (d) 2005
5. HCCI combustion is similar to
   (a) S I engine
   (b) C I Engine
   (c) Is a hybrid of both S I and C I Engine
   (d) Wankel engine
6. Lean burn concept is more ideal for
   (a) C I engine
   (b) S I Engine
   (c) Free piston engine
   (d) Wankel engine

7. Stirling engine is noted for
   (a) Quiet operation
   (b) High efficiency
   (c) Compatible with alternative and renewable energy
   (d) All of the above
8. Charge stratification can be achieved by
   (a) Injection
   (b) Carburetion
   (c) Injection as well as carburetion
   (d) Lean burn technology
9. Variable compression ratio can be used in
   (a) S I engine
   (b) C I engine
   (c) Wankel engine
   (d) All of the above
10. Wankel engines
    (a) have valve trains
    (b) are lighter and simpler
    (c) has lower volumetric efficiency
    (d) has lower sfc compared to reciprocating engine
11. Stratified charge engines
    (a) are more prone for knock
    (b) have multifuel capabilities
    (c) have lot of throttling losses
    (d) uses overall rich mixture
12. CRDI
    (a) increases the controllability
    (b) improves fuel atomization
    (c) helps in saving fuel
    (d) all of the above

13. HCCI engines

    (a) emits high NOx and soot
    (b) have large power range
    (c) efficiency is comparatively less
    (d) pre-catalyst hydrocarbon emissions are higher.

14. Stirling engine

    (a) uses a multi phase working fuel
    (b) are extremely nonflexible
    (c) requires only small temperature difference
    (d) none of the above

15. Wankel engine

    (a) is a rotary external combustion engine
    (b) has less time to complete the combustion
    (c) as a longer operating cycle
    (d) is more expensive

Ans:					
	1. – (d)	2. – (a)	3. – (d)	4. – (a)	5. – (c)
	6. – (b)	7. – (d)	8. – (c)	9. – (a)	10. – (b)
	11. – (b)	12. – (d)	13. – (d)	14. – (d)	15. – (c)

Index